LAND LAW

Third Edition

Land Law

Patrick J Dalton **LLB**

Barrister-at-Law & Head of Department of Law,
Birmingham Polytechnic

Pitman

PITMAN PUBLISHING LIMITED
128 Long Acre, London WC2E 9AN

PITMAN PUBLISHING INC
1020 Plain Street, Marshfield, Massachusetts 02050

Associated Companies
Pitman Publishing Pty Ltd, Melbourne
Pitman Publishing New Zealand Ltd, Wellington
Copp Clark Pitman, Toronto

First published in Great Britain 1972

Third edition published by Pitman Books Limited, 1983

British Library Cataloguing in Publication Data
Dalton, Patrick J.
Land law.—3rd ed.
1. Real property—England
I. Title
344.2064'3 KD829

ISBN 0-273-01858-2

Text set in 9½/10½pt Linotron 202 Imprint, printed and bound in Great Britain at The Pitman Press, Bath

To my brave friend
PATRICIA JANE WOODWARD

Preface

ONE OF THE principal aims of the first edition of this book was to explain the doctrines of land law by reference to reason rather than to history. That approach is retained in this third edition with a strengthened conviction that history can be a barrier to an understanding of the modern law on the part of beginners. It is no longer enough, however, merely to suppress dead principles. Some living law is still given prominence in teaching programmes long after it has declined in social importance. Meanwhile, new problems of great urgency queue up for attention. These new issues are not only more relevant to our age but are frequently much more intellectually challenging in an educational setting. A modern practitioner is unlikely to be confronted with, for instance, an entailed interest. He *is* likely to encounter very many disputes over matrimonial homes and they will all present him with different problems. Some other features and objectives of this book might be mentioned briefly.

Its structure has been further simplified and streamlined. The chapters have been reduced from twenty-four to eighteen. The Contents pages now show at a glance a cohesive plan of the subject. The overall length of the book has been increased by more than fifty pages.

Important modern developments have been given greater emphasis. Examples are the ownership and occupational rights of spouses and co-habiting persons, including questions of domestic violence, leases, licences, other occupational rights and the modern building society mortgage. On the other hand, discussion of entailed interests and the powers of life tenants under settlements has been abbreviated. The original emphasis on general principles has been maintained because these still underlie much of the subject. However, a forward glance has been attempted where appropriate. There are signs that the ancient and rigid doctrine of estates is becoming more flexible and that occupation of land as such increasingly invites statutory protection. A new chapter, 7, has been given over to discussion of this topic.

An attempt has been made to set the law in the practical and social contexts of everyday life. The domestic and residential environment is given prominence. Students will be familiar with such situations and this identification will assist the contextual approach I have aimed at. It will also help students to understand policy elements in judicial decisions. To this end an entirely new feature has been introduced. Study materials have been included at the end of chapters, illustrating some aspect of the subject which is of particular practical or social importance. Questions are provided to stimulate in the reader an inquisitive and critical approach to the subject. These materials are also intended to emphasize that the law is not a collection of static principles but a veritable laboratory in which policies and rules are tested and fashioned.

Land law is not only a most appropriate subject for academic study but in modern times has become a vital foundation for a growing number of other disciplines. For example, besides conveyancing, town and country planning, estate management and housing law also depend upon it. These specialized fields of knowledge are clearly beyond the scope of this book. The general balance of the text, however, takes account of this role of the subject.

I would like to express my thanks to all those who have given me so much kind help in writing this edition. I am indebted to students past and present. Patricia Woodward has been my constant guide and critic. Kay Sheriff has tirelessly deciphered and typed my manuscript with her usual clairvoyance, speed and accuracy. My brothers, Peter Dalton and Joseph Dalton, again gave me invaluable help in proof reading.

I thank the publishers for taking on this edition. I am grateful for the great professional care they have shown at every stage.

I have attempted to state the law as it stood on 1st January 1983. I accept any failure to do so as my own fault entirely.

Patrick J Dalton

Shirley, Warwickshire
9th May 1983

Contents

Table of cases

A

B

C

D

E

F

I

J

K

L

M

N

National Carriers Ltd. *v.* Panalpina (Northern) Ltd. [1981] AC 675; [1981] 1 All ER 161; [1981] 2 WLR 45 ***88***

National Provincial Bank Ltd. *v.* Ainsworth [1965] 2 All ER 472; [1965] AC 1175; [1965] 3 WLR 1; 109 SJ 415, HL ***116, 118, 327, 328, 333, 346***

National Provincial Bank Ltd. *v.* Hastings Car Mart Ltd. [1965] AC 1175; [1965] 3 WLR 1; [1965] 2 All ER 472; [1964] Ch. 665 ***325, 328***

National Westminster Bank Ltd. *v.* Allen [1971] 2 QB 718; [1971] 3 WLR 495; [1971] 3 All ER 201; 22 P & CR 1081 ***162, 211***

Neaverson *v.* Peterborough R.D.C. [1902] 1 Ch. 557; 71 LJ Ch. 378; 86 LTR 738; 66 JP 404; 50 WR 549; 18 TLR 360, CA ***268***

Neeld, *Re* [1962] Ch. 643; [1962] 2 WLR 1097; [1962] 2 All ER 335 ***70***

Newbury District Council *v.* Secretary of State for the Environment [1980] 1 All ER 731; [1980] 2 WLR 379; 78 LGR 306 ***54***

Newman *v.* Real Estate Debenture Corporation Ltd. and Flower Decorations Ltd. [1940] 1 All ER 131; 162 LT 183 ***85***

New Zealand Property Corporation *v.* H.M. & S. Ltd. [1981] 1 All ER 759; [1981] 1 WLR 870 ***86***

Newton Abbot Co-operative Society Ltd. *v.* Williamson & Treadgold [1952] Ch. 286; [1952] 1 TLR 283; [1952] 1 All ER 279 ***236***

Nickerson *v.* Barraclough [1981] Ch. 426; [1981] 2 All ER 369; [1981] 2 WLR 773 ***263***

Nielson-Jones *v.* Fedden [1974] 3 All ER 161 ***217***

Nisbet and Potts' Contract [1906] 1 Ch. 386 ***131***

Noakes & Co Ltd. *v.* Rice [1902] AC 24; [1900–3] All ER 34; 71 LJ Ch. 139; 86 LT 62; 66 JP 147; 50 WR 305; 18 TLR 196; 46 SJ 136 ***293, 294***

Noble and Wolf, *Re* [1949] OR 503 ***72***

North, *Re* [1952] Ch. 397; [1952] 1 TLR 674; [1952] 1 All ER 609 ***203***

Northern Counties of England Fire Insurance Co. *v.* Whipp (1884) 26 Ch.D. 482; 53 LJ 629; 51 LT 806; 32 WR 626, CA ***309***

Northern Development (Holdings) Ltd. *v.* U.D.T. Securities [1977] 1 All ER 747; [1976] 1 WLR 1230 ***319***

O

Oak Co-operative Building Society *v.* Blackburn [1968] Ch. 730; [1968] 2 WLR 1053; 112 SJ 172; [1968] 2 All ER 117; 19 P & CR 375, CA ***323***

Oakley *v.* Boston [1976] QB 270; [1975] 3 WLR 478; [1975] 3 All ER 405 ***265***

O'Brien *v.* Robinson [1973] AC 912; [1973] 2 WLR 393; 117 SJ 187; [1973] 1 All ER 583; 25 P & CR 239, HL ***86***

Oliver *v.* Hinton [1899] 2 Ch. 264; 68 LJ Ch. 583; 81 LT 212; 48 WR 3; 15 TLR 450; 43 SJ 622, CA ***309***

Osborn's and Easton's Application (1978) 38 P & CR 251 ***243***

Ough *v.* King [1967] 1 WLR 1547; 111 SJ 792; [1967] 3 All ER 859; 19 P & CR 40, CA ***271***

Owen *v.* Gadd [1956] 2 QB 99; [1956] 2 WLR 945; 100 SJ 301; [1956] 2 All ER 28, CA ***84***

P

Q

R

S

T

U

V

W

Y

Z

Table of statutes

1952 Intestates' Estates Act [15 & 16 Geo. 6 & 1 Eliz. 2 c.64]
s.1(4) **202**

1954 Atomic Energy Authority Act [2 & 3 Eliz. 2 c.32] **47**

1954 Landlord and Tenant Act [2 & 3 Eliz. 2 c.56] **169**
s.51 **93**
Part II **52, 105**

1957 Housing Act [5 & 6 Eliz. 2 c.56]
s.4 **85**
s.6 **85**
s.151 **241**
s.165 **243**

1957 Occupiers' Liability Act [5 & 6 Eliz. 2, c.31] **278**

1958 Variation of Trusts Act [6 & 7 Eliz. 2 c.53] **70, 154**

1959 County Courts Act [7 & 8 Eliz. 2 c.22]
s.191 **92**

1959 Rights of Light Act [7 & 8 Eliz. 2 c.56] **271**

1959 Mental Health Act [7 & 8 Eliz. 2 c.72] **156**
ss.102–5 **12**

1960 Charities Act [8 & 9 Eliz. 2 c.58] **12**

1961 Land Compensation Act [9 & 10 Eliz. 2 c.33] **51**

1961 Trustee Investments Act [9 & 10 Eliz. 2 c.62] **153**

1961 Housing Act [9 & 10 Eliz. 2 c. 65]
s.32 **86, 276, 279**
s.33 **86**

1962 Building Societies Act [10 & 11 Eliz. 2 c.37]
s.36 **302**

1963 Water Resources Act [1963, c.38] **47, 48**
s.23 **48**
s.31 **48**

1963 Matrimonial Causes Act [1963, c.45]
s.5(1) **227**

1964 Perpetuities and Accumulations Act [1964, c.55] **178–9, 191, 198–9**
s.1(2) **194**
s.2 **191, 197, 200**
s.2(4) **192, 200**
s.3 **193, 194, 200**
s.3(1) **191**
s.4 **193**
s.4(3) **192**
s.4(4) **192**
s.5 **193**
s.6 **196**
s.7 **184**
s.8 **190**
s.9(1) **195**
s.9(2) **195**
s.10 **195**
s.12 **68, 195**
s.13 **196**
s.14 **197**
s.15(5) **184, 194**

1964 Law of Property (Joint Tenants) Act [1964, c.63] **219**

1965 Compulsory Purchase Act [1965, c.56] **51**

1965 Commons Registration Act [1965, c.64] **283, 322**
s.16 **282**

1965 Race Relations Act [1965, c.73] **89**

1966 Land Registration Act [1966, c.39] **331**

1967 Agriculture Act [1967, c.22]
s.26 **102**

1967 Matrimonial Homes Act [1967, c.75] **118, 121, 211, 321, 338**
s.1 **119**
s.1(5) **119**
s.2(5) **120**
s.2(7) **120**

1967 Leasehold Reform Act [1967, c.88] **52, 87, 103–4, 234, 338**

1969 Family Law Reform Act [1969 c.46]
s.1 **9, 197**
s.14 **66**

Table of rules and regulations

Chapter One

Introduction

Subject-matter of land law

Land law deals with the kinds of rights you can enjoy in land. Conveyancing deals with the transfer of these rights to others. If I am the owner of 'Blackacre' and have a right of way over my neighbour's property, 'Whiteacre', land law tells me how I may use my own land and in what way I may exercise the right of way over my neighbour's property. If we both retain our properties, land law continuously governs our behaviour to our own and each other's property. My neighbour might wish to build a greenhouse across that part of his land where I exercise my right of way; I might wish to build a high wall on my land which would threaten the flow of light to his kitchen; my oak tree might be sending branches and roots into his property; perhaps I have failed to pay my mortgage instalments. Land law provides the answers to the problems raised by all these circumstances.

Now let us say that my neighbour decides to sell his land to *P*. The problems that arise on the transfer of the property are dealt with by the rules of conveyancing. *P* will insist on proof that my neighbour really owns the land and so will investigate his title to it by examining the recent history of its ownership and use. He will also wish to know about any restrictions imposed upon the land such as the right of way. He might wish to raise the purchase money by means of a mortgage. In any case, he will want to ensure that the ownership is transferred to him in the manner demanded by the law. All this involves not only examining existing documents of title but also drafting new ones. This process is called conveyancing and is clearly of occasional occurrence only. The relationship between the two subjects is nevertheless very close and the study of land law frequently crosses the boundaries of conveyancing.

The rights in land with which land law is concerned are of two types. Firstly, there are those rights which enable you to enjoy the land itself. Examples are absolute ownership, tenancies and life interests. In all these cases you may take exclusive possession of the land. Secondly, there are those rights which, while not empowering you to occupy the land itself, place restrictions on someone else's land in your favour: for example, the right of way over my neighbour's land, mentioned above, which is known as an easement. Other examples would be a right to prevent him carrying out certain activities on his land (a restrictive covenant), and a right to fish in the stream at the bottom of his garden (a *profit à prendre*). Both these kinds of rights are known as 'interests', although absolute ownership and tenancies are also called 'estates' in land. This use of the word 'estate' is peculiar to land law and must be distinguished from the everyday use of the word to mean a particular geographical portion of land.

History has exerted a powerful influence in land law and a few words are necessary to explain its role. Many of the statutes and cases which are still binding are old and untouched or only modified by modern legislation. The Prescription Act 1832 and the case of *Wheeldon* v. *Burrows* (1879) are examples from the law of easements. These are not mere history but living law and must be appreciated as such. This obvious statement is intended to counteract a common early impression that a completely new law of land was created by the great property statutes of 1925. However, the effect of these Acts was more akin to the restoration of an old building than the construction of a new one. Although many cobwebby attics and passages were cut away, much of the building still stands, although refaced and modernized in many places. In fact, much of the modernization carried out in 1925 was aimed at the kitchen where the conveyancing is done. The reforms here were radical. Over much of the house however, the structure is old and you must not be surprised to find the motor car in the stable.

Another application of history in land law is the study of old but now defunct law for the purpose of understanding the evolution of doctrines and terminology. History in this sense has been traditionally much pressed into service in the study of land law. Its role will be curtailed here, and a rational rather than narrative account of doctrines and terms will be attempted. This will enable the reader to save his energies for the living law. Such an approach will, at times, demand a faithful acceptance of the quaint at its face value. One example may be given together with a readily comprehensible analogy from everyday life. The vehicle used for consolidating new road surfaces is still referred to by the unpedantic as a steamroller. Yet everyone knows that it works on diesel fuel, not on steam. When the roadman drives it, or when the mechanic services it, they do not do so less efficiently because they know nothing of steam engineering. In the same way in land law we shall find that the interest which entitles a person to the fullest ownership of land is called the fee simple absolute. The reason for the use of this term lies in history, as in the case of the steamroller, and both statutes and lawyers continue to use the term rather than 'ownership'. Yet there is no difference between the meanings of the two expressions.

Common law and equity

Some of the rights mentioned above were developed by the common law courts and some by the courts of equity. Originally, only the common law courts decided and enforced rights in land and such rights were frequently narrow in scope and dependent upon technicalities. On the other hand, when title to interests in land was based on these 'legal' rights the degree of protection given was high, for they were enforceable against everyone, not merely against particular individuals. They were known as rights *in rem*, or real rights, that is rights to the land itself, as opposed to rights *in personam*, or personal rights, such as contractual rights, enforceable only against specified individuals.

Sometimes a person would be given such an interest in land on the understanding that he would, despite his own legal rights, allow someone else to enjoy the benefit of the land. This arrangement was known as a 'use', or, in modern times, a 'trust'. The common law courts ignored it. Since all they were concerned with was the question 'Who has the legal interest or estate in the land?' only the conscience of the person who held that interest protected the intended beneficiary. Later the Lord Chancellor and then the courts of equity did protect such a beneficiary by enforcing the arrangement. When this protection came to be granted regularly and as a matter of course, the beneficiary was said to have the equitable right to the land.

Thus arose the trust. One person might have a legal interest in land but must allow a person having the equitable interest to enjoy possession of it. For historical reasons this was sometimes a convenient arrangement. If *A*, for instance, wished to make a gift of land to *X* who was a minor, he was faced with the problem that a minor could not hold a legal interest in land. He might overcome this difficulty, however, by transferring the legal interest in the land to *T* and directing that he hold it in trust for *X*, who would thus have the equitable interest. This would entitle *X* to the enjoyment of the land and, when he came of age, he would be able to demand that *T* should convey the legal interest to him. Even now that the courts of common law and equity have been merged, this distinction is still with us and gives us a 'two-faced' land law. A legal interest, if held in trust for another, gives no enjoyment of the land but merely imposes the duty to allow the beneficiary who has the equitable interest to enjoy it. A person who holds a legal interest in land not upon trust for another but for his own purposes might without artificiality be considered as holding both the legal and the equitable interests in the land. In short, when you find that someone has a legal interest in land you have only half the story. You must also ascertain who holds the equitable interest.

There have always been some differences between the enforceability of legal and equitable interests. Legal interests were perfectly secure and enforceable against all. Equitable interests became enforceable against more and more people but never reached the state of inviolability of the legal interest. At first, equity enforced them only against the person who was originally given the legal interest on trust, but later enforced them against all others whose consciences ought to be affected by the trust, like, for example, a purchaser of the legal interest who knew of the trust. Clearly it would be unfair and unconscionable to allow him to take the land freed from the interest of the beneficiaries even though the latter could take action against the trustee. The purchaser would therefore be obliged to hold his legal interest on trust for the beneficiaries and thus involuntarily became a trustee. The scope of enforceability was widened as trusts became more common, the test again being that of good conscience and fairness, until the equitable interest was enforceable against nearly every person. This means that everyone who came to the land as donee or purchaser had to give effect to the trust. But equity stopped short of enforcing against a purchaser in good faith of a legal interest in the land for valuable consideration who had no notice of the trust. To deprive such a person of the enjoyment of the property would be as unfair as allowing the beneficiaries to lose their interest in the land. So, in such a case, the purchaser was allowed to hold the legal interest absolutely for himself. The land became discharged of the trust and the beneficiaries had to pursue personal remedies against the trustee. Furthermore, this discharge was permanent, so that if the purchaser resold the land to *X* who knew of the trust, *X* nevertheless took the land free of it.

Sometimes, however, the very terms of the trust are that the land should be sold and that the resultant purchase-money should be divided amongst the beneficiaries. In these cases the purchaser takes the legal interest free from the trust although he knows of it because that is the purpose of the trust. Special provision is made for the protection of the purchase-money.

So an equitable interest gives much more than a personal right, but just less than a real right. The position is unchanged today and all that need be added at this stage is that the expression 'the purchaser in good faith of a legal interest for value without notice' referred to above has been carefully developed and defined in meaning by both case law and statute. It must be emphasized that, in enforcing rights unknown to the common law, equity nevertheless paid full respect to the doctrines of the common law. It recognized legal rights, but merely directed that in some circumstances they should be exercised in favour of others. We shall see how, in fashioning the different types of interest which might be enjoyed by a beneficiary, it followed the law. Thus there were life interests in equity as at law. In some cases, equity went further and invented new interests in land unknown to the law. An example is the restrictive covenant.

Tenure

There was a time following the Norman Conquest when only the King owned land. It was his because he had conquered it. All other persons enjoying land merely held it of him on certain conditions and, if these conditions were not fulfilled, the land could be reclaimed by the King; rather like, as between landlord and tenant today, the landlord might have the right to end the lease if the tenant breaks a condition in it. This conditional holding of land was called 'tenure'. Several types of tenure developed and were named according to the conditions to be obeyed. The performance of these conditions amounted to a kind of rent. Thus tenure by knight service entailed supplying the King with soldiers for his army. Others were 'frankalmoign', 'serjeanty', 'copyhold' and 'socage'. All had their different types of rent as conditions but in time they tended to conform more to the pattern of socage, which came to have a money rent rather than services in kind. All these different forms of tenure have now been converted into socage by statute, and furthermore, with a few exceptions to be mentioned in the next chapter, all the conditions and rents have been abolished. Since no such conditions exist to be broken, it follows that the monarch can never take the land back.

Although all land is in theory 'held' of the Queen on socage tenure, it is now quite proper to speak of owning it, or, to use the lawyer's phrase, which means the same thing, 'owning the fee simple' in land. There is still one type of relationship which, although not feudal in origin, is called tenure. This occurs when the owner of land leases it to a tenant. Finally, it may be remarked that although the monarch does not own all land she is as capable of owning land in her private capacity as her citizens are.

The doctrine of estates

So 'tenure' told the 'conditions' on which land was held, and is now, apart from the case of leaseholds, obsolete. The words 'estate' and 'interest' tell us for how long a person may enjoy land. This is extremely important today. When no time limit is placed upon your enjoyment of land, clearly you have absolute ownership of it.

This is the 'fee simple' estate. It is the largest estate you can have in land in that it is potentially inexhaustible in duration. You may deal with it in the same way in which you may deal with an object absolutely owned by you. You may alienate it during your lifetime or leave it by will. If you die intestate it will pass to your close relations in the same way that your motor car will. Laymen refer to the fee simple as 'the freehold'.

If you own the fee simple estate you can make grants of the enjoyment of the land to others for limited periods. Rights to enjoy land for these lesser periods are also called 'estates' or 'interests', and, like the fee simple estate, they have their own names to describe their duration. Examples are the 'life interest' and the 'term of years' or 'leasehold'. Since the fee simple is of infinite duration any number of lesser interests may be granted by its owner. *C* may give a life interest to *A*, followed by a life interest to *B*. This would mean that *A* could occupy the land, to the exclusion of all other persons including the fee simple owner, for his lifetime. On *A*'s death, *B*, if still living, would be entitled to do the same. On the death of *B*, *C*, the fee simple owner, would again be entitled to enjoy the land. If he had died by that time the right would belong to the person to whom the fee simple has been conveyed by him or devised by his will. No matter how many lesser interests a fee simple owner grants, the fee simple remains his and will ultimately give the right to possession once again. In short, its owner is like the owner of a tap. Any number of buckets or barrels of water might be taken from it by various people but the ownership of the tap is unchanged, even though its owner may temporarily be denied the right of enjoying its water. This position only alters if he gives away the tap itself. Similarly the only way in which the owner of a fee simple can divest himself of it is to grant someone else the fee simple and not one iota less.

When an interest in land is owned by a person but does not entitle him to present possession, it is said to be 'in reversion' if it is owned by the person who granted the lesser interest and 'in remainder' if it is owned by someone else. Thus in the example above, during *A*'s life *A*'s interest is in possession, *B*'s is in remainder and *C*'s is in reversion. When *A* dies, *B*'s interest becomes an interest in possession and so on. The important point is that even if your interest is still in remainder or in reversion you presently own an interest in land which you can sell or give away. Thus during the lifetime of *A*, *B* may sell his life interest to *P*. Upon *A*'s death *P* will then be entitled to possess the land for as long as *B* lives. In the same way *C* could sell his fee simple in reversion. The grant of successive interests in this way will create a 'settlement' which will be more exactly defined later.

While terminology is being discussed, two terms, 'freehold' and 'leasehold', frequently seen on advertisement boards, ought to be explained. The 'freehold', as we have seen, simply means the fee simple or absolute ownership. All land in England is freehold because someone somewhere always owns the fee simple of a particular piece of land. When that person has leased it, for instance for fifty years, and only the leasehold interest is being offered for sale, the land may be referred to as 'leasehold'. There is a freehold to the land also. It consists of the landlord's fee simple, which of course is in reversion and will not entitle him to possession again until the lease has expired. Meanwhile, however, it does entitle him to receive the rent from his tenant. This freehold can be sold even while the lease is still running, whereupon the purchaser acquires the right to receive the rent for the remaining years of the lease and then the right to possession.

Why reform was necessary

Land law was well suited to the purposes for which it was originally most required, that is family endowment in a subsistence economy. Before 1926 there were three ways in which a person could settle his land for this purpose if, to take a very simple example, he wished to benefit his wife *W* and his son *S* only.

(1) He could grant legal estates to both as follows: 'to *W* for life and then to *S* in fee simple'.
(2) He could pass the legal fee simple to trustees and direct them to hold it for the benefit of *W* for life and then for *S* in fee simple. Here *W* and *S* have equitable interests for life and in fee simple respectively.
(3) He could do exactly the same as in (2) above but order the trustees to sell the land and allow *W* and *S* to enjoy their interests out of the proceeds of sale. This arrangement is a 'settlement by way of trust for sale'. The life interest is satisfied after sale by allowing the owner of the life interest to take the annual investment income from the proceeds of sale for the period of his life. The capital sum in the form of investments represents the fee simple interest and in the present example will pass entirely to *S* after *W*'s death.

In these ways the needs of various members of a family can be satisfied as long as they live. Another example, however, will show that land law was not nearly so well suited to the world of commerce, which after the eighteenth century made increasing demands on land. What would be the position in the case of land settled as described above, if *X*, proposing to build a factory, wished to buy some of the land for that purpose? Certainly he would want land of which he could take immediate possession and which he and his successors could occupy for a very long time. He would therefore require either a fee simple in possession or a very long term of years in possession.

Suppose in this instance that the land was settled by the first method mentioned above, as was often the case in eighteenth-century England. There is no person who can offer *X* the kind of interest he wishes to buy. *W*'s interest is of too indefinite duration. What is the good of building a factory on land and then being unable to use it because *W* has died? On the other hand if he purchased *S*'s interest it might not give the right to possession for many years. In fact *X*'s purpose could only be achieved if both *W* and *S* were willing to sell their interests, or unless, as was often the case in well-drafted settlements, special powers of sale had been included.

Even if the land could be sold, the purchaser would have the expense of investigating not only his vendor's title to the land, but possibly that of several other owners of legal estates in the land. Even in the rudimentary example given above, both *W* and *S* might have dealt with their own interests in some way such as by sale or mortgage. Finally in those cases where the land was rendered unsaleable by settlements, this inability to sell might be as harmful to the beneficiaries and to the land itself as it was inconvenient to the prospective purchaser, for there might be too much land and too little money to develop it. None of these difficulties existed, however, if the land had been settled by the third method. There was power, indeed a duty, to sell the fee simple owned by the trustees; a purchaser would have only the trustees' legal title to investigate and each has an identical title. The interests of the beneficiaries could be ignored by the purchaser since they were intended to be satisfied out of the purchase money paid to the trustees.

There were other reasons why land law was in need of an overhaul. Before 1926 it contained too many outmoded rules and fictions, such as the doctrine of tenure. Furthermore, the gulf between the law of freehold land on the one hand and that of leaseholds and ordinary objects on the other was unnecessarily wide. For instance, when a person died intestate, his freehold land went to his 'heir', which was usually his eldest son, whereas land which he held on lease went to his 'next-of-kin', who constituted a much wider class.

Reform did not come in one rush in 1925. Changes had been made throughout the nineteenth century. The Settled Land Act 1882 gave power to the owner of a life interest in possession under a settlement to sell the fee simple even though he did not own it. This helped to solve the problem of the unsaleability of land illustrated above. The life tenant of course could only take his life interest out of the resultant purchase money, the capital of which had to be carefully safeguarded for the other beneficiaries. This translation of rights in land into rights in the purchase money on sale is known as 'overreaching'. Other reforms were carried out which were radical enough to have been left alone by the 1925 legislation. The Acts passed in 1925 were the culmination of the process but left a vast body of old law intact. They were primarily aimed at facilitating conveyancing but this involved changes in land law of a major kind. Further amendments and new principles of law have been brought into force by statutes passed since 1925. The changes made in that year, however, were so far-reaching that the next chapter will be devoted to a summary of their more fundamental effects. The detailed provisions of the Acts will be dealt with in the following chapters as and when they become appropriate to the particular topic under discussion.

Constant development of land law

Land fulfils so many needs in society that the law must constantly develop to balance those needs. Sometimes this evolution is reflected in entirely new codes of rules. The Rent Act 1977 and the Town and Country Planning Act 1971 are just two modern examples. They both respond to the problems of a large urbanized population in a highly industrialized country. But sometimes changes are more difficult to discern. They occur over a long period of time through judicial decisions or legislation less spectacular than that mentioned above. Changing values in society often affect judicial policy in the appellate courts. A few examples are mentioned below, though the topics are discussed in detail in later chapters.

(1) There are signs that the rigid distinction between interests in land and personal rights relating to land is breaking down.
(2) Occupation of property as a home attracts growing judicial and legislative protection. The Rent Acts provide an example.
(3) While the married state still enjoys the greatest privileges under the law, other forms of cohabitation receive more recognition than formerly.
(4) The impact of marital breakdown on home ownership and occupation is having a profound influence on land law.

The account of land law which follows attempts to provide a foundation of general principles, not only as a basis for the study of conveyancing but for the other specialized subjects which have sprung up in response to the modern role of land in our society. It is not possible to discuss these specialized codes in any detail in a book of this length. It is essential to an appreciation of land law as a living force, however, to recognize their enormous importance and to take account of new social needs and interests which might affect the future policy of judges and Parliament. It is also necessary to observe how existing legal rules are sometimes used for purposes for which they were not designed, by persons wishing to avoid certain legal consequences.

Yet it is possible to see strong connections between the old and the new. Freehold possession was protected over several centuries for the sake of peace and stability, pending some more permanent resolution of disputed ownership. This favour for the person presently under some roof continues today. Eviction of tenants by landlords, for instance, is generally prohibited, except through court order, even though the tenancy has ended. Preservation of minor injustices can sometimes, paradoxically, keep a society at peace better than a too dynamic furtherance of abstract justice.

How property is acquired

Brief mention may be made here of how interests in land can be acquired and created. Further details will be given when those various interests are dealt with. Some methods of acquisition are of general application. Others are peculiar to certain interests only.

All interests in land, whether they give rights to the land itself or to rights in or over land belonging to another person, may be created or transferred by deed, which is simply a document authenticated by the signature and seal of the person making the deed. If some other person, such as a purchaser, agrees to perform some act, then he must also sign and seal the deed. Thus if I convey the fee simple in 'Blackacre' to you, I must sign and seal the deed of conveyance. If you agree to do something in regard to 'Blackacre', however, such as not to use it for industrial purposes and this is expressed in the deed, you also must sign and seal the document. The transaction is completed by delivering the deed to the person in whose favour the interest has been created. A deed of conveyance is shown on pages 10 and 11.

If the law insisted severely upon the general rule that the appropriate way of creating an interest is by deed, unjust results would sometimes follow. Additional methods have therefore been allowed. Two of these apply to all interests in land. Firstly, contracts must be considered. Although a valid contract to transfer or create an interest in land can save a transaction from being a nullity, it does not transfer the interest in question, but places the intended transferee in a position to demand that this be done. Sometimes such agreements are intermediate transactions only. Conveyances of land, for instance, are generally preceded by contracts to convey. Sometimes, however, an owner will purport actually to convey his interest by a document not under seal. The law has been indulgent in such cases and treats such documents as contracts to convey the interests in question.

The second general exception concerns the doctrine of proprietary estoppel. This doctrine is discussed in Chapter 7 in regard to licences, since it has been particularly active in that field. Yet the principle can apply to the acquisition of any interest in land. It must be emphasized, however, that this is an exceptional manner of acquiring an interest. It is sufficient to note here that where an owner permits another person to spend money or to alter detrimentally his position in the expectation that he will enjoy some privilege in that land, the owner will be prevented by the court from acting inconsistently with this expectation, and might also be ordered to convey an interest in the land commensurate with that expectation.

Alternative methods to the deed sometimes apply only to certain types of interest. Certain short leases for instance can be created by mere writing or even orally. Easements and profits can be created by long enjoyment of the activity in question. Once again, the acquiescence of the landowner and the expectations of the person exercising the particular activity over his land lie at the foundations of the principle. Finally, interests giving rights to the land itself can be acquired by long possession adverse to the owner's rights. This principle has long been recognized by statute. The law on the topic is now contained in the Limitation Act 1980. This topic is discussed more fully in Chapter 8.

Capacity

Certain classes of persons are disabled from exercising some of the normal incidents of ownership over their property. The prohibition is usually imposed because the persons affected are considered to be in need of protection. This calls for discussion of minority, mentally disordered persons, corporations and charities.

Under the Family Law Reform Act 1969, a minor is a person who has not reached the age of eighteen (s.1). The following are the main restrictions upon a minor's powers in regard to land.

(1) *Legal estates*. A minor cannot hold a legal estate in land (Law of Property Act ('L.P.A.') 1925, s.1(6)). He can however own equitable interests. An attempt to convey a legal estate to a minor, or to two or more minors jointly, operates as an agreement for valuable consideration to execute a settlement in their favour and meanwhile to hold the land in trust for them (Settled Land Act 1925, s.27(1)). An attempt to convey a legal estate to a minor jointly with one or more other persons of full age vests the legal estate in those others on a statutory trust for sale for themselves and the minor as co-owners in equity (L.P.A. 1925, s.19(2)). These matters are dealt with in Chapter 9.

(2) *Wills*. A minor cannot make a will unless he is a serviceman in actual military service or a 'mariner at sea' (Wills Act 1837, s.7). The laws of intestacy apply to his property in the ordinary way except that under the Administration of Estates Act 1925, s.51(3), if a minor dies without having married and entitled to an equitable interest in fee simple, he is deemed to have died owning an entailed interest. Entailed interests are discussed in Chapter 5. This provision is designed on the assumption that the settlor would have, in such a case, preferred a reversion to himself rather than to have the property pass to a distant relation of the minor.

A mentally disordered person is generally capable of holding property. If, however, he is incapable of understanding the effect of a disposition, then a transaction by him is void if not made for valuable consideration (*Manning* v. *Gill* (1872) L.R. 13 Eq. 485). If the disposition is made for value, it seems

THIS CONVEYANCE is made the 9thday of May 1983 BETWEEN JOHN QUINCE of 20 Athenia Wood Road Arden Warwickshire ("The Vendor") and MARY MOTH of 10 Starveling Lane Lysandford Warwickshire ("the Purchaser").

WHEREAS the Vendor is seised of the property hereby conveyed for an estate in fee simple absolute in possession free from incumbrances and has agreed with the Purchaser for the sale thereof to her for the sum of £30000.

NOW THIS DEED WITNESSETH as follows:

1. In pursuance of the agreement and in consideration of £30000 now paid by the Purchaser to the Vendor (receipt hereby acknowledged) the Vendor as beneficial owner hereby conveys unto the Purchaser ALL THAT property known as 20 Athenia Wood Road Arden Warwickshire and for the purpose of identification only edged by thick lines on the plan annexed hereto TO HOLD unto the Purchaser in fee simple.

2. The Purchaser hereby covenants with intent that this covenant shall enure to the benefit of the Vendor his successors and assigns and others claiming under him to that property owned by him adjoining the property hereby conveyed and known as 18 Athenia Wood Road Arden aforesaid that the property hereby conveyed shall not be used for the purposes of the trade of carpentry.

3. IT IS HEREBY CERTIFIED THAT the transaction hereby effected does not form part of a larger

transaction or a series of transactions in respect of which the amount or value or the aggregate amount or value of the consideration exceeds £30000.

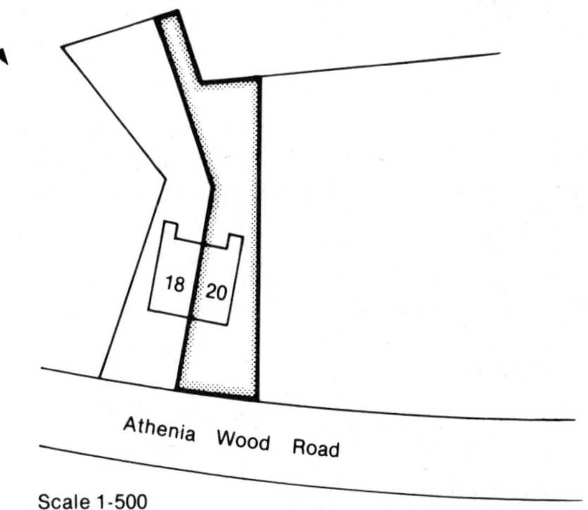

IN WITNESS whereof the parties hereto have hereunto set their hands and seals the day and year first before written.

Signed Sealed and Delivered by JOHN QUINCE — John Quince

in the presence of:- R Bottom
14, Wild Thyme Bank
Arden
Warwickshire

Signed Sealed and Delivered by MARY MOTH — Mary Moth

in the presence of:- C. Mustardseed
2, Willowshop Pool
Lysandford

This form is 'Conveyancing 23B—Lease (Lessor repairs outside of premises)', produced by the Solicitors' Law Stationery Society, Ltd and is reproduced here with their permission.

that its validity will depend upon the circumstances of the case. The authorities upon this last point are unsatisfactory and inconclusive. (For a discussion of this topic see 79 L.Q.R. 502.) A will made by a mentally disordered person during a lucid interval is valid and on principle this ought to apply to other transactions.

Under the Mental Health Act 1959, s.105, a receiver may be appointed under the order of a judge for a person suffering from a mental disorder. While the order is in force, the control of that person's property is in the hands of the receiver, so that any purported disposition *inter vivos* will be void, even if it occurs during a lucid interval. A will made in such circumstances, however, is valid. Very wide powers of management over the patient's property are available to the judge under the Act and these may be granted to the receiver (see ss.102–105 and, for example, *Re C. M. G.* [1970] 2 All E.R. 740). Under the Administration of Justice Act 1969, the court may make a will for a mental patient.

Statutory corporations are subject to the *ultra vires* rule and therefore their powers to hold and deal with land must be discovered from their constitutions. Subject to this, corporations may acquire and dispose of land in the same way as natural persons.

Under the Charities Act 1960, restrictions are placed upon the disposal of land held by charities as part of their permanent endowment property.

Study material: the deed of conveyance

On pages 10 and 11 is a simple example of a deed of conveyance. You will notice that it contains a restrictive covenant because the Vendor wishes to protect neighbouring property retained by him against competition in the carpentry trade which he carries on in that property. Since the Purchaser is making the covenant she must also sign and seal the deed.

The statement under Clause 3 of the conveyance is known as a 'certificate of value'. Stamp duty is payable on all property transactions in excess of £25,000. The clause certifies that the transaction is a truly separate one and has not been broken up in order to evade this duty.

Questions

1. *What is the importance of tenure in modern land law?*
2. *O, the legal owner in fee simple of land, created a restrictive covenant, an equitable interest, in favour of his neighbour, N. Later, O sold his legal fee simple in his land to P. Advise P as to whether he is bound by the restrictive covenant.*
3. *O, the owner in fee simple of 'Blackacre', created the following interests in that land:*

   A life interest in favour of A, to be followed by
   A life interest in favour of B, to be followed by
   A life interest in favour of C.

   Describe the nature of O's interest in 'Blackacre' as a consequence of these transactions.
4. *Why was English land law deficient in face of the requirements of land transfer in the middle of the eighteenth century?*
5. *Attempt to draft a deed transferring the fee simple in 'Blackacre' from John Smith to Jane Brown for £30,000.*

Chapter Two

The general effects of the 1925 legislation

THE FOLLOWING ACTS comprise 'the 1925 legislation'

The unrepealed parts of the Law of Property Act 1922
The unrepealed parts of the Law of Property Act 1924
The Law of Property Act 1925
The Administration of Estates Act 1925
The Settled Land Act 1925
The Land Charges Act 1925
The Trustee Act 1925
The Land Registration Act 1925

All these came into force on 1st January 1926. The Acts of 1922 and 1924 contained many preliminary radical reforms but most of their provisions were repealed before they came into force and absorbed into the Acts of 1925. As can be seen from their titles, each deals with a particular subject, with the Law of Property Act 1925 occupying a central position in the scheme of reform. Various amendments have been made to these Acts since 1925, but they will be mentioned later when the particular matters to which they refer are dealt with. The Land Charges Act 1925, as amended, has now been consolidated in the Land Charges Act 1972 and the Local Land Charges Act 1975.

The general manner of interpretation of the Acts was discussed by the House of Lords in *Grey* v. *Inland Revenue Commissioners* [1960] A.C. 1, at p. 13. Although they are consolidating Acts, and the presumption is that consolidating Acts do not change the law, this presumption does not apply because they consolidate Acts which were themselves amending Acts. Accordingly the Acts of 1925, like the Acts of 1922 and 1924, must be construed simply so as to give each word 'the meaning proper to it in its context'.

The Acts achieved the following general effects: the final emasculation of the doctrine of tenures; the closer approximation of land law with the law of personalty; the reduction in number of legal estates in land; the extension of the systems of registration of charges and registration of title; and the abrogation of miscellaneous outmoded rules.

The final emasculation of the doctrine of tenures

As explained in Chapter 1, apart from leaseholds, there is now only one tenure, socage. This was achieved by the Administration of Estates Act 1925 (s. 56), which abolished frankalmoign, already a dead letter, and the Law of Property Act 1922 (s. 128), which enfranchised all copyhold land by converting it into socage tenure. The other forms of tenure had already been abolished long before 1926. It has already been explained that, since the conditions and services on which land might be held had disappeared, and therefore land could not be claimed by the Crown for their non-performance, tenure is now obsolete and land may be considered as being susceptible to absolute ownership. It has been mentioned, however, that there are a few exceptional cases where incidents remain today. These must now be dealt with.

Some of the conditions or 'incidents' subject to which copyhold land was held before 1926 were, unlike other tenures, still very valuable either to the person who held the land or to the person of whom it was held. To have abolished all these peremptorily would have been an unjust act of confiscation. Some were extinguished at once and others were allowed to continue for a few more years, and all have now disappeared. The Act provided for the payment of compensation where appropriate. A third class, however, was allowed to continue permanently unless the persons entitled to the benefit and burden of the incidents agreed in writing in particular cases to discharge them upon payment of compensation. This class comprises

(1) Any commonable right such as a right of pasture attached to the enfranchised land. Thus if such a right existed over other land in favour of copyhold land before 1926, it continues today, despite enfranchisement, until otherwise agreed between the parties.
(2) Any rights or liabilities existing in favour of or against the land in respect of mines, minerals, or rights of entry and way to win or search for minerals. The minerals in question may be under the enfranchised land or other land.
(3) Any liability of the enfranchized land to incidents in respect of fairs, markets, hunting or the taking of game, fish and fowl.
(4) Any right or liability in favour of or against the enfranchised land relating to the construction, maintenance or cleansing of any dykes, ditches, canals, sea or river walls, ways and other works for the protection of land or preventing nuisances on them.

It should not be assumed, whenever rights and liabilities of the types mentioned above are met, that the land concerned was necessarily copyhold before 1926. Such rights may be created by landowners by ordinary private negotiation, in which case the Act does not apply. It only applies to these rights and liabilities when they are attributable to the fact that the land was once copyhold.

These are the only substantial remnants of the doctrine of tenure. Detached and inconsequential rootlets may still be unearthed which have a curiosity value (see 51 L.Q.R. 347 and 361 and *Re Lowe's W.T.* [1973] 2 All E.R. 1136). We may now put the whole question of tenure to bed in the following way. All land in England may be absolutely owned. The only vestige of tenure is that there may be certain rights and liabilities, as described above, attaching to land which used to be copyhold. Enquiry must be made when buying land. There is now no question of land being forfeited as a result of them, though, of course, like any other legal liability, they must be observed.

The further approximation of land law to the law of personalty

Land law, so important in feudal society, developed precociously in comparison with other branches of law. But early development sometimes means early obsolescence and English land law in the nineteenth century still betrayed its feudal origins, whereas the law of personal property wore a more modern aspect. However, one part of land law, the law of leaseholds, developing later and outside feudal influence, refected more of the modern rules. Indeed, even today, leaseholds are classified as personalty, though this strange classification merely reflects their historical origin and its implications do not go very deep. It is important mainly for descriptive purposes. Thus a gift by will of 'all my personal property' will carry land held by the testator on a lease. It does not mean that a leaseholder has a merely personal or contractual right to the land. Emphatically he has a real right, good against the whole world.

Complete identity of land law with the law of personalty is hardly possible considering the difference in subject-matter, but the 1925 legislation represents the culmination of the attempt to go as far in that direction as possible. The following steps were taken, although the significance of some of these may not be fully appreciated at this early stage of study.

(1) *Descent on intestacy*. For centuries before 1926 a man had been able to dispose of land as well as personalty by will as he chose. Yet the destination of the two types of property differed if he died intestate. Personal property was distributed amongst the next of kin, which included a range of close relations, though the spouse and children were preferred. In the case of land, excluding leaseholds, special rules of inheritance, which were feudal in origin but developed by common law and statute, dictated that it should descend upon the 'heir', a technical term which should never be used loosely. Suffice it to say here that they usually favoured the eldest son to the exclusion of all others including the wife and younger children of the deceased.

Section 46 of the Administration of Estates Act 1925, as later amended, now applies a new code of distribution on intestacy to realty and personalty alike. It takes account of the close relations and in particular the surviving spouse and children. In the absence of such relations, property goes to the Crown as *bona vacantia*. The rules of inheritance, however, have been retained to govern the intestate succession to the entail (which interest will be described later), in deference to the traditions of aristocratic families who have employed entails in order to keep land descending to a single owner instead of being divided.

(2) *Methods of mortgaging the fee simple and the term of years*. Mortgages of both types of interest are now carried out by conveying a term of years to the lender of the money as a security for the debt (L.P.A. 1925, ss.85 and 86). In the case of a mortgage of a term of years this is achieved by creating a sub-lease, which is a term of years granted by the owner of a term of years and which is of less duration than the term he himself owns. The mortgage of a fee simple is carried out by granting the lender a term of, say, 3,000 years, while the mortgage of a term of, say, 100 years' duration is effected by granting the lender a sub-term of, say, 99 years and fifty-one weeks. A new alternative method of mortgaging land called a 'charge by way of legal mortgage' is now possible under the Act and applies to mortgages both of the fee simple and of the term of years. This new method has gradually supplanted the mortgage by grant of a term of years. Before 1926 the fee simple was mortgaged by conveying the fee simple itself to the lender as a security until repayment of the debt.

(3) *Personalty can now be entailed.* Before 1926 an entail could not be created in leasehold or other personal property. It may now be created in any form of property (L.P.A. 1925, s.130). Here, therefore, the older law provided the example for reform.

(4) *General abolition of the need for words of limitation.* When a fee simple or entail was conveyed by deed before 1926, special technical words, known as 'words of limitation', had to be used. A mistake could mean that the interest would fail to pass. In the transfer of other forms of property, what mattered was the intention of the grantor as gathered from the words used; no special form of words was necessary. Section 60 (1) of the Law of Property Act 1925 provides that words of limitation are no longer necessary and that, on a conveyance of freehold land, the fee simple or other whole interest which the grantor had power to convey shall pass unless the contrary intention appears. The old strict rules have however been retained for the entail.

The reduction of legal estates to two

The difficulties caused by splitting the legal fee simple were considered in the previous chapter. Where land was granted 'to *A* for life with remainder in fee simple to *B*', there was no person for the time being independently capable of selling the absolute ownership of the land. The difficulties could be overcome however by conveying the fee simple to trustees with a direction or power to sell and to allow *A* and *B* to take equivalent benefits from the purchase money.

The policy of the 1925 legislation was to make it impossible to split the legal fee simple, so that the absolute ownership would always be available for sale. Accordingly s.1(1) of the Law of Property Act 1925, elemental in modern land law, enacts

> The only estates in land which are capable of subsisting or of being conveyed or created at law are:—
> (a) An estate in fee simple absolute in possession;
> (b) A term of years absolute.

So far as rights to the land itself are concerned, all others such as life interests, entails and even fees simple not in possession (such as *B*'s in the example above) may only exist in equity. The term of years absolute will be dealt with later, but the result is that there is always a fee simple presently available for sale in any land.

The part played by the Settled Land Act 1925 may be illustrated by referring again to the example above. The legal fee simple absolute in possession is held by a trustee in trust for *A* for life and for *B* in fee simple. Both *A*'s and *B*'s interests are equitable. This trustee holds and can, if desirable, sell what a prospective purchaser will want to buy—the absolute ownership. If a sale occurs, these equitable interests are satisfied out of the purchase money and no longer affect the land in the hands of the purchaser. They are overreached. The doctrine of overreaching was thus extended as a necessary corollary to the reduction in legal estates that may exist. Such a simplification of the law was achieved at a price. It clearly means that when land is settled there is no guarantee that the beneficiaries will enjoy the land in specie.

The Law of Property Act 1925, s.1(1) only refers to rights to the land itself. Certain rights in or over the land of another which may still exist both as legal and equitable interests are listed in subs.(2). Easements are an example.

These interests, however, may not be legal unless they are created to endure for the equivalent of a fee simple absolute or a term of years; that is, they must be perpetual or for a definite time. Thus an easement to last for a lifetime must be equitable, while one to endure for ten years may be legal. As a matter of terminology, it is convenient to call the two rights in land named in subs. (1) 'estates' and all other rights to the land itself, necessarily equitable, together with all rights in or over the land of another, whether legal or equitable, 'interests'. An easement to last 100 years, therefore, is a legal interest; a right to occupy land for life is an equitable interest. The Act does not however stick scrupulously to this nomenclature. Finally, while the only estates which can be legal are the two in subs (1), the Act does not say they must necessarily be legal. Both may be equitable. Thus a fee simple absolute in possession may be held by trustees on trust for *A* absolutely, in which case *A* will have an equitable fee simple absolute in possession.

Section 1 is fundamental to a mastery of modern land law. It must be applied word for word with the utmost rigour. If this is done it will be found to be a wonderful guide. Its implications are never contradictory.

Development of a system of registration of land charges

One weakness of an equitable interest is that it does not bind a purchaser in good faith for value of a legal estate in the land without notice of the equitable interest. A legal interest is, however, enforceable against all. In establishing whether a person had notice of an equitable interest the courts employed tests which were difficult to apply. These rules were somewhat modified by statute. Notice could be of three kinds, namely: 'actual notice', 'constructive notice', or 'imputed notice'.

'Actual notice' is almost self-explanatory. It simply means that the purchaser knows of the equitable interest. This knowledge however must be from a source sufficiently authentic to 'operate upon the mind of any rational man or man of business and make him act with reference to the knowledge he has acquired' (*Lloyd* v. *Banks* (1868), 3 Ch.App. 488, at p.491). Statements made in casual conversation, therefore, do not impart actual notice. Even though a person has no actual notice, however, the circumstances may affect him with constructive notice.

'Constructive notice' is knowledge which would have been revealed 'if such inquiries and inspections had been made as ought reasonably to have been made' (L.P.A. 1925, s.199). Thus a purchaser has constructive notice of all rights which would have come to light if he had investigated the title to land for the period specified by the law for those cases where the parties to the transaction have not agreed otherwise. This period is a minimum of fifteen years (L.P.A. 1925, s.44, as amended by L.P.A. 1969, s.23). A prudent purchaser should inspect the land as well as the vendor's title to it. The presence of a tenant might well be notice of the tenant's interest, whether he inspects the land or not. Of course, a tenant's interest will often be a legal one in any case and so will not be susceptible to the doctrine now under discussion. In short, the rules as to constructive notice prevent a purchaser merely turning a blind eye so as to escape actual notice. On the other hand, the restricted form in which s.199 of the Law of Property Act 1925, is expressed suggests that the doctrine will not be further expanded.

'Imputed notice' is the actual or constructive notice which an agent acting for a purchaser in that transaction receives in his capacity as agent (L.P.A. 1925, s.199). Knowledge gained in this way by a solicitor acting for me in the purchase of a house, for instance, will be deemed to be notice to me. If an agent acts for both parties in a transaction, such notice to the agent is normally imputed to both parties to the transaction.

Although these tests are based on sound ethical foundations, and have worked justly in many cases, they do lack precision and certainty. The Land Charges Act 1925, therefore introduced what was virtually a new system of safeguarding certain rights in land, and where it applies it dispenses with these tests. A state register—the 'Land Charges Register'—was opened, and the registration of certain eligible interests in it is deemed to constitute notice to the whole world (L.P.A. 1925, s.198). For instance, if a restrictive covenant was imposed on my neighbour's land before the Act, preventing him from building, and this covenant was intended to protect the amenities of my land, the covenant amounts to an interest of mine in the land of another, my neighbour. As we shall see later, it is an equitable interest. If my neighbour sells his fee simple to *P*, who gives value and has no notice of the covenant, *P* will take the land free of it and may therefore build upon it. Generally *P*'s notice will come from an inspection of the title deeds.

If, however, the covenant had been made after the Act, I could register it. Such registration would constitute permanent notice of my interest to all, so that no one will be able to buy my neighbour's land free of the covenant. Prospective purchasers of land, therefore, always search at the Land Charges Registry before completing a purchase. The request for a search is a simple process which may be carried out entirely by post for a small fee. Even if a purchaser does not carry out a search, he is nevertheless deemed to have notice of any entries against the land on the register. On the other hand, if a registrable interest is not registered a purchaser will not be prejudiced by his own knowledge of that interest. We may therefore say that the fact of registration or non-registration at the time of the completion of purchase is conclusive as to notice.

In this way, precision and certainty were achieved, for whether an interest is registered or not permits no argument. They were gained, however, at the cost of some ethical principle, for it is now possible to take unscrupulous advantage of a person's carelessness in failing to register an interest. The process and effects of registration will be dealt with when the particular registrable interests are discussed, and a more comprehensive account will be given separately in Chapter 17. But the following matters must be mentioned at this stage. Firstly, not all equitable interests are registrable and in these cases the old doctrine as to notice continues to apply, unless the interest is one which can be overreached, such as a life interest under a settlement. Equitable interests under a trust like this do not need the protection of the register because the Acts dealing with trusts provide their own special protection. We have already seen that a purchaser may take land free of such interests even though he knows of them, for they may be overreached and transferred to the purchase-money.

Secondly, a few legal rights are now registrable. Legal rights were always secure whether a purchaser of land knew of them or not, so that the system of registration was applied here not as a substitute for an existing doctrine of notice, but in order to provide a prospective purchaser with readily accessible information about third-party rights of which he might otherwise be unaware. Since the results of failing to register those legal rights which are registrable are similar to the results of failing to register eligible equitable interests, the position of such legal interests has been weakened by the Act. As failure to register them may result in a purchaser of the land taking free of them, this newly imposed risk might be considered a sharp incentive for the owners of such interests to make their existence known to the unwary purchaser through registration.

Finally, the Land Charges Act 1925, even created variations in the concept of the purchaser of the legal estate for value without notice. Sometimes the purchaser must take a legal estate in the land in order to take free of an unregistered interest; sometimes it is enough that he purchases any interest in the land, legal or equitable. Sometimes the price he pays must be 'valuable consideration'; sometimes it must be 'money or money's worth'. The application of these formulae will be considered later when the various registrable interests are being discussed.

'Money or money's worth' means all forms of consideration and also the payment of an existing debt. The consideration, however, need not represent the full value of the interest purchased. The consideration of marriage is not included. 'Valuable consideration' is a wider term including all that is meant by 'money or money's worth' together with the consideration of a future marriage. When a future marriage is the consideration given it is deemed to have been given not only by the parties to it, but also by the issue, as, for instance, grandchildren (*Macdonald* v. *Scott* [1893] A.C. 642, per Lord Herschell, L.C., at p.650).

The purchaser can be affected by a registration entered at any time before completion of the purchase. A purchase is not completed until the interest is finally transferred to the purchase and, where the consideration consists of money or other payment, this has been paid over.

The further development of the system of registration of title

The Land Registration Act 1925, continued and developed the policy, begun in the last century, of applying by degrees the system of registration of title to the whole country. At this point the opportunity will be taken of giving a most elementary account of conveyancing, firstly because it is necessary to an understanding of land law in any case, and, secondly, so that the new system of registered conveyancing may be appreciated.

Conveyancing is the transfer of interests in land. The study of conveyancing concerns the various methods of transferring these interests, the precautions that should be taken before they are purchased, and their protection after purchase. Ordinary chattels may be transferred from one person to another simply by delivery. Interests in land, however, are transferred by words. Sometimes these words must be contained in a deed under seal but sometimes mere writing or even oral words may be enough. Let us take the common cause of the transfer of a fee simple from *A* to *B*. All that is necessary is that a deed should be written stating '*A* hereby conveys unto *B* "Blackacre" in fee simple'. *A* then executes the conveyance by putting his name to it with a seal and delivers it to *B*, whereupon the property passes. In practice, of course, the deed contains other information for the purposes of clarity, such as the full names and addresses of the parties, an accurate description of the property, the date, the purchase price and, preferably, a ground plan. Other matters are frequently added because they are part of the arrangement agreed between the parties. In short, while a conveyance primarily passes property, it may also be the occasion for other transactions and declarations.

Before *B* commits himself to buying the land, however, he will wish to be sure of two things. Firstly he will require proof that the fee simple is *A*'s to sell, for even though *A* is living in the property he may only own a life interest or a lease. Secondly, he must know whether there are any third-party rights already existing in or over the land, such as an easement. To a lesser extent, the same may apply when a chattel is purchased, but in that case much greater assumptions are made. If a person is in possession of a chattel and states that he owns it, then, unless there is positive ground for suspicion, you readily accept that he is owner. As for third-party rights over chattels, these are uncommon and may, in ordinary circumstances, be discounted. You cannot, for instance, have a right of way over a grandfather clock, and even if it is used as security for a debt, the creditor will not usually allow the owner to remain in possession of it.

Therefore what *B* will insist on seeing, before he buys the land from *A*, is proof that it was conveyed in the past to *A* by a conveyance and, to dispel doubt as to whether even the person who conveyed it to *A* owned it himself, a complete record of all the conveyances up to that time for such a period as to raise an irrebuttable inference that *A* really owns the land. Considering that the Limitation Act 1980, and similar statutes in the past, place a time limit on the recovery of land by a true owner, a purchaser does not really need to investigate the title, as outlined above, over a very long period. The vendor and purchaser can agree whatever period of investigation they like, but unless they agree otherwise the period is fifteen years (L.P.A. 1969, s.23). This minimum period, however, must commence with some particular transaction called the 'root of title' so that in practice the period investigated might be considerably greater. As *B* also wishes to know of all third-party rights in or over the land he will make a search at the Land Charges Registry and will also wish to know the full contents of the deeds, but as noticed above, some rights in land are acquired even without writing, and do not require registration. *B* must therefore ask searching questions of *A* as to the existence of these.

Finally, there are many restrictions on land use which are imposed under statutory authority. Local authorities have power to refuse permission for developing land, to purchase property compulsorily and to require living accommodation to conform to certain standards. These matters are discussed in Chapter 4. A purchaser of land will wish to discover the extent of such restrictions before entering any agreement. Many such restrictions can be discovered by arranging for a search in the local land charges register which is maintained by the local district council. Such 'local searches' will be accompanied by a questionnaire seeking information about such matters as responsibility for maintenance of roads adjoining the property, proposals for new roads in the vicinity, town and country planning decisions, proximity of sewers, building regulations, slum clearance plans and smoke control.

In regard to the inspection of the deeds, *A* does not simply hand them over to *B* for inspection, for *B* might use them for a fraudulent purpose. Instead, *A* will summarize the contents of all the deeds in an 'abstract of title', which is a kind of pedigree of the land. Before completing the purchase, *B* will check the accuracy of the abstract against the deeds and will take possession not only of the deed of conveyance to him from *A*, but also of all the earlier deeds and other documents.

The following example may help to illustrate the main process in a conveyance of the fee simple in 'Blackacre', which is unregistered land. First we will set out the modern history of the land by showing the transactions that have occurred

1920	*A* conveys 'Blackacre' to *B*	Deed 1
1930	*B* conveys 'Blackacre' to *C*	Deed 2
(*C* makes a restrictive covenant in favour of *B*)		
1950	*C* conveys 'Blackacre' to *D*	Deed 3
1971	*D* conveys 'Blackacre' to *E*	Deed 4
1975	*E* conveys 'Blackacre' to *F*	Deed 5

G now wishes in 1983 to buy 'Blackacre' from *F* for £20,000. In very broad outline this is how he goes about it:

He sees the land advertised, decides he would like it and approaches *F*, who says that he will accept £20,000 for it. Such an agreement is not made binding at that moment, but is simply a settlement of price. *G* and *F* now instruct their solicitors to act. The principal stages thereafter are as follows

(1) A search is made of the Land Registry index map to ensure that the title really is unregistered, for if the title to the land is registered, a different system of conveyancing is followed, as we shall shortly see. This is explained in Chapter 18 and need not detain us now.
(2) An application for a mortgage will be made to a building society if *G* needs a loan.
(3) A list of fairly standard questions ('Enquiries Before Contract') are sent to *F*'s solicitor. The questions seek general information regarding boundaries, insurance policies, drainage and other services, shared facilities, adverse rights, fixtures, outgoings, possible completion date and other matters not likely to be revealed by searches and other enquiries mentioned later.
(4) The land should be visited and inspected. Professional inspection of buildings will be required by building societies before they advance money.
(5) A 'local search' is made together with enquiries of the district council.
(6) A search is made at the Land Charges Registry by the purchaser's solicitor.
(7) *F*'s solicitor draws up a draft contract and sends it to *G*'s solicitor for approval. Most contracts for the sort of transactions we are considering here are in one of several standard forms, such as the Law Society's Conditions of Sale. These provide for such matters as the obligation of *F* to prove title, the deposit on purchase price, completion date, apportionment of outgoings, delivery of preliminary documents, date from which proof of title shall commence and other specially added conditions which the vendor wishes to impose.
(8) If there is nothing in the answers to all the enquiries, searches and the terms of the draft contract to deter *G*, then the draft contract may be approved. Note carefully, however, that this does not yet signify the existence of a contract—merely that the terms are acceptable. A purchaser should

never enter a contract until he has money available to finance the purchase price. Generally this means that the building society must have approved his application for a loan and, if he wishes to sell his present home, that the prospective purchaser has contracted to buy that property.

(9) Assuming satisfactory responses to all *G*'s enquiries and applications, and that *F* is likewise ready to proceed, both parties may now sign their duplicate parts of the contract. When these are delivered to each other's solicitors, the contract is binding, provided that *F* can prove title to the land. Thus the parties are bound to buy and to sell; yet time is allowed for further work preparatory to sale. Upon exchange of contracts the purchaser generally pays 10 per cent of the purchase price as deposit. The abstract of title is now delivered by *F*'s solicitor to *G*'s solicitor. Unless otherwise agreed, *F* must show fifteen years' history of the land's title ending with the conveyance to himself and beginning with a good root of title. The links in that title must be continuous. Since the proof of title must start with some transaction, on most occasions more than fifteen years of ownership will be shown. In the present case, *F* may start with the 1950 conveyance. He must show how the land passed from *C* to *D*, from *D* to *E*, and from *E* to himself. If his proof simply showed the land passing from *C* to *D* and then from *D* to *E*, but no more, it would be unacceptable. He does all this by summarizing these deeds in the abstract. He must also provide full information about the restrictive covenant even though it was entered into in 1930, for this will still be binding. Although it was initially entered into in 1930, a recital of its existence will probably be given in subsequent conveyances. If it was registered, as it should have been, under the Land Charges Act 1925, *G* will have to accept the burden of it. He will not be surprised by it because the preliminary investigations mentioned above will have revealed it. Such a matter should have been mentioned in the draft contract.

The establishment of contractual obligations by the exchange of signed duplicates can cause problems of timing in land transactions. Frequently nowadays 'chain transactions' demand a sharper definition of the time of acceptance of an offer. A chain transaction occurs when *P* is willing to buy 'Blackacre' once he possesses a signed acceptance for the purchase of his present home, 'Pinkacre'; and *V* is only willing to sell 'Blackacre' when he has a signed acceptance of his offer to buy 'Violetacre'. Such chains can involve several persons in regard to the properties of both the vendor and purchaser. It is clear that the whole line of vendors and purchasers can only safely conclude contracts when all are satisfied that their immediate vendors and purchasers are also ready to commit themselves to contractual obligations.

Where contract exchange depends upon the ordinary principle of 'last postage', there might be a failure by one party to post, thus causing a failure of contract. Meanwhile another party might have committed himself by postal acceptance. Such a person might be obliged to sell, but is legally incapable of buying, thus becoming homeless. To avoid such catastrophes the law has developed the refinement of 'telephonic' exchanges which avoids this problem. The problem and its partial resolution are fully explained in *Domb* v. *Isoz* [1980] 2 W.L.R. 565.

(10) *G*'s solicitor might now ask further questions by way of clarification of the title ('Requisitions on Title'). The abstract might, for instance, have shown a certain person as 'Florence White' in one transaction and as 'Florence Black' in another. The explanation will probably be that she married John Black at

some time between the two transactions. The matter must however be cleared up.

(11) If all matters of title appear to be in order the solicitors for both parties will arrange for completion on a certain day. The purchaser's solicitor will repeat his search at the Land Charges Registry shortly beforehand. The significance of this is explained in Chapter 17.

(12) *G*'s solicitor meanwhile will have prepared a draft of the proposed conveyance. We will assume that this has been approved by *F*'s solicitor and that *G*'s solicitor has 'engrossed' the draft, that is typed it in final form on durable paper.

(13) On completion day, *G*'s solicitor will visit the office of *F*'s solicitor. The deed of conveyance transferring the ownership from *F* to *G*, which has been executed by *F*, is handed over in return for the purchase-money or the balance if part of the purchase-money was paid by way of deposit when the contract was completed. Thus another deed and link in the continuous chain of title is added and will be used in the future as the final link when *G* sells the land. The deed of mortgage will also have been prepared for this occasion. For the sake of simplicity explanation of this will be delayed until the mortgage is discussed in Chapter 15. Besides this deed conveying the land from *F* to *G* all the other deeds and documents relevant to the title are handed over to *G*'s solicitor. You will notice that *F* did not need some of the deeds, namely deeds 1 and 2, in order to prove his title. One of these, however, contains the restrictive covenant and is therefore of use for an indefinite period. It is clear, nevertheless, that some deeds become unnecessary as proof of title to land, as is the case with deed 1 here. The transaction is thus completed and *G* may enter the property.

The above account will suggest some of the shortcomings of this system. While new links in the title are being added at one end as transactions take place, and links at the early end gradually become redundant, nevertheless, on successive sales substantially the same documents are repeatedly investigated by different solicitors. This is wasteful of time and money. Furthermore, the purchaser's solicitor has to glean the information he requires in a cumbersome way and from various sources. Finally, proof of title through documents held in private custody is a system which might lend itself to fraud.

For these reasons a new system of conveyancing has been introduced and will gradually be extended to all parts of the country. This policy was begun in Acts going back to the middle of the last century, but, apart from the London area, little momentum was gained until the Land Registration Act 1925, came into force. Only a basic outline of the system need be considered here.

In those areas where registration has become compulsory, the fee simple must be registered on its first sale following the introduction of registration. Thus, in the example above, if *G* is required to register his title, he would do this after investigation and purchase in the ordinary way, by submitting the documents of title to the Land Registry where the title is inspected for the last time. If this is satisfactory to the Registry then the land is given a title number for identification and is placed on a register in the name of *G*. A certificate is then sent to *G* which henceforth constitutes his sole document of title to the land. The deeds are cancelled by the Registry. The state now guarantees the title, and any future conveyances of the land will be by a simple form of transfer. No investigation of title is necessary. All that is required is an inspection of the register to check who owns the land. The Registry not only records a person's right to the land itself, but also certain rights of other persons in or over the land. In this latter respect the Land Registry takes over the functions of the Land Charges Registry where registered land is concerned. In short, the Land Charges Registry is only used for registering rights in or over the land the title to which has not been registered. It may be mentioned here that while the Land Charges Registry is at Plymouth, the Land Registry has its headquarters at Lincoln's Inn Fields but it operates from various branch offices throughout the country.

While the system represents a considerable improvement in the method of transferring land, it must not be assumed that it is a perfect one. Some interests, for example, are not registrable, and a purchaser must still make an inspection of the land and search in the local land charges register. Indeed, it possesses many complexities of its own. It must be stressed that the Land Registration Act does not, where it is in operation, change land law. It merely facilitates the mode of transfer of interests in land. It does not affect the nature of those interests. The system is discussed in more detail in Chapter 18. There we shall see that leasehold title to land can also be registered.

The abrogation of miscellaneous outmoded rules

The 1925 legislation abolished a considerable number of rules which could not justify their place in modern land law and which in some cases produced unexpected and unfair results. To describe these rules would be contrary to the spirit of that legislation, which in this instance was to bury. Walk over the cemetery therefore by all means but there is no need to dig into the graves. Here we shall not even remove the moss from the headstones to reveal the names, but shall pass on.

We are shortly to proceed to a detailed study of the interests which give a right to the land itself. Before that, however, it is necessary to describe the meaning of a word which, up to this point, has been taken for granted, that is, the very subject-matter of these interests—'land'.

Study material: Law of Property Act, section 1 (as amended)

Legal estates and equitable interests

1.—(1) The only estates in land which are capable of subsisting or of being conveyed or created at law are—

(a) An estate in fee simple absolute in possession;
(b) A term of years absolute.

(2) The only interests or charges in or over land which are capable of subsisting or of being conveyed or created at law are—

(a) An easement, right, or privilege in or over land for an interest equivalent to an estate in fee simple absolute in possession or a term of years absolute;
(b) A rentcharge in possession issuing out of or charged on land being either perpetual or for a term of years absolute;
(c) A charge by way of legal mortgage;
(d) . . . and any other similar charge on land which is not created by an instrument;

(e) Rights of entry exercisable over or in respect of a legal term of years absolute, or annexed, for any purpose, to a legal rentcharge.

(3) All other estates, interests, and charges in or over land take affect as equitable interests.

(4) The estates, interests, and charges which under this section are authorised to subsist or to be conveyed or created at law are (when subsisting or conveyed or created at law) in this Act referred to as "legal estates", and have the same incidents as legal estates subsisting at the commencement of this Act; and the owner of a legal estate is referred to as "an estate owner" and his legal estate is referred to as his estate.

(5) A legal estate may subsist concurrently with or subject to any other legal estate in the same land in like manner as it could have done before the commencement of this Act.

(6) A legal estate is not capable of subsisting or of being created in an undivided share in land or of being held by an infant.

(7) Every power of appointment over, or power to convey or charge land or any interest therein, whether created by a statute or other instrument or implied by law, and whether created before or after the commencement of this Act (not being a power vested in a legal mortgagee or an estate owner in right of his estate and exercisable by him or by another person in his name and on his behalf), operates only in equity.

(8) Estates, interests, and charges in or over land which are not legal estates are in this Act referred to as "equitable interests", and powers which by this Act are to operate in equity only are in this Act referred to as "equitable powers".

(9) The provisions in any statute or other instrument requiring land to be conveyed to uses shall take effect as directions that the land shall (subject to creating or reserving thereout any legal estate authorised by this Act which may be required) be conveyed to a person of full age upon the requisite trusts.

(10) The repeal of the Statute of Uses (as amended) does not affect the operation thereof in regard to dealings taking effect before the commencement of this Act.

Questions

1 *Discuss the significance of the words 'personalty' as applied to leaseholds interests.*

2 *What was the general effect of the Administration of Estates Act 1925 upon the law of intestacy?*

3 *How did the Land Charges Act 1925 facilitate the sale of land?*

4 *Why does a sale of land demand more preliminary investigations than a sale of chattels?*

5 *What is meant by a good 'root of title'?*

6 *What are the principal disadvantages of the unregistered system of conveyancing?*

Chapter Three

The meaning of land

THE PRINCIPAL MESSAGE of this chapter is simple to state though difficult to apply. The meaning of the word 'land' is not fixed but varies according to the context in which it is found.

The appellate courts frequently find that words have been misinterpreted by judges at first instance. Such misinterpretations are not necessarily 'mistakes'. They might merely show a divergence in policy between one judge and another. This is particularly so with words in new statutes, where the first tracks of precedent are being put down. Sensitivity to the meaning of recently enacted words is thus built up.

The word 'land' has been appearing in a host of statutes, cases, wills, deeds, contracts and other transactions for centuries. Lawyers therefore should have achieved considerable knowledge of it. Before proceeding further, let us examine a modern decision of the Court of Appeal.

The facts of *Cedar Holdings Ltd.* v. *Green* [1979] 3 W.L.R. 31 were as follows. *H* and *W*, husband and wife, were joint owners of their home. After their divorce, *H* wished to mortgage the house and, by concealing the interest of *W*, appropriate all the loan proceeds. He therefore represented another woman, *X*, as being *W*. *H* and *X* thus purported to mortgage the house to *M* as a security for a loan. *M* later sought a declaration that the house was subject to a mortgage of *H*'s share in the property. It was conceded that the total interest in the house had not been effectively mortgaged because *X*, however convincing the deception, could not mortgage, sell or give away that which she did not own. That is a brute fact of property law, subject to very few exceptions. Therefore, the question really in issue was whether *H*, though failing in his scheme to mortgage the total interest, had at least mortgaged his half-share. This was really a matter of intention, since he clearly was capable of dealing with his very own share.

In an attempt to prove this intention, s. 63(1) of the Law of Property Act 1925 was invoked. This reads as follows

> Every conveyance is effectual to pass all the estate, right, title, interest, claim, and demand which the conveying parties respectively have, in, to, or on the property conveyed, or expressed or intended so to be, or which they respectively have power to convey in, to, or on the same.

A conveyance includes a mortgage.

The crucial part of the judgment of Buckley L.J. on page 38 at D reads as follows

> In my judgment, upon the true construction of section 63 a beneficial interest in the proceeds of the sale of land held upon the statutory trusts is not an interest in that land within the meaning of the section and a

> conveyance of that land is not effectual to pass a beneficial interest in the proceeds of sale.

We shall see in Chapter 11 that interests in co-owned property are not interests in 'land' but interests in 'personalty'. This arises from a fictional, but sometimes useful, doctrine of equity. But the significant point is that Buckley L.J. refers to 'land'. Yet that word is not mentioned in section 63; instead 'property' appears. That would not matter if the two words were synonyms, but they are not. The definition of land in section 205 of the Act expressly excludes co-owned property by the insertion of 'but not an undivided share in land'. This, uncontroversially, alludes to co-ownership. However, the definition of 'property' in the same section includes 'anything in action and any interest in real or personal property'. It is also uncontroversial that 'personal property' may include interests in co-owned property. All this will become clearer after co-ownership has been studied.

The only matter presently demonstrated is that a judge of the Court of Appeal assimilated 'land' with 'property', where both words possessed immediately relevant available and different definitions.

Following this caution, the next part of this chapter will be devoted to explaining why it is important to know whether a particular entity is land or not, and the second part to discussing how such a decision is reached.

The significance of the word 'land'

The Law of Property Act 1925, section 40 (I)

This provides that

> no action may be brought upon any contract for the sale or other disposition of land or any interest in land, unless the agreement upon which such action is brought, or some memorandum or note thereof, is in writing, and signed by the party to be charged or by some other person thereunto by him lawfully authorized.

The next subsection then adds, however, that this 'does not affect the law relating to part performance or sales by the court'.

This rule was originally created by the Statute of Frauds 1677, upon which some of the leading cases were decided. Its purpose is to present fraudulent claims based upon supposed oral agreements.

Once given that the subject-matter in question is 'land', then any contract for its sale or other disposition is caught by the section. 'Other disposition' includes a lease or a mortgage. It applies not only to contracts for disposing of existing interests, but also to contracts for creating new ones. So if I agree to grant an easement over my land in favour of my neighbour, we must ensure that the agreement is evidenced in writing. So long as a sufficient memorandum comes into being at some time before any action is brought upon the contract (*Lucas* v. *Dixon* (1889), 22 Q.B.D. 357), the section is satisfied. Thus, a recital, in a post-nuptial settlement, of an agreement made before marriage was held to be sufficient in *Re Holland* [1902] 2 Ch. 360. Furthermore, as Stirling L.J., added, 'the note need not be given for valuable consideration nor have any particular form' (at p. 383). The courts have accepted a will, a letter and an affidavit as evidence and indeed the memorandum may be made quite inadvertently.

On the other hand, it must contain all the main terms of the contract, including a description of the property, sufficient identification of the parties, the nature of the interest and of the consideration and any other terms of importance and be signed by the party to be charged or his agent. An unimportant term which is missing from the memorandum may be waived by the plaintiff if it is for his benefit only (*Hawkins* v. *Price* [1947] Ch. 645). Whether the converse is true, so that he may acquiesce in the insertion of an unevidenced term which is solely for the benefit of the defendant, is controversial. In *Martin* v. *Pycroft* (1852), 2 De G.M. & G. 785, the section was held to be no bar when the plaintiff offered to pay a premium on a lease when this premium had not been evidenced in writing. This decision has been followed (see *Scott* v. *Bradley* [1971] 1 All E.R. 583). A discussion of conflicting cases may be found at 67 L.Q.R. 299.

While the memorandum must be an accurate and unambiguous record, it is enough that it provides a formula or key which enables a particular term to be ascertained by oral evidence. This formula, however, must be such that it renders identification a merely mechanical process and leaves no room for real doubt. In *Plant* v. *Bourne* [1897] 2 Ch. 281, the land was described in the memorandum as '24 acres of land at Totmonslow in the parish of Draycott'. This was held to satisfy the section on proof that only twenty-four acres of land were owned by the vendor at that place. If such a key is provided, therefore, it must be capable of opening only one door. This was stressed in *Coombs* v. *Wilkes* [1891] 3 Ch. 77, where the vendor's name was missing and he was merely described as the 'landlord', which did not conclusively point to the defendant. In the same way, the description 'vendor' may not unequivocally point to one person, for a sale of property may, in some circumstances, be carried out by a mortgagee of that property, as well as by its proprietor.

Two or more documents may be joined to form a complete memorandum. Parol evidence may be given to identify a document expressly referred to in another, so long as one of them is signed, and may also be permitted to identify a document the existence of which is clearly implied in the signed document. Parol evidence is not admissible, however, to explain the link between two or more documents (*Timmins* v. *Moreland Street Property Co. Ltd.* [1958] Ch. 110, an important case. See also *Griffiths* v. *Young* [1970] 3 All E.R. 601). Thus, if a memorandum of a contract of sale is typed with a carbon copy, as in *Stokes* v. *Whicher* [1920] 1 Ch. 411, and the vendor and purchaser each sign a different part of this duplicate record, the very existence of the carbon may suggest and then identify the top copy, so that the two may be read together as one.

The only signature necessary is that of the defendant, or his agent, and the word 'signed' has been loosely construed. The signature may appear in any position and may be printed or even in the form of initials. On the other hand, it must have been written by way of authentication, and the fact that the defendant happens to have written his name as part of the narrative of the transaction is insufficient.

Although a memorandum may be effective even though it was made quite inadvertently, it cannot constitute evidence to satisfy the section if it denies the very existence of a contract (*Thirkell* v. *Cambi* [1919] 2 K.B. 590). Two modern cases, however, conflict on whether the memorandum must not only evidence the contents of the agreement but also the very existence of it.

In *Law* v. *Jones* [1973] 2 All E.R. 437 the Court of Appeal held, Russell, L.J., dissenting, that, assuming an oral agreement has been concluded and that there is sufficient evidence of the contents of its terms, the fact of agreement need not be evidenced in writing. When, therefore, one party has unjustifiably included such words as 'subject to contract' in a subsequent memorandum of the agreement, these words do not prevent that memorandum from being used as evidence of it. Furthermore, even if the words have been included justifiably, because the parties really intended their arrangement to be in suspense, then oral evidence is admissible to prove that the parties later agreed that it should no longer be subject to contract.

In *Tiverton Estates* v. *Wearwell Ltd.* [1974] 1 All E.R. 209 the Court of Appeal disapproved and refused to follow this decision, and held that the memorandum must, either expressly or impliedly, acknowledge the fact that agreement has taken place. Consequently the inclusion of such expressions as 'subject to contract' in that memorandum disqualifies it as evidence. The court hoped, by its decision, to quieten the anxieties of practitioners who feared that their correspondence during conveyancing transactions might, despite being marked 'subject to contract', unwittingly render enforceable arrangements which hitherto had not been so.

Two remarks may be made against this latter view. Firstly, if no oral contract had been concluded originally, no mere memorandum of what has occurred will change that position. Neither party can enforce it. Secondly, if an oral contract has already been made, then it is only just and honourable that it should be enforceable. It was not the policy of the Statute of Frauds that oral contracts relating to land should be avoided or evaded. On the contrary, its aim was to ensure that contracts should be performed and not be endangered by unscrupulous conduct. In any case, until the House of Lords decides which view is correct, any feelings of reassurance are misplaced because they are precarious. In *Cohen* v. *Nessdale* [1981] 3 All E.R. 118, a High Court case, Kilner Brown J. showed preference for the decision in *Tiverton Estates* v. *Wearwell Ltd.* On grounds of practical convenience this view will probably prevail.

Once a satisfactory memorandum has existed it may, if lost, be proved, as in the case of other lost documents, by oral evidence (*Barber* v. *Rowe* [1948] 2 All E.R. 1050). A final example may illustrate the general operation of the section. If John has orally agreed to take a lease of 'Bag End' from Peter, who has now changed his mind, John cannot enforce the contract against him. If, however, Peter writes to John in the following terms, John will surely have enough written evidence to satisfy the section and bring an action.

> Dear John,
>
> I am writing to say that I have decided not to lease you Bag End at Hobbiton after all on July 1st because I believe £100 per annum is too small, considering that it was to have been for seven years. Consider our agreement ended therefore.
>
> Yours sincerely,
>
> Peter.

The section allows two exceptions to the requirement of writing and one of these, the doctrine of part performance, must be examined. This was developed by equity following the Statute of Frauds and has now been given statutory recognition. The doctrine was created to prevent the Statute, which was aimed against fraud, becoming 'an engine of fraud'. If *L* orally agreed to grant a lease of a house to *T*, on condition that *T* carried out alterations, and *T* gave up an existing tenancy, moved in and carried out the work, it would be an unjust misuse of the statute for *L* to refuse to execute the lease by taking cover behind the Statute (*Rawlinson* v. *Ames* [1925] Ch. 96). If such a case comes before the court, there are two just alternatives open to the judge if an unfair result is to be avoided. The contract has already been partly performed and so in order to balance the scales of justice he may either order the remainder of it to be performed, or order the part which has been performed to be undone. Sometimes the latter is possible. If, for instance, one party has simply paid money to the other, its repayment will restore the parties to their original positions. If, however, one party has entered possession of the property, the alteration of his position cannot so easily be corrected, and therefore an order for the completion of the contract would be more fitting. When this choice is taken, the courts justify their apparent evasion of the Statute of Frauds by explaining that 'the defendant is really "charged" upon the equities resulting from the acts done in execution of the contract, and not (within the meaning of the statute) upon the contract itself' (per Lord Selborne in *Maddison* v. *Alderson* (1883), 8 App. Cas. 467, at p. 475). However, since the doctrine is now incorporated into s. 40, this is more useful for assessing its true spirit than for justifying its right to exist.

Where the doctrine applies, oral evidence is admissible of the contract, which is then enforced despite the lack of written memorandum. The constituents of part performance have been strictly defined, however, and they are as follows.

Firstly, the act of part performance must have been done by the plaintiff. Secondly, the acts 'must be unequivocally, and in their own nature referable to some such agreement as that alleged' (per Lord Selborne in *Maddison* v. *Alderson*, above, at p. 479). This means that the act would lead a casual observer to one reasonable conclusion, namely that it is attributable to a contract. In *Steadman* v. *Steadman* [1974] 2 All E.R. 977, the House of Lords corrected a common impression that the standards set by this test are almost impossibly severe. All the circumstances must be considered, leaving aside all evidence of the oral contract, to see whether the acts relied upon were done in reliance of a contract and the onus of proving this was simply, as in all civil matters, whether it was more probable than not. Nor is there any general rule that payment of money can never constitute part performance. The acts of part performance need not show the precise terms of the contract, for these can be proved by other acceptable evidence, once it has been shown in accordance with the doctrine that some contract must have existed which is consistent with the one alleged. To what extent the acts of part performance must indicate the general nature of the contract, as opposed to its details cannot be taken to be settled. There are inconsistencies in some of the cases decided during the long history of the doctrine and, while Steadman's case does not resolve them all, it appears to indicate a less technical approach for future decisions. In fact, in almost all cases, the only act that has been held to constitute an act of part performance is a change of possession. Mere retention of possession by a tenant after a lease is not sufficient, for it is not unequivocally referable to the granting of a new lease. It is equally compatible with him holding over improperly. If he pays an increased rent, or carries out improvements in addition, however, there will be a sufficient act of part performance.

A change of possession is not always necessary, provided that Lord Selborne's test is satisfied, for otherwise, it would be hard on persons who had contracted orally to sell or lease where the purchaser or tenant defected. In *Rawlinson* v. *Ames* [1925] 1 Ch. 96 the plaintiff had carried out alterations to a flat owned by her, under the supervision and instructions of the defendant, who had agreed to take a lease of it. The agreement was insufficiently evidenced in writing but it was held that the acts of the plaintiff constituted part performance. In *Wakeham* v. *Mackenzie* [1968] 2 All E.R. 783 an elderly man orally promised a widow that, if she would give up her council flat and move into his house to look after him for the the rest of his life, the house would be hers when he died. This she did, but he did not leave her the house by will. It was held that her acts amounted to part performance of a contract. The circumstances of the case make this a laudable decision because the woman certainly intended to create legal obligations, but the court will always closely scrutinize such claims made after a person's death. In the earlier case of *Maddison* v. *Alderson* above, a woman continued to act as housekeeper to a man in reliance on his promise that if she did so he would leave her a life interest by will. Unfortunately, his will was improperly executed so that she had to rely upon the oral promise. It was held that, even if there had been a valid contract, which was not so, there had been no act of part performance. The case may be distinguished on the latter point from *Wakeham* v. *Mackenzie* in that there had been no change of possession, merely a retention of it. As to the question whether a contract arises at all in such cases, clearly all the circumstances must be examined and these may lead to opposite decisions in different cases.

The third requirement for part performance is the rather obvious one that the oral contract must be proved to have been made, and must be valid in all respects. Fourthly, the contract must be one in respect of which equity would grant specific performance. Since this is an equitable remedy, it will be denied if the plaintiff has been guilty of fraud or long delay, or if it will involve inflicting hardship. In such cases the plaintiff cannot, of course, recover damages either, though he may recover any money paid because of failure of consideration.

Although an option to purchase is a contract to create an interest in land, a right of pre-emption, that is, a 'right of first refusal', was held in *Murray* v. *Two Strokes* [1973] 3 All E.R. 357 not to be a contract for the sale or other disposition of an interest in land and therefore not caught by s. 40. Perhaps we can justify this distinction by saying that the grant of a right of first refusal is a contract not to create or dispose of such an interest. This decision, though not followed at first instance in *Pritchard* v. *Briggs* [1978] 2 W.L.R. 317, was confirmed in the Court of Appeal where Goff, L.J. held that a right of pre-emption can never be an interest in land and Templeman and Stephenson, LL.J. held that it could only be such as from the time when it becomes exercisable, that is when the owner takes some step in which he indicates his desire to sell. Finally, in order to set the requirements of s. 40 in perspective, we should note that contracts for the sale of interests in land are in practice almost invariably contained in one of the standard printed forms.

Requirement of deeds for legal interests

The second reason why it is important to know whether the subject with which you are dealing is 'land' is that the transfer of ownership in it, or of any other legal interest in or over land, can generally be carried out only by deed. Furthermore, even if the interest is not a legal one, its creation or disposal must be in writing. Likewise declarations of trusts of land must be proved by writing, though this rule does not apply to the creation of resulting, implied or constructive trusts (L.P.A. 1925, s.53; and see *Hodgson* v. *Marks* [1970] 3 All E.R. 513). The significance of this will be appreciated later when we see how wide the definition of land is, but it may be mentioned, by way of example only, that deeds are necessary for the transfer of a fee simple, the grant of a lease or the grant of an easement. Furthermore, once a lease has been granted, the transfer of it to someone else must also be effected by a deed. An important exception to the rule is the grant of certain short leases which may be carried out by writing or orally. These will be discussed later along with leases in general, but it should be noticed that while the grant of such leases may be oral, contracts for this grant must nevertheless be evidenced in writing for the purposes of the Law of Property Act.

If an attempt is made to dispose of or create interests in land otherwise than by deed, equity will, in certain circumstances, regard the transaction as a contract to convey the interest, for 'equity treats that as done which ought to be done'. This is only so, however, if the transaction is for value and satisfies either the requirements of s.40 of the Law of Property Act 1925.

Wide rights carried by a conveyance

If *V* sells his land to *P*, *P* would certainly expect the house standing upon it to pass to him along with the fences and the trees. Equally certainly and correctly, he would not expect the car which happens to be standing in the garage to pass to him. Nevertheless, the definition of land we are shortly to discuss is such that *V* may well be surprised at what rights would pass unless he took positive steps to exclude them from the sale at the contract stage. Otherwise, to give but a few examples, his prize-winning rose bushes may pass to *P*, and on the other hand *P* may be in for an unpleasant surprise when he finds that neither the greenhouse nor the valuable antique birdbath, which *V* always takes from house to house with him, are his on completion.

The Law of Property Act 1925, s.62, names the different classes of objects and rights which pass on a conveyance and it should be studied carefully. Some of the items, however, such as 'fixtures' are mentioned without explanation and call for discussion. It may seem odd that while 'land' is defined in s.205(1)(ix) of the Act, a separate section, namely 62, should state what is deemed to pass on a conveyance of 'land' and proceed to give an independent, though similar, list of things and rights. Perhaps we can say that s.205 helps us to classify the totality of our property whereas, s.62 gives us a more magnified definition of a particular piece of physical property which is admittedly land.

Nomenclature in documents distributing a variety of property

The last paragraph stressed the importance of the distinction between land and other forms of property when land only is being conveyed. When, however, the whole or a wide variety of a person's property is being distributed according to his or another person's instructions, and the word 'land' is used to describe one of the classes of property, even more serious results may follow from a misunderstanding of its meaning. Thus, if I make a will leaving my 'land' to *L* and the 'rest of my property' to *R*, I shall certainly expect 'Blackacre', of which I own the fee simple, to pass to *L*, and it is perhaps not too catastrophic if I failed to realize that a particular object would go his way too, but my plans will go seriously wrong if I used the word 'land' without qualification, not realizing that it includes a rentcharge of, say, £2,000 owned by me at death and payable out of someone else's land, yet perhaps not land which is subject to a trust for sale. A rentcharge is a periodical sum of money charged on land and is classified as land by s.205. If land is held upon trust for sale, equity, regarding that as already done which ought to be done, considers it to be, for some purposes already sold. An interest in it, therefore, might be caught by the description 'personalty' but not 'land' (*Re Kempthorne* [1930] 1 Ch. 268). This rule is an example of the doctrine of conversion, which applies whenever there is a binding obligation to convert freehold land into money by a sale. The duty to convert may rise under a trust, as mentioned above, under a contract or under a statute. The topic will be further discussed later in this chapter.

This is a convenient place to note that the expression 'real property' or 'realty' means the same as 'land' except that, for historical reasons, leaseholds are excluded. Leaseholds, therefore, though not 'realty', are 'land'.

Equitable interests arising from contracts

> The moment you have a valid contract for sale the vendor becomes, in equity, a trustee for the purchaser of the estate sold and the beneficial ownership passes to the purchaser, the vendor having a right to the purchase money, a charge or lien on the estate for the security of that purchase money, and a right to retain possession of estate until the purchase money is paid . . . (per Jessel, M.R., in *Lysaught* v. *Edwards* (1876), 2 Ch.D. 499, at p. 506).

The same principle applies to agreements for the creation or disposition of other interests in land such as leases or easements. The effect of this will be examined in the context of the various interests when they are dealt with later. A decree of specific performance will usually be granted to compel a recalcitrant vendor to pass the legal estate.

This doctrine does not apply to contracts for the sale of goods, for specific performance is applied much more sparingly since damages are usually an adequate remedy. On the other hand, the legal ownership in goods frequently passes at the time of the contract under the Sale of Goods Acts.

Application of various other special rules of land law

Finally, it is important to distinguish between land and other property because there are still large areas of law which apply to land and not to goods and vice versa. One important one, namely s.40 of the Law of Property Act 1925, has been noted already but others will be met. One example may be given here. If I settle 'Blackacre' on *A* for life and on *B* in fee simple in remainder, the technical rules of the Settled Land Act 1925, apply. If I made a similar settlement of my shares it would not. Similarly, the Sale of Goods Act 1979 applies to goods but not to land, though there is a slight skirmishing for territory on the boundaries of these two empires.

What is 'land'?

The meaning of 'land' varies according to its context. That context can be a particular statute, deed, will or other transaction, or a particular line of judicial decisions. Its meaning might even vary within a single statute. An example will demonstrate this.

The definition of 'land' for the purposes of the Law of Property Act 1925 is contained in s.205(1)(ix).

> Land includes land of any tenure, and mines and minerals, whether or not held apart from the surface, buildings or parts of buildings (whether the division is horizontal, vertical or made in any other way) and other corporeal hereditaments; also a manor, an advowson and a rent and other incorporeal hereditaments, and an easement, right, privilege, or benefit in, over, or derived from land; but not an undivided share in land.

We noticed earlier in this chapter that beneficial interests in co-owned property are considered for certain purposes not to be 'land' but personalty. The words 'undivided share' in the statutory definition simply refer to co-owned property. That definition as it stands above therefore appears to exclude such co-owned property from any provision in the Act which refers to 'land'.

Next, turn to s.40 of the Act, which was discussed earlier in this chapter. It requires contracts for the sale or other disposition of interests in 'land' to be evidenced in writing. The result of a rigid interpretation would be to produce the absurd result that if a single owner contracts to sell his house he is caught by the section, whereas a co-owning married couple would not be. If that fixed meaning were carried beyond the Act to other statutes, even stranger consequences would occur. The single owner would be obliged to apply for permission under the Town and Country Planning Act 1971 if he wished to develop his 'land', whereas the co-owning couple would be free of such restraints.

The reason why such results do not occur is that 'land' has a flexible meaning. The preamble to s.205 reads: 'In this Act unless the context otherwise requires, the following expressions have the meanings hereby assigned to them . . .'. Clearly the context of s.40 requires an extended meaning of 'land' so as to embrace co-owned property. (See *Cooper* v. *Critchley* [1955] 1 All E.R. 520). In the case of the Town and Country Planning Act 1971, the Act provides its own definition of land which similarly embraces both types of interest.

The word 'land', therefore, must be interpreted sensitively in the context of the particular statute in which it appears. Sometimes there will be a statutory definition; sometimes there will not be. The general purpose of the Act must be considered in all cases.

If the word appears in a deed or will or other instrument the same approach is necessary in order to discover the true intention of the parties. Surely one of the fundamental purposes of law is to protect lawful designs, not to frustrate them. In short, an interest might be 'land' for some purposes and not for others. The subject is further discussed in relationship to co-ownership in Chapter 11.

Turning from the potential meaning of 'land' in law, recognizing the importance of the Law of Property Act 1925 to land law, we must briefly examine the meaning of the word in that particular Act, remembering however that its meaning even within that Act can vary.

In modern terms, this definition contains two categories. The first part of the definition mentions the cases where the subject matter of the ownership or other interest is physical. These are the things which the layman would expect to be within the meaning of 'land'; the ancient legal term for this class is 'corporeal hereditaments'. 'Hereditament' is simply an archaic word for 'land'. In short, the soil and its accoutrements are 'land'.

The second part contains the cases, such as easements, where the subject of ownership or other interest is not physical. These items are called 'incorporeal hereditaments' because you cannot see or touch them. Yet they are either so inseparably linked in their use with land, or imitate its characteristics so closely, that they are treated as land. What matters today is that the full force of land law, as described in the first part of this chapter, applies as much to incorporeal as to corporeal hereditaments. This twofold division will now be used for a more detailed explanation, but since the incorporeal matters can be treated more briefly, they will be taken first. 'Land', therefore, consists of the following.

Incorporeal hereditaments

These constituted a large class in the old law. The only important examples today are easements, profits and rents, with tithes and manors occupying a minor position. These are to be discussed individually later but a few general remarks may be made here. A rent includes a rent service, which is the rent received by a landlord from his tenant. Since the leasehold itself is included amongst corporeal hereditaments, both landlord and tenant own 'land'. Rent also includes other periodical payments made out of land such as rentcharges. Tithe has a curious history but today its only significance is that on a change of ownership of land which is subject to tithe, a sum of money may be payable to the Inland Revenue, whereupon the charge disappears from the land forever. It does not affect the owner or occupier until that time, and, as such, it is a conveyancing topic rather than one of land law. A 'manor', so far as modern land law is concerned, is the right to those incidents still existing against land which was copyhold before enfranchisement. These were dealt with in the previous chapter. A proprietor of such rights, therefore, owns land even though he owns no physical land.

Corporeal hereditaments

This second category concerns physical land. It does not spell out, but takes for granted, much of the meaning given to the expression by the common law. Its full meaning will therefore be explained by reference to the decided cases and also to s.62 of the Law of Property Act 1925.

In the first place it means the earth itself to an indefinite depth and also the air space to such height as is necessary for the ordinary use and enjoyment of the land and structures upon it, not above that (see *Bernstein (Baron)* v. *Skyviews and General Ltd.* [1977] 3 W.L.R. 136). This includes all the natural and permanent features, ranging from minerals and ponds to trees and buildings. Even horizontal or other sections of this earth or space are land, whether or not they are owned separately from the surface. Thus, I can sell a seam of minerals in fee simple to *P*, who thereupon owns land. More quaintly, such a section may be carved out above the surface. If I build a three-storey block of flats on my land I can convey the upper two in fee simple to *A* and *B* and retain the ground floor flat myself. In this case, all three of us own land, even though I am the only one who owns any soil. Enjoyment of land above the earth in this way by means of 'flying freeholds' is clearly dependent on the existence of easements of support and way, which, however, would readily be implied by law. Also included in the meaning of land are growing things generally such as grass and shrubs, but not annual crops such as corn.

Next, 'there is no doubt that the general maxim of the law is that what is annexed to the land becomes part of the land . . .' (per Blackburn, J., in *Holland* v. *Hodgson* (1872), L.R. 7 C.P. 328, at p.334). An object which, by such attachment to land, becomes part of that land is hereafter called a 'fixture'. The test whether it has become a fixture is not simply this physical one, and Blackburn, J., gave classic expression to it in that case in the following way at p.334.

> When the article in question is no further attached to the land, than by its own weight, it is generally considered to be a mere chattel. . . . But even in such a case, if the intention is apparent to make the articles part of the land, they do become part of the land . . . . On the other hand, an article may be very firmly fixed to the land, and yet circumstances may be such as to show that it was never intended to be part of the land, and then it does not become part of the land.

In short, two matters have to be examined in the following order: (1) the degree of annexation and (2) the purpose of annexation. The first is a question of fact only and raises a presumption. If the object is attached otherwise than by its own weight, it is *prima facie* land; if it is merely resting by its own weight, it is *prima facie* a chattel. Whatever presumption is thus raised may be rebutted by showing what the intention was of the person who placed it: that is, whether, in the case of an object merely resting, it was intended to benefit the land, or whether, in the case of annexation, it was only so annexed the better to enjoy it as a chattel.

The same object may indeed be chattel or land according to the circumstances (see *Rogers (Inspector of Taxes)* v. *Longsdon* [1967] Ch. 93). For instance, let us say I own a statue of Venus which I have always taken with me when I have moved house. It is a massive statue for outdoor use. In the house

I presently own, the terrace is very uneven so that I have had to screw the base to the ground for security. *Prima facie*, the statue is a fixture, but this presumption is clearly rebutted once the second test is applied. Conversely, if in planning my new garden I place a statue of Venus as part of the landscape on a balustrade, and find that it stands quite securely there by its own weight, then, although on the first test it is *prima facie* a chattel, this is reversed on applying the second, for the intention was to enhance the land as such.

Although the test of degree of annexation is applied first, 'it is not always the most important—and its relative importance is probably not what it was in ruder times' (per Lord Macnaghten in *Leigh* v. *Taylor* [1902] A.C. 157, at p.162). In that case, a tapestry was fastened to a wooden frame which was then screwed into a wall. It was held that it remained a chattel, for the intention was to fix it to the wall the better to enjoy it as a chattel. In other circumstances a tapestry might well be part of the land, as for instance the tapestry in Coventry Cathedral. In a Canadian case, a fitted carpet was held to be a fixture in an hotel although annexation was slight (*La Salle Recreations* v. *Canadian Camdex Investments* [1969] 4 D.L.R. (3d) 549). It is important to note, particularly in view of modern building techniques, that a superstructure might remain a chattel, while its base becomes a fixture. Thus in *Dibble* v. *Moore* [1970] 2 Q.B. 181, greenhouses standing on concrete dollies merely by their own weight were held not to be fixtures, particularly in view of evidence that it was customary to move such greenhouses to fresh sites every few years. The law of fixtures was invoked in an unusual context in *Simmons* v. *Midford* [1969] 2 Ch. 415, where the owner of 'Blackacre' had, with his neighbour's permission, laid a drain under that neighbour's land. Some years later the ownership of the drain was contested. It was held to be the property of the present owner of 'Blackacre'; because, said Buckley, J., it was 'appurtenant to' 'Blackacre.' Unfortunately for our present purpose, he did not have to determine whether the drain was land or personalty. He did, however, find that it had not become part of the land in which it was embedded, but had either remained a chattel or become part of the land it served, rather like a protruding limb upon that land, to which, however, it was connected. This latter suggestion is, of course, consonant with the definition of land, which embraces horizontal sections of it.

Finally, where one object, which is part of a series or system fulfilling a common purpose, has become land, it does not follow that other parts of the apparatus have done so, even though they are physically connected with it. For instance, in *Jordan* v. *May* [1947] 1 All E.R. 231, a generating plant set in concrete was held to be a fixture but a battery helping to run it was not.

Some of the practical results of these rules might now be considered. The owner of land may, of course, detach any fixture, whereupon it becomes a chattel again. If, however, he devises land to *L*, and leaves the rest of his property to *P*, all fixtures will pass to *L* and neither *P* nor the personal representatives may detach them (*Re Whaley* [1908] 1 Ch. 615). Similar principles apply between vendor and purchaser. No fixtures existing at the time of the contract may be removed by the vendor. If he wishes to do so, he must reserve the right in the contract. If land is mortgaged, all fixtures are affected by the mortgage, as are any later added fixtures (*Monti* v. *Barnes* [1901] 1 K.B. 205). This last rule may create serious difficulties these days when much valuable equipment belonging to third parties is taken onto mortgaged premises under a hiring or hire-purchase agreement. It might be thought that the existence of the agreement would show a contrary intention sufficient to prevent the machinery becoming a fixture, and so allow its original ownership to continue. A view that this is not, however, borne out by the decided cases, but that, where the agreement gives the hirer the right to seize the object on breach of the agreement, an equitable interest arises in his favour, may be found at 27 Conveyancer 30.

The rules as to annexation might have worked great injustice to the owners of limited interests in land, such as life tenants or lessees. A tenant would certainly be discouraged from annexing valuable objects to the land if there were no exception to the rule that on annexation they become part of the land and must enure to the benefit of the owner. The law has therefore long given the right for lessees and life tenants, under certain conditions, to remove some classes of fixtures annexed by them. This does not mean the objects have not become fixtures. It means that such tenants may detach certain parts of the land. These rights will be discussed when those interests are dealt with.

Study material: *Berkley* v. *Poulett* (1976) 241 Estates Gazette 911; 242 Estates Gazette 39

The judgment of Scarman L.J. is given below. Stamp L.J. agreed with Lord Scarman's conclusions but gave a separate judgment. Goff L.J. dissented.

This was an appeal by Rowland John Berkley, the sub-purchaser of Hinton House, part of Earl Poulett's estate at Hinton St George, Somerset, from the decision of Sir Anthony Plowman, then Vice-Chancellor, dismissing his claim for the delivery up of pictures and other objects, which he alleged to be fixtures passing to him on the sale of the house, and for compensation for loss and damage, and other relief. The respondents were the 8th Earl Poulett (and after his death his personal representatives), Sothebys and T R G Lawrence & Son, Crewkerne, Somerset.

P J Millett QC and B Marder (instructed by Ward Bowie, agents for Clarke, Willmott & Clarke, of Yeovil) appeared for the appellant, and N C H Browne-Wilkinson QC and L A Tucker (instructed by Eland, Hore, Patersons) represented the respondents.

Giving the first judgment, SCARMAN LJ said: In opening the appeal for the plaintiff Mr Millett QC said that the basic issue in the case was whether some pictures, some prints, a statue and a sundial were fixtures or chattels. If fixtures, they passed, he submitted, to the subpurchaser when Hinton House was sold: if chattels, he conceded they did not. The case has many complexities, which counsel have done their distinguished best to unravel, but ultimately we have to return to the issue identified by Mr Millett in the first few words of an address which, though it took five and a half days, lasted not a moment too long.

On November 11 1971 Mr Berkley (the plaintiff and appellant) issued a writ naming Earl Poulett, Sothebys, and a firm of surveyors, T R G Lawrence & Son, who practise in Crewkerne, Somerset, as defendants. Put briefly, the claim was for delivery up of certain fixtures which it was claimed passed with Hinton House when Lord Poulett sold the house, compensation for the loss of, or damage to, the fixtures, together with appropriate consequential relief. The claim was, and remains, strongly contested by all the defendants. Lord Poulett died in 1972, since when his personal representatives have carried on as defendants in his place. The plaintiff was a subpurchaser of Hinton House. He bought from Lord Poulett's purchaser. The history of the sale was as follows. Lord Poulett, the 8th Earl, decided to put up for sale by public auction his ancestral estate at Hinton St George in Somerset. Hinton House, with its gardens and grounds comprising some 23 acres, was part of the estate and included in the sale. The Poulett family had lived in the house for 500 years. The south wing, said to have been designed by Inigo Jones, was built for the reception of a queen who never arrived—Queen Anne. The wing includes two rooms which feature in the case, the Queen's Dining Room and the Queen's Ante-Room. The Queen's Dining Room is described in the auction particulars as follows: "The Queen's Dining Room, facing south and measuring about 39 ft 3 in by 29 ft, with oak panelling around picture recesses; open stone fireplace; magnificent moulded and decorated ceiling with egg and dart cornice and large casement windows overlooking the sunken garden." The Queen's Ante-Room is described in the same particulars as follows: "The Queen's Ante-Room, facing south and measuring about 28 ft 9 in by 27 ft 6 in, with oak panelling around picture recesses; large open stone fireplace; three-quarter glazed doors to sunken garden; doors to staircase hall and two communicating doors."

In the Queen's Dining Room there were six pictures, which the plaintiff claims passed with the house on its sale to him. These pictures were firmly fixed into the recesses in the panelling of the room. They were: a framed oil painting of Marquis of Hamilton, attributed to Mytens; a framed oil painting of Elizabeth, Countess of Essex, attributed to Mytens; a framed oil painting, said (but not believed) to be of James II, attributed to Kneller; a framed oil painting of the 1st Duke of Leeds, attributed to Gibson; a framed oil painting of Montague, Lord Willoughby, attributed to Old Stone; a framed oil painting of "The return of the Poulett family from the war," artist unknown.

In the Queen's Ante-Room, there were a number of pictures, only two of which were affixed to a wall, namely two portraits by Wood, of the 7th Earl and his countess respectively, each in coronation robes. The plaintiff claims them because, like the pictures in the Queen's Dining Room, they were fixed into the recesses of a panelled wall. On the first floor of the house there is a suite of rooms known as the Chinese Suite. These rooms contained a number of Chinese prints done on rice paper and stuck to the wall. It is conceded that these were fixtures and passed with the house. Finally there were in the grounds two objects which the plaintiff claims: a white marble statue of a Greek athlete, weighing approximately half a ton and standing on a plinth which was (and remains) fixed into position on the West Lawn; and a sundial which rested on a stone baluster (or pedestal) outside the South Wing. Neither the statue nor the sundial nor any of the eight pictures came to the plaintiff. He did get the Chinese prints all tattered and torn—severely damaged by someone who had tried unsuccessfully to remove them intact from the wallpaper to which they were stuck. The plaintiff's case is that all these items were fixtures; that they passed to him, the purchaser, by subpurchase of the house, garden and grounds; that he is entitled to their delivery up in good condition, damages for their detention, and compensation for their loss or damage.

The Hinton St George Estate was put up for sale by auction on August 2 1968. The auctioneers were Knight Frank & Rutley, who prepared the particulars of sale. There were 24 lots. Hinton House with its gardens, grounds and entrance lodge was lot 1, approximately 23 acres. The plaintiff was interested in lot 1 and also lot 4 (the park, 40 acres). A company, Effold Ltd, was prepared to bid for the whole estate, but was particularly interested in the forestry. A tenant farmer was interested in buying his farm. Such was the coincidence of their interests that, not surprisingly, a syndicate was formed. Mr Simon Lawrence was instructed to bid on their behalf. Mr Lawrence is a partner in the third defendants but at the auction sale on August 2 was acting for the syndicate which included the plaintiff and Effold. On the morning of the sale (which itself took place in the afternoon) the plaintiff contracted with Effold to buy lots 1 and 4 from them if their bid for the whole estate was successful. Later, by mutual agreement, he withdrew from the purchase of lot 4. Effold's bid for the estate was successful at a figure of £225,000 whereupon the plaintiff's contract to buy the house and grounds (lot 1) from Effold became unconditional. Effold were due to complete on

September 30, but completion was delayed until November 4.

Meanwhile there occurred other events of some importance. On August 5 the plaintiff, having told Lord Poulett that he was the purchaser of the house, paid a visit to the house. The plaintiff's reason for buying the house and grounds was that he hoped to be able to develop Hinton as a tourist attraction; Longleat was in his mind's eye. Naturally he wanted to secure as many of its historic ornaments as he could. On his visit he sought to discuss with Lord Poulett the possibility of buying the contents of the house, or some of them. But the Earl would not be drawn.

The Earl had in mind not only an auction of the contents but also the sale by private treaty or otherwise of such of the treasures as he might be advised to sell separately, that is to say, otherwise than at a contents auction. He arranged for an auction on October 23, with October 22 as the viewing date. The plaintiff did not visit the house between August 5 and October 22—almost certainly because Lord Poulett did not wish him to do so. On August 14 upon the Earl's instructions, five of the six paintings were taken from the Queen's Dining Room, namely: "Lord Willoughby" removed by Rogers instructed by Sothebys (subsequently, that is to say on February 19 1969, sold by Sothebys at auction for £100); "Duke of Leeds" removed by Rogers instructed by Sothebys (who subsequently, on June 11 1969, sold it at auction for £180); the alleged "King James II" removed by Rogers instructed by Sothebys (who subsequently, on June 11 1969, sold it by auction for £250); "Elizabeth Countess of Essex" removed by Rogers instructed by Sothebys (not sold); "Marquis of Hamilton" removed by Rogers instructed by Sothebys, who sold it by auction on March 5 1969 for £550. "The Return" was left in position.

On October 22 the plaintiff, armed with a sale catalogue, the contents of which had disturbed him, came to view. He found the two Poulett coronation portraits in place in the Queen's Ante-Room but the five pictures gone from the Queen's Dining Room: only "The Return" was in its place. The statue was on its plinth on the West Lawn, but the sundial had been removed from its baluster. In the Chinese Suite he noticed that several prints were missing. The catalogue upset him because it listed for sale "The Return," the two coronation portraits, the statue, the sundial, and a chandelier (about which there is no longer any dispute). He made complaint and sought advice the upshot of which was that Mr Simon Lawrence, now acting for Lord Poulett as auctioneer of the contents, withdrew from the sale the two coronation portraits and the plinth but not the statue which stood on it. The sundial and the statue were sold at the auction on October 23. So also was "The Return"; its frame was also sold on the same day to the same purchaser, but privately. A few days later the plaintiff went again to Hinton House only to find that all he claimed had gone save the Chinese prints, and these he found in bad shape. He refused to complete his subpurchase on the day agreed for completion that is to say October 31. We now know that "The Return" and its frame were removed on October 24 by a local builder, Mr Ash, after being sold (total price £700) by Mr Simon Lawrence on the 23rd; that the coronation portraits were also removed by him on Mr Lawrence's instructions; that the statue was sold for £225 at the auction and removed shortly thereafter by the purchasers; and that the sundial was sold at the auction for £40 and taken away by the buyer.

Despite the plaintiff's claims, of which Lord Poulett and Effold had notice before their completion, Effold completed their purchase of the whole estate without reservations or conditions on November 4, and the plaintiff, likewise, his purchase of the house and grounds on February 19 following. Thus all the objects (other than the Chinese prints) which the plaintiff claims as his property were removed on Lord Poulett's instructions after sale and before completion by Effold. The conveyances which followed were silent as to the matters in dispute.

I have recited enough of the history to show that, if the pictures, statue or sundial, or any of them, be fixtures, very difficult questions arise as to the entitlement of the plaintiff to sue the head vendor, Lord Poulett. But if none of them was a fixture, the plaintiff is non-suited at the outset, save for his claim in respect of the Chinese prints, which are admitted to have been fixtures and did come into his possession. The first question, therefore, is whether the objects (other than the Chinese prints) were fixtures. On this preliminary, but fundamental, issue I confess that my mind has wavered. But at the end of the day, after listening to prolonged and painstaking argument upon the facts and reflecting upon counsel's submissions in the course of the tranquillity obtained by reserving judgment, I find myself in agreement with the Vice-Chancellor. None of the objects (other than the Chinese prints) was, in my judgment, a fixture. I shall now endeavour to explain how I have reached this conclusion. Lord Poulett sold as an absolute owner. He was in a position to decide what he would offer for sale and what he would exclude from his offer. One turns therefore first to the contract of sale for the terms of his bargain. They are to be found in the following documents: a memorandum of agreement signed by the purchasers, Effold Ltd, and dated August 2 1968; printed stipulations which were bound up with the auctioneers' particulars of sale; some printed special conditions of sale; and the National Conditions of Sale (17th ed) with one or two express modifications. Effolds bought the whole estate (lots 1 to 24). Lot 1 was the house, garden and grounds. The particulars of sale contained a description of the lot, but, as is usual, the particulars were not incorporated into the contract. The printed stipulations, which were of contractual force, included the following clause:

Fixtures and fittings. Fixtures and fittings usually denominated tenant's fixtures and fittings belonging to the vendor shall be taken by the purchaser, according to an inventory to be prepared by the auctioneers and paid for at a valuation to be made in the usual way and the decision of the valuer or umpire as to what are tenant's fixtures and fittings shall be conclusive in the event of any dispute. Certain items are however specifically excluded from the Sale—see Special Conditions of Sale No 14.

I need not read the rest of the stipulation. Special condition no 11 reserved to the vendor the right to sell by auction at Hinton House "household goods, effects, chattels or . . . other possessions of the vendor" prior to completion. Special condition no 14 specifically excluded certain items from the sale—two sets of tapestries, two statues, some ornamental stonework, some bookcases and the cornice cupboards and curtain rails of the Grand Saloon. None of the items in dispute was specifically excluded under this condition. The contract was therefore for the sale of the realty—Hinton House, garden and grounds; certain specifically mentioned fixtures were excluded, but an inventory was to be prepared of "tenant's fixtures," which were to be taken by the purchaser and paid for at a valuation. No inventory has in fact ever been taken and, though the point is mentioned in the respondents' notice, no submissions based on this provision have, as I understand the litigation, been advanced to this court by either side. In my judgment, since the contract was silent as to the items in dispute, it is necessary to determine whether under the general law they are to be considered as fixtures, which pass with the realty, or as chattels, in which event they remain the property of the vendor.

As so often, the difficulty is not the formulation but the application of the law. I think there is now no need to enter into research into the case law prior to *Leigh v Taylor* [1902] AC 157. The answer today to the question whether objects which were originally chattels have become fixtures, that is to say part of the freehold, depends upon the application of two tests: (1) the method and degree of annexation; (2) the object and purpose of the annexation. The early law attached great importance to the first test. It proved harsh and unjust both to limited owners who had affixed valuable chattels of their own to settled land and to tenants for years. The second test was evolved to take care primarily of the limited owner, for example a tenant for life. In *Leigh v Taylor* the House of Lords invoked it to protect the interest of the tenant for life who had affixed large and valuable tapestries to the walls of the house for the purpose of adornment and enjoyment of them as tapestries. As I read that decision, it was held that she had not made them fixtures. "They remained chattels from first to last," said Lord Lindley at p 164 of the report. In the law of landlord and tenant the law's protection went further: even if the chattel affixed by the tenant must be held to have become a fixture, that is to say part of the realty, a rule was evolved that it was to be treated as the property of the tenant and could be removed by him if it fell into a class recognised by law as "tenant's fixtures," that is to say if it be a trade, agricultural, or an ornamental fixture. We are not concerned, on the view I take of the case, with "tenant's fixtures." The governing relationship with which this case is concerned is that of a beneficial owner of the legal estate selling the freehold to a purchaser. Such a seller can sell as much or as little of his property as he chooses. Lord Poulett excluded certain named objects from the sale, but the contract was silent as to the objects claimed by the plaintiff. I think it was conceded by the defendants—certainly I so read the contracts of sale—that, if the pictures, statue, and sundial were fixtures at the time of the contract, they were included in it as part of the freehold (subject of course to a valuation if they should prove to be tenant's fixtures). The preliminary, and basic, question is therefore whether these objects were at that time fixtures.

Since *Leigh v Taylor* the question is really one of fact. The two tests were explained in that case by the Lord Chancellor (see the report at pp 158 and 159), who commented that not the law but our mode of life has changed over the years; that what has changed is "the degree in which certain things have seemed susceptible of being put up as mere ornaments whereas at our earlier period the mere construction rendered it impossible sometimes to sever the thing which was put up from the realty." In other words, a degree of annexation which in earlier times the law would have treated as conclusive may now prove nothing. If the purpose of the annexation be for the better enjoyment of the object itself, it may remain a chattel, notwithstanding a high degree of physical annexation. Clearly, however, it remains significant to discover the extent of physical disturbance of the building or the land involved in the removal of the object. If an object cannot be removed without serious damage to, or destruction of, some part of the realty, the case for its having become a fixture is a strong one. The relationship of the two tests to each other requires consideration. If there is no physical annexation there is no fixture. *Quicquid plantatur solo solo cedit.* Nevertheless an object, resting on the ground by its own weight alone, can be a fixture, if it be so heavy that there is no need to tie it into a foundation, and if it were put in place to improve the realty. *Prima facie*, however, an object resting on the ground by its own weight alone is not a fixture: see *Megarry and Wade*, p 716. Conversely, an object affixed to realty but capable of being removed without much difficulty may yet be a fixture, if, for example, the purpose of its affixing be that "of creating a beautiful room as a whole" (Neville J in *In Re Whaley* [1908] 1 Ch 615 at p 619). And in the famous instance of *Lord Chesterfield's Settled Estates* [1911] 1 Ch 237 Grinling Gibbons carvings, which had been affixed to a suite of rooms 200 years earlier, were held to be fixtures. Today so great are the technical skills of affixing and removing objects to land or buildings that the second test is more likely than the first to be decisive. Perhaps the enduring significance of the first test is a reminder that there must be some degree of physical annexation before a chattel can be treated as part of the realty.

When one seeks to apply the law to the facts of this case, it is necessary to discriminate between what is relevant but not decisive and what is decisive. Investigatory expertise of a high order has been devoted by both sides to discovering how the pictures were affixed to the panelling and the wall in the two rooms. Fascinating though the investigation was, its conclusion (whether it be, as Mr Millett contended, that the pictures were really put up as an integral part, with the panelling, of the wall-covering, or, as Mr Browne-Wilkinson contended, were put into recesses left for them) is not, in my judgment, decisive. It is enough to say that the pictures were firmly fixed and that their removal needed skill and experience if it were to be done without damage to the wall and panelling. Certainly they were firmly enough fixed to become fixtures if that was the object and purpose of their affixing. But, if ordinary skill was used, as it was, in their removal they could be taken down, and in the event were taken down, without much trouble and without damage to the structure of the rooms. The decisive question is therefore as to the object and purpose of their affixing. Pictures had hung in the two rooms for centuries. "The Return" had been in the anteroom for a very long time—perhaps ever since it was painted. The 7th Earl decided in the early part of the 20th century to install in the two rooms the panelling and so designed it that there were recesses for pictures. It is this feature which lends plausibility to the suggestion that the pictures, fitted into the recesses left for them, were not to be enjoyed as objects in themselves but as part of the grand architectural design of the two rooms. The Vice-Chancellor rejected this view. So do I. When the panelling was installed in the two rooms the design was either panelled walls with recesses for pictures to be enjoyed as pictures, or rooms having walls which were a composite of panelling and pictures: in other words, the pictures were to be part of a composite mural. I think the former was the truth. The panelling was Victorian, the pictures a heterogeneous collection. According to Sothebys' expert they were of different dates in the 17th and 18th centuries, of different styles, by different hands, the sort of set anyone could put together at any time—very different, I would comment, from that unity of design, the "Elizabethan Room" in the case of *In re Whaley*. There was a particular Poulett family interest in "The Return" and in the two coronation portraits, but this interest focused attention not on the design of the room but on the pictures themselves. Notwithstanding the painstaking and attractive arguments of Mr Millett for the plaintiff, I find, applying the second test, that the pictures were not fixtures. They were put in place on the wall to be enjoyed as pictures. The panelling presented a technical problem in putting them up. The way the carpenter, or whoever it was, solved the problem is not decisive in determining their legal character. But the purpose in putting them there is.

The statue and the sundial give rise in my judgment to no difficulty. Neither was at the time of the sale physically attached to the realty. The sundial was a small object and, once the Earl had detached it (as he did many years earlier) from its pedestal, it ceased to be part of the realty. The statue was heavy. It weighed 10 cwt and stood 5 ft 7 in high on its plinth. There is an issue as to whether it was cemented into the plinth or rested on its own weight. The question is not decisive, for, even if it was attached by a cement bond, it was (as events proved) easily removable. However, upon the balance of probability, I agree with the Vice-Chancellor in thinking it was not attached. The best argument for the statue being a fixture was its careful siting in the West Lawn so as to form an integral part of the architectural design of the west elevation of the house. The design point is a good one so far as it goes: it explains the siting of the plinth, which undoubtedly was a fixture. But what was put upon the plinth was very much a matter for the taste of the occupier of the house for the time being. We know that at one time the object on the plinth had been a sundial. At the time of the sale it was this statue of a Greek athlete. The plinth's position was architecturally important: it ensured that whatever stood on it would be correctly positioned. But the object it carried could be whatever appealed to the occupier for the time being. Sundial or statue—it did not matter to the design, so long as it was in the right place—a result ensured by the plinth which was firmly fixed into the ground. Being, as I think, unattached, the statue was, *prima facie*, not a fixture, but, even if it were attached, the application of the second test would lead to the same conclusion.

As for the Chinese prints, I agree with the Vice-Chancellor. Even if the plaintiff could prove a title to sue in conversion, detinue or trespass, there is no evidence that it was by the hand or upon the instructions of Lord Poulett that the prints were damaged. And, if the plaintiff's case is put in equity as a breach of trust by a vendor when he was constructive trustee for the purchaser, the plaintiff (always assuming he can prove his entitlement to sue the head vendor, a question upon which I express no opinion) has failed to prove any act or omission by the defendant which could amount to a breach of trust.

Accordingly, I agree with the Vice-Chancellor. The action fails *in limine*. The plaintiff cannot show either that the pictures, statue and sundial were fixtures or that

Lord Poulett, his executors, or anyone acting on their behalf were guilty of any acts or omissions in respect of the Chinese prints which, assuming the plaintiff could make title, could amount either to trespass, conversion or detinue or to breach of trust. Accordingly, I would dismiss the appeal.

After I had prepared this judgment, I had the advantage of reading the judgment about to be delivered by Goff LJ. I would make two comments. First, without in any way disagreeing with the possibility, in logic, of drawing the distinction I understand my brother to be making between chattels and removable fixtures, I think it would be illogical to overlook the possibility that an object fixed to realty may yet remain a chattel. In my judgment, the pictures, statue and sundial did so remain. Secondly, upon my understanding of the way the case has been fought, Mr Millett for the plaintiff submitted that these objects were fixtures and part of the realty, while the defendants submitted that they were chattels. Having declared myself in favour of the defendants on this issue, I have not thought it necessary to consider the possibility of the objects being fixtures but not part of the realty, that is to say removable fixtures.

Extract reproduced by permission of the Estates Gazette, Ltd.

Questions

1 *John co-owned 'Oak House' in fee simple with his wife Jane. It was their home. He also independently held a lease of 'Blythe Meadows' which had fifty years to run. He had built a wooden shed at 'Oak House' in which he carried out his hobby of pottery making. He recently died. His will, which he had made without legal advice, contained only the following dispositions:*

'1. I would like Jane to take all my land.

2. I would like all my money and other goods to go to my friend Peter.'

Who is entitled to 'Oak House', 'Blythe Meadows,' the shed, and the rest of his property?

2 *Compare the merits, from the point of view of the practitioner, of Tiverton Estates v. Wearwell Ltd. [1974] 1 All E.R. 209 and Law v. Jones [1973] 2 All E.R. 437.*

3 *What exceptions are there to the general rule that legal interests in land can only be created by deed?*

4 *Compare the meanings of 'land' and 'realty'.*

5 *Consider the policy influences possibly operating in the case provided in the study material.*

Chapter Four

Limitations on the enjoyment of land

THE LEGAL restraints upon land use today are sometimes nostalgically contrasted with the freedom of former ages. The validity of the comparison depends upon which former age is considered. If the Middle Ages are chosen the criticism is surely misplaced. Communal agriculture, subsistence economy and formidable agrarian custom would have inclined an entrepreneur to deal with goods rather than land. Yet such choice of time is a little unfair. Enormous liberation of land use occurred during the hundreds of years which elapsed before Victorian times. This is when modern memory begins. Let us however go back to 1750 as our point of comparison. Villages were mostly tuned to agriculture still partly communal in nature. Sowing, weeding and harvesting tolled the year. Economics, though even then gravely affected by national and international events, still had a distinct local role. The problems of public health were unrealized. The houses of a few dozen families clustered together enjoyed the benefits of community and security. Aesthetic judgements were probably not so visually biased as our own. Indeed aesthetic appreciation was perhaps not so distilled a value as for us. The prevalence of settled traditions, with unconscious local variations, produced a balanced even static environment. It has been remarked that twelve hovels can be a delight, but twelve thousand a menace.

Spaced through these hamlets were market towns. Stratford, Derby and a hundred others supplied the more sophisticated elements of business. Finally, there were a few towns where commercial and socially activities were much more intense. London, Bristol, Oxford and a few others were centres of metropolitan stature to the counties surrounding.

The important common factor in this society, however, was that all these communities were of centuries-old growth and common experience. Slow growth bred long tradition. The countryside was still nearby. There was little mobility of population. The influence of large landowners was strong and lasting. 'Welfare' was largely a private matter.

Then, in the second half of the eighteenth century, came the industrial revolution, inclining the angle of industrial, social and intellectual development so steeply that, two centuries later, we have not caught up with the problems posed by it. The intensive growth of industry, migration to the towns and the sudden incompetence of medical and sociological management to cope with it, brought up problems of such size that only the state could influence events. Twelve thousand hovels bred not only cholera but also grave moral problems. Reformists persuaded Parliament to pass Acts concerned with public health, factories and the urban environment.

Much of that legislation has now been overtaken by later Acts. What is significant is that the habit of social legislation, once seized by Parliament, has never been put down. The subject matter of that legislation has however, moved on to new fields. Education, social security and the provision of a huge range of other benefits are the stuff of modern politics and administrative law. Land law has been crucially affected by it.

It seems that rapid growth and mixture of population must be associated with an increase in legislation and regulation. Perhaps this is not only because of the physical problems caused by large numbers of people living close together, but also because the powerful bonds of custom and tradition no longer hold sway. Any contrast drawn between the freedom to enjoy land in 1750 and the restrictions in force today should take account of the destruction of the environment which occurred when both social and legal restraints were lacking during the eighteenth century.

Uninhibited enjoyment of property is also sometimes incompatible with wider public needs. Once it is decided, for instance, that education shall be available for everyone, it follows that authorities must be empowered to buy land for schools compulsorily. Similarly, if we demand healthy towns and the preservation of our countryside, some restrictions on the use of land must be accepted. It is in this field of administrative law that enormous incursions into property rights have been made during the last century.

The rest of this chapter is given over to some of the more important restrictions on the enjoyment of land which affect all occupiers, whether they own fees simple or lesser interests. Owners of lesser interests are bound not only by these rules but often by further restrictions which prevent them abusing the land to the detriment of the absolute owner in reversion. The restrictions placed upon land use by these developments are sometimes complex and quite beyond the scope of a book of such general aims as this. Some of the subjects, such as planning, compulsory purchase, housing and security of tenure amount to statutory codes. The following accounts are therefore little more than signboards pointing in their directions. Yet the first constitutional principle must not be neglected. A landowner may do what he wishes with his property except insofar as the law positively restricts him from so doing.

Restrictions affecting the owners of all interests in land

Self-imposed restrictions

A landowner may voluntarily inhibit the use of his land by private transaction with another owner. He may, for instance, grant his neighbour the right to lay a drain through his property, or agree not to build on certain parts of the land. Such transactions, if carried out in the correct way, frequently affect the land permanently, even when the ownership changes. Important examples are restrictive covenants and easements.

The law of tort

A landowner must not use his land so as to commit a tort against another person. He must not, for example, commit nuisances such as allowing harmful vapours to escape from his property (*St. Helen's Smelting Co.* v. *Tipping* (1865) 11 H.L.C. 642), or permit the accumulation and escape of mischievous things generally (*Rylands* v. *Fletcher* (1868), L.R. 3 H.L. 330).

Neither must he deny his neighbour the natural rights in his own land. One of these is the right of support of that neighbour's land against his own at their respective natural levels. This applies whether the two properties are vertically adjacent or horizontally so, as in the case of a separately owned mine (*Backhouse* v. *Bonomi* (1861), 9 H.L. Cas. 503). This duty does not, however, extend to supporting buildings or structures or the extra stresses they cause on land. In *Wyatt* v. *Harrison* (1832), 3 B & Ad. 871, a man who dug foundations for his house so close to his neighbour's house that the walls of the latter sank was held not liable. An injunction is the appropriate remedy to prevent an infringement of such rights. Yet this might not be granted on the simple terms that the damage should be completely reinstated if this would cause injustice. Thus, in *Redland Bricks Ltd.* v. *Morris* [1969] 2 All E.R. 576 the quarrying of clay had caused adjacent land to slip. This adjacent land was worth £12,000, whereas the cost of stabilizing it completely would have been £30,000. It was held that the county court judge should have ordered specific works to be done, rather than have granted an unqualified mandatory injunction. Although support for artificial structures is not a natural right, it can come into being by act of parties as an easement as mentioned in the section on self-imposed restrictions above, either expressly or by implication.

Another example of a natural right, needing no act of parties for its creation, is the right to have a stream that has always flowed through land continue to do so, subject to the water rights of other riparian owners. Diversions and obstructions would be obvious examples of infringement of this right.

Nationalization of certain minerals

The Crown has long been entitled to gold and silver occurring in land. Natural petroleum vested in the Crown under the Petroleum (Production) Act 1934, and coal in the National Coal Board under the Coal Act 1938, and the Coal Industry Nationalisation Act 1946. Under the Atomic Energy Act 1946, and the Atomic Energy Authority Act 1954, the Minister may order the vesting in himself, or the United Kingdom Atomic Energy Authority, of the right to win from any land any mineral from which uranium, thorium, plutonium, neptunium, or other producers of atomic energy might be obtained.

Restrictions on the use of water

Water which stands on land, as in a pond or lake, is part of the land and belongs to the owner of the land (L.P.A. 1925, s.62). Water which is moving through land, whether in defined channels above or below the surface, or merely percolating, is ownerless, though it is capable of ownership when drawn off. The owner of land containing water has the following rights of abstraction.

(1) *Standing water*—The owner may use this without limit. The Water Resources Act 1963, dealt with below, does not apply since static water does not constitute a 'source of supply'. Even small groups of such waters which

are interconnected are exempt from its provisions if they do not discharge out of the group.

(2) *Percolating water.* Subject to the Water Resources Act the landowner may abstract as much percolating water as he pleases. Thus in *Chasemore* v. *Richards* (1859), 7 H.L. Cas. 349, the use of the Wandle stream was lost to a millowner because an adjoining owner sank a well and intercepted oozing water before it could reach the stream. In *Langbrook Properties Ltd.* v. *Surrey County Council and Others* [1969] 3 All E.R. 1424, a similar decision was given when percolating water had been taken to such a degree that it had desiccated neighbouring land and caused settlements in buildings there.

Abstraction of percolating water now, however, is subject to the Water Resources Act 1963. This Act, which aims at safeguarding the water supply of the country for the future, forbids abstraction without a licence granted by the water authority. There are some exceptions to this requirement, including abstractions not exceeding 1,000 gallons, or for the occupier's domestic uses (see 33 Conveyancer 14).

(3) *Flowing water.* A riparian owner, who is a person owning land which is both reasonably close to a river and abutting upon it at least at one point (*Attwood* v. *Llay Main Collieries* [1926] Ch. 444), may take water in unlimited quantities for 'ordinary' purposes connected with the riparian tenement. These purposes include drinking, washing, cooking and the needs of cattle on the land. Provided that these conditions are fulfilled, it does not matter that the use exhausts the stream. Secondly, he may take water for 'extraordinary' purposes connected with the riparian land, provided that the use is reasonable and that it is returned to the river substantially undiminished in both quality and quantity. Such purposes include ditch irrigation and manufacturing. In *McCartney* v. *Londonderry Rly.* [1904] A.C. 301 it was held that a railway company may not take water from a stream simply because locomotives were standing on their land nearby. Such a use was not connected with the riparian land at all, for the water would have been used over many miles of railway, not merely on that land. These principles were explained in the leading case of *Swindon Waterworks Co.* v. *Wilts & Berks Canal Co.* (1875), L.R. 7 H.L. 697.

In *Rugby Joint Water Board* v. *Walters* [1966] 3 All E.R. 497 it was held that large-scale spray irrigation was not an ordinary use. Neither was it a valid extraordinary use, because the water was not returned in substantially undiminished quantity. Buckley, J., however, remarked that no judge had yet attempted to define 'ordinary' use. It is to be hoped that when the opportunity for sharper definition arises the court will not induce it merely from the precedents of a technologically primitive society but will recognize that the ox has now yielded to the motor.

Apart from these rules, the use of flowing water is subject to the Water Resources Act 1963. The same rules apply generally as apply to percolating water, but a further exemption from licences exists. A riparian owner does not need a licence for taking water for agricultural purposes other than spray irrigation.

Licences under the Act may extend as well as restrict the common law right of extraction and may affect the defences available in civil actions between landowners for interference with water rights (see ss.23 and 31).

The same rules apply to the abstraction of water from an underground river as from one on the surface, provided that it is a reasonable inference from known facts that the water keeps to a bounded course. This knowledge must be present at the time when any act complained of was committed, and not merely established before the hearing. Entry of a stream below ground and its later re-emergence are an example of facts from which such inference may be made (*Bleachers Association Ltd.* v. *Chapel-en-le-Frith R.D.C.* [1933] Ch. 356, per Luxmoore, J., at p.363).

Other restrictions on the use of water include the public right of navigation in tidal waters up to the ebb and flow point of the mean tides. In non-tidal waters this right only exists where it can be proved to have arisen by immemorial use or under statute. Where it does exist, the riparian owner must not interfere with it either by physical obstruction or by abstraction of too much water. Thus in *Att.-Gen.* v. *Terry* (1874), L.R. 9 Ch. App. 423, the extension of a wharf by three feet into a navigable width of sixty feet was held unlawful.

Although strictly a conveyancing question, a few words may be added about the ownership of river beds and shores. The bed of a tidal river is vested in the Crown or its grantee up to the normal ebb and flow point; so is the foreshore. Boundaries which vary as a result of natural forces, such as the shift of a shoreline over the years, pose the question whether there can exist a 'movable fee simple'. It seems that there can be (see *Baxendale* v. *Instow P.C.* [1981] 2 All E.R. 620). As to the non-tidal parts of rivers, a riparian owner may in the nature of things own to the near bank, to some point under the river or to the far bank. It is a simple question of how much was conveyed to him and his predecessors in title. Frequently, however, a river is the boundary of property and such boundaries have, in the past, been all too vaguely drawn or described in conveyances. Where there is lack of positive evidence in such cases there is a useful presumption that the owner of each bank owns up to the midstream point in the bed. It is, however, a presumption only. The change of course of a river does not affect the ownership of land.

Objects and living things

The general rule is that if an object is embedded in the land so as to become a fixture it belongs to the landowner. As to objects that remain chattels, there is probably a presumption that the occupier is entitled against all but the true owner unless the circumstances show that he intended to exercise no control over them. The question should be pursued in the books on tort (see, for instance, *Re Cohen* [1953] Ch. 88). In any event the following exceptions stand aside from this general principle.

(1) *Treasure trove*. Under common law, the Crown has a prerogative right to treasure trove. An object is treasure trove only if it consists of gold or silver in the form of bullion, coin or trinket, if it has been hidden as opposed to having been abandoned or merely lost, and if the true owner is unknown. The second of these conditions, since it relates to an intention, must be inferred from the circumstances. It will readily be fulfilled for instance where several valuable objects are found placed together. Thus in *Att.-Gen.* v. *Trustees of the British Museum* [1903] 2 Ch. 598, gold ornaments lying together underground inside a hollow collar and dating from about A.D. 300 were held to be treasure trove. Speculation upon intention, however, tends to open the door

to extravagant arguments 'more suited to the poem of a Celtic bard than the prose of an English law reporter.'

(2) *Wild animals and birds*. These are ownerless unless they are too young to move away, or have been tamed. The landowner, however, or the person to whom he has granted sporting rights, has the exclusive right to catch them or to take eggs, whereupon they become his property. This is so even though they are killed by a trespasser (*Blades* v. *Higgs* (1865), 11 H.L. Cas. 621). White swans, unmarked and in open rivers, belong to the Crown. Apart from these and 'royal fish', any prerogative right of the Crown to wild creatures was abolished by the Wild Creatures and Forest Laws Act 1971. These remarks, of course, relate merely to ownership. The taking of wild animals and birds is also subject to the game laws and the laws protecting wild life (see, for instance, the Wildlife and Countryside Act 1981).

(3) *Fish*. Fish in rivers and sea, with a few exceptions, are ownerless. The owner of the river bed has, however, the exclusive right to catch them. The public have no such right even though there is a public right of navigation. The public have, however, a right to fish in tidal waters. All these rights must be exercised subject to the general law relating to fishing.

(4) *Plants*. These belong to the landowner. Again attention is drawn to legislation protecting certain species of growing things.

Interference with air space

The Civil Aviation Acts 1949 and 1971 empower aircraft to fly over property at a reasonable height. These provisions must be taken to give a defence against actions in nuisance rather than in trespass, since considering the height at which even low-flying aircraft fly, no trespass would be committed. A landowner's rights of property are no longer believed to go beyond the height necessary for ordinary use of enjoyment (*Bernstein (Baron)* v. *Skyviews Ltd.* [1977] 3 W.L.R. 136). In other cases of interference, as for instance by projections or missiles such as bullets from a rifle range, actions will lie in nuisance and trespass (see *Clifton* v. *Bury* (1887), 4 T.L.R. 8; see also *Woolerton and Wilson Ltd.* v. *Richard Costain Ltd.* [1970] 1 All E.R. 483).

Control of activities on land

This head of restraint is not intended to be exclusive since some types of such control have already been mentioned, and others, in particular planning control, will shortly be dealt with separately. However, some examples of the huge residue of inhibitions are given here to illustrate the social responsibility which now attaches to land ownership. An activity is controlled in order to protect interests which might be quite external to the land. Riding schools, for instance, must conform to certain statutory standards for the welfare of horses. An owner or prospective purchaser of land cannot afford to ignore these laws even though they have not always been considered part of land law. It is much more important today for the ordinary landowner to be acquainted with certain aspects of public health law than with some of the more remote sidings of the Settled Land Act 1925.

The details of some of these subjects amount to codes in themselves. Furthermore, legislation is generally active on these fronts, quickly outdating ordinary textbooks. Fortunately publishers have produced loose-leaf encyclopaedias on some of the topics to which anyone seeking detailed information should refer. Some of the most important of these subjects are the laws of: housing; public health (property aspects); pollution and health and safety at work. Yet some of the most specialized uses of land are also controlled by the law. From pub to private nursing home Parliament has been active. Finally, local bye laws often have a bearing on land use.

Compulsory disfigurement of land

Certain statutes give authorities power to enter land and place apparatus there. Thus local authorities and water authorities may, after notice and subject to compensation, lay sewers through land under the Public Health Act 1936 (s.15) (but see *Hutton* v. *Esher U.D.C.* [1972] 3 All E.R. 504). Pylons may be erected by the Board under the Electricity (Supply) Act 1919 (s.22).

Compulsory purchase

A host of statutes enable various authorities to acquire land compulsorily for their purposes. These range from the provision of housing accommodation to the building of aerodromes. Like all administrative powers, they are strictly subject to the *ultra vires* rule. While the powers of acquisition are to be found scattered in many statutes, the procedure for acquisition is laid down as a common code for most of these cases in the Acquisition of Land Act 1981. Briefly this is as follows: The authority makes a compulsory purchase order and notifies the owners of all interests in the land and the general public of the order and of the time limits for objections. It then submits the order to the Minister for confirmation. If there are objections, the Minister must hold a local enquiry, and may then confirm or refuse the order. If it is confirmed, the authority serves a notice to treat under the Compulsory Purchase Act 1965, which invites the owner to make a claim for compensation. If the price is agreed, this agreement, together with the notice to treat, constitutes the contract of sale. Thereafter the procedure follows that of an ordinary conveyance. The district valuer, an independent person, normally assists agreement, but, failing this, the compensation is settled by the Lands Tribunal.

The principles of compensation are complex but are based on the open market value of the land, compensation for disturbance or other matters not based on the value of land and compensation for severance of lands. Detailed rules for assessment are contained in the Land Compensation Acts 1961 and 1973. In 1980, 90 per cent of all compulsory purchase orders submitted were concerned with housing.

Protection of tenants

In this century, three classes of tenants have been given a large measure of security of tenure so that their tenancies continue indefinitely, despite the terms of their leases, unless landlords can prove specified reasons for termination. In some cases the rent that may be demanded is controlled. These classes are most business tenancies under the Landlord and Tenant Act 1954, Pt. II, most agricultural tenancies under the Agricultural Holdings Act 1948, and certain residential tenancies under the 'Rent Acts'. Furthermore, under the Leasehold Reform Act 1967, certain tenants can demand either to buy the freehold reversions to their leases or to be granted new leases of fifty years. These Acts are of a technical nature and are considered in general outline in Chapter 6. They are mentioned here to show that in a very large number of tenancies indeed contractual freedom has been greatly restrained, so that their landlords are restricted in their dominion over land.

Town and country planning

This is the most important of all the influences on land use discussed in this chapter.

The account of the law given below amounts to little more than a thumbnail sketch of the complex body of rules, now principally contained in the Town and Country Planning Act 1971, the Town and Country Planning (Amendment) Acts 1972 and 1977, the Local Government Planning and Land Act 1980 and the large volume of delegated legislation. Even a detailed knowledge of the legal rules, however, would provide a very incomplete understanding of the subject. A real appreciation can be gained only by examining the purpose of planning and by recognizing that the balancing of conflicting aims, sometimes private, sometimes public, turns more upon political, social and economic factors than upon law. The discretions exercised by planning authorities are enormous, and can seldom be controlled by law. For such an open-textured approach, see *Land Law and Planning* by Patrick McAuslan (Weidenfeld and Nicolson, 1975).

The local planning authorities are now the councils of counties and districts. Each planning authority had to prepare a 'development plan' for its area and periodically to review it. These reviews, like the plan, were subject to confirmation by the Minister. The plan forecasts the kind of development envisaged for the future and allocates areas for residential, industrial, cultural and other uses and may earmark areas for comprehensive redevelopment. It also forecasts the staging of such development. These plans are now being superseded by 'structure plans' and 'local plans'. The new provisions will come into force progressively as the Secretary of State makes orders applying them area by area. The structure plan will outline the large-scale development policy for the area, including traffic management and improvement of environment, and relate this policy to the policies of other authorities. The local plan will consist of a map and a more detailed description of development proposals for land use in that area. The structure plan, consisting of a written statement with diagrams only, as opposed to the detailed maps of the old system, is less precise and therefore attracts few objections. Its approval is thus subject to less delay.

Before submitting its structure plan to the Secretary of State for confirmation, the county council, which is the planning authority for this purpose, must advertise the results of a preparatory survey, so that representations might be made in regard to it by members of the public and various bodies.

After this stage, the council puts the plan into its final form for submission. The Secretary of State then conducts a public examination at which matters he considers ought to be discussed are considered. Only persons who are invited by him to participate may do so. He may then approve the plan, with or without modification, or reject it. The validity of the plan may be tested in the High Court within six weeks of approval on the grounds either that it is partly or wholly *ultra vires*, or that some procedural requirement has not been complied with.

The authority for the preparation of the local plan is, unless the structure plan provides otherwise, the district council. When the structure plan has been made, this authority must consider whether to make a local plan for any part of its area. It must, in any case, make such a plan if the Secretary of State orders it to do so, or, if the structure plan has defined any part of the area as an 'action area', that is, due for comprehensive development. The preparatory stages of the local plan are similar to those of the structure plan. In certain circumstances a local enquiry must be held to consider objections. Finally, the authority sends a copy of its plan to the Secretary of State who may order that it be submitted for approval. Otherwise the authority may adopt it.

The disclosure by these plans that land is destined to be compulsorily acquired by some public authority might make it very difficult or impossible for the owner to sell, except at a much reduced price. The 1971 Act (ss.192–196), therefore, entitles certain owner occupiers, in the circumstances laid down, to serve a 'blight' notice on the authority requiring them to purchase it. Machinery is provided for the authority to object and for the ultimate resolution of the dispute by the Lands Tribunal if necessary.

So far as the landowner is concerned, the essence of the 1971 Act is that it controls 'development'. The meaning of this word is defined by the Act and is most important. Development is 'the carrying out of building, engineering, mining or other operations in, on, over or under land, or the making of any material change of use of any building or other land' (s.22).

There are thus two distinct facets to 'development', namely, 'operations' and 'uses'. 'Operations' are acts which change the physical characteristics of the land or what is under or over it (see *Cheshire C.C.* v. *Woodward* [1962] 1 All E.R. 517 and *Planning Law and Procedure* by A. E. Telling). 'Use' denotes the purposes to which property is put. A change of use can therefore occur without any physical change in the land (see *Sunbury-on-Thames U.D.C.* v. *Mann* (1958), 9 P. & C.R. 309). For clarification, certain matters are declared to constitute development, such as the tipping of waste or the use of a single dwelling-house as more than one separate dwelling, and certain other matters are stated not to be development, as, for instance, internal improvements to a house, the use of land for agriculture or forestry, road repairs and improvements, or a change from one use to another within any of the 'use classes'. These use classes have been set out in a statutory instrument—the 'Use Classes Order' (see S.I. 1972, No. 1385). This provision enables owners to change from one use to another one similar in kind without permission. An example might illustrate the operation of these. Class I, for instance, consists of shops of various types including those used for hairdressing and travel agency, but not including petrol stations. This means that a change of use from hairdressing to travel agency is not development but a change to that of a petrol station might be.

The Minister is empowered to grant blanket permission for activities which do constitute development. This he does through statutory instruments known as 'General Development Orders' (see, for instance, S.I. 1977, No. 289). This is known as 'permitted development'. Examples of permitted development are the erection of a fence up to two metres high, or up to one metre where it abuts on a vehicular road, the use of land for any purposes, except as a caravan site, on not more than a total of twenty-eight days in a calendar year, or the erection of buildings within the curtilage of and incidental to the enjoyment of a dwelling-house. It should be added as a caution here that these permissions are subject to conditions mentioned in the Order. The legislation itself must be consulted in this, as in other planning matters, for it is an extremely detailed code. Mere work of demolition will not normally constitute development but the view that it can never do so has been proved wrong (*Coleshill and District Investment Co. Ltd.* v. *Minister of Housing and Local Government* [1969] 1 W.L.R. 746 and *Newbury D.C.* v. *S.O.S.E.* [1980] 1 All E.R. 731). Special development orders may also be made. These are limited to particular areas or subjects. It is possible that these will increase in importance in the future (see 1981, J.P.L. 545).

Apart from permitted development, no development is lawful without consent. Application for consent is made to the local planning authority, who, having regard to the development plan and other material considerations, may either grant permission with or without conditions, or refuse it. The details as to how and to whom application should be made are set out in the General Development Order of 1977. A fee, payable to the district councils, may now be prescribed for applicants. Some applications, such as for development likely to affect local amenities, require advertisement. Certain applications for the erection of industrial buildings must be accompanied by an industrial development certificate from the Department of Industry. All planning permissions are now by statute subject to the condition that development shall commence within five years, but the planning authority may expressly impose a less or greater period. As to conditions generally, although the authority may impose them as it 'thinks fit', they must relate to the development in question and must not have an ulterior aim. Neither must they contravene the general law (*Pyx Granite Co. Ltd.* v. *Ministry of Housing and Local Government* [1958] 1 Q.B. 554).

An appeal against the decision of the local planning authority or its failure to give a decision within two months of the application, lies to the Secretary of State, who, after considering the written representations of both sides, or holding a local enquiry, may dismiss or allow the appeal or substitute his own decision. In specified types of appeal, the decision can be made by the inspector hearing the enquiry (S.I. 1972, No. 1652, Sch. I). A further remedy is available if the owner can show that, as a result of a refusal of consent or the imposition of conditions, the land has become incapable of reasonable beneficial use. He may then serve a purchase notice on the district council demanding that it buys his interest. If this is not accepted the Secretary of State decides the matter.

Control of development is exercised in other ways, too. Unauthorized development is remedied by means of 'enforcement notices' in the long term and by 'stop notices' in the short term. Such notices must be served within four years of its occurrence in the case of building, engineering or mining operations, or the failure to comply with any conditions regarding such operations. Even authorized development may be removed by a 'discontinuance order' but compensation is then payable. Appeals lie to the Secretary of State in all these cases. Special kinds of control are provided for the preservation of certain kinds of amenities in town and country. There is a code for the control of advertisements. Trees can be protected by 'tree preservation orders', which may apply to single trees or woods. Such orders may provide for replanting after felling operations where these have been permitted under the order. Lists of buildings of special architectural or historic interest are compiled or approved by the Secretary of State, and the demolition, alteration or extension of such 'listed buildings' requires consent. Planning applications affecting their setting require special publicity. Every planning authority must determine which areas are of special architectural or historic interest. There is machinery for their designation as conservation areas. Within these areas no building may be demolished without consent. Proposals for the preservation and enhancement of such areas must be publicized by the authority. There is special protection for trees in these areas. Orders to abate may be served where waste land is seriously spoiling amenity.

Restrictions which may affect the owners of limited interests

Subject to the heavy restrictions described above, a fee simple owner can use land as he pleases. He may pull valuable buildings down and neglect the land. Legally he has only himself to consider. When a person has a lesser interest, however, other people must be considered. If land is settled on *A* for life with remainder in fee simple to *B*, and that land holds a fine house, an oak forest and a seam of unnationalized minerals, it would be unjust if *A*, unless specially authorized by the settlor, cut down and sold the trees, won and sold the minerals and misused the house, so that on his death all that passed to *B* was a shack in a blasted landscape. The law has, therefore, developed rules calculated to balance the accounts fairly when limited owners are in possession. This is not to say that these rules always necessarily apply. A settlor may, if he wishes, countenance the result described above. The rules merely categorize certain acts and omissions as constituting a permanent alteration in the character or value of land, leaving it to the settlor or lessor to decide whether the owner of the limited interest be allowed to indulge in them. These rules are known as the laws of 'waste'. Whether or not the owner of a limited interest is liable for, or, to use the technical term, 'impeachable for' waste, he is nevertheless bound by the general restrictions on the enjoyment of land described in the first part of this chapter. How to discover whether a particular limited owner is impeachable for waste will be discussed when the various limited interests in land are dealt with. There are three kinds of waste. Finally it should be borne in mind that one large class of limited owners, namely lessees, may suffer special restrictions on the use of land imposed under the lease.

Voluntary waste

This is the commission of any positive act which results in a change in the character of the land or injury of a lasting kind. Examples are pulling down or altering buildings, opening new pits or mines (though not merely working those already opened), and changing the course of husbandry, as for instance by changing woodland into arable land by cutting timber.

Acts which, though technically waste, have a beneficial effect on the land constitute 'ameliorating waste' and will not be actionable. Thus an injunction was refused in *Doherty* v. *Allman* (1877), 3 App. Cas. 709, where a tenant converted an old storehouse into a dwelling. Under the general law 'timber' is oak, ash or elm from the age of twenty upwards but not so old that they cannot provide 'a good post' (per Sir George Jessel, M.R., in *Honywood* v. *Honywood* (1874), L.R. 18 Eq. 306, at p.309). Other trees may be timber, however, by local custom, as for instance birch in Yorkshire. Custom may also provide a different qualifying age, or even require that girth should be the test. The cutting of other trees is not waste unless it amounts to such an improvident act, such as felling trees which would be timber when mature, as to constitute 'equitable waste', dealt with below.

In three cases, however, even the cutting of timber is not waste. Firstly, in the case of timber estates, the taking of the proper periodic crop is not waste, because there will be a planned rotation of cropping and replanting which ensures constant replenishment of the trees. Secondly, there may be a local custom to cut timber in the ordinary course of husbandry (*Dashwood* v. *Magniac* [1891] 3 Ch. 306) and then proper cutting of it is not waste. Thirdly, it is not waste to take 'estovers', which consists in the reasonable and thrifty cutting of timber for the following present needs, namely 'housebote' for fuelling and repairing houses, 'ploughbote' for making and repairing agricultural implements, and 'haybote' for repairing boundaries.

Permissive waste

This is a mere failure to act which results in buildings and lands falling into decay. Failure to cultivate, however, does not constitute permissive waste (per Parke, B., in *Hutton* v. *Warren* (1836), 1 M. & W. 466, at p. 472).

Equitable waste

A limited owner who was not impeachable for either of the types of waste mentioned above had considerable scope for abusing his position by committing improvident and wanton acts for which there was no remedy at common law. Equity, therefore, developed restraints which are now recognized by statute (L.P.A. 1925, s.135).

Examples of equitable waste are stripping or pulling down a house (*Vane* v. *Barnard* (1716), 2 Vern. 738), and cutting ornamental timber, unless of course there is good horticultural reason.

Restrictions imposed by leases

A tenant's use and enjoyment of land may be considerably curtailed by the terms of his lease, which might, for instance, forbid him to use the premises for business purposes, or to play musical instruments there after midnight.

Study material: extract from McAuslan's *Land Law and Planning*

Patrick McAuslan, *Land Law and Planning* (Weidenfeld and Nicolson, 1975) p. 94:

Decision making: an introduction

It is easy to underestimate the complexity of the process of decision making. For lawyers the typical decision-making process is the judicial decision, publicly made after carefully phrased oral and written submissions, and based on a finding of the 'facts' of the case, followed by the application of law to those facts. We may be aware that beneath the surface, things are not quite what they seem, but apart from discussions of the finer points of precedent, we rarely explore beneath the surface. Yet we must try to do so in this book, because the typical decision-making process in planning takes place not in a court, but in a local authority committee or a department, and involves the interaction of experts with experts, experts with amateurs, amateurs with amateurs, and the bringing to bear of a host of considerations, both relevant and irrelevant, all of which we must try to take account of in assessing the efficacy of the planning process. The comments which follow are no more than the barest introduction to administrative decision making, designed to highlight the following points:

(a) Making a decision is not something which takes place in a short space of time, in an afternoon committee meeting for instance. Much evidence shows that the typical decision is made by a gradual process of whittling down alternatives, of perceiving issues with greater clarity, of taking up positions from a variety of motives, not all of them rational, or possibly respectable, and of responding to outside pressures over a period of time. Thus the people who appear to the public as being those who have 'taken the decision' are almost always at the end of a chain of lesser decisions which have crucially shaped the final decision. Decisions, in other words, are not and cannot be taken in isolation from what has gone before, or what is likely to transpire, from the values of the decision makers, and from what Simon has called organisational loyalties, that is the values of the group or organisation to which the decision makers belong. Indeed as Brown emphasises, 'Decisions in large organisations belong to the organisation as a whole and are not attributable to any one individual. . . . The negotiations between individuals, the communication system, the formal rules – these and other factors interact to produce the decisions of the organisation.

(b) Both civil servants in a department and officers in a local authority are engaged in a process in which clear lines between policy and administration, and between policy making and fact finding are not easy to perceive. Nor are rules about the responsibility of ministers or local councillors for decisions they have taken clear to perceive, let alone base controlling devices or reforms of organisational structures on. The literature on decision making stresses the difficulty of pin-pointing who makes decisions, yet the theory of control over the administration is that some*one* can and must be held responsible for decisions that are taken, otherwise people at large will cease to have any say in their daily lives or any influence over the decisions that affect them. Part of the drive behind public participation in planning and in other fields is precisely because there is a general *feeling* that traditional methods of control of administrative decision making are less effective than of old at a time when more and more vital decisions are being taken which will affect our future. Is the problem that the controlling devices have failed to increase in scope and sophistication as fast as decision-making processes, or that potential controllers, and the public at large, are too easily mesmerised by the jargon of decision makers into believing that decisions are in some way inevitable and therefore uncontrollable?

(c) Taking this last point further, what is the role of the Minister and local councillor in the typical administrative decision-making process? How realistic is it to talk of ministerial responsibility for planning decisions when the minor decisions never reach the Minister, and the Minister can never hope to see more than a part of the information on the major ones before he announces 'his' decision? If anything, it is more difficult to see the role of the local councillor in decision making. Friend and Jessop's study of decision making in Coventry provides one of the clearest and most sympathetic accounts of local authority decision making that has been produced for some time, and that certainly makes a case out for the influence of councillors on decisions and the manner in which they are reached, but the general conclusions of the Maud Report on the Management of Local Government are less sanguine. My own view, based admittedly on very little experience, is that one can exaggerate the helplessness of the average councillor. However, there is no substitute for local councillors (and ministers for that matter) becoming familiar with a particular field, and then being prepared to spend a great deal of time on the major issues and problems in that field, and their effect on the councillors' locality so that they can hold their own with the officers. This is a counsel of perfection – it may even be thought rather naïve – and unlikely to be realised except in a very small number of cases, but at least it will serve as an antidote to the 'Bains' philosophy which is sweeping local government: that a reorganisation of the management structure of local authorities to take account of the corporate approach to their activities is the key to more effective and accountable local government. Arguably, the corporate management approach to government was behind the reforms that led to the DoE; while that might result in a more co-ordinated approach by the administration to the problem of the cities, will it lead to more accountability to Parliament and the electorate at large?

(d) The last point to bear in mind arises not so much from the readings that follow as from what has gone before. We must add to our awareness of the general complexities of decision making our awareness that in planning, as in other spheres of government, particular legal constraints and constitutional conventions and practices exist and have to be followed; some reforms might not be possible because they conflict with the law or the conventions, neither of which can, as a matter of practical politics, be altered; some reforms might be introduced which are thought to be necessary politically, but do not always make sense from the point of view of the student of decision making. Law and politics in short affect the procedures of planning as much as they do the substance; an obvious point, but one that is sometimes overlooked by lawyers and planners alike.

Extract reproduced by permission of Professor J. P. W. B. McAuslan.

Questions

1 *How does a solicitor acting for a prospective purchaser of land discover the extent to which the restrictions on land use discussed in this chapter affect that land?*

2 *Advise the owner of a retail grocery shop whether he requires planning permission in order to change the use of the shop to that of a laundrette.*

3 *Consider the influences which might operate when local planning authorities make decisions in respect of applications to develop land.*

4 *Advise a market gardener whose premises are adjacent to a river as to his rights, if any, to use river water for irrigating crops; centrally heating greenhouses; and selling it in containers to purchasers of plants requiring the particular mineral qualities of the water.*

Chapter Five

Freehold interests

The fee simple absolute in possession

Apart from the lease, this is the only interest giving a right to the land itself which can be a legal estate (L.P.A. 1925, s.1).

To qualify, the description 'fee simple absolute in possession' used in s.1 must be perfectly satisfied. The expression, therefore, must be closely examined. Then the nature and the method of transfer of this estate will be described.

The meaning of 'fee simple absolute in possession'

(1) *Fee simple.* The meaning of this may be disposed of quickly. It means ownership. In short, it is, of the interests we are now discussing, the only one which has no time limit placed on its potential endurance.

(2) *Absolute.* This means free from any determining event or condition. It may seem strange, after establishing that 'fee simple' means ownership, to suggest that limitations may be placed on its endurance, but it is possible to give ownership to a person yet provide that this ownership shall pass to someone else on the happening of a particular event. If, for instance, I give my land to *X* in fee simple 'so long as it is used for agricultural purposes' the interest passed is potentially of infinite duration. If, however, the use of the land is changed, then the interest ends and the land will pass back to me or my successor. Such an interest is not a legal estate because it is not 'absolute'. Qualified fees simple like these are of two types, 'determinable' and 'conditional'. They are dealt with later in this chapter. What must be emphasized now is that any inhibition, however slight, on the endurance of a fee simple prevents it from being a legal estate. Since it is, therefore, an equitable interest (L.P.A. 1925, s.1(3)), it involves a trust.

A person who grants a fee simple subject to a condition may do so in such a way that the ownership automatically shifts on the occurrence of the event, as in the case of a grant 'to *A* in fee simple but, if he should marry *X*, then to *B* in fee simple'. In other cases, the shift in ownership does not happen automatically, for the grantor reserves to himself the right to take the land back on the breach of the condition, which he may or may not decide to exercise. This reservation is known as a right of re-entry. The former method is usually used in cases of family endowment, the latter in ordinary commercial conveyances.

Since the meaning of 'absolute' is so crucial, s.7 of the Act, as amended, resolves possible doubt in three cases. Firstly, statutes enabling authorities to acquire land compulsorily for certain purposes frequently provide that, if the land is not used by the authority for those purposes, it shall revest in the original owner or the owners of the land adjoining (see *Pickin* v. *British Railways Board* [1972] 3 All E.R. 923). This possibility of the determination of the fee simple in the hands of the authority might seem to have prevented the interest from being absolute. The section, however, declares that it is absolute. It was held in *Re Clayton's Deed Poll* [1979] 2 All E.R. 1132 that when such use by the authority ceases, the legal estate is immediately held upon trust by that authority for the person entitled under the reverter provision. Secondly, and on the same principle, a fee simple vested in a corporation which is liable to determine by reason of the dissolution of that corporation is declared to be absolute. The third case was not originally envisaged by the section and had to be clarified by amending legislation. In parts of England, particularly Manchester, it is often the practice, on the sale of a fee simple, to take the purchase money not as a lump sum but as a permanent annual payment. To secure the prompt payment of this a right of re-entry is reserved in the grant. As explained above, this means that the vendor may take back the fee simple, if that sum is not paid. Following the enactment of the Law of Property Act 1925, such a fee simple clearly was not absolute. Being equitable, it attracted all the machinery of a trust, which was contemplated neither by the parties nor by the legislators, for the circumstances lacked all the ordinary characteristics of a trust. The Law of Property (Amendment) Act 1926 (Schedule), accordingly enacted that 'a fee simple subject to a legal or equitable right of entry or re-entry is for the purposes of the Act a fee simple absolute'.

The terms of the amendment appear wider than was necessary to remedy the particular difficulty. The Schedule applies whenever a condition is secured by a right of entry or re-entry, whether the condition is the payment of a rentcharge or some other obligation or factor. In the opinion of some (see, for example, Megarry and Wade, *The Law of Real Property* (Stevens & Sons Ltd, 3rd edn, 1966, pp. 143, 324), it embraces all cases of determining factors expressed in the form of conditions, since the imposition of a condition gives rise to a right of re-entry. This view appears to be modified in the 4th edition (1975; see pp. 138–139). It is suggested that this is not so since it is based on principles which have been overtaken by the 1925 legislation. If the view is correct it would mean that, in the case of a grant 'to *A* in fee simple but if he remarries then to *B* in fee simple', *A* has a legal estate, whereas, as we shall see when settlements are discussed, the Settled Land Act 1925, s.1(1)(ii)(b), clearly marks out such a disposition as a settlement. The 1926 Act was aimed at commercial arrangements which had been inadvertently transformed into trusts, not at settlements which were admittedly and consciously intended to be trusts.

Finally, 'absolute' does not mean that the land is free from the rights of other persons. The fact that it is subject to a mortgage for instance does not prevent it from being absolute.

(3) *'In possession'*. A fee simple, even though absolute, cannot be legal unless it is in possession and not in remainder or reversion. Thus if a grant is made 'to *X* for life with remainder to *Y* in fee simple', *Y*'s interest, during *X*'s life, is equitable. 'Possession', however, has unexpectedly wide meaning, for under the Law of Property Act 1925, s.205(1)(xix), it means not only physical occupation but also 'receipt of rents and profits or the right to receive the same, if any'. If *A* owns a fee simple, therefore, and has leased the land to *L*,

who is in occupation, *A*'s fee simple is in possession because he has the right to receive any rent payable. If the land is subject to a trust, and the fee simple is vested in trustees, the fact that those trustees do not themselves enjoy physical occupation of the land does not prevent their fee simple being in possession, for legally they have the right to possession even though equity directs that they exercise their rights in favour of the beneficiaries.

General

For every square inch of land in this country, someone holds the fee simple absolute in possession, even though there may be another person in occupation of that land. The case of a lessee in possession has just been explained. If possession is being enjoyed by the owner of a life interest, entail, or other limited interest, the fee simple absolute resides in one or more trustees in trust for that person in occupation, whose interest of course is merely equitable. The case of a person owning the fee simple absolute in possession for his own purposes, and not in trust for anyone else, is one of the commonest situations in land law. It is the case of the ordinary 'owner occupier'.

A person who owns such an estate can create any number of lesser interests out of it, as was illustrated in Chapter 1. These are examined below.

Method of transferring the fee simple absolute in possession

No special words are necessary to pass the estate to another person, whether by deed or by will (L.P.A. 1925, s.60). If I own such an estate in 'Blackacre' and execute a deed in which I 'hereby convey "Blackacre" to *P*', the fee simple absolute passes unless the contrary intention appears. In practice the words 'in fee simple' are added after the description of the property to avoid any doubt.

The life interest

Nature and creation

A life interest is an interest which lasts only for so long as a particular person lives. No special words are needed to create it, either by deed or by will, though the intention to do so must, of course, be apparent. The grant of a merely personal privilege to occupy land is inconsistent with such an intention, for a life interest is property and has the essential characteristic of alienability possessed by all interests is land (see *Binions* v. *Evans* [1972] 2 All E.R. 70 where the judgment of Lord Denning, M.R., is surely to be preferred upon this point). Such words as 'to *A* for life' will leave no room for doubt. In home-made wills, however, the intention may have to be gleaned from the instrument as a whole. Instructions such as 'I give my house to my son but he must allow my widow to live there, if she wishes, for the rest of her days' might well create a life interest in favour of the widow, the son taking the fee simple in remainder. The owner of a life interest is usually referred to as a 'life tenant'. The use of the word 'tenant' has no connection with its use in the relationship of landlord and tenant. It simply means 'owner' of a life interest. Life interests can only be equitable (L.P.A. 1925, s.1).

Usually the life which measures the length of time for which the interest is to endure is that of the grantee. Thus, in a grant 'to *A* for life', *A*'s life does this. Other lives may be used, however, as in a grant 'to *A* for the life of *B*'. In this case, *A*'s interest will last as long as *B* lives, whether or not he outlives *A*. *B* takes no interest in the land but is used only in the capacity of an egg-timer. He is called a '*cestui que vie*'. Such life interests are called 'interests *pur autre vie*'. An interest *pur autre vie* also arises where the owner of a life interest, say *A*, assigns it to *B*. *B*'s interest will last as long as *A* lives. It is not within the power of *A* to assign more because that is all he has to assign. Life interests may, though rarely these days, arise by operation of law in the form of 'curtesy' which is relevant only to entails.

A life tenant may dispose of his interest as he pleases during his lifetime. When he dies, however, his interest ends, so that there is nothing for him to leave by his will. In the case of a tenant *pur autre vie* the position is different if the *cestui que vie* is still living at the death of the tenant. Thus, if land is granted to *A* for the life of *B*, then *A* may on his death dispose of his interest as he pleases, or allow the laws of intestacy to act upon it. The beneficiary will then be entitled to enjoy the land for the rest of *B*'s lifetime.

The rights and duties of a life tenant

Rules are necessary to regulate the beneficial enjoyment of land by a life tenant for two reasons. Firstly, his behaviour towards the land might otherwise prejudice the remainderman. Of course, this might well be within the contemplation of the person who settled the land, and in practice he often empowers the life tenant to act in this way. Secondly, and conversely, his interest being of uncertain duration, he might spend money of a capital nature on the land which, if no special rules existed, would fall undeservedly into the lap of the remainderman to the detriment of the life tenant's next-of-kin. In short, he has certain special duties and he, or his personal representatives, have certain special rights which must now be dealt with.

(1) *Duties of a life tenant.* The nature of these duties is governed primarily by the instrument of creation, for it is quite open to a settlor creating the interest to decide what these duties shall be, even though in the outcome the remainderman is prejudiced. After all, the latter is receiving his interest, too, from that settlor. The weight of these duties will usually be described by reference to the law of waste. The settlor may make the life tenant impeachable, or otherwise, for the various types of waste as he thinks fit. As a matter of construction, 'without impeachment of waste', without more, will be interpreted so as to allow the life tenant to commit both permissive and voluntary waste. Some additional and clear words will be necessary if equitable waste also is to be allowed (L.P.A. 1925, s.135).

If the instrument of creation is silent on the question the general rules as to impeachability must be invoked. These are that a life tenant is liable for equitable and voluntary waste but not for permissive (*Re Cartwright* (1889), 41 Ch.D. 532). He will, however, be liable even for repairs if his life interest is in leasehold property and the lease contains a covenant to repair (*Re Betty* [1899] 1 Ch. 821). This kind of settlement will be explained shortly. In any case, this is not strictly a question of waste.

We shall see later that the Settled Land Act 1925, empowers life tenants, even when impeachable for waste, under certain conditions, to cut and sell timber (s.66) and to grant mining leases (s.41), but since any profits of these transactions are deemed to represent the products of the land the fundamental basis of impeachability remains undisturbed. Thus on a sale of timber by an impeachable life tenant, three-quarters of the proceeds are set aside for the benefit of the remainderman in fee simple. The purposes of the power is to enable land to *be* exploited to its best advantage in the absence, for the time being, of a beneficial absolute owner.

(2) *Rights of a life tenant and his personal representatives.* The life tenant has the right, subject to his responsibilities to the remainderman described above, to occupy the land and enjoy its profits. If the land has been leased, he is usually entitled to the whole of the rent, for this is only a vicarious way of enjoying occupation. Two special rights, however, must be explained. They arise on the death of the life tenant and so will be exercisable by his personal representatives unless he is a tenant *pur autre vie*, in which case they may be exercised by the life tenant himself.

The first is the right to emblements. This is the right to enter the land after the end of the life interest and take crops which the tenant sowed. It extends only to annual crops such as corn and not to fruit trees. Only one growth of each crop may be taken. See generally *Graves* v. *Weld* (1833), 5 B. & Ad. 105. Since the right is based on the principle that the end of a life interest cannot be foreseen, it cannot be exercised where the life tenant ends his interest by his own act. This might happen in the case of determinable life interests, dealt with later in this chapter, when, for instance, land is granted 'to *A* for life until he marries' and *A* later marries.

The second of these rights is the right of the next-of-kin, or the tenant himself if he is a tenant *pur autre vie*, to take certain fixtures from the land after the end of the life tenancy. The meaning of 'fixtures' was explained in Chapter 3. A life tenant may bring objects to the land in such circumstances that they become fixtures. The general rule is that all these must be left for the person next entitled to the land, since they have become 'land'. Such a rule would work unjustly, however, if applied without exception. It would certainly discourage a life tenant from improving the property if he thought he was making a gift of such improvements to a remainderman who might be a complete stranger to him, while his widow, who might be entitled to his property generally, would be unable to touch them. We shall see later that a similar problem arises between landlord and tenant and it is in that sphere that the law developed exceptions which make large inroads into the general rule. These exceptions, apart from one, that of agricultural fixtures, apply equally to life tenancies. Certain objects may be detached from land notwithstanding that they have become fixtures, during and at the end of the tenancy. These are trade, ornamental and domestic fixtures.

Trade fixtures are those fixtures attached by the life tenant for the purposes of carrying on his trade (*Poole's Case* (1703), 1 Salk. 368). Such items are too numerous to list but machinery (*Re Hulse* [1905] 1 Ch. 406) and petrol pumps at a garage (*Smith* v. *City Petroleum Co. Ltd.* [1940] 1 All E.R. 260) are examples. Agricultural fixtures may not be removed on a life tenant's death because they are not trade fixtures. Market gardening is, however, classified for this purpose as a trade, and so fixtures used in connection with it, such as shrubs (*Wardell* v. *Usher* (1841), 3 Scott. N.R. 508), may be removed. Ornamental and domestic fixtures have been held to include a wide assortment of objects ranging from ornamental chimney-pieces to panelling (*Spyer* v. *Phillipson* [1931] 2 Ch. 183). A less indulgent approach is taken by the courts to ornamental and domestic fixtures, so that they cannot be removed if substantial damage would be caused. In any case the person removing must reinstate damage caused by removal and restore a similar article where the fixture has been placed by way of substitution. Redecoration is not, however, necessary (*Re De Falbe* [1901] 1 Ch. 523).

A new role of the life tenant

So far we have been considering the beneficial position of the life tenant. The Settled Land Act 1925, perfecting earlier legislation, now casts him in the role of land manager. Since the very existence of a life tenant, or other limited owner, means that there is no absolute owner in occupation for the time being, many of the important decisions affecting the land and the persons entitled under the settlement such as sale, leasing and mortgaging could not be taken for a very long time. The Act, therefore, gives a wide range of such powers to the life tenant or certain other limited owners in possession. These powers do not affect the life tenant's beneficial position, for he is not entitled to the money accruing from such transactions. They are simply powers of decision-making given to the person who ought to be in the best position to make such a decision, the man on the spot in occupation.

Subject-matter of life interests

A life interest ordinarily results from a grant by a fee simple owner of land. It is possible, however, for the owner of a long lease, say for 150 years, to grant it to one person for life, and then for the remainder of its duration to another. Furthermore, it is even possible for pure personalty to be settled in the same way. I may, for instance, settle £10,000 on *A* for life and then to *B* absolutely. In that case, the money must be invested and the annual dividends of the investment represent the life interest, whereas the invested capital awaits the absolute owner, *B*, who may take it on *A*'s death. It will now be apparent how the owners of successive interests in land enjoy those interests when a sale of that land has taken place under the powers given the life tenant by the Settled Land Act 1925, and described above.

The entail

Nature

This is an interest in land which lasts as long as the donee or any of his descendants live. Its origin lies even before the statute De Donis 1285, which perfected it, and it has been admitted into the twentieth century, by the 1925 legislation, still clanking much of its medieval armour. Its complexities rather outweigh its usefulness, for it is seldom met now. It can exist only as an equitable interest (L.P.A. 1925, s.1) and so involves a trust. It is the only interest of inheritance left and represents the only context of any importance in land law in which the term 'heir' may properly be used. Since it does not end until the donee's descendants die out, it is an interest of indefinite duration but, of course, a lesser interest than a fee simple because a break in that chain of descent assuredly brings it to an end. It is, moreover, an unstable interest in that it can be ended by 'barring' with rather startling results as will be seen later. On an intestacy it does not go to the next of kin, as a fee simple and a motor car do, but to the descendant heir. As long as there exists a descendant heir unto whom it can descend, the entail will continue. It is important, therefore, to establish what the rules of descent are for this interest.

The rules of descent

(1) *Descent is traced from the original donee.* On the death of the owner of an entail descent is not necessarily traced from that owner but from the first owner even if the grant was originally made a very long time ago.
(2) *Males have priority.* Where there are members of both sexes in equal degree in the class from which the heir is to come, males are preferred to females unless special provision is made to the contrary in the terms of the grant. Thus, if a grant is made to *A* in tail and he has two children, a girl and a boy, the boy will be the heir irrespective of seniority. These rules can be varied.
(3) *Primogeniture.* Where there are two or more males of equal degree the oldest takes exclusively as heir. If there are no males then a female may inherit. If there are two or more females, however, they all take together as 'coparceners'.
(4) *Representation.* This important rule enables descendants to represent a deceased ancestor *ad infinitum*. Thus, if *A* has two sons, B^1 and B^2, and B^1 has died leaving a son, C^1, then on *A*'s death C^1 represents his deceased father B^1, who would have inherited had he lived. C^1, therefore, inherits and not B^2.

The diagram below may illustrate the operation of these rules. *D* denotes a daughter, *S* denotes a son, *GS* a grandson and so on. Age in a particular degree, that is a family of children, diminishes from left to right. *A* has just died and we must find his heir. He was the original donee, so that descent must be traced from him. His heir would have been *S*, had he lived, because, being male, he would have been preferred to his older sister *D*. *S*, however, is dead himself, but the representation rule may be applied, which brings us to GS^1, who would have been preferred to GS^2 and GS^3 because he was older. GS^1 is dead but he is represented by his heir GGS^1. The heir of *A* is therefore GGS^1 despite the existence of older descendants of *A*. If GGS^1 dies childless, descent will again be traced from *A* and GS^2 will be the heir.

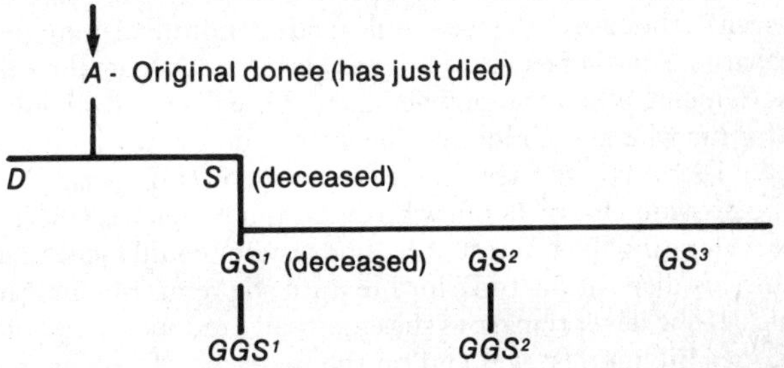

The right of an illegitimate child to succeed, on the intestacy of its parents, to the property of those parents, contained in s.14 of the Family Law Reform Act 1969, does not apply to entails. Fuller discussion of the entail is to be found in the reference books on land law. The rarity of the interest today requires us merely to notice its principal characteristics.

Principal characteristics

(1) *Creation*. While words of limitation for all other purposes have been rendered unnecessary (L.P.A. 1925, s.60), the rules have been tightened for entails. There are sound reasons for this. The entail is uncommon today and if its existence could be implied from informal expressions there would be a danger of it arising in cases where it was not intended. The ordinary testator will hardly wish to employ such an aristocratic method of disposing of his property. The person who wishes to use it will not make his will without legal advice. The rules for the creation of entails after 1925 are contained in the Law of Property Act 1925, s.130.
(2) *The right to bar the entail*. Under the Fines and Recoveries Act 1833, a tenant in tail of full age in possession can execute a deed of disentailment which has the effect of converting the entail into a fee simple absolute (s.15). The result is that the interests not only of his own descendants but also any subsequent interests, including those of the fee simple owner in reversion or remainder are defeated. The Act merely rationalized a fiction which had facilitated this confiscatory act since the Middle Ages. A tenant in tail of full age in remainder can bar his own descendants only. His resultant interest is called a 'base fee', which will endure for so long as descendants of his survive, even though they are of course disentitled. A base fee is convertible to a fee simple absolute once events have occurred which would have brought the entail into possession if it had not been thus partially barred.

Entitlement to an entail thus provides potential for present or future ownership of the fee simple absolute estate in the land. The role of the entail however has been that of dissolving and recasting family interests during the heyday of the strict settlement of land.

Determinable interests and interests upon condition subsequent

Nature

Fees simple and life interests are sometimes made subject to special provisions which might bring them to a premature end. One reason for doing this was seen in the case of the fee simple made conditional upon the payment of a rentcharge. Another example might now be added from the sphere of the family settlement. When a landowner makes his will he will obviously wish to provide for his wife and children. This he can do by leaving the land to his wife, *W*, for life and then in fee simple to his son, *S*. If *W* remarries, however, she will be provided for by her new husband and in that case there is a strong case for accelerating the interest of *S*. The testator could take account of this by framing his disposition 'to *W* for life until she remarries and then to *S* in fee simple'. If she never remarries she enjoys the land for the rest of her life; if she does, her life interest will end on the marriage. There are many other reasons, which will be seen from the decided cases, why fees simple and life interests are sometimes modified in this way.

The law has developed rules governing the nature and effect of these modifications, but, in doing so, has classified them into two types, namely, 'determinable interests' and 'interests upon condition subsequent'. Both types contain a terminating factor, but the way in which this factor is expressed decides whether a particular interest is classified as one or the other. There are some crucial differences between the two types of interest, so it is essential to know how to distinguish them.

The distinction between the two types of interest

In the case of an interest on condition subsequent, which will now be called a 'conditional interest', the terminating factor is expressed as a confiscatory proviso, as in a grant 'to *A* for life on condition he does not remarry'. The interest is granted in its ordinary full terms but might be interrupted before its course is run. In the case of a determinable interest, the terminating event is used to mark the natural end of the interest, as in a grant 'to *A* for life until he remarries'. Conditional interests are usually created by such expressions as 'on condition that' and 'but if', whereas determinable interests are created by 'until', 'during', 'while', and 'for as long as'. In short, in conditional interests the terminating event interrupts and is confiscatory, whereas in determinable interests it delineates and expresses duration. There is of course no difference between the intentions of the grantors in the examples of the gifts to *A* above, although their motives may differ. Remarriage in both cases is to end the interests. It is the mere mood of the language used which is effective. However, this can reflect motive so the distinction between the two types of interest is not entirely verbal or arbitrary.

Now that the identifying features have been highlighted, the differences in the law applying to the two types of interest must be explained.

Effects of conditional and determinable interests

(1) *Time of determination.* There seems to be no conclusive modern authority as to whether all conditional interests become merely voidable, as opposed to void, on the occurrence of the terminating event. No doubt they are voidable only in the case of fees simple on condition supported by a right of re-entry. On breach of the condition, the interest is not divested until the grantor, or his successor in title to the right of re-entry, re-enters. This type of conditional fee simple does not involve a trust (Law of Property (Amendment) Act 1926). Many conditional interests, however, operate by way of gift over to another person rather than by re-entry (see *Re Dugdale* (1888), 38 Ch.D. 176, at p.179, per Kay, J.), as, for instance, in a grant 'to *A* in fee simple, but if he remarries to *B* in fee simple', in which case, we shall see, there is a settlement and, therefore, a trust. Once a trust has been constituted, the interest of a remainderman, such as *B* in the example above, can hardly be dependent on the whim of the grantor. It is submitted, therefore, though without positive judicial authority, that it is only in the case of conditional fees simple caught by the 1926 Act that the interest is merely voidable after

the happening of the terminating event, and that in all other cases the interest ends spontaneously.

In the case of determinable interests the position is clear. They end automatically when the event occurs. This is to be expected, for that event is used as part of the limitation and serves to measure the time for which the property may be enjoyed. Just as an interest granted 'to A for life' ends naturally on *A*'s death, so one given 'to *B* for life until marriage' ends naturally upon *B*'s marriage without any steps being taken by anyone.

(2) *Existence at law.* A fee simple on condition subject to a legal or equitable right of entry or re-entry may, provided it is in possession, exist as a legal estate (Law of Property (Amendment) Act 1926). Other conditional interests must be equitable.

A determinable interest must always be equitable (L.P.A. 1925, s.1).

(3) *Effect of void terminating event.* It will be explained below that the events used to mark the ending of determinable and conditionable interests may sometimes be void. Here we are only concerned to notice that the results of such voidness vary according to whether the interest is conditional or determinable. In the case of a conditional interest the result is to make the interest absolute. This is also the case if the condition is or becomes impossible (*Re Croxon* [1904] 1 Ch. 252). Thus, a grant 'to *A* for life, but, if he fails to murder his wife this year, to *B* for life', creates an unconditional life interest in *A*. In the case of determinable interests, the result is to make the whole interest fail (*Re Moore* (1888), 39 Ch.D. 116). This is a rational result of the function that the terminating event performs in the two different cases. Pluck out the void event from a conditional interest and that interest still has a beginning and an end. Do the same with a determinable interest and you have taken its end away so that the whole fails.

The one exception to this is that if the event is void because it infringes the rule against perpetuities then even a determinable interest becomes absolute (Perpetuities and Accumulations Act 1964, s.12). This problem is dealt with in Chapter 10.

(4) *Grounds for voidness of terminating events.* These will be noticed primarily in relation to conditional interests, which they affect more, and any differences applying to determinable interests will be pointed out in each case.

(a) Repugnancy to the interest granted—It is really self-contradictory to grant an interest in land and then to take away some of the natural characteristics of ownership. These characteristics include the right of alienation, the availability of the property for the satisfaction of debts and the right to the fullest enjoyment of the land in those cases where the doctrine of waste has no application. In the case of an entail it includes the right to bar (*Mildmay's Case* (1605), 6 Co. Rep. 40a). Originally all forms of repugnancy to these principles may have been void, but exceptions have developed which are difficult to classify and give rise to unforeseeability (per Pearson, J., in *Re Rosher* (1884), 26 Ch.D. 801). One of the commonest forms of such repugnancy is a restriction on alienation. In the nature of things, such a restriction may apply either to the form of alienation, to the period of time before alienation shall be free or to the classes of persons to whom the land may be alienated. The present state of the law may be somewhat glibly summed up by saying that any condition which substantially affects the power of alienation is void, though partial restrictions may be valid. A few examples, beginning with the more restrictive and tapering to the less restrictive, may provide at least a rough guide. A condition against all forms of alienation either voluntary or otherwise was held void in *Re Dugdale* (p. 67 *ante*); one against alienation to all but the donee's brothers, who were of course a small and diminishing class, was held void in *Re Brown* [1954] Ch. 39; a condition that the property should be divested on bankruptcy was held void in *Re Machu* (1882), 21 Ch.D. 838. So were restrictions on particular kinds of alienation. On the other hand, partial restraints have been held valid. Probably the widest which has been allowed was a devise to *A* 'on condition he never sells out of the family' (*Re Macleay* (1875), L.R. 20 Eq. 186). This was criticized in *Re Rosher* (above), though it should be noticed that only one form of alienation, namely, sale, and not others such as leasing and mortgaging, was forbidden, and then only for the lifetime of *A*. Furthermore, he was not restricted from selling to his own family. There might be a distinction between limiting alienation to named persons and merely to an indeterminate class, because the numbers of the former are bound to diminish with time and reduce the market to such an extent as to lower the ordinary selling price, thus denying all real chance of selling (see 70 L.Q.R. 15).

Determinable interests, however, are almost completely free from the doctrine of repugnancy. Thus a grant 'to X until he attempts to alienate or becomes bankrupt' is valid, for during the subsistence of the interest no restrictions can be said to have been imposed. This advantage is used in the 'protective trust', discussed in a later chapter. There is, however, one exception. Although a person may grant his property to another so that the interest terminates naturally on bankruptcy or attempted alienation, and may even settle his own property upon himself until attempted alienation, he cannot, even by a determinable limitation, limit his own property to himself until his bankruptcy so as to defeat his creditors (*Re Brewer's Settlement* [1896] 2 Ch. 503).

It has been assumed above that the restriction has been framed as a condition which, if valid, would confer a right of re-entry or cesser of the interest granted. If, however, it has been expressed as a covenant only, giving the covenantee no more than the right to damages on its breach, it is not repugnant to the interest granted (*Caldy Manor Estate Ltd.* v. *Farrell* [1974] 1 W.L.R. 1303.

(b) Uncertainty—The condition must, said Lord Cranworth in *Clavering* v. *Ellison* (1859), 7 H.L. Cas. 707, at p.725, 'be such that the court can see from the beginning, precisely and distinctly, upon the happening of what event it was that the preceding vested estate was to determine'. Not only must the language in the limitation be clear, but the operation of the terminating event must be susceptible of reasonably certain observation. The following examples may illustrate the standard of certainty needed, but it should not be assumed that decisions on the same subject-matter in the future must follow these decisions, for not only circumstances but also the meaning of words are liable to change over many years. A condition that the donee should 'provide a home' for a certain person has been held too vague, for a home is something more than a mere protection from the weather and the other elements implicit in the expression were too elusive (*Re Brace* [1954] 2 All E.R. 354). The same decision was reached in the case of conditions requiring donees 'to conform and be members of the Church of England' (*Re Tegg* [1936] 2 All E.R. 878), and to 'continue to reside in Canada' (*Sifton* v. *Sifton* [1938] A.C. 656).

On the other hand, the courts are usually practical rather than pedantic in their insistence upon reasonable certainty, so that a condition that a donee should become 'a convert to the Roman Catholic faith' was held to be valid in *Re Evans* [1940] Ch. 629, since baptism is necessary for conversion in the ordinary usage of the expression, and there can be no reasonable doubt as to whether a person has been baptised. A condition requiring the assumption of a surname was upheld in *Re Neeld* [1962] Ch. 643, because use of a name is a discernible fact. Finally, in *Bromley* v. *Tryon* [1952] A.C. 265 a condition to operate when the beneficiary became entitled to 'the bulk' of certain other property was not void for uncertainty because 'the bulk' was taken to mean any proportion greater than 50 per cent.

Since breach of a condition brings about forfeiture of the interest it may be that a higher standard of definition is required of the terminating event than in the case of a determinable interest but in matters of definition and construction it is dangerous to venture sweeping statements.

(c) Contrariness to public policy—A condition will be void if it provokes an illegal or immoral act, or prevents or discourages a person from carrying out his legal or moral duty, but the meaning of public policy embraces demands even beyond those of the law and morals. Thus, a condition aimed at preventing marriage altogether will be void, although this will not be so if the intention is merely to provide for a person until marriage (*Jones* v. *Jones* (1876), 1 Q.B.D. 279). Partial restraints on marriage, such as conditions against marrying certain persons or forbidding second marriages, are always valid (see, for instance, *Jenner* v. *Turner* (1880), 16 Ch.D. 188). Other examples of conditions being against public policy are those which might induce spouses to separate (*Re Moore* (1888), 39 Ch.D. 116) or influence parents' duties in the upbringing of children.

In this context may be mentioned an unusual application recently made under the Variation of Trusts Act 1958, which empowers the court to order the rearrangement of trust provisions in favour of future beneficiaries under certain conditions. The court ordered the removal of a condition against practising the Roman Catholic religion on proof that its removal would benefit those on whose behalf the application was made. The condition was held to be 'undesirable' (*Re Remnant's Settlement Trusts* [1970] 1 Ch. 560). The condition would not of course have been void as being against public policy.

An infringement of the rule against perpetuities is one which needs special watchfulness in drafting settlements. Racial discrimination in itself would not be unlawful for the reasons now being discussed, although a limitation framed with that motive might often fail for uncertainty.

Determinable interests are affected by the rules of public policy in the same way as conditional interests, except that they are completely free of the rules regarding marriage. An interest granted until marriage is valid in all circumstances and is often used in settlements.

Beneficial position of owners of modified interests

The owner of a determinable or conditional interest may enjoy the land to the same extent as if he owned the equivalent absolute interest. Thus, in the case of a determinable life interest, his position is controlled by the law of waste, subject to any express provision in the instrument of creation, and in the case of a modified fee simple, he may use the land in the same way as the owner of a fee simple absolute, except that equitable waste will be restrained if there is a gift over to another person following a breach of condition (*Re Hanbury's Settled Estates* [1913] 2 Ch. 357, per Eve, J., at pp.363 and 365). If there is no gift over but the grantor reserves a right of re-entry, the reasons for restraining equitable waste do not seem to be so strong. If there is no gift over or right of entry reserved in the instrument of creation, the court might be led to construe an expression as a mere request to the grantee rather than a condition of forfeiture (*Re Evans*, p.61, *ante*).

Apart from these beneficial rights, the owner of a conditional or determinable interest will often be in the position of a 'land manager', as we saw, earlier in this chapter, is the case with a tenant for life. This will be discussed with the settlement.

Interests upon condition precedent

Interests upon condition subsequent have been discussed above and their outstanding feature is that they are liable to be ended on the occurrence of a particular event. The main characteristic of an interest upon condition precedent is that the interest does not arise at all until the occurrence of an event, whereupon the interest which arises behaves just like other interests of its kind. Thus in a grant 'to *A* in fee simple when he marries' *A* owns no interest at all until he marries, but then the fee simple absolute which has sprung up in his favour is no different from any other fee simple absolute. Any interest in land may be subject to a condition precedent. They are sometimes called 'contingent interests'.

The condition itself must not be void for any of the reasons mentioned in relation to conditions subsequent. If a condition precedent is void the interest fails to take effect. Just as a determinable interest fails if its terminating event is void because it then possesses no end, so an interest subject to a condition precedent is deprived of its beginning once a void condition is struck out, and therefore collapses completely. A common cause of voidness in conditions precedent is infringement of the rule against perpetuities.

Study material: (1954) 70 L.Q.R. 15

Re Macleay (1875) L.R. 20 Eq. 186 belongs to the group, select and small, of those decisions of Sir George Jessel M.R. which have not been approved by posterity. Land was devised to a brother of the testator "on the condition that he never sells it out of the family." The Master of the Rolls held that the condition did not infringe the rule against total restraint upon alienation because it bound only the devisee personally, it applied only to sales and not other modes of alienation, and within the "family" (an expression which was construed as meaning "blood relations," and comprehended many persons) even sales were permissible. The judgment was somewhat critical of the decision of Sir John Romilly M.R. in *Attwater* v. *Attwater* (1853) 18 Beav. 330, but in turn Pearson J. In *Re Rosher* (1884) 26 Ch.D. 801 was critical of *Re Macleay*. As John Chipman Gray pointed out, in *Re Macleay* "there was no argument of opposing counsel," and he added that "the obvious ease of evading such a condition, if allowed to exist, renders it doubtful whether Sir George Jessel will have a following in this matter, beyond what he already has in the Province of Ontario" (*Restraints on the Alienation of Property* (2nd ed., 1895) pp.28, 43: for a modern Ontario instance, see *Re Noble and Wolf* [1949] O.R. 503, in which, incidentally, *Re Drummond Wren* [1945] O.R. 778 (noted (1948) 64 L.Q.R. 19) came under fire). On the other hand, Professor Glanville Williams has attacked the whole basis of the doctrine that total restraints against alienation are bad for repugnancy to the interest given, urging that any such invalidity should be based on grounds of public policy rather than repugnancy: (1943) 59 L.Q.R. 343.

In *Re Brown* [1953] 3 W.L.R. 877, the point arose again. The testator gave land to trustees in trust for his widow for life, and thereafter (subject to an intermediate trust) in trust for his four sons as tenants in common. The will then provided that if any son executed any assurance whereby his share might become vested in any person except one or more of his brothers, that son's share should be held on certain discretionary trusts for the son, his wife and his children. Harman J. held that the doctrine laid down for realty applied equally to the son's interests under the trust for sale which would arise on their mother's death (a point upon which it is useful to have authority), and then proceeded to a discussion of the cases. As between *Attwater* v. *Attwater* and *Re Macleay*, the learned judge plainly inclined in favour of the former; but although the headnote records that *Re Macleay* was "not followed," it could be said that in reality that case was distinguished. "It is pertinent that a number of named persons as in this clause is in essence different from a class consisting, for instance, as Sir George Jessel's did in *Re Macleay*, of members of the family, which he said was a large indeterminate class of people and might, of course, increase as time went on; whereas, if alienation be restricted to three or four or five named persons, the class is bound to diminish as death takes its toll of the members" (p. 885). The proviso accordingly in substance amounted to a general prohibition against alienation, so that both on the authorities and in accordance with the increasing modern tendency to curtail the extent to which the dead hand of a testator may rule the living, it was held to be void. This conclusion accords with the decision in a somewhat similar Australian case which does not seem to have been cited. In *Grayson* v. *Grayson* [1922] Q.S.R. 155, a testator specifically devised certain lands to his four sons, subject (inter alia) to a condition against any son during his life selling any of the land except to one or more of the other sons. After a full examination of the authorities and literature on the subject, McCawley C.J. (at p. 163) said that the power of alienation was "restricted within limits so narrow as to constitute a substantial taking away, not of the whole power of alienation, but of a valuable portion of it, subjecting it to fetters which inevitably, by limiting the market, diminish the ordinary selling value of the land, and which might, in fact, destroy all opportunity of selling." The condition involved "such a substantial restriction of the power of alienation" that it could not be regarded as falling within any recognised exception to the rule against such restrictions, and so was void.

R.E.M.

Questions

1 *What is meant by 'in possession' in the expression 'fee simple absolute in possession' as used in the Law of Property Act 1925, s.1?*

2 *Under what circumstances might a fee simple subject to a condition subsequent be an equitable interest?*

3 *Explain the nature of the doctrine of 'repugnancy to the interest granted' and its limits in regard to determinable interests and interests upon condition subsequent.*
4 *Can you discern the reason for any distinctions made by the 1925 legislation between family and commercial interests in land?*

Chapter Six

Leasehold interests

THE LEASE is the final interest to be discussed which gives a right to the land itself. 'Lease', 'tenancy', 'demise', 'term of years', and 'leasehold interest' have the same meaning, although 'tenancy' is often used to describe a lease of shorter duration. The order of treatment of leases will be their nature, types, creation and contents, the remedies of landlords and tenants, the remedies of assignees of landlords' and tenants' interests and the determination of leases. Finally, the statutory protection of certain classes of tenants is considered.

The nature of a lease

Definition

A lease is the grant of the right of exclusive possession of a defined piece of land for a fixed maximum period of time, or series of fixed periods of time, with the intention that the grantee shall have an estate in the land. Some of the elements of this definition must now be examined.

(1) *The right of exclusive possession.* There can be no lease unless the right of exclusive possession is granted. The tenant must have the right to exclude all persons including the landlord himself. In a true lease, the landlord commits trespass if he enters the property without authority. Where the grantor retains some degree of authority over the land therefore, or where he has the right to enter at will, or where the grantee has not true dominion but merely the right to use the land for a certain limited purpose, possession is not exclusive. Thus a lodger is not usually a tenant (see *Wells* v. *Kingston-upon-Hull Corporation* (1875), L.R. 10 C.P. 402). Restrictions imposed by the lease or otherwise against using the property for certain purposes are, however, quite compatible with exclusive possession; so is a right reserved by the landlord to enter at times for certain purposes, such as to view the state of repair.

Yet an owner granting possession for profit will sometimes wish to represent the transaction as a licence rather than a tenancy since, as we shall see later in this chapter, a tenant's occupation and rent is generally protected by the Rent Acts, whereas in the case of a licensee this is generally not so. Superficial attempts to this end, such as the use of words denoting licences, have long failed to convince the courts, who ask whether the parties really intended that the grantee should enjoy exclusive possession, not whether some sham words theoretically allow the owner to impose himself on some other person as joint possessor.

The possible gulf between express words and real intention is crucial. One owner might really intend to reserve the right to share possession; another might wish merely to exclude the Rent Acts. In such a broth of uncertainty the personal policies of particular judges can become rather fertile. Two recent cases illustrate this.

In *Somma* v. *Hazelhurst* [1978] 2 All E.R. 1011 the Court of Appeal held that the reservation by the grantor of possession of a right to share possession with the grantee denied the intention to give exclusive possession. In *Walsh* v. *Griffith-Jones* [1978] 2 All E.R. 1002, where the facts were substantially similar, it was held by a county court that a non-exclusive agreement was a sham, so that a tenancy resulted. This case can be distinguished from the former on the grounds that the grantees of possession were informed that the reservation of the right to possession was a legal formality only. On the other hand, it was stated in Somma's case that there is nothing to prevent a grant of exclusive possession by a licence rather than by lease, provided that this was the common intention of the parties and that a lease was not merely masquerading as a licence.

This must surely mean that it is now possible to contract out of the Rent Acts. This is not so heretical as it appears, since intention is also vital in the establishment of another characteristic of a lease, namely the intention to create an estate, shortly to be discussed.

While exclusive possession is a necessary characteristic of a lease, it does not serve to distinguish it from other interests giving rights to the land itself. Furthermore, exclusive possession is often given in the grant of a mere licence, which is dealt with below (see *Hughes* v. *Griffin* [1969] 1 All E.R. 460).

(2) *Defined piece of land.* There can be no lease unless the property is defined. If the land or premises which are to be used are determinable from time to time by their owner there is no lease but merely a contract or licence. This might be the case, for instance, where a resident in a house is obliged by his agreement to change his rooms when asked to do so (see *Interoven Stove Co. Ltd.* v. *Hibbard* [1936] 1 All E.R. 263).

(3) *Fixed maximum period of time.* The duration of a lease may be as long or as short as the parties wish, but it must have a certain beginning and a certain maximum duration, though it is enough that these requirements are satisfied before the lease takes effect, even if they are not settled when the lease is executed (see *Harvey* v. *Pratt* [1965] 1 W.L.R. 1025). These dates may be expressly stated or determined collaterally as in a lease to *L* 'to commence upon his birthday this year'. If either of these two events is uncertain the transaction is void. Thus, an attempt to make a lease 'for the duration of the war' failed in *Lace* v. *Chantler* [1944] K.B. 368.

Provided that the maximum duration is ascertained, an intermediate terminating event, which itself might happen at an uncertain time, does not invalidate the lease. A grant to *T*, for instance, for fifty years, terminable upon his marriage, is good.

Two forms of occupation which bear the name of 'tenancy' are difficult to reconcile with this aspect of the definition. Firstly, a 'tenancy at will' has no ascertainable duration. It arises when a person occupies land, supposedly as tenant, on the understanding that either he or the owner may determine the occupation at any time. Despite the violence the suggestion does to accepted legal terminology, this form of occupation is better considered to be no tenancy at all. It is essentially a licence, that is a personal permission to occupy land which negatives trespass. The fact that it mixes in the company of tenancies, in that it sometimes arises before or after true leases, does not make it one itself. Nevertheless, for the purposes of the Limitation Act, 1980, it must be distinguished from a licence (see *Cobb* v. *Lane* [1952] 1 All E.R. 1199). Perhaps the tenancy at will is now obsolescent and the only purpose it can serve is as a midwife, in certain circumstances, to a periodic tenancy (*post*, p. 80, see *Heslop* v. *Burns* [1974] 1 W.L.R. 1241 and *Hagee* v. *Erickson* [1976] Q.B. 209).

Secondly, there is a 'tenancy at sufferance'. This arises where a person whose tenancy has ended continues in possession of the property without the consent of the owner and without statutory authority. Clearly the maximum duration of such occupation is uncertain. Once again we can say that this is not a tenancy at all. Since under the Limitation Act, 1980, time begins to run against the owner from the inception of this form of occupation, it is clearly a simple case of adverse possession.

(4) *Series of fixed periods*. Some leases are granted for a single fixed period such as for ten years. Others are granted on a periodic basis as from month to month or from year to year. These continue indefinitely until ended by a notice to quit. Thus a monthly tenancy might last twenty years and then be terminated by a month's notice. The requirement of certainty of duration is satisfied in these cases provided that the periodic unit itself has fixed bounds. The chain's length might be uncertain but the link must be measured. This is so even if restrictions have been placed on the right to serve notice to quit, such as that it may only be served by the tenant and not by the landlord. In such cases, however, even though the term itself is valid, the clause restricting determination might be held repugnant to the interest granted (*Centaploy Ltd.* v. *Matlodge Ltd.* [1973] 2 All E.R. 720 and see 89 L.Q.R. 457).

(5) *Intention to create an estate*. An estate in land gives a right to the land itself and not merely a right against particular persons. A person who owns an estate owns property which is defensible and recoverable *in specie*, and which is valid against the whole world. An estate is not restricted to the grantee, for it may be alienated both during his life and on death. This contrasts with a mere personal permission to use land either to the extent of full occupation or for some limited purpose, which amounts to a licence only, whether unilateral or contractual. The effect of such a licence is to create a relationship only betweeen the parties to it. It is not contemplated that it shall give rights of property defensible against the whole world. Neither is it intended to be alienable like an estate.

Licences are, in most cases, easily distinguishable from leases but there have been several cases in the last century in which, in particular circumstances, they have been held to be binding upon third parties (see for instance *Errington* v. *Errington and Woods* [1952] 1 K.B. 290). Where limited occupation is given, or when possession is merely transitory as when, for instance, you allow your neighbour to repair his car in your garage, the factors distinguishing them from leases stand out clearly: There is either no exclusive possession, or no definite duration. Since it is however now settled that licences may possess both these attributes (see *Marcroft Wagons Ltd.* v. *Smith* [1951] 2 K.B. 496), the really critical distinction between a lease and a licence must now be isolated. The distinction is that in a lease there is the intention to create an estate in land with the effects described above. This intention must be deduced from what the circumstances show the parties wished substantially to achieve, rather than from the terms in which they clothed the transaction. Some cases must be examined to illustrate this test. Firstly, exclusive possession raises a presumption of a tenancy. Secondly, this presumption may be rebutted by circumstances showing a contrary intention.

In *Errington* v. *Errington and Woods*, above, Denning, L.J., said

> Although a person who is let into exclusive possession is *prima facie* to be considered to be a tenant, nevertheless he will not be held to be so if the circumstances negative any intention to create a tenancy. Words alone may not suffice. Parties cannot turn a tenancy into a licence merely by calling it one. But if the circumstances and the conduct of the parties show that all that was intended was that the occupier should be granted a personal privilege, with no interest in the land, he will be held to be a licensee only.

In a licence the intention is to accommodate a particular person only in particular circumstances, and this intention does not embrace other persons, such as alienees. Thus in *Crane* v. *Morris* [1965] 1 W.L.R. 1104, a farm worker was allowed to occupy a cottage so long as he remained an employee. Later he went to work elsewhere. It was held that he was a licensee only, or 'service occupant', and therefore denied the protection of the Rent Acts.

The same conclusion was reached in *Abbeyfield (Harpenden) Society Ltd.* v. *Woods* [1968] 1 All E.R. 352 n., where a resident in an old people's home had exclusive possession of a room. The provision of services, meals and other attention, including that of a housekeeper, led to the inference that the occupation was personal in nature despite the use of the words 'rent' and 'tenancy' in the agreement. (See also *Binions* v. *Evans* [1972] 2 All E.R. 70.) To highlight the distinction, we might imagine the surprise of the owners of the home if that resident had attempted to assign his occupancy to a person aged sixteen. An inference that a licence only was intended is also likely in cases of family arrangement (see *Cobb* v. *Lane*, p. 151, *ante*). The question of intention must be explored anew in each case and the deductions made from the circumstances of one case cannot be applied automatically to another one exhibiting similar conditions.

Legal and equitable leases

(1) *Legal*. A lease can exist as a legal estate only if two conditions are satisfied. It must be 'a term of years absolute' under the Law of Property Act, 1925, s.I(I), and be created in the way laid down by ss. 52 and 54 of that Act. The creation of leases is separately discussed below.

The expression 'term of years absolute' is not as demanding as it appears and is defined in s. 205(I) (xxvii). The effect is that if a grant satisfies the test as to duration outlined above it is a term of years. A monthly tenancy and one for 100 years are equally 'terms of years', for the definition includes terms of less than a year. The word 'absolute' seems to have no meaning, for the definition expressly includes terms which are liable to terminate through notice to quit, by operation of law, or by re-entry. A right of re-entry by the landlord is inserted in a lease in order to bring about its premature forfeiture for breach of some covenant. In short, factors which would prevent a fee simple being absolute do not do so in the case of a lease.

There is no requirement that a lease shall be in possession. Thus a lease granted today to take effect in possession next year may be a legal estate. A sub-lease may equally be a term of years absolute and therefore a legal estate. These are described below. Several legal estates can therefore exist in land at the same time (L.P.A. 1925, s.I(5)).

(2) *Equitable*. Equitable leases may arise in two ways. Firstly, a specifically enforceable contract for a lease creates an equitable lease which will be described below under creation of leases. Secondly a lease, like any property, may be held upon trust by trustees for a person, in which case the beneficiary holds an equitable interest in it

Sub-leases

If a lessee transfers to another person the whole of the unexpired term, the transaction is called an 'assignment' (see *Milmo* v. *Carreras* [1946] 1 All E.R. 288). Thus, if *L* leased land in 1960 to *T* for twenty years and in 1970 *T* transferred all the remaining term of ten years to *A*, an assignment has been made. *A* now becomes the owner of the lease and holds of *L*.

If, however, *T* transfers to a person something less in duration, even by a single day, than the unexpired term which he holds, he has granted a sub-lease out of the lease. If in 1970 *T* granted to *S* a term of nine years, or even ten years minus one day, *S* would take a sub-lease. In that case *S* would hold of *T*, who would continue to hold of *L*, although only *S* would be entitled to present possession of the land. In such circumstances *L*, if he owns the fee simple, is said to hold the 'freehold reversion', while *T* holds a 'leasehold reversion', although it is, in this case, only of one day's duration. If *L* assigns his interest the transaction is a conveyance of his fee simple subject to *T*'s lease, which entitles the purchaser to receive the rent from *T*, or from *T*'s assignee if *T* has assigned his interest.

Types of leases

There are now two types of lease. Firstly, there is a lease for a fixed term such as two years or 200 years. This kind does not normally end before the end of the specified period, unless a right to end it is expressly reserved. Secondly, there is the periodic tenancy, which might be granted on a monthly, quarterly, annual or other such periodic basis. These tenancies continue indefinitely until ended by notices to quit. Certain other types of grant were possible before 1926, but these have been brought into line with the two types mentioned above. These cases, together with certain other related restrictions upon the types of lease which may be created, must now be considered.

Leases for life or until marriage (Law of Property Act 1925, section 149(6))

A lease at a rent, or for a fine for life or lives, or for a term of years determinable with life or lives or the marriage of the lessee, or a contract therefor, now takes effect as a lease, or contract therefor, for ninety years. It is, however, terminable after such death or marriage by either party—by one month's written notice to determine it on one of the quarter days applicable to the tenancy—or, if there are none, on one of the usual quarter days. A fine is a premium.

The general effect is simply to equip such leases with a formal fixed duration, without affecting the substantial intentions and rights of the parties. In a few cases, however, the effects might interfere in a way probably not contemplated by the section. An example would be if the lessor only wished to make a grant of a few years to a person who he thought would not live long. Thus a lease for five years to *T*, if he should live so long, might not be terminable until more than that period has elapsed if *T* should outstay his welcome.

The application of this principle only where a rent or fine is payable is aimed at drawing a sharp line between a profit-making life term which leaves the fee simple still 'in possession', and one which is a truly gratuitous endowment, returning no profit, which therefore pushes the fee simple into remainder, thus creating a real element of succession. In the latter case, such as a grant 'to A for 100 years if he should live so long' free of rent or fine, a settlement arises. Such a lease is clearly equivalent in every substantial way to a life interest. The lessee becomes the life tenant under s.20(iv) of the Settled Land Act, 1925. (But see *Re Catling* [1931] 2 Ch. 359). This will be discussed further in Chapter 9.

Perpetually renewable leases (Law of Property Act 1922, section 145)

A perpetually renewable lease is one which contains a clause entitling the tenant to a new lease on the same terms as the old one, including the clause for renewal, thus entitling the tenant to stay in the property forever. This must be distinguished from a lease which is 'simply' renewable, for in that case the original lease does not give the right to demand a lease which is the mirror image of itself, but simply another lease, without the renewal clause.

Perpetually renewable leases existing at the end of 1925 were converted into leases for 2,000 years, calculated from the time when the existing term began. Fines payable on renewal became payable as additional rent. A purported grant of or contract for such a lease after 1925 takes effect as a term of 2,000 years, or contract therefor, but free from any obligation to pay renewal money (see *Caerphilly Concrete Products Ltd.* v. *Owen* [1972] 1 W.L.R. 372). These statutory terms are subject to the terms of the original lease but with the addition of the following provisions:

(1) The lessee for the time being may end the lease by giving at least ten days' notice in writing before any date at which it would have expired had there been no conversion and if it had not been renewed.
(2) The lessee must register every assignment or devolution with the lessor or his agent within six months of its occurrence.
(3) A lessee who assigns the term ceases to be liable on the covenants even though privity of contract still exists between him and the lessor.

Once again it should be observed that the substantial position of the parties is unchanged. The lessee has complete control over his future occupation, for the landlord is not entitled to serve the notice mentioned above. (See *Barnett Ltd.* v. *Barclay*, 1980, *The Times*, 19th Dec.).

Reversionary leases

A reversionary lease is one which is expressed to commence at some future date. Formerly, there was no limit as to this time lapse between creation and commencement. Under the Law of Property Act, 1925, s. 149(2), any term at a rent or for a fine, limited after 1925 to take effect more than twenty-one years from the date of the instrument purporting to create it, or any contract to create such a term, is void. The subsection does not apply to leases taking effect in equity under a settlement.

Thus a lease limited under an instrument executed in 1970 to take effect in 1992 is void. A contract for a lease is not void merely because the lease takes effect more than twenty-one years after the date of the contract, so that the exercise at the end of the lease of a right of renewal in a lease for 100 years is valid, because there will be no unlawful lapse between the execution of the lease and its operation (*Weg Motors Ltd.* v. *Hales* [1962] Ch. 49). A contract, however, to grant a lease which when granted will not become effective for more than twenty-one years is void. Where contracts and options are in question, the rule against perpetuities must also be borne in mind.

Duration of renewed leases (Law of Property Act 1922, section 145)

A contract for the renewal of a lease or sub-lease for a term exceeding sixty years from the end of that lease or sub-lease is void. This provision affects simple renewals and must not be confused with the rules as to perpetual renewals mentioned above.

The creation of leases

All leases, legal or equitable, must conform to the essential requirements of a lease mentioned earlier. That being so, however, there are certain formalities necessary in the creation of some leases, upon the observance of which will depend whether a legal or equitable lease, or indeed any interest at all, arises. Frequently, however, the parties enter the landlord and tenant relationship under a contract for a lease only, and never contemplate the formation of a legal lease. Such equitable leases have most, though not all, of the attributes of legal leases. Finally, there are certain conditions which result in the formation of both legal and equitable leases of different durations simultaneously between the same parties in the same land. This happens because the formalities required for legal and equitable leases differ. The problem in these cases as to which of the two conflicting leases shall prevail has now been settled.

The subject of creation will therefore be discussed in the following order: the creation of legal leases; the creation of equitable leases; the solution of conflicts between them; and the advantages of a legal lease over an equitable one.

The creation of legal leases

A periodic tenancy such as a monthly or annual one may be created, and is in fact presumed, merely by a tenant going into possession and the landlord accepting rent. If, however, it is clear that the parties intended to create some other relationship, such as a tenancy at will, even the payment of rent on a periodic basis will not override this intention (*Manfield & Sons Ltd.* v. *Botchin* [1970] 3 All E.R. 143). The particular period which is applicable will depend upon the period by reference to which the rent is calculated and not upon the mere frequency with which it is paid. Thus no formalities are required for these tenancies, a common-law principle now preserved by statute (L.P.A. 1925, s.55(c)).

Next, under s.54(2) of the Act, a lease taking effect in possession for a term not exceeding three years, whether or not the lessee is given power to extend the term, at the best rent which can be reasonably obtained without taking a fine, may be created orally. Of course, as is the case with periodic tenancies, the parties may carry out the transaction in writing or by deed if they wish. The three elements present in this rule should be carefully noted. A reversionary lease, for instance, no matter how short, can never qualify. On the other hand, these requirements do not affect the periodic tenancies mentioned above, which may be created by possession and payment of rent, even though they eventually last for more than three years.

Finally, all other legal leases must be created by deed (L.P.A. 1925, s.52(1)).

The creation of equitable leases

An equitable lease is created by an enforceable agreement for a lease. Two matters are essential to enforceability. Firstly, and this is a question of the ordinary law of contract, the parties must have reached final agreement upon the essential terms (see *King's Motors (Oxford) Ltd.* v. *Lax* [1970] 1 W.L.R. 426). Secondly, as stated in Chapter 3, an agreement for the sale or other disposition of land, or any interest in land, cannot be enforced by action unless it is supported either by a signed memorandum or some sufficient act of part performance (L.P.A. 1925, s.40). A contract for a lease is clearly caught by the section.

Provided that these rules are satisfied, in most cases the agreement can, if desired, be specifically enforced by the court, in which case a legal lease must be executed. In some cases, however, a decree of specific performance might not be granted because the party seeking it has infringed the maxim that 'he who seeks equity must do equity'. A tenant who has entered a specifically enforceable contract for a lease has an equitable lease, pending the grant of specific performance. He frequently seeks no legal lease.

The only formalities necessary for the creation of an enforceable equitable lease therefore are those contained in s.40 of the Act. On the other hand the section applies to all contracts for leases no matter how short in duration. Ironically, while a legal lease for one year may, under certain conditions, be created orally, a contract for a lease of one year's duration must always satisfy s.40 before it can be judicially enforced.

Finally, although there is clearly a distinction between the intention to grant a lease and the intention to make a contract for a lease, it is quite settled that a purported lease which fails to create a legal estate, because it is not by deed under seal, may be treated as a contract for a lease, provided that it embodies sufficient memorandum to satisfy s.40, or is supported by sufficient act of part performance. Since specific performance can be decreed of such an 'agreement' and a legal lease created (*Parker* v. *Taswell* (1858), 2 De G. & J. 559), it is clear that the flank of s.52(1) of the Law of Property Act 1925, discussed above, can easily be turned. Nevertheless such a lease, created in writing and not under seal, remains equitable only until a legal lease is executed.

Where contradictory legal and equitable leases result, the equitable lease prevails

The discrepancy between the methods of creating legal and equitable leases can lead to contradictory results. This conflict and its solution is illustrated by *Walsh* v. *Lonsdale* (1882), 21 Ch.D. 9. *L* agreed in writing to lease a mill to *T* for seven years with a term that on demand *T* should pay a year's rent in advance. No deed was executed in accordance with this, but *T* took possession and paid rent quarterly. The question arose whether *L* could demand a year's rent in advance and use the remedy of distress to enforce it.

Clearly the possession coupled with payment of rent was sufficient to create a legal yearly tenancy; equally clearly the written agreement created an equitable lease for seven years. It was argued that distress was a legal and not an equitable remedy, and that the only legal interest *T* held was an annual tenancy, subject to those terms of the agreement that were consistent with such a tenancy. The payment of a year's rent in advance was not consistent with it because a yearly tenancy can be ended by half a year's notice. This being so, it was pressed, the advance payment could not be demanded because it was not a term of the legal tenancy.

It was held, however, that there were not two separate interests created by two independent codes of rules, as was the case before the fusion of the courts of equity and common law. The court must apply all the rules, legal and equitable, but if there should exist any incompatibility between them, the rules of equity must prevail. Therefore, *T* was holding under the equitable and not the legal lease, and since equity treated that as done which ought to be done, *T* and *L* must have all the rights and responsibilities which would have been theirs if the seven years' lease had been granted by deed. In short, the distress was lawful.

The case may be cited to support two propositions. Firstly, if there is an enforceable equitable lease, this will stifle any legal tenancy which would otherwise have arisen from the incidents of possession and payment of rent. Secondly, a contract for a lease is for many purposes as good as a legal lease. This doctrine will be discussed below. However, the first of these propositions pre-supposes that the equitable lease is valid and enforceable. If for some reason it is not—because, for example, specific performance will not be granted—then advantage may nevertheless be taken of any legal tenancy that arises through taking possession and paying rent.

So, if *T* enters possession of land and pays rent upon a monthly basis after *L* has purported to grant him a term of five years under an unsealed written document, his rights and duties will be those expressed in that document, because the imperfect lease is treated as a contract for a lease: that is an equitable lease for five years. If, however, he has failed to perform some covenant in that document, he might not be able to claim specific performance. In that case, he would not be entitled to a lease for five years, although he might be entitled to sue *L* for damages for breach of contract. He would, however, have the advantage of a legal monthly tenancy.

The advantages of legal leases over equitable leases

Despite the doctrine of *Walsh* v. *Lonsdale*, there are some important differences between a legal lease and an equitable lease arising from a contract for a lease. They are as follows:

(1) *Specific performance is a discretionary remedy*. The doctrine in *Walsh* v. *Lonsdale* presupposes that specific performance would be ordered of the contract. There are cases, however, when it might be refused (see *Coatsworth* v. *Johnson* (1886), 55 L.J.Q.B. 220 and *Warmington* v. *Miller* [1973] 2 All E.R. 372). The parties will then be left with the mere right to sue upon the agreement for damages. Of course, in many cases a legal periodic tenancy will have arisen and they may then fall back on their rights under that.

(2) *A contract for a lease does not create privity of estate*. There exists between a lessor and lessee under a legal lease 'privity of estate', a relationship which continues to exist between all assignees of the lease on the one hand and all assignees of the reversion on the other. Its importance is that some of the most important covenants in a lease are binding not only as between persons enjoying privity of contract, but also between persons who have privity of estate, and that the liabilities as well as the rights under such covenants pass into the hands of assignees. In the case of a contract for a lease, however, no privity of estate exists between the parties or their assignees, so that the ordinary rule of contract applies (except insofar as statute has altered this position) that the benefit but not the burden of the covenant may be assigned (*Purchase* v. *Lichfield Brewery Co.* [1915] 1 K.B. 184). This difference, however, has perhaps now disappeared. It will be considered further shortly.

(3) *Equitable leases are liable to be overridden*. We have already seen that a legal interest is a real right, good against all persons. A legal lease, therefore, prevails against any purchaser of any interest in the land, whether or not that purchaser has notice of it and whether or not he gives value. This is not so with an equitable lease, which may in some circumstances be overridden by purchasers of legal estates in the land. Their position has been modified by the 1925 legislation if the contract was entered into after that date.

If the contract was made before 1926, and there has been no assignment after 1925, the equitable lease will be overridden by a purchaser for value of a legal estate in good faith for value without notice. Possession under the lease, however, constitutes notice. A contract for a lease entered into after 1925 is registrable as an estate contract under the Land Charges Act 1972, or, in the case of registered land, as a minor interest. If it is not registered, it is void against a purchaser for money, or money's worth, of a legal estate in the land—even though that purchaser had actual or constructive notice of the lessee's rights. If the interest is registered, therefore, it is quite as secure as a legal estate.

(4) *Section 62 of the Law of Property Act, 1925, does not apply to a contract*. It will be explained in a later chapter that this section may operate in a 'conveyance' to convey unexpectedly wide rights in the form of easements or

profits to a purchaser unless its effects are excluded by the conveyance. A contract for a lease, however, is not a 'conveyance' for this purpose, whereas legal leases, provided that they are in writing, are (see L.P.A. 1925, s.205(i)(ii), and *Borman* v. *Griffith* [1930] 1 Ch. 493).

The rights and duties of the parties under a lease

The rights and duties of the parties under a lease are governed by two factors. Firstly, there are certain rights and duties of a fairly rudimentary kind which apply when no express agreement has been made between the parties, beyond such really essential matters as the duration of the term, without which indeed the lease could not exist at all. Some of these may be displaced by express terms but others apply in certain circumstances, even in the face of express terms to the contrary. Secondly, it is open to the parties over a wide field to fix their own rights and duties by express covenants. Nevertheless, in view of the wide application of certain important statutory rules, which prevail irrespective of express terms, there is some truth in the observation that the relationship of landlord and tenant now owes much less to contract than it used to do, and much more to statute.

Such restrictions upon freedom of contract illustrate a more general protection of the consumer in the modern state. The development has affected contracts of employment and dealings with goods and mortgages. Later we shall examine how that has profoundly curtailed contractual freedom to end tenancies and determine rents.

Rights and duties in default of effective express covenants upon the issue

Rights and duties are correlative notions and for simplicity they will be considered from the point of view of the tenant.

(1) Rights of the tenant

(a) *Implied covenant for quiet enjoyment*—Even if there is no express provision dealing with the matter, there is implied in every tenancy a covenant that the lessor shall put the lessee into possession and then shall not himself make, nor authorize any other person nor permit any person claiming under him to make, physical interference with the enjoyment of the premises (*Browne* v. *Flower* [1911] 1 Ch. 219, at p.228). There is no liability, however, for the acts of persons claiming by a paramount title such as that of a superior landlord. Examples of breach of this right are the erection of scaffolding in front of the access to a shop (*Owen* v. *Gadd* [1956] 2 Q.B. 99), conduct threatening physical eviction and removing belongings of the tenant (*Kenny* v. *Preen* [1962] 3 All E.R. 814). Even an easement granted for the enjoyment of the property may be within such an implied covenant (*Miller* v. *Emcer Products Ltd.* [1956] Ch. 304). On the other hand, mere interference with personal comfort by noise or invasion of privacy does not constitute a breach.

There is no room for the implication of such a covenant if there is an express term covering the matter (*Line* v. *Stephenson* (1838), 4 Bing. (N.C.) 678), but the doctrine applies to all kinds of tenancies, whether created by deed, by writing, orally, or by agreement only (*Markham* v. *Paget* [1908] 1 Ch. 697).

(b) *The right to enjoy his grant without derogation.* The terms and circumstances of the grant of a lease will determine the total rights to which a lessee is entitled, including any easements to be enjoyed with the premises and the purposes for which the property is let. This might involve difficult problems of construction, but it is a general principle applying to all grants that the grantor must not later derogate from that grant by acts which contradict or are inconsistent with it, so that the grantee cannot enjoy it to its full extent.

The doctrine is concentric with that of the implied covenant for quiet possession, in that breaches of the latter will constitute a derogation from grant, but the doctrine of non-derogation from grant is wider and may include obligations beyond the reach of the covenant for quiet possession. There is no need, for instance, to prove any physical interference with the property leased. It is frequently invoked in cases where the landlord retains property nearby and frustrates the enjoyment of his tenant's premises by the use of his own. There must, however, be some act which renders the property 'unfit or materially less fit to be used for the particular purpose for which the demise was made' (*Browne* v. *Flower,* above, per Parker, J., at p.226). (See also *Port* v. *Griffith* [1938] 1 All E.R. 295).

Examples of breach of this obligation are a landlord building on adjacent land so as to obstruct ventilation to land leased to a timber merchant, thus interfering with the drying of wood (*Aldin* v. *Latimer Clark* [1894] 2 Ch. 437); changing the environment of a flat leased for residential purposes by subsequently letting the surrounding flats for business purposes (*Newman* v. *Real Estate Debenture Corporation Ltd.* [1940] 1 All E.R. 131); and even the prevention of a tenant from entering the landlord's land to carry out repairs upon the leased property (*Ward* v. *Kirkland* [1966] 1 All E.R. 609, at p.617).

(c) *Implied covenants for repair and fitness for habitation in certain residential lettings.* The general rule is that there is no implied covenant by the landlord to repair or even that the property is fit for habitation. There are, however, three exceptions to this.

Firstly, in the absence of an agreement to the contrary, there is an implied condition that, upon the lease of a furnished house, it is fit for human habitation (*Collins* v. *Hopkins* [1923] 2 K.B. 617). Breach of the obligation entitles the tenant to repudiate the tenancy. There is no implied covenant, however, that the house shall remain habitable, provided that it was so at the beginning of the tenancy. The principle could be justified under the doctrine of non-derogation from grant but seems to lead an independent existence.

Secondly, under the Housing Act 1957, s.6, there is an implied condition, which cannot be excluded by the parties, that, on the letting for human habitation of a house at a rent not exceeding £80 a year in London, or £52 elsewhere, the house is fit for human habitation at the beginning of the tenancy and will be kept so by the landlord throughout it. The rule does not, however, apply to leases which are not terminable within three years and under which the tenant is obliged to make the house fit for human habitation. If the letting was made before 6th July 1957, smaller maximum rentals apply. The Act provides tests for deciding whether a house is fit for human habitation (s.4). The landlord is not in breach of the implied covenant unless he knows of the defect in question. Few houses are now within these provisions.

Finally in any tenancy of a dwelling-house made after 24th October 1961, for a term of less than seven years, there is an implied covenant by the landlord to keep in repair the external fabric of the house, the installations for supplying water, gas, electricity and sanitation, and for space heating or heating water (Housing Act 1961, ss.32 and 33). (See *Brown* v. *Liverpool Corporation* [1969] 3 All E.R. 1345). A term is to be treated as a term of less than seven years if it is 'determinable at the option of the lessor before the expiration of seven years from the commencement of the term'. 'Determinable' has been held to mean determinable irrespective of the happening of any event (*Parker* v. *O'Connor* [1974] 1 W.L.R. 1160). A landlord, therefore, who makes the option exercisable only upon some event which is theoretically uncertain, but practically certain, avoids the responsibilities laid down by the Act.

The landlord's obligation does not arise until he knows of the need for repairs or at least has been put on enquiry as to such need (*O'Brien* v. *Robinson* [1973] 1 All E.R. 583). The parties cannot contract out of these obligations but the county court may modify them if it is reasonable to do so.

Under s.4 of the Defective Premises Act 1972, when a landlord owes a duty of maintenance or repair to a tenant he also owes a duty to all persons, who might reasonably be expected to be affected by defects in the premises, to take reasonable care that they are reasonably safe from personal injury or from damage to their property caused by a failure in his duty under the tenancy of which he knows or ought to know. This provision applies whether the obligation to repair arises by agreement or by virtue of statute.

(d) *Implied covenant for repair of easements necessary to a demise*. This doctrine was recently established by the House of Lords in *Liverpool City Council* v. *Irwin* [1976] A.C. 239. In the absence of contrary agreement, a landlord has a duty to maintain to a reasonable standard those parts of the premises retained in his possession over which the tenant has easements necessary to the enjoyment of his tenancy, such as stairways and lifts in high-rise lettings, and rubbish chutes.

(e) *The right to estovers*. A tenant for years has the right to take estovers. This right was explained in Chapter 4.

(f) *The right to remove certain fixtures*. A tenant has the right to remove trade, ornamental and domestic fixtures during, though not after, the term. Where a lease terminates by operation of law, such as by effluxion of time, rather than by act of parties, and even though replaced by a new lease, then, assuming the original lease is silent on the point, it is inferred that it was intended that the tenant does not give up his right to fixtures installed by him. (*New Zealand Property Corporation* v. *H.M. and S. Ltd.* [1981] 1 All E.R. 759). The right of removal in those respects is the same as in the case of a life interest, which was dealt with in Chapter 4. A further right is given to tenants of agricultural holdings by the Agricultural Holdings Act, 1948, s.13. Agricultural fixtures annexed by the tenant may be removed before or within two months after the end of the term, provided that one month's written notice is given to the landlord before the end of the tenancy (upon which the landlord acquires the option to purchase the fixtures at a fair price), and that the tenant has performed all his covenants.

(g) *The right to security of tenure and restriction of rent in certain cases.* As mentioned in Chapter 4 most agricultural and business tenants enjoy a large measure of security of tenure under statute and many residential tenants have both security of tenure and protection against rent increase. These statutory rights cannot be excluded by the parties. Finally the Leasehold Reform Act 1967, gives certain classes of lessees the right to buy the freehold or to demand an extended lease. These topics are considered in outline later in this chapter.

(2) Duties of the tenant

The duties for which a tenant will be liable even when there is no express agreement upon the matter are as follows. (In the case of rent there must, of course, be agreement between the parties as to the amount payable.)

(a) *The duty to pay rent, rates and taxes.* These payments must be made by the tenant except insofar as statute provides that a tax must be paid by the landlord.

(b) *The duty to use the premises properly and in certain cases to repair.* In the absence of express covenants the tenant's duties in this field are governed by the doctrine of waste. A tenant for a fixed term of years is liable for both voluntary and permissive waste and thus has a duty to keep the property in repair (*Yellowly* v. *Gower* (1855), 11 Exch. 274).

A periodic tenant is liable for voluntary waste but not for permissive waste (*Warren* v. *Keen* [1954] 1 Q.B. 15), except that a yearly tenant probably has a duty to keep the premises wind and water tight (*Wedd* v. *Porter* [1916] 2 K.B. 91), though this was doubted by Somervell, L.J., in *Warren* v. *Keen*. Weekly and probably other periodic tenancies of less than a year only carry a duty to use the property 'in a tenant-like manner' (*Warren* v. *Keen*). This duty merely involves doing those things which a good housekeeper would do and which, if left undone, could lead to a deterioration of the premises. Examples are sweeping the chimney, unblocking the sink and turning the water off when going away in the winter. A tenant at will is not liable for permissive waste but the commission of voluntary waste terminates his tenancy.

(c) *The duty to allow a landlord to view, if liable for repairs.* The landlord generally has no implied right to enter the demised property to view the state of repair. If, however, he is under a contractual or statutory obligation to repair, such a right is implied.

Rights and duties of the parties where there are express covenants

It is not possible in a book of this length either to deal with all the covenants commonly used in leases today, or even to make a detailed study of those which are mentioned. The covenants in leases for specialized purposes might extend to several pages. Here we shall restrict ourselves to some general remarks about some of the more common covenants.

(1) *Covenant to pay rent.* The rent payable by a tenant is called 'rent-service' because there is tenure between him and the person to whom it is paid, his

landlord. It may be expressed in money or in kind. Unless otherwise provided, it is payable in arrear at the end of each period with regard to which it is calculated (see *Coomber* v. *Howard* (1845) 1 C.B. 440). Payment is overdue if the tenant has failed to pay by midnight at the end of the day upon which the rent fell due.

It was formerly considered that the duty to pay the rent is absolute and continues despite the occurrence of some catastrophe which renders the property unusable, such as destruction by fire. Thus, in *Cricklewood Property and Investment Trust Ltd.* v. *Leighton's Investment Trust Ltd.* [1945] A.C. 221, rent was held to be payable in respect of a building lease although government restrictions had made building impossible.

There is yet no reported case of the doctrine of frustration being applied to the lease itself and therefore to the rent covenant. Until recently, the prevalent view was that it could not apply. This view has now been dispelled by the House of Lords in *National Carriers Ltd.* v. *Panalpina Ltd.* [1981] 1 All E.R. 161. The lessee in that case was, on the particular facts, unsuccessful in his submission that a ten years lease of a warehouse had been frustrated by the closure for about two years of the highway leading to it. It was held, however, that the doctrine is capable of applying to leases if frustrating events prevented any substantial use of the property permitted by the lease and in the contemplation of the parties.

Their Lordships noted that events qualifying as frustrating factors in the case of leases are likely to be rare; the 'never' school of thought has given way to the 'hardly ever' principle. Yet Lord Wilberforce's rejection of the argument that the floodgates of litigation might be opened was surely most welcome. 'It is said that to admit the possibility of frustration of leases will lead to increased litigation. Be it so, if that is the route to justice' (at p.172).

It is appropriate to note here that, within strictly confined limits, a tenant may recoup out of forthcoming rent the cost of repairs where the landlord has breached his duty to repair (see *Parker* v. *Izzet* [1971] 3 All E.R. 1099).

(2) *Covenant to repair*. Apart from the statutory duty of the landlord to repair in certain cases, the parties may make what arrangements they wish regarding repairs. Unless otherwise agreed, this covenant also imposes an absolute duty so that the defaulting party will be liable even though he is prevented from carrying out the repairs by circumstances outside his control, such as by the refusal of a building licence (*Eyre* v. *Johnson* [1946] K.B. 481), for he can always pay damages.

While the duty to repair does not involve any obligation to rebuild, it does demand replacement of parts of a building even if those parts are sizeable, but an ordinary covenant to repair does not include reinstatement so substantial as to be out of proportion to the value of the premises (see *Brew Bros. Ltd.* v. *Snax (Ross) Ltd.*, [1970] 1 Q.B. 612). The standard of this repair depends upon the character of the premises and the nature of the locality at the time of the letting. This does not mean that after a long lease the property must be in the same condition as when it was first let. It means that it must be retained in a condition in keeping with that type of property, accepting the fact that its age will show (see *Anstruther-Gough-Calthorpe* v. *McOscar* [1924] 1 K.B. 716). It would, for instance, be contrary to this duty to replace a worn-out oak door with one of cheap deal which, though effective, was out of character with the building.

In all cases, the extent of the duty of repair is a matter of construction of the words used in the lease. The use of expressions, however, such as 'good repair' or 'tenantable' repair are not taken to add anything to the simple duty to repair. One qualification of the duty is that 'fair wear and tear' are excepted. This exempts the party concerned from liability for damage which results from ordinary use of the premises or from the weather. A tenant need not, for instance, repair floorboards worn away near a door, or point mortar which has been eroded by rain. Yet if damage occurs through such a cause and, if left unattended, will cause further serious damage, the exemption will not exonerate a person who allows the original damage to remain unrepaired. Thus, if a tile falls from a roof as a result of ordinary wear and tear, a tenant will be responsible for the consequent damage to the interior of the building (*Regis Property Co. Ltd.* v. *Dudley* [1959] A.C. 370).

The measure of damages for breach of a repairing covenant is governed by the Landlord and Tenant Act 1927, s.18. In no case are the damages to exceed the diminution in value caused to the reversion. If, at the end of the term, the lessor intends that the premises are to be pulled down or to undergo such structural alterations that the repairs contemplated by the covenant would have been valueless, no damages are recoverable (see *Hibernian Properties Co. Ltd.* v. *Liverpool Corporation* [1972] 3 All E.R. 1117).

(3) *Covenant against assignment or underletting*. Unless otherwise provided in the lease, a tenant may assign, sub-lease or grant a licence. This covenant is therefore frequently included in case the possession should come into the hands of an undesirable person. Such covenants are of two types. Firstly the covenant might be absolute, in which case the tenant cannot assign or sublet unless the landlord waives the benefit of the covenant. This he may refuse to do and his decision, however unreasonable, is binding.

Secondly, the covenant might be qualified in that assignment and subletting are only forbidden without the landlord's consent. Such covenants are, except in the case of agricultural holdings, subject by statute, despite any agreement to the contrary, to the proviso that the landlord's consent is 'not to be unreasonably withheld' (Landlord and Tenant Act 1927, s.19). The result is that, if a landlord unreasonably refuses consent, the tenant commits no breach if he assigns or sub-lets. If, however, he fails to ask for consent, the tenant commits a breach no matter how unreasonable it would have been for the landlord to refuse.

Whether the grounds for refusal must concern either the personality of the sub-lessee or assignee, or the purposes for which he intends to use the property, or whether it may be for some other reason, is uncertain (see *Swanson* v. *Forton* [1949] Ch. 143). Unless the terms of the covenant are qualified in some way, the latter view is probably preferable (see *Tredegar* v. *Harwood* [1929] A.C. 72, at p.79). It is of course open to the parties to restrict the grounds of refusal to narrower or broader reasons than these by an express qualification to that effect. The crucial question is whether the landlord's refusal is designed to achieve the true purpose of the covenant (*Bromley Park Garden Estates Ltd.* v. *Moss* [1982] 2 All E.R. 890). Under the Race Relations Act 1965, however, it is unreasonable to refuse consent on grounds of colour, race or ethinic or national origin. This does not apply where part of a dwelling-house is let and part of the house is shared with the landlord. It is of course possible to evade the effect of the Act if an absolute covenant against assignment and sub-letting is included in the lease, and discrimination then exercised by waiver. In *Bickel* v. *Duke of Westminster* [1976] 3 W.L.R. 805 it was held by the Court of Appeal that refusal of an assignment which would afford the assignee, unlike the assignor, the benefit of leasehold enfranchisement was reasonable. In *Adler* v. *Upper Grosvenor Street Investment Ltd.* [1957] 1 W.L.R. 227 it was held by the Court of Appeal that a covenant requiring a tenant to offer to surrender the lease to the landlord before seeking consent to assignment or sub-letting was not caught by the section and was thus enforceable (see *Bocardo* v. *S. and M. Hotels Ltd.* [1980] 1 W.L.R. 17). The correctness of this decision was doubted by the Court of Appeal in *Green* v. *Church Commissioners for England* [1974] Ch. 487. The latter case was, however, decided on different grounds. Many leases today contain such covenants because they are intended to enable landlords to take advantage of a rise in rents. It is, therefore, important that the question should be settled in the near future.

Finally the covenant is not breached by a bequest of the lease nor by involuntary alienation such as occurs upon bankruptcy.

(4) *'The usual covenants'*. In agreements for leases the parties sometimes summarize their intentions by declaring that the lease is to contain 'the usual covenants'. What covenants are included in this description depends upon the circumstances of the case, trade practice and local custom (*Flexman* v. *Corbett* [1930] 1 Ch. 672). The question is one of fact and to be solved by examining the nature of the premises, their situation and the purpose for which they are being let. The evidence of conveyancers, including their books of precedents, is therefore in point. (*Chester* v. *Buckingham Travel Ltd.* [1981] 1 All E.R. 386.)

It has been suggested that what is essentially a question of fact can in particular cases, through notoriety and judicial knowledge, attain the status of law. Such elevation would often enable a court to reach a speedy decision and would screen many claims from the courts (97 L.Q.R. [1981] 385). In that case the list mentioned above must be supplemented by reference to current case law in regard to the many forms of specialized leases. Reported precedents are however scarce. Fifty years elapsed between the decisions in *Flexman* v. *Corbett* and *Chester* v. *Buckingham*. In any case it appears from the latter case that the same test will be applied in deciding what covenants are usual whether the question arises in relation to an express reference to 'usual convenants' in a lease or contract, or in relation to cases where the term is implied.

The following covenants, however, are certainly included in such a description, namely covenants by the tenant to pay the rent, rates and taxes, to keep and deliver up the premises in repair, and to allow the landlord to view the state of repair, a condition that the landlord may re-enter if the rent is not paid, and a covenant by the landlord for quiet possession.

Remedies

We must now examine the remedies which are available when covenants are broken. The remedies for breach of a rent covenant differ from those for breach of all other types of covenant and will therefore be dealt with separately.

Remedies for breach of rent covenant

(1) *Action for arrears*. No action may be brought to recover arrears of rent after the expiration of six years from the date when it fell due (Limitation Act

1980, s.19). Where, however, the tenant makes an acknowledgement of the claim or makes a payment of part of the rent, the six-year period runs from that time. Rent under a lease continues to fall due no matter how long a time has elapsed since the last payment and no matter how much rent has been rendered irrecoverable under the statute. If however the rent has been paid for twelve years to some third person who claims the reversion, as opposed merely to not being paid at all, the landlord's rights are determined.

(2) *Distress*. Distress is a remedy which entitles the landlord to take and ultimately to sell chattels present upon the demised land, and to satisfy his claim out of the proceeds. The rules of distress are complicated and only a certificated bailiff can execute this remedy. Only a few brief remarks will therefore be made here.

A landlord cannot levy distress and bring an action for arrears at the same time. In all cases he must own the reversion both at the time the rent falls due and when the distress is levied. Only six years of arrears may be recovered (Limitation Act 1980, s.19). In the case of an agricultural tenancy only one year's arrears are recoverable (Agricultural Holdings Act 1948, s.18).

(3) *Re-entry under an express proviso for re-entry or for breach of condition*. A breach of covenant does not itself enable a landlord to end a lease prematurely. Of course, in the case of a periodic tenancy, he may serve a notice to quit upon an unsatisfactory tenant, but if the lease is for a fixed term this will not be possible. Since it would be very inconvenient to bring successive actions against a persistently defaulting tenant, special provisions are included in most leases to enable landlords to end them prematurely by forfeiture. This may be achieved in two ways.

Firstly, the duty in question may be expressed as a condition, in which case the lease may be forfeited when a breach of the obligation has occurred. Whether a duty amounts to a condition or not depends upon the intentions of the parties and might involve difficult problems of construction. Secondly, if the duty has been expressed as a covenant only, the right of forfeiture only follows upon its breach if the lease contains an express proviso for re-entry upon breach of those covenants to which it is expressed to apply. If the terms of the lease confer upon the landlord the right to serve notice to quit in case of breach of covenant, this right has the character of a right of forfeiture and the tenant may seek relief as described below (*Richard Clarke & Co.* v. *Widnall* [1976] 1W.L.R. 845).

In either case the landlord may waive his right of forfeiture either expressly or impliedly. Waiver will only be implied, however, if the landlord both knows of the facts constituting the breach and

> does some unequivocal act recognising the continued existence of the lease . . . . Therefore, though an act of waiver operates with regard to all known breaches, it does not operate with regard to breaches which were unknown to the lessor at the time when the act took place (*Matthews* v. *Smallwood* [1910] 1 Ch. 777, per Parker, J., at p.786 and see *David Blackstone* v. *Burnetts* (West End) [1973] 3 All E.R. 782).

Neither does it operate as a waiver of future breaches (L.P.A. 1925, s.148). Typical examples of acts which imply waiver are demands for or acceptance of rent accruing after the breach and distress for rent whenever it fell due. No waiver can be implied, however, if the landlord does not know of the breach at the time of the alleged act of waiver. Furthermore, a statement or act by the landlord not communicated to or not having any impact on the tenant will not constitute waiver (*London and County (A. & D.) Ltd.* v. *Wilfred Sportsman Ltd.* [1970] 3 W.L.R. 418, per Russell, L.J., at p.427) Once a landlord has, moreover, finally taken a step to forfeit the lease, such as by bringing an action for possession (see *Canas Property Co. Ltd.* v. *K.L. Television Services Ltd.* [1970] 2 All E.R. 795), acts which would usually constitute waiver do not amount to waiver. A landlord may, however, waive his rights by accepting rent even though it was stipulated that any waiver must be in writing (*R.* v. *Paulson* [1921] 1 A.C. 271).

Before proceeding to forfeiture, the landlord must make a formal demand for the rent unless he is exempted from doing so either by the terms of the lease or by statute. A formal demand is one made upon the demised premises between sunrise and sunset specifying the amount due. This requirement is usually excluded by the lease by the provision that forfeiture will ensue if rent is in arrear for more than a specified time 'whether formally demanded or not'. Even if there is no such provision, however, no formal demand is necessary if 'one half year's rent shall be in arrear' and there is not sufficient distress on the premises (Common Law Procedure Act 1852, s.210).

The exercise of a power of forfeiture can bring harsh results but equity gave relief against it—provided that the tenant paid the rent due together with interest and any costs which had been entailed to the landlord; for then a just position had been restored and it could be said that forfeiture was unnecessary. This jurisdiction has been regulated by the Common Law Procedure Act 1852 (ss.210–212), the Supreme Court of Judicature (Consolidation) Act 1925 (s.46), and the County Courts Act 1959, s.191. Under the 1852 Act, if the landlord brings an action for forfeiture and the tenant makes the payments mentioned above to the landlord or into court before the trial, all proceedings are stayed. It was held in *Standard Pattern Co. Ltd.* v. *Ivey* [1962] Ch. 432 that, because of the unfortunate drafting of the three sections, this relief cannot be claimed by a tenant unless 'one half year's rent shall be in arrear'. (For a criticism of this result see 78 L.Q.R. 168.) This restriction only applies, however, to actions in the Supreme Court.

If the tenant does not make payment, so that judgment is given against him he can still apply for relief within six months after the execution of the judgment, and the court may then grant him relief subject to the same conditions as to rent and costs as could formerly be imposed under the equitable principles employed by the former Court of Chancery. There is thus a discretionary power to refuse relief in light of the conduct of the tenant or the possible hardship to the landlord. For instance this might be so where the tenant has delayed his application until so late within the six months period that the landlord has changed his position upon the assumption that forfeiture was to ensue (see *Stanhope* v. *Haworth* (1886), 3 T.L.R. 34). It seems to be a corollary of the Standard Pattern case that the six months time limit would not apply to a tenant who has less than 'one half year's rent' in arrear.

The landlord might enforce forfeiture by re-entry rather than by action. In that case, relief may still be granted (*Howard* v. *Fanshawe* [1895] 2 Ch. 581).

Presumably the application must be made within six months of the re-entry as it must under the 1852 Act. All this must be read subject to the general restriction upon re-entry without court order where premises are let as a dwelling-house (Protection From Eviction Act 1977, s.2).

Finally, when relieved, the tenant holds under the terms of the original lease. An underlessee may also apply for relief from forfeiture when a head lessor is proceeding against that underlessee's own landlord, whereupon the court may vest the property in that underlessee for part or the whole of the remainder of the term upon such conditions as it thinks fit (L.P.A. 1925, s.146(4)).

Remedies for breach of covenants or conditions other than rent

(1) *Action for damages, injunction or specific performance.* The landlord can sue for damages or for an injunction if the tenant breaks a covenant. In the case of a covenant to repair premises other than an agricultural holding, where the lease is for seven years or more, of which at least three are unexpired, the landlord must first serve a notice upon the tenant under the Leasehold Property (Repairs) Act 1938, as amended by the Landlord and Tenant Act 1954, s.51, specifying the breach, requiring it to be remedied, if that is possible, and asking for compensation. The tenant may then serve a counter-notice within twenty-eight days, in which case the landlord cannot proceed with an action without the leave of the court.

The remedy of specific performance can be awarded where appropriate. Its incidence as between landlord and tenant, however, is not necessarily mutual. Thus, while it is available to a tenant against a landlord who has broken a repairing covenant, a landlord could not obtain it against a tenant for such a breach (*Jeune* v. *Queens Cross Properties Ltd.* [1973] 3 All E.R. 97).

(2) *Re-entry under express proviso for re-entry or breach of condition.* As in the case of a rent covenant, the remedy for forfeiture cannot be used unless there is an express proviso for re-entry relating to the covenant in question, or unless the obligation is expressed as a condition. The rules discussed above governing waiver of the right of forfeiture apply equally here. The provisions for relief against forfeiture are different; for equity only assisted where the covenant breached was for payment of rent. Eventually, relief was made available by statute. The law is now contained in the Law of Property Act 1925, s.146; this section operates despite any stipulation by the parties to the contrary (*Plymouth Corporation* v. *Harvey* [1971] 1 All E.R. 623).

Before enforcing a right of forfeiture by action or otherwise, the landlord must serve a notice specifying the particular breach, requiring it to be remedied, if it is capable of remedy, and requiring the lessee to make compensation. In the cases to which the Leasehold Property (Repairs) Act 1938, applies, the landlord cannot take any proceedings without the leave of the county court if the tenant serves a counter-notice. This was explained above in relation to an action for damages, to which it also applies.

As to the three factors to be specified in the notice, the breach must be described sufficiently to enable the tenant to know with reasonable certainty what he has done wrong. The landlord need not however demand compensation if he does not want it, nor ask for the breach to be remedied if it is not remediable. Thus, in *Rugby School (Governors)* v. *Tannahill* [1935] 1 K.B. 87, where premises had been used for prostitution, it was held that omission to demand compensation did not invalidate the notice, for the landlord understandably would not wish 'to touch money coming from a tenant in such circumstances'.

Furthermore, there was no need to require the breach to be remedied, for mere cessation of such a use would not cure the bad reputation which the property would have acquired in the neighbourhood. A breach of covenant by unlawful sub-letting has been held not to be capable of remedy for it is a breach once and for all and not a continuing breach. Accordingly, no time need be given for its remedy and the tenant's only recourse will be to apply for relief (*Scala House and District Property Co. Ltd.* v. *Forbes* [1973] 3 All E.R. 308).

Where the unlawful use is by a sub-tenant, and the head landlord is proceeding against the tenant for allowing the breach, it does not follow that the breach is incapable of remedy so far as the tenant is concerned, provided that he had no previous knowledge of it and takes steps, including forfeiture proceedings, against the sub-tenant (*Glass* v. *Kencakes Ltd.* [1966] 1 Q.B. 611).

After service of the notice, the landlord must allow the tenant 'a reasonable time' to remedy the breach and then may proceed to forfeiture if no remedy is forthcoming. When he is proceeding to enforce forfeiture, by action or otherwise, the tenant may, either in the landlord's action or in proceedings brought by himself, apply for relief which the court may grant or refuse as it 'thinks fit', considering the conduct of the parties and all other circumstances. Unlike the case of rent covenants, there is no power to grant relief after forfeiture has been accomplished. On the other hand, the provision enabling sub-lessees to apply for relief applies equally here (s.146(4), as amended by the Law of Property (Amendment) Act 1929, s.1). Furthermore, this applies in the exceptional cases mentioned below where the tenant himself cannot apply for relief.

These exceptional cases under the section in which the landlord need serve no s.146 notice but may proceed immediately to forfeiture, and where no relief may be granted, are as follows:

(a) Breach of covenant for inspection of records, machines or workings in the cases of a mining lease.

(b) Breach of condition against bankruptcy of the tenant or the taking of his interest in execution where the lease is of agricultural land, mines, a public house, a furnished house, or any property with respect to which the personal qualifications of the tenant are important in preserving its value or character or important because the landlord or other tenants of his have premises nearby (see *Earl Bathurst* v. *Fine* [1974] 2 All E.R. 1160).

In all other cases of breach of condition against bankruptcy, apart from those mentioned above, relief may be applied for at any time at all provided that the lease is sold within one year of the bankruptcy. If it is not sold within the year, then no relief may be sought after the expiration of that year. These rules are designed to give the trustee in bankruptcy a reasonable chance to decide whether to sell the lease and, in case of sale, to give the purchaser the chance to have his title confirmed.

Finally, quite apart from statutory provisions and the Rules of the Supreme Court, the rules of natural justice demand that notice of proceedings must be given to a tenant when a landlord is seeking possession in the courts (*Fleet Mortgage and Investment Co. Ltd.* v. *Lower Maisonette, 46 Eaton Place Ltd.* [1972] 2 All E.R. 737).

The persons as between whom the covenants are enforceable

Before mentioning the persons by and against whom the covenants in a lease are enforceable, certain terms which are necessary to an understanding of this topic must be explained.

When a lease is made two major legal results occur. Firstly, an estate in land is created. This is the only estate today which involves tenure in that land is held of a landlord in return for a rent and upon certain agreed conditions. The fact that a lease may be free of rent does not disturb this doctrine of tenure. This estate can of course be transferred to other persons, as can the landlord's reversion. The relationship between the persons entitled, at any particular time, to the reversion and to the lease, whether they are the original parties or not, is called 'privity of estate'. In the case of transfer of the landlord's and tenant's estates there is only privity of estate between the transferees, however, if there is an assignment of the whole of the unexpired term of the lease or the entire reversion. Thus, if *L* leases land to *T* for ten years and on the next day *T* grants *S* a term of nine years there is no privity of estate between *L* and *S*, because *S* only takes a sub-lease and not an assignment of the whole term of the lease. Successful adverse possession against a lessee under the Limitation Act 1980, does not operate to 'assign' that lessee's title to the claimant. The Act does not transfer titles but merely extinguishes them, leaving claimants to establish their own independent titles (*Tichborne* v. *Weir* (1892), 67 L.T. 735).

The second result of the creation of a lease is that the covenants contained in it are contractual between the parties to it. The original parties to a lease are bound together by privity of contract. This privity of contract continues between them throughout the term of the lease even though the estates of both the parties are transferred to other persons. The transferees of these estates neither interrupt nor partake of this privity of contract of the original parties. A diagram might illustrate these relationships.

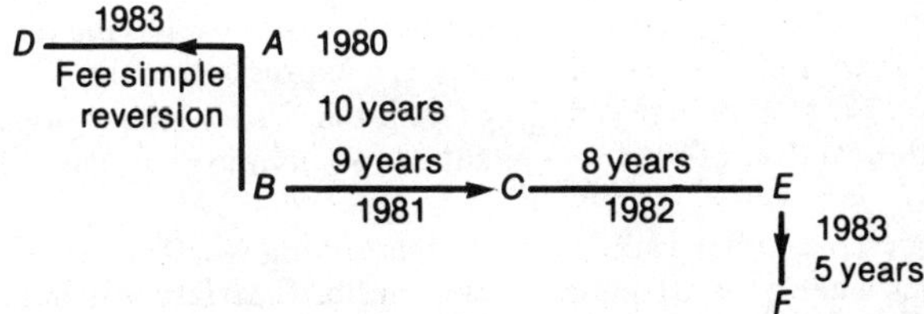

In 1980, *A* leased land to *B* for ten years. Between these two at that time there exists both privity of contract and privity of estate. In the next year *B* assigned the whole of the unexpired lease to *C*. At this stage there is privity of contract between *A* and *B* but no privity of estate. Between *A* and *C* there is privity of estate but not of contract. In the next year *C* assigns the lease to *E*.

There is still privity of contract between *A* and *B* but no relationship between *A* and *C* either in estate or contract. Privity of estate exists however between *A* and *E*.

Finally, let *E* sub-lease to *F* and *A* assign the reversion to *D*. Privity of contract continues between *A* and *B*. There is privity of estate between *D* and *E* since one holds the lease and the other holds the reversion to it. There is neither privity of contract nor privity of estate between *D* and *F* because *F* does not hold the lease of which *D* has the reversion. The same result would follow if *F* had been a mere licensee or trespasser upon the land. A new relationship, however, has sprung up. *E* now enjoys both privity of estate and privity of contract with *F*, for a sub-lease is just as much a lease as a head-lease is.

In short, persons only enjoy privity of contract in regard to the covenants in a lease if they are the original parties to that lease. Yet this privity lasts throughout the lease. They only enjoy privity of estate if one holds the entire unexpired term of the lease while the other holds the reversion to it. This relationship does not outlast the period for which they are simultaneously held.

We are now in a position to consider to what extent the covenants contained in a lease are binding between the various persons who might be concerned with the property.

(1) *If privity of contract exists between the parties, all the covenants in the lease are mutually enforceable.* The original parties to a lease can enforce against each other all the covenants in the lease. This rule is the ordinary law of contract and the only restriction therefore is that the covenant must not be illegal. Thus if *L* leases property to *T*, who assigns the lease to *A*, *T* remains liable to *L* upon all the covenants even though he no longer occupies the land. So, if the liquidator of a company disclaims a lease which has been assigned to the company, the original lessee remains liable for the rent falling due even after the assignment (*Warnford Investments Ltd.* v. *Duckworth* [1978] 2 W.L.R. 741). The principle applies equally if *L* assigns his interest.

(2) *If privity of estate exists between the parties, covenants 'having reference to the subject-matter of the lease' are mutually enforceable.* Where there is no privity of contract but only privity of estate between the parties in question, only covenants 'having reference to the subject-matter of the lease' are mutually enforceable. If this requirement is satisfied, however, it does not matter whether the covenant is positive or negative. The phrase 'having reference to the subject-matter of the lease' is the modern expression of the requirement used by the Law of Property Act 1925 (ss.141 and 142), and is preferable to the older description of such covenants as 'touching and concerning the land'.

A test which has judicial approval for ascertaining whether a covenant is of such a kind is whether it 'affects either the landlord *qua* landlord or the tenant *qua* tenant'. A covenant may have reference to land without being referable to the lease (*Breams Property Investment Co. Ltd.* v. *Stroulger* [1948] 2 K.B. 1, at p.7). Furthermore, covenants which, though included in a lease for convenience, are of a merely personal nature do not satisfy the requirement. Examples of covenants which do satisfy it are to pay rent, to repair, not to assign or under-let, to use property in a certain way, to buy beer from the landlord for sale on the demised premises and to renew the lease. On the other hand, examples of covenants which do not satisfy the requirement are to sell the reversion and not to open another public house near the demised property.

If the covenant has reference to the subject matter of the lease in this way, then both the benefit and burden pass to the assignee either of the tenant (*Spencer's Case* (1583), 5 Co. Rep. 16a), or of the landlord (L.P.A. 1925, ss.141 and 142). The liability of the assignee is limited, however, to breaches committed while he holds the lease or the reversion. His right to sue for breaches is limited in the same way except that in the case of an assignment of the reversion the assignee is the only person who can sue, even though the breach occurred before the reversion came into his hands, unless the damage is suffered by the assignor exclusively (*Re King* [1963] Ch. 459). The new reversioner is also entitled to remedy such breaches of covenant occurring before assignment by any right of re-entry contained in the lease provided that the right has not been waived. The assignment of the reversion, 'subject to and with the benefit of' the lease, does not impliedly waive previously committed breaches by admitting that the lease still exists, for the words are merely performing a mechanical conveyancing function (*London and County (A. & D.) Ltd.* v. *Wilfred Sportsman Ltd.* [1970] 3 W.L.R. 418).

There is now no need for the lease to be under seal for the covenants to run with the estates in this way. In a case concerning an assignment by the tenant, the judge said: 'I assume that it does not matter that there was here only an agreement under hand and not a lease by deed, since the tenant took possession under the agreement' (per Evershed, M.R., at p.242 in *Boyer* v. *Warbey* [1953] 1 Q.B. 234). Probably therefore a specifically enforceable contract for a lease suffices and it may now be that no writing at all is necessary in those cases in which tenancies can be created orally. Similar relaxed rules apply equally when the landlord assigns, for the word 'lease' used in ss.141 and 142 includes a 'tenancy' (see s.154).

Where part only of a reversion is assigned the covenants and any conditions or rights of re-entry are apportioned and remain enforceable by the owners of the severed parts of the reversion against the lessee. If *L* leases houses numbered 1, 2, 3 and 4 to *T* and then assigns the reversions of numbers 1 and 2 to *A*, *L* could enforce a repairing covenant, for instance, against *T*, in respect of numbers 3 and 4, and *A* could do likewise in respect of numbers 1 and 2 (L.P.A. 1925, s.140).

The operation of the two doctrines of privity of contract and privity of estate might give a lessor the choice of two defendants in the event of a breach of covenant. He may sue the original lessee, because the privity of contract continues throughout the lease, and, assuming that the covenant has reference to the subject-matter of the lease, he may also sue an assignee who holds the lease at the time of the breach, because of his privity of estate with that assignee. In such cases, however, the lessor can only recover once and, furthermore, it is the assignee who is primarily liable. The original lessee, if sued, may claim indemnity from the guilty assignee. Lessees frequently took an express covenant for indemnity from their assignees at the time of assignment and those assignees would similarly cover their own contractual liability by taking covenants of indemnity from persons to whom they later assigned.

Such an indemnity against all breaches of covenant in the future is implied in any assignment for valuable consideration made after 1925 (L.P.A. 1925, s.77(1)(c) and Sched. 2, Pt. IX). Thus if *A* leases property to *B*, who assigns to *C*, who assigns to *D*, who assigns to *E*, who commits a breach, *A* can sue either *B* or *E*. If he sues *B*, the latter can join *C* in the action because of the implied indemnity. Likewise, *C* can then join *D* and *D* can join *E*, so that ultimately liability is satisfied by the person who was in breach of the covenant in the lease.

(3) *If there is neither privity of contract nor privity of estate between the parties, covenants are enforceable only if they run with the land.* Before explaining what covenants 'run with the land', we must notice in what circumstances there might be neither privity of contract nor privity of estate between the parties. Neither form of privity exists between landlord and sub-lessee, nor between a landlord and the licensee of his tenant, nor between a landlord and a person who is a trespasser or an adverse possessor upon the demised premises. Yet all these persons might do acts which are contrary to the terms of the lease and, although the landlord might have his remedy against his tenant, it might often be more convenient to proceed directly, if possible, against the wrongdoer himself.

In such cases, it is not sufficient that the covenant 'runs with the estate' under *Spencer's Case*, because none of these persons takes the estate of the lease. What we must ask is whether there are any covenants which 'run with the land', so that persons coming to the land, though not the estate, through whatever right or claim, will be bound by them. There are indeed covenants which are so enforceable in certain circumstances and are effective even outside the sphere of leases as, for instance, when *A* sells land to *B* in fee simple and *B* later sells the land to *C*. The role of covenants in land law generally, and not merely in the province of leaseholds, is dealt with in Chapter 12. It is sometimes possible for *A* to enforce covenants contained in the conveyance to *B* against *C*, even though neither privity of contract nor privity of estate exists between *A* and *C*. Before mentioning those covenants, we must notice one other method, of particular importance in the law of leases, by which remedies are available against persons irrespective of privity of contract or estate.

A right of re-entry in case of breach of covenant in, or in respect of, a lease may be a legal interest in land (L.P.A. 1925, s.1(2)(e)). As such, it is effectively enforceable against all occupiers of the land, even though there is no privity of contract or privity of estate between the parties concerned: a landlord may enforce it against a sub-lessee who has done acts which are contrary to a covenant to which the right of re-entry relates.

Restrictive covenants are discussed in Chapter 12. It is sufficient for present purposes to say that a restrictive covenant creates an equitable interest in land and is enforceable against persons irrespective of privity of contract or estate. They may be created on the sale of land or by independent transactions. They may also be created by a landlord and tenant within a lease. Since they are capable of running with the land itself, as opposed to the estate of the lease merely, they affect persons coming to the land irrespective of privity of contract or estate and thus may be enforced, for instance, by the landlord against sub-lessees and licensees under the rule in *Tulk* v. *Moxhay*.

Determination of leases

Leases may end through effluxion of time, forfeiture, surrender, notice to quit, merger, enlargement (see L.P.A. 1925, s.153) and disclaimer. The last two are of minor importance and will not be considered here. Forfeiture has already been discussed. The death of one of the parties does not determine a lease even in the case of an ordinary short periodic letting, such as a weekly tenancy. The personal representatives must serve notice to quit in order to end the tenancy (*Youngmin* v. *Heath* [1974] 1 All E.R. 461).

Effluxion of time

A lease for a fixed period of years ends naturally at the end of that term and no notice to quit is necessary unless expressly stipulated. This general principle has, however, been greatly affected by modern legislation which has given security of tenure to certain classes of tenants even though the contractual term of the lease has ended.

Surrender

A surrender is a return of the estate to the landlord immediately in reversion, whereupon it is extinguished by merger with that reversion. Surrender may be express or by operation of law. It will occur by operation of law, if, for instance, the tenant gives up possession of the premises to the landlord and the landlord accepts this or the parties otherwise show by their conduct their intention to end the lease. If express, surrender must be by deed (L.P.A. 1925, s.52). If the transaction is supported by consideration and sufficient memorandum in writing to satisfy s.40 of the Act, or by part performance, however, specific performance would no doubt be ordered.

Notice to quit

Periodic tenancies may be ended by notice to quit which must conform to any agreement made by the parties to the tenancy as to its length and form, subject of course to mandatory statutory provisions. It must name the date of the termination of the tenancy or refer to it in such terms that it can be ascertained without doubt (*Addis* v. *Burrows* [1948] 1 K.B. 444), and there must be no ambiguity as to its purpose, which is to end the tenancy. Conditions in the notice will therefore invalidate it unless they can be construed as merely offering a new tenancy, as where it is stated that the tenancy may nevertheless continue if a new rent is paid. On the other hand, provided that the landlord's intentions are made clear, he is not prejudiced merely because he makes concessions to the tenant. Thus in *Dagger* v. *Shepherd* [1946] K.B. 215 a notice to quit 'on or before the 25th March next' was construed as an unambiguous notice to quit upon the day mentioned coupled with an offer to accept an earlier termination.

We must now discuss the length of notice necessary to end the various types of periodic tenancy. Firstly, quite apart from the statutory protection of tenure mentioned above, there is a general provision that no tenancy of a dwelling-house, whenever let, may be ended by less than four weeks' notice to quit (Protection from Eviction Act 1977, s.5). All dwelling-houses and not merely those otherwise protected by the Rent Acts are affected by this.

Unless otherwise agreed, a yearly tenancy may be ended by not less than half a year's notice. If the tenancy began on one of the usual quarter days the period of notice must be at least two quarters, so that a tenancy begun on Midsummer Day, 24th June, may be ended by a notice served on or before Christmas Day. If, however, the tenancy began on some other day, the period of notice must be at least 182 days. Agricultural tenancies stand outside these rules.

The date upon which a tenancy should be ended is the day before the anniversary day of its commencement or the anniversary day itself. A tenancy begun on Lady Day, 25th March, should therefore be required by the notice to end on 24th or 25th March, for which purpose the notice should be served on Michaelmas Day, 29th September, at the latest.

Other periodic tenancies can be ended by notices governed by similar principles except that the period of notice is not half the duration of the period in question but the full duration: unless otherwise agreed, a weekly tenancy begun on a Saturday may be ended by a notice given on or before a Friday requiring the tenancy to end on the following Friday.

Merger

A lease signifies a relationship between two people. A person cannot hold land of himself. When the lease and the reversion become vested in one person in the same right, therefore, the lease becomes merged in the greater estate and disappears. This does not happen if the person who takes the two interests intends otherwise.

The statutory protection of tenants

In modern times, Parliament has been prepared to combat social and economic problems by legislation over a wide field. We noticed in Chapter 4, where limitations on the use and enjoyment of land were discussed, that, under various statutes, many tenants enjoy considerable security of tenure and sometimes protection against increases in rent. This topic will now be considered in outline, but it must be emphasized that this account is given only for the purpose of a general appreciation of the subject. The legislation is complex and at times highly developed by case law, so before any practical problem is considered, reference should be made to the books which deal with it in detail and, of course, to the primary sources of the law.

The Rent Acts

A chronic housing shortage during this century, sharpened by war, caused Parliament to intervene by passing the first of the 'Rent Acts' in 1915. This was the first of a series of Acts controlling rent and providing security of tenure for large numbers of residential tenants. The present law is mainly contained in the Rent Act 1977 and the Housing Act 1980. References to parts of Acts are to the Rent Act 1977, as amended, unless otherwise stated. The Acts divide the cases which they affect into two categories. They will be referred to below as 'protected tenancies' and 'restricted contracts'.

Protected tenancies

With certain exceptions, the Act applies to every dwelling-house or part of one, of a rateable value described below, which is let as a separate dwelling.

The Act does not apply where the landlord is either the Crown, a local authority, a new town development corporation or one of certain types of housing association, or where the tenancy is free of rent or at a rent of less than two-thirds of the rateable value (see s.5), or includes payments for board or attendance and these payments form a substantial proportion of the rent. Neither does it apply in certain cases where the landlord resides in part of the same building. These are caught by Part V of the Act. Lettings made for the purposes of holidays and lettings made by specified educational institutions to students are also expected. Finally, certain types of premises are exempted, including premises licensed to sell liquor for consumption on the premises and most agricultural holdings (see ss.4–16).

The Act provides protection in two alternative ways, still reflecting the rambling development of the law over the years. Recent amendments accentuate the need for simplification.

(1) *Controlled tenancies*. With certain exceptions, these were of small properties and were almost all converted to regulated tenancies by the Housing Act 1980, s.64. This category will not receive further attention.

(2) *Regulated tenancies*. Regulated tenancies are tenancies where the rateable value in the valuation list of 1st April, 1973, did not exceed £1,500 in Greater London or £750 elsewhere or, on 22nd March, 1973, did not exceed £600 in Greater London or £300 elsewhere, or in the case of premises first rated before 23rd March, 1965, did not exceed £400 and £200 respectively. The recent introduction of these higher values extends the system of regulation to almost all tenanted accommodation.

A tenant protected by the Act has the right to continue in occupation, even after termination of the tenancy by notice to quit, until the court makes an order for possession against him on the grounds mentioned in the Act or until he abandons occupation. This phase of occupation, protected by the Act, is known as a 'statutory tenancy'. If the tenant dies, any member of his family who has resided with him for at least the previous six months is entitled to replace him as statutory tenant. If that person dies, there is a similar privilege for a member of his family, but after the death of the second statutory 'successor' there can be no further transmission.

A landlord seeking possession must satisfy the court on one or more of the available grounds against any protected or statutory tenant (s.98), and if a contractual tenancy still exists, that tenancy must first be terminated by notice to quit. A court order for possession is necessary in all cases. Some of the grounds are mandatory; some are within the discretion of the court (see s.98 and Schedule 15).

(a) Discretionary grounds—Possession will not be granted unless firstly the court considers it reasonable to do so and either:

(i) the court is satisfied that suitable alternative accommodation is available to the tenant or will be available when the order takes effect, or

(ii) the circumstances are as specified in any of the cases in Part I of Schedule 15. Very briefly, these are that there has been breach of covenant, including failure to pay rent or misuse of the property; that the landlord has acted prejudicially to himself as a result of the tenant's notice to quit; that the tenant has assigned or sublet without consent, whether or not such consent is required under the contractual tenancy; that the premises are needed by the landlord for a full-time employee and were originally let to the tenant because he was an employee; that the landlord needs the premises for himself or for a member of his family; that the tenant has sublet part of the premises at an excessive rent. Possession is in fact seldom recovered even when the grounds exist.

(b) Mandatory grounds—The court must make an order for possession in certain cases, provided generally that the landlord had notified the tenant before the commencement of the tenancy that he would require possession on one of the relevant grounds. These grounds are specified in Part II of Schedule 15. Again briefly, they are that the landlord was an owner-occupier who wishes to recover possession under one of the conditions laid down in Part V of Schedule 15, paragraphs (a) and (c) to (f), for residence by himself or a member of his family; that the house is required as a retirement home for the landlord or a member of his family; that the house was let as a holiday home for a term not exceeding eight months; that the house was let as a student residence within the last twelve months; that the house is required as a residence for performance of duties of a minister of religion; that the house is required for an agricultural employee in certain circumstances; that amalgamation for agricultural purposes has been approved under s.26 of the Agriculture Act 1967; that the house is required for an agricultural worker under specified circumstances; that the house has been let by a member of the regular armed forces as specified in the Schedule; or that the house was let under a 'protected shorthold tenancy'.

A protected shorthold tenancy is defined by section 52 of the Housing Act, 1980, as a protected tenancy granted for a term certain of not less than one year, nor more than five years, which cannot be terminated by the landlord before the expiry of the term, except by forfeiture for breach of covenant; which is notified to the tenant before commencement as being such a tenancy; and in respect of which a fair rent is registered at the appropriate time.

The purpose of this provision was to encourage owners to let residences by facilitating ultimate recovery of possession. The safeguards for the tenant mentioned above are seriously undermined however by section 55 of the 1980 Act which authorizes the court to dispense with the requirement of some of the safeguards where it is 'just and equitable' to make an order for possession.

Protected tenants are protected in regard to rent as well as in regard to tenure. The rent recoverable is generally the last rent payable. Under s.67, however, the landlord and tenant may apply separately or jointly to the area rent officer for the registration of a 'fair' rent. Once registered this rent becomes the maximum rent recoverable by the landlord. If the parties do not agree with the rent officer's decision, a rent assessment committee may make a final ruling. This limit will generally be binding for two years. The criteria for determining a fair rent are laid down by s.70. Evasion of the Act through the exaction of premiums and loans is prohibited by s. 119.

Restricted contracts

A restricted contract is a contract whereby one person grants to another the right to occupy a dwelling as a residence in consideration of a rent which includes payment for the use of furniture or for services (s.19). Licences are thus included, provided that exclusive possession is enjoyed. Certain other arrangements for occupation not caught by the definition in section 19 are brought within the ambit of restricted contracts by express separate provision. The most notable is that of the landlord who resides in the same building as the tenant and that building is not a purpose-built block of flats. Such a tenancy is declared not to be protected (s.12). It is however declared to be a restricted contract (s.20).

Certain contracts otherwise falling within the definition are expressly excluded however, such as where the lessor is a Government Department, where the rateable value exceeds certain limits, or where the rent includes payment for board and the value of the board forms a substantial proportion of the whole rent (see generally s.19).

The security of tenure under a restricted contract depends upon whether the contract was created before or after the commencement of the Housing Act 1980. The former case will be mentioned first.

The protection of tenure only exists as ancillary to an application by a tenant to a rent tribunal for the registration of a rent. In such a case, if the landlord has served a notice to quit upon the tenant, that notice shall not take effect until six months after the tribunal's decision, or such shorter period as the tribunal decides. If the landlord serves notice to quit before such application, the tenant may apply to the tribunal for extension of the period of notice up to a maximum of six months (s.104).

In the case of contracts entered into after the 1980 Act, the tenant's position is weakened. The jurisdiction to postpone the effect of a notice to quit is vested in the court, which may, on the making of an order for possession, postpone possession for no longer than three months (s.106A). A court order is however necessary for eviction in case of all residential occupation under the Protection from Eviction Act 1977 as amended.

Protection in regard to rent under restricted contracts, as intimated above, is afforded by rent tribunals. Either the landlord or tenant or local authority may refer the contract to a rent tribunal for the determination of a reasonable rent (ss.77 and 78). This is recognized to be on a higher level than a 'fair rent' fixed by a rent officer.

The Leasehold Reform Act 1967 (as amended)

This Act gives the opportunity to certain leaseholders at low rents to buy the freeholds or to obtain extensions of their leases by fifty years. The conditions under which an application may be made under the Act are as follows. The Act in no way affects the ordinary free negotiation of a sale of the freehold reversion or a grant of an extension of a lease by a landlord and his tenant.

(1) The rent must be less than two thirds of the rateable value specified in the Act.
(2) The rateable value must not exceed that laid down in section 1 as amended by the Housing Acts of 1974 and 1980.
(3) The lease must have been granted for a term of more than 21 years.
(4) The property must have been occupied by the lessee as his main or only house of residence for the last three years or for periods totalling three years in the last ten years.

(5) The lease must be of the whole house. The Act does not apply to flats or maisonettes, though it does apply in certain cases where the house has been sub-let. The Act should be consulted carefully on these matters. There is machinery for the transmission of the lessee's rights under the Act in certain circumstances.

A qualified lessee has the following alternative rights:

(1) After serving a notice he may acquire the freehold at a price based on the assumption that the existing lease has to run for a further fifty years. In cases of disagreement as to price the matter is settled by the Lands Tribunal.
(2) He has the right to an extension of his lease by fifty years with a rent revised and based on the letting value of the site. This rent may be reviewed after twenty-five years. Once again, disputed cases are settled by the Lands Tribunal.

A landlord may resist applications of both kinds if he reasonably requires the house as a residence for himself or for a member of his family and, in certain cases where he owned a housing estate, could apply to the High Court for a scheme under which he retains powers of control over houses on the estate in the interests of the estate as a whole; the time for such applications has now passed. He may resist an application for an extended lease on the additional ground that he wishes to demolish or reconstruct the house. A Crown tenant cannot apply under either head and certain public authorities may apply to the Government for exemption if the land will be required for development within ten years.

Agricultural holdings

During the present century, the economic difficulties of the farmer and the crises of food supply produced by two world wars have made governmental influence in agriculture inevitable. Here we are concerned only with that aspect of the resulting legislation which has affected the farmer's security of tenure and the rent he pays. The law is now contained principally in the Agricultural Holdings Act 1948, as amended by the Agricultural Holdings (Notices to Quit) Act 1977.

An agricultural holding is one let and used for the business of farming, horticulture, fruit growing or market gardening. If the tenancy was created substantially for one or more of those purposes the Act applies, even though the land or parts of it can be put to uses of a subsidiary nature. A notice to quit is invalid if it attempts to terminate the tenancy before the expiration of twelve months from the end of the current year of tenancy. A tenancy or licence for a period of one year certain or less becomes a tenancy from year to year under the 1977 Act.

Security of tenure

With some exceptions, a periodic tenancy can only be ended by twelve months' notice to quit expiring at the end of a tenancy year.

If, however, the tenant, within one month of receiving such a notice to quit, sends the landlord a counter notice, he has security of tenure unless one or more of the following conditions apply, in which case the notice to quit is effective. The notice to quit must specify the grounds:

(1) Where the Agricultural Land Tribunal has given prior consent to the notice.
(2) Where the land is stated to be required for some non-agricultural use for which planning permission has been given or is, with certain exceptions, not required.
(3) Where the Tribunal has, on application within the previous six months, certified bad farming.
(4) Where the tenant has failed, within certain time limits, to remedy in full a breach of contract after the landlord has notified him of it.
(5) Where the landlord's interest has been materially prejudiced by breach of some term which is incapable of remedy.
(6) Where the tenant has become bankrupt.
(7) Where the tenant, or the last survivor of joint tenants to whom the property was originally let, has died within three months of the notice. There is however provision for members of the deceased tenant's family to apply to the Tribunal for succession.
(8) Where the Tribunal consents to the notice to quit. If none of the seven grounds mentioned above applies and the tenant serves a counter notice the matter is resolved by the Tribunal, which must allow the notice to take effect if one of the following grounds exists, unless satisfied that a fair and reasonable landlord would not insist on possession.
 (a) That the landlord's purpose in requiring possession is in the interests of good farming.
 (b) That the purpose is in the interests of the sound management of the estate.
 (c) That the purpose is in the interests of agricultural research, education, experiment or demonstration or for the provision of allotments or small holdings.
 (d) That greater hardship would be caused by withholding consent than by giving it.
 (e) That the land is required for some non-agricultural use not falling within (2) above.

Rent

On the granting of a tenancy, the parties may agree on what rent they please. Either party may, however, submit the matter not more than once every three years to an arbitrator who may increase or decrease the rent as from the time the tenancy could be ended by a notice to quit served when the request for arbitration was made. No revision is therefore possible where the tenancy is for a fixed term.

Business tenancies

Part II of the Landlord and Tenant Act 1954, as amended, affords protection in the two ways described below, where the property or part of property comprised in a tenancy is occupied by the tenant for the purposes of any trade, profession or employment. There are some exceptions such as agricultural holdings, public-houses, mining leases, certain service tenancies and tenancies of not more than six months. 'Business' has been interpreted widely by the courts and may even apply to clubs and land where no buildings stand.

(1) *Security of tenure*. Business tenancies continue under the Act even after the expiration of the term, unless ended in accordance with it or ended by a tenant's notice to quit, by surrender or by forfeiture.

To end the tenancy, the landlord must give not less than six nor more than twelve months' notice in the form required, expiring no earlier than the tenancy would have ended apart from the Act, or could have been ended by notice to quit. If the tenant serves a counter notice within two months informing the landlord that he is not willing to give up occupation, he may, not less than two nor more than four months after the landlord's notice, apply to the court for a new tenancy. There is an alternative procedure under which tenants for fixed terms exceeding one year can initiate matters by serving a statutory request for a new tenancy (see generally ss.25 and 26).

A new tenancy must be granted by the court unless the landlord establishes one of the following grounds mentioned below (s.30). The new term is not to exceed fourteen years; the rent is based on market value; and the other terms are, in default of agreement between the parties, to be settled by the court. The statutory protection described above in no way affects the competence of the parties to negotiate a new lease without having recourse to the Act. The grounds for possession are:

(a) Breach of repairing covenant.
(b) Persistent delay in payment of rent.
(c) Other breaches of covenant or mismanagement of the property.
(d) Reasonable offer of alternative accommodation by the landlord.
(e) The applicant is a sub-tenant of part of the premises and the whole could be let substantially more profitably than the parts.
(f) The landlord intends at the end of the tenancy to demolish or reconstruct the whole or a substantial part of the premises and could not reasonably do so without obtaining possession. There is no obligation on the landlord, however, to carry out his plans once he obtains possession.
(g) The landlord wishes to occupy the premises wholly or partly for his own business or for his own residence. In this case, however, the landlord must not have purchased his interest nor must his interest have been created within five years before the end of the term. This provision protects tenants against speculative purchases of reversions of business tenancies when the terms have but short times to run.

(2) *Compensation*. The Act provides for modest compensation where possession is granted on one or more of the last three grounds and, in certain cases, for improvements made by evicted tenants.

Public sector tenancies

Formerly, public sector residential tenants were excluded from the protective legislation described above. This exception was numerically of great importance, considering that council tenants were thus beyond the reach of the Rent Acts. Under the Housing Act 1980, they now enjoy a position analogous to the 'protected tenancy'. They occupy a status of 'secure tenancy'. The details of this protection cannot be explored here but s.32 describes its basis.

A secure tenancy is either a weekly or other periodic tenancy or a tenancy for a term certain but subject to termination by the landlord. It cannot be brought to an end by the landlord except by obtaining an order of court for possession. Grounds for possession are provided under s.34. They are comparable with, but somewhat wider than, those which apply in the case of private sector tenants.

Study material: the lease

On pages 108–9 is an example of a lease.

Questions

1 *Who is responsible for the external repairs of the property?*
2 *Peter Wall has sublet the property without the landlord's permission. Advise the landlord as to his rights.*
3 *Suppose that Peter Wall has sublet the property with the landlord's permission and that the subtenant receives planning permission to use the house for business purposes. Will he be liable for breach of any covenant in the lease?*
4 *Explain to a tenant under a lease for five years of residential property what is his legal position if he fails to pay his quarterly rent.*

THIS LEASE made the 9th day of May 1983 between John Snug of 14 Theseus Way Arden Warwickshire (hereinafter called "the Landlord") and Peter Wall of 9 Philomel Creek Arden aforesaid (hereinafter called "the Tenant")

WITNESSETH as follows:-

1. The Landlord hereby demises unto the Tenant ALL THAT property known as Humblebee Cottage Shirley Warwickshire TO HOLD the same unto the tenant from 9th day of May 1983 for the term of 2 years in consideration of the yearly rent of £1000 clear of all deductions payable by equal instalments twice yearly on the 1st day of November and the 31st day of March in each year of the tenancy.

2. The Tenant hereby covenants with the Landlord as follows:-

    (i) To pay the rent on the days mentioned and all rates taxes assessments and other outgoings payable in respect of the property during the term.

    (ii) At the Tenant's cost to repair and paint the interior of the property during the last six months of the tenancy.

    (iii) At the expiration or sooner determination of the tenancy to yield up the property to the Landlord.

    (iv) To use the property only as a dwelling house.

    (v) Not to assign charge underlet or part with the possession of the property without the previous written consent of the Landlord.

3. The Landlord hereby covenants with the Tenant as follows:-

(i) That the Tenant paying the rent hereby reserved and observing the covenants on his part shall enjoy peaceable possession of the property during the tenancy without disturbance on the part of the Landlord.

(ii) That the Landlord will keep the property insured against loss or damage by fire in the sum of £20000 and if the property is destroyed or damaged by fire will reinstate the property fit for habitation within 6 months of the occurrence of the fire.

4. PROVIDED ALWAYS and it is hereby agreed that if the rent or any part thereof shall remain unpaid for 21 days after becoming payable (whether formally demanded or not) or if any covenant on the part of the Tenant shall not be performed or if the Tenant shall become bankrupt the Landlord may at any time thereafter re-enter upon the property and the tenancy shall absolutely determine.

IN WITNESS whereof the parties hereto have hereinto set their hands and seals the day and year first before written.

Signed Sealed and Delivered by John Snug
JOHN SNUG

in the presence of:- Fred Flute
9, Moonshine Glade
Monks' Walk,
Warwickshire

This is a model lease prepared by the author based on commonly used forms.

Chapter Seven

Occupational rights without estate

Introduction

During the thousand years of history of English land law there has been a slow evolution of personal rights to estates. The principal features of an estate or interest in land are enforceability against all or most persons and assignability. To illustrate the former, suppose that a fee simple owner *F* grants a lease to *L* and later sells his fee simple to *P*. If *L* then sells his lease to *X*, the latter can enforce his interest against *P* and vice versa, whether or not either knows of the rights of the other. There is no need to prove any personal nexus.

No doubt, in the early days of feudalism rights in land were of a personal nature, that is enforceable only between grantor and grantee. The relationship of loyalty implied that the grant was personal and that free alienation was not contemplated. In practice, however, since land was the basis of the national economy as well as the object of political fealty, assignment of interests was later allowed. Thus arose estates in land enjoying the distinguishing features mentioned above.

This accolade of estate was bestowed on a limited range of grants, the fee simple, the entail, the life interest and the variants of these. The reason was that feudal land law was created by and for the aristocracy. The events which tolled the passage of aristocratic life were births, deaths and marriages. Estates were fashioned for the family.

The lease enjoyed a similar but later career. At first it sounded only in contract. It concerned only the landlord and his tenant. If the landlord assigned the fee simple and the new owner refused to confirm the lease, the tenant's only remedy lay in damages and not for recovery of occupation. Yet just as the social and economic factors of feudal England shaped the first estates, so did the developing commercial influences of the fifteenth century allow the lease to graduate from contract to estate. The tenant; usually a farmer and a stalwart of the economy, needed security of tenure against all persons for his term. The calendar rather than family events registers time for the trader. The leap to estatehood was brought about through technical developments in the law centred around the writ of ejectment.

We might also anticipate how social and economic need in the nineteenth century enabled the restrictive covenant to make that same leap with the guiding hand of equity.

Since the eighteenth century, Britain has changed from a centuries-old agrarian society to a community of such complex family and work patterns that it would be strange to find the old system of estates unrestrained by new influences. Human activity continuously outgrows the law which constantly tries to catch up upon, classify and control it. Examples of such influences in contemporary Britain are divorce and marital separation, cohabitation on the part of unmarried people, mobility of the population, greater incidence of home ownership, state protection of the under-privileged, the housing shortage and the leisure industry.

A complicating factor in regard to the relationships we are about to discuss is that they have not made any uniform leap towards estatehood. Sometimes enforceability of an arrangement has expanded beyond the immediate parties, but falls short of affecting all persons. Often the power of assignment is absent. Only time will confirm whether they will attain the two hallmarks of interests in land. Perhaps, however, this classical concept of the estate is outmoded and a more finely graduated system of occupational rights is called for. Between the rigid bone of estate and the soft muscle of contract there is needed, and is growing, a cartilaginous sinew which combines the capacity for youthful flexibility with some capacity for endurance.

Sometimes these rights have developed through precedents; sometimes they have been enacted. As to the former, while they are disparate they appear to spring from very general equitable principles. In *Re Sharpe* [1980] 1 All E.R. 195, Browne-Wilkinson, J. remarked at page 201

> I do not think that the principles lying behind these decisions have yet been fully explored and on occasions it seems that such rights are found to exist simply on the ground that to hold otherwise would be a hardship to the plaintiff.

Here two elements of justice confront each other. The law ought to be reasonably certain and foreseeable; on the other hand, it should respond to the infinitely variable circumstances of the case in issue.

Land law has been accustomed to distinct interests with distinct names. These modern rights to occupy land possess some but not all the features of the older interests. Consequently they tend to be classed as merely personal rights, the result only of the brake of equity being applied to prevent the owner of an 'interest' asserting his full 'rights' against some person. The old legal maxim 'Where there is a right there is a remedy' is clearly appropriate where rights are precisely defined and well established. Yet what is a right but the claim to a remedy? The even older truth that 'Where there is a remedy there is a right' is appropriate in regard to these new relationships to land. Merely because the remedy is available against a narrower range of persons or for a shorter time than in the case of the older interests surely ought not to forbid their classification amongst rights to land.

It is, however, permissible to distinguish them from the older interests provided that we remember that the differences are of degree only. The scheme will be first to describe the nature of each right then to silhouette it against the two hallmarks of estatehood, range of enforceability and assignability.

Licences

Nature

A licence gives permission to do some act, otherwise unlawful, in regard to land belonging to another. The permission might be express or implied. An example of the latter is the implied consent of a householder to members of the public to call at his door to make lawful enquiries, provided that he has not signified that such calls are forbidden. Licences generally lack the hallmarks of interests in land, namely assignability and enforceability against third parties. They merely authorize the licensee to do some act which would otherwise be a tort. During this century, however, it has become clear that in certain circumstances licences can possess these attributes.

The subject matter of licences is universal, spanning activities which are compatible with the existence of leases, easements, life interests and even profits, as shown below.

Leases	*Profits*	*Easements*
Exclusive possession	Taking things from the land	Doing acts on the land
	Licences	

A licence may authorize taking your seat in the cinema, going to a friend's house for a drink, putting an advertisement sign on another person's property or even enjoying exclusive occupation of land for an indefinite period. In short, any act can be the subject matter of a licence. In practice, the two interests from which it is important to distinguish it are leases and easements.

A licence is distinguishable from an easement in that the latter exists for the benefit of another piece of land, whereas the former exists for the benefit of a person only. This factor also distinguishes it from a profit which, we shall later see, is an interest in land analogous to an easement.

Generally there will be no confusion between a licence and a lease because licences usually concern doing some act upon land, whereas a lease demands exclusive possession. It is now beyond question, however, that a licence can confer exclusive possession (see *Errington* v. *Errington and Woods* [1952] 1 K.B. 290), so that when this is present some conclusive test must be applied. The test is that, if exclusive possession is given, then *prima facie* there is a lease: but if the circumstances and conduct of the parties show that only a personal privilege, not an interest in land, was intended, then there is only a licence (per Lord Denning L.J. in *Errington's Case*).

The criterion, imprecise though it might be, is that of the intentions of the parties. This intention must be deduced from all the circumstances. The label which the parties place upon the transaction is by no means conclusive, for sometimes what is in substance a lease is called a licence with the motive of evading the Rent Acts or some other rules which affect leases. The question to ask therefore is whether what was intended was an estate, which is impersonal and assignable, or merely a special privilege for some particular individual. Thus,

> in all cases where an occupier has been held to be a licensee there has been something in the circumstances such as a family arrangement, an act of friendship or generosity or such like to negative any intention to create a tenancy (*Facchini* v. *Bryson* [1952] 1 T.L.R. 1386, per Denning L.J. at p.1390).

Association with land law and its precisely defined estates has fostered some prematurely rigid classification of licences. An attempt to distinguish them according to their range of enforceability has, however, produced a fourfold classification which is rooted only in mode of creation, namely bare licences, contractual licences, licences coupled with grants and estoppel licences. It is submitted that this classification is spurious as to its intended purpose and has been a principal cause of the confusion in this subject. It has failed to detect the true reasons why the courts have afforded durability to some licences but not to others.

The classification has failed fully to observe that a licence is a means only and, unlike an estate or interest, not an end in itself, whereas the remedies supplied by the courts have frequently been tuned to the ultimate aims of the parties.

A licence is merely one means through which occupation of land occurs. Its end or purpose must be sought by examining the precise terms of each individual licence and all the circumstances surrounding its offer and acceptance. Its mode of creation is not without significance but constitutes only one of these surrounding factors. A licence can, for instance, lead to the licensee becoming entitled to an estate in land. This is so in the case of proprietary estoppel. Such licences are more appropriately considered as means through which interests in land are acquired. They are accordingly dealt with as such in Chapter 1. Here we are only concerned with licences which confer rights of occupation falling short of 'interests', as described at the beginning of this chapter. Speaking in terms of remedies, such rights attract 'negative' injunctive relief, whereas the positive relief of specific performance is more appropriate in the case of interests.

There are signs that the rigid fourfold classification is crumbling in the face of modern authorities. The dictum of Browne-Wilkinson J. noted on page 111 illustrates a more general approach. The older classification will be described below when the range of enforceability of licences is discussed. This is done not only because its rationale, faulty though it might be, is enshrined in high judicial authority, but also because the manner of creation possesses some genuine significance in attracting equitable remedies. More detailed criticism of the older approach will be reserved for that discussion.

It is submitted that general equitable principles and remedies ultimately measure all licences irrespective of manner of creation but according to all the circumstances of the case.

Range of enforceability of licences

(1) Enforceability against the licensor.
This is a question of revocability.

(a) *Bare licence.* This is a licence given otherwise than for consideration and not coupled with a grant of property in the land. It is revocable at the will of licensor at any time, even if given by deed. The licensee must however be given a reasonable time to leave. Subject to that he becomes a trespasser (see *Minister of Health* v. *Bellotti* [1944] 1 K.B. 298).

The grant of exclusive occupation to a person, for example a mistress, with the intention of providing security of occupation even for a long period, may nevertheless be merely a bare licence, devoid of the contractual element qualifying it to be dealt with under (c) below. Even an

intention that ownership shall pass will not alter this position if no conveyance of the property has been made (*Horrocks* v. *Forray* [1976] 1 W.L.R. 230). While some of the constituents of contract might be present, such as agreement to terms, the intention to create legal obligations might be absent.
(b) *Licence coupled with a grant*. If the licence is ancillary to the grant of some proprietary right in the land or chattels on the land, such as a permission to enter and take a tree or a heap of bricks which the licensor has sold or given to the licensee, then it is irrevocable (*James Jones and Sons Ltd.* v. *Tankerville* [1909] 2 Ch. 440).
(c) *Licence for value*. This is simply an ordinary contract and revocability depends upon the particular terms. Whether the right to enter the land is the primary purpose of the contract or is merely secondary is immaterial (*London Borough of Hounslow* v. *Twickenham Gardens Development Ltd.* [1970] 3 All E.R. 328, at p.343). Examples are admissions to cinemas and sportsgrounds for payment and entry upon property to do building or other work. Sometimes the contract will expressly state how long the licence is to last; sometimes it will clearly imply it.

In the earlier days of this century the rights of the licensee rang only in contract. The licence could be revoked at any time, the licensor being liable in damages only if revocation amounted to breach of contract. There could be no damages in tort. Damages in tort would depend upon the licensee having an interest in land, which, being property, is irrevocable by the grantor. If the licensee's rights were merely contractual, however, the licence could be revoked effectively though wrongfully. The consequence would be breach of contract only.

This doctrine has been changed by modern developments, notably by the willingness of the courts to apply equitable remedies. In *Winter Garden Theatre (London) Ltd.* v. *Millennium Productions Ltd.* [1948] A.C. 173 Lord Uthwatt said at page 202 'The settled practice of the courts of equity is to do what they can by an injunction to preserve the sanctity of a bargain'. His statement was *obiter*, however, because the licence in question was held to have been properly revoked.

In *Hurst* v. *Picture Theatres Ltd.* [1915] 1 K.B. 1 it was held by the Court of Appeal that the ejection of the plaintiff from a cinema on the mistaken grounds that he had not paid for his ticket amounted not merely to breach of contract but to assault. The basis of the decision was that he had gained an interest in the land through his contract, for in equity he would have been entitled to decree of specific performance of his contract. Notionally, a Chancery judge was sitting by his side at the performance. The comparative age of this case is reflected by the old-fashioned requirement of an interest for securing occupation of the land itself, and the inference that, although contracting parties 'may' not break their contracts, they nevertheless 'can' do so. See *Wood* v. *Leadbitter* (1855) 13 M. & W. 838. The *dicta* from the Winter Garden case cited above, although *obiter* only, point to a more sophisticated formula for modern development. A right to the land itself results from a remedy and not vice versa.

The view of Megarry J. in the Hounslow case at page 343 that 'I find it difficult to see how a contractual licensee can be treated as a trespasser so long as his contract entitles him to be on the land' surely points the way for the future. In short, revocation depends upon the terms of the agreement.

(d) *Estoppel licence.* The principle upon which this licence rests is that if an owner permits another person to spend money or detrimentally to alter his position in the expectation that he will enjoy some privilege in the land, the owner will be prevented from acting inconsistently with this expectation.

Thus, relief has been given against an owner where a person was allowed to spend money on a watercourse running through the owner's land (*Duke of Devonshire* v. *Eglin* (1851), 14 Beav. 530), where a territorial concession was made in the expectation of a right of way (*Ives Investment Ltd.* v. *High* [1967] 1 All E.R. 504), and where a son was encouraged to build a bungalow on his father's land, partly at his own expense, with the expectation of living there as long as he wished (*Inwards* v. *Baker* [1965] 2 Q.B. 29). While none would disagree with the justice of these decisions, the nature of the remedy and the rationalization of the right by the judges have varied. The remedy has sometimes been of a positive kind, where the anticipated right has in reality amounted to a quantifiable interest in land. Thus, in *Dillwyn* v. *Llewelyn* (1862), 4 De G.F. & J. 517, where the facts were similar to those of *Inwards* v. *Baker*, it was held that the son, having built the house, was entitled to a conveyance of the land. This decision was, however, criticized in the Court of Appeal in *Dodsworth* v. *Dodsworth* (1973), 228 E.G. 1115, where it was remarked that such a positive remedy might sometimes presuppose wider rights than contemplated by the parties. Similar problems might arise from the recent development of 'rental purchase' of property when the purchaser pays the price by instalments while in occupation. Such purchasers are sometimes referred to in their contracts as licensees (see 36 Conveyancer 325). In other cases, with which this chapter is more concerned, the remedy has been of a negative kind, the court ruling that the licence has created a proprietary estoppel which the licensor is not allowed to deny (*Ives Investment* v. *High*, above). The court looks at all the circumstances of each case to decide by what kind of remedy the equity can be satisfied (see *Plimmer* v. *Wellington Corporation* (1884), 9 App. Cas. 699). Thus in cases such as *Ives Investment* v. *High*, above, where decrees of specific performance are not appropriate because the substantive right is unenforceable through failure to register, the court may give negative procedural protection which is not founded upon a positive right. As to the rationalization of the right to protection, it would surely be possible to classify these cases as contracts. The licensee has acted to his detriment in return for an undertaking by the licensor which amounts to a promise not to obstruct the licensee when he has altered his position. The question of consideration should cause no difficulty since it is clearly established that this only requires a detriment to the promisee, and not necessarily a benefit to the promisor. This is one of the branches of land law which needs bracing with stronger and clearer concepts. If the medieval lawyers had been concerned with the licence, things might have been different (see, generally, 37 Conveyancer 402).

This class of licence has often received separate treatment in the decided cases. There appears to be no good reason for this. Estoppel licences have been classified as 'equities', as for instance in the judgment of Lord Scarman in *Chandler* v. *Kesley* [1978] 2 All E.R. 942. Yet the two features entitling them to be so called can apply equally to contractual licences.

These are susceptibility to equitable remedies and the capability, in appropriate circumstances, of binding third parties. To the extent that they can claim these characteristics all licences are 'equities'.

(2) Enforceability against third parties.

(a) *Bare licence.* This is not binding on third parties.

(b) *Licence coupled with a grant.* If the subject-matter of the grant is an interest in the land, and the legal interest has passed, then the licence, like the interest itself, will be binding on all third parties. If there is merely a contract to create such an interest, then presumably its enforceability against third parties will depend upon whether this has been registered as an estate contract under the Land Charges Act 1972. If the grant is one of chattels, then, according to R. H. Maudsley and E. H. Burn in their *Land Law: Cases and Materials* (Butterworth, 1980, 4th edn, p.438), if the ownership of the chattels has passed, the licence is binding on all persons, although clear authority is lacking. This seems reasonable, though possession of another person's chattel does not usually justify the owner's entry upon land for its recovery.

(c) *Contractual licence.* On the principle that since contractual licences can, in appropriate circumstances, enjoy protection through equitable remedies in the same way as estoppel licences do, they ought to bind third parties to the same degree as the latter. This would mean that they are enforceable against third parties other than purchasers for value of a legal estate in the land without notice. There appears to be no good reason why contractual licensees, as such, should be denied this stability for their rights. They are as vulnerable and deserving of protection as estoppel licensees. The only distinction is that they act to their detriment at the time of the licensor's promise, whereas the estoppel licensee acts to his detriment after it.

It would appear fairer if the distinction between the two categories were forsaken and all forms of relief were based on the substantial merits of the case. The basis of relief could be developed by precedent to the point only of reasonable certainty yet so as to retain some elasticity. The law of tort managed to burst out of technical categories into broader standards of liability in the development of negligence. Perhaps this is an example to be followed. The existing authorities on the question however are less promising. The older cases infer that contractual licences do not bind third parties (see *King* v. *David Allen and Sons, Billposting Ltd.* [1918] 2 A.C. 54 and *Cloe* v. *Theatrical Properties Ltd.* [1936] 3 All E.R. 483). Yet in *Errington* v. *Errington* [1952] 1 K.B. 290 the Court of Appeal held that a contractual licence bound a third party volunteer and it was suggested that it might also bind a third party purchaser. The authority of this decision is weakened by dicta of the House of Lords in *National Provincial Bank* v. *Ainsworth* [1965] A.C. 1175 and by the fact that it can be considered as a case of estoppel licence. (See also the judgment of Lord Denning, M.R., in *Binions* v. *Evans* [1972] 2 All E.R. 70 and (1972), 35 M.L.R. 551 and *D.H.N. Food Distributors* v. *Tower Hamlets* [1976] 1 W.L.R. 852). It is clear that mode of creation is obscuring the more fundamental question of whether all the circumstances of the case invoke a remedy in specie rather than mere damages. The need for a resolution of these difficulties was stressed by Browne-Wilkinson J. in *Re Sharpe* [1980] 1 All E.R. 195.

(d) *Licence by estoppel.* In *Errington* v. *Errington*, a father bought a house with the aid of a mortgage from a building society, paying part of the purchase price as a down-payment, and leaving the rest on mortgage. He let his son and daughter-in-law live in it, telling them the house would become theirs when they paid off the building society instalments. Before these were fully paid off the father died, leaving the house to the widow. The Court of Appeal held that the married pair were licensees with an equitable right to remain in the house as long as the instalments were paid, whereupon they would have an equitable title to the house itself. Accordingly the widow had no right to the house. The case is clear authority for the enforceability of this type of licence against third parties other than purchasers for value of a legal estate in the land without notice. Once again, the question must be asked why this problem cannot be considered as one of ordinary contract. The rights under it would be registrable as an estate contract, though upon the facts of *Errington* v. *Errington* this would not have been necessary as against the widow, who was not a purchaser.

In the case of registered land, there appears no good reason why such licences to occupy should not constitute overriding interests. The unsettled state of the law makes difficulties for a landowner who wishes to grant occupation to a person without creating a commercial arrangement or a life interest. It has been suggested that the solution is to grant a short periodic tenancy rent-free with an absolute covenant against assignment and sub-letting and with the landlord contractually postponing his right to serve notice to quit (36 Conveyancer 266). This appears, however, to be open to two objections. Firstly, persons attempting to accommodate friends and relations in this way frequently do not take legal advice and might not even be aware of the problem. Secondly, the highly personal nature of the terms and relationships might still lead the court to find that, despite the terms, a licence was intended rather than an estate.

Assignability of licences

Up to this point, we have been discussing the enforceability of licences against third parties. A brief word may now be added as to whether the benefit of a licence may be assigned by the licensee. A bare licence clearly cannot be assigned without the consent of the licensor. A licence coupled with a grant may be assigned along with the grant. As to contractual licences, the ordinary rule of contract law that the benefit is assignable applies, subject to the exclusion of this factor, expressly by the terms of the licence, or impliedly by the nature of the contract. Similar principles probably apply to licences by estoppel. There is a shortage of authority on the subject generally. The range of possibilities can be appreciated by a comparison of *Inwards* v. *Baker* [1965] 2 Q.B. 29 and *E. R. Ives Investment Ltd.* v. *High* [1967] 2 Q.B. 379.

A table representing the enforceability and assignability of licences might be helpful in conclusion. The orthodox categorization of licences has been adopted.

Type of licence	*Revocable by licensor*	*Enforceable against third parties*	*Assignable by licensee*
Bare licence	Yes	No	No
Licence coupled with a grant	No	Yes, in certain circumstances	Yes
Contractual licence	No	Possibly, but some doubt here	Yes
Estoppel	No	Yes, in certain circumstances	Yes

Occupational rights of spouses

A spouse may be entitled to occupy the matrimonial home, irrespective of his or her status of husband or wife, because of a proprietary interest in the property. This will be so where spouses co-own the property. It is shown in Chapter 11 that this proprietary right exists, even though the legal estate is improperly vested in one of the spouses only, provided that it can be established that there is co-ownership in equity. The circumstances under which equitable co-ownership arises need not be repeated here. A proprietary right of occupation similarly arises where the spouses take a joint lease. In such cases, the right of occupation of a spouse is a result of the ordinary principle of co-ownership which was illustrated in another context by *Bull* v. *Bull* [1955] 1 Q.B. 234.

We must now consider the right of a spouse to occupy the matrimonial home by virtue of the status of spouse, even if that spouse has no proprietary interest in the property.

At common law, a husband is under a duty to his wife to allow her to occupy the home he has provided for her unless he provides suitable alternative accommodation for her (see *Lee* v. *Lee* [1952] 2 Q.B. 489). Where it is necessary to protect the wife's right, the court may compel the husband to leave the matrimonial home, pending divorce proceedings, even though he owns it or is a tenant of it (*Jones* v. *Jones* [1971] 2 All E.R. 737). This right is *sui generis* and is not a species of licence or 'an equity' (*National Provincial Bank Ltd.* v. *Ainsworth* [1965] A.C. 1175). Even a husband who, during the subsistence of the marriage, remains in the matrimonial home after his wife has left, does not become a trespasser (even though the home is owned by her) until the court has determined that he has no right to stay (*Morris* v *Tarrant* [1971] 2 All E.R. 920).

Ainsworth's case (above), which settled that the right was not enforceable against third parties, placed the deserted wife who held no proprietary interest in the home in a vulnerable position. If her husband disposed of the property, her right of occupation could not be enforced against the purchaser, even though an injunction might prevent the dealing in appropriate cases when the wife, knowing of the intended transaction, acted in time. To mitigate these harsh consequences the Matrimonial Homes Act 1967, was passed.

However, a right to occupy the matrimonial home can be futile if one of the partners suffers under a threat of violence from the other. Recognition in recent years of the scale of violence in the family has resulted in the Domestic Violence and Matrimonial Proceedings Act 1976. The provisions of that Act have an influence upon the right to occupation of the matrimonial home. The two Acts will be dealt with separately.

The Matrimonial Homes Act 1967 (as amended by the Matrimonial Homes and Property Act 1981)
The principal provisions of this Act are as follows:

(1) Where one spouse is entitled to occupy a dwelling-house by virtue of any estate or interest or contract, or under any enactment, and the other spouse is not, then the spouse not so entitled has a right, if in occupation, not to be excluded from occupation of any part by the other spouse without a court order, and, if not in occupation, the right, with the leave of the court, to enter possession of the house. Where these 'rights of occupation' exist, either spouse may apply to the court for an order 'declaring, enforcing, restricting or terminating those rights or regulating the exercise by either spouse of the right to occupy the dwelling house' (s.1).

Section 1 clearly could not as it stood be invoked in cases where the spouses are co-owners. If both spouses hold legal estates they have no such need for protection, though problems of a different kind might still arise, such as the spouses finding it intolerable to live under the same roof (see *Phillips* v. *Phillips* [1973] 2 All E.R. 423). Then the court might order one spouse, even though a part-owner, to leave the property (see [1973] C.L.J. 227). If one spouse merely has an equitable interest, while the other alone holds the legal estate, there is clearly a danger that the one with only an equitable interest might have his rights overridden upon a sale by the other. Accordingly, the owner of an equitable interest in the house who does not hold a legal estate is now empowered to claim the protection of the Act (Matrimonial Proceedings and Property Act 1970, s.38). In exercising this jurisdiction, the court may have regard to the conduct of the spouses, their needs and financial resources, the needs of any children and all the circumstances of the case and make such order as it thinks just and reasonable.

(2) The effect of the statutory right of occupation is that of a charge on the interest of the spouse owning the estate or interest in the house, having priority as if it were an equitable interest created at the date of the acquisition of the estate or interest upon which it is charged, or the date of the marriage, or the commencement of the Act, whichever is the latest. The right is registrable. A deserted spouse in occupation, who has not registered, need not be joined in an action for possession by a prior chargee so as to give the opportunity of paying off the debts of the other spouse (see s.1(5)); such a deserted spouse would, of course, have no other means of retaining possession as against the prior chargee (see *Hastings and Thanet Building Society* v. *Goddard* [1970] 3 All E.R. 954). The charge lasts for the duration of the marriage, unless the court directs otherwise in the event of a matrimonial dispute, and is void against a purchaser of the property, or of any interest in it, unless it is registered before the completion of the purchase. Furthermore it is void against the trustee in bankruptcy of the spouse who owns the estate

or interest, whether registered or not (s.2(5)). The right of a spouse not in occupation to re-enter is a continuing one and, though it is only to be exercised with the leave of the court, may be registered at all times, even when still conditional in this way (*Watts* v. *Waller* [1973] 3 All E.R. 257).

(3) If the owner-spouse contracts to sell the house with vacant possession, a statutory term is implied in the contract that he or she will procure the cancellation of the charge, but breach of this implied term will not entitle the person who has agreed to purchase to obtain a decree of specific performance, since an owner will not usually be required to embark on a difficult and uncertain litigation (*Wroth* v. *Tyler* [1973] 1 All E.R. 897). If the protected spouse knowingly stands by or assists while the owning spouse contracts to sell with vacant possession, that protected spouse may, however, be estopped from asserting the rights of occupation under the Act.

(4) Where the title to the property is registered, a spouse's right of occupation may be protected by a notice under the Land Registration Act, 1925 (Chapter 18, *post*). The registration of a class F land charge would be of no avail (*Miles* v. *Bull* [1968] 3 All E.R. 632). Rights of occupation do not constitute overriding interests (s.2(7) and Matrimonial Homes and Property Act 1981 s.4(1)).

(5) The rights of occupation will only be binding on a mortgagee of the home if registration occurs before the mortgage is made. Such registration will not often take place. When it does, it might well discourage a prospective mortgagee from lending on the security of the home.

(6) The Act also provides for the payment of rent by a spouse protected by the Act, where the other spouse is a tenant, for Rent Act protection when the tenant spouse has enjoyed such protection and for the tender of mortgage instalments and other outgoings. The details of these provisions cannot be dealt with here.

(7) Rights of occupation are not assignable.

The Domestic Violence and Matrimonial Proceedings Act 1976

Recognition in recent years that violence in the home is common led to the passing of this Act. Even before the Act, the divorce court occasionally granted injunctions excluding a spouse from the home for this reason, but the jurisdiction was exercised only incidentally to substantive matrimonial proceedings. The criminal law has not been effective as a deterrent since the police are reluctant to interfere in any but the more serious assaults between spouses.

Section 1(1) enacts

> Without prejudice to the jurisdiction of the High Court on an application by a party to a marriage a county court shall have jurisdiction to grant an injunction containing one or more of the following provisions, namely:
>
> (a) a provision restraining the other party to the marriage from molesting the applicant;
>
> (b) a provision restraining the other party from molesting a child living with the applicant;
>
> (c) a provision excluding the other party from the matrimonial home or a part of the matrimonial home or from a specified area in which the matrimonial home is included;

(d) a provision requiring the other party to permit the applicant to enter and remain in the matrimonial home;

Whether or not any other relief is sought in the proceedings.

Section 1(2) enacts:

> Subsection (1) above shall apply to a man and a woman who are living with each other in the same household as husband and wife as it applies to the parties to a marriage and any reference to the matrimonial home shall be construed accordingly.

In *Davis* v. *Johnson* [1978] 2 All E.R. 1132 an unmarried couple cohabited as joint tenants of a council flat. The man had been violent to the woman. She therefore left the flat, but wished to move back. She applied to the county court for an injunction excluding the man from the flat. The House of Lords held that such an injunction could be granted. It had been argued that the Act was procedural only in its effect and could not affect property rights. The House held that the Act did not affect property rights but did affect the way in which such rights could be enjoyed. Lord Scarman stated that the injunction confers a 'right of occupation which can for a period override the property rights of her family partner' (at p.1156).

Discussion upon the interpretation of the Act, the procedures to be followed and the matters weighed by the court in deciding whether to grant an injunction must be sought in the textbooks on family law. The Domestic Proceedings and Magistrates' Courts Act 1978 should also be consulted. The significance of this legislation to land law is the nature of the right which accrues to a person who successfully applies for an injunction. In the first place, the injunctive relief is of short term duration only, a few months during which the relieved party can secure accommodation.

Of course, this prolonging of the status quo as against the other spouse or cohabitee is an augmentation of the original rights of the applicant in the scale of time. The Act does not, however, enlarge such rights in the 'horizontal' spheres of enforceability against third parties or disposability. In these last respects they remain what they were before. If an applicant spouse, for instance, has statutory rights of occupation under the Matrimonial Homes Act 1967 which, being registered, are enforceable against third parties, these rights remain so. If the rights of a cohabitee did not enjoy this capacity before the grant of injunction, presumably they will not acquire them under the grant.

The effect of an injunction is to put existing legal relations into a temporary freeze, not to change the right which is put into that freeze. Land law must surely be concerned with the rights to enjoy land, however precarious, as well as the rights to sell it. The effect of the Act is comparable with Acts which confer security of tenure in the field of landlord and tenant.

Condominium and time-sharing

The topics considered in this chapter show that important changes are taking place in the content and emphasis in land law. Even a short book such as this should greet new developments briefly, although they are only on the horizon.

In some parts of the world, notably in America and parts of Continental Europe, new kinds of community ownership are growing fast. Causes have been diverse. Sometimes the single family dwelling in its own grounds has become too expensive; sometimes the need to share the costs of purchasing and maintaining holiday accommodation enjoyed for only brief periods of the year has become crucial. The principal methods of meeting these difficulties have emerged during the last twenty years or so. They offer a challenge to expand our existing pattern of estates and licences.

(1) *Condominium*. A condominium is an area of land of which a part is designated for separate ownership and part for common ownership by the owners of the separate parts. In the context of a residential condominium, an owner might enjoy exclusive use of a house or apartment together with rights in common with other owners over gardens and other places of resort comprised in the holding. In the United States, condominia are run under statutory provisions which facilitate their management and funding. In the more complex structures, social organization approaches the municipal function of local government.

Certain features of these schemes, such as multiple ownership by legal tenants in common and the running of positive covenants with land, present considerable technical difficulty to the introduction of condominium to England. (For general reading see [1979] J.P.L. 505).

(2) *Time-sharing*. Some applications of this concept have already reached this country in the context of holiday accommodation. Participants in a time-sharing scheme purchase the right to occupy an apartment and to enjoy the use of surrounding facilities for a limited period in recurring years. Matters such as insurance, rates and property maintenance are cared for by a management team. These rights can be transferred, let or bequeathed by the purchaser. Despite the description of 'interval ownership' sometimes applied to such arrangements, the legal title of the units will generally be vested in a company which is responsible for general management.

Although such schemes vary considerably in detail, generally the participants purchase a bundle of contractual rights including assignable licences to occupy the land during a particular week or weeks in each year. The general intention of assignability suggests a new form of lease or sub-lease. Alternatively, we must accept an expanded view of the contractual licence as a transmissible right.

Statutory tenancies

We have seen in Chapter 6 that the Rent Acts protect the occupation of the tenant in the case of certain types of residential tenancies, even after the contractual tenancy has ended. Although such a right of occupation is called a 'statutory tenancy' it is really no tenancy at all. A true tenancy is an estate in land characterized not only by enforceability against all persons but also by assignability. A statutory tenancy is not assignable, though it is to a limited extent transmissible upon death, and a sub-tenancy can be granted out of it.

It is therefore classified amongst the rights discussed in this chapter. However, since it is found in the context of the lease it is considered more fully in Chapter 6.

Study material: *Somma* v. *Hazelhurst* [1978] 2 All E.R. 1011

3rd March. **CUMMING-BRUCE LJ** read the following judgment of the court, prepared by him, at the invitation of Stephenson LJ. In February 1976 two young people, Mr Martin Hazelhurst and Miss Savelli (herein called H and S), were looking for accommodation in which to live together in London. He was an educated man employed as a computer programmer, a job involving some mathematical qualifications. She also had a job. They were not married. On Wednesday, 18th February, they saw an advertisement in the *Evening Standard* in the column headed 'Flats and Maisonettes to Let' which read: 'ACTON/HAMMERSMITH West Kensington. Double bedsits & flatlets. All amenities. Near Tubes. £13 to £19 per week 602 5464.' They telephoned the number given and by appointment visited a house at 4 Cornwall Mansions, W14, which belongs to Miss Somma. The house is divided into four flats, subdivided into four rooms and two maisonettes. There they met Mr Ritter, resident managing agent for Miss Somma. Mr Ritter showed them a room 22 feet by 18 feet on the third floor, with two beds in it which he described as a double room. They looked at it and went away. On Friday, 20th February, they returned, saw Mr Ritter again and said they wanted to take the room and to move in next day. Mr Ritter gave each of them a printed form of agreement into which he wrote the appropriate detail in the blank spaces. They each read the form they were given. H asked a few questions including a query about the clauses which indicated that they would have to share with a third person described as the licensor. They each signed their agreement before they moved in, and though they had not thought out the legal implications of the contracts they urgently wanted accommodation and, in the judge's phrase, understood what they were letting themselves in for. The agreements were identical save the name of the licensee, and we have set forth as an example the agreement signed S on 21st February 1976. I herein set forth and include in this judgment that licence in extenso:

> 'THIS LICENCE is made the 21st day of Feb., 1976. One thousand nine hundred and seventy-six Between I. Somma or Agent of 7, Agate Road, W.6 (hereinafter referred to as "the Licensor") of the one part and R. Savelli of Milan, Italy (hereinafter referred to as "the Licensee") of the other part.
>
> WHEREAS the Licensor is not willing to grant the Licensee exclusive possession of any part of the rooms hereinafter referred to.
>
> AND WHEREAS the Licensee is anxious to secure the use of the rooms notwithstanding that such use be in common with the Licensor and such other licensees or invitees as the Licensor may permit from time to time to use the said rooms.
>
> AND WHEREAS this Licence is entered into by the Licensor and the Licensee solely upon the above basis.
>
> By this Licence the Licensor licenses the Licensee to use (but not exclusively) all those rooms (hereinafter referred to as "the Rooms") on the 3rd Floor Double B/Sit floor of the building known as and situate at Flat 4, Cornwall Mansions, W.14 (hereinafter referred to as "the Building") together with the use of the entrance hall and lift (if any) the staircase outer door and vestibule of the Building and the furniture fixtures and effects now in the Rooms (more particularly set out in the Schedule of Contents annexed hereto) from 21.2.76 until 15.5.76 (Twelve weeks) for the sum of £116.40 on the following terms and conditions:
>
> '1. THE Licensee agrees to pay the said sum of £116.40 by 4 weekly instalments of £38.80 commencing on the 21st day of Feb. 1976 next and thereafter on Saturday of each 4th week until 15.5.76.
>
> '2. THE Licensee shall be responsible for the payment of all gas electric light and power which shall be consumed or supplied in or to the Rooms during the Licensee's occupation thereof and the amount of all charges made in respect of the telephone installed therein or in the Building so far as the same relates to his use thereof.
>
> '3. THE Licensee shall use his best endeavours amicably and peaceably to share the use of the Rooms with the Licensor and with such other licensees or invitees

whom the Licensor shall from time to time permit to use the Rooms and shall not interfere with or otherwise obstruct such shared occupation in any way whatsoever.

'4. THE Licensee shall keep the interior of the Rooms and all fixtures and fittings and fixtures therein in good and clean condition and complete repair (fair wear and tear and damage by accidental fire only excepted) and immediately replace all broken glass.

'5. THE Licensee shall preserve the furniture and effects in the said Rooms from being destroyed or damaged and make good pay for the repair of or replace with articles of a similar kind and of equal value such of the furniture and effects as may be destroyed lost broken or damaged (fair wear and tear thereof only excepted).

'6. THE Licensee shall leave the furniture and effects at the expiration or sooner determination of this Licence in the Rooms or places in which they were at the commencement hereof.

'7. THE Licensee shall pay for the washing (including ironing or pressing) of all counterpanes blankets and curtains which shall have been soiled during the Licensee's occupation (the reasonable use thereof nevertheless to be allowed for).

'8. ON notice in writing being given to the Licensee by the Licensor or her Agent of all wants of repair cleansings amendments and restorations to the interior of the Rooms and of all such destruction loss breakage or damage of or to the furniture and effects as the Licensee shall be bound to make good found therein the Licensee shall repair cleanse amend and restore or make good the same within two months of the giving of such notice.

'9. THE Licensee shall not remove any furniture and effects from the Rooms without the previous consent in writing of the Licensor.

'10. THE Licensee shall not carry on or permit to be carried on in the Rooms any profession trade or business whatsoever.

'11. THE Licensee shall not do or suffer to be done in the Rooms any act or thing which may be a nuisance cause of damage or annoyance to the Licensor and the other occupiers or users of the Rooms or the Building or of any adjoining premises or which may vitiate any insurance of the Building against fire or otherwise or increase the ordinary premium thereon.

'12. THE Licensee shall not affix to the windows of the Rooms externally or internally any venetian blinds except of such colour and construction as shall be previously approved in writing by the Licensor or her Agent.

'13. THE Licensee shall not hang or allow to be hung any clothes or other articles on the outside of the Rooms or the Building.

'14. THE Licensee shall clean all the windows of the Rooms once at least in every month during his occupation.

'15. THE Licensee shall not deposit any store of coal elsewhere than in the cellar or other receptacle provided for the purpose and shall not keep any combustible or offensive goods provisions or materials in the Rooms.

'16. THE Licensee shall not cause or permit any waste spoil or destruction to the Rooms or to the Building.

'17. THE Licensee shall not pull down alter add to or in any way interfere with the construction or arrangements of the Rooms without the previous consent in writing of the Licensor.

'18. THE Licensee shall not keep any animals or birds in the Rooms Nor shall the Licensee permit any child or children to reside or stay in the Rooms.

'19. THE Licensor shall not at any one time permit more than one other persons to use the Rooms together with the Licensor and the Licensee.

'20. UNLESS prevented by any cause not under his control the Licensor shall keep the entrance hall staircase vestibule and lift (if any) clean and properly lighted.

'21. THIS Licence is personal to the Licensee and shall not permit the use of the Rooms by any other person whatsoever.

'22. UPON the Licensee being in breach of any of the conditions referred to above this Licence shall immediately determine without prejudice to any other remedies of the Licensor and the Licensee shall immediately cease his use of the Rooms and the Building as permitted hereunder.

SIGNED by the above-named Licensor or Agent } S. Ritter

SIGNED by the above-named Licensee: } Savelli Rossella

The Licensee hereby states having received a copy of this contract

SCHEDULE OF CONTENTS

If an Electric Meter is installed the rent will be reduced by 25 pence per week.

S. Ritter
Savelli Rossella'

Extract reproduced by permission of the All England Law Reports.

Questions

1 *Was the agreement a lease or a licence? The judgment should be further consulted for an answer to this question.*

2 *Attempt to reconcile the decision with Walsh v. Griffiths-Jones [1978] 2 All E.R. 1002.*

3 *Consider the effect of this litigation upon the security of tenure provided for tenants by the Rent Act (see Real Property and Real People by K. J. Gray and P. D. Symes, Butterworth, 1981, pp.428–430).*

4 *Doreen, wife of Darren, arrives at your office in distress. Darren has often been violent to her during their marriage. Today he evicted her from their home. She has nowhere to go. The legal title to the home is in Darren's name only. What action do you propose to take?*

Chapter Eight

Extinguishment of interests in land under The Limitation Act 1980

Introduction

Entitlement to land in English law is based upon priority of possession. If *A* possesses land he has a better right to it than anyone else, except one who can prove a superior right by showing previous possession of the land or its profits. If *A* occupies land and *B* dispossesses him, *A* has a superior right based upon previous possession and may retrieve the land. However, if *A* does not do this, and later *C* dispossesses *B* and then *D* dispossesses *C*, *C* may evict *D* because of his superior title. Similarly *B* may recover the land as against both *C* and *D*, and *A* has the best right of all these persons.

Since land exists permanently, the life story of a particular plot might, if discoverable, reveal several such acts of dispossession over the centuries. It might show that even *A*'s title was based upon the dispossession of *X* over a hundred years ago. Perhaps the persons who today would have been entitled to the land through *X* under the laws of succession have now learned of these events. If there were no restrictions on the doctrine that possession is the basis of title, then ancient claims of this kind would constantly empower speculators to disturb long-accepted rights to land, so that indeed no fee simple owner could sleep tight in his bed at night. There is a social need for certainty of title to land.

For centuries, therefore, statute has placed a limit on the time after which a claimant to an interest in land may bring an action to establish it in the face of the possession of another person holding under a later title. The present law is contained in the Limitation Act 1980. The general effect of the Act is not to confirm any particular claim to land but merely to extinguish stale titles to it. In the example given above, the title of *X* would be extinguished simply, leaving *A*'s claim as superior. It is most important to realize that the Act does not transfer *X*'s title to *A* (see *Tichborne* v. *Weir* (1892), 67 L.T. 735). A man of ninety suddenly finds himself the oldest man in the village not necessarily because he is ninety but because a man of ninety-one died yesterday. The scythe of time creates superiority of title as it does seniority of age. Title is never extinguished because of its age, of course. Quite the contrary. It is only extinguished or 'barred' because the claim it gives to land has been allowed to remain unpressed for a long time in face of a rival title.

Thus the effect of the Act is to eliminate. This is in contrast to the Prescription Act, which is acquisitive in its approach to easements and profits. Even though the Limitation Act works negatively, once a person, through his own occupation and that of his predecessors in title, can show possession for such a time and in such circumstances that the risk of a successful rival claim may be discounted, the element of relativity of title disappears for practical purposes, and that person may consider that he has an absolute title to the land.

It might appear that while the law punishes theft of chattels it rewards theft of land but acquisition of title under the doctrine, is seldom attributable to a single and conscious act of confiscation. In many cases there has been misunderstanding as to boundaries, perhaps due to mistakes or lack of definition in conveyancing documents. The role of the Act in quietening claims and rendering title certain in such instances is clearly beneficial.

It is sometimes suggested that when an owner, *A*, is dispossessed by *B*, both *A* and *B* own fee simple estates in the same land, only one of which will prevail of course if the parties put their rights before a court. Inviting though the notion is for the speculative thinker, it is surely misconceived. The fee simple estate simply denotes ownership. There cannot be two conflicting ownerships of the same piece of land; neither can there be two fee simple estates in the same land at the same time. What there can be is two or more rival claims to one fee simple estate or to ownership. One claimant only owns it. The other is a trespasser as against that person (see 80 L.Q.R. 63).

The length of the limitation period

The general rule under s.15(1) is that

> no action shall be brought by any person to recover any land after the expiration of twelve years from the date on which the right of action accrued to him or, if it first accrued to some person through whom he claims, to that person.

The period for recovery by the Crown or by a charitable corporation or corporation sole is thirty years from the date when the right of action accrued to it, or, if it first accrued to some person through whom it claims, to that person. The period for the recovery of foreshore by the Crown is sixty years (see s.15(7)).

The point from which the limitation period runs

The fundamental rule is that the period runs from the date of the accrual of a right of action against some person. The identification of that date is dealt with in Part I of Schedule 1 of the Act.

Initially, two provisions must be examined. Paragraph 1 enacts

> Where the person bringing an action to recover land, or some person through whom he claims, has been in possession of the land, and has while entitled to the land been dispossessed or discontinued his possession, the right of action shall be treated as having accrued on the date of the dispossession or discontinuance.

Paragraph 8(1) provides

> No right of action to recover land shall be treated as accruing unless the land is in the possession of some person in whose favour the period of limitation can run (referred to below in this paragraph as "adverse possession"); and where under the preceding provisions of this Schedule any such right of action is treated as accruing on a certain date and no person is in adverse possession on that date, the right of action shall not be treated as accruing unless and until adverse possession is taken of the land.

In short, there must be some person in possession and that possession must be 'adverse'. No right of action can accrue, for instance, if land is merely vacated by the owner. The meaning of 'adverse' has been the subject of some controversy.

In *Leigh* v. *Jack* (1879), 5 Ex. D. 264, land on the south side of a proposed road was conveyed by *O* to *D* who built a factory on it. In 1857, *O* conveyed land on the north side of the road to *X*, who conveyed it to *D* in 1872. *O* had retained ownership of the strip of land proposed for the road, but it was never dedicated as a highway. From 1854 *D* placed industrial materials on this strip, so that no vehicles could pass. In 1865 he enclosed part of it and in 1872 fenced in the whole. It was held that the owner's title to it had not been barred under the Real Property Limitation Act 1883. The acts done by *D* were not inconsistent with the enjoyment of the land for the purpose for which the owner intended to use it; that is to make it a highway. *D*'s possession was not 'adverse', merely concurrent.

In *Treloar* v. *Nute* [1977] 1 All E.R. 230 it was emphasized that whether possession has occurred, quite apart from whether possession is adverse, is a question of fact in each case, depending on the particular circumstances, including the nature of the property and the suitable mode of using it. It was held that merely grazing a few beasts on a small plot was an insignificant act. Yet the filling in of a gulley on the site did support a finding of possession in the circumstances. There was no evidence of the original owner having any special purpose in mind for the future use of the land, although to leave land as a wilderness for the benefit of wild life might be a purpose in itself.

The general effect appears to be as follows. Exclusive possession is necessary, as opposed to minor acts of trespass or casual use. This simple requirement has been adapted however in the special case of a specific future use on the part of the owner. In that case the present use must be inconsistent with that proposed use in order to be adverse.

Formerly there was a doctrine developing that when a person takes possession of land and the owner intends some particular use in the future, then the user of that person

> is to be ascribed to the licence or permission of the true owner. By using the land, knowing that it does not belong to him he impliedly assumes that the owner will permit it: and the owner, by not turning him off impliedly gives permission (per Lord Denning M.R. in *Wallis's Cayton Bay Holiday Camp Ltd.* v. *Shell-Mex B.P. Ltd.* [1975] Q.B. 94 at 103.)

Such an implication, if generally applied, could empty the notion of adverse possession of any meaning.

However, paragraph 8(4) of Part I of Schedule I of the Act enacted

> for the purpose of determining whether a person occupying any land is in adverse possession of the land it shall not be assumed by implication of law that his occupation is by permission of the person entitled to the land merely by virtue of the fact that his occupation is not inconsistent with the latter's present or future enjoyment of the land.
>
> This provision shall not be taken as prejudicing a finding to the effect that a person's occupation of any land is by implied permission of the person entitled to the land in any case where such a finding is justified on the actual facts of the case.

The doctrine of the implied licence therefore remains available as a possible channel of judicial policy in relation to squatters; but the channel now runs only through the medium of fact, not law. In *Hyde* v. *Pearce* [1982] 1 All E.R. 1029, the Court of Appeal held that the possession of a person who had been in occupation of land for fourteen years following a contract to purchase never completed by conveyance, was not adverse because he had a defence to any action for possession. This seems to suggest that only trespassers can enjoy adverse possession. In that case one of the functions of the Limitation Act, that of ironing out little problems based on informal agreements, will be thwarted. (See 46 M.L.R. 89).

Adverse possession is therefore necessary before an action can accrue. Provided that it is present, the Act identifies the time when actions shall accrue, and the period thus begin running, for various types of circumstances as follows. (The Act should be consulted, however, for an exhaustive list of these).

(1) *Present interests.* We have seen that when the person bringing the action was in possession of the land and either was dispossessed or abandoned his occupation, and this abandonment was followed by another person taking possession, the right of action accrues when that act of adverse possession takes place. When a person is in occupation at his death, however, and a squatter takes the land after his death, the right of action accrues at the date of death and not at the time when the adverse possession begins. (Schedule I Part I para. 2).

(2) *Future interests.* When the adverse possession occurs while an interest is in reversion or remainder, and the owner of the prior interest was in possession when that prior interest ceased, the right of action accrues on the determination of the preceding interest. If the person entitled to the preceding interest, not being a lease, was not in possession at the determination of that interest, then two alternative periods are available during which the owner of the remainder or reversion may bring an action, namely, twelve years from the time when the right of action accrued to the owner of the preceding interest, or six years from the date when the right of action accrued to the person entitled to the remainder or reversion, whichever is the longer. (S.15(2) and Schedule I, Part I, para. 4).

(3) *Trust property (s.18).* A trustee's title to trust property is not barred until the rights of all the beneficiaries have been barred. Thus twelve years' adverse possession against a tenant for life will bar his title to the life interest, but will not affect his right to the legal estate so long as the interest of any remainder-man still exists and is unbarred. Trustees can never bar the interest of the beneficiaries by adverse possession no matter how long. This of course applies to statutory trusts for sale as well as to express trusts and therefore affects cases of co-ownership. (See 35 Conveyancer 6). Neither can a beneficiary under a strict settlement or trust for sale extinguish the title of any trustee, statutory owner, life tenant or other beneficiary under the trust.

(4) *Leases (Schedule I).* The right of action does not accrue to a reversioner until the end of the lease, even though a right of forfeiture has occurred before that time and has not been enforced. If a tenant is dispossessed, although his title to the lease may be extinguished after twelve years, time will not begin to run against the landlord until the end of the lease (see *Fairweather* v. *St.*

Marylebone Property Co. Ltd. [1963] A.C. 510). Failure by a tenant to pay rent does not, with one exception (see L.P.A. 1925, s.153), affect his landlord's title to the reversion unless, in the case of a lease in writing under which a yearly rent of at least £10 is reserved, it is received by some other person wrongfully claiming the reversion. In this case the reversioner's right of action is deemed to accrue at the time of the first wrongful payment (para. 6).

In the case of a tenancy at will the cause of action accrues against the landlord at the end of one year after its beginning or after its determination, whichever event occurs first. (But see *Hughes* v. *Griffin*, [1969] 1 All E.R. 460). In the case of a tenancy at sufferance it accrues at its beginning because the possession is immediately adverse. Where there is a periodic tenancy but no written lease, it accrues at the end of the first period (para. 5). If there is a written lease, however, it accrues upon the determination of the tenancy.

Extension, postponement and recommencement of the period

The normal running of the limitation period is modified in certain special circumstances as follows.

(1) *Extension of the period (s.28).* If the person to whom a right of action accrues is a minor, or suffering from a mental disability when it accrues, the period is extended to six years, from the cessation of the disability or his death, whichever event occurs first, notwithstanding that the ordinary period of limitation has expired. In no case, however, is the period to be extended for more than thirty years from the date when the right of action accrued.

This privilege does not apply to a disability which occurs after the right of action accrues, such as when a person becomes a mental patient after dispossession, but it may be claimed where one disability succeeds another in the same person, provided that there is no interval between the ending of one disability and the beginning of the next. When a disabled person dies while still suffering from a disability, the person next entitled must bring any action within six years of that death, even though he himself was under a disability upon his succession to his interest.

(2) *Postponement of the period.* Section 32(1) enacts that where

> (a) the action is based upon the fraud of the defendant; or
> (b) any fact relevant to the plaintiff's right of action has been deliberately concealed from him by the defendant or
> (c) the action is for relief from the consequences of a mistake;
> the period of limitation shall not begin to run until the plaintiff has discovered the fraud, concealment or mistake (as the case may be) or could with reasonable diligence have discovered it.

There is protection for innocent third parties.

(3) *Recommencement of the period (s.29).* The period of limitation may be stopped in two ways and, in both cases, if adverse possession recurs, the period of time which has already run is discounted and time must start afresh.

Firstly, the owner may end the period by taking back possession of the land or by bringing an action for its recovery.

Secondly, the period is ended if a written signed acknowledgement of title is made by the person in possession of the land to the person whose title is being acknowledged, or if any part-payment of principal interest or rent is made by the person from whom it is due to the person to whom it is due (s.29) (see *Edginton* v. *Clark* [1964] 1 Q.B. 367). Once the period of limitation has run its course, no repossession, acknowledgement or part-payment can revive the rights of the person against whom it has run, for his title is extinguished.

Finally no recommencement of the period occurs if a person enjoying adverse possession transfers his possession to another either *inter vivos* or by will, or even if he himself is dispossessed. In all such cases the new occupier may aggregate the original period of possession with his own as against the owner (*Asher* v. *Whitlock* (1865) L.R. 1 Q.B. 1), but if adverse possession is abandoned and later another enters the land, the limitation period must start afresh.

The nature of the title acquired by possession

The general effects of acquisition of title by possession and the elimination of title under the Limitation Act have already been considered. Certain qualifications of these principles must now be discussed briefly.

Firstly, even if an adverse possessor or 'squatter' acquires a supreme title to the land, rights in or over that land which existed before his possession will continue to affect it unless they are ended independently by some form of extinguishment to which they are susceptible. Thus a restrictive covenant will remain in force, for a squatter is not a 'purchaser' and therefore cannot override even such an equitable interest (*Re Nisbet and Potts' Contract* [1906] 1 Ch. 386).

Secondly, when the title to a lease is extinguished by a squatter, that lease nevertheless remains valid as between the lessor and lessee, so that the latter can repossess the land if the squatter leaves, and the lessor can re-enter to enforce forfeiture for breach of covenant if the lease allows this (*Fairweather* v. *St. Marylebone Property Co. Ltd.* [1963] A.C. 510). In such circumstances, the effect of the Act is considerably diminished (see 37 Conveyancer 85).

Section 75 of the Land Registration Act 1925 enacts that the Limitation Act shall apply to registered land in the same way as to unregistered land, except that when an interest would have been extinguished in the case of unregistered land, then in the case of registered land it shall not be extinguished, but shall be deemed to be held on trust by the proprietor for the person who has acquired title against him. This provision was not intended to affect the substantive position of the parties but merely to provide machinery to apply the law to registered land (per Lord Denning in the *Fairweather* case at p.548). In *Spectrum Investment Co.* v. *Holmes* [1981] 1 All E.R. 6 however, Browne-Wilkinson J. held that if a squatter registered his rights under the Land Registration Act 1925, once the limitation period has run, those rights could not be defeated by subsequent surrender of the lease between the original documentary lessee and the landlord. In the *Fairweather* case the House of Lords held that a surrender of the lease enabled the landlord forthwith to evict the squatter. It was not open to the House however to consider the effect of registration of a squatter's title.

Remedies

Possession may be recovered by an owner, before his title is barred, under R.S.C. Ord. 113 in the High Court and under C.C.R. Ord. 26 in the county court. The procedure is swift. Squatting in residential premises is, under certain circumstances, a criminal offence under the Criminal Law Act 1977 (see s.7). It is also an offence to use or threaten violence to gain entry into premises where there is known to be someone present and therein opposed to such entry (see s.6). This provision applies to owners re-entering as well as to squatters entering, though there are certain defences, in particular, in favour of a displaced residential occupier.

Study material: *Wallis's Cayton Bay Holiday Camp Ltd.* v. *Shell-Mex and B.P. Ltd.* [1975] 1 Q.B. 94

Lord Denning's judgment in the Court of Appeal is given in full below. Then follows an extract from the dissenting judgment of Stamp L.J. Which judgment do you prefer? Are the differences between the two approaches still important, considering the abrogation of the doctrine of the implied licence by the Limitation Act 1980?

Lord Denning M.R. This case concerns a small piece of land—only one-and-a-third acres—in Yorkshire. It is near the sea at Cayton Bay. It has a frontage to the main road from Scarborough to Filey. Nearby there is a big holiday camp with hundreds of caravans. Next door to it there is a garage. Now there is a dispute as to who owns it. The plaintiffs, Wallis's, the caravan company, claim a squatter's title by 12 years' possession.

In 1957 the disputed land was part of the farm. But the county council were proposing to build a big new road behind the garage and the disputed land. They had actually bought the site of the proposed road from the farmer. The garage proprietor thought it would be a good thing to have a stretch of land next to the new road. So he bought the disputed piece (1·33 acres) from the farmer for £1,000.

In April 1961, Wallis's too thought the time appropriate to get more land. They had their big holiday camp with caravans beside and behind the garage. So they bought up the rest of the farm from the farmer. It was the farm-house and 107 acres. They bought it for £35,700. But the conveyance clearly *excluded* the line of the proposed new road (which had been sold to the county council) and the disputed land of 1·33 acres (which had been sold to the garage proprietor). But there was nothing on the land itself to mark the boundaries. No fences. Nothing. If cattle were put in the fields, they could stray without hindrance on to the line of the proposed new road and on the disputed land.

In September 1961, the defendants, Shell-Mex and B.P. Ltd., also saw good prospects ahead. They bought the disputed land (1·33 acres) from the garage proprietor for £5,500. So in four years its value had gone up from £1,000 to £5,500. Shell, too, had an interest in the garage. They supplied all the petrol and oil for it.

But neither the county council nor Shell-Mex had any immediate use for their pieces of land. So they did not put up any fences. The Wallis's having bought the farm (through their family farming company) farmed it as before. Seeing that there were no fences, they cut the grass, not only on their own land, but also on the site of the proposed new road, and on the disputed land. They put their cattle out on to their own fields and let them stray on to the site of the proposed new road and on to the disputed land. (In one subsequent year they even ploughed up the fields and cropped them with wheat.) They got a licence to do all this—on the site of the proposed new road—from the county council. But they did not ask Shell-Mex for a licence for the disputed land. They just treated it as if it was their own. Indeed they came to think it was their own.

That went on for 10 years from April 1961 to 1971. Then the Wallis's (through their caravan company) took over the whole area. They treated it as if it was a playground for the holiday camp. They cut the grass, they collected litter, they put a football field on the proposed new road, they used the disputed land as a visual frontage amenity for their holiday camp, they painted the old outer fence (next to the main road) white, like the other fences of the camp.

But 12 years had not yet elapsed. After only 11 years, in 1972, the county council abandoned their proposals for a new road. So Shell-Mex revised their plans. They thought they would not want the disputed land. It was surplus to their requirements. So they decided to sell it. On October 20, 1972, the secretary to Shell-Mex wrote this letter to Wallis's:

> "I have pleasure in enclosing a plan showing, edged red, an area of land owned by this company and adjoining your own property which is surplus to requirements.
> "I should be pleased to learn whether your company would be interested in purchasing the land, and, if so, to receive your best offer for consideration."

They enclosed with that letter a plan which clearly showed the disputed land (1·33 acres) and that it was owned by Shell-Mex.

On receiving that letter, Wallis's went to their solicitor and received legal advice. We do not know what that advice was. But it is easy to guess. The solicitor looked up the deeds and told Wallis's that on the title deeds the disputed land belonged to Shell-Mex and not to Wallis's. The solicitor also told them, so we may assume, that if they remained in possession for 12 years, they might get a squatter's title. At any rate, as a result of the lawyer's advice, Wallis's did not reply to the letter from Shell-Mex.

On December 14, 1972, Shell-Mex wrote again. They asked for a reply to their earlier letter and wished to learn whether Wallis's would be interested in purchasing the land. Still Wallis's did not reply. The 12 years had not yet run. On April 5, 1973, Shell-Mex wrote again on the same terms. Still no reply. There were then only nine days to go to complete the 12 years. These nine days passed before Shell-Mex got wise to what was happening.

Two months later, in June 1973, Shell-Mex began to wonder what Wallis's were up to. They smelt a rat. They took action. Out it came. So on June 27, 1973, they begun to fence off their boundary on the disputed land. On the very next day, Wallis's came at last into the open. Their solicitor wrote claiming the disputed land. He said that his clients "have a possessory title to the same."

If this contention be right, Wallis's have done exceedingly well by not replying to the letters. They have acquired this valuable strip of land—next to the main road—for nothing. It is now worth over £8,000. Yet by lying low since October 1972 they have acquired an absolute title to it—when they knew perfectly well that it did not belong to them, but belonged to Shell-Mex. The judge put it neatly when he said:

> "I cannot believe they were too busy to answer and on balance of probabilities can only conclude they were playing for time to sit out the final months of the 12-year period."

The judge rejected Wallis's claim to the land. Wallis's appeal to this court.

Wallis's stake their claim on actual possession for 12 years. They farmed the land as their own for 10 years and used it as their own for another two years. They say that Shell-Mex ought to have brought an action for possession during those 12 years: and that not having done so, Shell-Mex are barred: and Wallis's have a possessory title under the Limitation Act 1939.

There is a fundamental error in that argument. Possession by itself is not enough to give a title. It must be *adverse* possession. The true owner must have discontinued possession or have been dispossessed and another must have taken it adversely to him. There must be something in the nature of an ouster of the true owner by the wrongful possessor. That is shown by a series of cases in this court which, on their very facts, show this proposition to be true.

When the true owner of land intends to use it for a particular purpose in the future, but meanwhile has no immediate use for it, and so leaves it unoccupied, he does not lose his title to it simply because some other person enters on it and uses it for some temporary purpose, like stacking materials; or for some seasonal purpose, like growing vegetables. Not even if this temporary or seasonal purpose continues year after year for 12 years, or more: see *Leigh* v. *Jack* (1879) 5 Ex.D. 264; *Williams Brothers Direct Supply Ltd.* v. *Raftery* [1958] 1 Q.B. 159; and *Tecbild Ltd.* v. *Chamberlain* (1969) 20 P. & C.R. 633. The reason is not because the user does not amount to actual possession. The line between acts of user and acts of possession is too fine for words. The reason behind the decisions is because it does not lie in that other person's mouth to assert that he used the land of his own wrong as a trespasser. Rather his user is to be ascribed to the licence or permission of the true owner. By using the land, knowing that it does not belong to him, he impliedly assumes that the owner will permit it: and the owner, by not turning him off, impliedly gives permission. And it has been held many times in this court that acts done under licence or permitted by the owner do not give a licensee a title under the Limitation Act 1939. They do not amount to adverse possession: see *Cobb* v. *Lane* [1952] 1 T.L.R. 1037; *British Railways Board* v. *G.J. Holdings Ltd.*, March 25, 1974; Bar Library Transcript No. 81 of 1974 in this court.

Take this very case. In October 1972, Shell-Mex wrote to Wallis's asking them if they would like to buy this land. If Wallis's had written back in October 1972, as any good neighbour would: "we know it is your land but do you mind if we go on using it until you want it" Shell-Mex would have replied: "Of course, we don't mind. You can use it until we sell it." The subsequent user would be by licence. Wallis's would get no title. Or if Wallis's had written back the truth, and said: "We know it is your land but we are going to use it for another six months so as to oust you and get a possessory title" Shell-Mex would at once have put up a fence and stopped them acquiring a title. But Wallis's simply did not reply at all. I cannot think that Wallis's can get a good title by deliberately not replying to letters. By not replying, they put themselves in the wrong. Even if they were in possession for 12 years, a court of equity would not allow them to enforce their strict rights under the Limitation Act 1939. There is a broad principle of equity dating back for at least 100 years that where a person, by his words or conduct, leads another to believe that his strict rights at law will not be enforced—and the other acts on it—the person who otherwise might have enforced those rights will not be allowed to enforce them where it would be inequitable having regard to the dealings which have taken place between the parties: see *Hughes* v. *Metropolitan Railway Co.* (1877) 2 App.Cas. 439, 448, *per* Lord Cairns L.C. That principle carries out the very object for which equity was first introduced—to mitigate the rigours of the law. It has been applied in recent years so as to preclude a party to a contract from enforcing his strict rights under it: see *Central London Property Trust Ltd.* v. *High Trees House Ltd.* [1947] K.B. 130. I see no reason why it should not be applied so as to preclude a squatter from enforcing his strict rights under the Limitation Act 1939. By not replying to the letters Wallis's were plainly doing wrong. They were deliberately trespassing on the land of Shell-Mex—lying low and saying nothing—so as to acquire a title for themselves. They knew full well that it was not their land. Yet they seek to take advantage of their own wrong to say that it is now their land. The judge would not allow them to do this. He said that it was "contrary to equity and natural justice." I agree with him. I would dismiss this appeal.

Stamp L.J. said, at p. 107, 'Were it not for the two decisions of this court which I will have to consider I would be content to leave the matter there, holding that on the facts which I have related the plaintiffs or the farming company were throughout for upwards of 12 years in possession and enjoyment of the land not only, as the judge called it, de facto but also within the meaning of the Limitation Act 1939. De facto possession is what the statute is about, and there were in my judgment facts upon which the judge could properly find, as he did, that the plaintiff company was in de facto possession for the full period of 12 years. Possession cannot be divided and if the plaintiffs or the farming company was in possession, the defendants were not.'

The county court judge, however, found that the defendants' intention in purchasing the land was to extend the garage filling station once the new road was constructed; and, as I understand it, the submission that the defendants were for the purposes of the Limitation Act 1939 never out of possession rests upon that foundation. Since the defendants did not acquire the land until after May 1961, it is not clear to me how the existence of that intention could operate to put the defendants into possession of the land they bought; but I am prepared to assume that Avis had that same intention.

There are passages in the judgments in *Leigh* v. *Jack*, 5 Ex.D. 264, and cases which followed it which, taken out of their context, might lead to the conclusion that where an owner of land has acquired it for a particular purpose and does not immediately require it for that purpose, he is not, so long as that intention remains in existence and cannot be carried into effect, to be taken, as against a squatter, to be out of possession of the land for the purposes of the statute.

I agree, however, with counsel on behalf of the plaintiffs that to understand the judgments in *Leigh* v. *Jack* it is necessary to call attention to the facts of that case. The period of limitation was then 20 years and the plaintiff brought his action against the squatting defendant in April 1876. In 1854 Leigh conveyed to Jack a piece of land in a township lying to the south of Grundy Street and to the west of a triangular piece of land called "Napier Place." Grundy Street and Napier Place were portions of waste land belonging to Leigh which he had contemplated dedicating to the public as streets. Leigh in 1857 conveyed the land to the north of Grundy Street to the Mersey Dock Trustees. The northern boundary of Grundy Street was fenced off. From 1854 down to 1872, Jack, by placing a quantity of waste from his foundry—old graving dock materials, screw propellers and boilers and other refuse—rendered the surface of Grundy Street and Napier Place, which were, as the court held on the construction of the deeds, Leigh's property, impassable for horses and carts. In 1865 (less than 20 years before action brought) Jack enclosed part of Grundy Street and in 1872 enclosed the rest of it and Napier Place. It is to be noted first that there the disputed land was waste land which could not be put to any beneficial use by Leigh, second, that there was no enclosure by Jack until less than 20 years before action brought, third, that the facts relied on by Jack as constituting possession were the placing of his waste materials on the disputed land and that in this regard Cockburn C.J. took the view that these acts were those of a man who did not intend to be a trespasser or to infringe upon another's rights. "The defendant," he said at p. 271, "simply used the land until the time should come for carrying out the object originally contemplated." The facts were thus widely different from those in the present case. Here the disputed land was throughout the 12-year period enclosed. Here the disputed land was not waste land but land which the owner could, as did the North Riding County Council, in respect of their strip of fields O.S. Nos. 194 and 196, obtain payment for its use as part of field 194. Here the acts relied on are not the mere dumping of waste materials. Here, unlike the case of *Leigh* v. *Jack*, the disputed land was occupied as of right and with animus possidendi.

It was in the context of the facts of that case that Bramwell L.J. in *Leigh* v. *Jack* made the remarks on which so much reliance is placed by the defendants in this case. He said, at p.273:

> "I do not think that there was any dispossession of the plaintiff by the acts of the defendant: acts of user are not enough to take the soil out of the plaintiff and her predecessors in title and to vest it in the defendant; in order to defeat a title by dispossessing the former owner, acts must be done which are inconsistent with his enjoyment of the soil for the purposes for which he intended to use it: that is not the case here, where the intention of the plaintiff and her predecessors in title was not either to build upon or to cultivate the land, but to devote it at some future

> time to public purposes. The plaintiff has not been dispossessed, nor has she discontinued possession, her title has not been taken away, and she is entitled to our judgment."

Cockburn C.J., as I have already indicated, took a similar view, remarking, at p. 271: "If a man does not use his land, . . . he does not *necessarily* discontinue possession of it."

The facts in *Williams Brothers Direct Supply Ltd.* v. *Raftery* [1958] 1 Q.B. 159, which followed *Leigh* v. *Jack*, 5 Ex.D. 264, were also widely different from those in the instant case. Williams Brothers bought some land at Edmonton in 1937. They put up a row of shops with maisonettes above them. At the back of the shops they made a roadway and between the roadway and the remaining land they put up a fence. They intended to develop the land at the rear but the outbreak of war interrupted their plans. In 1940, one Heydon during the "dig for victory campaign" marked out with a line of bricks and cultivated a patch of land which was not adjacent to nor part of any land of his and was 13 feet wide and 110 feet long. Others did the same thing, some with permission of Williams Brothers. Raftery in 1943 took the place of Heydon. He occupied a maisonette in the block and he thought he was entitled in right of this occupation to use the little strip of land.

He put in shrubs and bulbs. Two of his neighbours gave up in 1947, but he continued to grow potatoes. Then in 1949 when the place had become overrun with weeds he went in for greyhounds, first putting up a shelter, and later built sheds and a fence to keep the dogs in. He said in his evidence (see p. 162): "Not trying to take over land, not really. Exercising rights I thought I had as tenant of these premises . . . I did nothing to keep the plaintiffs off."

It was held first (accepting the conclusion of the judge in the court below) that the plaintiffs had not "discontinued" their possession, Hodson L.J. taking this view that they had done all that they could do in the circumstances (see p. 167), being landlords who intended to use the land for no other purpose than to develop it, and who had been prevented by circumstances hitherto from so doing. Morris L.J. taking the same view called attention at p. 171 to the fact that in 1953 the plaintiffs had actually dumped "some rubbish, on the land, which they were saying was their land" and that it had been pointed out in *Leigh* v. *Jack* that the smallest act was sufficient to negative a discontinuance. It was held, second, that there was no evidence on which the judge in the court below could properly find that the defendant had dispossessed the plaintiffs. Applying the test laid down in *Leigh* v. *Jack*, Hodson L.J. said, at p. 169:

> "I cannot see that any act which the defendant did is capable of being treated as sufficient to dispossess the plaintiffs. The defendant never even thought he was dispossessing the plaintiffs; he never claimed to do more than work the soil, as he thought he was permitted to do. He had some vague idea in his head, derived from a source which is not clear on the evidence, that it was quite all right for him to work it; but he never, so far as I know, had any intention, nor claimed any intention of asserting any right to the possession of this piece of ground."

Hodson L.J. said he would have left the matter there but for *Marshall* v. *Taylor* [1895] 1 Ch. 641 which had been relied on by the judge; and after referring to the facts of that case he continued, at p. 170:

> "I think it is sufficient, to distinguish this case, to point out that in that case the defendant had completely enclosed the property in question by a hedge and made it entirely part of his garden, which was a property of the same kind and of the same nature as the garden of the plaintiff alongside. The plaintiff was excluded from access to the defendant's garden unless he had chosen, as Lord Halsbury pointed out [1895] 1 Ch. 641, 645, to creep through the hedge; whereas in this case there was nothing of the kind. No attempt was made by the defendant here to fence off his piece of ground so as to exclude anyone from it; all he did was to work

the ground in the period before the sheds were built, and in 1949, within the 12-year period, he put up these sheds which have been, in the end, the reason why this action has been brought."

Morris L.J. also thought that the evidence showed that there was user of the land, but not user amounting to dispossession (see p. 173).

Reading the judgments in *Leigh* v *Jack*, 5 Ex.D. 264, and *Williams Brothers Direct Supply Ltd.* v. *Raftery* [1958] 1 Q.B. 159, I conclude that they establish that in order to determine whether the acts of user do or do not amount to dispossession of the owner the character of the land, the nature of the acts done upon it and the intention of the squatter fall to be considered. Where the land is waste land and the true owner cannot and does not for the time being use it for the purpose for which he acquired it, one may more readily conclude that the acts done on the waste land do not amount to dispossession of the owner. But I find it impossible to regard those cases as establishing that so long as the true owner cannot use his land for the purpose for which he acquired it the acts done by the squatter do not amount to possession of the land. One must look at the facts and circumstances and determine whether what has been done in relation to the land constitutes possession.

One of the facts that distinguishes this case from those cases is the fact that here, as in *Marshall* v. *Taylor* [1895] 1 Ch. 641, the property in question was enclosed, and, to apply the words used by Hodson L.J. in *Williams Brothers Direct Supply Ltd.* v. *Raftery*, at p. 170, made "entirely part" of the squatter's field or farm. The defendants were excluded from access to it unless one of their representatives had, as Lord Halsbury pointed out in *Marshall* v. *Taylor*, chosen to creep through the hedge or fence, whereas in *Leigh* v. *Jack*, 5 Ex.D. 264, and *Williams Brothers Direct Supply Ltd.* v. *Raftery* [1958] 1 Q.B. 159 there was nothing of the kind. Here the land was not waste land. Here it was land believed by the plaintiffs to be owned by them, occupied as of right and with the necessary animus possidendi.

Nor in my judgment does *Tecbild Ltd* v. *Chamberlain*, 20 P. & C.R. 633 take the matter any further. As Sachs L.J. remarked in that case, at p. 641, "each case naturally depends on the nature of the land in issue and the circumstances in which it is held," while Cairns L.J. described the use of the land, at p. 646, "as trivial acts of trespass." It is the undoubted fact as pointed out by Lord Denning M.R. that acts done under licence do not amount to adverse possession, but here I can detect no licence.

Holding, as I do, that, immediately prior to the writing of the letter by the defendants offering to sell the disputed land, the plaintiffs were in possession of it, did the writing of that letter operate to interrupt that possession? I think not. So to hold would in my judgment be to fly in the face of authority.

Pennycuick J. in *Bligh* v. *Martin* [1968] 1 W.L.R. 804, 812 I think summarised the law correctly, when, discussing a contention that whenever the true owner puts foot on the land in the possession of another then he is to be treated as having taken possession so that adverse possession ceases, he said that in the ordinary case of adverse possession one has to find that "the true owner took possession in the ordinary sense of that word, to the exclusion of the wrongful occupier." See also, e.g., *Doe* d. *Baker* v. *Coombes* (1850) 9 C.B. 714. Once a wrongdoer is in possession a claim by the true owner that he is the rightful owner unaccompanied by the retaking of possession does not operate to interrupt the wrongdoer's possession.

It was faintly argued that when in 1971 the farming company's occupation gave way to that of the plaintiffs there was a break in the adverse possession which operated as an interruption and prevented the statute from running in favour of the plaintiffs. In face of the passages from *Megarry and Wade, The Law of Real Property*, 3rd ed. (1966), pp. 1006 and 1007, which I have always understood to state the law, this submission was not pursued. If a squatter who has been in possession for less than the full statutory period transfers the land, he can give the transferee a right to the land which is as good as his own and the latter can add the former's period of possession to his own. It is for this reason that I have not thought it necessary to consider whether during the first 10 years the possession was that of the plaintiffs or the farming company.

There was in my judgment ample evidence upon which the county court judge could properly find as a fact that the plaintiffs (or the farming company) were in de facto possession of the disputed land for the full 12-year period and he was, in my view, in coming to his further conclusion, misled by his understanding of the true effect of *Leigh* v. *Jack*, 5 Ex.D. 264, and *Williams Brothers Direct Supply Ltd.* v. *Raftery* [1958] 1 Q.B. 159.

Some hard things have been said regarding the failure of the plaintiffs to answer the letters of October 20 and December 14, 1972, and that of April 5, 1973, and I accept the implication that having looked at their title deeds and discovering for the first time that the disputed land had not been conveyed to them, they hoped that the full statutory period of 12 years would run before the defendants brought an action or moved in and expelled them. I am, however, not wholly without sympathy for a party who, having had in the full light of day the full and exclusive use of property for some 11½ years in the belief that it was his, discovers that another has a lawful claim to it. Had the full period of 12 years elapsed before the letter of October 20 was written it could hardly have been suggested that the plaintiffs were acting inequitably in relying on a statute designed by Parliament to confer a good title upon them. And whatever may be said about their conduct I cannot see that it was more inequitable than that of any defendant in an action for tort or breach of contract who lies low or plays for time in the hope that the appropriate limitation period will expire before action brought: a course which, however reprehensible, is adopted very often.

We know not all the circumstances giving rise to the belief of the plaintiffs that they had purchased the disputed land. It cannot, however, be doubted that if, when the defendants did purchase it, they had taken the elementary step of inspecting it and insisted either on marking out its boundary or on some acknowledgment of its rights in the form of some, perhaps trivial, annual payment, the plaintiffs would have then appreciated the mistake. And it may be—I do not suggest for the moment that it was so—that the plaintiffs would then have had some action, now long since statute-barred, against one of those who advised in relation to its purchase.

But however reprehensible you may characterise the conduct of the plaintiffs, I cannot share the view either that the plaintiffs are to be regarded as getting a good title by not replying to the letter or that their failure or refusal to do so led the defendants to believe that the plaintiffs would not rely on the Statute of Limitations. It was not in my judgment because they failed to reply to the letter that they got a good title but because they remained in possession until the end of the statutory period of limitation. I cannot accept that the plaintiffs' silence raised any equity in the defendants such as to preclude the plaintiffs from setting up the statute. No such equity was pleaded or relied upon in argument.

I would allow the appeal.

Questions

1. *The doctrine of the implied licence has been abrogated by the Limitation Act 1980. The possibility of a licence being implied from the facts has been preserved however. Discuss whether this enactment commits the question too openly to the personal proclivities of the judge.*
2. *Patience has occupied 'Folornacre' for thirteen years, so that Peregrine, the original owner, has lost his title. Patience now discovers that Peregrine entered into a restrictive covenant fifteen years ago with the neighbouring*

landowner, Green, not to build. The covenant was registered at the Land Charges Registry at the time of its creation. Advise Patience as to whether she is bound by the covenant.

3 *A group known as 'occupants militant' consult you as to their rights if they break into and occupy an empty dwelling-house owned by Owen. Advise them generally.*

4 *'Greyacre' is a strip of land between 'Blackacre' and 'Whiteacre'. 'Blackacre', owned by Black, is grazed by beasts. 'Whiteacre', owned by White, is under the plough. There is no fencing between 'Blackacre' and 'Whiteacre'. 'Greyacre' has long been unused because it comprises steep inclines into a central ditch. Black now wishes to claim 'Greyacre'. What investigations will you make?*

Chapter Nine

Settlements

IN CHAPTER 5, we were concerned with various interests in land and the problems they raised individually. When two or more of these interests occur consecutively, new kinds of difficulty arise. These will be examined in this chapter. Leases, however, do not raise the same difficulties and may be left out of the account at this stage. When interests in land, other than leases, occur consecutively, the whole structure of interests is called a 'settlement'. A grant as simple as 'to *A* for life, remainder in fee simple to *B*' creates a settlement, but some of the settlements met in practice are of great complexity. There are two kinds of settlement, strict settlements and settlements by way of trust for sale. The former is dealt with by the Settled Land Act 1925, the latter by the Law of Property Act 1925. Since they are mutually exclusive it is vital to distinguish them. That is easy. In a settlement by way of trust for sale the settlor gives an instruction to sell the land. This instruction must be mandatory; a mere power of sale is insufficient. In a strict settlement this instruction is absent.

Strict settlements

Strict settlements reached their heyday in the classical England of the eighteenth and early nineteenth centuries, the England of the gavotte, Mr Capability Brown and Bath. In those days a single settled estate might consist of thousands of acres, for not only was land a most secure form of wealth, but affection for the country life was strong. Yet a strict settlement can arise at the present time from a home-made will disposing of a tiny cottage. Although applying equally to large and small estates, the special body of law which applies whenever there is a strict settlement contemplates sizeable ones, so here the machinery employed in the traditional strict settlement of a large estate will be described, but in a much simplified way.

Let us say that *O*, owner in fee simple of a large estate, intends to marry shortly and wishes to endow future members of his family. He would find the doctrine of estates admirably suited to his purposes, and could dispose of his fee simple absolute in the following way. First *O* himself would take the fee simple until his marriage, a determinable fee simple, then, upon marriage, a life interest, which is contingent of course. Next, an entail would be limited to his first son, and then, in case that son should die without an heir, entails would be limited to other sons in order of age. These entails are contingent because no sons yet exist. All these provisions are made in a single grant and their purpose is to keep the land in the family for as long as possible. *O* wishes to provide for other members of the family too, so the settlement also includes an annual rent-charge, known as a 'jointure', payable out of the profits of the land to *O*'s wife, if she should survive him, and capital sums, known as 'portions', payable to younger children of the family. These are secured on the land. Despite the grant of all these interests, the fee simple absolute still remains to be disposed of. The final limitation in the instrument therefore is that the ultimate reversion in fee simple shall belong to *O*. After the failure or exhaustion of all the other interests, the land will pass absolutely to him or his successors in title, who would, of course, be identified by the general law without reference to the settlement. It has been the tradition in the case of large settlements to resettle the land before such a result occurs. In this way, the property is kept within the family for generation after generation.

Whether a settlement is of a complex nature, or as simple as 'to *A* for life, remainder to *B* in fee simple', the greatest problem it has presented is that of inalienability. Sometimes a power of sale was included in a settlement, but since the fee simple was in reversion, where it was not there was no person who owned what the ordinary purchaser wished to buy, namely, a fee simple absolute in possession. The Settled Land Act 1882 brought reform and many of the cases still relevant to the subject were decided on that Act. It has now been re-enacted and perfected in the Settled Land Act 1925, which will be our starting-point.

The essence of the reform is that all the beneficial interests under a settlement are now equitable following the Law of Property Act 1925, s.1. The fee simple absolute in possession is held on trust for the various beneficiaries, can never be divided in any way, and is always available for sale. On sale, the interests of the beneficiaries are overreached and are satisfied out of the purchase-money. Furthermore, powers of leasing, mortgaging, improvement and management are also given to the life tenant by the Settled Land Act; otherwise he would not be able to carry out a transaction of this nature which transcended his own life interest. A prospective lessee, for instance, would think little of a lease which would end suddenly on the life tenant's death. If these powers are to be granted, a strict and delicate machinery is necessary to safeguard the interests of all the beneficiaries. Trustees are needed to take care of purchase-money and their appointment and duties require regulation; rules for the management of the land during a minority must be provided, together with the control of many other activities. In short, a special and elaborate code of rules is necessary to govern all the activities of a settlement. This is contained in the Settled Land Act 1925. These rules must now be discussed systematically, beginning with the crucial question of how to diagnose a settlement, for it is the existence of a settlement only which invokes these rules. Statutory citations, unless otherwise stated, will be from the Settled Land Act 1925.

Definition of a settlement

Under s.1, a settlement exists when land is

(1) limited in trust for any persons by way of succession; or

(2) limited in trust for any person in possession:

  (a) for an entailed interest, whether or not capable of being barred or defeated;

  (b) for an estate in fee simple, or for a term of years absolute, subject to an executory limitation, gift, or disposition over, on failure of his issue or in any other event;

(c) for a base or determinable fee or any corresponding leasehold land;
(d) being an infant, for an estate in fee simple or for a term of years absolute; or

(3) limited in trust for any person for an estate in fee simple or for a term of years absolute contingently on the happening of any event; or
(4) charged, whether voluntarily or in consideration of marriage or by way of family arrangement, and whether immediately or after an interval, with the payment of any rentcharge for the life of any person, or any less period, or of any capital, annual or periodical sums for the portions, advancement, maintenance, or otherwise for the benefit of any persons, with or without any term of years for securing or raising the same.

This definition need not intimidate. It could have been expressed in much shorter form, but the Act, in order to save doubt in the minds of busy practitioners, spells out the individual occasions which produce settlements. If we go to the root of the section and understand its policy, there will be no need to memorize it. Its purpose is to round up all the cases which produce the problem of inalienability, in preparation for the treatment in store for them in the Act. On examination, this inalienability is caused in most cases by the beneficial interest, that is the equitable fee simple absolute, being put into remainder by the creation out of it of limited interests. Thus, if a grant is made to *A* for life, with remainder in fee simple to *B*, there is, for the present, no single person capable of offering for sale the type of interest a purchaser will wish to buy, for *A*'s interest might end suddenly and early, whereas *B*'s does not give possession at all for the moment. In short, the common element in all the cases mentioned in the definition except (2)(d) and (4) is that of succession. Apart from these two, all the other instances are implicit in (1) and are really superfluous. A few examples will illustrate this.

Take, for instance, (2)(a), the entail. Whenever an entail exists, there must be an element of succession because its grant does not exhaust the grantor's ownership. There must be a fee simple owner in reversion or remainder. One interest is thus followed by another. Secondly, take (2)(b), which is a conditional fee simple. An example of this would be a grant 'to *A* in fee simple, but, if he shall remarry, to *B* in fee simple'. Although the interest of *B* is only contingent on *A* remarrying, it constitutes a clear possibility of one interest following another. Finally, in the case of (3), there is an element of succession. This is a contingent interest and an example would be a grant 'to *A* at the age of thirty in fee simple'. Here we must ask what happens to the land during the time before *A* has reached thirty. The answer is that it remains with the grantor, *G*, so that a description of the interests really reads, 'to *G* in fee simple until *A* reaches thirty and then to *A* in fee simple', whereupon the elements of succession becomes obvious. So we can both shorten and rationalize all this part of s. 1 by deducing that, leaseholds apart, whenever any person is entitled to any interest less than a fee simple absolute in possession there exists a settlement, for in all such cases there must be an interest in remainder or reversion, and therefore an element of succession. This does not embrace fees simple on condition subject to rights of entry or re-entry, because these have been declared absolute by the Law of Property (Amendment) Act 1926. However, these must be sharply distinguished from conditional fees simple subject to gifts over, which do create settlements under (2)(b) above.

The two additional cases where settlements arise must now be explained, and firstly that of minority under (2)(d). Minority does not involve succession, but it does involve a problem of inalienability. A person under eighteen years of age cannot hold a legal estate. Thus, if I grant the fee simple absolute in possession of 'Blackacre' to *A*, a minor, while he alone is entitled to enjoyment because he owns the land absolutely in equity, he himself cannot sell the land because he cannot own it at law. Since minority posed this problem of inalienability in common with the cases where there was an element of succession, it was constituted a settlement by the section so that it could partake of the same solution for its problems provided by the Act. Next is the case of charges under (4). The requirement that they are voluntary and are for no consideration unless it be marriage or other family arrangements divides them sharply from the rentcharges which are sometimes payable as the result of the purchase of a fee simple estate. In those cases, there is clearly consideration. Settlements are instruments of family endowment, not commercial transactions, and the Act follows this natural boundary. The presence of land charged in this particular way in the settlement fold can be justified in two ways. Firstly, such a charge is a natural and common incident of settlements. Secondly, and more significantly, land subject to charges may be difficult to sell if those charges are to continue to affect the land. If, however, they can be overreached and be satisfied out of the purchase-money, this problem can be overcome. Since a settlement must contain all the necessary machinery for overreaching, including trustees, it was a convenient solution to classify these cases as settlements (*Lord Henry Bruce* v. *Marquess of Ailesbury* [1892] A.C. 356, per Halsbury, L.C., at p.361).

While this provision would serve usefully where the land had been rendered difficult to sell, it did impose a burden where the existence of the charge did not have this effect, because all the elaborate rules which must be observed when settled land is sold applied. To release vendors from compliance with these rules, where purchasers are willing to buy the land even subject to the charge, the Law of Property (Amendment) Act 1926, therefore enacted that an estate owner may sell subject to the charge as if the land were not settled (s.1). Of course this privilege only applies when the existence of the charge is the only reason why a settlement exists, and not where there are other grounds too, such as the presence of a life interest.

Before summing up the total effect of these remarks, it should be explained that the existence of a lease does not create an element of succession so as to constitute a settlement. It is true that strictly speaking the right to possession of a tenant is followed by that of his landlord, but since the right of the landlord to receive the rent, if any, amounts to 'possession' under the Law of Property Act 1925, s.205(1)(xix), there is no 'succession' for present purposes, and the landlord's fee simple remains absolute and 'in possession'. Yet a lease can be instrumental in the creation of a settlement in two ways. Firstly, it might be a lease itself which is settled, as, for instance, if I, the owner of a hundred years' lease, bequeath it to *A* for life with remainder of the term to *B*. Here, the subject-matter of the settlement is a lease, and the fee simple is unaffected. Secondly, if a fee simple owner grants land to a person for a term of years determinable on death, and no rent is payable, this creates a settlement of the grantor's interest. This is really only a foreshortened life interest rather than a lease, because no one is receiving rent and presumably the fee simple in reversion is not 'in possession'.

In short, a settlement exists whenever any person is entitled to any interest less than the fee simple absolute in possession, and, even if entitled to the fee simple absolute in possession, if he is a minor or if the land is subject to charges of the type described above.

The life tenant in possession holds the legal estate

We have seen that, apart from leases, no limited interest in land can exist at law, and that such interests as determinable fees simple and life interests can exist only in equity (L.P.A. 1925, s.1). It was explained in Chapter 2 that effect is given to these equitable interests by vesting the legal fee simple absolute in possession, or term of years absolute if a leasehold is being settled, in some trustee who holds it on behalf of the various beneficiaries. Thus, the absolute ownership is always available for sale in the hands of one person. This trustee is the person who is currently entitled in possession to the life interest or other interest under the settlement (Settled Land Act 1925, s.4). Where, for instance, land stands settled on *A* for life, then to *B* for life and then to *C* in fee simple, the legal fee simple absolute in possession is held by *A*. A few remarks must be made about this rather surprising rule.

Firstly, he is given the legal estate because the legislature designated him the land manager and as such he may take decisions on major matters such as the sale, leasing, mortgage or improvement of the land, which will affect not only himself but future beneficiaries under the settlement. When you consider that he will often be the father, husband, or grandfather of many of the other beneficiaries, his claims to this role are clearly stronger than those of an outsider with no interest, beneficial or otherwise, in the land. Secondly, although the life tenant thus finds himself in two capacities, these are quite distinct. As to the legal estate, he holds it only as trustee for himself and the other beneficiaries, and his own beneficial entitlement is not altered in the least. In disposing of it in any way, he is strictly bound by the terms of the Act. His life interest is his very own, and he can dispose of it as he wishes. Thirdly, while it is, in view of certain safeguards provided by the Act, quite safe to allow him to hold the fee simple absolute while the land remains unsold, it would be dangerous to allow him to hold the purchase money on sale, for a person can abscond with money, though not with land. Because of this, in every settlement there must be special trustees for the purposes of the Act. This trusteeship is quite distinct from the trusteeship of the life tenant. Such trustees have many functions to perform, but the main one is to hold the purchase and other capital moneys which result from the sale or other disposition of the land. They never, as such, hold the legal estate in the land, although we shall see that they do, in certain other capacities, hold it temporarily when there is presently no life tenant, or when it is in transit on the termination of a life tenant's interest.

There are two exceptions to the rule that the legal estate and its associated statutory powers must be held by the tenant for life.

(1) *Where the life tenant is a minor.* A minor cannot hold a legal estate and

the Act is concerned to ensure that there is no abeyance of the power to dispose of the land. The legal estate is therefore vested in the 'statutory owner', a term used to describe the makeshift body who exercise the statutory powers in such an interim period (see s.117(1)(xxvi)). The beneficial interest of the minor is affected in no way. The statutory owner in this case is

> (a) if the settled land is vested in a personal representative, the personal representative, until a principal vesting instrument has been executed pursuant to the provisions of this Act; and (b) in every other case, the trustees of the settlement. (s.26)

An example of (a) would be if a landowner settled his land by will, for then the legal estate would vest in his personal representative. If the first person entitled is a minor, that personal representative is a statutory owner, but under s.26(2) the trustees may require him to vest the legal estate in them and meanwhile he shall give effect to the directions of the trustees, irrespective of their 'proprietary', provided that they appear to be legal. Finally, the section does not apply if the minor is one of joint life tenants and one of the others is of full age, for then the person of full age may hold the legal estate.

(2) *Where there is no life tenant presently entitled.* An example of this would be if, as in *Re Frewen* [1926] Ch. 580, land is settled upon trust to pay *A* two-thirds of the income, the other third to go on different trusts, for, as we shall see, *A*'s interest does not amount to a life interest. Once again, to enable the land to be dealt with, the statutory owner is brought to the helm. In this case, under s.23, this is: '(a) any person of full age on whom such powers are by the settlement expressed to be conferred; and (b) in any other case, the trustees of the settlement'.

Who is the tenant for life?

It is the policy of the Act that the legal estate and the wide statutory powers of disposal and management of the land should be in the hands of the tenant for life. It is essential therefore to know who this very important person is. Since the intention was to confer these powers upon the person beneficially entitled in possession, the 'tenant for life' would ordinarily be too narrow a term to use for this purpose, for a person might be in possession, for instance, by virtue of an entail. Sections 19 and 20 bestow these powers not only on the tenant for life properly so called, but upon other persons interested in possession. To save laboriousness of reference, these are all called 'tenants for life' (s.117 (xxviii)). This does not in any way affect their various beneficial interests and perhaps 'land manager' would have been a happier description. As in the case of the definition of a settlement, these sections are rather superfluous in their expression and the general characteristic present here is that all the persons described are presently entitled to possession or to the whole of the net income of the land. More specifically, however, the tenant for life may be one of the persons mentioned below, provided he is of full age, and presently and beneficially entitled under the settlement (*Re Jemmett and Guest's Contract* [1907] 1 Ch. 629). It was held in *Re Johnson* [1914] 2 Ch. 134 that the personal representative of a deceased beneficiary is beneficially entitled so as to have the powers of a tenant for life, provided, of course, that the interest of the beneficiary is one which is not extinguished by his death. Finally, an assignee of a life tenant's beneficial interest does not take 'under the settlement', so that the legal estate remains in the hands of the life tenant, even though he is no longer beneficially entitled (*Re Earl of Carnarvon's Chesterfield Settled Estates* [1927] 1 Ch. 138).

(1) The person entitled to possession of the land for life. This refers to the owner of an ordinary life interest. It was held in *Re Anderson* [1920] 1 Ch. 175 that where a person had been given an option to take possession of property, or part of it, she would not become a tenant for life until she had exercised the option by informing the trustees of her intention to take up possession.
(2) A tenant in tail in possession.
(3) An owner of a fee simple or lease subject to a gift over. An example would be 'to *A* in fee simple, but if he marries *B*, to *C* in fee simple'.
(4) An owner of a determinable or base fee or a corresponding interest in leasehold land.
(5) A tenant for years determinable on life, not holding merely under a lease at a rent. The Act aims at cases of endowment, not of profit return. This was strictly applied in *Re Catling* [1931] 2 Ch. 359, where a woman was given such a term at a nominal rent of £1 per year. It was held that she was not a tenant for life. Where rent is payable in this type of lease terminable upon 'family' events, such as death and marriage, the interest is converted into a ninety year lease under the Law of Property Act 1925, s.149(6). In that case, there is no settlement at all. This was considered under leasehold interests.
(6) A tenant for the life of another, not holding merely under a lease at a rent.
(7) A tenant for his own or other life, or for years determinable on life, whose interest is liable to cease in any event during that life, or is subject to a trust for accumulation of income.
(8) A tenant by curtesy.
(9) A person entitled to the income of land for his own or other life, whether or not subject to expenses of management, or to a trust for the accumulation of income, or until some other event. Thus a person who is not entitled to physical possession of the land, because, for instance, it is leased, but only to its income, becomes tenant for life and can demand the legal estate. It does not matter if this income is reduced by outgoings such as repairs (*Clarke* v. *Thornton* (1887), 35 Ch.D. 307) and annuities, even though they exhaust the income as they did in *Re Jones* (1884). 26 Ch.D. 736, where the beneficiary was held to have the powers of a life tenant, even though he received no benefit; but he must have the right to the whole net income, not merely even a large fraction of it (*Re Frewen* [1926] Ch. 580) or a hope only that a discretion will be exercised in his favour (*Re Atkinson* (1886), 31 Ch.D. 577). If, on the other hand, the net profits are divisible between two or more beneficiaries, this will constitute them joint life tenants (*Re Bennett* [1903] 2 Ch. 136).
(10) A person entitled to a fee simple or lease subject to any estates, interests, charges, or powers of charging, subsisting or capable of being exercised under a settlement. If land is charged under a settlement with the payment of charges and the fee simple absolute belongs beneficially to *X*, then *X* has the powers of a life tenant and has a right to the legal fee simple absolute and to exercise the powers of a life tenant. We have seen, however, that if he does not wish to overreach the charges, but to sell subject to them, he can deal with the land irrespective of the Act (Law of Property (Amendment) Act 1926, s.1).

Despite such a wide range of eligible life tenants, there might still be circumstances where, for the time being, there is no life tenant. One example is during a minority. Another is in the circumstances presented by *Re Frewen*, above, where the beneficiary was entitled only to two-thirds of the income of land, the other third going on different trusts and not to another person so as to constitute joint life tenants. In such cases, the statutory owner holds the legal estate and statutory powers.

Who are the trustees?

The trustees are a vital part of the furniture of a settlement and without them none of the major statutory powers granted to the life tenant may be exercised. Section 30 provides who they shall be and in what order of precedence. We must follow that 'queue order' rigidly.

If the settlement arises under a will or intestacy and there are otherwise no trustees, then the deceased's personal representatives may be trustees until others are appointed. If there is only one personal representative, not being a trust corporation, he must appoint another trustee to act with him. If the settlement is created *inter vivos* and otherwise there are no trustees, an application may be made to the court under the Trustee Act 1925, for appointments to be made. These last two provisions are for use as a last resort, but they ensure that a settlement need never be crippled through lack of trustees.

Formalities of creation

It was seen in Chapter 1 how simple a deed of conveyance can be, but it can be complicated by further additions, such as covenants, which will affect the purchaser and future owners. At one time, a further complicating factor was the existence of a settlement, because all the various interests and charges occurring under it were recited. This was so even when a power of sale existed, despite the fact that such family interests were of no interest to the purchaser, because they would be overreached. As a result he had to examine large quantities of material which were to him irrelevant, in order to find the comparatively small amount of information which concerned him. The nuisance to him may be compared with that presented to a motorist who, travelling along a fast major road to his destination, suddenly finds in the middle of the journey that he has to drive through a busy town, full of minor roads and culs-de-sac which do not concern him and present him with confusion. How much more convenient if the town can be by-passed by the major road. The policy of the Settled Land Act is to by-pass the settlement because now, under its provisions, all the family interests arising thereunder can be overreached. This it achieves by providing that only matters necessary to the proof of the legal title, or otherwise concerning the purchaser, shall appear on the deed of conveyance, and that the interests which are overreached and concern only the beneficiaries shall be contained in a separate document which need not, and in most cases cannot, be inspected by the purchaser. This is known as the 'curtain principle'.

Accordingly, s.4 enacts that every *inter vivos* settlement of a legal estate shall be made by two deeds, a principal vesting deed and a trust instrument, and if effected in any other way, shall not transfer the legal estate. Under s.6, if a settlement is created by will, the will becomes the trust instrument and the personal representatives must, when required, convey the land to the person entitled to the legal estate by a vesting assent, which is tantamount to a vesting deed except that, being made by personal representatives, it needs no seal. Sections 4 and 5 lay down what these two instruments must contain.

The principal vesting deed or assent must:

(1) Describe the settled land.
(2) Declare the land to be vested in the person to whom it is conveyed, or in whom it is declared to be vested, upon the trusts of the settlement. This rather strained expression covers not only cases where the settlor conveys to another person as tenant for life, but also where he himself is to be the first tenant for life and the legal estate is thus already vested in him.
(3) Name the trustees.
(4) Name the persons empowered to appoint new trustees.
(5) Describe any powers conferred in addition to those provided by the Act.

Additional land is brought into a settlement by a subsidiary vesting deed (see s.10).

In short, the vesting instrument is like an ordinary conveyance except that it advertises that a settlement exists, even though its terms do not appear. The purchaser is therefore alerted to pay the purchase-money to the trustees, whose identities are also discoverable from the deed. He can see what land has passed from whom to whom. He has need for no more. The trust instrument must:

(1) Declare the trusts. This refers to the detailed beneficial provisions of the settlement.
(2) Appoint the trustees.
(3) Contain any power to appoint new trustees.
(4) Set out any powers granted in addition to those in the Act.
(5) Bear any *ad valorem* stamp duty which is normally carried by a conveyance.

Some of the information is common to both instruments, and in these cases the vesting instrument is merely recording something effected by the trust instrument.

A diagram might illustrate the effects of the sections.

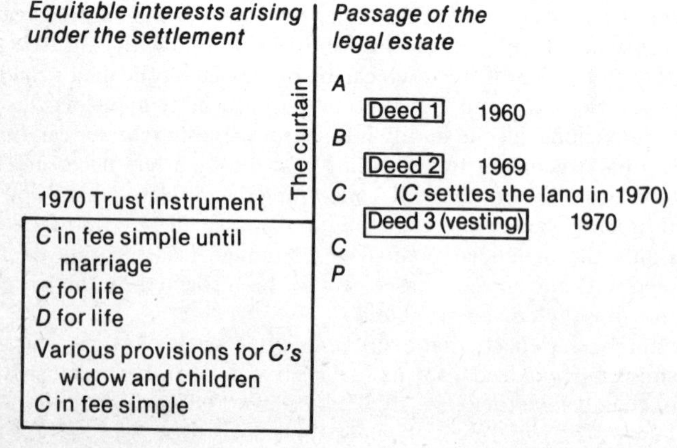

P, a purchaser, now wishes to buy the settled land from *C*, the tenant for life. He will require proof of title from a root at least fifteen years old. This root will be provided by the conveyance of 1960, which was before the settlement. The title is traced in the ordinary way by inspection of deeds 1, 2 and 3. The settlement provisions are by-passed and overreached on sale, so that the trust instrument is not seen. Deed 3 announces the existence of the settlement because it is a vesting deed, so that *P* pays the purchase-money to the trustees named in it, or to their successors.

Absence of vesting instrument

The Act had to provide sanctions if the requirement that all settlements must be created by two instruments was to be observed. These are provided by s.13, known as 'the paralysing section', although, as we have already seen, s.4 prevents the legal estate passing in cases where it is not obeyed. Section 13 enacts that once a tenant for life or statutory owner has become entitled to have a vesting instrument executed in his favour, then, until this is done, any purported disposition *inter vivos* by any person of the legal estate shall operate only as a contract for valuable consideration to carry out the transaction after the vesting instrument has been executed. In short, no legal estate passes; but there are the following exceptions to the provision:

(1) Personal representatives may pass the legal estate even if a principal vesting instrument was not executed in favour of the person entitled. So if *C*, above, had created the settlement only by one instrument, and then died, his personal representatives would nevertheless be able to deal with the land.
(2) If a person purchases the legal estate without notice that the tenant for life or statutory owner has become entitled to a vesting instrument, then s.13 does not apply. For instance, if *C* had made his settlement by one instrument and then concealed from a purchaser that he had settled the land, by showing him deeds 1 and 2 only, the purchaser would take the legal estate (Law of Property (Amendment) Act 1926, Sched.). The language of s.13 is not really satisfactory here, because in referring to a purchaser of 'the legal estate', it presupposes the exception which the section itself created.
(3) If the settlement has ended before a vesting instrument has been created, s.13 does not apply. In *Re Alefounder's Will Trusts* [1927] 1 Ch. 360 it was held that a tenant in tail in possession, with no prior trusts or incumbrances which could independently keep the settlement alive, could, on disentailment, dispose of the land, although he had obtained no vesting deed.
(4) Where land is settled land merely because it is subject to family charges— it has already been seen that the land may be conveyed, still subject to the charges, as if it were not settled land (Law of Property (Amendment) Act 1926, s.1).

Where an *inter vivos* settlement is attempted by a single document, this document becomes the trust instrument. The general effect, therefore, of s.13 is not to invalidate a settlement, but to immobilize it until it has been regularized by the execution of a vesting instrument. However, a settlor who has lapsed in this way cannot correct his own mistake. Under s.9, it is the trustees who must then execute the deed.

The curtain principle

A purchaser of a legal estate in settled land cannot, with a few exceptions, demand to see the trust instrument (s.110 (2)). Furthermore, he is bound to assume that the facts recited in the vesting deed are correct, although the Act provides no solution to the problems which might arise if they are not. The exceptions under which a purchaser may look behind the curtain include the case of the imperfectly constituted settlement which was originally created *inter vivos* by a single deed. Here the purchaser may look at the trust instrument to make sure that the corrective vesting deed is faithful to the original act of settlement, which, though formally incorrect, is the authentic record of the transaction.

Subsequent transfer of the legal estate within the settlement and at the end of it

The essential difference between an ordinary conveyance and a vesting deed is simply that the latter, by showing the existence of a settlement, flashes a warning sign to prospective purchasers. Since such a warning is necessary throughout the subsistence of the settlement, then when one life tenant gives way to another, the legal estate must be passed to the next person entitled by an instrument which continues to transmit this warning, namely, by a further vesting instrument. We must see how, and on what occasions, this need arises (see s.7).

(1) *Death of a life tenant.* The legal estate devolves upon the special personal representatives, who are the trustees of the settlement under the Administration of Estates Act 1925, s.22, and when required, they must convey it to the next person entitled, either by vesting deed or vesting assent.

(2) *Termination of life tenant's interest before death.* An example would be if, under a settlement upon '*A* for life until he marries, then to *B* for life with remainder in fee simple to *C*', *A* married, thereby ending his beneficial interest. The settlement, of course, continues, and *A* must convey the legal estate to *B* by a vesting deed.

(3) *Minor reaching full age.* During his minority, a life tenant cannot hold a legal estate. When he reaches full age, the person in whom it is vested, usually the statutory owner, must convey it to him by the appropriate vesting instrument.

(4) *Person of full age absolutely entitled.* An example would be when, under a settlement on '*A* for life, remainder to *B* in fee simple', *A* dies. Provided that there are no charges, powers of charging or other limitations, the settlement ends, for *B* is beneficially entitled to the fee simple absolute in possession. In this case, the legal estate vests in the general personal representatives of the deceased, and not in the trustees as special personal representatives (*Re Bridgett and Hayes' Contract* [1928] Ch. 163). They must now convey the land to the person entitled by an ordinary conveyance or assent, and not by a vesting instrument. Since the land can now be dealt with outside the terms of the Settled Land Act, the warning sign to purchasers is, so to speak, turned off. The same is true if the person last entitled is entitled as a trustee for sale, personal representative or otherwise.

Requirement of deed of discharge

It will be explained later that although the tenant for life holds the legal estate, he cannot dispose of it just as an absolute owner can, but only as laid down in the Act (s.18). Furthermore, purchase-money must be paid to the trustees and not to the life tenant. The vesting deed makes a purchaser aware of this. We have seen how, when a settlement ends on a death, the legal estate is transmitted to the person entitled by an ordinary assent, and this does not mention trustees. The purchaser may then assume that the person holding that legal estate owns it absolutely and not upon trust (s.110(5)). The same rule applies if the settlement ends with an ordinary conveyance; where land is settled on *A* for life until marriage, then to *B* in fee simple, and *A* marries. *B*'s title will derive from an ordinary conveyance from *A*. In such cases, the inhibiting effect of the last vesting instrument is thereby cancelled. Similarly, if a settlement ends before a vesting deed has been executed, the legal estate may be freely dealt with, because there is no vesting instrument to inhibit dealing (*Re Alefounder's*, p. 149, *ante*).

In some cases, however, even when a settlement has ended, the last document of title is a vesting instrument; an example being if land stood limited to *E* in tail in possession and there were no prior interests existing but a vesting deed has been executed in *E*'s favour. If *E* now barred the entail, the settlement would be at an end. Yet, since the land is still subject to a vesting deed, s.18 makes any dispositions subject to the stringent terms of the Act, including the necessity of paying the purchase-money to the trustees. The person absolutely entitled may require the trustees to execute a 'deed of discharge', which has the result of cancelling the restraining effect of the vesting deed by declaring that all the trusts are discharged (s.17). He may then deal with the land as an ordinary absolute owner and the deed of discharge will be proof of this to a purchaser.

Duration of settlements

Section 3, as amended by the Law of Property (Amendment) Act 1926, s.7, hardly adds anything new to s.1, which defines a settlement, but emphasizes that not until the final wisp of its tail has disappeared is the settlement over. It enacts that land remains settled so long as:

(1) any limitation, charge, or power of charging under the settlement subsists, or is capable of being exercised; or
(2) the person who, if of full age, would be entitled as beneficial owner to have the land vested in him for a legal estate is an infant, provided in either case that under the terms of the settlement a trust for sale has not come into operation. If land has been settled on *A* for life, then to *B* for life, then to *C* in fee simple with a power given to *X* and *Y* to charge the land in favour of the widow of *B*, and *A* and *B* have both died, then, even though *C* is of full age, the power given to *X* and *Y* keeps the settlement alive.

Ultra vires transactions

Although the life tenant or statutory owner holds the legal estate, he holds it as trustee. Unlike a person who owns it beneficially for himself alone, he cannot deal with it as he wishes, but only as authorized by the Act, unless wider powers are given under the settlement or by the court. In short, he is subject to the *ultra vires* rule. Section 18 defines his position, where the land is still subject to a vesting instrument and the trustees have not been discharged.

(1) Any disposition not authorized by the Act or other statute or made under additional powers mentioned in the vesting instrument 'shall be void' except for the purpose of disposing of his equitable interest.
(2) If capital money is payable in respect of a transaction, the transaction only takes effect if it is paid to or by the direction of the trustees, or into court. Notwithstanding anything to the contrary expressed in the settlement, such payment shall not be to less than two trustees unless a trust corporation has been appointed.

These restrictions do not affect the right of personal representatives to deal with the land for the purposes of administration, or the right of a person who has become absolutely entitled at the end of a settlement to have the land conveyed to him. The relationship between ss.13 and 18 is as follows. Section 13 prevents, with a few exceptions, any dealings at all with the legal estate until a vesting instrument has been executed. Section 18 prevents any dealings with the legal estate beyond the limits authorized by statute or by the settlement, even when a vesting deed has been executed. Section 13 places a muzzle upon the goat so that he cannot graze at all. Section 18 fixes a tether on him which confines him even when that muzzle is off. The extent of his pasture will be described in the next section.

The operation of s.18 is well illustrated by *Weston* v. *Henshaw* [1950] Ch. 510. *G* sold land to *F*, his son, who later sold it back to *G*. *G* then settled it upon *F* for life, then to *F*'s son, *S*. *F* then purported to mortgage the land to *M*. He presented himself not as a tenant for life, who can mortgage the settled land only for the purposes mentioned in the Act, but, by concealing all the documents of the settlement and the deed of conveyance from himself to *G*, as absolute beneficial owner, which of course he once had been. His motive was to raise money for his own purposes. After his death, the question arose whether the mortgage to *M* was good as against *S*, both of whom were innocent of the fraud. It was held that the mortgage was void as against *S*. The fact that *F* could show a deed which once vested the land in him absolutely was a matter of mere history and no longer entitled him to deal with the land at all, because it had since been reconveyed to *G*. His only power to dispose of a legal estate in the land, therefore, was by virtue of his status of tenant for life under the settlement. Since, however, his purpose was not one of those listed in the Act for which a life tenant may deal with the legal estate, but his own personal purpose only, the mortgage was void under s.18. The doctrine of the purchaser of the legal estate without notice is not in point in such cases, because the legal estate itself does not pass at all. It should be noted that this situation can arise only in relation to unregistered land.

The powers of the tenant for life

The extent of the life tenant's powers must now be discussed. These rules confining his powers of dealing with the legal estate do not affect his right to dispose of his beneficial interest. This he can do in any way he wishes, because it is his very own and not held upon trust for anyone else.

As a safeguard against abuse of his powers, the tenant for life must, before exercising most of his powers, give notice to the trustees (*Wheelwright* v. *Walker* (No. 1) (1883), 23 Ch.D. 752), and in a few cases he must obtain the permission of the trustees or a court order. Where notice is necessary it must be given by a registered or recorded delivery letter to at least two trustees, or all of them if there are more than two, or a trust corporation, and to the solicitor to the trustees if known, at least one month before the transaction or the contract for it. A person dealing in good faith with the tenant for life is not concerned to enquire whether such notice has been given (s.101(5)). A general notice that the life tenant intends from time to time to exercise his statutory powers is enough, except in the case of a mortgage or charge. However, the trustees may demand information as to completed or impending transactions (s.101). On the other hand a trustee may, by writing, accept less notice or waive it altogether. In authorizing the following transactions, the Act confers powers, not duties, so that if there are joint life tenants, one life tenant cannot, at least in the absence of bad faith on the part of the other, insist upon a transaction against the wishes of the other (*Re 90, Thornhill Road, Tolworth* [1970] Ch. 261).

It is not the function of a textbook concerned with general principles to reprint statutory provisions. Signposting only of these powers will be given here therefore. What must be emphasized is that the powers authorized by the Act can only be exercised to the extent and in the manner allowed by the Act. The tenant for life can exercise most of the powers of an absolute owner of land but only in the way permitted by the Act. These powers include sale (ss.38–40); exchange (ss.38 and 40); leasing (ss.41–48); acceptance of leases (s.53); mortgaging (s.71); granting options (s.51); improvement of settled land (ss.83–89, Sched.3); investment of capital money (ss.75 and 73) and see also the Trustee Investments Act 1961; and some minor powers.

Enlargement of powers

We shall see that the life tenant's statutory powers cannot be inhibited in any way. They can, however, be increased in two ways:

(1) *Under the settlement.* Section 109 provides that powers wider than or additional to those conferred by the Act may be granted to the tenants for life, and when the settlement authorizes such greater powers, they are exercisable as if they were conferred by the Act. Furthermore, any power, other than a power of appointment or revocation, which the settlement attempts to give to the trustees or any other person, whether or not provided for in the Act, becomes exercisable by the life tenant or statutory owner (s.108 (2)). If, for instance, powers of mortgaging, whether or not for one of the purposes authorized by the Act, were in terms conferred upon the trustees by the settlement, they would be exercisable by the life tenant.

(2) *Under an order of court.* Section 64 empowers the court to authorize the life tenant to carry out any 'transaction', not being one which is authorized by the Act or the settlement, concerning the settled land or other land, if, in its opinion, it would be for the benefit of the settled land or the persons interested under the settlement, provided that it is a transaction which could validly be effected by an absolute owner.

The section, as amended, gives a wide meaning to the word 'transaction', so that besides its more obvious meanings such as leasing, it includes a covenant, an application of capital money, a purchase and any compromise or other arrangement. Its provisions have been used, for instance, to permit a mortgage for the purpose of paying debts incurred in running the estate (*Re White-Popham Settled Estates* [1936] Ch. 725). It can even be used to authorize schemes on behalf of persons under a disability or who are unborn, which would change the beneficial interests under the settlement. The motive will frequently be the saving of tax. (See also *Re Simmons' Trusts* [1956] Ch. 125). It has, however, been largely overtaken in this role by the Variation of Trusts Act 1958.

The inviolability of the life tenant's powers

The policy of the Act in choosing the life tenant to exercise the statutory powers, and in making these powers inviolable, is reinforced in several ways.

(1) The Act prevails (s. 108)
While nothing in the Act restricts powers given to the life tenant and while the powers in the settlement and in the Act are cumulative, if the Act and the settlement conflict, the Act shall prevail. So if a settlement purports to make the consent of another person necessary before a life tenant or statutory owner can sell, there is a direct conflict between the settlement and the statutory power of sale, and the life tenant may sell without consent (*Re Jefferys* [1939] Ch. 205).

(2) Inhibiting provisions void (s. 106)
Section 108 above deals with cases where there is an express or overt conflict between the Act and the settlement, but a life tenant might be prejudiced against exercising his powers by the use of indirect provisions in the settlement which dissuade rather than forbid or restrict. If a settlor wished, for instance, to prevent a sale of the settled land, he might provide that on its sale some other benefit given to the life tenant under the settlement should terminate. Section 106 develops the theme set in s. 108 and enacts in its first subsection that if any provision is inserted in a settlement:

> (a) purporting or attempting, by way of direction, declaration, or otherwise, to forbid a tenant for life or statutory owner to exercise any power under this Act, or his right to require the settled land to be vested in him; or
>
> (b) attempting, or tending, or intended, by a limitation, gift, or disposition over of settled land, or by a limitation, gift, or disposition of other real or any personal property, or by the imposition of any condition, or by forfeiture, or in any other manner whatever, to prohibit or prevent him from exercising, or to induce him to abstain from exercising, or to put him into a position inconsistent with his exercising, any power under this Act, or his right to require the settled land to be vested in him;
>
> that provision, as far as it purports, or attempts, or tends, or is intended to have, or would or might have, the operation aforesaid, shall be deemed to be void.

This strong and rather difficult section should be studied with the help of decided cases. In *Re Ames* [1893] 2 Ch. 479, a fund was left for the maintenance of the settled land and any surplus income was to be given to the tenant for life, unless he ceased to be entitled to possession of the land, whereupon that fund was to be denied to him. It was held that even after sale of the settled land, he would still be entitled to the income. Otherwise, he might be discouraged from exercising his statutory power by the prospect of losing this benefit. The section strikes at such inhibiting factors even if they involve property apart from the settlement or are expressed in documents outside the settlement. Thus in *Re Smith* [1899] 1 Ch. 331 there was a provision in a settlement that, if the land were sold, personalty settled under a different settlement should not go to the life tenant of the land, but to someone else. It was held that the gift over was ineffectual.

The section is often infringed by conditions in settlements that the life tenant's interest shall determine when he ceases to live on the settled land. Clearly the prospect of enjoying no interest in the purchase money could dissuade him from exercising any powers such as the power to sell which must result in his giving up possession. In *Re Simpson* [1913] 1 Ch. 277, a leasehold house was bequeathed to *W* during her widowhood, and rents, taxes and repairs were to be paid for out of a general fund by trustees during her occupation. It was held that there was no infringement of s.106, because the fund was from the beginning bestowing a benefit on the land, not on the tenant for life, and therefore was not a deterrent to the exercise of the statutory powers, because *W* would suffer no direct loss on a sale of the property. The fact that the provision of the fund in the first place might obliquely deter her from selling because in her new home she would have to pay her own outgoings did not invoke the section.

This distinction made by the judge may perhaps be further explained by remarking that all the settlor did was to leave her a desirable property which she might be reluctant to leave. If this had been a transgression of the section, it might have been argued with equal strength that the grant of a life tenancy in a house so beautifully situated and appointed that a person would never wish to move from it would also infringe it. A leading modern case which discusses this and other decisions is *Re Aberconway's Settlement Trusts* [1953] Ch. 647. In all such cases, however, if the life tenant decides to leave the property for some reason other than that he wishes to exercise his statutory powers, the forfeiture condition is effective and his interest ends (*Re Trenchard* [1902] 1 Ch. 378). The rather cynical moral to be drawn by a life tenant who is subject to such a condition and who, while not wishing in any case to reside on the settled property, yet wishes to retain a live interest in the purchase money, is that he should exercise the statutory power of sale.

To the extent that a provision deters exercise of the statutory powers, it is an illegal determining factor, whether employed in a condition subsequent or in the delineation of a determinable interest. Such illegal conditions were dealt with in Chapter 5, but it may be added here that its illegality does not cause a determinable interest to fail, as illegal terminating events usually do.

(3) A life tenant cannot relinquish his powers (s.104)

A life tenant cannot assign or release his powers or contract not to exercise them. Even when he assigns his beneficial interest, or when assignment of his interest occurs by operation of law, it is he and not the assignee who may exercise them. Only in three exceptional cases do they become exercisable by someone else. These are dealt with below. If the assignment of the interest occurred after 1925, no consent of the assignee is needed. If the assignment so provides, or if it takes effect through bankruptcy and the trustees have notice of this, the assignee's consent is required for the application or investment of capital money affected by the assignment, unless the investment is to be in trustee securities. Notice of intended transactions must be given to the assignee unless otherwise provided in the assignment. On sale of the land, the rights of the assignee are transferred to the purchase-money just as the life tenant's rights would have been if he had not transferred his interest. The exceptional cases where the statutory powers cease to be exercised by the life tenant are as follows:

(a) *Surrender of life tenant's interest to next remainderman (s.105).* When the life tenant's interest has been assured, with intent to extinguish it to the next person entitled under the settlement (see *Re Maryon-Wilson's Settlements* [1969] 3 All E.R. 558), the powers become exercisable as if he were dead. In *Re Shawdon Estates Settlement* [1930] 2 Ch. 1, the trustee in bankruptcy sold a life tenant's beneficial interest to the next remainderman and it was held that there had been such an assurance. Indeed, the language of the section is in the passive voice, so that the assurance need not be by the life tenant, and the intention to extinguish need only be that of whoever assigns. Accordingly, he has to execute a vesting deed in favour of the remainderman.

(b) *Tenant for a life mental patient.* In this case, the powers may be exercised by the life tenant's Receiver under the provisions of the Mental Health Act 1959.

(c) *Court order under s.24.* If the life tenant has by reason of bankruptcy, assignment, incumbrance or otherwise ceased, in the opinion of the court, to have a substantial interest in his estate or interest in the land or part of it, and either has unreasonably refused to exercise any of the statutory powers, or consents to an order under the section, the court may, on the application of anyone interested in any part of the land affected, make an order authorizing the trustees to exercise any of the powers in the name and on behalf of the life tenant, either generally or in such way or for such period as it thinks fit.

While the order is in force, the life tenant must not exercise his powers, but a person dealing with him is not affected unless it is registered under the Land Charges Act 1972 (s.6), or, in the case of registered land, by a notice or caution. The legal estate and the powers remain vested in the life tenant, for the words of the section merely forbid and do not disable him. The combinations of factors which will satisfy the section should be carefully noted. Thus, even a deplorable failure to exercise his powers is not enough. He must also have ceased to have a substantial interest in the land and either unreasonably refused to exercise the powers or consented to an order. (See generally *Re Thornhill's Settlement* [1941] Ch. 24). Finally 'substantial interest' relates to the right to proprietary enjoyment of the land and not to a concern for its welfare, so that a life tenant who merely neglects or absents himself from the property is no candidate for the section for those reasons.

(4) Legal Estate Remains in Life Tenant even on Bankruptcy (s.103)

Even though his beneficial interest may be taken in bankruptcy, the legal estate of a life tenant does not vest in the trustee bankruptcy as long as the settlement subsists. This is a further illustration of the general inviolability of his statutory powers.

The life tenant as trustee (section 107)

This section enacts that a life tenant or statutory owner, in exercising his statutory powers, shall 'have regard to the interests of all parties entitled under the settlement' and 'be deemed to be in the position and to have the duties and liabilities of a trustee for those parties'.

Two views have been expressed as to the extent to which the section enables the court to examine the motives of a life tenant in exercising his statutory powers. The first favours an objective view. Provided that the terms of the Act are obeyed in such matters as obtaining the best price reasonably obtainable on a sale, the court cannot inquire into motives, which might even be malicious. To take an example, if the life tenant wished to sell, in order to thwart the remainderman who he knew was anxious to enjoy the land in specie, the court could not interfere, provided that the transaction was properly carried out (*Wheelwright* v. *Walker* (No.1) (1883), 23 Ch.D. 752, per Pearson, J.). The weakness of this view is that s.107 is just as much part of the Act as are the more specific sections regulating the exercise of the powers and its language seems capable of supporting the second view.

This view is that the life tenant must consider all interests, whether they are pecuniary or sentimental, and mere compliance with the more particular statutory obligations is not in itself enough. This would allow the court to make a more subjective approach to a life tenant's decisions. Perhaps the two views may be compromised. Both accept that, to whatever extent the interests of other beneficiaries must be considered, once they have been considered they may be overridden by the life tenant, although it could be argued that the beneficiaries may thus find themselves at the mercy of an autocrat.

The operation of the section may be illustrated by *Middlemas* v. *Stevens* [1901] 1 Ch. 574, where a woman, entitled for life until her remarriage, proposed to grant a lease to her intended husband. She was restrained by an injunction on proof that her sole purpose was to ensure that she could continue to live in the property after her marriage. Where the life tenant wishes the statutory powers to be exercised in favour of himself in his private capacity, for example where he wishes to buy the settled land, special provision is made so that his trusteeship does not place him in an ambivalent position. Section 68 enacts that in such cases the trustees shall have all the powers of the life tenant in negotiating and completing the transaction (see *Re Pennant's Will Trusts* [1969] 2 All E.R. 862).

Protection of purchasers (section 110)

The Act has greatly facilitated dealings with settled land, but of course such transactions are subject to more rules than dispositions by an ordinary absolute owner. The purchase price must be the best reasonably obtainable, capital money must be paid to trustees and the obligations regarding vesting instruments and notice must be obeyed. Such complications might well deter a person from buying settled land if the Act did not exonerate him from establishing whether they had all been observed. Otherwise, he might be placed in a false position. For example he can hardly be expected to ensure that the best price reasonably obtainable is paid, since his purpose is clearly to acquire the land as cheaply as possible. Section 110, therefore, provides as follows:

(1) On any disposition, a purchaser dealing in good faith shall, as against all the beneficiaries, be conclusively taken to have given the best price, rent, or other consideration reasonably obtainable by the life tenant, and to have complied with all the requisitions of the Act (subs. (1)). The subsection applies even though the purchaser does not realize he is dealing with a tenant for life. It applies to executory as well as to completed transactions (*Re Morgan's Lease* [1971] 2 All E.R. 235). Section 101 more specifically enacts that a person dealing in good faith with the life tenant is not concerned with the question whether notice of an intended transaction has been given to the trustees.
(2) With some exceptions, mentioned earlier in this chapter, the purchaser of a legal estate may not call for the trust instrument, and is entitled to assume that statements made in the vesting instrument are correct.
(3) If a conveyance or assent relating to land formerly settled does not state who are the trustees, a purchaser of the legal estate may assume that the person in whom it was thereby vested was entitled to the land free of the settlement, and that the facts in the conveyance are correct.

Although this is, in the ordinary case, a reassuring section to a purchaser, it operates on the assumption that every statement is correct. It does not provide for cases where mistakes or misrepresentations are made, such as where the person stated to be life tenant in the vesting deed, although originally entitled, has ceased to be life tenant (see Megarry and Wade, *The Law of Real Property*, 3rd edn, p.315, and 22 Conveyancer 78).

The duties of Settled Land Act trustees

The various duties of the trustees have been mentioned from time to time in this chapter. It may be convenient to collect them at this point for appreciation, but without further comment: (i) to receive capital money; (ii) to receive notice of transactions; (iii) to consent to certain transactions; (iv) to execute deeds of discharge; (v) to act as statutory owner; (vi) to negotiate transactions when a life tenant takes a disposition of the settled land; (vii) to exercise the statutory powers in the name of the life tenant under s.24; (viii) to act as special personal representatives; (ix) to execute vesting deeds in imperfectly constituted settlements; (x) to oversee the settlement and to intervene in cases of illegality or where responsible initiative is desirable, as for instance under s.24 (see, however, s.97).

Overreaching of interests (section 72; see also Law of Property Act, section 2)

The meaning of overreaching has already been explained. It must now be explained in more detail what interests can be overreached when a life tenant completes a transaction under the Act, whether by way of sale, mortgage, lease or other disposition. The broad policy is to overreach all the beneficial interests under the settlement and a few others arising independently of it where they lose nothing by being expressed in money. The following interests are overreached:

(1) 'All the limitations, powers, and provisions of the settlement and all estates, interests and charges subsisting or to arise thereunder', with the following exceptions:

(a) legal estates and charges by way of legal mortgage prior to the settlement;

(b) legal estates and charges by way of legal mortgage created for securing money actually raised at the date of the disposition by the life tenant;

(c) all leases, easements, profits or other rights which are at the date of the disposition binding on the successors in title of the life tenant and protected by registration, if registrable.

(2) Limited owners' charges, general equitable charges and certain annuities, whether arising under the settlement or prior to it, and whether or not they are registered.

An example may illustrate the working of the section:

1960—*O*, absolute owner of land, creates a general equitable charge, such as an equitable mortgage not protected by deposit of deeds in favour of *A*.
1970—*O* creates a restrictive covenant in favour of *B*.
1972—*O* settles the land upon *C* for life and *D* in fee simple in remainder.
1977—*C*, under statutory powers, creates a lease in favour of *E*.
1981—*C*, under statutory powers, sells the land to *P*.

The interests of the following will be overreached: *A* under (2) above; *C* under (1); *D* under (1). The interests of the following will not be overreached: *B* under (1)(c); *E* under (1)(c); so that *P* will not be entitled to occupy the land during the lease, but will be entitled to receive the rent from *E*.

The strict settlement in modern times

The strict settlement has lost most of its attractions as a means either of family endowment or of ensuring that a particular landed estate should remain in the ownership of members of one family. Its role has largely been taken up by the settlement by way of trust for sale. Modern tax legislation has been partly the cause of decline in the first of these purposes, and, as we have seen, the statutory powers given to the life tenant might often frustrate the latter. Ironically, it is easier to ensure that land remains unsold by creating a settlement by way of trust for sale, for the persons holding the legal estate may in that case be instructed to obtain consents before selling land: this will be explained below. This obligation cannot, of course, be imposed upon a life tenant under a strict settlement, even though he might be a poor land manager.

Another disadvantage of the strict settlement is the cumbersome machinery imposed by the Act. These complicated and expensive safeguards might perhaps be expected where a large estate is being settled, but they apply equally to land of the smallest dimensions and testators might be completely unaware that they are creating strict settlements. As remarked at the beginning of his chapter, a simple gift of a cottage to a testator's widow for life and then to his son attracts all the provisions of the Act, including, for instance, those regarding vesting deeds, trust instruments, trustees and deeds of discharge.

Since the only difference at inception between a strict settlement and a settlement by way of trust for sale is that the latter contains a mandate to sell, and since the words used by a settlor might not always make it clear whether such an imperative instruction is being given, there is the possibility of confusion. Such confusion could be very inconvenient, for the two categories are governed by very different rules.

These considerations have led to the suggestion that the two types of settlement ought to be fused, or that the trust for sale should be the only method allowed for settling land (see 54 L.Q.R. 576).

Settlements by way of trusts for sale

Nature

If, in a strict settlement, the settlor were to give one additional instruction, namely that the land must be sold, a trust for sale and not a strict settlement would arise. So a simple statement in a will such as 'I wish "Blackacre" to be sold and its rents and profits until sale, and the proceeds after sale, applied for the benefit of my wife *W* during her life, and then for my son *S* absolutely', creates a settlement by way of trust for sale. This small addition has extremely important results, for a completely different code of rules applies to a trust for sale.

Trusts for sale are wider in their scope than strict settlements, for they can exist even when there is no element of succession in the disposition, nor a minority, nor a family charge in existence. For instance, land can be ordered to be held upon trust for sale for *A* absolutely. Such are the advantages of a trust for sale, that statute has copied from it and imposed some of its basic rules upon certain transactions where there is no express instruction by the settlor to sell. These are called 'statutory trusts for sale' and do not concern us here. Those we are now to examine are called 'express trusts for sale', because the sale has been expressly ordered by a settlor. The hallmark of an express trust for sale is simply an imperative instruction by the settlor to sell the land.

The trust for sale came into common use in the nineteenth century. Because it was used by the new rich rather than by the aristocracy, it was known as the 'trader's settlement'. When a successful businessman wished to settle his wealth upon his family he would naturally look for some secure and profitable investment wherein his money would be protected against the constant fall in the value of the pound while his family grew up. In those days land satisfied these requirements admirably, for, provided its site was wisely chosen, it was in growing demand in a rapidly advancing industrial society.

The land chosen, however, might differ sharply from that subject to a strict settlement, because the settlor was only interested in its potential value on sale and did not intend that the beneficiaries should live there. It was simply a treasure chest for his wealth and might consist of some very unattractive and undeveloped areas near towns which would soon be ripe for development. Such land would be purchased and conveyed to trustees upon trust that they should sell it and hold the proceeds for the beneficiaries of the trust. This did not oblige the trustees to sell at once. Indeed, such an exercise would have been pointless. The purpose was that they should sell when they considered it profitable to do so.

The usual disposition of interests under a trust for sale is quite different from that under the traditional strict settlement. Since land held on trust for sale is personalty, because of the doctrine of conversion, the entail could not be used in such a trust before 1926; the reason for this being that personalty could not be entailed until that time. Although it is now possible to entail personalty, it is unlikely that anyone would wish to so under a trust for sale, for the modern approach is to divide the settled property equally between the issue. Under a typical trust for sale there would probably be a determinable interest to *H* until marriage, then to *H* for life, then to his wife *W* for life, if she should survive him, and then absolutely to such of their children or other issue in such shares as *H* and *W* should appoint, or, in default of appointment, to the children equally on reaching a specified age or on marriage. In case there were no children there would be an ultimate limitation to *H*, the settlor.

A device frequently used in trusts for sale is the protective trust, which is a combination of limitations designed to safeguard a family in case the life tenant becomes bankrupt or attempts to alienate his interest. It hinges on the use of the determinable interest. For instance, if property is being settled on a husband, *H*, and his family, *H* would be granted a life interest determinable on his bankruptcy or attempted alienation. In that event, the trustees are given a discretion as to how they will then apply the income during the rest of *H*'s life amongst certain specified beneficiaries, which will include *H* himself, his wife *W* and the children. After *H*'s death the property will probably be limited to pass to *W* for life, if she should survive *H*, and finally to the children or other issue in such shares as *H* and *W* shall appoint, and in default of appointment to the children equally, with ultimate remainder, if there should be no children, to the settlor. The protective nature of this trust may now be appreciated. When a husband is granted the first life interest under a settlement, although the interest is legally speaking entirely his own, it is naturally anticipated that he will maintain his wife and children out of it. There is always the risk, however, that this means of support will be snatched away from the family either by the husband's bankruptcy or by his capitalization of it by a sale. Once a steady income is thus converted into a lump sum there is obviously a danger that it might soon be dissipated, leaving the family without its main source of income for the rest of the husband's life. In a protective trust this cannot happen. Any attempted alienation or a bankruptcy automatically ends his interest, so that there is no longer anything to sell, or anything which can be taken into bankruptcy. Therefore the husband has no longer any property in the trust, but merely the hope that the trustees will from time to time exercise their discretion in his favour. This they will usually do, but it is only the subject matter of each of these individual applications of income which falls into the ownership of the husband. Of course, a person cannot settle his own property upon himself until bankruptcy and then upon another, as this would be contrary to the bankruptcy laws. This was explained in Chapter 5.

The protective trust has been used so frequently that a settlor need not now set out its detailed machinery. If he declares that any periodical payment shall be held on 'protective trusts' for any person, s.33 of the Trustee Act

1925 now provides a model similar to that described above, the terms of which are incorporated into a trust by such a reference. These terms of course may be varied as the settlor wishes by a contrary provision in the settlement. Trusts of this nature have been used in recent years to save estate duty.

The machinery of trusts for sale

The detailed rules as to the operation of trusts for sale are to be found mainly in statutes, in particular in ss.22–23 of the Law of Property Act 1925. The definition of a trust for sale is contained in s.205 of that Act. These detailed rules will be considered later in this chapter. At this point, two of the outstanding features of a trust for sale must be considered. Throughout the remainder of this chapter, references to sections will be from the Law of Property Act 1925, unless otherwise stated.

(1) *The legal estate is held by trustees.* The settlor constitutes the trust by conveying the legal estate to trustees who are instructed to hold it upon trust for sale and to give effect to the beneficial interests described. The legal estate remains with the trustees throughout the trust. There is no provision, as there is in the case of strict settlements, requiring or allowing a life tenant to hold it. In practice, the trust has always been created by two instruments, the one conveying the land to the trustees stating that it must be held on the trusts which are declared in a second instrument. This second deed contains the beneficial interests. The advantage in this is that since the trust envisages the satisfaction of these interests out of the proceeds of sale, and since they therefore do not concern a purchaser, they do not appear in the documents of legal title. Conveyancing is thus simplified. It was this practice in trusts for sale which provided the example for the introduction of vesting deeds and trust instruments in the case of strict settlements under the Settled Land Act 1925, but strangely there is still no statutory provision that a trust for sale shall be constituted by two instruments.

The fact that in strict settlements the legal estate must be vested in the life tenant, whereas in trusts for sale it must be vested in the trustees for sale, provides just one of the several important reasons why the two categories must be sharply distinguished. Since it remains with the trustees in the case of trusts for sale, the death of life tenants or the cessation of their interests calls for no transfers of the legal estate. Conveyancing is thus facilitated.

(2) *The doctrine of conversion applies.* Under the principle that equity treats that as done which ought to be done, the interests of the beneficiaries are considered to be interests in the purchase-money from the very creation of the trust, even before the land is sold (see *Irani Finance Ltd.* v. *Singh* [1970] 3 All E.R. 199, but distinguish *National Westminster Bank Ltd.* v. *Allen* [1971] 2 Q.B. 718). The settlement therefore is one of personalty. This is known as the doctrine of conversion and will be explained in Chapter 11.

We shall see later that when the trustees eventually sell the land the purchaser takes it free from the interests of the beneficiaries. In the case of strict settlements this process is known as overreaching because these interests are transferred from land to money. In the case of trusts for sale, however, it is hardly correct to use this expression because, since the interests are in money from the beginning, there is no such transference and therefore no overreaching in the real sense. The purchaser takes the land free of the interests because they never affected the land at all. Nevertheless the fact that the result, if not the cause, is the same in both cases has led to the somewhat improper use of the term 'overreaching' even in the case of trusts for sale.

The definition of a trust for sale (section 205 (I) (xxix))

Although the distinguishing feature of an express trust for sale is the instruction to sell, we must now take a much closer look at the nature of this obligation by examining the definition in the Act, which enacts that a trust for sale in relation to land means:

> An immediate binding trust for sale, whether or not exercisable at the request or with the consent of any person, and with or without a power at discretion to postpone the sale.

Some of the elements of this definition must now be discussed.

(1) *'Trust for sale'*. As is sometimes unfortunately the case in the 1925 legislation, this definition attempts to describe something by reference to itself. Leaving that aside however, the word 'trust' means that there must be a duty to sell as opposed to a mere power. Unless the very phrase 'trust for sale' is used by the settlor, the matter is one of construction and the whole instrument must be examined to discover whether he was issuing an imperative instruction to sell. The difficulty will be most commonly met in home-made wills, because few testators even know that there is such a thing as a trust for sale. A person making a will might vaguely feel that a sale of certain property would be wise, but perhaps is not even sure himself. He might therefore write in his will: 'I think it would probably be a good idea if "Blackacre" were sold' or '"Blackacre" is a valuable property; sell it if you think fit'. In short it might sometimes be difficult to decide whether a duty is being imposed.

The Act does assist in just one case of difficulty of interpretation and that is where the settlor leaves the scales so equally balanced that it would, without such help, be impossible to decide whether a duty is conferred. Section 25(4) enacts that in instruments coming into force after the Act 'a trust either to retain or sell land' shall be construed as a trust for sale, though with power to postpone the sale.

(2) *'Immediate'*. The fact that the trust for sale must be immediate does not mean that there must be a duty to sell the land immediately, for, as we shall see, there may still be a trust for sale when there is power to delay sale, or even when consents have to be obtained before sale. It means that the mandate to sell is presently operative and capable of exercise, even though some person may have the discretion to delay it, and is not merely to arise at some future date. If land is settled upon *A* for life, then upon trust for sale, with *X*'s consent, for *B* for life, and then to *C* in fee simple, there is a strict settlement followed by a future trust for sale (*Re Hanson* [1929] Ch. 96). The strict settlement persists throughout *A*'s life because during that time there is no duty to sell, only a power to do so under the Settled Land Act. The legal estate must therefore be vested in *A*. The terms of settlement clearly show, however, that on *A*'s death the duty to sell arises. At this point, the trust for

sale becomes 'immediate' so as to satisfy the definition. This is so despite the need for *X*'s consent, which might indeed be long delayed. After *A*'s death the legal estate must therefore be vested in the trustees for sale.

Thus the trust for sale is immediate if the duty to sell is presently exercisable apart from the power to delay given to any persons.

(3) *'Binding'*. This word has given rise to conflict of opinion amongst judges and writers. Probably the word was inserted to emphasize the mandatory character which a trust for sale must possess, so as to distinguish it from cases where a mere power of sale is given. Some have been unable to accept this natural interpretation because, since the word 'trust' itself imports imperative duty, the word would become mere surplusage (see *Re Leigh's Settled Estates* [1926] Ch. 852; *Re Parker's Settled Estates* [1928] Ch. 247; Megarry and Wade, *The Law of Real Property*, 4th edn, p.360). Yet the 1925 legislation, masterly though it is, contains many superfluous words and phrases. Furthermore, if it had been intended to bear the meaning that some judges have given it, the legislature would surely not have allowed this one frail and somewhat ambiguous word to stand alone. It would have been out of character with the Act, which is not self-consciously concise but mindful of the busy practitioners who have to operate it. Nevertheless, the view persists that a trust for sale does not exist unless there is power to overreach all interests affecting the land. Insofar as this incompetence might be caused by a previous strict settlement, however, the continuance of the latter is secured by s.7 of the Law of Property (Amendment) Act 1926, discussed on page 151.

(4) *Consents, requests and power to postpone*. Provided that there is a duty to sell, neither the need for requests or consents before the duty may be exercised, nor the power to postpone the sale indefinitely, prevent a trust for sale from arising. Thus if land is conveyed upon trust to sell when the consents of *A, B, C, D, E* and *F* have been obtained, and to hold the profits pending sale and the proceeds after it for the benefit of *X* for life and then for *Y* absolutely, there is a presently operative trust for sale even before any consents are given. It is thus possible for a settlor to ensure that a beneficiary in remainder can enjoy the land in specie if he wishes, by making his consent necessary to a sale (*Re Herklot's Will Trusts* [1964] 2 All E.R. 66). This of course cannot be done in a strict settlement because the life tenant's powers cannot be restricted. The requirement for such a consent may even be implied from the tenor of the instrument.

The power to postpone sale (section 25)

It has just been explained that this is quite compatible with a trust for sale, and this section enacts that this useful power to postpone sale is implied in every trust for sale unless the contrary intention appears. Furthermore, subject to any express directions to the contrary in the instrument, the trustees are not liable in any way for their exercise of this discretion. Neither is a purchaser of a legal estate concerned with any directions regarding postponement of sale.

An example of a contrary intention is provided by *Re Rooke* [1953] Ch. 716, where land was devised to trustees with the instruction to sell it 'as soon as possible after my death'. It was held that this prevailed over the trustees' desire to delay sale. Even where there is a power to postpone sale, moreover, the trustees must be unanimous in their decision to exercise it. If only one wishes to sell, then in the absence of bad faith the land must be sold. All must agree before a power may be exercised, whereas one can insist upon a duty being carried out (*Re Mayo* [1943] Ch. 302). If a settlor, therefore, wishes to allow one person to delay a sale, he would be advised to make that person's consent necessary.

The power to retain the land unsold for an indefinite period has helped to make the trust for sale a more popular way of settling land than a strict settlement.

Consents to sale (section 26)

It has been explained that the need for prior consents to sale is compatible with a trust for sale. We must now consider whether there are any limits upon the need for consents. When consents are made necessary, they may be the consents of beneficiaries, of trustees, or of persons quite external to the trust. The question of limitation of consents necessary may be considered under two heads.

(1) *From the standpoint of the trustees.* The rule is that the trustees must obtain all the consents specified, no matter how many in number and how difficult to secure. If this is not done before sale they will be guilty of a breach of trust, and of course will be restrained by the court if the transaction has not been completed. This rule is however relaxed in two instances. Firstly, if a person whose consent is necessary is subject to a disability, or is a minor, then the trustees must obtain a consent of the receiver, if any, in the case of the former and the parent or testamentary or other guardian in the case of the latter. Secondly, if any requisite consent cannot be obtained, 'any person interested' may, under s. 30, apply to the court, which may make 'such order as it thinks fit'.

(2) *From the standpoint of a purchaser.* If the consent of more than two persons is required by the trust, then, in favour of a purchaser, the consent of any two of these will be enough. The same applies if more than two consents are needed for the exercise of any other powers vested in the trustees by statute or otherwise. Furthermore, a purchaser is not concerned at all with the consent of a person who is a minor or under a disability.

Thus, if the consents of *A, B*, and *C* are required under an instrument, and *B* is a minor and *C* is a mental patient, the trustees must obtain three consents, namely those of *A*, *B*'s parent and *C*'s receiver. A purchaser, however, needs simply to ensure that *A*'s consent has been given.

Other powers of the trustees besides sale (section 28, as amended)

The possible need for consents and the power to delay sale will frequently mean that the land will remain unsold for a considerable period of time. It is clear therefore that powers to make interim dispositions of the land less than sale and to manage the property pending sale are desirable. These are generally bestowed upon the trustees, as holders of the legal estate, by the Act.

The trustees have, in regard to both the land and the proceeds of sale, all the powers of a life tenant under the Settled Land Act 1925, together with those of the settlement trustees, including the powers of management exercisable during a minority. The section (which was amended by the Law of Property (Amendment) Act 1926, s.7 and Sched.) incorporates by reference the wide powers dealt with in the previous chapter. These include, for example, leasing, mortgaging and making improvements within the limits described in the Settled Land Act, and all the powers also which a life tenant under a strict settlement could only exercise with the consent of the trustees. Furthermore, the powers of Settled Land Act trustees under s.102 of that Act are available to trustees even though no minority exists, whereas under a strict settlement they are only exercisable where there is a minority. Such powers include entering into possession and cutting timber, rebuilding and repairing property and continuing the working of mines and quarries which have usually been worked.

These powers must be exercised with the consents of any persons whose consents would be required for a sale of the land, and presumably the same provision for vicarious consents and the relaxations in favour of purchasers also applies. With strict settlements, the powers are capable of enlargement under statute. Firstly, it was held in *Re Simmons' Trusts* [1956] Ch. 125 that the incorporation of Settled Land Act powers included the power to seek a court order under s.64 of that Act. The wide powers given by this section, which even enable the court to adjust beneficial interests, have been considered in connection with strict settlements. Secondly, a further provision is available in the case of trusts for sale which does not apply to strict settlements, but which, however, does not countenance variation of beneficial interests. This is the Trustee Act 1925, s.57, under which the court may authorize the trustees to carry out a wide range of transactions where power to do so is not otherwise available to them, where this is expedient for the trust.

Subject to any express provision to the contrary, all capital money arising from the exercise of these powers must be treated in the same way as proceeds of sale, unless applied for a purpose authorized by the Settled Land Act.

An interesting illustration of the operation of the section is provided by *Re Wellsted's Will Trusts* [1949] Ch. 296, where it was held that after trustees for sale had sold the land they could invest the proceeds of sale in the purchase of other land because this was within the powers of the life tenant and trustees under the Settled Land Act (see ss.75 and 73).

Finally, there remains the question whether these statutory powers may be curtailed in any way by the trust. We have seen that they may be subjected to consents. Such restrictions are valid because the Act says they are. As to other kinds of restrictions, since the trustees are given 'all the powers of a tenant for life . . .', presumably these powers have the same protection in the hands of trustees for sale as they have in the hands of the life tenant under a strict settlement. So s.106 of the Settled Land Act applies, and such other types of restriction are invalid. There is no direct authority on the point, though the problem was touched upon in *Re Davies' Will Trusts* [1932] 1 Ch. 530.

Delegation of certain powers by the trustees (section 29)

The Act recognizes that the beneficiary presently entitled to the income of the land is likely to take a keen interest in its management. That is why the

Settled Land Act chooses the life tenant to exercise the wide powers contained in that Act. In the case of a trust for sale, some outlet is provided in this respect for the beneficiaries, although the legal estate remains vested in the trustees.

The section enables the trustees, revocably and in writing signed by them, to delegate from time to time to any person of full age, other than a mere annuitant, for the time being beneficially entitled in possession to the net rents and the profits of the land during his life or for any less period, the powers of and incidental to leasing, accepting surrenders of leases and management. When delegated, such powers are exercisable only in the names and on behalf of the trustees delegating the powers, but it is the person exercising the powers, and not the trustees, who is liable for any consequences of their exercise. He is deemed to be in the position of a trustee for this purpose. In the absence of express powers, the trustees could not delegate these powers to a beneficiary under a discretionary trust because his enjoyment of any benefits or even of occupation of land derives not from 'entitlement' but from the changeable wish of trustees.

Although these powers may be delegated, there is no obligation for the trustees when they exercise their powers and duties to consult any beneficiaries unless the trust provides that they shall do so.

Satisfaction of the beneficial interests (section 28 (2))

Subject to any contrary direction in the trust, the net rents and profits of the land until sale, after keeping down outgoings such as repairs, are to be applied in the same way as income from investments would be payable after a sale of the land. If, however, some transaction has been carried out under Settled Land Act powers and this has produced capital money, such proceeds must be treated as capital.

If all the potential beneficiaries are of full age and capacity and have become absolutely entitled to the property, they may decide to put an end to the trust altogether, and direct the trustees not to sell but to convey the land according to their wishes (see s.23). Such a direction may ultimately give rise to a division of the land between the beneficiaries, who will each own a part absolutely, or to a strict settlement. The former would occur if the beneficial ownership became entirely vested in two or more as co-owners. The latter would occur if the persons entitled to the entire beneficial interest were entitled in succession, as, for instance, where *A* had a life interest and *B* the absolute ownership in remainder. In the latter case a vesting deed would be necessary to give *A* the legal estate. The difficulties which might be caused by such an instruction given to trustees, and the solution to them provided by the Act, are dealt with below.

Duration of trusts for sale (section 23)

If a prospective purchaser knew that all the beneficiaries were of full age and capacity he might be unwilling to take a conveyance without the agreement of the beneficiaries in case a direction of the kind described above had been given to the trustees, thus terminating the trust for sale. It is therefore provided that as regards the safety and protection of a purchaser, a trust for sale shall be deemed to continue until the land has been conveyed to or under the direction of the beneficiaries. In short, if the legal title is still in the trustees, purchasers are protected and they may accept this fact at its face value. This however is without prejudice to an order of court restraining a sale.

Enforcement of duties and powers (section 30)

We have seen that the Act gives trustees for sale certain powers. Further powers of giving or withholding consents to sales might also be given to the trustees or other persons by the trust. It is the nature of a power that the person to whom it has been given may decide to exercise or not to exercise it according to his own discretion. In this way it differs from a duty which must be carried out irrespective of a person's private opinion. Nevertheless, a decision not to exercise a power might sometimes have serious effects on the well-being of the settlement and there should be some ultimate means of resolving deadlock. This is provided by the section, together also with appropriate machinery for enforcing duties as follows.

If the trustees refuse to sell, or to exercise their powers of management or dealing with the land under the Settled Land Act, or to exercise their powers of delegation under s.29, or, as we have already noticed, any consent cannot be obtained, any person interested may apply to the court, which may make such order as it thinks fit.

Overreaching (sections 2 and 27, as amended)

Since the interests of the beneficiaries under a trust for sale are, under the doctrine of conversion, interests in the purchase-money from the outset, a purchaser of the land takes free of these interests without reference to the doctrine of overreaching. This is so even if the interests appear on the documents of legal title. Section 27 declares that a purchaser of a legal estate from the trustees shall not be concerned with the trusts affecting the proceeds of sale or the rents and profits pending sale. It then provides (as amended by the Law of Property (Amendment) Act 1926, s.7 and Sched.), that, notwithstanding anything to the contrary in the terms of the trust, the proceeds of sale or other capital money shall not be paid to or applied by the direction of fewer than two trustees unless a trust corporation is trustee. This does not affect the right of a sole personal representative to give receipts. If no capital money is involved in a transaction there is need only for one trustee. If a purchaser fails to comply with these provisions he will not take the land clear of the rights of the beneficiaries, although it would be better if the Act had expressed itself more clearly at this point.

There is no power to overreach any interests other than those mentioned above. If, however, the trustees were appointed or approved by the court or are a trust corporation, certain prior interests can be overreached under s.2 (as amended by the 1926 Act, s.7 and Sched.). This device, usually called an '*ad hoc*' trust for sale, is little used. Under the Settled Land Act '*ad hoc*' settlements may be created by absolute owners of land for the purpose of overreaching certain equitable interests to which this land is subject. This also is little used. In any case even under *ad hoc* settlements and *ad hoc* trusts for sale certain prior equitable interests can never be overreached.

Apart from the *ad hoc* arrangements under s.2, the 'overreaching' effect under a trust for sale is thus less than that under a strict settlement, under which certain prior interests may be affected.

Study material: *Re Morgan's Lease* [1971] 2 All E.R. 235

12th March. **UNGOED-THOMAS J** read the following judgment. This summons raises the question whether a tenant's option to renew a lease of settled property was varied and was duly exercised and the resulting contract is now enforceable by specific performance.

By a document of 12th November 1960, and described as a lease, David William Morgan purported to demise four rooms on the ground floor of 16 and 18 Pier Street Aberystwyth, to the plaintiffs for the term of seven years from an unspecified day of November 1960, at a yearly rent of £475 exclusive of rates and charges; and he purported to covenant with the plaintiffs that he would, on their written request made three months before the expiration of the term, grant to them a lease for a further term of seven years from the expiration of the original term, and containing the same provisions, with the exception of the covenant for renewal. The document was signed by the parties over a 6d stamp. The plaintiffs had been in possession with another under a 1950 lease to the three of them. That lease expired on 12th November 1960, and thereafter the plaintiffs continued in possession and paid the rent of £475 in accordance with the 1960 document. The rooms are shop premises and at all relevant times the plaintiffs have carried on the business of drapers there.

In March 1962, Mr Morgan died and the legal estate in reversion of the property vested in his daughter, the first defendant, as administratrix of his estate. In August 1965, she executed a vesting assent to herself and the other three defendants on trust for sale. The plaintiffs, in accordance with the provisions of the 1960 document, duly gave notice for the further lease from the expiration of the current lease, i.e. commencing 12th November 1967. Before that date the plaintiffs commenced proceedings in the county court for a new tenancy to avoid losing the protection of the Landlord and Tenant Act 1954; but those proceedings were stayed pending the decision of this action.

Apart from any question of adequacy of rent it is common ground that: (1) the 1960 document is void as a lease, but operated as an agreement for a lease, taking effect as a present demise in equity (see, in particular, the Settled Land Act 1925, s 42 (1), the Law of Property Act 1925, ss 52 (1) and 152 (1)); (2) on service of the notice exercising the option, an executory contract arose in accordance with the terms of the option.

Consequently the case turns principally on s 110 (1) of the Settled Land Act 1925. It provides:

> 'On a sale, exchange, lease, mortgage, charge, or other disposition, a purchaser dealing in good faith with a tenant for life or statutory owner shall, as against all parties entitled under the settlement, be conclusively taken to have given the best price, consideration, or rent, as the case may require, that could reasonably be obtained by the tenant for life or statutory owner, and to have complied with all the requisitions of this Act.'

The questions which arise are: (1) Assuming good faith within the meaning of the subsection, are the plaintiffs, as against the defendants, to be taken to have given the best rent that could reasonably be obtained by the tenant for life? (2) If the answer to (1) is Yes, then have the defendants shown absence of good faith, within the meaning of the subsection, on the part of the plaintiffs? (3) If the answer to (1) is No, (a) with reference to what date is such best rent to be ascertained? and (b) have the plaintiffs proved that the option rent is such best rent at such date?

Three issues arose on the first question. First, whether the section can be relied on only if there is no defect in the transaction apart from insufficiency of rent. The defendants raise this issue on the basis of *Kisch v Hawes Brothers Ltd*[1]. In that case a lease granted by a tenant for life was exposed to attack on two grounds under the Settled Land Act 1925, s 42, ie (1) that it did not reserve the best rent that could reasonably be obtained; and (2) that it did not take effect in possession not later than 12 months after its date. Farwell J at first instance, assumed for the purposes of his judgment that the Law of Property Act 1925, s 152, would defeat the second ground of attack[2]. That left the first ground of attack, and in reply to that the lessee sought to rely on s 54 of the Settled Land Act 1882, replaced, with immaterial alterations for present purposes, by s 110 of the Settled Land Act 1925. Farwell J observed[3]:

> 'It is essential, in my judgment, for the defendants to prove that apart from the fact that the lease is to take effect more than twelve months after its date it is otherwise such a lease as Mrs. Ramus [the tenant for life] could properly have granted on December 25, 1919, and in this respect s. 54 of the Settled Land Act, 1882, does not assist them.'

This observation is so compressed as to have caused difficulties. It was made in circumstances in which the lease was, on its face, granted by a tenant for life in contravention of the Settled Land Act 1882, because it was not to take effect in possession not later than 12 months after its date, with the result that the lessee did not satisfy the good faith required by s 54 (now s 110 of the 1925 Act). This appears quite clearly from counsel's submission[4] followed by Farwell J's interlocutory observation. Counsel, in the course of his argument as reported, said[4]:

> '. . . the lease granted by Mrs. Ramus is invalid, since it is one which was to take effect more than twelve months from its date . . . s. 54 of the Settled Land Act, 1882, does not assist the lessee where the lease on the face of it is in contravention of the Act. The defendants say the lease takes effect in equity, and it is for them to show that the rent reserved was the best rent.'

Then comes immediately Farwell J's interlocutory observation[5]:

> 'The lease of 1919 was a lease which Mrs. Ramus could not have granted, and it is on the face of it an invalid lease: the burden of proof is therefore on the defendants.'

The interpretation of this case for which the defendants contend was frowned on by Somervell and Romer LJJ in *Davies v Hall*[6]. Romer LJ said[7]:

> '. . . the tenant could not rely on s. 110 of the Settled Land Act, 1925, because, as I have already said, it could not be said of him that he was a person acting in good faith, the lease, on the face of it, being an improper one . . . Certainly I do not think that [FARWELL J] was suggesting as a general proposition that where an attack is made on a lease which has been granted by a tenant for life for reasons other than insufficiency of rent, the lessee cannot rely on s. 110. In my opinion, he could do so, provided that he had acted in good faith.'

I respectfully agree.

The second issue on the first question was whether s 110 is only available where the transaction has been completed and is not still the subject of a contract which is

---

1 [1935] Ch 102, [1934] All ER Rep 730
2 [1935] Ch at 109, 110, [1934] All ER Rep at 733, 734
3 [1935] Ch at 109, [1934] All ER Rep at 734
4 [1935] Ch at 105, 106
5 [1935] Ch at 106
6 [1954] 2 All ER 330, [1954] 1 WLR 855
7 [1954] 2 All ER at 334, [1954] 1 WLR at 861

executory. The defendants urged that in the clauses of the definition subsection of the Settled Land Act, i e s 117 (1), the clauses do not, in terms, extend to include or cover an executory contract in the definitions of the words 'lease' or 'disposition' appearing in s 110 (see s 117 (1) (x) and (v)), or to include or cover a person who falls short of acquiring an interest in settled land in the definition of 'purchaser' (similarly appearing in s 110) under s 117 (1) (xxi). So, if the defendants' submission were correct, the plaintiffs would not, in this case, be within the express words of the clauses defining the words 'lease', 'disposition' and 'purchaser' which appear in s 110 (1).

Wilberforce J in *Re Rycroft's Settlements, Rycroft v Rycroft*[8] decided that the 'agreement for a lease', included in the definition of 'lease' in s 117 (1) (x), meant such an agreement as takes effect in equity as a present demise, to the exclusion of an executory contract for a lease. It appears to me, however, that in accordance with the decision of the Court of Appeal in *London and South Western Ry Co v Gomm*[9], and especially from the observations of Sir George Jessel MR[10], the contract created by the exercise of the option would create an assurance of the interest in the property and, subject to good faith, constitute the plaintiff purchasers as persons who acquired an interest in settled land for value and thus fall within the words 'disposition' and 'purchaser' within s 110 (1).

The defendants sought to rely on the past tense appearing in s 110 in 'have given' and 'have complied with' as indications of a transaction that had been completed before the section spoke. But these clauses are not exclusive definitions, and each of the two words 'disposition' and 'purchaser' is described in its clause as a word which 'includes' what is thereafter stated; and the clauses themselves are governed by the introductory words of s 117 (1), which provide that the expressions in the clauses have the meanings assigned to them 'unless the context otherwise requires'. Further, 'have given' must, in the context, be capable of including future payment, since a lessee cannot be said to have given the rent not yet due; and 'to have complied with is capable of referring to having complied with whatever requisitions are applicable as at the date of the occurrence contemplated by the section.

This brings me back to the opening words of s 110 (1), and in particular: 'On a sale . . . lease . . . or other disposition'. 'Sale' is not defined by the Act, but in the Settled Land Act 1882 'on a sale' are words which similarly appear in s 54 (corresponding to s 110 of the 1925 Act), and in s 5. Section 5 provided for transfer of incumbrances from settled land sold to settled land retained; and in *Re Knight's Settled Estates*[11] it was indicated that 'on a sale' in that section was not limited to cases where a sale had been made, and could even include a contemplated or intended sale. Certainly it appears to me that the words 'on a' governing sales and other transactions, as in ss 5 and 54 of the 1882 Act, and s 110 of the 1925 Act, do not merely mean 'after' a sale. If 'after' was meant then it would certainly have been clearer to have said so. 'On a' sale is a vague and wide expression; and presumably deliberately so. It bears, to my mind, a significance approaching more nearly to 'in connection with' or 'on the occasion of' than 'after', and is not limited to a completed sale; and 'on the occasion of' is one of the meanings given by the Oxford English Dictionary for 'on'. 'On a' lease or other disposition would have a corresponding meaning, and would include an executory contract for a lease.

The defendants, however, suggested that s 110 should be narrowly interpreted so as to be limited to completed transactions, on the ground that otherwise it would do what a court of equity would not do in any specific performance action, i e treat as best price or rent what was not so; and achieve performance of a contract in breach of

---

8 [1961] 3 All ER 581 at 584, [1962] Ch 263 at 268
9 (1882) 20 Ch D 562
10 (1882) 20 Ch D at 580, 581
11 [1918] 1 Ch 211, [1916-17] All ER Rep 662

a life tenant's trust duty. Words in Fry on Specific Performance[12], were relied on in support of this proposition on specific performance. But those words are cautiously phrased:

> 'The Court will not generally exercise its extraordinary power in compelling a specific performance, where to do so would necessitate a breach of trust.'

Nor do the authorities quoted in support of the proposition in terms fully establish it. I need not and do not dissent from the quoted passage as a general proposition. It is not, however, directed specifically at all to the Settled Land Acts; nor, even more particularly, to the duties of the tenant for life under the Settled Land Act 1925 (or duties under its predecessor). The purpose of the 1925 legislation is, of course, to facilitate dealings in settled land, and it provides a complete scheme for that purpose. The terms of s 110, which I have analysed, the history of the section into which no such limitation as the defendants suggested has been imported by legislation or judgment, the meaning which the section on its face, so it appears to me, carries, and the omission to include such a limitation into a section which forms part of the comprehensive scheme which the Act establishes, convince me that s 110 should not be restricted to completed transactions as the defendants submit.

I come now to the third issue on the first question, whether s 110 only applies if the purchaser knows that the other party to the transaction is a tenant for life. The defendants' submission was founded on *Weston v Henshaw*[13]. I will now follow and paraphrase the headnote so far as material for present purposes. In 1921 a father sold certain property in fee simple to his son who, in 1927, sold it back to him in fee simple. By his will made in 1931 the father settled that particular property on his son for life with a remainder over. In 1944 the son charged the property by way of legal mortgage to secure certain advances, the charge reciting that he was seised in fee simple of it, and the schedule to the charge describing it and stating that it had been conveyed in fee simple to him by a conveyance dated 29th July 1921. In an action by the grandson for a declaration that the charge and further charges were void as against him, Danckwerts J observed[14]:

> 'I am satisfied, however, that that sub-section [i e s 110 (1)] applies only to a person who is dealing with the tenant for life or statutory owner as such, whom he knows to be a limited owner, and with regard to whom he might be under a duty.'

The passage, unfortunately, does not set out the reasoning which led to the conclusion, and I confess to some difficulty in appreciating what was the relevant duty which the person dealing with the life tenant might be under to the life tenant, as contrasted with the limitation which was imposed on the purchaser by the section. Unfortunately, too, *Mogridge v Clapp*[15] was not brought to the judge's notice. The headnote of *Mogridge v Clapp*[15], so far as I need read it, states:

> 'In October, 1884, one *H.*, purporting to demise as absolute owner (which he believed himself to be), granted a building lease of certain land to the Plaintiff for the term of ninety-nine years. The Plaintiff made no inquiry as to *H.'s* title but assumed that he was the absolute owner of the land demised. The Defendant afterwards agreed to purchase the lease of the demised land from the Plaintiff; but, on investigating the title, he discovered that the land had, under a will, belonged to *H.'s* deceased wife, and that *H.* was only tenant by the curtesy. A tenant by the curtesy has, under sect. 58, sub-sect. (1) (viii.), of the *Settled Land Act*, 1882, all the powers of a tenant for life; but the lease, though complying with

12 6th Edn, para 407
13 [1892] 3 Ch 382
14 [1950] Ch at 519
15 [1950] Ch 510

> the enabling sections of the *Settled Land Acts*, contained no reference thereto; and at its date there were no trustees of the will, to whom the notices, required by sect. 45 of the *Settled Land Act*, 1882, in the case of a lease by a tenant for life, could be given.'

Kay LJ referred to s 54 of the 1882 Act, the predecessor of s 110 of the 1925 Act and said[16]:

> 'Sect. 54 provides that on a sale, lease, &c., a purchaser or lessee, dealing in good faith with a tenant for life, shall, as against the parties entitled under the settlement, be conclusively taken to have given the best price or rent "and to have complied with all the requisitions of this Act". This section confirms the view that in the case of a lessee dealing in good faith the remedy, if any, of the persons entitled under the settlement for any neglect of the provisions of the Act is to be against the tenant for life in his fiduciary character, not against the lessee, and is not to affect the validity of the lease . . . If the lessee knew that there were no trustees, or that the tenant for life had not given the trustees notice, he might, by accepting the lease under such circumstances, be implicated in the breach of fiduciary duty by the tenant for life. It might be said that he was not dealing then in good faith with the tenant for life. Good faith in that connection must mean or involve a belief that all is being regularly and properly done; and if the lessee has not that belief, it may be said that sect. 54 of the Act of 1882 does not protect him against an action by other persons entitled under the settlement . . . my present opinion is that if the lease were otherwise unobjectionable it could not be set aside because the lessee knew there were no trustees . . . it is not necessary to give a decided opinion on this point, because I do not think that the lessee in this case had either knowledge or notice such as to make his acceptance of the lease a dealing not in good faith with the lessor.'

Here Kay LJ, sitting in the Court of Appeal with Lindley and Bowen LJJ, seems to me to treat it as self-evident that a person dealing with a life tenant without knowing that he was a life tenant would be entitled to rely on s 110; and, with the greatest respect for the decision in *Weston v Henshaw*[17], that is the conclusion to which I would come independently of authority. There is, in the section, no express provision limiting its benefit to a purchaser who knows that the person with whom he is dealing is a tenant for life. On its face it reads as free of limitation and as applicable to a person without such knowledge as to a person who has it. There is a limitation, i e that the purchaser must act in good faith; but that limitation reads as applicable to a purchaser with such knowledge as without. So, despite the insertion of the limitation of good faith on the part of the purchaser, there is no insertion of the limitation for which the defendants contend. Thus my conclusion is that s 110 applies whether or not the purchaser knows that the other party to the transaction is tenant for life. That disposes of the first question.

The second question is whether the defendants have shown absence of good faith, within the meaning of s 110 (1), on the part of the plaintiffs. The defendants have rightly disavowed any suggestion of dishonesty on the part of the plaintiffs. Quite clearly there was none whatsoever. It is submitted that the plaintiffs knew, in 1960, that the £475 rent provided for in the option was less than was or would be obtainable under a lease in the terms of the option lease. I am, however, satisfied that this is not so for reasons which, I trust, will sufficiently appear from my consideration of question 3 (b) when I deal with the quantum of rent. However, assuming that the defendants' submission so far is correct, they then, on that footing, suggest that it follows that the plaintiffs were not dealing in good faith. But the plaintiffs did not know that the life tenant was a life tenant, and thought that he was absolute owner. Therefore even if

16 [1892] 3 Ch at 400, 401
17 [1950] Ch 510

they thought that the option rent was or would be less than would be obtainable under a lease on the terms of the option lease, that would clearly not establish any lack of good faith on their part; and if, contrary to my view, knowledge that they were dealing with a person who was tenant for life was required to bring the plaintiff's within s 110 (1), then they were not within it and this question does not arise at all.

It follows from the answers to questions 1 and 2 above that the plaintiffs are entitled to rely on s 110, and their option to renew the lease has been validly exercised and is enforceable by specific performance. Question 3, therefore, does not arise, but it may be helpful if I state briefly my conclusions on question 3(a) and deal at greater length with the questions of fact arising on question 3(b).

Question 3(a): at what date is the best rent to be ascertained? In 1887, in *Gas, Light and Coke Co v Towse*[18] it was decided that where there was a covenant for renewal in a lease made under a power of granting leases in possession at the best rent, the best rent has to be ascertained as at the date of the new lease made under the covenant, and not at the date of the covenant. As I read the case, it turned on the construction of the power and the best rent to which it referred.

In 1889, the Settled Land Act 1882 was amended to enable any building lease, and any agreement for a building lease, to contain an option, exercisable within ten years, to purchase the land leased at the price fixed at the time of the making of the lease or agreement for the lease, and to be the best price reasonably obtainable. This seems to me to state clearly, in express terms, that the price is fixed at the time of the lease, or the agreement for a lease, and not at the time of the exercise of the option to purchase or of the purchase. Section 51 of the Settled Land Act 1925 replaces s 2 of the Settled Land Act 1889, and extends it to options to take leases whilst preserving the ten year period, and the requirement of best price or, under the 1925 Act, rent 'fixed at the time of the granting of the option'. In *Re Rycroft's Settlements*[19] Wilberforce J held, on the construction of s 90 (1) (iii), which empowered the tenant for life to contract to make a lease 'but so that the lease be in conformity with this Act', that it related to executory agreements, but that the lease had to be in conformity with the Act when it came to be granted. This decision was made in accordance with *Gas, Light and Coke Co v Towse*[18], to which Wilberforce J referred. It was not concerned with, and did not refer to, s 51 of the 1925 Act, or its predecessor, s 2 of the 1889 Act.

However, it follows from these cases, and the wording of s 90 (1) (iii) of the Settled Land Act 1925, that an executory contract for a lease can only be made if the lease conforms with the Act in respect of (inter alia) best rent reasonably obtainable when the lease is granted. Section 51, however, deals specifically with options and best price or rent under them, as contrasted with the more general provision of s 90 (1) (iii) applicable to executory contracts and the requirements for leases thereunder. For my part, I have little difficulty in reading s 51 apart from, or if need be in the case of options, as prevailing over s 90 (1) (iii). It is not difficult to see business considerations which would be to the advantage of those interested under the settlement in thus treating options exercisable subject to the safeguard of a limited period for their exercise. So my conclusion is that the best rent is to be ascertained as at 1960, when the option was granted.

Question 3(b): was the option rent the best rent at 1960? I had the advantage of evidence from two valuers, Mr Griffiths for the plaintiffs and Mr Hackett for the defendants. [His Lordship then reviewed the evidence of the valuers and concluded:] To estimate the best obtainable rent is certainly not free from difficulty, but doing the best I can I, for my part, conclude that £475 in 1960 satisfies the

---

18 (1887) 35 Ch D 519

19 [1961] 3 All ER 581, [1962] Ch 263

requirement of the Settled Land Act 1925, s 42 (i) (ii) as being 'the best rent that can reasonably be obtained, regard being had . . . to the circumstances of the case'.

Order for specific performance.

Solicitors: *Horace W Davies & Co,* agents for *D Emrys Williams & Co,* Aberystwyth (for the plaintiffs); *Batchelor, Fry, Coulson & Burder*, agents for *E G Seagroatt & Co*, Birmingham (for the defendants).

Jacqueline Metcalfe Barrister.

Questions

1 *What is the authority of Weston v. Henshaw [1950] Ch. 510 in view of Re Morgan's Lease [1971] 2 All E.R. 235?*
See G. C. Cheshire and E. H. Burn's Modern Law of Real Property (Butterworth, 13th edn, 1982) p.760.

2 *What would be the advantages of merging the categories of the strict settlement and the settlement by way of express trust for sale?*

3 *Discuss the extent to which the 1925 legislation, as it affected strict settlements, was principally aimed at facilitating conveyancing.*

4 *John, sole fee simple owner of 1 Railway Crescent, has recently died. His will, drafted without legal advice, states: 'I would like my wife Lucy to stay on at the Terrace for as long as she wishes. After that it shall go to my daughter Isobel'. What are the rights of Lucy and Isobel?*

Chapter Ten

The rules against perpetuities and accumulations

Introduction: reasons for the rules

The difference between vested and contingent interests

Where Peter, Joseph and John live there is a tennis court. Some time ago, Peter and Joseph were given a tennis racquet each. John was promised one if he passes an examination next year. At the moment Peter is playing tennis on the court with a friend. Joseph would like to play with his friend also, but since there is only one court he must wait until later in the day. If I ask who owns a tennis racquet Peter and Joseph will both answer yes. John will say no. Now return to land law.

Suppose the land is settled upon Peter for life with remainder for life to Joseph and remainder in fee simple to John when he marries, with ultimate remainder over. If I ask who owns an interest in the land at this moment, Peter and Joseph will answer 'yes' and John 'no'. It is true that Joseph is not entitled to possession of the land yet, by virtue of that interest, because Peter is now in occupation, but his interest is none the less a present interest. He can, for instance, sell or mortgage it to another person, just as surely as he could sell or pawn his tennis racquet even though there is someone else in possession of the court. John, however, has no interest at all in the land at the moment and might never have, in the same way that he has no tennis racquet. In both cases, his acquisition of those things depends upon contingencies, namely, passing an examination and getting married. A mere prospect of having an interest in land in this way is called a 'contingent interest'.

When, in the example given above, Peter dies, Joseph's interest comes into, or 'vests' in possession. When John marries his interest springs into being or 'vests' in interest. This is the very nativity of his interest which he now for the first time owns, even though the law has long recognized that even a prospect of an interest is a saleable asset and may be disposed of (L.P.A. 1925, s.4). When the word 'vests' is used without additional words it bears the latter of these two meanings and it will be so used throughout this chapter. In short, 'vested' means the opposite of 'contingent', that is free of any conditions precedent to an interest coming into being. It will be explained how vitally important it is to know whether an interest is contingent and that special strict rules apply to such interests; the first task, however, is to learn how to discover whether an interest is contingent or not. In the example above, John's interest clearly is so, but in some cases the element of contingency is less obvious.

An interest is contingent unless three requirements are satisfied. Firstly, the identity of the beneficiary must be ascertained. Secondly, the size of the interest which he is to take must be finally settled. Thirdly, any conditions precedent imposed upon the grant of the interest must have been satisfied. These must now be discussed.

(1) *The beneficiary must be identified*. It is not enough that the beneficiary is alive. He must be able to show that in every way he satisfies the description of the beneficiary used in the gift. Thus in the case of a grant to 'the survivor of *A* and *B*', neither owns the interest until the other has died. Similarly, if a grant is made to *A* for life with remainder for life to any wife he might marry, the second life interest does not arise until *A* has married even though he plans to marry *B* in a week's time.
(2) *The quantum of the interest must be finally settled*. Two factors constitute the quantum of an interest in property. Firstly, there is the nature or duration of the interest itself. This is lacking in a limitation such as 'to *A* for such interest as *X* shall appoint'. Not until *X* appoints a particular interest such as a life interest does *A*'s interest vest. Secondly, although the nature of the interest might be established, it might have to be shared amongst a certain class of beneficiaries. In that case, the size of the share of each will not finally be known until it is known how many persons will make up the class: if a gift is made 'to all the children of *A* equally for life', the size of each share will depend on how many children *A* ultimately has. Not until all his children are born, therefore, does the gift vest in favour of any of them.
(3) *Any conditions precedent must be satisfied*. An example of this type of contingency was given above in the limitation to John in fee simple upon his marriage. The interest remains contingent until that condition is satisfied. Another common example of a condition precedent is the grant of an interest to a person when he reaches a certain age.

A gift might be subject to more than one of these three kinds of contingency. In that case it does not vest until the last of them has been satisfied. Sometimes, however, the one event might accomplish this, as in a grant 'to the first son of *A* to marry'. Here the marriage of a son identifies the beneficiary and fulfils the condition. When several interests follow each other consecutively each limitation must be separately and rigorously tested by applying all the three tests described above. Provided that this is done the diagnosis of a contingent interest is a simple matter.

The problem created by contingent interests

We have seen that in the past when successive interests were created in land a serious problem of inalienability could result because a long time might elapse before there was a person capable of disposing of the fee simple absolute in possession. So far as the land itself is concerned, the problem was solved by providing for the overreaching of those interests and by equipping the life tenant with a power of sale which cannot be fettered.

Overreaching does not eradicate the problem of inalienability; it merely transplants it from the land to the purchase-money and the investments which represent it, so that the capital cannot be dealt with by anyone as absolute owner for a very long time, even though it may be dealt with by trustees. The general policy of the law has always been against removing property of any kind from free commerce for too long a period. Some examples of this policy have already been discussed, such as the barring of the entail and the illegality of conditions subsequent which prevent alienation. Before considering a further example which is the subject of this chapter, it must first be shown that where successive interests are created in property it is the contingent rather than the vested interests which cause serious inalienability.

In the case of vested interests the beneficiary is always in being and identified—see the first rule as to vesting discussed above. This means that there is a practical limitation upon the extent to which successive vested interests may be created and, therefore, upon the extent to which the property may be tied up. For instance, if a settlor wishes to keep property within his family for an indefinite time it is not through the grant of vested interests that he can do so. Having granted life interests to his sons and such grandsons as are already living, he has reached the limits to which he can go. If he wishes to grant any interest to unborn persons it follows that they must be contingent interests. That is not to say that there is any numerical limit to the number of vested interests which may be granted; he can give a life interest to *A*, followed by a life interest to *B* and so on successively to *Z*. All these twenty-six interests are vested; only possession is postponed in twenty-five of them. But the very fact that they are all given to living people necessarily means that they will all be exhausted in the space of an ordinary lifetime, give or take a few years, for twenty-six people do not live substantially longer than one or two. Many of them might not live to enjoy their interests in possession, but the application of the three tests clearly shows that even the interest given to *Z* was vested from the beginning.

While vested interests tie property up they cannot do so for a very long time. In the example above, if the ultimate remainder to *Z* had been granted to a living person, the property would have been fully disposable again within a human life span. The use of contingent interests, however, which have no such natural time boundaries, may, if unrestricted, cut deep into the future and tie land up indefinitely. One single example is enough to show this. A settlor might attempt to grant property 'to my son *A* for life, then to his eldest son for life, then to the eldest son of the eldest son of *A* for life . . .' and so on. The first interest to *A* is vested but, if *A* has no son yet, the next and all the following gifts given by reference to the formula of successive eldest sons are contingent because the intended beneficiary is unborn in each case. Such a settlement might delay the final vesting of the property in a beneficiary absolutely for hundreds of years and therefore constitute a most serious problem of inalienability.

The law has developed a rule designed to prevent this, known as 'the rule against perpetuities'. In so doing, it has recognized that settlors justifiably wish to endow their families, and that some kind of compromise as to the limits to which property may be fettered in this way is desirable. Since vested interests do not raise a serious problem of inalienability the rule does not apply to them at all. The rule took many years to develop, but the case of *Cadell* v. *Palmer* (1833), 1 Cl. & F. 372, brought it to maturity. Some of the technicalities of the rule, however, have proved a trap and have caused hardship to beneficiaries. Some of these have been radically dealt with by the Perpetuities and Accumulations Act of 1964 so that, although the substance of the rule is still the same, the considerable reforms justify us in referring to the changed law as the 'new rule'. Since the Act applies only to instruments coming into operation after 15th July 1964 (with the exception of two retrospective provisions), the old rule will be still needed for many years to come for assessing the validity of instruments operating before that date. Furthermore, the new reforms are engrafted onto the stock of the old rule, which must be mastered for this reason also. Both rules apply to all forms of property.

The old rule will be first considered; then the new rule will be examined separately, but by reference to it. Finally, the related subject of accumulations will be explained.

The old rule against perpetuities

The rule

An interest which is capable of vesting later than twenty-one years after the end of some specified life or lives in being when the instrument creating it came into operation is void. The two main components of the rule must now be analyzed. The meaning of the word 'vest' has already been explained.

(1) *Life or lives in being*. The period allowed by the rule is a compromise based on the ordinary settlement; a lifetime and the period of minority have been familiar working units of time in family affairs. All persons who are alive or conceived when the instrument creating the interest comes into operation are eligible lives in being (see *Long* v. *Blackall* (1977), 7 Term. Rep. 100). A will only comes into operation on the death of the testator, even though it was executed many years before that. Only human beings and not animals or corporations may be lives in being (*Re Kelly* [1932] Ir. R. 255).

Although all persons are eligible to be lives in being, the only people who may be considered in testing the validity of a gift are those who are expressly so designated in the grant, or whose length of life has such a bearing on the time at which the interests of the beneficiaries will vest that they are lives in being by implication; in short, those whose lives validate the gift (see 86 L.Q.R. 357, at p.363). A person who is only casually mentioned in a grant may not be considered as a life in being. On the other hand, a person may be a life in being whether or not he is also a beneficiary under a particular limitation. For the purposes of the rule a conceived child may be treated as a life in being.

There is no limit to the number of lives in being that may be appointed or implied and persons of any age may be chosen, for it has been remarked that a hundred candles lit together will not significantly outlast one single candle. Thus in *Re Leverhulme* (No.2) [1943] 2 All E.R. 274 under a will coming into operation in 1925, the lives designated were those descendants of Queen Victoria living at the testator's death. These numbered over one hundred. The appointment was held valid. This particular device, used because it is relatively easy to ascertain whether royal persons are alive or dead, is known as the 'Royal lives clause'. If, however, so many are designated that it becomes 'substantially impracticable to ascertain the date of the extinction of the lives' there will be a failure for uncertainty (see the remarks of Astbury, J., in *Re Villar* [1929] 1 Ch. 243). If there are no valid express or implied lives in being the period for vesting is twenty-one years only. Where there are such lives the period lasts for twenty-one years from the death of the last survivor. These principles must now be illustrated by examples.

An example of expressly designated lives in being would be a grant 'to all the grandchildren of *X* who are alive twenty-one years after the death of the survivor of *A*, *B*, *C* and *D*'. Here the lives are clearly used to control the time at which the gift shall vest. But the mere mention of a person's name in a gift does not necessarily constitute him a life in being, as for instance where it appears merely casually or for some other function. In a gift 'to the first of my children to break *A*'s record for the hundred metres', *A* is not a life in being, even though he is alive, for his name is used to describe a standard of performance and not to control a time of vesting. Frequently there will be no express designation of lives in being and indeed sometimes this will not be necessary, for the persons in question, whether mentioned or not, will be very clearly involved by implication. If a testator leaves property 'to all my grandchildren equally', his children will all be lives in being, for they must all have been born by the time of his death and the reference to grandchildren presupposes children. There is no need for him to state the obvious by writing 'to such of my grandchildren as are born during the lives of my children'. Of course, such persons must be in existence at the time of the instrument coming into operation so that in a similar gift *inter vivos* children born after that time would not be lives in being.

In the same way a gift 'to the children of *A*' would constitute *A* a life in being, because his death is the event which finally enumerates the beneficiaries and marks the vesting time. Further examples will appear throughout this chapter.

(2) *Incapability of the interest vesting outside the period.* The strangest characteristic of the old rule is that it is not enough that the interest vests within the perpetuity period; it must, from the very date on which the instrument came into operation, bear no possibility, no matter how remote or curious, of ever vesting outside the period. Even though you are examining the limitation many years after that date, you have to transport yourself back in time to the date when the instrument came into operation, ignore all subsequent events, and ask: 'Is there one single chance of this interest not being vested by the end of the period?'. If there is such a chance, the gift is void even though it did in fact vest within the period. In short, it is possible, not actual, events which count and you cannot 'wait and see' whether vesting takes place within the period. The vigour with which this principle is applied and the absurd results which it can produce can only be appreciated by examining some of the decided cases.

In *Re Wood* [1894] 3 Ch. 381 a gift was made to such of the testator's issue as should be living when certain quarries were worked out. The gift was held void even though in the event they were worked out within six years. The lives in being by implication were his children. The contingency of the gift lay in the fact that the beneficiaries would not be identified until the quarries were exhausted. Ignoring the fact that the quarries were finished inside the perpetuity period, the judge, from the standpoint in time of the testator's death, had to ask whether there was a possibility, however remote, that the workings would not be completed during the lifetimes of these lives in being and a further twenty-one years, for not until that event occurred would the gift vest. There clearly was such a possibility.

The remoteness of the possibility was even more pronounced in *Re Dawson* (1888), 39 Ch.D. 155. The relevant part of the gift was to such of the grandchildren of *A* as should reach twenty-one. The gift was clearly contingent until all the grandchildren which *A* could possibly have had either reached twenty-one or died before that age, because not until the last born had done one or other of these would the shares of any beneficiary be finally ascertained. Your approach in testing the validity of limitations should be to discover just one single possibility of the gift vesting outside the period. One is enough to avoid the gift as one prick will collapse a whole balloon. Let us apply this method to this case.

If *A* had been dead at the date of the grant, the gift would have been good. All her children would have been implied lives in being, and, since she was dead, there would have been no chance of her having any more children after the date of the grant who would not have been lives in being. We could then have said that all the grandchildren must have been born within the lifetimes of the lives in being who were their parents. It follows that the contingency, the attaining of majority by the youngest of these, must have occurred within twenty-one years after the death of the last life in being.

A, however, was not dead at the date of the gift; so it was possible that she might have a child, *X*, after the date of the gift who would, therefore, not be a life in being. It was also possible that *A* and all the other lives in being might die, leaving *X* only alive. *X* might some time later have a child. Such a child, who would be a grandchild of *A*, clearly might not reach twenty-one until more than twenty-one years after the death of the last life in being, for *X* himself would not be a life in being. Even such a remote possibility of vesting outside the period made the gift void. Yet the case provides even more spectacular illustration that it is possibilities, not probabilities or even actualities, that count. The real cause for the failure of gifts to the grandchildren of a living person is, as shown above, that this living person might have a child after the gift who would not constitute a life in being. In *Re Dawson* it was argued that, although alive at the date of the gift, *A* could not have another child because she was in her sixties. The argument was rejected, but strangely, although under the old rule the law ignored physical impossibilities it takes account of legal ones, so that a person under sixteen years of age is considered incapable of having children since it is not lawful to marry under that age (*Re Gaite's Will Trusts* [1949] 1 All E.R. 459).

A limitation which has frequently caused gifts to fail is that used in *Re Frost* (1889), 43 Ch.D. 246. Land was devised to *A* for life, then to any husband she might marry for life, and then in remainder to such of their children as should be living at the death of the survivor of these two. Each gift must be scrutinized in the light of the rule. The gift to *A* is vested since none of the three elements of contingency is present. The beneficiary and the quantum of the interest are identified and there are no conditions precedent to be fulfilled. The second limitation is contingent because the beneficiary was not identified at the date of the instrument. The event which will cause the gift to vest is the marriage of *A*, for then a husband of *A* will exist. We must now ask whether this might possibly occur outside the period. The only life in being is *A*, who is so by implication. Her future husband is not a life in being, firstly because he might not even be born at that time, but also because even if born, he is not identified in the instrument. The gift cannot vest outside the period because the marriage of *A* cannot take place outside her lifetime. So, although contingent, the second limitation is valid. This validity, it need hardly be added, means only validity from the viewpoint of the perpetuity rule, for if *A* never marries at all, clearly no one benefits from the grant.

The third limitation is contingent because the beneficiaries do not even exist at the date of the instrument. Their identification will only be complete when *A* and the husband she might marry are both dead. The grant does not contemplate all the children of the marriage necessarily benefiting, but only those outliving both parents. This means that even after the death of one parent, the class is not finally enumerated because reductions might occur before the death of the survivor. *A* is the only life in being for the same reasons as stated above. The vesting event is the death of the survivor of *A* and her possible future spouse. The question is whether there is the remotest possibility of the survivor of the two dying more than twenty-one years after *A*'s death. There clearly is. *A* might marry *B* and they might have children. *A* might die first, thus reducing the perpetuity period to a further twenty-one years only. *B* might then die twenty-two years later, thus for the first time identifying the eligible children. This third limitation was, therefore, void.

If the third limitation had been simply in favour of 'the children of such marriage', rather than the children who survived both parents, it would have been valid. The vesting event would have been the birth of the last child of the marriage, and this, or, of course, its conception, must occur within the lifetime of *A*, who is a life in being. All the children, and hence all the shares, will be identified at that time. It is quite true that the children will not be able to enjoy their share until their father's life interest has run its course, and this might not occur until outside the perpetuity period. The rule against perpetuities is, however, completely unconcerned with the time at which interests fall into possession (*Re Garnham* [1916] 2 Ch. 413).

Since a gift is not vested until the quantum of the interest is finally established, it follows that, in the case of class gifts, if there is any chance of the number of beneficiaries in a class being increased or decreased outside the period, the whole gift is void even though most of those beneficiaries must have been identifiable within the period. In other words, a class gift cannot be partly good and partly bad. It must either vest entirely within the period or be totally void. Some of the examples given above illustrate this. Careful drafting of instruments however can produce the effect of severing the gift and ensuring that those beneficiaries who must fulfil all the required conditions within the period can take an interest. Thus if, instead of leaving property 'to the grandchildren of *A*', which is a void gift if *A* is still living, the grant is limited to 'such of the grandchildren of *A* who shall be born within twenty-one years after the death of the last survivor amongst *A* and the children of *A* who are now living', it would be valid because by its own terms it only contemplates beneficiaries born within the period.

Even if this intention to limit the class is not express, a class gift might sometimes be construed to have been intended in this way. This construction might occur under the class-closing rules based upon the doctrine in *Andrews* v. *Partington* (1791), 3 Bro. C.C. 401. These rules are no part of the rule against perpetuities, but are a convenient means through which a confined interpretation may be placed upon the class of beneficiaries intended to be benefited, with the aim not of making the gift valid under the perpetuity rule, but of distributing the property as soon as possible. The essence of the rule is that the class is closed when the time for distribution has arrived through one member of the intended class of beneficiaries having fulfilled all conditions for possession. Suppose property is devised to the grandchildren of *A*, a living person, at twenty-one. If a grandchild has reached twenty-one at the death of the testator, then all grandchildren then living will be entitled to benefit provided they reach twenty-one. Those born later will be excluded. With the class severed in this way, an accidental by-product of the interpretation will be that the gift is also good from the standpoint of the perpetuity rule. If, however, no grandchildren have reached twenty-one at the testator's death, then all grandchildren must be taken to constitute the intended class, whenever born. This would make the gift void.

The rationale of the rule may be said to be the solution of a dilemma caused by the appearance of two inconsistent intentions of the settlor. On the one hand, he seems to wish to benefit the whole class; on the other hand, he can hardly wish for the effects of his gifts to be stultified by having to wait for an inordinate period before all the beneficiaries are identified (*Re Kebty-Fletcher's Will Trusts* [1969] 1 Ch. 339). Since the rule is one of construction, it may be excluded expressly or impliedly by the settlor. The strength of the policy underlying the rule means that it is only excluded if the tenor of the gift is inescapably incompatible with it (*Re Clifford's Settlement Trusts* [1980] 1 All E.R. 1013 at 1016). Independently of this rule, moreover, where there is a limitation which offers two possible and unstrained constructions, one of which would lead to an infringement of the perpetuity rule and one of which would not, the latter one should be followed (*Re Deeley's Settlement* [1973] 3 All E.R. 1127). Finally, if the share to be given to each member of a particular category is specified there is not a true class gift and some of the associated problems will not arise. Thus if a person grants ten acres of land to 'each of my children for life', the gifts can vest as soon as each child is born and before the settlor dies.

Even under the old rule, there is an exception to the principle that it is possible, not actual, events which must be considered, and where it is permitted to 'wait and see'. This occurs when a gift is subject to two alternative and separately expressed contingencies, one too remote under the rule, and the other valid. Such a gift is not void from the beginning and will remain good if the valid contingency is the one which actually happens. If property is granted to 'the first son of *A* to become a clergyman, but if *A* should either have no son who becomes a clergyman, or have no son at all, then to *B*' the first contingency is too remote, for it might not be finally known whether a son becomes a clergyman or not until more than twenty-one years after *A*'s death. *A* might, for instance, have a son after the date of the instrument, who would not be a life in being. That son might then become a clergyman twenty-two years after his father's death. The second contingency, however, cannot occur outside the period. On the death of *A*, a life in being, and not later, we shall certainly know whether he has a son or not. The validity of the gift to *B* will therefore not be settled until *A*'s death. If he dies without a son at all, the gift to *B* is good; if he dies leaving a son, then the gift to *B* is void, even though that son never becomes a clergyman.

However, this privilege is only extended to limitations where the two alternatives are explicit and not where they are merely implicit, as in a gift to 'the first son of *A* to become a clergyman, but, if he should have no such son, to *B*' (*Proctor* v. *Bishop of Bath and Wells* (1794), 2 Hy. Bl. 358).

Validation of gifts by reduction of age

The condition that a beneficiary should reach a certain age before becoming entitled to a gift was such a common cause of voidness under the rule that the Law of Property Act, s.163, made special provision for it. If a gift would otherwise be void for a beneficiary or class of beneficiaries because it is dependent upon them reaching an age greater than twenty-one, then the age of twenty-one may be substituted for that age.

This relaxation only applies to age and not to a period of time which does not refer to age. If, therefore, a grant is made 'to the youngest son of *A* twenty-two years after the death of *A*' the gift is still void if *A* is alive at the date of the instrument of grant. If the gift, in similar circumstances, is to 'the youngest son of *A* at the age of twenty-two' then the age of twenty-one may be substituted and the gift will be valid. If *A* is dead at the time of the grant and his youngest son is then one year old the limitation is valid without reference to the section, which therefore cannot be used. The gift will not vest until the child is twenty-two. When the section applies the reduction is always to the age of twenty-one, never more, never less. Although the section has now been repealed and replaced, the work it has already done is undisturbed, so that it will be employed in litigation for some time to come when the instrument in question came into force after 1st January 1926, and before 16th July 1964.

Application of the old rule to powers of appointment

The way in which the rule applies to powers depends upon whether the power in question is general or special. Since the meanings of 'general' and 'special' have been statutorily defined for the purposes of the rule, all other classifications of powers must be ignored in this context. Furthermore, since that definition, contained in s.7 of the Perpetuities and Accumulations Act 1964, is retrospective (s.15(5)) it must be applied to all powers, no matter when the instruments of creation came into operation. This means that it is part of the old rule. This vital definition must first be discussed and then the application of the old rule to the two types of powers of appointment will be explained.

(1) *Definition (s.7)*. A power is only general if:

> (A) in the instrument creating the power it is expressed to be exercisable by one person only, and
>
> (B) it could, at all times during its currency when that person is of full age and capacity, be exercised by him so as immediately to transfer to himself the whole of the interest governed by the power without the consent of any other person or compliance with any other condition, not being a formal condition relating only to the mode of exercise of the power:

> Provided that for the purpose of determining whether a disposition made under a power of appointment exercisable by will only is void for remoteness, the power shall be treated as a general power where it would have fallen to be so treated if exercisable by deed.

All other powers are special. The principle of division taken by this definition is that in the case of a general power, the appointor can sit down and make the property his own by a mere stroke of a pen. This does not mean that he must appoint to himself; it simply means that he must be able to do so. By this test, some powers which might well be special powers for other purposes are general. Thus a power given to *A* to appoint amongst the children of *B* will be a general power if *A* is himself one of *B*'s children, because he could appoint to himself. The rationale of the definition is that whenever a person has complete powers of alienation over a particular interest there is nothing contrary to the rule against perpetuities because the interest is not tied up in any way (see *Earl of Coventry's Indentures* [1973] 3 All E.R. 1). This is also the principle which operates in the proviso to the section. A person who is given complete freedom of appointment except that he can exercise the power by will only, has, during his life, no power of disposal at all, because a will only becomes effective on death; therefore during the appointor's life the power is special because the property is inalienable. At the moment of death, however, the appointor has complete freedom to give the property to any person in the world, provided the power would have been general if exercisable by deed. In short, the fact that at that time the fetters drop away from the interest, even though momentarily, means that it may then be treated as a general power. This type of testamentary power therefore changes its character, once executed.

(2) *Application of the rule to general powers.* The rule applies to general powers in two ways.

(a) The powers must be incapable of first becoming exercisable outside the perpetuity period beginning with the date when the instrument creating the power came into operation.

(b) The interest eventually created by the appointment must be incapable of vesting outside the perpetuity period commencing with the date when the appointment was made. An example will illustrate these rules.

Suppose that in 1950 *T* devised 'Blackacre' 'to such person as my son *S* shall appoint after his marriage', and that immediately after his marriage in 1960 *S* appointed 'to my first son to reach twenty-one years of age in fee simple'. First, the power must be classified and this is done by reference to the 1964 Act, which is retrospective on this particular point. It is clear that from the moment the power is expressed to begin, namely, the marriage of *S*, until it is exercised, *S* could appoint to himself, if he wished, without referring to any other person or fulfilling any condition. This would not be so of course if the power had been given jointly to him and another person. The power may be exercised either by deed or will, for there is no requirement that it should be exercised by will only. The power is therefore general.

The next question is whether the power must become exercisable, if at all, within the period. The 1964 Act can now be tossed aside because, since the instrument in question came into operation in 1950, the old rule applies. In 1950, *S* was a life in being and the power was to become exercisable upon his marriage. This event clearly could not occur outside the lifetime of *S* and a further twenty-one years. The first rule set out above is therefore satisfied. Once *S* marries and the power becomes exercisable, since the power is general, it is tantamount to absolute ownership, so that the rule does not demand that *S* must actually exercise the power within the period. It is enough that he can exercise it as he likes, for at this time the property is out of its fetters and the perpetuity rule therefore loses interest in it (see *Re Fane* [1913] 1 Ch. 404, at p.413).

However, in exercising the power, *S* might do so in such a way that the interest created is contingent, as in the example given. The rule against perpetuities must be applied afresh, but since the property came out of its fetters completely on the marriage of *S*, who then acquired complete powers of alienation, the period may begin anew. Since the instrument creating the contingent interest came into force in 1960, the old rule still applies. On the other hand, we can take advantage of any lives in being expressly or impliedly so designated who are in existence in 1960, and we are not concerned with the 1950 instrument for this purpose. *S* is still the only life in being and to test the appointment we therefore ask whether it is possible for a son of *S* to reach twenty-one more than twenty-one years after the death of *S*. That is obviously not possible and the appointment is therefore valid.

(3) *Application of the rule to special powers.* The rule applies to special powers also in two ways: to the power itself and to the resultant appointment, but in a more stringent way than is the case with general powers.

(a) The power must be incapable of being exercised outside the perpetuity period commencing with the date of the instrument creating the power (*Re De Sommery* [1912] 2 Ch. 622).

(b) The appointed interest must be incapable of vesting outside the perpetuity period beginning with the date when the instrument creating the power came into operation. If a power is special merely because it is exercisable by will only, the period commences afresh and runs from the date of the appointment, as in the case of general powers.

The first requirement is more severe than in the case of general powers, for not only must a special power be incapable of becoming exercisable outside the period, but it must be incapable of being exercised outside it. Thus if property is left 'to such of the grandchildren of *A* as the first-born son of *B* shall appoint' and *B* is childless at the date of the grant, the power is void. It is true that it cannot become capable of exercise after the lifetime of *B*, who is a life in being, and a further twenty-one years. This would have been sufficient in the case of a general power. The power may, however, be capable of being actually exercised outside the period, for the first-born son of *B* might wait until more than twenty-one years after *B*'s death before deciding to exercise it. Once again it is possible, not actual, events which matter. The reason for this additional demand of a special power is that even when the power becomes exercisable the interest does not become absolutely disposable as in the case of ordinary ownership, for *B*'s son can only appoint to *A*'s grandchildren. In short, the property might be fettered not only during the period before it is capable of exercise but also during the period when it is capable of exercise but before the appointment is made. Accordingly the rule stretches its control over this period too.

On the other hand, the fact that it would be possible to make an invalid appointment under the special power does not invalidate it. Provided that the power itself is good, it is only the appointment made which must be considered, another concession to the 'wait and see' principle even under the old rule. Here again, the rule is stricter than it is for general powers, for the appointment must obey the rule from the standpoint of the instrument creating the power. Once again the reason is that in the case of special powers there is a continuing problem of inalienability from the time the power is created until the interest appointed itself vests. There is no intermediate hiatus of absolute freedom of alienation as with a general power and so there is no justification to begin a new period to run for the appointment. The following example will illustrate this.

Let us say that in a will operating from 1950 property was left 'to such of my children and upon such terms as my brother *B* shall appoint' and that in 1960 *B* appointed to child *C* 'when he marries'. The power itself is good, for since it is given to a life in being, *B*, an appointment cannot be made outside the period which begins in 1950. The interest of *C* must now be tested, but since the period for this purpose also begins in 1950 and not in 1960, only lives in being under the 1950 instrument may be used. Since the testator is dead, all his children are included in these. The appointment made may only be one which could validly have been made in 1950. The question to be asked is whether the testator himself in 1930 could have left the property 'to my child *C* on his marriage'. Since *C* was a life in being under the 1950 instrument he could do so, for *C* is incapable of marrying outside his own lifetime. The appointment, therefore, is good. (See also *Re Brown and Sibly's Contract* (1876), 3 Ch.D. 156.)

Although the appointment is considered to be an extension to the instrument of creation and is said to be 'read back' into it, and although only lives in being under the original instrument may be taken into account, nevertheless factual circumstances existing at the date of the appointment may be considered. Thus in *Re Paul* [1921] 2 Ch. 1, *T* left property to his daughter *D* for life and then to such of her children as she could appoint. *D* later by will appointed to her son *S* on attaining the age of twenty-five. *S* was not a life in being at *T*'s death, but was eighteen years of age at *D*'s death. The court held the gift to the son to be valid and took into account the fact that he was eighteen. *T* could have left property to his daughter *D* for life and then to her son at twenty-five 'provided that he should reach twenty-five within twenty-one years of his mother's death'. Similarly, if the appointment to *S* had been made conditional upon his marriage and he had married by the time the appointment came into operation, it would have been valid. If, however, he had been still single at that time, the gift would have been void even though he had married shortly afterwards.

Finally, an example may illustrate the proviso to s.7 of the 1964 Act. Suppose that in 1950 property was granted 'to such a person as *A* shall by his will appoint', and that in 1960 *A* died having by his will appointed to 'the last survivor of all my children'. The power is special because, since it is exercisable by will only, *A* cannot appoint to himself. Applying the appropriate test to this power, we find that, as *A* is a life in being in 1950 and since it is incapable of being exercised later than his death, the power itself is valid, but the only factor which prevented the power qualifying as a general one was that it was only exercisable by will. If it had been exercisable by a deed it would have constituted a general power. Under the proviso, having tested the power itself as special, we may now treat the appointment as if it had been produced under a general power. This enables us to take advantage of a new perpetuity period commencing in 1960. At that time all *A*'s children must have been born and were implied lives in being under *A*'s will. It follows that the death of the last-but-one child, the event which will identify the beneficiary, must occur during the period and the appointment is valid.

Before leaving the subject of powers of appointment, the application of the perpetuity rule to protective trusts should be mentioned. It was explained earlier that in such trusts the trustees are given a discretion to apply the income in favour of specified beneficiaries, usually upon the termination of a prior life interest. This power to apply income is akin to a power of appointment. Its exercise on one particular occasion does not once and for all exhaust the power however. Each application may be considered as a separate exercise of it. This must be borne in mind when deciding whether the power is capable of being exercised outside the period. If a life interest in property is given to *A*, and after his death trustees are to have a discretion to make grants of income to any widow he may leave, the latter disposition is void because the trustees might choose to make such applications in favour of *A*'s widow more than twenty-one years after his death. Of course, if a simple life interest had been granted to such a widow it would have been valid because it would vest, if at all, upon *A*'s death. On the other hand, if the right to an interest which consists of periodic payments must vest within the period it is not objectionable that the quantum of each payment might be variable outside the period (*Beachway Management Ltd.* v. *Wisewell* [1971] 1 All E.R. 1, but see *Re Whiteford* [1915] 1 Ch. 347).

Exceptions to the old rule against perpetuities

The general principle is that the rule applies to all contingent interests in property. Thus the grant of an easement to use drains not only presently passing under land but also 'hereafter to pass' is void because it contemplates easements through drains which might be constructed outside the perpetuity period (*Dunn* v. *Blackdown Properties Ltd.* [1961] Ch. 433). The rule, therefore, must be borne in mind when drainage and other easements are being negotiated preparatory to the construction of large estates which will take a long time to complete. The rule does not, however, apply to the duration or divesting of interests, but merely to their commencement. This is an integral part of the rule, and not an exception to it, but there are two cases in which, at first sight, the rule does not appear to apply to the duration of an interest.

The first is that the rule does apply to the determining event in an interest upon condition subsequent (*Re the Trustees of Hollis' Hospital* [1899] 2 Ch. 540; and see L.P.A. 1925, s.4(3)). An example of such an interest is a grant to '*A* in fee simple provided that the land is always used for agriculture'. When the condition is void under the rule, the effect is to make the interest absolute and not to invalidate it. Herein lies the justification for the application of the rule. What is a condition subsequent to the owner of one interest is really a condition precedent to the owner of the interest expectant upon it, and this is substantially so whether the second interest operates by way of gift over or by right of entry. If land is granted to '*A* in fee simple but if the land should ever become part of Warwickshire then to *B* in fee simple', the rule is attacking the commencement of *B*'s interest, and not the duration of *A*'s.

Whether the old rule applies to determinable interests is controversial, but in one case it was certainly held to do so. In *Hopper* v. *Liverpool Corporation* (1944), 88 Sol.J. 213, property was conveyed in fee simple until it should cease to be used as a library. It was held that the terminating event was void under the rule, that the possibility of reverter expectant upon it was void and that the fee simple accordingly became absolute. This decision presents no exception to the rule, for once again the terminating event is susceptible to the rule not because it marks the end of the determinable interest but because it marks the commencement of the possibility of reverter. Now the true exceptions to the rule must be mentioned.

(1) *Interests following entails.* Since an entail may be barred so as to defeat all subsequent interests, the latter cannot cause property to be inalienable. To enjoy this privilege, the interest must be incapable of vesting after the end of the entail, as in a grant to '*A* in tail and in default of such issue to such of the descendants of *B* then living'. The rule applies in full force to the grant of the entail itself, though not of course to the inheritance of it once it is vested. Thus a grant in tail to the first child of *A* upon his marriage would be void if *A* has no child at the time of the grant.

(2) *Certain gifts to charities.* The rule applies to all original contingent gifts to charities such as 'to Charity *A* when it moves its premises to London'. If there is a gift over from one charity to another, such as a grant to Charity *A* to go to Charity *B* if Charity *A* fails to repair a family vault, then the gift over to the second or subsequent charity is exempt from the rule (*Re Tyler* [1891] 3 Ch. 252).

(3) *Certain rights of entry.* These include a right to re-enter and determine a lease for breach of covenant and certain remedies for enforcing rentcharges (L.P.A. 1925, s.121(6)). We have already seen that the terminating event in an interest upon condition subsequent is subject to the rule and so a right of entry exercisable upon breach of such a condition is not an exception to the rule. Where, however, the condition is the payment of a rentcharge, the right of entry is not subject to the rule and may be enforced even though exercisable in perpetuity (see L.P.A. 1925, s.4(3)).

(4) *Obligations arising from privity of contract.* Between the original parties contractual obligations are not subject to the rule, even though they create contingent interests in land such as an option to purchase it in the future (*Hutton* v. *Watling* [1948] Ch. 398). But where a contract does create a contingent interest in land in this way, and the land is sold to a third person, then if the promisee attempts to enforce against that third person, he is basing his claim not upon a privity of contract but upon an interest in land alone. The existence of such a contingent interest of course attracts the rule. In *Woodall* v. *Clifton* [1905] 2 Ch. 257 it was held that a covenant in a 99-year lease to purchase the fee simple in reversion at any time during the lease was not enforceable by the assignee of the lease against the assignee of the reversion since the option was exercisable outside the perpetuity period.

(5) *Covenants to renew leases.* Despite what has been said above, covenants contained in leases giving rights of renewal of such leases are exempt from the

rule as between both the original parties and assignees (*Weg Motors Ltd.* v. *Hales* [1962] Ch. 49). This valuable and practical exception should be sharply distinguished from a right in a lease to purchase the reversion, which is dealt with above and is not an exception.
(6) *Mortgages.* The rule against perpetuities does not apply to the postponement of the right to redeem a mortgage.
(7) *Administrative powers.* The rule does not apply to any administrative powers such as those of sale, lease, exchange or otherwise disposing of property for full consideration, which are sometimes conferred upon persons under settlements, in addition to their statutory powers, for the purposes of the better administration of the trust. Such powers, administrative only in nature, and not affecting beneficial interests, must be distinguished from powers of appointment, which are dispositive and do affect beneficial interests. This exemption was introduced by s.8 of the 1964 Act but, being one of the two retrospective provisions in that Act, applies to the old rule.

The consequences of voidness under the old rule

A gift which infringes the rule is itself void but we are now concerned with any effect this might have on other limitations in the grant. Firstly, we can say that an invalid limitation has no effect on prior interests. It might be anticipated that subsequent interests are also unaffected and can take effect provided they themselves do not infringe the rule. This unfortunately is not true in all cases, although conflicting decisions and dicta and the imprecise nature of the rules applied make the formation of any principle difficult. However, the following classification of subsequent interests into three categories is generally accepted.

(1) *Vested.* If the subsequent interest is vested then it is always good no matter what limitation precedes it. An example would be 'to the first of my descendants for life who shall join the Royal Navy, remainder to *A* in fee simple' (see *Re Hubbard's Will Trusts* [1963] Ch. 275).
(2) *Contingent but independent.* If the contingency upon which the subsequent gift depends must not only occur within the period, but is quite unassociated with the void contingency in the prior gift, then the subsequent gift is good. Thus in *Re Coleman* [1936] Ch. 528 property was left on discretionary trusts to *A* for life, then on similar trusts to any widow he might leave for life, then to *A*'s children equally at the age of twenty-one. The discretionary trust to the widow was void but the gift to the children was good. The events upon which their shares were to vest could not occur outside the period and were not connected in any way with the void contingency of the prior gift. *Re Backhouse* [1921] 2 Ch. 51 is a decision which runs contrary to this but is probably bad in law.
(3) *Contingent but dependent.* If the subsequent gift is contingent and also dependent or expectant upon a prior void gift, it is itself invalid even though it is incapable of vesting outside the period. This is sometimes called the rule of 'infectious invalidity'. The difficulty in distinguishing cases which fall under this class from those falling under (2) above is considerable because no precise objective meaning has been given to the word 'dependent'. A clear example would be 'to the youngest son of *A* on his marriage in fee simple, but

if *A* should have no such son to *B* for life'. Although the gift to *B*, being for life only, is incapable of vesting outside the period because *B* is a life in being, the vesting event is clearly linked to that of the prior gift. The gift is therefore void. If the subsequent gift is capable of vesting outside the period, as would be the case if the second gift above had been for an interest in fee simple, it would have been void quite apart from the infectious invalidity principle (see *Proctor* v. *Bishop of Bath and Wells*, 184 *ante*).

In short, whether a limitation is placed in the above category (3) and therefore rendered void, even though good in itself, or is classified as independent, is to a large extent a matter of construction for the judge, who will place it in the present category if he considers the gift was only to take effect upon the exhaustion of the prior interest (see the judgment of Buckley, J., in *Re Hubbard's Will Trusts*, above).

The new rule against perpetuities

Important changes have been made to the rule by the Perpetuities and Accumulations Act 1964, which affects all instruments coming into effect on or after 16th July 1964. The order of treatment below will, as far as practicable, follow that of the old rule, so that these changes can be appreciated more conveniently.

The rule

An interest which is capable of vesting outside the perpetuity period shall be void only if it does not in fact vest within the period prescribed by the Act. The implications of this statement must be examined.

(1) *Actual vesting within the period is sufficient.* This is a result of s.3(1), which introduces the 'wait-and-see' rule under which actual, and not possible, events decide whether a gift is valid. A gift will no longer be void merely because it might vest outside the period; it is to be treated as valid until it is clear that it must vest outside the period. The new rule has no application unless the gift would have been void, although some slight differences in drafting could have made this preliminary reference to the old rule unnecessary (see 86 L.Q.R. 357, at p.370). Thus, if a testator leaves property 'to my youngest son on his marriage' there is no need to wait and see because the gift is clearly good in any case. This illustrates how the new rule merely places a superstructure upon the old. If the gift does turn out to be void because, after waiting and seeing, it does not vest within the period, any advancement or application of intermediate income earned by the property is not thereby invalidated. Unless otherwise provided by the settlement, therefore, this income may generally be applied to the contingent beneficiary without fear that such application will be falsified by the subsequent failure of the capital gift to vest.

Recognizing that all gifts must first be judged under the old rule, the Act seeks to prevent the need to invoke the 'wait-and-see' rule by negativing one of the most extravagant possibilities recognized by the old rule. It may now be presumed that a female can only have a child between the ages of twelve and fifty-five inclusive, and that a male can only do so over the age of fourteen (s.2). These presumptions, where applicable, will enable a gift to be valid from the beginning without reference to the 'wait-and-see' rule. They may be rebutted positively or negatively by evidence to the contrary in the case of living persons. An example would be proof that a fifty-six-year-old woman was expecting a child.

'Having a child' for the purposes of the presumption, includes having one by adoption, legitimation or 'other means' but for the purposes of rebutting the presumption only includes physically bearing or begetting one (s.2(4)). A woman of sixty may rebut the presumption that she cannot bear a child by conceiving one, but not by merely showing that she might adopt one. It may be remarked in passing here that in any disposition coming into force after 1st January 1970, any reference to the children of a person is presumed, unless the contrary intention appears, to include illegitimate children (Family Law Reform Act 1969, s.15).

These provisions clearly enable property to be distributed without reference to the 'wait-and-see' rule, and events might prove the presumptions, generous though they are, to have been wrong. In such a case, the court may make 'such order as it thinks fit' for making a just restoration of the position of a beneficiary. As to whether reversible sterilization will create problems in this field in the future we shall have to wait and see.

The application of the new rule to class gifts must now be examined. Firstly, the old class-closing rules based upon *Andrews* v. *Partington*, are not affected. They must, as rules of construction, be applied in the first instance, before invoking the Act. If they operate to limit the intended beneficiaries in such a way as to conform with the old rule the gift is good and there need be no reference to the Act. If they do not so limit the meaning of the class, and if as a result the gift would be void under the old rule, then the 'wait-and-see' principle must be applied under the Act. If the class is incapable of increase at the end of the period the gift is obviously completely saved. It might happen, however, that when the end of the period arrives there are potential class members who are either yet unborn or who still have to fulfil some condition. To meet this event, the Act introduces a class-closing rule in the true sense of the word without taking refuge in the subject of construction.

It provides in s.4(3) and (4) that those potential members in whose favour the gift has failed to vest at the end of the period shall be excluded from the class. Thus if a grant is made to the grandchildren of *A*, and *A* is still of child-bearing age, the gift is *prima facie* void, unless of course *Andrews* v. *Partington* operates to save it, so that the 'wait-and-see' principle must be used. If, at the end of the period, three grandchildren exist, these alone take, to the exclusion of any grandchildren born later.

Finally, the Act provides for a new alternative form of perpetuity period which, like the 'Royal lives clause', may be used collaterally to a gift and thus make it incapable of vesting outside the period, and therefore necessarily valid from the standpoint of the law without reference to the 'wait-and-see' rule. It is now possible under s.1 to specify a number of years not exceeding eighty. If used, this period should be expressly and clearly designated and cannot be combined with lives in being. An example of its use would be a gift to 'such of my great grandchildren who shall be alive eighty years from now which I hereby specify as the perpetuity period'. Such a gift is, through its own self-limiting drafting, valid from the beginning and needs no help from the 'wait-and-see' rule for this purpose, although of course the time must elapse before any distribution can take place.

(2) *The duration of the 'wait-and-see' period*. In determining the validity of the gift initially, in order to discover whether it will be necessary to wait and see, the perpetuity period is the same as at common law, subject to the alternative period of eighty years. Once it has been found that it is necessary to 'wait and see', because the gift is void under the old rule, the lives in being which may be used for this purpose are those provided by the Act in s.3 and no others. Frequently, the lives in being so identified will be the same as at common law but this is not necessarily so. These statutory lives must not only be in existence but ascertainable at the time when the instrument comes into operation. If there are no lives in being under the section, the period during which you can wait and see is twenty-one years only. The persons mentioned by the section are as follows:

(a) The donor.

(b) The beneficiaries, their parents and grandparents. In the case of class gifts this includes any member or potential member. In the case of conditional gifts to individuals, any person who has satisfied some of the conditions and may in time satisfy the others is included.

(c) Objects of a special power of appointment, their parents and grandparents. Where there is only one object and he is ascertainable only on certain conditions being satisfied, any person who has satisfied some of the conditions and may in time satisfy the others is included.

(d) A person on whom any power, option or other right is conferred.

(e) The owner of an immediately prior interest.

Though all these persons must be alive and ascertainable to be eligible, parents and grandparents of beneficiaries under (b) and (c) qualify if their children or grandchildren respectively would be beneficiaries or objects when born, even if not born at the date of the gift. Of course, the parent or grandparent himself must be alive at that date.

Long though this list is, there is one common type of disposition to which it lends insufficient help. This is a gift 'to *A*, a bachelor, for life, remainder to any wife he might marry for life, remainder equally to such of their children as should be living at the death of the survivor'. The final limitation is void under the old rule (*Re Frost*, p. 181 *ante*). If the wife of *A* dies before *A*, the gift to the children will now be saved by the Act under the 'wait-and-see' principle, for *A* is a life in being. If *A* dies first, however, even this new rule would not necessarily save the gift. For the wife, not being ascertainable at the date of the gift, even though alive, is not a statutory life in being and she might die more than twenty-one years after *A*. Section 5 therefore provides that in this latter event the gift may be treated as if it had been limited by reference to the end of the perpetuity period. In short, if the 'wait-and-see' period has elapsed and the wife is still alive, all the children then living share the gift. This will not of course vest in possession until their mother's death; her life interest is unaffected and valid to the end of her life.

Validation of gifts by reduction of age

Section 4 replaces s.163 of the Law of Property Act 1925, for instruments coming into force on or after 16th July 1964, and provides a rule for age reduction which is more capable of respecting a settlor's intentions. Where it is clear at the end of the 'wait-and-see' period that a disposition, limited by reference to the attainment of a specified age exceeding twenty-one years by any person, would otherwise be void merely because of the requirement that an age greater than twenty-one must be reached, then that age may be reduced as much as is necessary to save the disposition. A flaw in the drafting of this provision has now been corrected by the Children Act 1975, Schedule 3, para.43.

Though the age still cannot be reduced below twenty-one, it need not now be reduced arbitrarily to twenty-one, but only to such age (nearest to that specified by the settlor) as will save the gift. The rule applies not only to cases where the beneficiaries themselves are required to reach a certain age, but where they are only to take when some collateral person does so. Now that the three major relaxations permitted by the Act have been explained—the 'wait-and-see' principle, the class-closing provision and the rule now under discussion—an example may be given to show how they operate together.

Suppose that property was granted in 1965 to the grandchildren of *A*, a living person, at the age of thirty. The gift is void under the old rule so that the 'wait-and-see' rule may be invoked. The lives in being for this purpose must be ascertained from s.3. At the death of the last of these, a further twenty-one years must elapse. However, since no grandchild born after this date will be capable of reaching even twenty-one, below which the qualifying age cannot be reduced, they will not be eligible beneficiaries. The extent to which the age must be reduced may now be determined. Let us say three grandchildren exist aged ten, eight and five. The age must be reduced for the whole disposition and not merely for each individual, unless separate ages are specified for different classes of beneficiaries. This means that the age requirement must be reduced for all three beneficiaries to twenty-six, for that is the age which even the youngest will be capable of reaching. Since no later born grandchildren can even reach twenty-one they must now be excluded from the gift under the class-closing principle. In short the rules are applied in the following order: wait and see; reduce the age; close the class.

Application of the new rule to powers of appointment

The definition of general and special powers has already been discussed. It may simply be added that all the general reforms brought about by the Act apply equally to powers. Thus the 'wait-and-see' rule may be applied to the question whether a power will become exercisable or will actually be exercised within the period, as well as to the appointed interest when created. A few further matters of more special application to powers must be mentioned.

Firstly, if the eighty-year period or less is specified by the instrument creating the power, that period will also apply to any disposition made under the power as well as to the power itself (s.1(2)). Next it is important to remember that an instrument made in the exercise of a special power of appointment attracts the new rule only if the instrument creating the power does (s.15(5)), for it is deemed to come into force when its parent instrument did. If an instrument coming into force in 1950 gave a power to *A* to appoint to such of the grandchildren of *B* as he thought fit, and in 1970 *A* appointed to grandchildren G^1 and G^2, the rule against perpetuities must be applied in the following way. Firstly, the power must be classified as general or special by reference to the 1964 Act because on this matter it is retrospective. Whether the power must become exercisable, if at all, and be exercised, if at all, within the period, must be decided under the old rule because the power was created in 1950. Furthermore, the appointment to G^1 and G^2, though made in 1970, attracts the old rule only, because it was executed in response to a 1950 instrument and the power was a special one. In such cases no advantage can be taken of the 'wait-and-see' rule.

Exceptions to the new rule against perpetuities

The new rule applies, like the old, only to the commencement of interests and not to their duration. As explained above, the application of the old rule to determinable interests and interests upon condition subsequent does not breach this principle. The new rule applies to both these interests and also to resulting trusts (s.12), and so the controversy as to the application of the rule to determinable interests is now settled for the future and the case of *Hopper* v. *Liverpool Corporation* (189 *ante*) is confirmed. When the new rule applies, the 'wait-and-see' rule may of course be used to decide whether the terminating event is valid.

The effect of the Act upon the exceptions to the rule against perpetuities at common law must now be examined. Firstly, the exceptions relating to entails, charities, covenants of renewal in leases and mortgages are unaffected, and of course the retrospective exception relating to administrative powers introduced by the Act applies under both the old and new rules. The other two exceptions have been affected in the following way.

(1) *Rights of entry*. Section II broadens and clarifies s.121(6) of the Law of Property Act 1925, by enacting that the rule shall not apply to any powers or remedies for recovering or compelling the payment of rent charges. As to the right of entry exercisable on breach of condition in an interest on condition subsequent, the rule still applies in the same way as it did under the old law, but of course the 'wait-and-see' rule may be applied.
(2) *Obligations arising from privity of contract.* Firstly, the Act has applied the rule even as between the original contracting parties to contracts *inter vivos* which create interests in land (s.10). Secondly, options to purchase any interest in land for valuable consideration are now, with the exception mentioned below, subject to a restricted perpetuity period of twenty-one years only. Neither lives in being nor the eighty-year period can be used, although once again the 'wait-and-see' rule applies (s.9(2)). Thirdly, one class of option is now totally exempt from the rule. This is an option to purchase for valuable consideration the reversion, immediate or otherwise, on a lease, provided that (a) it is exercisable only by the lessee or his successors in title and (b) it ceases to be exercisable at or before the expiration of one year after the end of the lease (s.9(1)). The length of the lease is immaterial and the section applies to agreements for leases as well as to leases.

The consequences of voidness under the new rule

An important reform has been introduced by the Act. An interest is no longer to be void because it follows and is dependent upon a void limitation, and the voidness of the prior gift is not to prevent the acceleration of the later one (s.6). Of course, there might be other factors preventing acceleration. Thus the infectious invalidity rule is abolished and every limitation must be considered entirely on its own merits.

The rule against accumulations

The rule against perpetuities is one manifestation of a wider principle that property shall not be rendered inalienable. A further example must now be considered. Wealthy persons sometimes direct that the income derived from property shall be re-invested and accumulated for a very long period of time and finally shared out amongst beneficiaries. This might be done so that the vesting of the shares must take place within the perpetuity rule. Even though the rule might thus not be infringed, huge sums of money might be rendered inalienable for a very long time. A separate and even more severe rule has therefore been developed to place limits upon the period during which such accumulations, whether total or partial, may be ordered. If the instrument directing the accumulation came into force before 16th July 1964, the settlor may select one only of the periods permitted by the Law of Property Act 1925, s.164. If it came into operation on or after that date there are two additional possibilities available under the Perpetuities and Accumulations Act 1964, s.13.

The accumulation periods

The periods provided by the 1925 Act are as follows:

(1) The life of the grantor or settlor.
(2) A period of twenty-one years from the death of the grantor, settlor or testator.
(3) The duration of the minority or respective minorities of any person or persons living or *en ventre sa mere* at the death of the grantor, settlor or testator.
(4) The minority or respective minorities only of any person or persons who under the limitations of the instrument directing the accumulations would, for the time being, if of full age, be entitled to the income directed to be accumulated.

The two additional periods available for instruments coming into effect on or after 16th July 1964 are as follows:

(5) A period of twenty-one years from the making of the disposition.
(6) The minority or respective minorities of any person or persons in being at that date.

The fourth period includes persons who might not even be born at the death of the settlor (*Cattell* v. *Cattell* [1914] 1 Ch. 177). Susceptibility of a disposition to the accumulations rule, however, does not confer immunity from the perpetuities rule, and the vesting of a gift must obey the old or new rule as appropriate. If the purpose of the accumulation is that of purchasing land, then the fourth period alone may be chosen (L.P.A. 1925, s.166), though this does not apply to accumulations to be held as capital money under the Settled Land Act 1925. Finally, under the Family Law Reform Act 1969, s.1, 'minority' denotes an age less than eighteen, but this provision is not to invalidate any direction for accumulation in any instrument made before its commencement date (Sched. 3).

The effects of excessive directions to accumulate

If the duration of the accumulation ordered exceeds the ordinary perpetuity period of a life or lives in being and twenty-one years the direction is completely void (*Curtis* v. *Lukin* (1842), 5 Beav. 147). This requirement is quite separate from the general rule that all interests must vest within that period which was mentioned above. However, if the accumulation is confined within that period, but is to exceed the statutory period which according to the construction of the instrument the settlor must be deemed to have selected, the direction is only void to the extent of the excess (see *Re Ransome's Will Trusts* [1957] Ch. 348, at p.361). The process of ascertaining which of the periods is applicable is necessarily rather an artificial one. If *S* orders the accumulation of income during the lifetime of *X*, the second or fifth period will most nearly fit his designs so that accumulation may last for twenty-one years. Which of these two is invoked depends upon whether the settlement was by deed or will. The first period is not appropriate because it is that of the lifetime of the settlor only. (See also *Re Watt's Will Trusts* [1936] 2 All E.R. 1555.)

Finally, if at the end of an accumulation period the beneficiary is a minor, the further accumulation necessary pending his majority is not aggregated to the original accumulation and so will not cause an infringement of the rule (L.P.A. 1925, s.165).

The right to stop accumulations

Under the doctrine in *Saunders* v. *Vautier* (1841), 4 Beav. 115, where a beneficiary has an absolute and vested interest in property, but there is a direction to accumulate the income from it for him during a certain period, he may end the accumulation and call for a transfer of the property to himself, when he reaches his majority.

Since it is based upon the principle that because no other person is interested in the property he must be allowed to have full control over it if he wishes, it follows that if there is more than one such beneficiary, they may do the same, provided that together they constitute the total number of persons who have any interest, contingent or otherwise, in the property. There is no right to stop an accumulation if the class of beneficiaries is still capable of growing. In the case of instruments coming into operation on or after 16th July, 1964, however, beneficiaries may take advantage of the presumptions relating to the ability to bear children contained in s.2 of the 1964 Act (see ss.14 and 2). If the beneficiaries in question are 'the children of *A*' and three such children have reached their majority, then if there are no other young children, and *A* is a woman of 56, the three children can claim that together they constitute the entire class of beneficiaries. They will accordingly be entitled to end an accumulation provided that the other requirements of the doctrine are fulfilled.

Exceptions to the rule against accumulations

Directions to accumulate income for the following purposes are exempt from the rule (L.P.A. 1925, s.164(2)).

(1) *Payment of debts.* Accumulations for this purpose need not be restricted either to an accumulation period or to the perpetuity period. Furthermore, the debts may be those of the settlor, the testator or any other person.
(2) *Raising of portions.* If the portions are to be raised for any children or remoter issue of any grantor, settlor or testator, or any children or remoter issue of a person taking any interest under any settlement or other disposition directing the accumulations, or to whom any interest is thereby limited, a direction to accumulate need not be confined to a statutory period. No satisfactory definition of the meaning of 'portions' has been settled in the decided cases and in practice the word is used in several different senses in different branches of law.
(3) *Timber or wood.* A direction to accumulate the produce of timber or wood is exempt from the accumulations rule but must be confined to the perpetuity period (*Ferrand* v. *Wilson* (1845), 4 Hare 344). Various reasons have been suggested for this exception, such as that it is intended to encourage tree planting. There are certain other forms of accumulation which are not caught by the Act, which operates on dispositions or settlements of property only. Such exceptions lie outside the range of land law. Finally a direction to apply income for the upkeep of property is not a direction to accumulate at all, though its effect must be confined to the perpetuity period.

Question

A testator who died in 1963 left a will by which he gave property on trust for all Jane's grandchildren, whenever born, who should attain twenty-one. At the testator's death, Jane was sixty years old and all her children were dead, but she had one grandchild, Rebecca, aged eighteen. Consider whether Rebecca is entitled to the trust property. Would your answer be the same if the testator had died in 1983?

Specimen answer

This question concerns the rule against perpetuities which represents one of several different ways in which the law generally ensures that property shall not become inalienable. The rule was reformed by the Perpetuities and Accumulations Act 1964, though, with minor exceptions, only for instruments coming into effect after 15th July 1964. If the testator died in 1963, the dispositions attempted by his will must be considered in the light of the unreformed common law rule, whereas if he died in 1983 the new rule will apply.

The old rule, perfected by *Cadell* v. *Palmer*, 1833, requires that an interest in property must be incapable of vesting outside the lifetime or lifetimes of some life or lives in being at the time when the instrument attempting to create the interest came into operation plus a further twenty-one years.

'Vesting' means the precipitation of the right of an ascertained beneficiary to a defined piece of property or share of property. It demands that the beneficiary and the size of the interest be ascertained and that any conditions precedent imposed upon the gift be fulfilled necessarily within the period. In short, vesting means ceasing to be contingent. In the case of a class gift, the class of persons must be incapable of expansion outside the period because an increase in numbers must mean a reduction in the share of the other members. The lives in being may either be expressed or implied in the limitation. An example of the former would be 'to all my descendants living twenty-one years after the death of the last lineal descendant of King George V now living'. Such lives must, however, be ascertainable (*Re Villar*, 1928). An example of the latter would be a gift by will to all the testator's grandchildren, when all his children would be lives in being by implication. By definition, lives in being must be persons whose duration of life concerns and governs the vesting of the gift. In applying these principles, the rule at common law is that it is possible not actual events which count. If there is even the slightest theoretical possibility of the gift vesting outside the period the gift is void and the fact that it does eventually vest inside the period must be disregarded. Thus in *Re Dawson*, 1888 a testator left property to his daughter and then after her death, *inter alia*, for her grandchildren at the age of twenty-one. It was held that the gift was void. The daughter, herself of course a life in being, might have had a further child after the testator's death and that child would not have been a life in being. The other lives in being at the testator's death might then have died leaving perhaps the youngest child to have a child which would not reach twenty-one until more than twenty-one years after the death of the last life in being. That possibility prevented the shares of the existing members of the class from being finally ascertained within the period. The absurd stringency of the rule is, however, highlighted by the fact that the daughter was in her sixties at the testator's death. The court, regarding the authorities, refused to recognize, for the purposes of the rule, that she could have no more children and that the possibility mentioned above did not exist.

Applying these common law principles to this question, Jane is a life in being. She must be considered capable of having more children with the same results as were pointed out in *Re Dawson*. Sometimes, such a gift can be saved because of the limited construction placed by the court on the words used by the donor under the class closing rules, known as the rules in *Andrews* v. *Partington*. Then the class of beneficiaries is a restricted one, the effect of which might be that no further beneficiary can enter it outside the period. In the present case unfortunately, the testator has ruled out such a confined interpretation because he has made the gift to all his grandchildren 'whenever born'. Therefore Rebecca is not entitled to the property. If the testator had died in 1983, then the will must be considered in the light of the Perpetuities and Accumulations Act 1964. This Act brought several important changes, but only some of these need be considered in the case of this question. Quite apart from the Act it may be mentioned that, if Jane had died between 1963 and 1964, the gift to Rebecca would be valid because there would not be even a theoretical possibility of children having been born to her after the commencement of the period.

Section 2 of the Act introduces the presumption that a female over the age of fifty-five cannot have a child, though this presumption is rebuttable by evidence that she would be able to do so. When this presumption has been acted upon, and has then been falsified by subsequent events, the High Court is empowered to make 'such order as it thinks fit' for placing the persons interested in the property 'so far as is just' in the position they would have held if the question had not been so decided. 'Having a child' generally means both having or begetting one physically or having one by adoption or legitimation or 'other means', but in the case of the presumption now being discussed its rebuttal can only be achieved by physically having or begetting one (s.2(4)). This means that it may be presumed that Jane will have no more children. There can therefore be no more grandchildren, so the gift will be valid from the standpoint of the perpetuity rule. Rebecca will be entitled to all the property, but only if she reaches twenty-one, which she will clearly do within the period if at all.

In the most unlikely event of Jane giving birth to another child after Rebecca has received her share and of that child having a child, recourse may be had to section 2 mentioned above. If Jane has another child after the testator's death, but before the distribution of the property, then the personal representatives must not of course operate the presumption in s.2. Yet there will be a possibility of the birth of more grandchildren outside the period. Two further provisions in the Act may, however, be invoked.

Firstly, the introduction of the 'wait and see' rule by s.3 has abolished the rule that possible not actual events must be considered. It is enough now that the gift actually vests fully within the period. The section specifies the lives in being available for this purpose which largely, though not completely, correspond to those available at common law. For present purposes, they would be Jane and Rebecca only, since no subsequently born child or grandchild of Jane would have been alive and ascertainable at the commencement of the period as demanded by the section.

The personal representatives may therefore wait until the dropping of these two lives and then establish how many grandchildren Jane has, for these will be capable of reaching twenty-one within the next twenty-one years. Any grandchild born after the death of the last life in being must be excluded, since section 4, which introduces a true class closing rule, enacts that any potential member of a class whose inclusion would prevent the disposition vesting fully within the period must be excluded. However, no grandchild of Jane may take until the age of twenty-one.

Chapter Eleven

Co-ownership

WE HAVE SEEN that several persons may be interested in land consecutively. It is also possible for two or more persons to be interested concurrently. A fee simple, life interest or other interest may be granted to *A* and *B* so that they both enjoy that interest together at the same time. A common case of co-ownership of a fee simple estate is that of husband and wife in the matrimonial home. Frequently, of course, the matrimonial home is not co-owned but is owned by only one of the spouses.

Types of co-ownership

There are three different types of co-ownership: joint tenancy, tenancy in common and coparcenary. The first two of these are much more important than the third, which is rarely met today. The word 'tenancy' here has nothing to do with leases and simply means 'ownership'. (It is quite possible of course for a lease, like any other interest, to be co-owned.)

It is crucial to distinguish between joint tenancy and tenancy in common because the doctrine of survivorship operates in joint tenancy but not in tenancy in common. This doctrine will therefore be explained first. Survivorship here means the coalescence, on the death of one joint tenant, of the entire interest in question in the surviving joint tenants. The joint tenants together constitute one single legal personality, rather like a body corporate whose existence remains unimpaired by the removal of one member. Thus a joint tenant does not own a share or proportion of value of the property as a tenant in common does. The group of joint tenants as such own it all. Despite this principle, however, the profits and enjoyment of the land are the property of all the joint tenants to the same extent.

If an interest in property is granted to *A*, *B*, *C* and *D* as joint tenants and *D* dies, the interest passes entirely to *A*, *B* and *C* and no part of the interest passes either under the will of *D* or upon his intestacy. When *C* dies the interest survives in *A* and *B* only. If *B* dies, the joint tenancy is ended and the interest belongs to *A* absolutely. If such a result is not desired, a joint tenancy can be converted into a tenancy in common by a joint tenant during his lifetime, though not by his will, since a will operates only immediately after death and upon that event survivorship will have already operated. On the other hand, the doctrine works very conveniently for certain other purposes such as trusteeships. When property is vested in trustees it is done by way of joint tenancy so that on the death of one trustee the entire interest survives in the remaining trustees, for it would obviously be undesirable if a share of the interest were to pass to the trustee's personal representatives.

When the doctrine operates it might sometimes be very important to know which of two or more joint tenants died last so as to ascertain who became entitled to the property by survivorship. To take an example: if joint tenants in fee simple, *A* and *B*, both die in circumstances where it is not known who died first—such as in a motor accident—there is the question whether the next-of-kin of *A* or *B* become entitled to the property. The rule is that if ordinary evidence can prove that one died before the other, even though by only a few seconds, this proved fact must predominate, for the doctrine does not require one to have survived the other by any substantial time. If, however, positive evidence fails to prove which survived the other then, subject to any order of court, the younger is presumed to have survived the elder (L.P.A., 1925, s.184). Presumably such an order of court would be used where it is unknown which is the elder. In *Hickman* v. *Peacey* [1945] A.C. 304 the rule was applied to discover survivorship where two persons were killed by a bomb. It seems therefore that the courts will not entertain the possibility of completely simultaneous deaths, because such an event is incapable of proof.

The rule is of general application and is not restricted to the establishment of priority of death in the case of joint tenants only. In the case of joint tenancies it applies even as between husband and wife, despite the exception introduced by the Intestates' Estates Act 1952, s.1(4), for the purposes of intestate succession generally as between husband and wife.

How to distinguish between joint tenancy and tenancy in common

A joint tenancy only exists if the answers to all the following questions are positive. Otherwise there can only be a tenancy in common. The questions should be asked in the following order:

(1) Are the four unities present?
(2) Are words of severance absent?
(3) Is the transaction in question free of all the three characteristics any one of which would, on equitable principles, raise the presumption of a tenancy in common?

Of course what originated as a joint tenancy might later have been converted to a tenancy in common, so this must also be checked. The first two questions mentioned above can be answered by examining the face of the document creating the co-ownership. In the case of the third it will be necessary to go behind the instrument to discover the true nature of the transaction. These three matters must now be discussed in detail.

(1) The four unities

The principle explained above that joint tenants are in many ways in the position of a single tenant necessarily means that there must be unity between them in the following four ways.

(a) *Unity of time.* The interest of each tenant must vest at the same time. Some exceptions however grew up in this rule and it does not apply to wills, so that joint tenancy may arise on a devise 'to my grandchildren' even though the births and therefore the vesting of the interests of the beneficiaries might occur at different times.

(b) *Unity of title.* The title of all the co-owners must derive from the same instrument or, in the case of title based on adverse possession, under a contemporaneous commencement of possession.

(c) *Unity of interest*. The interest of each co-owner must be identical. Thus if one interest is leasehold and the other freehold, or if one is vested and the other contingent, this unity does not exist.

(d) *Unity of possession*. Each co-owner is entitled to enjoy possession of every part of the property, yet cannot exclude any of the others from the same enjoyment. None of the co-owners can identify any particular part as his, for this would amount to separate independent ownership by them. If several persons are joint tenants of property they might, and probably will, allow each other to occupy certain parts exclusively for the sake of their own privacy, but this does not affect their predominant right to universal possession. This unity is common to all forms of co-ownership. The right to possession must be distinguished from actual possession. Co-ownership can exist even though one or more of the co-owners is not in occupation. A co-owner out of occupation cannot generally claim rent from his fellow co-owners in occupation. If, however, one co-owner has been ousted by the other, the former is entitled to such compensation as could be claimed by a beneficiary against a trustee who had taken sole possession of trust property. The purpose to which the trustee has actually put the property in such cases is therefore irrelevant. (*Dennis* v. *McDonald* [1982] 1 All E.R. 590).

(2) Words of severance

Even if all the unities are present, there will still be a tenancy in common and not a joint tenancy if there are any words in the instrument creating the co-ownership which suggest that the co-owners are to take distinct shares in the interest. This does not mean that possession of particular divided parts must be intended, for that would amount to grants of separate ownership of various parts, and we have seen that unity of possession is necessary even in tenancy in common. It means that even the allocation of a proportion of value of the whole will be incompatible with a joint tenancy. In fact, any words which individualize shares necessarily deny the essential molecular singleness which joint tenancy demands. Examples of such words are 'equally', 'divided between', and 'as to one-third', etc. The sensitiveness of the rule is illustrated by *Re North* [1952] Ch. 397, where land was granted to two persons on condition that they 'should pay in equal shares' ten shillings a week to another person. This identification of separate personalities was held to create a tenancy in common. A clear express provision, however, indicating that one form of tenancy or the other is intended will prevail despite the presence of words which are capable of producing severance. If this provision does not record the true intentions of the parties taking the conveyance, rectification of the conveyance can be obtained from the court (*Re Colebrook's Conveyances* [1974] 1 All E.R. 132).

(3) Equitable presumption in favour of tenancy in common

Equity preferred equality and justice to the element of chance operating in joint tenancy through the doctrine of survivorship, and has left its mark upon co-ownership. Even though the four unities are present, and even though there exist no words of severance, tenancy in common will still be presumed in three cases. The presumptions can of course be rebutted.

(a) *Purchase by business partners*. When two or more persons purchase land for the purposes of business or some other enterprise aimed at making profit, there is a presumption that the land is held by them as tenants in common because clearly such arrangements are not compatible with the rule of survivorship. Thus in *Lake* v. *Craddock* (1732), 3 P.W. 158, the principle was held to apply where several persons had purchased land in order to improve it by drainage.

(b) *Loan by co-mortgagees*. When a person lends money on the security of land the borrower, or mortgagor, conveys to the lender, or mortgagee, a lease in the land or, alternatively, creates a legal charge in his favour, which, we shall see in Chapter 15 produces the same effect as a lease. The mortgagee will not ordinarily take possession under the lease, for its purpose is merely to endow the lender with what is one of the best forms of security, a legal estate in the land. When the money is repaid the mortgage ends, and it contains special provisions to this effect. When several persons together advance money to a borrower they take a conveyance as co-mortgagees. It is convenient for them to do so as joint tenants rather than as tenants in common so that if one mortgagee dies survivorship will make it unnecessary to involve his personal representatives in the discharge of the mortgage when the loan is eventually paid. This is often made quite clear on the face of the mortgage deed by the inclusion of a 'joint account clause'. There is, however, a presumption that where several persons advance money in this way, whether in equal or unequal shares, a tenancy in common is intended, because, as in the case of business enterprises, survivorship is clearly not intended to operate. But these apparently conflicting factors can live side by side. Under the Law of Property Act 1925, s.111, the money lent is, as between the mortgagees and mortgagor, deemed to belong to the mortgagees on a joint account, so that surviving mortgagees can give a valid receipt and discharge. However, this does not affect the presumption that there is a tenancy in common, as between the mortgagees themselves. In short, the right to discharge is joint, but the beneficial interest in the land and the repaid money is in common.

(c) *Purchase-money provided in unequal shares*. If land is purchased with money provided by two or more persons in unequal shares, there is a presumption that these persons are tenants in common even though there are no words of severance in the conveyance and the four unities are present. Their shares in the interest purchased will be in proportion to the amounts they advanced. There is no such presumption if the money is advanced in equal shares. This absurdity has not been consciously created by equity. It intervened where it could on the grounds of presumed intention, but in the case of equal advancement there was no initial fissure in the face of the unities to provide it with an occasion for severance. These circumstances raise presumptions of intention which may be rebutted by proof of contrary intention. Such contrary intention may be expressed in the conveyance itself by a declaration of the beneficial shares of the co-owners. If the conveyance does declare the beneficial shares, this will be conclusive unless it is proved that the document, through fraud or mistake, does not faithfully record the true intentions of the co-owners at the time of the conveyance (see 34 Conveyancer 156).

Up to this point, in distinguishing between joint tenancy and tenancy in common, it has been assumed that the co-ownership is at least expressed in the conveyance in that all the co-owners are mentioned. There are two circumstances where co-ownership arises in favour of a person without this. Firstly, coparcenary arises only on intestacy and so there is no instrument of creation at all. This will be dealt with later. Secondly, persons sometimes advance money with which land is purchased and the conveyance is taken by one or some of the persons and no mention is made in the instrument of the others. In these cases co-ownership may arise by implication of law. It most commonly occurs in the case of husband and wife.

The problem is well illustrated by *Bull* v. *Bull* [1955] 1 Q.B. 234. A mother and son provided the purchase-money for a house in which they were to live, the son advancing the greater proportion. The property was conveyed into the son's name only. After domestic strife the son tried to evict his mother by a notice to quit, as if she were his lessee only. It was held that they were both tenants in common in equity and so until sale both were entitled to possession. The mother was a co-owner and a notice to quit was quite out of place. We shall shortly see that in such cases the property cannot be sold, however, until a further trustee is appointed. The requirement under the Law of Property Act 1925, s.53(1), that interests in land must be created in writing does not prevent co-ownership arising by implication in this way, because it does not apply to constructive, implied or resulting trusts. See also *Hussey* v. *Palmer* [1972] 3 All E.R. 744. The inferred trusts now to be discussed will be termed 'implied trusts' in order to emphasize that they are based on the intention of the parties. They are however often classified as 'resulting trusts'.

This inference of co-ownership in equity is not difficult where a direct contribution is made to the purchase price in circumstances which suggest that the persons contributing intend to take interests in the property, even though the conveyance is made into the name of one legal owner only. In recent years, however, in disputes as to ownership between husband and wife, the courts have inferred co-ownership when the contributions by one spouse have been of an indirect kind. A contribution might be made by one spouse to the general household expenses so as to leave the other spouse free to pay the mortgage instalments, or money might be spent upon improving the property, or personal time and skill might be spent carrying out alterations which would ordinarily be done by professional tradesmen. Indeed, there is at least moral strength in the argument that a wife, by spending her time in running the house and looking after her husband so as to enable him to earn the money with which to pay for the house, is equally deserving of a share in the property. In recent years the principle of the implied trusts, a 'cold legal question' of property law, has been strained in order to do substantial justice to a spouse who will be poorly provided for on the breakdown of a marriage which might have lasted many years.

Such provision is, however, more properly the function of the divorce court and should not be allowed to slur the lines of property law, according to *Gissing* v. *Gissing* [1970] 2 All E.R. 780. In that case, the doctrine of the implied trust was returned to its native vigour and held to be based on the common intention of the parties at the time of purchase. Yet the conduct of the parties in relation to the payment of the mortgage instalments may be no less relevant to the proof of this common intention than their conduct in relation to the cash deposit (per Lord Diplock, at p.791). The House of Lords held that such an intention cannot be imputed to the parties where in reality it did not exist, no matter how much one party might evoke sympathy. What is required is evidence of the whole conduct of the parties from which it can be inferred that there probably was an agreement or common intention to share in the property. (See for instance *Smith* v. *Baker* [1970] 2 All E.R. 826.) The quantum of the share, however, is to be determined not immediately on the acquisition of the property but when it is disposed of (*Cooke* v. *Head* [1972] 2 All E.R. 38).

The nature of this common intention is to be deduced on objective grounds as a reasonable man would discern it from words and conduct. (For an interesting though earlier insistence by the court upon original intention, see *Tinker* v. *Tinker* [1970] 1 All E.R. 540.) Little purpose is served by discussing what evidence will or will not suffice to satisfy this test because it is the total inference in every individual case which weighs. Rules of thumb are sucker growths that enfeeble sound broad principles. Thus there is no distinction in law between a direct and an indirect contribution. In weighing contributions by a husband, there is little place in these days of women's liberation for the old presumption that they are intended as a gift to his wife (*Falconer* v. *Falconer* [1970] 3 All E.R. 449). (See 86 L.Q.R. 98.) Furthermore, the mere fact that the quantum of contribution is difficult to assess does not justify taking refuge in the maxim 'equality is equity', for a fair estimate amounting to some other fraction might be a preferable allocation of shares in the property. (See also *Pettit* v. *Pettit* [1969] 2 All E.R. 385).

If express agreement can be shown, evidence of subsequent conduct might not be necessary, for the transaction might be effective by way of settlement rather than by purchase. Unlike a 'purchase' agreement this would not require consideration. An express trust is not effective unless proved by writing, as required by section 53 of the Law of Property Act 1925. Yet equity would count such an arrangement as a constructive trust, and therefore exempt from this requirement, if it would be unconscionable to allow the legal owner to take refuge in the fact that the legal interest had been conveyed to him alone. The scope of the trust and the quantum of the shares of the parties in such cases would depend entirely upon the terms of the agreement actually made, and not upon the inference to be drawn from the subsequent conduct of the parties. (See *Re Densham* [1975] 1 W.L.R. 1519 and 92 L.Q.R. 489).

Unfortunately, the judgments given by the House of Lords in *Gissing* v. *Gissing* vary in their statements of principle. Lord Diplock considered that where one party has made no initial contribution to the deposit and legal costs, and no direct contribution to the mortgage instalments, and has made no adjustment to her contribution to other household expenses which are referable to the purchase of the house, there is, in the absence of an express agreement, no material to justify the inference of a common intention to share the ownership (at p.793). Yet in *Hazel* v. *Hazel* [1972] 1 All E.R. 923, Lord Denning, M.R. held in the Court of Appeal that it was enough that the party claiming a share had made a 'substantial contribution' to the family expenses, and that there need be no agreement, express or implied. He said that he was well aware that some speeches in the House in *Gissing* v. *Gissing* were to different effect so that he had to choose between them, and he would follow Lords Reid and Pearson. Yet Lord Pearson had stated, only a few lines before his passage cited by Lord Denning, that contributions of a substantial nature would raise 'a presumption as to the intention of the parties . . .' (at p.

787), thus indicating that a common intention was always necessary. Lord Denning's interpretation of the case is wide enough to deny it any importance as a precedent.

The implied trust arises from the common intention of the parties to own the property together. It might be the intention of the parties, however, that the contribution of a sum of money by one party is only to be by way of loan. The distinction is important, since repayment of a loan will be satisfied by return of the sum advanced plus interest. The lender will not be entitled to the possibly vastly inflated sum represented by a proportionate share in the proceeds of sale of the property. Constructive trusts on the other hand are imposed by the law, irrespective of the intentions of the parties, where justice and good conscience require it. There are often good reasons for imposing such a trust, but to do so in terms which assimilate implied (or resulting) trusts with constructive trusts surely runs contrary to the principles laid down in *Gissing* v. *Gissing*. This is based on common intention. An example of this confusion can be found in the judgment of Lord Denning M.R. in *Hussey* v. *Palmer* [1972] 3 All E.R. 744 at 747

> Although the plaintiff alleged that there was a resulting trust, I should have thought that the trust in this case, if there was one, was more in the nature of a constructive trust; but this is more a matter of words than anything else. The two run together. By whatever name it is described, it is a trust imposed by law whenever justice and good conscience require it.

The principle in *Gissing* v. *Gissing* applies to all cases of implied co-ownership. Between husband and wife though, the possible harshness of its effects has been nullified by the Matrimonial Proceedings and Property Act 1970 and the Matrimonial Causes Act 1973; this has happened in two ways. Firstly, under s.37 of the 1970 Act, a substantial contribution in money or money's worth by a spouse to the improvement of any property owned by the other spouse, or jointly owned, is to entitle the contributing spouse to a share, or an enlarged share, in the property. The size of the share is to be such as is agreed between them or—and this is wider than the principle stated in *Gissing* v. *Gissing*—as seems just to the court if there is default of agreement. Since, however, the contribution must be 'substantial' it does not follow that the particular facts of *Gissing* v. *Gissing* would lead to a different decision under the section (see 34 Conveyancer 390).

Secondly, s.25(1)(f) of the 1973 Act empowers the court, when making orders for financial provision or for the transfer, settlement or variation of settlement of property in cases of divorce, nullity or judicial separation, to have regard, amongst other matters, to the contributions made by the parties to the welfare of the family, including looking after the home or caring for the family. In substance, the 'warm question' which flew out of the window of equity has returned through statute's front door. The operation of this part of the 1973 Act has now been considered in detail by the Court of Appeal in *Wachtel* v. *Wachtel* [1973] 1 All E.R. 829.

This power is to be exercised so as to place the parties, as far as it is practicable to do so and, having regard to their conduct, just to do so, in the financial position in which they would have been if the marriage had not broken down, and each had properly discharged his or her own responsibilities towards the other. The conduct of the parties is to be taken into account only very broadly, that is only where failure to do so would be quite inequitable, having regard to the behaviour of the other party and the course of the marriage (*Harnett* v. *Harnett* [1974] 1 All E.R. 764). The court should not consider conduct in the sense of allocating blame for the breakdown of the marriage but only where it is of a gross obvious nature. The word 'gross' does not carry a moral meaning but means 'of the greatest importance' (*West* v. *West* [1977] 2 W.L.R. 933).

The court has jurisdiction, on an application for property transfer under the Act, to determine the rights not only of the husband and wife but also of third parties who have intervened in the application to claim an interest. Otherwise, it would be impossible for the judge to know the extent of the property in respect of which he could exercise his discretion (*Tebbutt* v. *Haynes* [1981] 2 All E.R. 238).

The flexible powers conferred by the subsection should not be confined by this or that decision or line of decisions, but the approach of the court in Wachtel's case may be summarized as follows. When a marriage ends, there will be two households instead of one and the 'family assets' acquired by one or both parties for the purposes of the marriage must be divided. These may be either capital assets, such as the matrimonial home, or revenue-producing assets such as the earning powers of the spouses. There must be some starting point in determining what division shall be made and this is that one third of the capital assets and one third of the joint earnings shall be granted to the wife. This starting figure has no legal basis and may vary upward or downwards according to all the circumstances. How this benefit will be realized and granted will also depend upon the circumstances. If, for instance, the wife leaves home and the husband stays, the matrimonial home will be probably be vested absolutely in the husband who will be liable for the mortgage instalments, but the wife should be compensated by a lump sum to enable her to acquire a home of her own by putting down a deposit. This sum can be raised by the husband by a further mortgage of the matrimonial home.

The wide and flexible authority given by the Act comes to much more than a device for dividing financial assets. The power to regard the requirements of the parties and to delay sale casts the judge in a paternalist role, more familiar to the administrative than the judicial function. His new acquaintance with housing provision and relief of need offers him some very 'warm questions' indeed. For an example see *Hanlon* v. *Hanlon* [1978] 1 W.L.R. 593. The question arises whether the legal profession plays too large and too early a part in marital conflict. Accustomed as it is to taking sides, claiming rights and representing the only route to the final demise of marriage, perhaps it is too naturally attuned to confrontation, upon which marital breakdown feeds. Perhaps reconciliation prospers best when there is no potential loser.

Questions as to the ownership of property concerning husband and wife can be settled by a convenient procedure of application under s.17 of the Married Women's Property Act 1882, as amended, by spouses or by persons whose marriages have been dissolved or annulled within three years before the application. The judge is empowered to make such order regarding the property 'as he thinks fit'. Despite previous doubt, this last phrase does not empower the judge to vary property rights as is the case under the 1973 Act. It is now settled that the jurisdiction is procedural only. The court's function is simply to unravel and discover confused existing rights and to give effect to them, or, where this is impracticable, to give a fair ruling (*Pettit* v. *Pettit*, above). It is to declare ownership and not to reallocate it.

In cases of divorce, nullity or judicial separation, it is now unnecessary to decide the property rights of the parties under s.17, since all appropriate orders can be made under the 1973 Act. Section 17 will still be appropriate in other cases such as where the parties are not seeking divorce, or where one of the parties is dead. Section 37 of the 1970 Act has a role to play here in assessing the shares in property to which a spouse is entitled.

The Law Commission's Third Report on Family Property (Law Com. No. 86) has now recommended that, subject to contrary agreement, spouses should become statutory equal co-owners of any interest in the matrimonial home.

The legal machinery of co-ownership

The problems of inalienability and complication in the investigation of title experienced in settlements existing before 1926 have already been discussed. The difficulties caused by successive legal interests were solved by making it impossible to split the legal fee simple and by giving the life tenant an inviolable right to sell it. These difficulties, which existed on the vertical plane in settlements, were present in even more acute form on the horizontal plane in co-ownership, for up to 1926 both joint tenancy and tenancy in common could exist either as legal or equitable interests.

Joint tenancy did not, however, cause hardship in conveyancing as tenancy in common did. An example will illustrate this. Suppose that *A*, *B* and *C* were legal joint tenants and *P* wished to buy the land. Since it is an unfailing characteristic of joint tenancy that there is unity of title, *P* would only have to investigate one title to the land. If, however, *A*, *B* and *C* were legal tenants in common this was not necessarily so and the title of each individual tenant had to be investigated. *A* might have died, leaving his share to his three children equally, *B* might have mortgaged his share and *C* might have sold his to another person. Any purchaser wishing to buy the land would in that case have to navigate his title through a delta of distributary legal interests.

The solution given by the Law of Property Act 1925 is, as in the case of settlements, of a twofold nature. Firstly, simplicity of investigation of title and disposability of the legal estate were achieved by enacting that tenancy in common can no longer exist at law, only in equity. Secondly, the Act rendered land more saleable by imposing a trust for sale in all cases of co-ownership, although there is power to retain the land unsold for an indefinite time. Furthermore, upon sale a purchaser takes a title freed from all the interests of the co-owners whether they all agreed to the sale or not, for these interests are overreached and satisfied out of the purchase-money. These provisions must now be examined in detail.

(1) *Legal tenancies in common abolished.* Section 1(6) enacts that 'a legal estate is not capable of subsisting or of being created in an undivided share in land . . .' The expression 'undivided share' simply means 'tenancy in common', which may continue to exist as an equitable interest behind a trust. Joint tenancies are unaffected and may exist at law or in equity. Striking though this provision is, its purpose is only that of a conveyancing device,

and exactly the same beneficial effects can be achieved after the Act as before it.

If, for instance, a grantor wishes to grant land to *A* and *B* as tenants in common he must convey the legal estate to trustees as joint tenants. These trustees may be *A* and *B*, the beneficiaries themselves. *A* and *B* then hold the legal estate according to the settlor's instructions, namely upon trust for themselves as tenants in common in equity. If he wishes to make them equitable joint tenants, he again conveys the legal estate to them, or other trustees, as joint tenants upon trust for them both as joint tenants in equity.

In either case, the number of trustees who hold the legal estate jointly must not exceed four (Trustee Act 1925, s.34(2)). Where an attempt is made to convey the legal estate to more than four persons as trustees, the first four named, who are able and willing to act, alone become trustees. Any attempt to constitute persons as legal tenants in common is blocked by the provision that this shall operate as if the land had been conveyed to them, or, if there are more than four, to the first four of them named in the conveyance, as joint tenants upon trust for all of them as tenants in common (L.P.A. 1925, s.34(2)). Thus, if a conveyance expresses that land is conveyed to *A*, *B*, *D*, *E* and *F* as tenants in common, the legal estate vests in *A*, *B*, *C* and *D* as joint tenants at law upon trust for sale for the benefit of *A*, *B*, *C*, *D*, *E* and *F* as tenants in common in equity.

This new machinery will cause no confusion provided you remember that the true position of the beneficiaries is reflected in the equitable interests only, that joint tenancies, whether legal or equitable, and tenancies in common are still true to their old natures, as described earlier in this chapter, and that the devolution of the legal and equitable interests must be plotted completely separately. The following table might help to show this.

Legal fee simple			*Equitable fee simple*	
1930	*ABCD*	J.T.	*ABCDE*	T.I.C.
1940 (*D* dies)	*ABC*	J.T.	*ABCXE*	T.I.C.
1950 (*C* sells beneficial interest)	*ABC*	J.T.	*ABPXE*	T.I.C.

This shows land conveyed for the benefit of *A*, *B*, *C*, *D* and *E* in 1930 as tenants in common. The legal title is vested in *A*, *B*, *C* and *D* only as legal joint tenants upon trust for all of them in equity as tenants in common. When *D* dies in 1940 survivorship operates on the legal joint tenancy but does not affect the beneficial interests. *D*'s share goes to his next of kin *X*. Of course, if the five persons had been granted beneficial joint interests, survivorship would have operated in equity as well as at law, so that *X* would take no interest on *D*'s death. On the other hand, when *C* sells his beneficial interest in 1950 to *P* the legal joint tenancy is not affected. *C* remains a joint tenant at law but when the land is sold he will take no benefit, nor will he enjoy any benefit before sale. The purchaser, however, will have the same single title to investigate as he would have done if he had bought the land in 1931. The changes in ownership mentioned above do not cause a ripple of disturbance on the surface of the legal title.

(2) *A trust for sale arises.* Secondly, with one exception to be mentioned later, a trust for sale arises in all cases where land becomes vested in co-owners. This type of trust for sale, imposed by the statute and not by act of parties, is called a 'statutory trust for sale'. In the case of joint tenancies, the Law of Property Act 1925, s.36(1), imposes the trust for sale in all cases in an unambiguous way. When beneficial tenancies in common are dealt with by s.34, the wording does not seem wide enough to embrace all cases in which such interests might arise. Subsection (2) imposes the trust for sale where land 'is expressed' to be conveyed to persons in undivided shares. The word 'expressed' seems to demand that the tenancy in common must be apparent on the face of the instrument. We have already seen, however, that tenancies in common can arise without being so apparent, as where there are no words of severance but the beneficiaries are partners, or advance purchase-money in unequal shares. Sometimes this even occurs when the legal estate is conveyed to one person only. This difficulty has not prevented the courts from finding that a trust for sale arises in all cases of tenancy in common. In *Bull* v. *Bull* [1955] 1 Q.B. 234, the court was able to justify this by having recourse to s.36(4) of the Settled Land Act 1925, which provides, almost parenthetically in the particular context, that an 'undivided share in land shall not be capable of being created except under a trust instrument or under the Law of Property Act 1925, and then shall only take effect behind a trust for sale'.

The mere imposition of a trust for sale in cases of co-ownership would not of itself assist the alienability of the land if the purchaser took it still subject to the equitable interests of the beneficiaries. The essence of the new principle is that he is enabled to take free of them. As with the express trusts for sale, the doctrine of conversion applies to the statutory trust so that the beneficiaries' interests are interests in personalty and not interests in land (*Irani Finance Ltd.* v. *Singh* [1970] 3 All E.R. 199, at p.203 but see *National Westminster Bank Ltd.* v. *Allen* [1971] 2 Q.B. 718) and the Charging Orders Act 1979 s.2(i)(ii). Therefore perhaps it is technically incorrect to say that these interests are 'overreached' on a sale. In any event, it is enacted by the Law of Property Act 1925, s.27, that the purchaser takes the land free of the rights of the beneficiaries—provided that the purchase-money is paid to trustees who must be at least two in number or a trust corporation. This raises difficult problems in those cases where the legal estate was irregularly conveyed to one of the owners only and the beneficial interest of the other or others does not appear on the face of the conveyance but arises by implication. The question arises whether the legal owner has either a right or power to pass the legal estate to a purchaser so that the latter takes free of the beneficial interests.

Firstly, it is clear that the sole trustee has no right to do so and may be prevented from selling or leasing the property if a beneficial owner takes the appropriate steps before the sale or lease is completed, even though the contract has been made. Thus in *Waller* v. *Waller* [1967] 1 All E.R. 305 an injunction was granted against a husband. The legal estate was vested in him alone, at the instance of his wife who was a co-owner in equity, to prevent him selling until the appointment of a second trustee had been made. If, however, the sale goes through without interference, and the purchaser knows nothing of the trust at the time of the sale, he takes free of the interests of the co-owners even though a breach of trust has been committed. In *Caunce* v.

Caunce [1969] 1 All E.R. 722, where a husband mortgaged a house which was in his name only to a bank, it was held that the latter, being a purchaser in good faith of a legal estate for value without notice of his wife's concealed co-ownership in equity, had priority of claim against the property. This would not be so if the purchaser took only an equitable interest, as where, for instance, there is only a contract to convey the interest. In short, although the interests of co-owners cannot be overreached on a sale by a sole trustee, they might well be overridden altogether (see 33 Conveyancer 240).

Whether a purchaser has actual or constructive notice of the equitable interest in these cases is a matter of great importance. In *Caunce* v. *Caunce* it was held that the mere presence of a person, such as a wife, in the property did not constitute notice, for wives or other members of a household frequently have no proprietary interest in the property, and to place the duty upon a purchaser of making enquiries as to whether they have interests would create too many practical problems. But sole occupation of the home by a wife would constitute notice. Formerly, this caused difficulties for spouses with proprietary interests in their homes where such interests did not appear upon the face of the conveyance, for those interests were not registrable. Even the Matrimonial Homes Act 1967 did not avail them, for this Act only allowed spouses to protect themselves against eviction by registering their rights of occupation where they arose merely out of the status of a spouse as such, and not where they were attributable to a proprietary interest. A spouse who had no interest in the house could register, but one who held a share could not. The Matrimonial Proceedings and Property Act 1970, s. 38, has now amended s. 1 of the 1967 Act so as to enable a spouse who has an equitable interest, but no legal estate, in the matrimonial home to register his or her rights of occupation. The general effect of the 1967 Act will be considered later.

In the case of registered land the position is quite the opposite. The House of Lords held in *Williams and Glyn's Bank Ltd.* v. *Boland* [1980] 2 All E.R. 408 that when a husband has been registered as sole proprietor, and the wife has by her contribution to its purchase acquired an equitable interest in the land, then, provided that she resides there, her rights constitute an overriding interest under section 70(i)(g) of the Land Registration Act 1925, which is binding on a purchaser of the legal estate from the husband, even though that purchaser knows nothing of the wife's interest. The principle does not appear to be restricted to matrimonial cases. Although, as we shall see in Chapter 18, the principles applying in such cases differ according as whether the land is registered or unregistered, nevertheless *Caunce* v. *Caunce* must now be considered to be a vulnerable decision. It certainly exemplifies the aims of the 1925 legislation in facilitating commercial conveyancing by the presentation of a clean title. It fails, however, to give sufficient protection of the enjoyment of land by occupiers.

We must remember that if the legal estate is vested in two or more beneficiaries the overreaching provisions of the 1925 legislation apply, but also that no surreptitious dealing with that estate can occur (see 1980 Conveyancer 191).

The operation of the statutory trust for sale

In the case of an express trust for sale, the fundamental rule is that the trustees carry out the instruction of the settlor who has ordered a sale. The timing of the sale will also depend upon such instructions, although statute provides guides if they are lacking. In the case of statutory trusts for sale, such a mandate will frequently be lacking because the co-owners are probably contemplating anything *but* sale. The trust for sale is an imposition of statute, which clearly ought to supply a formula to enable the trustees to decide when the land must be sold in the absence of any other guide. This formula will be mentioned below, but it should be borne in mind that the purpose of the statutory trust is not to enforce a sale but merely to provide conveyancing liquidity and resolve deadlocks. The formula is contained in the Law of Property Act, s.26(3), as amended by the Law of Property (Amendment) Act, 1926. It does not apply to express trusts for sale, unless of course it is incorporated by the settlor in his instructions to the trustees.

The trustees

> shall so far as practicable consult the persons of full age for the time being beneficially interested in possession in the rents and profits of the land until sale, and shall, so far as consistent with the general interest of the trust, give effect to the wishes of such persons, or in the case of dispute, of the majority (according to the value of their combined interests) of such persons . . .

The section contains two elements: firstly, the general purpose for which the land is co-owned, and secondly, the desires of the co-owners. The first predominates, although sometimes, even when it has been present, the second might provide evidence as to whether it still exists. If the first element is not present then the second one operates.

The first rule is that if the land was taken into co-ownership for some particular purpose, such as for a matrimonial home, or for business, the land must not be sold while this purpose subsists. Such 'collateral purposes' indeed account for the greater number of co-ownerships of land (see *Jones* v. *Challenger* [1961] 1 Q.B. 177; *Re Buchanan-Wollaston's Conveyance* [1939] Ch. 738). Cases of doubt may be tested by an application to the court under s.30 of the Act, when the court will judge whether the purpose still exists (*Jackson* v. *Jackson* [1971] 3 All E.R. 775). Since this section enables the court to make 'such order as it thinks fit', it is not restricted merely to deciding whether or not there shall be a sale, but may mould its decision to the circumstances, such as by ordering that, though the property may remain unsold and in the occupation of one co-owner, the other shall be entitled to periodical payments secured by a charge on the property, but shall lose all rights in the ownership. In *Re Holliday* [1980] 3 All E.R. 385 the sale of a former matrimonial home was postponed, even in face of the claims of the trustee in bankruptcy of one co-owner, so that the other owner and the children of the marriage might enjoy the home while the children grew up. Generally, however, the courts have preferred the interests of the trustee in bankruptcy.

The problem of deciding what order to make is capable of much variation in matrimonial cases, particularly in view of a husband's duty to allow his wife to enjoy accommodation he has provided for her (see Law Commission Working Paper No. 42, and 36 Conveyancer 99). In deciding whether or not to postpone sale, the court can take into account all the personal problems affecting the owners of the beneficial interests, such as the provision of a home for their children. The most important factor, whether or not there are children to be considered, is that everyone concerned should have a roof over his head (*Martin* v. *Martin* [1977] 3 W.L.R. 101). Questions involving the matrimonial home should now be disposed of by the Family Division under the Matrimonial Causes Act 1973. There is greater responsiveness on the part of today's judges to the use of property for family purposes.

If there is no collateral purpose the trustees must, so far as practicable, consult the persons of full age for the time being beneficially interested in possession in the rents and profits of the land until sale, and give effect to the value of their combined interests. Thus if land is devised to *A*, *B* and *C* in shares of three-fifths, one-fifth and one-fifth respectively, *A*'s wish must be followed even if *B* and *C* disagree with him. Section 30 may be invoked here also, if, for instance, trustees failed in this duty. The meaning of the words 'in possession' in the section is simply 'not in remainder' so that physical occupation is not necessary (see also *Re House* [1929] 2 Ch. 166).

Whether the duty to sell emanates from the first or the second of the two elements just discussed, a purchaser is not concerned to see that the provisions of s.26(3) have been complied with.

A short comparison of the duty to sell in express and statutory trusts for sale might be helpful at this point.

Express trust for sale—

(1) Obey the express terms, taking any necessary consents. If these cannot be obtained, or a co-trustee will not agree to sale, an application to the court may be made under s.30.

(2) If there are no instructions as to when to sell, the trustees may delay sale if they unanimously agree. There is no need to consult beneficiaries.

Statutory trust for sale—

(1) If there is a collateral purpose the land must not be sold while this subsists. Of course, if all the beneficiaries wish to sell, this would be conclusive that the purpose has ended. Cases of doubt can be tested under s.30, when the court will be guided by the existence or otherwise of such purpose.

(2) If there is no collateral purpose the trustees must be guided by the wishes of the majority of the beneficiaries according to value. If trustees do not obey this duty, s.30 can be used to force them to sell where applicable.

Apart from the duty to sell, the main features of a statutory trust for sale are similar to those of an express trust for sale. Thus the doctrine of conversion applies and the interests of the persons interested are 'overreached' upon sale. Property granted to persons in equal shares may, of course, be subject to an express trust for sale by the grantor, in which case his instructions must be regarded. In one case, a grantor ordered sale as a priority, since he only intended the beneficiaries to receive a distribution of the sale money. Their interests in such cases might only be in the proceeds so that possession of the land cannot be claimed (*Barclay* v. *Barclay* [1970] 2 All E.R. 676).

The differences between express and statutory trusts for sale also occur in relation to the right to occupy the land in question. In the case of express trusts, the doctrine has always been that the beneficiaries may only occupy the land at the discretion of the trustees, although they enjoy the right to receive the rents and profits pending sale. This principle reflects the managerial role to which trustees are appointed by a landowner setting up a settlement of what was lately his own property. Such a doctrine can hardly apply in the case of statutory trusts for sale for the following reasons. Firstly, before the 1925 legislation co-owners had an unqualified right to occupy the land itself. The application of the trust for sale to co-ownership by the Law of Property Act 1925 was a mere device aimed at conveyancing liquidity, but not intended to affect substantive rights. Secondly, the vast majority of co-owners have purchased the land for themselves and therefore must have intended to receive full managerial powers. Indeed, in most cases, the legal estate and the beneficial interests are held by the same persons (see *Bull* v. *Bull* [1955] 1 Q.B. 234 at 237).

A contrary view is put forward by the learned authors K. J. Gray and P. D. Symes in *Real Property for Real People* (Butterworth 1981, pp.262–273). The 1925 legislation indeed favoured land transfer at the expense, it now transpires, of land enjoyment. Suppose, for instance, that one co-owning spouse should sell his equitable share in the matrimonial home. May the stranger purchasing it move into possession with the spouse remaining in occupation?

Social developments in one decade sometimes carry their problems to the Court of Appeal in the next. The greater incidence both of divorce and home-ownership during the 1950s and 1960s gave rise to litigation which culminated in *Gissing* v. *Gissing* and the Matrimonial Proceedings and Property Act 1970. During the 1960s and 1970s another important social development occurred. Cohabitation without marriage, always present to some degree in most societies, increased considerably in this country. The problems arising on separation have gained litigiousness through the frequency of home-ownership by one or both parties. The waves of this development are now beginning to break upon judicial shores.

The Matrimonial Causes Act 1973 has no part to play in the settlement of property disputes of such unmarried couples, although we have seen that injunctive relief against molestation in the home may be afforded. At present property adjustment is not available. The court is restricted to declaring rights in such cases. Section 30 of the Law of Property Act 1925 is available, of course. Thus, sale of property may be delayed while illegitimate children of unmarried couples grow up during the separation of their parents (*Re Ever's Trusts* [1980] 3 All E.R. 399). Once marriage has taken place however, it appears possible, in appropriate circumstances, to take into account the circumstances prevailing during previous unmarried cohabitation in the judicial resolution of break-up (*Kokosinki* v. *Kokosinki* [1980] 1 All E.R. 1106).

The commencement of an implied trust in the case of unmarried persons accords with the general principles laid down in *Gissing* v. *Gissing*. To that extent, the legal principles are the same as in the case of married couples. The possibly different relationship between unmarried couples, however, might alter the factual inferences to be drawn from their behaviour (See *Bernard* v. *Josephs* [1982] 3 All E.R. 162 at 169). One extraordinary decision suggests that this trust ends spontaneously on separation of the parties. In *Hall* v. *Hall* (*The Times*, April 1st 1981) it was held that, as a result of this, the share of a wife who left the home had to be calculated as at the time of her leaving and not at the time of judgment. The decision infers that trusts can die as impliedly as they can be born, a novelty in English law. It also confirms the desire of judges to approve or disapprove of behaviour in particular cases without too much doctrinal constraint. That is certainly no novelty.

Conversion of joint tenancy into tenancy in common

Although the doctrine of survivorship which characterizes joint tenancy is convenient for some purposes, there will obviously be many instances when it is undesirable. It is possible, however, to convert a joint tenancy into a tenancy in common.

This process is known as 'severance'. It has already been explained that tenancy in common cannot exist at law so that severance cannot affect the legal estate (see also L.P.A. 1925, s.36(2)). What really matters is that the beneficial joint tenancy can be severed. Thus if *A* and *B* hold the legal estate jointly in trust for themselves jointly and *B* severs, the result will be that *A* and *B* still hold the legal estate jointly but on trust for themselves as tenants in common in equity. So although survivorship will operate upon the bare legal ownership, it will not affect the beneficial enjoyment of the interest: if *B* dies, his share will go to his next-of-kin or beneficiary under his will.

As a result of severance, the co-owner can for the first time say he holds a share in the property, whereas before he only had a potential share. This share is only a mathematical one, for even in tenancy in common there is unity of possession. This is why it is called tenancy 'in undivided shares'. The size of share which a severing tenant will own depends upon the number of co-tenants. If he is one of three he will own a third, if one of five a fifth and so on. The view expressed by Lord Denning, M.R., in the Court of Appeal in *Bedson* v. *Bedson* [1965] 2 Q.B. 666 that a spouse cannot sever a joint interest in the matrimonial home while the other spouse remains in possession is surely wrong (see L.P.A. 1925, ss.36(2) and 37, and 82 L.Q.R. 29, at p.31).

Yet the learned judge was seeking to avoid a difficult and practical dilemma. If, for instance, one spouse deserted the other and severed the beneficial joint ownership, selling his interest to a stranger, that stranger would be entitled to go into possession with the other spouse. Against this, it has been argued that ownership of the equitable interest does not entitle a person to possession, for the right to possession belongs to the owners of the legal estate as trustees, and the purchaser from the deserting spouse would not obtain the legal estate (37 Conveyancer 270). This argument can hardly be valid because the right of the trustee to possession is cancelled, and has been so for the last three hundred years, by his duty to allow the persons beneficially entitled to enjoy their interests. The stranger would therefore be entitled to possession or compensation. The ultimate solution would be a sale of the property, an outcome which might well have occurred if the deserting spouse had made an application under section 30 of the Law of Property Act 1925. In any case, a similar problem could arise if the original joint tenants were not husband and wife so that Lord Denning's remarks, aimed at co-ownership by spouses, hits all cases of joint ownership.

There are four ways of severing joint tenancy.

(1) *Inter vivos alienation.* If a joint tenant alienates his interest in equity, severance occurs and his potential share thereby precipitates out of the joint tenancy in favour of the alienee. If there is more than one other co-tenant,

however, their relationship between themselves is not changed. If there are three, *A*, *B* and *C*, and *C* sells his interest to *P*, *A* and *B* hold two-thirds as joint tenants as between themselves, but as tenants in common against *P*, who takes a one third share of the property, as tenants in common. The following diagram expresses the change in relationships between these co-owners caused by disunity of titles following alienation.

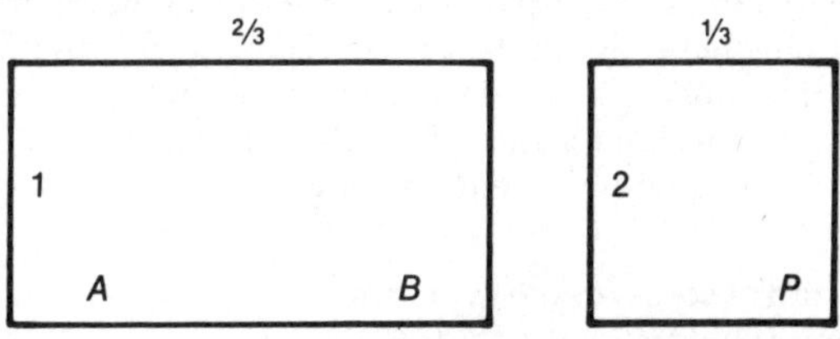

A and *B* are still joint tenants as to a two-thirds part so that survivorship will operate between them. If *A* dies, *B* will take a two-thirds share in common with *P*, who continues to own one-third. Severance also occurs upon other forms of alienation such as mortgage, and even upon contracts for alienation if specifically enforceable.

(2) *Later acquisition of another interest in the land.* If one co-owner acquires an additional interest, severance occurs as to his part, for the unity of interest is broken. Thus if *A*, *B* and *C* are joint life tenants and *C* subsequently acquires the fee simple in remainder, his life interest 'merges', that is coalesces, with his remainder. As in the example above, however, *A* and *B* continue to hold jointly as between themselves. Severance does not occur unless the additional interest is different in quantum from the one held in joint tenancy, neither does it result if the additional interest is granted at the same time as the joint interest, as in a gift to *A*, *B* and *C* jointly for life with remainder in fee simple to *C*.

(3) *Agreement by joint tenants to hold as tenants in common.* Such an agreement might be expressed or implied from the conduct of the co-owners (*Jackson* v. *Jackson* (1804), 9 Ves. 591). A merely unilateral declaration or a course of conduct falling short of alienation is not sufficient (*Nielson-Jones* v. *Fedden* [1974] 3 All E.R. 38), but if communication of intent is made it does not matter that the transaction in which it took place is otherwise legally ineffective, as, for instance, where there was an oral agreement for sale by one joint tenant of his share to the other lacking the requirements of section 40 of the Law of Property Act 1925 (see *Burgess* v. *Rawnsley* [1975] 3 W.L.R. 99). This doctrine has now been confirmed by statute which, since the section concerned also deals with severance by writing, is cited under (4) below.

(4) *Notice in writing (L.P.A. 1925, s.36(2)).*

> . . . where a legal estate (not being settled in land) is vested in joint tenants beneficially and any tenant desires to sever the joint tenancy in equity, he shall give to the other joint tenants a notice in writing of such desire or do such other acts or things as would, in the case of personal estate, have been effectual to sever the tenancy in equity . . .

(see *Re 88 Berkeley Road, London, N.W.9* [1971] 1 All E.R. 254 and *Holwell Securities Ltd.* v. *Hughes* [1974] 1 All E.R. 161).

Two points should be highlighted. Firstly, the language of the subsection requires that the legal owners and the owners in equity shall be exactly the same persons, as in the case of *A*, *B* and *C* holding the legal estate for *A*, *B* and *C* in equity. Severance by notice is perhaps not therefore possible by any co-owner where any person holds only at law, or only in equity, as where *A*, *B* and *C* hold the legal estate for *A*, *B*, *C* and *D* jointly in equity, or where trustees T^1 and T^2 hold the legal estate for *A* and *B* jointly in equity. The matter is open to doubt. Secondly, the provision excludes settled land. This topic will be mentioned later, but the result of the subsection is that co-owners, such as joint life tenants who hold land under a strict settlement, cannot sever a joint interest by written notice.

Determination of co-ownership of land

Co-ownership of land may end in the following ways:

(1) *Partition*. When all the co-owners, whether in joint tenancy or in tenancy in common, being of full age, are beneficially absolutely entitled to the net proceeds of sale, the trustees may partition the land, with the consents of the persons (if any) of full age who are interested in possession in the net rents and profits until sale. Each co-owner becomes sole owner of a separate part of the land. The details of the process are to be found in the Law of Property Act 1925, s.28(3) (see 34 Conveyancer 123). The subsection in terms only applies to tenancies in common, but in fact also applies to joint tenants because of the assimilating effect of s.36(1). Cases of deadlock can be resolved through applications under s.30.
(2) *Sale*. When the land is sold, we have seen that the purchaser takes it free of any of the interests of the co-owners, provided that the transaction is conducted in accordance with the Act. The co-ownership continues to exist in the purchase-money.
(3) *Union of beneficial interest in one person*. If a joint tenant becomes solely entitled in equity, either by survivorship or by acquiring the interests of his co-tenants *inter vivos*, or a tenant in common becomes similarly entitled by acquisition of the other shares, the co-ownership ends. In the two types of determination mentioned in (1) and (2) above, the end of the trust for sale will be marked by a conveyance from the trustees which will vest the land in the alienee as absolute owner and which will clearly purge the title of the trust. When the co-ownership ends through union, however (see *Re Cook* [1948] Ch. 212), it might not be so apparent as to satisfy a purchaser.

Suppose land was held both at law and in equity by *A*, *B* and *C* as joint tenants in fee simple, and that *B* and *C* both died. Survivorship will have vested both the legal and equitable interest in *A* only. The co-ownership has ended, and with it the trust for sale. *A* is therefore entitled to dispose of the land as an absolute owner, without appointing a trustee to act with him to receive purchase-money (see L.P.A. 1925 s.36(2), as amended by the Law of Property (Amendment) Act 1926).

Even though *A* can make an ordinary conveyance, the purchaser might have misgivings, If, for instance, either *B* or *C* has severed his tenancy before his death, a fact which might not be easy to discover at once, then the co-ownership and therefore the trust for sale still subsists. *A* would therefore have to appoint another trustee before making a sale. Even if no severance had taken place, this negative fact might be difficult to prove. This problem has now been remedied by the Law of Property (Joint Tenants) Act 1964, which is retrospective to 1st January 1926; this provides that, in favour of a purchaser of the legal estate, the survivor of two or more joint tenants shall be deemed to be solely and beneficially interested if he conveys as 'beneficial owner' or the conveyance includes a statement that he is so interested, unless before the date of the conveyance either: (a) a memorandum of severance has been indorsed on the conveyance which vested the legal estate in the joint tenants or (b) a bankruptcy petition or receiving order has been registered. The relevance of this latter provision is that bankruptcy brings about a severance of joint tenancy because it involves an alienation, even though an involuntary one, in favour of the trustee in bankruptcy. There are circumstances, however, in which the trustee in bankruptcy may have a claim even against the share of the person who is in co-ownership with the bankrupt (see the Bankruptcy Act 1914, s.42, and *In re Densham* [1975] 1 W.L.R. 1519). The Act does not apply to registered land. It is not stated what shall happen if a purchaser takes the legal estate with knowledge of a severance which has not been indorsed. In any case the owner who has severed will have an interest in the purchase-money.

The main effect of the Act is to give peace of mind to a purchaser. It does not endow a sole owner at law with any additional powers.

Co-ownership and strict settlements

If two or more persons become entitled under a strict settlement beneficially as joint tenants, they together constitute the tenant for life, if of full age, and the settlement continues (Settled Land Act 1925, s.19(2)). The subsection refers to beneficial entitlement for life, but presumably the same applies if the beneficiaries are entitled for some modified interest less in quantum than a fee simple absolute, such as a determinable interest. If, however, they hold for a tenancy in common, or in coparcenary, as in the case of life tenants in common, the strict settlement ends and the statutory trust for sale supervenes (Settled Land Act 1925, s.36(1)). The Settled Land Act trustees become the trustees for sale and can demand the legal estate. This is so even when the element of succession has been exhausted and the land would have ceased to be settled in any case. Thus if land is limited to *A* for life with remainder in fee simple to *X*, *Y* and *Z* equally, on *A*'s death his personal representatives must convey the land to the settlement trustees and not to *X*, *Y* and *Z*.

Coparcenary

Little need be said of this third antique and rare form of co-ownership except to identify it and to relate it to the other two types. Coparcenary can only now arise on the death intestate of the owner of an unbarred entail who leaves no sons but only daughters, or the representatives, male or female, of daughters. These daughters constitute together the single heir. Coparcenary has some of the characteristics of both joint tenancy and tenancy in common. Survivorship does not operate upon it. As mentioned above, it always brings about a trust for sale even when it arises out of a strict settlement, for, like tenancy in common, it carries undivided shares.

Party walls and structures

The status of a party wall must be ascertained as a fact in each individual case, but, in the nature of things, a wall might be claimed to be a party wall for one of four reasons.

(1) The neighbouring owners might own it as tenants in common.
(2) Each neighbour might own to the mid-point of its width.
(3) Each neighbour might own part as in (2) above but each half-width enjoys an easement of support against the other.
(4) The wall might be owned entirely by the owner of one property but subject to an easement in favour of the other to have it retained there.

The effect of the legislation discussed in this chapter would have been to impose trusts for sale on party walls in the first class, if special provision had not been included to prevent so whimsical a result. The Law of Property Act 1925, s.38, enacted that all party walls in the first category shall become converted to the third.

Study material: *Wachtel* v. *Wachtel* [1973] 1 All E.R. 829

Lord Denning delivered the judgment of the Court of Appeal. Note that Section 5(1)(f), cited on page 221 and subsequently has now been re-enacted in the Matrimonial Causes Act 1973 (s.25(1)(f)).

Cur adv vult

8th February. **LORD DENNING MR** read the following judgment of the court. Mr and Mrs Wachtel were married on 9th January 1954. They were both then 28 years of age. They have two children, a son now aged 14 and a girl of 11. The husband is a dentist in good practice. On 31st March 1972 the wife left the home. On 21st July 1972 there was a divorce on the ground that the marriage had irretrievably broken down. In consequence many things have to be settled. The parties have made arrangements for the children. The son is with the father. He is a boarder at Epsom College, where his fees are paid by his grandfather. The daughter is with the mother. She goes to day-school. There remain the financial consequences. The parties have not agreed on them. So they have to be settled by the courts.

On 3rd October 1972 Ormrod J ordered the husband to pay to his wife (i) a lump sum of £10,000, or half the value of the former matrimonial home in Norwood, South London, whichever be the less; (ii) a periodical payment of £1,500 per annum, less tax; and (iii) a further payment of £500 per annum, less tax, in respect of the 11 year old daughter. The husband appeals to this court.

The appeal raises issues of wide importance. This court is asked to determine, for the first time, after full argument, the principles which should be applied in the Family Division when granting ancillary relief pursuant to the powers conferred by the Matrimonial Proceedings and Property Act 1970 (in this judgment called 'the 1970 Act') following dissolution of marriage pursuant to the Divorce Reform Act 1969 (in this judgment called 'the 1969 Act'). We were told by counsel both for the husband and for the wife that it was hoped that this court might feel able, to quote the phrase used in the argument, 'to lay down some guide lines' which would be of help in the future. There are divergences of view and of practice between judge and registrars. Furthermore, counsel and solicitors are unable to advise their clients with a reasonable degree of certainty as to the likely outcome of any contested proceedings. It is very desirable to remove that uncertainty and to assist parties to come to agreement.

The parties separated on 31st March 1972. The husband's petition was filed on 18th April 1972, and alleged adultery by the wife with a doctor whose patient she was. By her answer dated 9th May 1972, the wife denied the adultery and cross-petitioned on the ground that her husband had behaved in such a way that she could not reasonably be expected to continue to live with him. Her answer was amended later to add two charges of adultery against the husband. The husband denied all the allegations against him. The co-respondent doctor also filed an answer denying the alleged adultery. These contested proceedings were heard before Ormrod J on five days between 3rd and 7th July 1972. The learned judge reserved his judgment at the conclusion of the hearing. He delivered the judgment on 21st July. He had, it seems, previously indicated to the parties that he was not satisfied that any relevant charge of adultery had been proved on either side, but he had given the husband leave to amend his petition so as to rely in the alternative on s 2 (1) (*b*) of the 1969 Act.

The learned judge granted cross-decrees to both parties under s 2 (1) (*b*) of the 1969 Act. He then proceeded to deal with the ancillary matters. He again reserved judgment, and delivered it after the Long Vacation, on 3rd October 1972[1]. It is against that second reserved judgment that the present appeal is brought.

The crucial finding of fact is that the responsibility for the breakdown of the marriage rested equally on both parties. The learned judge, having made that finding, determined that the only capital asset, namely the matrimonial home, should be divided more or less equally between the parties. Since the evidence before the judge showed that the equity of the house in Norwood (after discharging the outstanding mortgage amounting to some £2,000) was about £20,000, he ordered the husband to pay to his wife a lump of £10,000 or half the net value of the house if and when sold, whichever was the less. So far as the periodical payment of £1,500 per annum is concerned, the learned judge appears to have worked on an earning capacity on the part of the husband of £4,000 to £5,000 gross taxable income. He appears not to have allowed anything for the wife's earning capacity, at least in terms of monetary value. On this basis the £1,500 represents about one-third of the learned judge's assessment of the husband's earning capacity. But if one adds to that figure of £1,500 the further sum of £500 gross which the judge ordered to be paid by the husband to the wife in respect of the 11 year old daughter, the total is £2,000 gross, considerably more than one-third of the figure which the judge took as the husband's earning capacity.

The husband's appeal was founded on the ground that in effect he had been ordered to pay his wife one-half of his capital, and about one-half of his income. Particular criticism was levelled in this respect at an important passage in the learned judge's judgment[2] stating that Parliament had intended in the 1970 Act to bring about a shift of emphasis from the old concept of maintenance to one of redistribution of assets and of purchasing power. Counsel for the husband contended that the judge had but lightly concealed his view that the 1970 Act had brought about a new concept of community of property so that it was just to give every wife—or at least almost every wife—half the value of the matrimonial home on the break-up of the marriage, and about half her husband's income. If that were right in the case of a wife held equally to blame with her husband for the breakdown of the marriage, what, he asked rhetorically, was the position of a wife who was wholly innocent of responsibility for such a breakdown. He further asked this: if, as in the past, one-third of the combined available income of the parties had been regarded as proper maintenance for a blameless wife, with a reduction (we avoid the use of the word 'discount') in the case of a wife who was not free from blame, how could periodical payments totalling nearly one-half of the husband's earning capacity be justified in a case where the wife was found equally to blame with the husband for the breakdown?

Counsel for the husband also complained that the judge had really started from a presumption that equal division was right and had worked back from the starting point and, allowing nothing—or almost nothing—for 'conduct', had arrived at the determination we have stated. He contested the judge's view that it was right to disregard conduct where blame had been found to exist, especially as Parliament in s 5 (1) of the

1 [1973] 1 All ER 113, [1973] 2 WLR 84
2 [1973] 1 All ER at 116, [1973] 2 WLR at 88

1970 Act had enjoined the courts to have regard to the conduct of the parties. He also said that no, or no sufficient, account had been taken of the wife's earning capacity and that the £500 ordered to be paid for the child was in any event too high. He offered a lump sum of £4,000, together with a guarantee of any mortgage instalments which the wife might have to pay in connection with the acquisition of a new home for herself and the child. He urged this court in any event to reduce the £1,500 to £1,000; and the £500 to £300, or less.

Counsel for the wife supported the judgment on the broad ground that the long line of cases decided over the last century and more, which dealt with the issue of conduct, especially in relation to a guilty or blameworthy wife, were all decided when the foundation of the right to relief in matrimonial causes was the concept of a matrimonial offence. Now that concept had been swept away by the 1969 Act, the whole question of conduct in relation to ancillary relief required to be reconsidered, even though s 5 (1) of the 1970 Act preserved the obligation on the courts to have regard to the 'conduct' in language not easily distinguishable from that of the earlier statutes from 1857 onwards. Although judges and former judges of the present Family Division of great experience have recently said that s 5 (1) was only 'codifying' the preceding law and practice, counsel for the wife contended that that was wrong and that the new provisions contained in s 5 (1) (*f*) showed it to be wrong. Any approach to questions arising out of the 1970 Act founded on decisions before that Act and the 1969 Act were passed was wrong, since the 1970 Act ought not to be considered apart from the fundamental change wrought by the 1969 Act. Counsel for the wife particularly criticised the continued application of the so-called 'one-third rule' under present day conditions, and drew attention to the fact (as is undoubtedly the case) that in *Ackerman v Ackerman*[3], where this court recently proceeded on the basis that that so-called rule was still applicable to cases arising under the 1970 Act, it had done so without the matters which have been argued on this appeal having been argued. We will deal with these issues in order.

The conduct of the parties

When Parliament in 1857 introduced divorce by the courts of law, it based it on the doctrine of the matrimonial offence. This affected all that followed. If a person was the guilty party in a divorce suit, it went hard with him or her. It affected so many things. The custody of the children depended on it. So did the award of maintenance. To say nothing of the standing in society. So serious were the consequences that divorce suits were contested at great length and at much cost.

All that is altered. Parliament has decreed: 'If the marriage has broken down irretrievably, let there be a divorce'. It carries no stigma, but only sympathy. It is a misfortune which befalls both. No longer is one guilty and the other innocent. No longer are there long contested divorce suits. Nearly every case goes uncontested. The parties come to an agreement, if they can, on the things that matter so much to them. They divide up the furniture. They arrange the custody of the children, the financial provision for the wife, and the future of the matrimonial home. If they cannot agree, the matters are referred to a judge in chambers.

When the judge comes to decide these questions, what place has conduct in it? Parliament still says that the court has to have 'regard to their conduct': see s 5 (1) of the 1970 Act. Does this mean that the judge in chambers is to hear their mutual recriminations and go into their petty squabbles for days on end, as he used to do in the old days? Does it mean that, after a marriage has been dissolved, there is to be a post mortem to find out what killed it? We do not think so. In most cases both parties are to blame—or, as we would prefer to say—both parties have contributed to the breakdown.

It has been suggested that there should be a 'discount' or 'reduction' in what the wife is to receive because of her supposed misconduct, guilt or blame (whatever word is used). We cannot accept this argument. In the vast majority of cases it is repugnant

---

3 [1972] 2 All ER 420, [1972] Fam 225

to the principles underlying the new legislation, and in particular the 1969 Act. There will be many cases in which a wife (although once considered guilty or blameworthy) will have cared for the home and looked after the family for very many years. Is she to be deprived of the benefit otherwise to be accorded to her by s 5 (1) (*f*) because she may share responsibility for the breakdown with her husband? There will no doubt be a residue of cases where the conduct of one of the parties is in the judge's words[4] 'both obvious and gross', so much so that to order one party to support another whose conduct falls into this category is repugnant to anyone's sense of justice. In such a case the court remains free to decline to afford financial support or to reduce the support which it would otherwise have ordered. But, short of cases falling into this category, the court should not reduce its order for financial provision merely because of what was formerly regarded as guilt or blame. To do so would be to impose a fine for supposed misbehaviour in the course of an unhappy married life. Counsel for the husband disputed this and claimed that it was but justice that a wife should suffer for her supposed misbehaviour. We do not agree. Criminal justice often requires the imposition of financial and indeed custodial penalties. But in the financial adjustments consequent on the dissolution of a marriage which has irretrievably broken down, the imposition of financial penalties ought seldom to find a place.

The family assets

The phrase 'family assets' is a convenient short way of expressing an important concept. It refers to those things which are acquired by one or other or both of the parties, with the intention that they should be continuing provision for them and their children during their joint lives, and used for the benefit of the family as a whole. It is a phrase, for want of a better, used by the Law Commission, and is well understood. The family assets can be divided into two parts: (i) those which are of a capital nature, such as the matrimonial home and the furniture in it; (ii) those which are of a revenue-producing nature, such as the earning power of husband and wife. When the marriage comes to an end, the capital assets have to be divided: the earning power of each has to be allocated.

Until recently the courts had limited powers in regard to the capital assets. They could determine the property rights of the parties. They could vary any ante-nuptial or post-nuptial settlements. But they could not order a transfer of property from one to the other. They could not even award a lump sum until 1963. The way in which the courts made financial provision was by way of maintenance to the wife. This they often did by way of the 'one-third' rule.

Now under the 1970 Act the court has power after a divorce to effect a transfer of the assets of the one to the other. It set out in s 5 various criteria. It was suggested that these were only codifying the existing law. Despite what has been said, we do not agree. The 1970 Act is not in any sense a codifying statute. It is a reforming statute designed to facilitate the granting of ancillary relief in cases where marriages have been dissolved under the 1969 Act, an even greater measure of reform. It is true that in certain of the lettered sub-paras of s 5 (1) of the 1970 Act one can find reflections of certain earlier well-known judicial decisions. But this was not to ensure that earlier decisions on conduct should be slavishly followed against a different jurisdictional background. Rather it was to secure that the common sense principles embodied in the lettered sub-paragraphs, which found their origin in long standing judicial decisions, should continue to be applied where appropriate in the new situation. We regard the provisions of ss 2, 3, 4 and 5 of the 1970 Act as designed to accord to the courts the widest possible powers in readjusting the financial position of the parties and to afford the courts the necessary machinery to that end, as for example is provided in s 4. It must not be overlooked in this connection that certain of the provisions of the 1970 Act are

4 [1973] 1 All ER at 119, [1973] 2 WLR at 90

new. See for example s 7 (2). Further, so far as we are aware, the principles clearly stated in s 5 (1) (*f*) have nowhere previously found comparable statutory enactment.

The matrimonial home

The matrimonial home is usually the most important capital asset. Often the only one. This case is typical. When the parties married in 1954 they started in a flat. He was a dentist. She a receptionist. They both went out to work. They pooled such money as they had to get the flat and furniture and keep it going. Two years later, in 1956, they bought a house, 37 Pollards Hill North, Streatham, and moved in there. It has been their matrimonial home ever since. The purchase price in 1956 was £5,000. They did not put any money cash down, but bought it with a 100 per cent mortgage. It was taken in the husband's name. The husband paid the mortgage instalments. The mortgage over the years has been reduced from £5,000 to £2,000. The house has increased in value from £5,000 to £22,000, or more.

After they moved into the house in 1956, the wife continued to go out to work until the son was born in 1958. She then stayed at home and looked after the children. But she helped her husband in various ways in his practice, such as by filling in the National Health forms, and helping as a receptionist from time to time. He put down a salary to her as part of his expenses against tax. This continued for all the years until 31st March 1972 when the wife left the house.

During the divorce proceedings the wife took out a summons under s 17 of the Married Women's Property Act 1882 claiming that, by reason of her financial contributions, she was entitled to one-half of the equity in the house. Alternatively she claimed that, under s 4 of the 1970 Act, there should be a transfer to her of half the house or its value by way of a lump sum.

Before the 1970 Act there might have been much debate whether the wife had made financial contributions of sufficient substance to entitle her to a share in the house. The judge said[5] that it 'might have been an important issue'. We agree. But he went on to say[5] that since the 1970 Act it was 'of little importance' because the powers of transfer under s 4 enabled the court to do what was just having regard to all the circumstances. We agree. We feel sure that registrars and judges have been acting on this view; because, whereas previously we had several cases in our list each term under s 17 of the 1882 Act: now we have hardly any.

How is the court to exercise its discretion under the 1970 Act in regard to the matrimonial home. We will lead up to the answer by tracing the way in which the law has developed. Twenty-five years ago, if the matrimonial home stood in the husband's name, it was taken to belong to him entirely, both in law and in equity. The wife did not get a proprietary interest in it simply because she helped him buy it or to pay the mortgage instalments. Any money that she gave him for these purposes would be regarded as gifts, or, at any rate, not recoverable by her: see *Balfour v Balfour*[6]. But by a long line of cases, starting with *Re Rogers' Question*[7], and ending with *Hazell v Hazell*[8], it has been held by this court that, if a wife contributes directly or indirectly, in money or money's worth, to the initial deposit or to the mortgage instalments, she gets an interest proportionate to her contribution. In some cases it is a half-share. In others less.

The court never succeeded, however, in getting a wife a share in the house by reason of her other contributions; other, that is, than her financial contributions. The injustice to her has often been pointed out. Seven members of the Royal Commission on Marriage and Divorce presided over by Lord Morton of Henryton[9] said:

---

5 [1973] 1 All ER at 119, [1973] 2 WLR at 91
6 [1919] 2 KB 571, [1918–19] All ER Rep 800
7 [1948] 1 All ER 328
8 [1972] 1 All ER 923, [1972] 1 WLR 301
9 (1956), Cmd 9678, para 652, at p 178

> 'If, on marriage, she gives up her paid work in order to devote herself to caring for her husband and children, it is an unwarrantable hardship when in consequence she finds herself in the end with nothing she can call her own.'

In 1965 Sir Jocelyn Simon P[10] used a telling metaphor: 'The cock can feather the nest because he does not have to spend most of his time sitting on it.' He went on to give reasons in an address which he gave to the Law Society[11]:

> 'In the generality of marriages the wife bears and rears children and minds the home. She thereby frees her husband for his economic activities. Since it is her performance of her function which enables the husband to perform his, she is in justice entitled to share in its fruits.'

But the courts have never been able to do justice to her. In April 1969 in *Pettitt v Pettitt*[12] Lord Hodson said: 'I do not myself see how one can correct the imbalance which may be found to exist in property rights as between husband and wife without legislation.'

Section 5 (1) (f)

Now we have the legislation. In order to remedy the injustice Parliament has intervened. The 1970 Act expressly says that, in considering whether to make a transfer of property, the court is to have regard, among other things, to—

> '(*f*) the contributions made by each of the parties to the welfare of the family, including any contribution made by looking after the home or caring for the family'

Counsel for the husband suggested that there was nothing new in these criteria in s 5 (1) (*f*). He referred us to *Porter v Porter*[13], where Sachs LJ said: '. . . the court must always take into account how long the marriage has lasted and to what extent the wife has rendered her domestic services to the husband.' But in saying that, Sachs LJ was only anticipating the report of the Law Commission which was printed in the very week in which *Porter v Porter*[14] was reported. In their Report on Financial Provision in Matrimonial Proceedings[15] the Law Commission emphasised the importance of s 5 (1) (*f*) and the change which it would make. They said:

> '. . . we recommend that in the exercise of the court's armoury of powers to order financial provision it should be directed to have regard to various criteria. Among these there is one of outstanding importance in regard to the adjustment of property rights as between the spouses. This is the extent to which each has contributed to the welfare of the family, including not only contributions in money or money's worth (as in the determination of rights to particular items of property) but also the contribution made (normally by the wife) in looking after the home and family. This should meet the strongest complaint made by married women, and recognised as legitimate by the Morton Commission in 1955, namely that the contribution which wives make towards the acquisition of the family assets by performing the domestic chores, thereby releasing their husbands for gainful employment, is at present wholly ignored in determining their rights. Under our proposal this contribution would be a factor which the court would be specifically directed to take into account'.

---

10 Cited by Lord Hodson in *Pettitt v Pettitt* [1969] 2 All ER 385 at 404, [1970] AC 777 at 811

11 The Seven Pillars of Divorce Reform (1965) 62 Law Society Gazette at p 345

12 [1969] 2 All ER at 404, [1970] AC at 811

13 [1969] 3 All ER 640 at 644, [1969] 1 WLR 1155 at 1160

14 [1969] 3 All ER 640, [1969] 1 WLR 1155

15 (1969) Law Com No 25, para 69

It has sometimes been suggested that we should not have regard to the reports of the Law Commission which lead to legislation. But we think we should. They are most helpful in showing the mischief which Parliament intended to remedy.

In the light thus thrown on the reason for s 5 (1) (*f*), we may take it that Parliament recognised that the wife who looks after the home and family contributes as much to the family assets as the wife who goes out to work. The one contributes in kind. The other in money or money's worth. If the court comes to the conclusion that the home has been acquired and maintained by the joint efforts of both, then, when the marriage breaks down, it should be regarded as the joint property of both of them, no matter in whose name it stands. Just as the wife who makes substantial money contributions usually gets a share, so should the wife who looks after the home and cares for the family for 20 years or more.

The one-third rule

In awarding maintenance the divorce courts followed the practice of the ecclesiastical courts. They awarded an innocent wife a sum equal to one-third of their joint incomes. Out of it she had to provide for her own accommodation, her food and clothes, and other expenses. If she had any rights in the matrimonial home, or was allowed to be in occupation of it, that went in reduction of maintenance.

The one-third rule has been much criticised. In *Kershaw v Kershaw*[16] Sir Jocelyn Simon P spoke of it as 'the discredited "one-third rule"'. But it has retained its attraction for a very simple reason: those who have to assess maintenance must have some starting point. They cannot operate in a void. No better starting point has yet been suggested than the one-third rule. In *Ackerman v Ackerman*[17] Phillimore LJ said: '. . . the proper course is to start again. I would begin with the "one-third rule"—bearing in mind that it is not a rule.'

There was, we think, much good sense in taking one-third as a starting point. When a marriage breaks up, there will thenceforward be two households instead of one. The husband will have to go out to work all day and must get some woman to look after the house—either a wife, if he remarries, or a housekeeper, if he does not. He will also have to provide maintenance for the children. The wife will not usually have so much expense. She may go out to work herself, but she will not usually employ a housekeeper. She will do most of the housework herself, perhaps with some help. Or she may remarry, in which case her new husband will provide for her. In any case, when there are two households, the greater expense will, in most cases, fall on the husband than the wife. As a start has to be made somewhere, it seems to us that in the past it was quite fair to start with one-third. Counsel for the wife criticised the application of the so-called 'one-third rule' on the ground that it no longer is applicable to present-day conditions, notwithstanding what was said in *Ackerman v Ackerman*[18]. But this so-called rule is not a rule and must never be so regarded. In any calculation the court has to have a starting point. If it is not to be one-third, should it be one-half? or one-quarter? A starting point at one-third of the combined resources of the parties is as good and rational a starting point as any other, remembering that the essence of the legislation is to secure flexibility to meet the justice of particular cases, and not rigidity, forcing particular cases to be fitted into some so-called principle within which they do not easily lie. There may be cases where more than one-third is right. There are likely to be many others where less than one-third is the only practicable solution. But one third as a flexible starting point is in general more likely to lead to the correct final result than a starting point of equality, or a quarter.

There is this, however, to be noted. Under the old dispensation, the wife, out of her one-third, had to provide her own accommodation. If she was given the right to

---

16 [1964] 3 All ER 635 at 637, [1966] P 13 at 17
17 [1972] 2 All ER at 426, [1972] Fam at 234
18 [1972] 2 All ER 420, [1972] Fam 225

occupy the matrimonial home, that went to reduce the one-third. Under the new dispensation, she will get a share of the capital assets; and, with that share, she will be able to provide accommodation for herself, or, at any rate, the money to go some way towards it.

If we were only concerned with the capital assets of the family, and particularly with the matrimonial home, it would be tempting to divide them half and half, as the judge did. That would be fair enough if the wife afterwards went her own way, making no further demands on the husband. It would be simply a division of the assets of the partnership. That may come in the future. But at present few wives are content with a share of the capital assets. Most wives want their former husband to make periodical payments as well to support them; because, after the divorce, he will be earning far more than she; and she can only keep up her standard of living with his help. He also has to make payments for the children out of his earnings, even if they are with her. In view of these calls on his future earnings, we do not think she can have both—half the capital assets, and half the earnings.

Under the new dispensation, she will usually get a share of each. In these days of rising house prices, she should certainly have a share in the capital assets which she has helped to create. The windfall should not all go to the husband. But we do not think it should be as much as one-half, if she is also to get periodical payments for her maintenance and support. Giving it the best consideration we can, we think that the fairest way is to start with one-third of each. If she has one-third of the family assets as her own—and one-third of the joint earnings—her past contributions are adequately recognised, and her future living standard assured so far as may be. She will certainly in this way be as well off as if the capital assets were divided equally—which is all that a partner is entitled to.

We would emphasise that this proposal is not a rule. It is only a starting point. It will serve in cases where the marriage has lasted for many years and the wife has been in the home bringing up the children. It may not be applicable when the marriage has lasted only a short time, or where there are no children and she can go out to work.

The lump sum provision

In every case the court should consider whether to order a lump sum to be paid by her husband to her. Before 1963 a wife, on a divorce, could not get a lump sum paid to her. All that she could get was weekly or monthly payments secured or unsecured. By s 5 (1) of the Matrimonial Causes Act 1963 the court was empowered to make an order for the payment of a lump sum. This is now contained in s 2 (1) (*c*) of the 1970 Act. This court has decided many cases about lump sums. They will be found usefully set out in Mr Joseph Jackson's chapter on the subject in his book on Matrimonial Finance and Taxation[19]. The circumstances are so various that few general principles can be stated. One thing is, however, obvious. No order should be made for a lump sum unless the husband has capital assets out of which to pay it—without crippling his earning power.

Another thing is this: when the husband has available capital assets sufficient for the purpose, the court should not hesitate to order a lump sum. The wife will then be able to invest it and use the income to live on. This will reduce any periodical payments, or make them unnecessary. It will also help to remove the bitterness which is so often attendant on periodical payments. Once made, the parties can regard the book as closed. The third thing is that, if a lump sum is awarded, it should be made outright. It should not be made subject to conditions except when there are children. Then it may be desirable to let it be the subject of a settlement. In case she remarries, the children will be assured of some part of the family assets which were built up for them.

But the question of a lump sum needs special consideration in relation to the matrimonial home. The house is in most cases the principal capital asset. Sometimes

19 (1972), pp 116-131

the only asset. It will usually have increased greatly in value since it was acquired. It is to be regarded as belonging in equity to both of them jointly. What is to be done with it? This is the most important question of all.

Take a case like the present when the wife leaves the home and the husband stays in it. On the breakdown of the marriage arrangements should be made whereby it is vested in him absolutely, free of any share in the wife, and he alone is liable for the mortgage instalments. But the wife should be compensated for the loss of her share by being awarded a lump sum. It should be a sum sufficient to enable her to get settled in a place of her own, such as by putting down a deposit on a flat or a house. It should not, however, be an excessive sum. It should be such as the husband can raise by a further mortgage on the house without crippling him.

Conversely, suppose the husband leaves the house and the wife stays in it. If she is likely to be there indefinitely, arrangements should be made whereby it is vested in her absolutely, free of any share in the husband; or, if there are children, settled on her and the children. This may mean that he will have to transfer the legal title to her. If there is a mortgage, some provision should be made for the mortgage instalments to be paid by the husband, or guaranteed by him. If this is done, there may be no necessity for a lump sum as well. Furthermore, seeing that she has the house, the periodic payments will be much less than they otherwise would be.

Remarriage

In making financial provision, ought the prospects of remarriage to be taken into account? The statute says in terms that periodical payments shall cease on remarriage: see s 7 (1) (*b*). But it says nothing about the prospects of remarriage. The question then arises: ought the provision for the wife to be reduced if she is likely to remarry?

So far as the capital assets are concerned, we see no reason for reducing her share. After all, she has earned it by her contribution in looking after the home and caring for the family. It should not be taken away from her by the prospect of remarriage. In *Buckley v John Allen & Ford (Oxford) Ltd*[20] Phillimore LJ showed that it was a guessing game, which no judge was qualified to put his—or her—money on. His observations were disapproved by this court in *Goodburn v Thomas Cotton Ltd*[21]. But they have been vindicated by Parliament.

So far as periodical payments are concerned, they are, of course, to be assessed without regard to the prospects of remarriage. If the wife does in fact remarry, they cease. If she goes to live with another man—without marrying him—they may be reviewed.

The present case

Coming now to the facts of the present case. The matrimonial home belongs in law to the husband. On the figures before the learned judge, its gross value was about £22,000; and, as already stated, the equity is worth about £20,000. Counsel for the wife sought to reopen these figures. We saw no justification for allowing him to do so, since these figures could have been challenged before the learned judge had it then been desired to do so. But we allowed counsel for the wife to cross-appeal to argue that the judge, consistently with the principles which he sought to apply, should have ordered a lump sum payment of £10,000, or half the net value of the house, whichever was the greater, and not, as the learned judge in fact ordered, whichever was the less.

So far as the husband's earning capacity is concerned, we venture to think that the learned judge's findings are self-contradictory; for, if the husband was spending at the rate of £4,000 to £5,000 per annum without incurring debts and was, in fact, at the same time making savings, his gross taxable income must have been considerably more than the £4,000 to £5,000 found by the judge. We propose to proceed on the basis of the

20 [1967] 1 All ER 539 at 542, [1967] 2 QB 637 at 645
21 [1968] 1 All ER 518, [1968] 1 QB 845

husband's earning capacity (i e his gross taxable income) being not less than £6,000 per annum. This may well be too favourable to the husband who appears not to have disclosed part of his income as a dentist. We put the wife's potential earning capacity on part-time work as a dental nurse at £15 per week gross—say £750 per annum. The combined total earning capacity is thus £6,750 per annum gross, of which one-third (if that be the right starting point) is £2,250. If one deducts the £750 from that latter figure of £2,250, the result is £1,500—the same figure as the learned judge arrived at although he reached that figure by a different route.

The husband is presently living at the former matrimonial home. The son of the marriage, aged 14, is now at a boarding school at the grandfather's expense. The boy lives with his father in the holidays. The father has to clothe and maintain him in the holidays. Clearly this requires the father to maintain a home for the son. Both parties gave their ages as 46. Remarriage is thus a possibility, although not it seems an imminent probability. The wife undoubtedly contributed to the home for some 18 years and, so far as the evidence goes, was in every respect an excellent mother. This is clearly a case in which the wife has made a substantial contribution to the home, as of course the husband has out of his earnings.

Any lump sum ordered to be paid will, we were told, be raised by the husband by increasing the sum for which the house is mortgaged. To require him to pay a lump sum of £10,000 raised in this way might cost him around £900 per annum in interest; and, of course, he will have to repay the principal as well. If £900 is added to the total of £1,500, plus the £500 (i e £2,000), the result is the equivalent of an order for a periodical payment of almost half of what we have taken to be the husband's gross taxable income. We think an order for a periodical payment on this scale (omitting any consideration of a lump sum payment) would be too high, having regard to the wife's needs and to the husband's needs. But, even if the matter be approached by a different route, we still think the £10,000 figure is too high. The wife should be able to make a substantial deposit in order to purchase suitable accommodation (assuming she wishes to buy, and not to rent) with the aid of a considerably smaller sum; and, if the order for £1,500 as a periodical payment is upheld, there seems to us to be a margin within that figure beyond the requirements of ordinary living expenses out of which repayments of mortgage, principal and interest could be made. On the other hand, we think the husband's offer of £4,000 is too low in a period of notoriously inflationary house prices. The offer of a guarantee of the wife's mortgage repayments does not improve the wife's day-to-day position, although it might make the obtaining of mortgage facilities easier.

On the basis that the order for a periodical payment of £1,500 per annum is left untouched, we think the proper lump sum, taking everything into account that the 1970 Act requires, is £6,000, and we would vary the learned judge's order for £10,000 accordingly. We think the wife should have that sum, £6,000, free of any trust, or other terms.

We, therefore, see no reason to interfere with the order for £1,500 in favour of the wife on the basis of the figures we have just mentioned. But, with all respect to the learned judge, we think the figure of £500 for the child is considerably too high. We would substitute a figure of £300 per annum, which we would express as £6 per week so that the payment should be made gross of tax. We see no reason whatever on the facts of this case, as found by the learned judge, for making any reduction of any kind on the ground that the judge found the wife equally responsible with the husband for the breakdown of their marriage. To do so would be quite inconsistent with the principles which we think should be adopted in future in relation to conduct.

Looking at it broadly

In all these cases it is necessary at the end to view the situation broadly and see if the proposals meet the justice of the case. On our proposals here the wife gets £6,000 (nearly one-third of the value of the matrimonial home). She gets it without any conditions at all. This seems to represent a fair assessment of her past contributions, when regard is had to the fact that she will get periodical payments as well. She also gets £1,500 a year by way of periodical payments, which is about one-third of their joint incomes. She will also have the management of £300 a year for the daughter who is at a good school, and aged 11. These provisions are as much as the husband can reasonably be expected to make. It will mean that each will have to cut down their standard of living: but it is as much as can be done in the circumstances.

The appeal should be allowed to the extent indicated. The wife's cross-appeal will be dismissed.

Extract reproduced by permission of the All England Reports.

Questions

1 *Dylan and Dandelion, his girlfriend, do not believe in marriage. They wish to set up home together and to have children. They intend to pool their savings and buy 'Nettle Nook' as their family home, with the assistance of a loan from a building society secured upon that property. Dylan is a herbal scientist who intends to stay at home in order to carry out research into natural medicines. There is little prospect that he will earn any income. Dandelion is manageress of 'Fibrefoods Pantry', a very successful restaurant. Dylan is very domesticated but Dandelion has little time for household work. Advise them as to their material interests in the future if they should go ahead with their venture.*

2 *Discuss the effects of registration of title upon the rights of a spouse who has an equitable interest in the matrimonial home but who has no legal ownership.*

3 *Consider whether lawyers are suitable people to offer initial advice to married persons who contemplate divorce or separation.*

4 *Since cohabitation outside marriage is not forbidden by criminal law, should not the civil law be more ready to recognize unmarried unions?*

Chapter Twelve

Restrictive covenants

The role of covenants in land law

In Chapter 4 we noticed some of the principal controls and restrictions upon the enjoyment of land. The most important of these, town and country planning law, is of comparatively recent origin. Its purposes are many but include the protection of amenity. However, during the hundred years before the Town and Country Planning Act 1947, landowners had resorted to private covenants to restrain land use, in an effort to preserve local amenity against the urban squalor of the industrial revolution. The purposes of the Act and the landowner who employed such restrictive covenants had much in common.

Since the 1947 Act had a revolutionary effect on land enjoyment, so universal and far reaching were its effects, it might be expected that the restrictive covenant would decline in importance, its aims being achieved through a more powerful agent. This has not been the case. It has been noted that in the ten-year period ending in 1965 more than 600,000 sets of new restrictive covenants were entered in the Land Charges Registry in respect of unregistered land alone (see *Cases and Materials on English Land Law* by Michael Harwood, Professional Books 1977, p.344). Although some of these relate to very small units, such as a domestic landowner and a purchaser to whom he has sold part of his land, the majority concern much larger sweeps of land. Estate development is a most important feature of modern urban and rural building, both domestic and commercial.

The use of land after sale on such estates is almost invariably restrained by restrictive covenants. Such restrictions are designed to make ownership of property on the estate a more attractive or profitable proposition. The restrictive covenant can achieve many objectives which planning law generally cannot reach. A commonplace example might illustrate this.

'Oakesacre' is a new residential estate near Birmingham, one hundred acres in extent. It is a mile away from shops, so the developer applied for and received planning permission to build five retail shops on the estate. In Chapter 4, it was explained that under planning law it is generally lawful to change the use of a shop from one retail trade to another, with certain exceptions (see p.53). If the control of activities on the various residential and business premises on 'Oakesacre' had been left to the protection of planning law alone, the properties might have been less desirable than if restrictive covenants had been entered into by the purchasers. The developer wished to provide a balance of shops for the sale of goods of ordinary domestic kind. The intention was that each shop should restrict sales to one of five purposes. These were to be grocery, butchery, ironmongery, off-licence, and newsagency. There is a clear advantage both to the shopowners as a group and to the residents that no shopowner should change his business range to that of one of the other shopowners. If the grocer, for instance, changes his business to ironmongery, not only is the estate deprived of an amenity, but the ironmonger is likely to go out of business.

In fact the estate developer would find it more difficult to sell the shops if some permanent restriction upon the type of sales permitted by each shopowner could not be imposed. Yet under planning law each of the five shopowners could take up the trade of each of the others. Similar problems would arise in regard to the residential population. There are many activities which might be undesirable on a particular kind of residential estate which would be permitted under planning law. Examples are the building of fences and small structures and the keeping of farm animals.

In short, restrictive covenants can control areas of activity which are generally beyond the reach of planning law on one side or the law of tort on the other. Furthermore, enforcement can be more readily available to the private individual. No complaint to a public authority is necessary as in the case of breaches of planning law. This avoids the question of *locus standi*.

Before studying the detailed rules of restrictive covenants, we should first consider the general scheme of covenants affecting land. An owner or occupier of land frequently contracts with someone who may or may not have an interest in that land or other land. The subject-matter of such contracts varies considerably. It may, for instance, be that the occupier shall paint the property at certain intervals, or that he shall refrain from selling intoxicating drinks on the premises. Such duties are often enforceable without reference to the law of restrictive covenants. Our particular enquiry is to discover what role restrictive covenants play which cannot be achieved by ordinary covenants. The diagram below may help to illustrate their use.

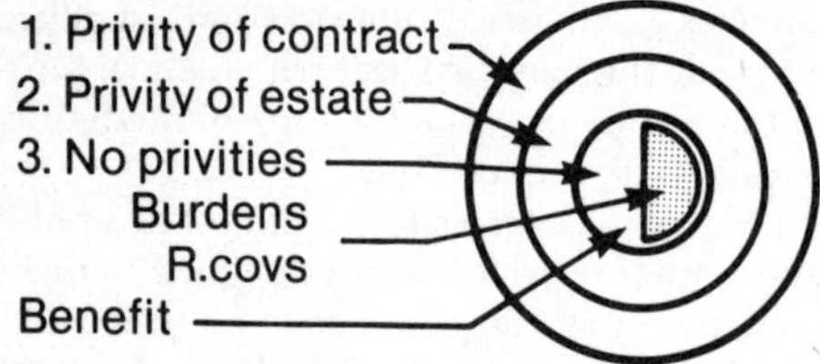

Circle 1. This large circle denotes cases where there is privity of contract between the person seeking to enforce the contract and the person against whom he is seeking to enforce it. In these cases, all kinds of rights may be enforced no matter what the subject-matter is or the circumstances are. In short, the ordinary rules of contract law apply. Thus, if *A* and *B* were the parties to the contract and *A* is seeking to enforce against *B*, it does not matter whether or not *A* has any interest in *B*'s land, or whether or not he has any interest in land whatsoever. Nor does it matter whether the covenant is positive or negative, or whether it touches and concerns the land, two factors which, we shall see, assume importance when there is no privity of contract. So even though the covenant in question ranks as a valid restrictive covenant because it conforms with the necessary rules, it can be enforced between the two original parties without reference to these rules and on the ordinary principles of contract.

Circle 2. This intermediate circle shows a more select set of circumstances. Here there is no privity of contract but merely privity of estate; that is, the landlord and tenant relationship exists between the person attempting to enforce the contract and the person against whom he is attempting to enforce it. Let us say that *L* has leased land to *T* for ten years and *T* has agreed in the lease to paint the property every five years. While *L* holds the reversion and *T* the lease, *L* can enforce the duty on the principle described above, namely, because there is privity of contract. But if *T* assigns the lease to *A*, and *L* wishes to enforce the duty against *A*, there is no privity of contract. Since, however, *A* has taken the lease of which *L* holds the reversion, there is tenure between them and therefore privity of estate. Notice that the assignment must be of the whole of the unexpired term of the lease if this result is to be achieved. Where there is privity of estate but not of contract, a narrower category of covenants only can be enforced by *L* against *A*. These are all covenants which have reference to the subject-matter of the lease. This is the only restriction. It does not matter that the covenant in question is negative or positive. Neither does it matter whether it is *L* or *T* who assigns his interest, for both the benefits and burdens of contracts in leases continue to apply when there is privity of estate.

Circle 3. The inner circle denotes cases where there is neither privity of contract nor privity of estate between the person seeking to enforce and the person against whom he is seeking to enforce. To illustrate this position, a few examples of the circumstances under which this arises might be given. Firstly, *L* might lease land to *T*, who then might sub-lease to *S*. Between *L* and *S* there is neither privity of contract nor privity of estate. If *L* then wishes to enforce covenants in the lease against *S* rather than *T*, he cannot do so on any principle mentioned above. Secondly, if *V* sold the fee simple in land to *P*, who covenanted to perform some act, and then *P* himself sold the land to *X*, we must look for some further route through which *V* might enforce the covenant against *X*. Thirdly, if *A* either sold or leased land to *B*, and *B* covenanted to do something, and either a licensee *L* or a trespasser *T* came into occupation of the land and ignored the covenant, a similar problem would exist as to the enforcement of the covenant against either *L* or *T*. Finally, it should be noticed that covenants may be imposed on the owners and occupiers of land by independent transactions without any proprietary interest in the land passing. Thus owner *A* might covenant with owner *B* not to build on his land. *A* might then sell to *P*, and *B* might wish to enforce against *P*. Briefly, the question is how can one enforce covenants against persons with whom there is neither privity of contract nor privity of estate. In such cases, the conditions for enforcement are more stringent and a distinction must be made between the benefit and the burden of the covenant.

The benefit of the covenant will pass under the following conditions: (i) it touches and concerns the land of the covenantee; (ii) the covenant must be created for the benefit of the legal estate of the covenantee; and (iii) the assignee must have the same legal estate as the covenantee, though in the case of covenants entered into after 1925 it is enough that he has an estate derived from this.

If such conditions are fulfilled the covenant is enforceable both at law and in equity. It does not matter whether this covenant is positive or negative (see *Smith and Snipes Hall Farm Ltd.* v. *River Douglas Catchment Board* [1949] 2 K.B. 500). These cases are represented by the whole of the inner circle.

The burden of the covenant, apart from the exceptional cases mentioned below, will pass only if the rules relating to restrictive covenants have been conformed with, and then only in equity. Certain types of negative covenants alone qualify. Thus the cases which the law will assist when there is neither privity of contract nor privity of estate and when the burden is sought to be enforced are still more select and represented by the shaded portion of the inner circle.

When there is a question of enforcing a covenant concerning land the order of attack should be as outlined above. First, check whether the covenant falls within the class of cases in circle 1; if so, proceed no further, for this is the zone most favourable for enforcement in that less rules have to be conformed with. If it does not, then move to circle 2; then to circle 3. If in the latter case, however, it is a question of the burden being transmitted, then the law of restrictive covenants must be invoked.

The place of restrictive covenants in the law relating to covenants is that they achieve something no other covenant can. Under them not only the benefits but also the burdens will be enforceable as between persons who are are in neither privity of contract nor privity of estate.

The exceptional cases referred to above are as follows:

(1) *Chain of covenants*. If *A* sells land to *B* who covenants to do some act and then *B* sells to *C*, *A* will not be able to enforce that covenant against *C* because there will be neither privity of contract nor privity of estate between him and *C*. He will, however, be able to enforce it against *B*, with whom he enjoys continuous privity of contract. *B* could have protected himself against such breaches of covenant by *C* by taking from him a covenant of indemnity when he sold him the land. By this means, the liability may be passed indirectly to the person who has broken the covenant. In theory, the chain might grow to indefinite length through subsequent sales of the land. The device is not a satisfactory means of imposing an enduring duty. It can only result in the remedy of damages and not an injunction and its clumsiness might obviously lead to a break in the chain of liability as the years go by.

(2) *Enlargement of long leases*. Section 153 of the Law of Property Act 1925 provides for the enlargement of certain uncommon types of long leases into fee simple estates in the circumstances described there. The lease must have been originally granted for at least 300 years, of which not less than 200 years must still be unexpired. There must be no trust or right of redemption, no rent of any value payable and no right reserved for re-entry for condition broken. The owner of such a lease is clearly substantially in the position of a fee simple owner anyway, so that the section is not performing any real act of confiscation from the reversioner.

The importance of the power for our present purposes is that the resultant fee simple is made subject to all the covenants of the lease before enlargement. Since these covenants might have been positive in nature, the Act provides a means by which the burden of positive covenants might exceptionally be enforceable between persons enjoying neither privity of contract nor privity of estate. The Leasehold Reform Act 1967 provides a similar machinery in those cases to which the Act applies (see s.8(3)).

(3) *The doctrine of Halsall* v. *Brizell [1957] Ch. 169*. A person who wishes to enjoy an advantage under some agreement must also perform any obligation

of a reciprocal nature. Thus if a conveyance permits owners to use a road or sewer on an estate and also obliges them to contribute to the cost of its maintenance, the enjoyment of the use of the facility will be conditional upon the payment of the costs. This obligation will affect successors in title who were not parties to the agreement.

(4) *Public law obligations*. Positive obligations are sometimes imposed by statute upon owners and occupiers of property. The burden of these duties affects successive owners. They are not, however, of a contractual nature.

Rules of restrictive covenants

We have just seen that where neither privity of contract nor privity of estate exists between the parties, the benefit of covenants may nevertheless be enforceable at law in certain circumstances. Equity generally followed the law in this but applied looser rules in certain circumstances, for the person seeking to enforce the benefit in such cases was not required to hold a legal estate in the dominant land. An equitable interest was enough. These rules may have fulfilled the needs of our society in the past, for they ensured that the most important covenants in leases were enforceable despite assignments of both leases and reversions. They even enabled the benefits of other covenants to be enforced by assignees of the dominant land if they 'touched and concerned' that land.

As towns grew rapidly in the nineteenth century, and the desire to maintain privacy and amenity for land became more urgent, the shortcomings of these rules were felt. If a landowner sold some of his land to *P* and continued to live on the rest, he might wish to impose some restriction on the land sold, such as that no building should be erected near to his boundaries. As between himself and *P*, a covenant to this effect would be enforceable on the ordinary principles of privity of contract. Furthermore, a purchaser of the rest of his land could enforce the covenant because, as explained earlier, the benefit was capable of passing. If *P*, however, sold his land to *X*, then not even the original vendor could enforce the covenant against *X* because before the nineteenth century the burden was only capable of being enforced where there was either privity of contract or privity of estate.

It has sometimes come about in our legal history that where some reasonable human aim could not be achieved under existing legal rules, the law has grown to accommodate that objective. Today it usually falls to Parliament to enact an appropriate statute. In the nineteenth century, the shortcomings in the law of covenants were mitigated by an organic development through cases decided in equity. The new doctrine, which went far beyond the existing law, is traditionally traced to the case of *Tulk* v. *Moxhay* (1848), 2 Ph. 744, but its origins lie before that date and its principles have developed much since then. Further developments may be expected. The remark of Megarry, J., in *Brunner* v. *Greenslade* [1970] 3 All E.R. 833, at p.842, that perhaps 'this is one of those branches of equity which work best when explained least' hints that the law, like the human personality, sometimes develops more quickly behind a mask of shyness. During its development as an interest in land, some of its concepts shadowed those of easements. Although the new element concerns the passing of the burden of a covenant, the law of restrictive covenants has now become a self-sufficient branch of law so that the rules governing the passing of the benefit will be dealt with too. These rules will now be considered.

The passing of the benefit

Firstly, irrespective of the rules given below, a person may take the benefit of a covenant even though he is not named as a party to it, provided that he falls within a class of persons named as parties. Such persons must be in existence at the date of the contract. If they are not in existence at that time they cannot take any benefit as parties, but they might do so as assignees. This is permitted by s.56 of the Law of Property Act 1925, as explained in *Beswick* v. *Beswick* [1968] A.C. 58. In the present context it means that, if a covenant touches and concerns land belonging to such a third party, then both he and his successors in title may enforce it. In such a case, the land must, of course, be adequately identified. In *Re Ecclesiastical Commissioners for England's Conveyance* [1936] Ch. 430, *V* sold land to *P*, who entered covenants expressed to be for the benefit, not only of land retained by *V*, but also of adjacent land owned by *X*, who was not a party to the deed. It was held that the benefit was effectively conferred. The conditions necessary for the passing of the benefit to persons other than the original beneficiaries under the covenant must now be considered. We shall see that restrictive covenants concern the relationship between two or more pieces of land. One of these, the 'dominant', enjoys the benefit of the covenant; the other, the 'servient', suffers the duty of obedience to it.

(1) *The covenant must benefit the dominant land.* This means that the value, amenity or convenience of the land is either preserved or increased in some way. If the covenant is contained in a lease and it is the landlord's reversion that is to be protected, it must concern the way in which the demised land is enjoyed. Examples are covenants by a neighbouring landowner either not to build at all or not to erect buildings of a particular description, or not to use premises for particular purposes. These may clearly enhance the amenities of the dominant land. It has been held that a covenant not to sell certain types of goods on the servient premises so as to allow the owner of the dominant land a greater monopoly of the trade satisfies the requirement (*Newton Abbot Co-operative Society Ltd.* v. *Williamson & Treadgold Ltd.* [1952] Ch. 286).

(2) *The assignee of the dominant land must be able to show that the benefit of the covenant has passed to him.* This can be done in one of three alternative ways:

(i) By original annexation of the covenant to the dominant land

The benefit of a covenant touching and concerning land will run with the land, provided that the language used shows a clear intention of bestowing a benefit upon the land as such, and not merely upon a particular covenantee. This is a question of construction. A formula that leaves no room for doubt is 'with intent that the covenant may enure to the benefit of the vendors their successors and assigns and others claiming under them to "Blackacre"'. It is enough, however, if it is expressed to be made with the dominant owner in his capacity as owner of the dominant land. In *Renals* v. *Cowlishaw* (1878) 9 Ch.D. 125, *P*, a purchaser, covenanted with the vendors and 'their heirs, executors, administrators and assigns' not to build. The vendors later sold the dominant land without mention of the covenant. It was held that the new owners could not sue. The word 'assigns' was taken to mean assignees of the covenant, which remained a separate entity from the land. Thus its benefit would only pass if assigned as such. If the language used had made it part of the land then it would pass with the land as an adjunct to it and without special mention. In *Rogers* v. *Hosegood* [1900] 2 Ch. 388 a covenant was expressed to be for the benefit of the dominant owners, 'their heirs and assigns and others claiming under them to all or any lands adjoining'. It was held that, when the dominant land was later conveyed, the benefit of the covenant passed naturally with it.

These two cases can be distinguished in the following way. Consider the benefit of the covenant to be quite a separate thing from the dominant land. In *Renals* v. *Cowlishaw* the dominant owner had, so to speak, the land in his right hand and the covenant in his left. When he conveyed the land in his right hand he made no reference to the covenant in his left. So there it remained and did not pass to the purchaser. In *Rogers* v. *Hosegood* the words in the covenant were such as to impress it as part of the very land, so that land and covenant were a single entity held in one hand. A later conveyance of that land therefore carried the benefit of the covenant as naturally as it carried the soil, the hedges and the ditches upon it. All this may be achieved by making the intention clear.

The words of annexation must, of course, identify the dominant land. The rules as to identification, however, have been relaxed in recent years and an implied reference will serve this purpose, provided that extrinsic evidence is available to complete this identification (Newton Abbot case, above).

There can be no annexation of the benefit of a covenant to land if the area of the alleged dominant land is greater than can reasonably receive some advantage from it. The original covenantee can enforce, but a purchaser from him cannot. In *Re Ballard's Conveyance* [1937] Ch. 473 annexation was attempted in favour of an estate of 1,700 acres. It was held that an alienee of the land could not enforce even in favour of those parts which could derive benefit, for other parts were too remote to enjoy any advantage. In short, the court refused to sever the covenant and attach its benefit to parts of the land. Yet if the parties themselves sever the covenant, as in *Zetland* v. *Driver* [1939] Ch. 1, so that it is expressed to be for the benefit not only of the whole but also of 'each and every part' of the land, then it may be enforced by alienees of any part which in fact benefits from it. It must not be concluded from this, however, that a restrictive covenant imposed upon a very small area is never capable of benefiting the whole of a large estate. It is a question of fact to be decided on all the evidence. Unless it is very clear that a covenant is incapable of benefiting particular land there is a presumption that the covenant is capable of doing so. (*Wrotham Park Estate Company* v. *Parkside Homes Ltd*. [1974] 1 W.L.R. 798 at 808).

Following *Marten* v. *Flight Refuelling Ltd* [1962] Ch. 115, it has been suggested that annexation can be implied from the circumstances in which a covenant is made and without the assistance of language (see *The Law of Real Property* by R. E. Megarry and H. W. R. Wade (4th edn, p.764)). This decision, however, does not seem to justify such an extension of the rules (see 36 Conveyancer 20).

The Court of Appeal has now held that the benefit of a covenant is automatically annexed to land, irrespective of the use of words of annexation, by force of section 78 of the Law of Property Act 1925, provided that the covenantee has land to which the covenant relates. Moreover, annexation is to every part of the land as well as to the whole. Intention is apparently irrelevant (*Federated Homes Ltd.* v. *Mill Lodge Properties Ltd.* [1980] 1 All E.R. 371 (C.A.).

Subsection (1) enacts

> A covenant relating to any land of the covenantee shall be deemed to be made with the covenantee and his successors in title and the persons deriving title under him or them, and shall have effect as if such successors and other persons were expressed . . . .

Brightman L.J. was impressed by the clarity of these words as a free standing enactment. This view however perhaps undervalues other factors:

(1) This part of the 1925 Act is a consolidating measure and should be construed as changing the law as little as possible. Section 78 replaces section 58 of the Conveyancing Act 1881 and passed through its Parliamentary Committee with no discussion. Section 58 was never held to annex the benefit of a covenant to land, merely to save the addition of the words 'his executors, administrators and assigns'. It is true that the wording of section 78 differs from that of section 58, but this difference was only intended to accommodate the changed rules of inheritance introduced by the 1925 Act (see 1982 J.P.L. p.295). Statute law, like common law, loses its innocence with age.

(2) Words of annexation perform an important policy function. They separate cases where there is a real intention to benefit land from those where there is no such intention, but where prolongation of a covenant's effect would achieve nothing but the unwanted incumbrance of land. *Kingsbury* v. *Anderson* [1979] 40 P.C.R. 136 had earlier emphasized that, even in the case of 'building schemes', in regard to which, we shall see, more flexible rules apply, whatever concessions are made in other respects, there must initially have been a covenant, not merely an allusion to one. This restraint is in the tradition of restrictive covenants. Enforcement of covenants where there is neither privity of contract nor privity of estate is a privilege. The Mill Lodge case loosens this tradition. Words of annexation acted as a corset on the proliferation of covenants. If the new doctrine prevails the principle of express assignment, discussed below, will become unnecessary.

Once annexed in accordance with the rules given above, the benefit of a covenant runs in favour of subsequent owners of any interests in the land without express mention and even if the parties are unaware of it.

By an express assignment of the benefit

If no annexation takes place in the ways just described, the covenant's benefit remains separate from the land. If it is to be passed to a purchaser of the land it must therefore be assigned independently, and this can be achieved by a statement in the conveyance that the benefit is to pass. It is, however, probably enough that all the circumstances show that this was intended. In fact, such an assignment may even occur by operation of law and the benefit may thus pass to the executors of a deceased dominant owner, and, since they would be bare trustees of the benefit, the devisee would be entitled to sue upon it in equity and to assign the benefit to purchasers without joining the personal representatives (*Earl of Leicester* v. *Wells U.D.C.* [1972] 3 All E.R. 77). Once the dominant land has been sold, it is too late to assign the benefit; the rather unconvincing reason being that if the land was saleable without it, then its purpose is spent. On the other hand, the covenant can be severed and dealt with in parts—in equity, though not at law—so if only part of the land has been sold, the benefit can be assigned with the parts retained on their eventual sale.

Whether the benefit of a covenant not originally annexed but contemporaneously assigned with the land passes on all future sales without express mention is open to doubt (see *Re Pinewood Estate, Farnborough* [1958] Ch. 280 and *Renals* v. *Cowlishaw*, above, at pp. 130–131).

By the existence of a 'building scheme'

Since the law of restrictive covenants developed to fulfil a social need, its growth was more precocious where that need was most pronounced. This was the case where a developer wished to build an estate and impose restrictions on the purchasers of the plots for their mutual benefit and to the general advantages of the estate. Such a scheme may be highly desirable in an area of intensive development. In such cases, even some of the new equitable rules, concessionary though they are, were somewhat too confining, so that further relaxations were made. Private law was aspiring to be public law at a time before town and country planning had received the attention of Parliament.

The result is that special rules apply if a 'building scheme' exists and these affect not only the passing of the benefit of covenants but also the burden, which is dealt with below. In fact, given that the covenant is negative these rules are almost self-supporting. Formerly, it was considered that some fairly rigid rules laid down by Parker J. in *Elliston* v. *Reacher* [1908] 2 Ch. 374 must be observed. Today it is enough that the outer perimeter of a scheme shall be defined and that the purchasers or lessees within the scheme shall purchase, or take leases, on the footing that the restrictions were to enure for the benefit of other plots in the scheme. The restrictions need not, however, apply equally to all the plots. The modern principles can be found in *Baxter* v. *Four Oaks Properties Ltd.* [1965] Ch. 816 and *Re Dolphin's Conveyance* [1970] Ch. 654.

The first of these requirements is to some extent subjective in nature and the difficulty of proving it may vary according to the availability of evidence. An express declaration that a scheme is intended or that the purchasers expect mutual enforceability is not necessary, though such 'internal' evidence is clearly a great advantage. It was explained in *Re Wembley Park Estate Co. Ltd.'s Transfer* [1968] 1 All E.R. 457 that, if 'external' circumstances sufficiently suggest a scheme, the inference will be readily drawn. Thus, if there is no express declaration to its effect, proof that the purchasers saw a plan of the estate might be given; but ignorance by them of the position will be fatal to a scheme. Failing an expressed intention, if no land is retained by the vendor, the intention of mutual benefit to the plots will be more readily inferred than if it is, for the latter might lead to the conclusion that he simply wished to benefit his own land. Yet the retention or otherwise of land by the vendor is by no means conclusive. Neither is the mere similarity of the covenants affecting the various plots. In short, rules of thumb should be spurned and all the circumstances considered when answering the broad question whether the developer intended and the purchasers expected reciprocal obligations and benefits within a defined estate.

The benefit and burden of covenants may even be transmitted under the doctrine to sub-purchasers where the original plot from which their own sub-plots are derived was part of a scheme of development. If the common vendor *V* of the plots *A*, *B* and *C* shown below intended a scheme of development for the three plots, aimed at preventing the erection of more than four houses on each, and took covenants to this effect from the purchasers, then when the purchaser of *A* has sold sub-plots *A2* and *A3*, the owners of these sub-plots may enforce the covenants between themselves, just as the owners of *A*, *B* and *C* can (*Brunner* v. *Greenslade* [1970] 3 All E.R. 833).

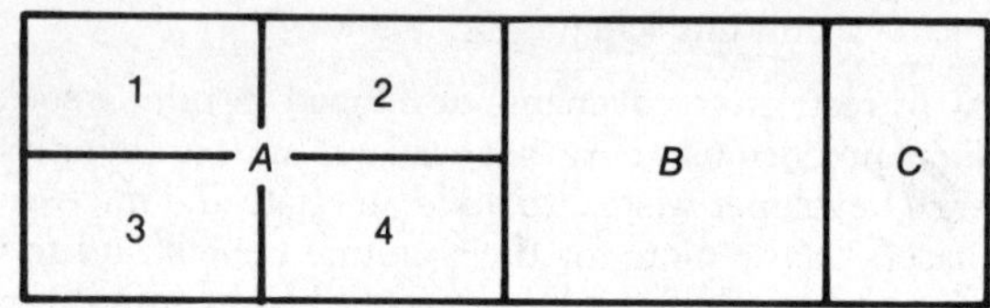

The same principle applies if some of the plots come into common ownership at a later stage by purchase and are then again sold to separate owners. The covenants remain enforceable by the new purchasers as between themselves, though it is open to the parties to show that the restriction is no longer to apply between them, either by express provision or by the circumstances of the transaction. It will, of course, still be enforceable by the owners of the other original plots and sub-plots in the scheme (*Texaco Antilles Ltd.* v. *Kernochan* [1973] 2 All E.R. 118 at p. 126).

The passing of the burden: conditions

If neither privity of contract nor privity of estate exists between the person seeking to enforce and the person against whom he is seeking to enforce, the burden of a covenant benefiting other land is enforceable if the following conditions prevail.

(1) *The covenant must be negative in substance.* This means that the covenant must not oblige the covenantor to carry out any act. Whether it is positive or negative in its language is immaterial. Thus in *Tulk* v. *Moxhay*, p. 235 *ante*, the covenant was to keep certain land uncovered with buildings. Though positive in form, this obviously amounted merely to an undertaking not to build. On the other hand, a covenant not to allow property to fall into disrepair is positive since it imposes a duty to repair. The test whether it involves expenditure of money is usually sound but not necessarily conclusive, for, while a covenant involving expenditure can never be negative, the reverse is not true. If the covenant contains both negative and positive elements, the positive part may be severed, leaving the negative part only enforceable. This occurred in *Tulk* v. *Moxhay*. Finally, a positive duty merely ancillary to a substantially negative obligation may be indirectly enforceable, as, for instance, in the case of a covenant not to build without first submitting plans.

(2) *There must be dominant land.* This will normally mean that the covenantee must retain land to take the benefit of the covenant. In the case of building schemes, and cases such as *Re Ecclesiastical Commissioners for England's Conveyance*, p.236 *ante*, where the benefit is bestowed upon another person's land, this need not necessarily be so. In all cases there must be dominant land for the benefit of which the covenant was taken, for the whole rationale of the doctrine is the protection of land as such. In *Formby* v. *Barker* [1903] 2 Ch. 539, *X* sold all his land, the purchaser entering a covenant restricting its use. It was held that *X*'s executors could not enforce against an assignee from that purchaser. If the covenantee does retain land, but later sells it, he cannot enforce the covenant against the servient owner in equity and so cannot obtain an injunction, for he cannot claim that it is protecting land. He could sue at law because privity of contract exists, but this would probably result in nominal damages only. We shall see, however, that a purchaser of such retained land can enforce the covenant in certain circumstances. The retention of a reversion behind a lease is equivalent to the retention of land, so that a landlord may enforce a restrictive covenant against a sub-lessee. There are, moreover, some statutory exceptions to the requirement that land must be retained, in favour of certain public authorities (e.g. Housing Act 1957, s.151).

Finally, the land or reversion retained must derive benefit from the covenant. It was said in *Kelly* v. *Barrett* [1924] 2 Ch. 379, at p.440, that 'covenants binding land in Hampstead will be too remote to benefit land in Clapham', but considering that a business interest in land is one which can be protected by restrictive covenants, physical proximity alone is a test to be applied carefully.

The effectiveness of restrictive covenants

It is clear that a restrictive covenant conforming to the principles described above is more than a personal right. It is an interest in land. It is capable not merely of running with an estate in land, as certain covenants made between landlord and tenant may do, but with the very land itself, so as to be capable of binding anyone who comes to that land whether as a purchaser of the fee simple, lessee, sub-lessee, mortgagee, licensee or trespasser. One might say that whereas landlord and tenant covenants having reference to the subject-matter of the lease, though lacking the ingredients of restrictive covenants, are 'pinned' to the lease and affect only persons who take that very lease, restrictive covenants are nailed to the gatepost on the land itself, so as to be capable of affecting anyone who comes to the land, whatever his interest in it may be. Landlord and tenant covenants may and quite frequently do qualify as restrictive covenants also. These principles are illustrated by *Mander* v. *Falcke* [1891] 2 Ch. 554, where a lessee covenanted not to disturb the enjoyment of the lessor's neighbouring property and then sub-leased. The reversion and sub-lease eventually came to *R* and *S* respectively. *S* did not occupy the property himself but allowed his father to use it as an oyster bar. In fact, the latter caused disturbance by using it as a brothel. It was held that the father was bound by the covenant, even though a mere licensee.

On the other hand, being creatures of equity, restrictive covenants create equitable and not legal interests in land, and, like all such interests, they have a frailty. A covenant created before 1926 cannot be enforced against a purchaser of a legal estate in the servient land for value without notice of it, nor against any person claiming through him. A covenant created after 1925 is void against a purchaser for money or money's worth of a legal estate unless it is registered under the Land Charges Act 1972, or on the charges register if the land is registered, before that legal estate is taken. Covenants made before 1926 and covenants between landlord and tenant whenever made, however, cannot be registered. A covenant in a lease may still come within this exception, even though the servient land is not the lease or the reversion but separate land altogether (*Dartstone Ltd.* v. *Cleveland Petroleum Co. Ltd.* [1969] 3 All E.R. 668). As to the former of these two exceptions, the old rules governing notice apply; as to the latter, a sub-lessee is taken to have notice of the covenants in the lease. The difference between 'valuable consideration' and 'money or money's worth' is that 'valuable consideration' includes marriage.

Unless otherwise agreed, a restrictive covenant is normally binding for ever. Nevertheless, even if it is perfectly valid under the rules described above, the court may refuse a remedy where it would be contrary to the principles of equity as, for instance, where the covenant has been openly breached for so long as to give the impression that it is no longer binding, or where it has become obsolete through changed surroundings and the action is not in good faith. Mere delay does not constitute acquiescence. The circumstances must be such that as a result of the delay, it would be unconscionable or dishonest for the person having the benefit of the covenant to seek to enforce it (*Shaw* v. *Applegate* [1977] 1 W.L.R. 970). It is clear, both from this and from the demanding nature of the rules applying to restrictive covenants, that whether a covenant is enforceable may sometimes be very uncertain. Important and expensive decisions may depend on the answer, such as whether to erect buildings. It is therefore provided by s.84 of the Law of Property Act 1925 that the court has power to make a declaration as to whether an alleged covenant affects freehold land. This power should be distinguished from the power, dealt with below, of discharging an admittedly binding covenant.

The extinguishment and modification of restrictive covenants

Power is given to the Lands Tribunal by the Law of Property Act 1925, s.84, as amended by the Law of Property Act 1969, s.28, on the application of any person interested in freehold land affected by a restrictive covenant, to discharge or modify the restriction in any of the following cases:

(1) Where the restriction ought to be deemed obsolete.
(2) Where it would impede some reasonable user and does not give any practical benefit or substantial value to the land, or is contrary to the public interest.
(3) Where those entitled to the benefit have expressly or impliedly agreed to the discharge.
(4) Where discharge will not injure anyone entitled to the benefit of the covenant. There is a provision for compensation under this head. This was somewhat paradoxical in view of the requirement that discharge shall not cause injury.

Modern Lands Tribunal decisions should be consulted for an appreciation of the operation of these provisions. The provision regarding the 'public interest' under (2), for instance, has not been generously interpreted. In *Re Osborn's and Easton's Application* [1978] 38 P. & C.R. 251 the President commented: 'It is one thing to say that a development is in the public interest and another to say that it would be contrary to the public interest if such development did not take place'. This view is significant in the inevitable conflict between private and public interests. Perhaps the central government might advise higher density residential development to ease the housing shortage; perhaps planning permission has been granted for such development in a particular case after consideration of this and other public and private considerations. Nevertheless, such development could be blocked by the refusal of the Lands Tribunal to discharge a covenant in restraint of that development.

Limited powers to modify the effects of restrictive covenants are given by section 165 of the Housing Act 1957 and section 127 of the Town and County Planning Act 1971 to county courts and to local planning authorities respectively.

General

Finally, the law of restrictive covenants is quite distinct from the law of town and country planning. A person wishing to develop land must ascertain that he may do so under both these branches of law. Thus the grant of planning permission does not entitle a person to breach a restrictive covenant.

Study material:

Law of Property Act 1925, section 78

> Benefit of covenants relating to land—(1) A covenant relating to any land of the covenantee shall be deemed to be made with the covenantee and his successors in title and the persons deriving title under him or them, and shall have effect as if such successors and other persons were expressed.
>
> For the purpose of this subsection in connection with covenants restrictive of the user of land 'successors in title' shall be deemed to include the owners and occupiers for the time being of the land of the covenantee intended to be benefited.
>
> (2) This section applies to covenants made after the commencement of this Act, but the repeal of section fifty-eight of the Conveyancing Act, 1881, does not affect the operation of covenants to which that section applied.

Federated Homes Ltd. v. *Mill Lodge Properties Ltd.* 1980 1 All E.R. 371 (C.A.)

Brightman L.J. at p.378:

Counsel for the defendants submitted that there were three possible views about s 78. One view, which he described as 'the orthodox view' hitherto held, is that it is merely a statutory shorthand for reducing the length of legal documents. A second view, which was the one that counsel for the defendants was inclined to place in the forefront of his argument, is that the section only applies, or at any rate only achieves annexation, when the land intended to be benefited is signified in the document by express words or necessary implication as the intended beneficiary of the covenant. A third view is that the section applies if the covenant in fact touches and concerns the land of the covenantee, whether that be gleaned from the document itself or from evidence outside the document.

For myself, I reject the narrowest interpretation of s 78, the supposed orthodox view, which seems to me to fly in the face of the wording of the section. Before I express my reasons I will say that I do not find it necessary to choose between the second and third views because, in my opinion, this covenant relates to land of the covenantee on either interpretation of s 78. Clause 5(iv) shows quite clearly that the covenant is for the protection of the retained land and that land is described in cl 2 as 'any adjoining or adjacent property retained by the Vendor'. This formulation is sufficient for annexation purposes: see *Rogers v Hosegood*[1].

There is in my judgment no doubt that this covenant 'related to the land of the covenantee', or, to use the old-fashioned expression, that it touched and concerned the land, even if counsel for the defendants is correct in his submission that the document must show an intention to benefit identified land. The result of such application is that one must read cl 5(iv) as if it were written: 'The purchaser hereby covenants with the vendor and its successors in title and the persons deriving title under it or them, including the owners and occupiers for the time being of the retained land, that in carrying out the development of the blue land the purchaser shall not build at a greater density than a total of 300 dwellings so as not to reduce the number of units which the vendor might eventually erect on the retained land under the existing planning consent.' I leave out of consideration s 79 as unnecessary to be considered in this context, since Mill Lodge is the original covenantor.

The first point to notice about s 78(1) is that the wording is significantly different from the wording of its predecessor, s 58(1) of the Conveyancing and Law of Property Act 1881. The distinction is underlined by sub-s (2) of s 78, which applies sub-s (1) only to covenants made after the commencement of the Act. Section 58(1) of the earlier Act did not include the covenantee's successors in title or persons deriving title under him or them, nor the owners or occupiers for the time being of the land of the covenantee intended to be benefited. The section was confined, in relation to realty, to the covenantee, his heirs and assigns, words which suggest a more limited scope of operation than is found in s 78.

If, as the language of s 78 implies, a covenant relating to land which is restrictive of the user thereof is enforceable at the suit of (1) a successor in title of the covenantee, (2) a person deriving title under the covenantee or under his successors in title, and (3) the owner or occupier of the land intended to be benefited by the covenant, it must, in my view, follow that the covenant runs with the land, because ex hypothesi every successor in title to the land, every derivative proprietor of the land and every other owner and occupier has a right by statute to the covenant. In other words, if the condition precedent of s 78 is satisfied, that is to say, there exists a covenant which touches and concerns the land of the covenantee, that covenant runs with the land for the benefit of his successors in title, persons deriving title under him or them and other owners and occupiers.

This approach to s 78 has been advocated by distinguished textbook writers: see Dr Radcliffe in the Law Quarterly Review[2], Professor Wade in the Cambridge Law Journal[3] under the apt cross-heading 'What is wrong with section 78?', and Megarry

---

1 [1900] 2 Ch 388, [1900–3] All ER Rep 915
2 (1941) 57 LQR 203
3 [1972] CLJ 157

and Wade on the Law of Real Property[4]. Counsel pointed out to us that the fourth edition of Megarry and Wade's textbook indicates a change of mind on this topic since the third edition was published in 1966.

Although the section does not seem to have been extensively used in the course of argument in this type of case, the construction of s 78 which appeals to me appears to be consistent with at least two cases decided in this court. The first is *Smith v River Douglas Catchment Board*[4]. In that case an agreement was made in April 1938 between certain landowners and the catchment board under which the catchment board undertook to make good the banks of a certain brook and to maintain the same, and the landowners undertook to contribute towards the cost. In 1940 the first plaintiff took a conveyance from one of the landowers of a part of the land together with an express assignment of the benefit of the landowner's successors in title; and there was no assignment of the benefit of the agreement. In 1944 the second plaintiff took a tenancy of that land without any express assignment of the benefit of the agreement. In 1946 the brook burst its banks and the land owned by the first plaintiff and tenanted by the second plaintiff was inundated. The two important points are that the agreement was not expressed to be for the benefit of the agreement in favour of the second plaintiff, the tenant. In reliance, as I understand the case, on s 78 of the Law of Property Act 1925, it was held that the second plaintiff was entitled to sue the catchment board for damages for breach of the agreement. It seems to me that that conclusion can only have been reached on the basis that s 78 had the effect of causing the benefit of the agreement to run with the land so as to be capable of being sued on by the tenant.

The other case, *Williams v Unit Construction Co Ltd*[6], was decided by this court in 1951. There a company had acquired a building estate and had underleased four plots to Cubbin for 999 years. The underlessors arranged for the defendant company to build houses on the four plots. The defendant company covenanted with Cubbin to keep the adjacent road in repair until adopted. Cubbin granted a weekly tenancy of one house to the plaintiff without any express assignment of the benefit of the covenant. The plaintiff was injured owing to the disrepair of the road. She was held entitled to recover damages from the defendant for breach of the covenant.

We were referred to observations in the speeches of Lord Upjohn and Lord Wilberforce in *Tophams Ltd v Earl of Sefton*[7] to the effect that s 79 of the Law of Property Act 1925 (relating to the burden of covenants) achieved no more than the introduction of statutory shorthand into the drafting covenants. Section 79, in my view, involves quite different considerations and I do not think that it provides a helpful analogy.

It was suggested by counsel for the defendants that if this covenant ought to be read as enuring for the benefit of the retained land, it should be read as enuring only for the benefit of the retained land as a whole and not for the benefit of every part of it; with the apparent result that there is no annexation of the benefit to a part of the retained land when any severance takes place. He referred us to a passage in *Re Union of London and Smith's Bank Ltd's Conveyance, Miles v Easter*[8], which I do not think it is necessary for me to read.

The problem is alluded to in Megarry and Wade on the Law of Real Property[9]:

> 'In drafting restrictive covenants it is therefore desirable to annex them to the covenantee's land "or any part or parts thereof". An additional reason for using this form of words is that, if there is no indication to the contrary, the benefit may be held to be annexed only to the whole of the covenantee's land, so that it will not pass with portions of it disposed of separately. But even without such words the

4 4th Edn (1975) p 764
5 [1949] 2 All ER 179 [1949] 2 KB 500
6 (1951) 19 Conv NS 262
7 [1966] 1 All ER 1039 at 1048, 1053 [1967] 1 AC 50 at 73, 81
8 [1933] Ch 611, [1933] All ER Rep 355
9 4th Edn (1975) p 763

> court may find that the covenant is intended to benefit any part of the retained land; and small indications may suffice, since the rule that presumes annexation to the whole only is arbitrary and inconvenient. In principle it conflicts with the rule for assignments, which allows a benefit annexed to the whole to be assigned with part, and it also conflicts with the corresponding rule for easements.'

I find the idea of the annexation of a covenant to the whole of the land but not to a part of it a difficult conception fully to grasp. I can understand that a covenantee may expressly or by necessary implication retain the benefit of a covenant wholly under his own control, so that the benefit will not pass unless the covenantee chooses to assign; but I would have thought, if the benefit of a covenant is, on a proper construction of a document, annexed to the land, prima facie it is annexed to every part thereof, unless the contrary clearly appears. It is difficult to see how this court can have reached its decision in *Williams v Unit Construction Co Ltd*[10] unless this is right. The covenant was, by inference, annexed to every part of the land and not merely to the whole, because it will be recalled that the plaintiff was a tenant of only one of the four houses which had the benefit of the covenant.

There is also this observation by Romer LJ in *Drake v Gray*[11]. He was dealing with the enuring of the benefit of a restrictive covenant and he said:

> '. . . where . . . you find, not "the land coloured yellow", or "the estate", or "the field named so and so", or anything of that kind, but "the lands retained by the vendor", it appears to me that there is a sufficient indication that the benefit of the covenant enures to every one of the lands retained by the vendor, and if a plaintiff in a subsequent action to enforce a covenant can say, "I am the owner of a piece of land or a hereditament that belonged to the vendor at the time of the conveyance", he is entitled to enforce the covenant.'

In the instant case the judge in the course of his judgment appears to have dismissed the notion that any individual plotholder would be entitled, even by assignment, to have the benefit of the covenant that I have been considering. I express no view about that. I only say this, that I am not convinced that his conclusion on that point is correct. I say no more about it.

In the end, I come to the conclusion that s 78 of the Law of Property Act 1925 caused the benefit of the restrictive covenant in question to run with the red land and therefore to be annexed to it, with the result that the plaintiff company is able to enforce the covenant against Mill Lodge, not only in its capacity as owner of the green land, but also in its capacity as owner of the red land.

For these reasons I think that the judge reached the correct view on the right of the plaintiff company to enforce the covenant, although in part he arrived there by a different route.

There remains only the question whether we ought to interfere with the remedy granted by the judge of an injunction against the building of the 32 extra dwellings. *Shelfer v City of London Electric Lighting Co*[12] is authority for the proposition that a person who has the benefit of a restrictive covenant is, as a general rule, entitled to an injunction on the trial of the action as distinct from an award of damages unless (1) the injury to the plaintiff's legal rights is small, (2) it is capable of being estimated in terms of money, (3) it can adequately be compensated for by a small payment, and (4) it would be oppressive to the defendant to grant an injunction. In my view, the first, third and fourth of these conditions have not been shown to be satisfied. I would, therefore, uphold the injunction and I would dismiss this appeal.

Extract reproduced by permission of the All England Law Reports.

---

10 (1951) 19 Conv NS 262
11 [1936] 1 All ER 363 at 376, [1936] Ch 451, at 465
12 [1895] 1 Ch 287, [1891–4] All ER Rep 838

Report of the Committee on Positive Covenants Affecting Land (Cmnd 2719, 1965)

10. We recommend, first, that the assignability and enforcement of positive covenants should, as far as possible, be assimilated to that of negative covenants. Broadly speaking, . . . in the case of positive covenants as in that of negative covenants the burden should run with the land encumbered, and the benefit should run with the land advantaged.

36. The recommendations we have made so far would go some way towards meeting the special needs of owners of flats or other parts of divided buildings to which we referred at the beginning of this Report; but they would not provide a complete answer. In such multiple units every owner is dependent for shelter and support on the maintenance and repair of adjoining, superjacent and subjacent units; and the amenities and services available in each unit (water, gas, electricity, central heating, telephone, ventilation, drainage, refuse disposal, etc.) may depend for their continuance on access through, and maintenance of the means of access in, other units or common parts in the building. In order to afford the occupants the fullest enjoyment of their own units and to preserve the value and integrity of each unit, there must therefore be a far higher degree of interdependence between adjoining properties than is normally the case between neighbouring land or buildings. Between flat owners compliance with mutual obligations is vital and consequently there is a special need for effective and rapid enforcement. To a lesser extent this is also true in regard to building estates consisting of individual houses where an area has been developed as one estate with substantial areas of land to be used in common by the owners of the individual properties. And even where the occupants are less interdependent the value of each property must to some degree be affected by the general state of repair of the remainder of the estate, the efficiency of the services provided and the maintenance of the common amenities.

38. In our opinion it is therefore important to ensure that at least the essential obligations will in future be imposed in every such development; and that facilities for imposing a more comprehensive scheme of mutual covenants and of management for the mutual benefit of the owners of units in multiple developments are so readily available that the developer will have every inducement to adopt it. But, if there are to be binding mutual obligations to repair and maintain divided buildings, it is also important to ensure that these mutual covenants will not have the effect of artificially prolonging the life of obsolete or decayed structures and so obstruct redevelopment . . .

Extract reproduced by permission of the Incorporated Council of Law Reporting for England and Wales

No legislation has been passed to implement the recommendations of the Report. The Law Commission is, however, preparing a more comprehensive series of reports on rights appurtenant to land.

Questions

1 *List as many of the problems suggested by the extracts above. Develop possible solutions to them. Then consult the full Report to assess your answers.*

2 *Has the amendment to s.84 of the Law of Property Act 1925 provided by s.28 of the Law of Property Act 1969 been futile?*

3 *Discuss the divergences between restrictive covenants and negative easements.*

4 *In what ways does the decision in Federated Homes Ltd.* v. *Mill Lodge Properties Ltd. [1980] 1 E.R. 371 (C.A.) run contrary to the established principles of restrictive covenants?*

Chapter Thirteen

Easements

Introduction

An easement is traditionally defined as a right to use or restrict the use of another person's land in some way. This definition is unsatisfactory because it misses the purpose of a definition, which is to distinguish and identify. It attempts to describe easements by reference to their subject-matter, whereas this is one of their least distinctive characteristics. There is no kind of advantage which one person can enjoy over another person's land by virtue of an easement which he cannot enjoy through some other means, even though the enforceability and stability of the right might be much more robust if achieved by an easement. Thus rights of ways and of light are commonly found as easements but may be enjoyed through licences or restrictive covenants respectively.

To give an analogy, I can go to a concert either on my bike or in my car. The concert will sound the same in either case. No one would describe a car by saying that it will take you to a concert, because so will a bike. To describe a car you must talk of the vehicle itself. Likewise, easements are vehicles, not destinations. It is true that there are some destinations I cannot reach by means of easements, just as there are certain destinations, such as mountain peaks, which are beyond the reach of my car. These forbidden destinations no more serve to identify easements than do the destinations they are capable of reaching.

Yet it is most important to know whether enjoyment of a particular advantage over another person's land is attributable to an easement as opposed to some other right, because, as mentioned above, the span of enforceability and the durability of the advantages will be affected by this. This is so because an easement is an interest in land. It may be a legal interest if it is to endure forever or for a certain term of years (L.P.A. 1925, s.1 (2)(a)) and has been created in one of the ways required for legal easements. These methods of creation are dealt with below. It is an equitable interest if it is to endure for any other period, such as for life, or has not been created in the form appropriate for legal easements, even though it is to endure for a period which would ordinarily entitle it to exist as a legal interest.

In other words, an easement is very much more than a personal right such as a licence. If it is a legal easement it can be enforced against anyone coming to the servient land whether he has notice of it or not, and no matter what interest he takes in the land. Furthermore, a legal easement needs no registration to secure it. Indeed, it cannot be registered. The benefit is, moreover, as sturdy as the burden. It passes without mention on a conveyance of the dominant land to another person (L.P.A. 1925, s.62). If it is an equitable easement then it possesses the Achilles' heel of all equitable interests and may be overridden by a purchaser of a legal estate in the servient land for value without notice. An equitable easement created after 1925, however, may be registered under the Land Charges Act 1972, as a Class D (iii) land charge or, in the case of registered land, as a minor interest under the Land Registration Acts. Once registered, it becomes universally enforceable just as a legal easement is. If not registered, it will be void as against a purchaser of a legal estate in the servient land for money or money's worth unless the principle of 'proprietary estoppel' can be invoked. This will be explained below.

An easement, therefore, is a means by which certain advantages may be enjoyed over the land of another person. It is the means, or vehicle, which must be examined. The subject will be approached in the following way, which reflects the order in which a particular claim to an easement should be analyzed so as to establish whether it really is an easement or some other right. Firstly, since there are certain advantages which cannot be enjoyed through the medium of easements, these must be considered at the outset, for if the subject-matter is not within the province of easements there is no purpose in exploring further. Secondly, given that the right can be achieved by an easement, certain conditions must exist before an easement can be created. Thirdly and finally, even if the first two conditions are satisfied, an easement can only be created in certain ways. The first requirement speaks of content, the second of conditions, and the third of form. To bake a pie the ingredients must be acceptable though the choice is wide, the oven must be correct, and the mixture contained within a dish.

So an easement is a means of acquiring against land, for the benefit of other land, a right which is enforceable as an interest in land.

Certain other rights which have some of the characteristics of easements must then be distinguished.

The subject-matter of easements

We may begin with the general principle that all kinds of advantages over another person's land can be the subject-matter of easements, except insofar as the law has imposed restrictions to the contrary. The precise limits of these restrictions have not been conclusively settled, for all the possibilities have not been litigated, but the broad principles of exclusion can be identified. Within this somewhat ill-defined framework, new kinds of easements are quite capable of emerging, and two judicial dicta on the question must not be taken as contradictory. On the one hand, Lord Brougham said in *Keppell* v. *Bailey* (1834), 2 My. & K. 517, at p.535, that 'it must not therefore be supposed that incidents of a novel kind can be devised and attached to property, at the fancy or caprice of any owner', while Lord St. Leonards remarked in *Dyce* v. *Hay* (1852), 1 Macq. 305, that 'the category of servitudes and easements must alter and expand with the changes that take place in the circumstances of mankind'.

The first dictum means that there are restrictions in principle upon the subject-matter of easements. These restrictions will be described below as precisely as the present condition of the law permits. The second statement means that, given that those principles of exclusion are not offended, new examples of easements are quite possible. Thus it is clear that the rights to drive a motor car over land or to attach a television aerial to a roof are both capable of being easements although obviously of modern origin.

Before examining these principles relating to subject-matter, some examples of established easements may be given. 'Positive' easements, which involve the dominant owner in doing some act, include rights of way whether on foot or otherwise; drainage through pipes; rights to fix boards; cables or other such items on or through property; to use a particular seat in church; to enter property of another in order to repair your own; to take water; to discharge roof water; to create nuisances such as emissions of liquids, gases or noises; the right to use a lavatory and many other rights of a miscellaneous character. These are only examples and reflect the activities of mankind in the past; they should not be taken to mark the boundaries of easements but rather to pave the way for new ones. Examples of 'negative' easements which do not involve the dominant owner in the doing of any act, but merely restrict the activities of the servient owner, are rights of support and light.

The restrictions placed upon the subject-matter of easements are as follows:

(1) *An easement cannot involve the servient owner in doing any positive act or expending money*. In *Jones* v. *Price* [1965] 2 All E.R. 625, at p.628, Willmer, L.J., said: '. . . properly speaking an easement requires no more than sufferance on the part of the occupier of the servient tenement . . .' and approved a statement in Gale on Easements that an easement is 'either a right to do something or a right to prevent something'. (C. J. Gale, *Law of Easements*, Sweet and Maxwell 1972). There is no known case where an easement has obliged the servient owner either to do any positive act or to spend money in relation to an easement. The relationship of landlord and tenant, however, might import a contractual duty to maintain and repair the subject-matter of an easement to a reasonable standard where that easement is necessary to the tenancy. Thus in *Liverpool City Council* v. *Irwin* [1977] A.C. 239 the House of Lords held that unless there was express provision to the contrary, the landlord must so maintain stairways, lifts and rubbish chutes where these are not part of the letting but retained by him.

If *A* has a right of way over the land of *B*, *B* is under no duty to maintain the path or road which is used by *A* for this purpose. Nor can the right to a supply of hot water be the subject-matter of an easement (*Regis Property Co. Ltd.* v. *Redman* [1956] 2 All E.R. 335). Similarly, if *A* has a right to support for his buildings against those of *B*, *B* need not repair his own property even though his failure to do so threatens that support. He must, however, allow *A* to carry out these repairs. On the other hand, the servient owner cannot remove the existing means of support without substituting an equivalent one (*Bond* v. *Nottingham Corporation* [1940] Ch. 429, at pp.438–439). Although an easement cannot itself impose a duty to do a positive act or to spend money, once it is created, its very existence can constitute a financial loss to the servient owner, since the useful enjoyment of the land subject to the easement may be rendered more expensive because of it (*Saint* v. *Jenner* [1973] 1 All E.R. 127).

A right to have fences, hedges, or boundary walls maintained is therefore said not to be a true easement, for it involves positive acts or expenditure of money by the servient owner. Yet when the conditions appropriate to the existence of easements exist, such a right enjoys enforceability similar to that of an easement. Although described as a 'spurious' easement, its status as a right analogous to an easement cannot now be questioned. (See *Jones* v. *Price*, above, and *Crow* v. *Wood* [1970] 3 All E.R. 425). Nevertheless, it offends the principle that an easement is a right against property as such and not against persons, for only persons can perform dynamic acts. The right is rare.

(2) *An easement cannot involve taking anything from the land apart from water.* A right which involves taking away part of the land or the produce of land cannot be an easement, although it may be a *profit à prendre*. Thus the rights to pasture cattle, or to take peat, sand or game cannot be easements, though they may be profits (see p.281 *post*). However, water is not for this purpose deemed to be part of land so that a right to take water may be an easement (*Polden* v. *Bastard* (1865), L.R. 1 Q.B. 156).

(3) *An easement cannot give exclusive possession of the servient land.* The four tests, described later, which define the conditions necessary to the existence of an easement, do not lay down to what extent the exercise of an easement may preclude the owner of the servient land from enjoying his land. Certainly all easements have this effect to some extent. A right of way, which can be an easement if anything can, may prevent an owner building on land. A right of way is a fairly elemental example and others must be examined to find out how near an easement may approach to an ouster of possession of the servient owner from his land.

In *Re Ellenborough Park* [1955] 3 All E.R. 667 it was held that the owners of several houses could enjoy such an easement over land nearby as entitled them to walk about in and have 'full enjoyment' of a pleasure garden. They were not restricted to a mere right of passage but could sit and linger. Of course, this did not exclude the owner, but it shows an easement of broader calibre than a mere right of way. Let us see how much broader it may be. In *Miller* v. *Emcer Products Ltd.* [1956] 1 All E.R. 237 the right to use another person's lavatory was held to be an easement. Here, we have an easement amounting to exclusive occupation, or so most people would expect. This represents a further stage towards ouster of the servient owner, but the exclusive use of the premises was of course temporary and occasional. Yet if there were many people residing at the dominant tenement their use of the lavatory might be so extensive as to be, if one might use the expression, an inconvenience to the servient owner. Still, it might be argued, even an ordinary right of way might, in its exercise, exclude the servient owner from a certain part of his land for the brief moment of time for which the dominant owner covered a given piece of land.

The next case is *Pye* v. *Mumford* (1848), 11 Q.B. 666, the facts of which are hardly more salubrious. The right of one farmer to enter the land of another to mix manure was held to be an easement. Here exclusive possession was taken of a part of land. The report tells us little except several different words for manure, and neither judge nor counsel gave any consideration to the point in question, although the dominant owner was held to be entitled to 'a certain small reasonable portion' of the close 'at all seasons'.

The next stage in the progression is the right to put small items on servient land on a permanent footing. Several rights of this type have been sanctioned by the courts as easements. One is the right to fix stones there to prevent earth erosion as in *Philpot* v. *Bath* (1905), 21 T.L.R. 634. There is some doubt as to whether the right to run telephone wires across another's land may be an easement, although one judge in *Lancashire Telephone Co.* v. *Manchester Overseers* (1884), 14 Q.B.D. 267, assumed it could be. In any case, this doubt is somewhat leapfrogged by the decision in *Moody* v. *Steggles* (1879), 12 Ch.D. 261, where it was held that the right to have a signboard fixed on a neighbouring property could be an easement. No mention was made that this amounted to exclusive and permanent possession of a small portion of that land. The same problem arises of course in the case of an easement of drainage through pipes. Is the easement merely the right to pass the effluent across the servient land, and the right to have the pipes there attributable to some other legal category? The pipe is necessary to prevent contamination of the land by sewage but does its presence turn a spasmodic and occasional activity into virtually permanent possession? Further complications may be caused by the question to whom does the pipe, as a physical thing, belong? Buckley, J., tangled with this latter problem in *Simmons* v. *Midford* [1969] 2 All E.R. 1269. The answer to it depends on the circumstances of the particular case, but has its home more in the law of fixtures than that of easements. In other words if *S* allows *D* to lay pipes under his (*S*'s) land, those pipes, according to the arrangements made of course, may be fixtures appurtenant to the land of *D*, not *S*. In short they become part of *D*'s land. There is nothing particularly strange in this, for back in 1879 James, L.J., in *Wheeldon* v. *Burrows* (1879), 12 Ch.D. 31, at p.60, discussing a similar problem, remarked

> '. . . the whole of the conduit through which the water ran was a corporeal part of the house, just as in any old city there are cellars projecting under other houses. They thought it was not merely the right to the passage of water, but that the conduit itself passed as part of the house, just like a flue passing through another man's house.'

This reasoning, however, would not justify the presence of things on another man's land where there is no physical connection between them and the dominant land.

In any case, two further cases suggest that an easement may go much beyond transient use and may amount not merely to a theoretical and inconsequential possession but to a considerable and territorially substantial and permanent one, which may even exclude the servient owner. In *Wright* v. *Macadam* [1949] 2 All E.R. 565, a decision of the Court of Appeal, it was held that the right to store coal in a shed belonging to another was an easement, despite the fact that this would deny possession of part of the property to the owner. Neither judges nor counsel addressed themselves to this factor. In *Att.-Gen. of Southern Nigeria* v. *John Holt & Co.* [1915] A.C. 599, a decision of the Judicial Committee of the Privy Council, *X* carried on business in Lagos from land of his which originally fronted directly on to the sea. Foreshore works, however, had enabled the recovery of the land between his land and the sea. He, believing this land to be his own, erected warehouses on it. It was held that, since the reclamation amounted to natural accretion, the land vested in the Crown but that an irrevocable licence should be presumed in his favour, allowing him to continue his business. There was held to be no easement, only a licence, but only because an easement can only be constituted over servient land which the dominant owner takes to be servient land—which was not so here. The Privy Council saw no objection to such a right being an easement on the grounds now under discussion.

Thus, on the cases so far considered, the fact that a substantial piece of land is permanently and to all intents and purposes exclusively possessed has not prevented a right being classified as an easement. But the next case, *Copeland* v. *Greenhalf* [1952] Ch. 488, a decision of the High Court, runs contrary to this. It was held that the right to store vehicle parts on part of a neighbour's land could not exist as an easement since it amounted to joint user. The remark by Upjohn, J., 'I say nothing of course as to the creation of such rights by deeds or covenants; I am dealing solely with the question of a right arising by prescription', should not be taken as meaning that he thought such a right could be an easement if created by express grant. It probably means no more than that it is open to parties to confer such rights by way of licence or contract. To conclude that the subject-matter of easements may vary according to the mode of creation would be dangerous since, fictionally, all easements are deemed to lie in grant.

Wright v. *Macadam* was not even cited in *Copeland* v. *Greenhalf*. The way is therefore open for reconciliation on the grounds that one was wrongly decided, rather than leaving as the only explanation that there is some hairline distinction between the two that will cause such a blurring of the boundaries of easements as has occurred between leases and licences.

Nevertheless, it must be faced that the difference between the right to do something on someone's land and the right to occupy is a matter of degree, for they both involve possession, and sooner or later the questions 'How much?' and 'For how long?' must be decided. In *Grigsby* v. *Melville* [1973] 3 All E.R. 455, Brightman, J. considering the problem to be one of degree, was not convinced that there was any inconsistency between the two cases because, while the claim in *Copeland* v. *Greenhalf* was to exclusive possession, it was not clear from the report of *Wright* v. *Macadam* that a right to the whole of the coalshed was asserted. It was not, however, necessary for him to express any final view on the question.

The problem is sometimes masked by authors who state that before a right can be an easement it must be 'within the general nature of rights capable of existing as easements'. This particular version is from the fourth edition of Megarry's *Manual of the Law of Real Property* (Stevens & Sons, 1975). It does not take a deep analysis to show that this falls into the trap of defining a thing by reference to itself. Occasionally things and ideas do not need defining because they are unique and no other things or ideas are proximate enough to need distinguishing. Thus there is no need to define a human being. But surely, in light of the cases mentioned above, this is not so with easements, which, it seems, may merge with licences and occupation.

(4) *The subject-matter of an easement must be reasonably definite*. Shortly we shall see that all easements, other than those arising under statute, must originate in grant. In many cases, however, such a grant is implied from the circumstances, or is presumed to have been made at some time in the past, when an alleged easement has been enjoyed for a long time, even though in reality there was no grant. This relaxation was developed in order to give legal validity to what had, by long user, become accepted as a fact.

The doctrine that the origin, real or fictional, of all easements lies in words has led to the contention that the subject-matter of easements must be reasonably definite. Lack of definition is clearly a justifiable ground for the failure of a claim to an easement, as it is indeed for the failure of a claim to any other legal right. Several cases are traditionally cited to support this view. In *Bryant* v. *Lefever* (1879), 4 C.P.D. 172, it was held that the flow of air in undefined channels could not be the subject-matter of an easement. In *Phipps* v. *Pears* [1964] 2 All E.R. 35 the right to have a wall protected against the weather by the retention of an adjacent though not contiguous building was held incapable of being an easement. Nor can the right to an unspoilt view be an easement.

On the other hand, the right to a flow of light to a window, as opposed to land in its natural state, is a well-established easement. In *Wong* v. *Beaumont Property Trust Ltd.* [1965] 1 Q.B. 173 the right to a flow of air through a defined channel was held to be capable of being an easement, as was the right to enjoy another person's garden in *Re Ellenborough Park* [1955] 3 All E.R. 667.

The reasons given by the judges in the cases of failure cited above do not always support the contention that certain kinds of rights are predeterminedly incapable of sufficient definition to be easements. Lord Denning's reason in *Phipps* v. *Pears* seems to have been that the right claimed 'would unduly restrict your neighbour in his enjoyment of his own land'. A right to sunshine, as opposed to disseminated light, now appears capable of being an easement, provided it is enjoyed through defined apertures (*Allen* v. *Greenwood* [1979] 1 All E.R. 819). Certainly an easement must be defined, but there seems no good reason for not even allowing a draftsman to try, particularly since the desired effect can in any case be produced by a properly drafted covenant (per Lord Denning in *Phipps* v. *Pears*, at p.38).

The rationale behind the exclusion of these rights from the category of easements is rather different from a congenital insusceptibility to definition. The truly common factor in the cases seems to be that, where an easement is being acquired by long user, the servient owner should be able to discern easily what rights are being obtained against him, so that he will be able to resist and nullify them before they become established as legal rights. This he is much less able to do in the case of a negative easement because its encroachment is not marked by events which strike the senses. A nascent positive easement, such as a way over the servient property, can be detected by seeing a man walking over the property, and therefore should not emerge insidiously and without warning as a fully fledged right. Perhaps this is why the right to use a garden, though open to the charge of indefiniteness, has been allowed to join the ranks of easements whereas 'the law has been very chary of creating any new negative easements' (per Lord Denning in *Phipps* v. *Pears*, at p.37).

Moreover, even a positive act must be identifiably adverse to the servient property to enable its owners to resist it. A blacksmith cannot acquire an easement to commit a nuisance in the middle of a barren moor, for his hammering will not constitute a nuisance until his neighbour develops his land (see *Sturges* v. *Bridgman* (1879), 11 Ch.D. 852, at p.858).

Yet even a negative right is only objectionable in this way when claimed through long user, for then a man's property might be besieged by a hundred emerging rights, such as those of his neighbour to light over all his property or to an unspoilt view. These the servient owner could neither individualize, nor indeed resist, unless he built up the whole of his land. Such negative rights, however, are hardly open to the same criticism if they are quantified and identified within the four corners of an express grant.

In short, the principle that certain kinds of rights are at the outset too indefinite to be easements ought only to be applied to the acquisition of negative easements by long user and should not affect positive easements by whatever means they are acquired, nor negative easements when they are acquired by express grant. In the case of positive easements, the acts of the dominant owner perform the act of definition. In the case of negative easements expressly granted, the skill of the draftsman should at least be allowed to have its tilt at moulding the right, no matter how intractable, into a definite form. If he fails, then let us say he failed because of faulty creation rather than because of ineligible subject-matter.

The problem might well assume greater practical importance in the future as living accommodation becomes denser and more interdependent. The lack of an easement for protection against weather, for instance, might be felt when a lower freehold flat depends for its weather-proofing upon the roof of the flat above (see 80 L.Q.R. 321).

On the basis of the present authorities, however, certain rights, negative in nature, are excluded from the category of easements because of their subject-matter, rather than their mode of creation. It is difficult to foretell what new rights will be admitted.

Conditions necessary to the existence of easements

An easement involves a relationship between two pieces of land and, even though the subject-matter of a right is eligible for the formation of an easement, it must also be shown that the particular right in question expresses such a relationship. If it does not, although capable in the abstract of being an easement, it cannot be one in the particular instance, even though it may be enforceable for some other reason, perhaps as a personal licence. The following conditions must be fulfilled before the right can be said to represent a relationship between two properties.

(1) *There must be a dominant and servient tenement.* There must be two properties concerned with the right, one enjoying the benefit of it, and one carrying the burden. Thus in *Hawkins* v. *Rutter* [1892] 1 Q.B. 668, a man claimed, as a member of the public, an easement to ground his barge on the bed of a river although he owned no land for the benefit of which the right was claimed. It was held that there was no easement because there was no dominant land. This requirement is sometimes expressed by saying that an easement cannot exist 'in gross'. In short, it is helpful to forget about persons altogether and imagine one piece of land having rights over another. Thus, if I give permission to the postman to cross my land so that he can more easily reach the next street, he enjoys a licence only, because the privilege was not given for the benefit of any land. The dominant tenement is usually physical land, but it may also be an incorporeal hereditament, so that there can exist, for instance, a right of way over land for the benefit of a fishing right in a river.

It has been argued that this doctrine has been accepted on too flimsy authority and could be an obstacle to reasonable land use in the future (see 96 L.Q.R. 557).

(2) *The easement must 'accommodate' the dominant tenement and must bestow some benefit upon the dominant land.*

> A right enjoyed by one over the land of another does not possess the status of an easement unless it accommodates and serves the dominant

> tenement, and is reasonably necessary for the better enjoyment of that tenement, for if it has no connection therewith, although it confers an advantage upon the owner and renders his ownership of the land more valuable, it is not an easement at all, but a mere contractual right personal to and only enforceable between the two contracting parties.

(per Evershed, M.R., in *Re Ellenborough Park*, p.254, *ante*, at p.677, approving a statement of the doctrine in Cheshire and Burn's *Modern Law of Real Property*, 12th edn (Butterworth, 1976).

The essence of this requirement is that the dominant land as such must benefit. While the dominant and servient properties will frequently be close together, this need not necessarily be so (*Pugh* v. *Savage* [1970] 2 All E.R. 353). It is possible, for instance, for a right of way to accommodate a dominant property, even though it does not lead all the way up to it. On the other hand, as remarked by Byles, J., in *Bailey* v. *Stephens* (1862), 12 C.B. (N.S.) 91, a right of way over land in Kent cannot accommodate land in Northumberland. Even this restriction, however, does not apply to all kinds of easements. A signboard on land facing a busy road in Kent advertising a holiday cottage in Northumberland might well accommodate the latter.

Hill v. *Tupper* (1863), 2 H. & C. 121, illustrates the principle. The owner of a canal leased land adjoining it to *L* together with the exclusive right to sail boats upon the canal. This right was held to be a contractual licence only and not an easement. Pollock, C.B., said: 'It is not competent to create rights unconnected with the use and enjoyment of land, and annex them to it so as to constitute a property in the grantee'. The result was that when a third party began to put boats on the canal, *L* could only sue his licensor in contract and not that third party, with whom he enjoyed no privity of contract, for *L* had no right of property in the canal. This highlights nicely the difference between a personal right acquired under a contract and real right enjoyed under an easement.

The reasoning in the decision seems to be that the land on the canal bank was really intended to serve an independent business enterprise upon the canal, rather than itself to be enhanced by the right of sailing. Far from being intended as the dominant land, it was subservient to the business venture. But the case must not be taken as deciding that the right to sail boats cannot accommodate land on the banks of water. In view of *Re Ellenborough Park*, above, such a right must surely be capable of being an easement.

It is not enough that the right increases the value of property unless it is also connected with the normal enjoyment of it (*Re Ellenborough Park*, at p.173). This does not mean that a property has a fixed mode of enjoyment; merely that the right must be restricted to the needs of that particular piece of land and not embrace some collateral purpose as where a right of way is granted 'for all purposes' (*Ackroyd* v. *Smith* (1850), 10 C.B. 164). The court will, if possible in the circumstances, construe 'for all purposes' as meaning all purposes connected with the dominant land. Perhaps the best test is to ask whether the right assists what goes on in the dominant property. The land in respect of which the easement is claimed and not merely some person or some other land must benefit, and this was not so in *Hill* v. *Tupper*, above.

Finally a right can accommodate a business on the dominant premises (see *Clapman* v. *Edwards* [1938] 2 All E.R. 507).

(3) *The dominant and servient tenements must not be both owned and occupied by the same person.* 'You cannot have an easement over your own land' (*Metropolitan Railway Co.* v. *Fowler* 1892 1 Q.B. 165, at p.171). This is really an obvious fact, for it is indeed impossible for a person to have a right of any kind against himself. However, mere occupation of both properties without ownership of both is quite compatible with the existence of an easement, which would simply lapse temporarily until the unity of occupation ended. Neither is ownership of both without occupation of both objectionable, although in that case the easement will not be of permanent duration, but will last only until the occupation of the second of the properties returns to the common owner.

Actions constantly exercised by an owner over part of his land are sometimes called 'quasi-easements', although they are really nothing more than habits. Thus a farmer might consistently choose to reach the road from his field 'Blackacre' by crossing another of his fields, 'Whiteacre'. The significance of such habits is that under certain circumstances they become easements if part of the land is sold off. 'Quasi-easements' is therefore not a satisfactory description for activities which are the simple result of ordinary ownership and which are, during that time, devoid of significance, but it is however widely used.

(4) *An easement must be capable of being made by a grant.* The rule that all easements, other than those of statutory origin, must be created by deed of grant naturally means that the right in question must, in all the circumstances of its creation, have been capable of being granted by deed. This is equally so in those cases where it is fictionally presumed that a grant was made at some time. The rule gives rise to the following requirements:

(a) There must have been a capable grantor and grantee—there can be no easement if at the time when it was alleged to have been created there was neither a person capable of making the grant on behalf of the servient land, nor person capable of receiving it on behalf of the dominant land. Thus in *Mulliner* v. *Midland Railway Co.* (1879), 11 Ch.D. 611, a claim to an easement alleged to have been granted by a railway company failed because a grant would have been *ultra vires* that body. Similarly, a vague or fluctuating body of people, such as the inhabitants of a village, cannot claim an easement, because they cannot receive a grant. They might, however, be able to prove some enforceable customary right, or a public right of way.

(b) The right must be reasonably well defined—the question of definiteness of subject-matter has already been discussed and the argument advanced that it would be preferable not to pre-judge the problem of definition by treating it as one of subject-matter, but to treat it as one of mode of creation. In any event there can be no controversy about the rule that an easement must actually be defined in its creation. It is strange that such a fundamental asset as certainty, which is surely as necessary to other kinds of rights as to easements, should be attributed to the rule that easements lie in grant. Perhaps the real answer lies in the 'thinginess' of English land law. Easements are property which can be conveyed. A right of way and the way itself, for instance, are both frequently referred to in one breath (see L.P.A. 1925, s.62). Both can be pointed to from a bedroom window. A negative right is hardly a thing in this sense and has only been allowed as an easement when it has geometric shape, such as a right of support or right of light to a window.

The creation of easements

Even though the subject-matter of the right in question is eligible to be an easement, and even though the right conditions exist for its formation as discussed above, there can be no easement unless the relationship between the two properties has been created in one of the legally accepted ways. These methods of creation are as follows.

By statute

Easements are occasionally created by statute. Such Acts are usually local ones.

By express grant

An express grant may arise in any of the following ways:

By direct grant
An easement will arise by a direct grant when the owner of the servient property grants the right in so many words in the deed of creation. This is a commonplace form of express creation and needs no further discussion.

By reservation
When a landowner sells part of his land, he might wish to retain an easement over the part sold in favour of the part retained. He can secure such a right in the deed of conveyance to the purchaser, for, like restrictive covenants, easements do not require separate independent documents for their creation, but may arise as subsidiary features in larger transactions. The purchaser need not execute the document for the easement (L.P.A. 1925 s.65(1)). Before 1925, reservations operated by way of implied re-grant to the vendor by the purchaser. Because the purchaser was granting a legal interest to the vendor, this had to be done by deed executed by the purchaser as grantor. Since 1925 this is not necessary, because the easement reserved is not now deemed to arise by way of an immediate re-grant (L.P.A. 1925, s.65).

Since the vendor is therefore the 'grantor' of this easement to himself, the rule that grants, including any reservations contained in them, are construed against the grantor might be taken to run against him. There is, however, reluctance to accept this view (*St. Edmundsbury and Ipswich Diocesan Board of Finance* v. *Clark (No. 2)* [1973] 3 All E.R. 902). The moral is that the vendor should precisely define and quantify any easements reserved by him upon sale, for he will not receive the benefit of any doubt (*Cordell* v. *Second Clanfield Properties Ltd.* [1968] 3 All E.R. 746).

Under Law of Property Act 1925, section 62
This section provides that on a 'conveyance' of land there shall, subject to any expressed intention to the contrary, be deemed to pass to the purchaser, besides all the buildings and other fixtures, all 'liberties, privileges, easements, rights, and advantages whatsoever, appertaining or reputed to appertain to the land . . . or any part thereof, or, at the time of conveyance'.

The operation of this section is dealt with here under express grants because it 'speaks' between the lines, as a word-saving section, in every conveyance—unless it is expressly excluded. The section is mainly concerned with a statement of what would normally be the intention of the parties. We would all expect a conveyance to include buildings, fences and water-courses upon the land, and nineteenth-century conveyancers, in their verbosity, expressly mentioned such matters. Now we are saved the trouble. Similarly, we would expect easements already existing for the benefit of the land that we purchase to pass to us in the conveyance. Hence the mention of easements. Thus if *V*, the common owner of 'Whiteacre' and 'Greenacre' in the diagram below, sells 'Whiteacre' to *P*, the benefit of the right of way over a neighbour's property 'Blackacre', which had been created perhaps many years previously, will pass to *P* without any mention, just as the buildings and fixtures on 'Whiteacre' will. To this extent, the provision is only a word-saving section.

Road

Blackacre | Whiteacre | Greenacre

Easement | Permission

Road

It is quite settled, however, that the later words of the section have a much wider effect than this and may create new rights, not contemplated by the parties, as well as transferring existing ones. Suppose that, before the sale of 'Whiteacre' by *V* to *P*, *V* had leased it to *P*, and later, as a matter of goodwill, had given *P* permission to cross 'Greenacre' to reach the road. The permission at this stage would be a mere licence revocable at the will of *V*. When *V* later sells 'Whiteacre' to *P*, however, the conveyance operates under s.62 to convert the licence into an easement in favour of 'Whiteacre'. This *V* can no longer revoke and it will permanently enure for the benefit of that property. Thus, in *Wright* v. *Macadam* [1949] 2 K.B. 744, *T* became tenant of a flat and was later allowed by her landlord to use his shed for storing her coal. Later he granted her a new tenancy making no reference to the shed. It was held that the grant of the second tenancy turned the hitherto precarious right in the shed into an easement. See also *Ward* v. *Kirkland* [1967] Ch. 194. The requirements of the section must now be examined in some more detail.

Firstly, there must be a 'conveyance'. Under s.205(1)(ii) of the Act this includes 'a mortgage, charge, lease, assent, vesting declaration, vesting instrument, disclaimer, release and every other assurance of property or of an interest therein by any instrument, except a will'. The weight of judicial opinion holds that some form of written document is necessary to constitute a conveyance, even in cases where a legal estate can be created orally. Some doubt remains, however (*Rye* v. *Rye* [1962] A.C. 496). It is settled that the document need not be under seal in those cases where mere writing is sufficient to pass the legal estate (*Wright* v. *Macadam*, above). A conveyance does not include an agreement for a lease or sale (*Borman* v. *Griffith* [1930] 1 Ch. 493), even though specific performance would be granted. Presumably this restriction only applies to truly executory agreements and not to those cases where the document embodies the final arrangements of the parties but uses the expression 'the landlord agrees to let'. In any case, the exclusion of agreements from the definition is somewhat surprising, because even an agreement effects an 'assurance of property', though only of an equitable interest.

Secondly, the liberty will not be transformed into an easement unless it is by virtue of its subject-matter capable of being an easement. There need not be any 'right' to do the act and even the most precarious of licences may be turned into easements (see *Goldberg* v. *Edwards* [1950] Ch. 247). Yet if permission has to be sought before every exercise of the act in question there will not even be a privilege in existence at the time of the conveyance upon which the section can operate, because each performance of the act exhausts the particular permission. Thus in *Green* v. *Ashco Horticulturist Ltd.* [1966] 2 All E.R. 232 a tenant of shop premises was allowed from time to time to use his landlord's adjacent entry, but frequently had to ask on individual occasions that the gates be opened. It was held that a renewal of his lease did not create an easement of way. The distinction seems to be as follows. In the case of privileges which are given for an indefinite period, though subject to withdrawal, the nature of the privilege is not changed by the section. It is simply made permanent. In cases like *Green* v. *Ashco Horticulturist Ltd.*, where there is no continuing privilege but merely a series of frequent independent concessions, the section is excluded because its effect would be to change the nature of the privilege itself. It has now been held that a right to have a fence maintained is capable of passing under the section (*Crow* v. *Wood* [1970] 3 All E.R. 425).

Thirdly, it was until recently by no means clear whether the section only operates where there has been, before the conveyance, diversity of occupation of the part sold and the part retained. If, in the example given above, *V* had not only owned but occupied the land before the sale to *P*, then no 'rights', 'privileges' or 'advantages' could have existed over 'Greenacre' in favour of 'Whiteacre'. It is true that *V* might have been in the habit of crossing 'Greenacre' from 'Whiteacre', but this would have been attributable to his ownership and occupation of 'Greenacre' itself and not merely to rights in or over it. Furthermore, as a matter of brute jurisprudence and common sense, a person cannot have a 'right', 'privilege' or probably even an 'advantage' against himself (Fry, J., in *Bolton* v. *Bolton* (1879), 11 Ch.D. 968). The clearest case in favour of this view was *Long* v. *Gowlett* [1923] 2 Ch. 177, where it constituted the *ratio decidendi*. Yet the question of diversity of occupation has been ignored altogether in other cases, so that doubt persisted (see *Godwin* v. *Schweppes Ltd.* [1902] 1 Ch. 926). These cases were decided upon s.6 of the Conveyancing Act 1881, which s.62 re-enacts (see 30 Conveyancer 346). It has now been confirmed in *Sovmots Investments Ltd.* v. *Secretary of State for the Environment* [1979] A.C. 144, that diversity of occupation is necessary to the operation of the section. We shall shortly see that quasi-easements may be converted into true easements under the doctrine of *Wheeldon* v. *Burrows* (1879), 12 Ch.D. 31 without previous enjoyment of the advantage by a second party.

As a fourth point, the section cannot operate to enlarge rights against third parties. The diagram on page 261 illustrates this principle.

If the owner of 'Blackacre', *B*, has been allowed by the owner of 'Whiteacre', *W*, to walk over 'Whiteacre', and *B* later sells 'Blackacre' to *P*, the licence never becomes an easement. The reason is that the only person capable of

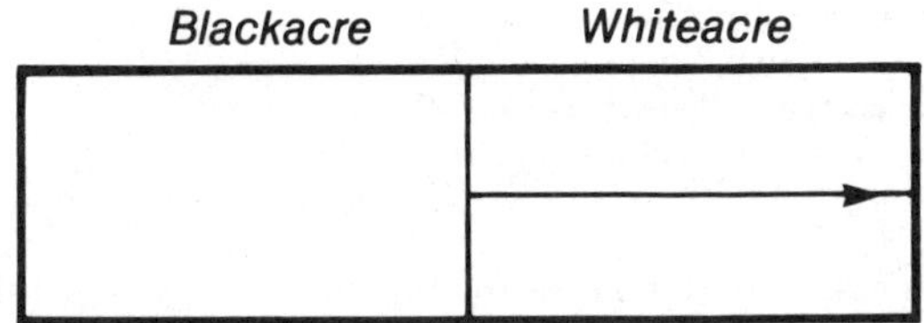

granting such an easement is *W*, and he has carried out no legal act whatsoever which can be taken to have done this, whereas when one person sells off part of his own land, the creation of an easement over the part retained is clearly within his power (*Quicke* v. *Chapman* [1903] 1 Ch. 659).

Finally, the drastic consequences of the section can be avoided by excluding its operation to the extent desired. Clear words are necessary (*Hansford* v. *Jago* [1921] 1 Ch. 322), although the circumstances preceding the conveyance may sometimes have the same effect.

Under an agreement for an easement

An easement must be created by deed (L.P.A. 1925, s.52), but under the doctrine of *Walsh* v. *Lonsdale* (1882), 21 Ch.D. 9, an equitable easement will arise where a purported grant is in writing only, or where there exists an agreement for an easement of which specific performance would be granted. There must be sufficient memorandum or act of part performance to satisfy s.40 of the Law of Property Act 1925. Thus where *A*, in reliance on *B*'s permission, laid waterpipes under *B*'s land, it was held that an equitable easement had been created although the permission was not granted under seal (*Duke of Devonshire* v. *Eglin* (1851), 14 Beav. 530; see also *McManus* v. *Cooke* (1887), 35 Ch.D. 681).

Equitable easements which have arisen after 1925 are registrable as Class D (iii) land charges under the Land Charges Act 1972 or, in the case of registered land, as minor interests. If not so registered, they are void against purchasers of legal estates in the land for money or money's worth (L.P.A. 1925, s.199). The practical effect of this rule can in certain circumstances be nullified where the owner of the servient property is estopped from denying the burden of an unregistered easement. In a modern case, the principle was described by Lord Denning in the following way

> When adjoining owners of land make an agreement to secure continuing rights and benefits for each of them in or over the land of the other, neither can take the benefit of the agreement and throw over the burden of it. This applies not only to the original parties but also to their successors

(*E.R. Ives Investment Ltd.* v. *High* [1967] 1 All E.R. 504, at p.507).

While no one would deny that even technical legal rules must be applied in the light of justice, one of the elements of justice is certainty, and such a decision can sap the confidence of both practitioners and laymen in their interpretation of apparently straightforward statutory provisions.

Remember, man, "The Universal Cause
Acts not by partial, but by general laws";
And makes what happiness we justly call
Subsist, not in the good of one, but all.
(Pope's *Essay on Man*, Epistle IV).

In the Ives case, *A* built flats the footings of which extended slightly under the neighbouring land of *B*. The latter, however, agreed not to insist upon his rights, provided that *A* allowed him in return to have a vehicular right of way over his land. *A* accepted this arrangement. The right of way was not granted by deed and *B* did not protect it by registration as an estate contract or an equitable easement. Later the successors in title to *A*, who purchased with knowledge of the right, sought to prevent its exercise. It was held that although they were purchasers of a legal estate they must, since they enjoyed the benefit of the agreement, submit to the right of way. Alternatively, it could be said that a 'proprietary estoppel' incapable of registration operated against them (see 32 Conveyancer 333).

Although the right had all the attributes of an easement, the court seemed at pains to steer it away from this category of right so that failure to register would not cause an unjust result. To achieve this, the arrangement between the original parties was substantially reduced by the court to mutual agreements not to sue, which would clearly have been incapable of registration. Alternatively we might say that, because of lack of registration, the easement was void against the purchasers, but because of the associated benefit they were enjoying, they were estopped from pleading lack of registration. The danger in the former explanation is that it could breed a species of right alongside easements; this might cause problems of identification as serious as in the case of leases and licences.

It is hardly surprising that the statutory code of registration should sometimes cause substantive rules to be warped. The old doctrine of notice was based upon good conscience, as is all sound law. The code of registration is not primarily so based. An honest layman is no more likely to be acquainted with that code than is a dishonest one. The same problem arose in regard to the requirement of written evidence for contracts concerning land under the Statute of Frauds 1677. The principle of part performance is perhaps as active today as it was then in scavenging injustice where rules of law fail to meet principles of justice.

By implied grant

When a landowner grants part of his land—or some interest in it—to another person, easements may sometimes be implied from the circumstances surrounding the transaction, even though there is no express mention of them. However, since a grant is usually construed against the grantor, they are implied more generously in favour of the grantee. The grantor must, with two exceptions, expressly reserve any easement which he wishes to exercise over the part sold.

Easements implied in favour of land retained by grantor

The two exceptional situations when easements will be implied in favour of the grantor are as follows:

(1) *Easements of necessity*. An easement will be implied in favour of the grantor if it is essential to the mode of enjoyment of the retained land at the time of the disposal of part of it. The most obvious such case is when the land retained is totally encircled by the land disposed of, or partly by this and partly by land belonging to third parties. A right of way will then be implied in favour of the grantor, who may choose, once and for all, its route. This easement is limited by the necessity existing at the time of the grant. For example, if an island of agricultural land is retained, a right of way can be claimed only for agricultural purposes and not for other kinds of use or development (*London Corporation* v. *Riggs* (1880) 13 Ch.D. 798). Furthermore, mere difficulty of access does not constitute necessity.

Other examples of necessity exist besides that of access. A right of support for buildings is probably better classified in this category than in the second of the exceptions mentioned below. In *Wong* v. *Beaumont Property Trust Ltd*. [1965] 1 Q.B. 173 an easement to maintain a ventilation duct through which to expel fumes from premises let for the purposes of a Chinese restaurant (and so comply with public health regulations) was implied in favour of a tenant against his landlord. This suggests that the necessity need not be a physical one but may be simply a legal one. This was an example of an easement implied in favour of the grantee, which will be mentioned below, but the principle of necessity is the same. The case also suggests that the doctrine of easements of necessity is perhaps not founded on the common intention of the parties because neither landlord nor tenant was aware of the necessity at the time of the letting. This factor, therefore, might separate true easements of necessity from the class mentioned below.

In *Nickerson* v. *Barraclough* [1981] 2 All E.R. 369, however, the Court of Appeal rejected public policy as the basis of the doctrine. The decision exposes potential problems for the future in this part of the law (see *Current Legal Problems 1981*, p.133).

(2) *Easements particularly intended by the parties*. If the circumstances are such as to raise a necessary inference that the common intention of the parties was to reserve to the grantor the right to exercise the right in question, an easement will be implied to this effect. Mere knowledge by the purchaser that the grantor was using the property disposed of in a certain way is not enough (*Re Webb's Lease* [1951] Ch. 808). (But see also *Simpson* v. *Weber* (1925), 133 L.T. 46, discussed in Webb's case).

Easements implied in favour of land taken by grantee

The easements implied in favour of the grantee are as follows:

(1) *Easements of necessity*. The principles discussed above in relation to the grantor apply equally in favour of the grantee. If the grantee takes a limited interest in the land the easement will of course be limited to that duration. Thus in *Wong* v. *Beaumont Property Trust Ltd*., above, a leasehold easement resulted in favour of the tenant.

(2) *Easements particularly intended by the parties*. Once again the same principles as discussed above apply in favour of the grantee.

(3) *Easements within the doctrine of Wheeldon v. Burrows (1879), 12 Ch.D. 31*. Easements are more liberally implied in favour of the grantee upon the disposition by an owner of part of his land. For, in addition to easements of necessity and of common intention, there will also pass to the grantee all those 'quasi-easements' previously exercised by the common owner which are 'continuous and apparent' and 'necessary to the reasonable enjoyment of the property granted' and which 'have been and are at the time of the grant used by the owners of the entirety for the benefit of the part granted'.

'Continuous and apparent' denotes some form of habitual enjoyment, the signs of which would reveal themselves on an inspection of the land by a person who is ordinarily capable of interpreting such signs. Examples are light going to windows, drains showing some marks on the land, and a made-up or worn path (*Hansford* v. *Jago* [1921] 1 Ch. 322). On the other hand, a route which leaves no indication of its use on the face of the land would not qualify. The word 'necessary' here is used in a softer sense than is 'necessity' in the term 'easements of necessity' and does not mean 'indispensable'.

The operation of the doctrine differs in several ways from that of s.62 of the Law of Property Act 1925. Section 62 only operates where there is a 'conveyance' and not, for instance, where an interest in land is passed by an agreement or by will. The doctrine of *Wheeldon* v. *Burrows* is not confined in this way. In *Borman* v. *Griffith* [1930] 1 Ch. 493, *L* agreed to lease *T* a house in a large park which contained a mansion reached by a main drive which also served as access to the house. The agreement did not reserve *T* any right of way over the drive. It was held that a right to use the drive passed, however, under *Wheeldon* v. *Burrows*, even though there had been no 'conveyance' to attract the operation of s.62.

It is also obvious that the doctrine in *Wheeldon* v. *Burrows* operates, even though immediately before the transaction there was no diversity of occupation. Quasi-easements exercised by the person who commonly owned and occupied both pieces of land are capable of passing. *Borman* v. *Griffith*, above, illustrates this.

On the other hand, s.62 embraces a wider class of potential easements than does the rule in *Wheeldon* v. *Burrows*. For instance, the section does not require that the advantage should be of a continuous and apparent nature. Thus a right which has left no evidence of its exercise upon the servient land—such as that of entering a neighbour's property in order to carry out repairs on your own building—will pass under s.62, but not under *Wheeldon* v. *Burrows* (see *Ward* v. *Kirkland* [1967] Ch. 194). When a conveyance is preceded by a contract, the rights of the parties are settled by the contract, and, unless otherwise agreed, easements will be implied in this contract as mentioned above. The conveyance should reflect these rights and s.62 should be excluded to the extent necessary to reflect the contract. These matters are often, regulated by the general conditions in the printed forms used on the sale or leasing of land.

When an owner makes contemporaneous grants of two or more pieces of land to different persons, each new owner takes the same implied easements over the land of the others as he would have done if his grant had been made first. In other words, *Wheeldon* v. *Burrows* applies. Conveyances will rarely be contemporaneous but gifts by will are governed by this rule. When the two conveyances are not contemporaneous but the order in which they are made is fortuitous, as in the sale of houses on an estate, the rule that only easements of necessity are implied in favour of the land reserved by the grantor works capriciously, for the vendor would often be surprised to learn that the purchaser of one plot has greater rights than another (see *Kwiatkowski* v. *Cox* (1969), 213 E.G. 34).

By presumed grant

All the methods of creating easements described so far allude to a grant on some particular occasion. Often, however, an advantage capable of existing as an easement has been enjoyed over another person's land for a long time but cannot be traced to any grant. In certain circumstances the law protects such advantages and presumes fictionally that a grant was made at some time, but that the record of it has been lost. This method of acquisition, justified by the acquiescence of the servient owner, is known as prescription. The fiction can appear flimsy. Thus in *Cargill* v. *Gotts* [1981] 1 All E.R. 682, the Court of Appeal considered that an easement could not be acquired through a criminal activity, even though recently made so by Act of Parliament (see also *Oakley* v. *Boston* [1975] 3 W.L.R. 478 at 490).

There are three forms of prescription, reflecting the development of the doctrine at common law and under statute over the centuries. The main difference between them is the period over which the enjoyment of the advantage must be proved. Long enjoyment alone, however, is not enough to found a claim under any of the three methods. The enjoyment must with a few exceptions, occur under certain conditions. It must be 'continuous' and 'as of right'. Furthermore, since with one exception it can only result in the formation of a perpetual easement, it must be such as to bind the owner of the fee simple of the servient land. These three conditions must be considered before we discuss the three forms of prescription in detail.

(1) *Enjoyment must be continuous*. Only advantages which require no personal participation, such as those of light, support or drainage, can strictly be said to be continuous, but this kind of continuity is not necessary in other cases. Moreover, there is no rule requiring any particular degree of frequency for individual types of advantages. It also seems that the site of a nascent easement need not, in certain circumstances, be constant during the prescription period (*Davies* v. *Whitby* [1973] 3 All E.R. 403, at p.405). Some kind of regularity in its exercise is necessary to suggest to the servient owner that a right of a permanent nature is being asserted rather than an isolated trespass or nuisance committed (see *Dare* v. *Heathcote* (1856), 25 L.J.Ex. 245).

(2) *Enjoyment must be 'as an easement' and 'as of right'*. The advantage must be enjoyed in such a way as would lead an observer, who is aware of the circumstances and behaviour of the parties, to the conclusion that an easement exists. This means that it must be enjoyed under a claim of an easement and not for some other reason, and that it must be enjoyed 'as of right'. This latter expression implies that, although the servient owner knows that the advantage is being enjoyed, and although he has given no permission for its

exercise, he acquiesces in it. In technical language, the enjoyment must be *nec vi, nec clam, nec precario*. These elements must now be discussed.

(a) Enjoyment 'as an easement'—The advantage must be exercised against one tenement for the benefit of another. The assumpiton of dominancy, necessary to the existence of an easement, cannot arise if the advantage is enjoyed by virtue of some other legal claim. Thus no easement will arise where, for instance, one owner uses another person's land in a certain way because he mistakenly believes he owns it himself (*Att.-Gen. of Southern Nigeria* v. *John Holt & Co.* [1915] A.C. 599). In such a case the advantage has been exercised not out of dominancy and serviency of two properties but out of sovereignty over one.

(b) Enjoyment 'as of right'—The enjoyment must be *nec vi, nec clam, nec precario*. '*Nec vi*' means without force. No easement can arise, therefore, if the user is exercised by force or in the face of clear and continuous protests or legal proceedings, for these would be incompatible with acquiescence, which is the basis of prescription. An observer would put the exercise down to trespass or nuisance.

'*Nec clam*' means not secretly. An owner cannot acquiesce in the exercise of advantages of which he does not know or which he cannot discern. Thus a secret discharge of liquids into a drain cannot found an easement by prescription. On the other hand, a person cannot claim ignorance of a fact of which a reasonably observant man ought to have been aware, such as that a building will normally demand some lateral support from adjacent ground (*Dalton* v. *Angus* (1881), 6 App. Cas. 740). Long user raises the presumption that the servient owner has knowledge, but this can be rebutted by proof that he did not know. When a servient owner employs an agent to act for him in relation to the property, the burden of proving the agent's knowledge or means of knowledge rests on the claimant and depends upon the nature of the duties delegated (*Diment* v. *N. H. Foot Ltd.* [1974] 2 All E.R. 785). An activity is also *clam*, even though known to an owner, if he has for the time being no means of resisting it. This 'constructive ignorance' is illustrated by *Sturges* v. *Bridgman* (1879), 11 Ch.D. 852, where a confectioner created noise which obtruded into the back garden of a physician. No actionable nuisance existed until the physician built a consulting room in the garden, for it was only then that the noise began to interfere with the use and enjoyment of his land. It was held that the long period during which the noise had been emitted before the consulting room was erected, counted as nothing towards prescription because the physician was powerless to prevent the confectioner's activities by action or otherwise.

In *Union Lighterage Co.* v. *London Graving Dock Co.* [1902] 2 Ch. 557, the support of a dock by means of rods sunk invisibly under a neighbour's land was held to be unenforceable as an easement since, although originally lawfully placed, the rods were unknown to the person through whose land they passed. However, in view of the modern case of *Simmons* v. *Midford* [1969] 2 Ch. 415, their retention could surely be justified on the grounds that they had become fixtures attached to the dock so as to become an extension of it. In short, the issue was simply one of land ownership, not one of easements (see the dissenting judgment of Vaughan Williams, C.J.).

'*Nec precario*' means without permission. The enjoyment of an advantage by a permission which the grantor may give or refuse is inconsistent with a claim to such enjoyment 'as of right'. A user which begins permissively may, however, become *nec precario* in certain circumstances, for example when the advantage is exercised after the permission originally given has exhausted its authority (*Healey* v. *Hawkins* [1968] 3 All E.R. 836). As a precaution against acquisition by prescription, a periodic payment is often demanded for the user to show clearly that permission is regularly sought and given. In *Gardner* v. *Hodgson's Kingston Brewery* [1903] A.C. 229, such a payment clearly showed that a woman's use of a way from her stables through an inn yard to a road was *precario* even though it had been enjoyed for sixty years. The principles now being discussed are concerned with the acquisition of easements by prescription. When easements are granted expressly, the very grant itself is a permission to do the act in question; and there is no objection in law to the exaction of a payment in consideration of that grant.

(3) *Only perpetual easements can be prescribed for.* Although easements may be expressly or impliedly granted for any periods of time, only perpetual easements can result from prescription. The reason for this is that the doctrine of prescription is based on immemorial enjoyment of a use. If the dominant tenement is occupied by the owner of a limited interest, such as a lessee, during some of the prescription period, the exercise of the advantage during this time still counts towards the development of a perpetual easement, and not for a leasehold one. The user is, so to speak, 'banked' for the benefit of the fee simple. We shall see later that there is an exception to this rule in the case of an easement of light.

Now that the conditions necessary for the operation of prescription have been explained, we must examine the three kinds of prescription.

(4) *Prescription at common law.* At common law it is presumed that an easement has been granted if the advantage has been enjoyed under the conditions described above since 'time immemorial'. The date fixed by the Statute of Westminster in 1275 for this purpose was 1189. It has remained unchanged. With the passing of the centuries the burden of proving user dating back to 1189 became so great that the courts presume that fact if proof is given of enjoyment for twenty years. Yet even this presumption can be rebutted if it is shown that the advantage was, at some time between 1189 and the present day, incapable of being exercised. Thus a claim to a right of way on foot exercised for many generations might be defeated by proof that the servient land lay under water until, say, the seventeenth century. This factor obviously spells death to claims to easements of support for buildings, since very few have stood since 1189.

(5) *Lost modern grant.* This doctrine, also evolved by the common law, remedies to some extent the frequently fatal flaw in common-law prescription that a claim fails if it can be demonstrated that there was a time after 1189 when user would have been impossible. If enjoyment is proved for twenty years or more, this intermediate impossibility is rendered irrelevant by the presumption that a grant of an easement was made at some later date but has been lost. This desperate fiction prevails, even though the court has no shadow of a belief that any such instrument ever really existed (see *Bryant* v. *Foot* (1867) L.R. 2 Q.B. 161, per Cockburn, C.J., at p.181). Although the presumption cannot be defeated by proof that a grant was never made, it probably can be rebutted by evidence that it could not have been made

because, for instance, there was no capable grantor, or because it would have been *ultra vires* (*Neaverson* v. *Peterborough R.D.C.* [1902] 1 Ch. 557). Furthermore, a person resisting a claim is entitled to know whether it is claimed that the lost grant was fictionally made before or after a certain date, so that he can more conveniently assemble his evidence to rebut the plea (*Tremayne* v. *English Clays Lovering Pochin & Co. Ltd.* [1972] 2 All E.R. 234).

(5) *Under the Prescription Act 1832.* The Prescription Act was passed to overcome the difficulties of proving user since time immemorial. Its main effect is to shorten the time of legal memory. It leaves intact prescription at common law and under lost modern grant, which are still available for the establishment of easements, but provides a third alternative and more desirable method of proof. The Act applies special rules to the easement of light which must therefore be discussed separately.

Easements other than light

The Prescription Act 1832 provides two new ways of establishing easements other than light.

Firstly, when an easement has been enjoyed as of right without interruption for twenty years next before some suit or action concerning the claim, it cannot be defeated by proof that it commenced after 1189, but may be defeated in any other way under the law. Secondly, where an easement has been enjoyed as of right without interruption for forty years next before some suit or action concerning it, the right to it shall be considered absolute and indefeasible, unless it appears that it was enjoyed by some consent or agreement expressly given or made for that purpose by deed or writing. In neither case is a break deemed to be an interruption, unless it has been submitted to or acquiesced in for one year after the party interrupted has had notice of it and of the person making or authorizing it (ss.2 and 4).

In both cases, the user must be 'next before some suit or action' so that an easement cannot be finally established under the Act until precipitated by an action. Since the user for twenty years or forty years must be immediately before that action, it follows that potential easements which have been exercised for either of these periods without being finally constituted in an action are dissolved if they are later interrupted. Thus in *Hyman* v. *Van Den Bergh* [1908] 1 Ch. 167, user was exercised as of right between 1877 and 1899 but then was enjoyed by consent of the owner of the servient land. It was held that the enjoyment for the period of twenty-two years was of no avail since it was not 'next before' the action, which commenced in 1906.

Next, although the user must be uninterrupted, no interruption counts unless it is acquiesced in for one year. Furthermore, interruption means obstruction by the servient owner and not mere non-user (*Smith* v. *Baxter* [1900] 2 Ch. 138, at p.143). In short, what must be proved to defeat a claim is an acquiescence lasting one year in an obstruction to the easement. A protest is enough to negative acquiescence and will be effective for this purpose for some time after it is made. If it is not repeated, silence and inaction may be interpreted as submission. The date when such acquiescence begins is a question of fact depending on all the circumstances (*Davies* v. *Du Paver* [1953] 1 Q.B. 184). Since an interruption is ineffective to defeat an easement unless it has lasted for one year, once an advantage has been enjoyed for more than nineteen years or thirty-nine years no interruption can prevent an easement being established, provided that the dominant owner clinches the right bringing an action as soon as the twenty or forty years have elapsed. Such an interruption could not then last one year even if acquiesced in. No action by the dominant owner, however, will be successful if commenced before the period in question has elapsed (*Reilly* v. *Orange* [1955] 2 Q.B. 112).

Prescription under both periods must be 'as of right', so that the enjoyment must be *nec vi, nec clam, nec precario* throughout those times. A permission given long before the prescription period begins to run will characterize the user even within the period as *precario*, for the principle is

> once permission has been given the user must remain permissive and not capable of ripening into a right . . . unless and until, having been given for a limited period only, it expires, or being general it is revoked or there is a change in the circumstances from which revocation may fairly be implied (*Healey* v. *Hawkins* [1968] 3 All E.R. 836, at p.841).

The only exception to this rule under the section is that in the case of the forty-year period a permission given before the period commences will not defeat a claim unless it was given in writing expressly for the purpose.

The effects of consents may be summarized in the following way which has been judicially approved (see *Healey* v. *Hawkins*, above, at p.840).

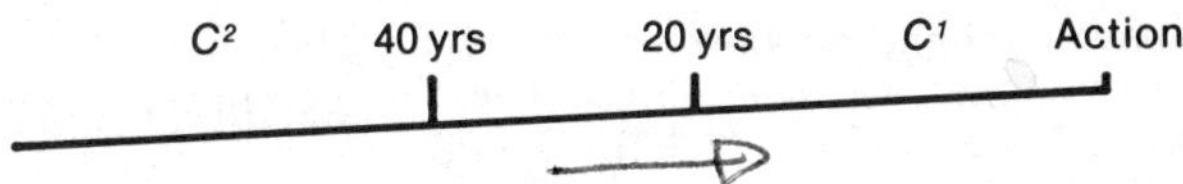

The diagram represents the time running up to an action at the present time. C^1 and C^2 represent oral consents. If a claim is brought on account of user for twenty years, it will be defeated by proof of either C^1 or C^2 unless the latter consent had expired for some reason. If a claim is brought supported by proof of user for forty years, it will be defeated by C^1 but not by C^2. A consent given at the stage when C^2 was given will only defeat a claim if it is in writing. In short, apart from this one exception in favour of the forty-year period, the section merely makes concessions as to the proof of the period of enjoyment and not as to the mode of enjoyment.

Finally, the Act recognizes that in certain circumstances the owner of the servient land might not be in a position to resist the accrual of an easement against his property and it makes allowances in the following way. Under s.7, the period during which the person entitled to resist a claim is a minor, a mental patient or a tenant for life or during which an action has been pending and diligently prosecuted must be deducted in computing the twenty-year period. A period of user enjoyed before such a deducted interval may, however, be aggregated with one enjoyed after it. Thus if fifteen years of user were enjoyed against a fee simple owner and then there followed ten years during which there was a life interest running and this in turn was followed by a further five years of enjoyment against a fee simple owner, a claim could be established.

Section 8 then enacts that any period during which the servient land has been held for a life interest or a lease exceeding three years shall be deducted in computing the forty-year period, provided that the claim is resisted by the 'reversioner' within three years after the determination of the life interest or lease. The section applies to any 'way or other convenient watercourse or use of water' but it is thought that the word 'convenient' is a misprint for 'easement'. If it is not a misprint, the scope of the section is considerably reduced. This problem, raised as long ago as 1881 (see *Laird* v. *Briggs* (1881), 19 Ch.D. 22, at p.33), is undecided even today. A strange result of the two sections should be noted. While periods for which the servient property was subject to a leasehold interest may be deducted in the case of a claim under the forty-year period, this is not so when a claim is made under the twenty-year period (see *Pugh* v. *Savage* [1970] 2 All E.R. 353).

Easements of light

Section 3 provides that

> when the access and use of light to and for any dwelling-house, workshop, or other building shall have been actually enjoyed therewith for the full period of twenty years without interruption, the right thereto shall be deemed absolute and indefeasible, any local usage or custom to the contrary notwithstanding, unless it shall appear that the same was enjoyed by some consent or agreement expressly made or given for that purpose by deed or writing.

An easement of light cannot be acquired for the benefit of open land. The section clearly shows that, as at common law, so under the Act, some building must exist for the benefit of which the right is prescribed for. Yet, provided that a window-opening exists, the fact that it was shuttered for long periods or that the house was uninhabited does not prejudice the dominant owner (*Cooper* v. *Straker* (1888), 40 Ch.D. 21).

The enjoyment must immediately precede the action, for s.4 governs s.3 as well as s.2, and an action is necessary to precipitate it into an easement. It need not, however, be 'as of right' because this requirement is significantly omitted from s.3. This is a most important factor which sets easements of light apart from other easements where prescription under the Act is concerned. Proof of the simple fact of actual enjoyment of the light over the period suffices, unless it is shown to be attributable to some written consent. Oral permissions are no obstacle to acquisition under the section (see *Mallam* v. *Rose* [1915] 2 Ch. 222). Similarly, the enjoyment may be '*vi*' or '*clam*' but these factors will have little practical application in the case of enjoyment of light.

The words of the section are strong and unqualified enough to enable a tenant not only to acquire an easement against another tenant of his landlord but also against the landlord himself (*Mallam* v. *Rose*, above). Indeed, the fact that the servient land is leased does not prevent the running of the period. Sections 7 and 8, discussed above, deal with disabilities and do not apply to prescription for the easement of light under the Act. On the other hand, unlike other easements, a right of light cannot be acquired against Crown lands, for s.3 does not bind the Crown.

Like all other easements established in this way, an easement of light acquired by prescription is of perpetual duration. This is so even when it is acquired by a tenant against another tenant of his landlord. Such a result can be prevented by the inclusion in the lease of a clause amounting to a written consent.

Section 3 requires that the period of twenty years shall be 'without interruption' and the remarks made above as to the meaning of this expression in regard to the acquisition of other easements apply also to the easement of light. Similarly, the period must be next before some suit or action (s.4). If the owner of the servient land seeks to obstruct the passage of light to the dominant land, an alternative method to that of erecting unsightly hoardings is now available to him under the Rights of Light Act 1959. He may register a notice as a local land charge in a prescribed form, which should describe by dimensions and location a hoarding notionally erected so as to interrupt the flow of light to the desired degree. The notice must be accompanied by a certificate from the Lands Tribunal stating that it has been given to all persons likely to be affected. The dominant owner is thereby placed in the same position that he would be in if the light had been physically obstructed. The Act should be consulted for further details, but it applies to acquisition of easements of light under all forms of prescription and not only under the Prescription Act.

The quantity of light which the dominant property is entitled to receive under an easement of light, by whatever means that easement is acquired, is no more than is sufficient to make a house comfortable or to enable any business to be carried on as beneficially as it was when the easement was created (see *Colls* v. *Home and Colonial Stores Ltd.* [1904] A.C. 179, at p.187). This means that a reduction of the flow of light by the servient owner will not be a violation of the easement unless it constitutes a nuisance. On the other hand, the amount of light which is considered sufficient for the purpose in question changes with human progress and higher minimum standards are expected today than formerly. The court can also have regard to the locality (*Ough* v. *King* [1967] 3 All E.R. 859). But see *Allen* v. *Greenwood* [1979] 1 All E.R. 819.

The extent of the easement acquired

When an easement has been acquired by one of the various methods discussed above, the owners of the dominant and servient lands will sometimes wish to know the extent to which the right can be exercised. Two factors are particularly important in assessing the limits of an easement: the mode of user and the intensity of user. If a right of way is granted over 'Blackacre', in favour of a house on 'Whiteacre', the question might arise as to whether the right of way is exercisable on foot only, or by means of horses, or vehicles. Such a question would be one of mode of user, but if the problem was how frequently the right could be exercised, it would relate to intensity. Both these considerations depend upon the circumstances under which the easement was acquired.

Under statute or express grant

The extent of an easement created by statute or by express grant is a simple question of construction. The language of the document must be consulted to define the rights of the parties. If, however, their intentions are not clear upon some particular matter, the rule that a grant is construed against the grantor must be applied (per Willes, J., in *Williams* v. *James* (1867), L.R. 2 C.P. 577, at p.581). One example only will be given here to serve as a caution when drafting easements. In *V.T. Engineering* v. *Barland and Co.* (1968), 19 P. & C.R. 890, a right of way was granted 'for all purposes' over a road which the dominant owner used for carrying large structural units. The servient owner later began to erect a building on stilts over the road. It was held that a right of way for all purposes granted over land open to the skies includes reasonable vertical, though not lateral, 'swing space'. An injunction was accordingly granted to prevent the obstruction of the easement.

Under implied grants

Insofar as easements created under implied grant are based upon the intention of the parties, similar principles apply here as under express grant. But since there are no words expressing them, these intentions must be discovered from the circumstances prevailing at the time of the transaction. Easements of necessity are not, however, so clearly attributable to the intentions of the parties and the extent of these might be defined strictly by the necessity existing at the time of the transaction.

Under presumed grants

The extent of an easement acquired by prescription is defined by mode of user in fact enjoyed during the period. Therefore, a right of way for agricultural purposes cannot be used for industrial purposes (see *Bradburn* v. *Morris* (1876), 3 Ch.D. 812). Though the mode of user is finally cast in this way, intensification of that user may take place both during the prescription period and after it, provided that the increase in intensity is not so extreme as to amount to a user of a different kind. Thus in *British Railways Board* v. *Glass* [1965] Ch. 538 a way to a caravan site, originally used for only six caravans, was being used for twenty-eight caravans immediately before the action. It was held that an easement had been acquired for this larger number. Furthermore, once an easement exists in favour of land, the identity of the persons making lawful use of it is immaterial (*Woodhouse & Co. Ltd.* v. *Kirkland (Derby), Ltd.* [1970] 2 All E.R. 587, at p.590). It is of course possible that a right of way for certain purposes might even become generalized into a right of way for all purposes in certain circumstances.

Easements acquired for certain purposes will usually be taken to include other purposes which are less onerous on the principle that the greater includes the smaller. Thus a vehicular right of way includes a right of way on foot, though the contrary is not so. Furthermore, the nomenclature of an easement is not itself a restricting factor; it is the substance of the enjoyment which matters. This enables owners to take advantage of modern methods of enjoying advantages over the land of others. Thus a right of way for coaches and horses granted 100 years ago would entitle the dominant owner to drive motor vehicles over the servient land today.

The question of the extent of the easement of light has already been dealt with.

The extinguishment of easements

By release

The dominant owner may extinguish an easement by releasing it. Release may be either express or implied.

(1) *Express release*. A deed is necessary for an express release, but if the servient owner has prejudicially altered his position in reliance on a release informally granted, he will be protected by equitable principles (*Davies* v. *Marshall* (1861), 10 C.B. (N.S.) 697).
(2) *Implied release*. Behaviour by the dominant owner which shows an intention to abandon the benefit of the easement will release the easement. It is a question of fact to be gathered from the circumstances of each case whether a particular act or omission shows an intention to abandon (see *Swan* v. *Sinclair* [1924] 1 Ch. 254, at p.266). Thus while mere non-user may be evidence of release, it is not in itself enough. In one context it might be explained as abandonment; in another merely as an interlude. In *Moore* v. *Rawson* (1824), 3 B. & C. 332, where the owner of a building enjoying an easement of light rebuilt it without a window to receive the benefit of the easement, it was held that there was a clear intention to release the right. Destruction of a building alone, however, is not conclusive, for there might be an intention to rebuild and to continue the easement

> Abandonment of an easement or of a *profit à prendre* can only, we think, be treated as having taken place where the person entitled to it has demonstrated a fixed intention never at any time thereafter to assert the right himself or to attempt to transmit it to anyone else (*Tehidy Minerals Ltd.* v. *Norman* [1971] 2 All E.R. 475, at p.492).

By unity of ownership and possession

If the dominant and servient properties fall into both the same ownership and possession the easement ends. Unity of ownership alone does not produce this result, for the easement continues in favour of, or against, the person who is enjoying possession without ownership. Neither is unity of possession enough, for then the easement is merely suspended during the time this unity lasts. There remains some doubt, however, as to whether this principle is of general application (see *Richardson* v. *Graham* [1908] 1 K.B. 39 and *Buckby* v. *Coles* (1814), 5 Taunt 311).

In any case, once an easement has been extinguished by unity of ownership and possession, it is not resurrected by a later alienation of one of the original tenements, although a new easement might arise under the doctrine of implied grant.

Rights to be distinguished from easements

We have already seen that, although there are some restrictions upon the subject-matter of easements, this factor does not serve to distinguish them from other advantages over land. Such distinction lies rather in the circumstances in which the advantage was created. A few of the more common rights which might be confused with easements because of the common subject-matter will now be very briefly distinguished from them. Some of these rights are separately discussed in other parts of this book.

Profits à prendre

Profits have many characteristics in common with easements. The factor which distinguishes them is that they give the right to take something from land, other than water.

Licences

A licence is a permission bestowed upon a person, whereas an easement is a right created in favour of a piece of land—the dominant tenement. It would indeed be quite possible for *A*, the owner of 'Blackacre', to give *B*, the owner of neighbouring 'Whiteacre', permission to cross 'Blackacre' and yet thereby create merely a licence, if the permission was personal only. There are other differences between the two rights which might sometimes be present in the comparison of particular examples of them, but this is the really telling difference.

Restrictive covenants

The elemental difference between an easement and a restrictive covenant is that a restrictive covenant imposes a duty not to do something whereas an easement imposes the duty to allow something to be done. There are several differences of more practical consequence which derive largely from the later advent of restrictive covenants into our legal system and from certain shortcomings in the law of easements. Firstly, the subject-matter of restrictive covenants, while negative only and narrower than that of easements, is complementary to it. Thus some of the effects which are denied to easements on the grounds of uncertainty of subject-matter mentioned above can be achieved through restrictive covenants. A right to an unspoilt view, for instance, cannot constitute an easement, but a restrictive covenant can forbid alterations to land. Secondly, the methods of creating the two rights differ. Thirdly, a restrictive covenant can only exist as an equitable interest.

Natural rights

Rights in law can arise in two ways. Firstly, they might exist because the law applies them to all persons except insofar as they voluntarily restrict them. Examples of such 'natural rights' arise under the laws of tort and intestacy. Secondly, parties may themselves sometimes manufacture their own rights and obligations, within the framework of the law. Examples are the law of contract and the law of wills. Easements come into this second class, being created, actually or fictionally, by act of parties. However, there are certain other rights against the land of others which come into the class of rights ever present by operation of law, except insofar as they are altered by act of parties. One or two of these might be confused with easements.

A landowner has, for instance, a natural right of support of his land by that of his neighbour, which extends only to the support of land in its natural state. Any support required for building upon the land must be acquired by act of parties as an easement (*Dalton* v. *Angus* (1881), 6 App. Cas. 740). Other examples of natural rights affecting land are the right to have water in a stream flow through land as it always has done, and the right not to have enjoyment of land spoilt by nuisances committed by other landowners. Once again, however, the natural right can be diminished by the acquisition of an easement to override it.

Public rights

Some public rights superficially resemble easements, such as the right to use a highway for passage, a river for sailing, or a park for recreation. The distinction between such rights and easements is that they are exercisable by all or certain sections of the public as such and without reference to any dominant land.

Customary rights

Customary rights which resemble easements are mentioned separately from public rights because, although they are often exercisable by a section of the public, their derivation is remarkable enough to earn special attention. A right can be established as a 'customary right' if it is certain, reasonable and applicable to a particular district, and if it has been exercised continuously since time immemorial (see *Mercer* v. *Denne* [1904] 2 Ch. 534). In practice, long use of the custom will raise the presumption of enjoyment since 1189, though this presumption can be rebutted.

Rights are from time to time established by custom which bear a resemblance to easements, such as the duty to fence against cattle on a common (*Egerton* v. *Harding* (1974), 118 Sol. J. 565), or the right for fishermen in a village to dry their nets on certain land (*Mercer* v. *Denne*, above) or to cross land to get to a church (*Brocklebank* v. *Thompson* [1903] 2 Ch. 344). These rights are of course not easements, because they benefit inhabitants of a particular area as such and have no reference to dominant land.

Rights arising from the doctrine of non-derogation from grant

This doctrine was discussed in Chapter 6. It applies to all grants, including easements. The importance of establishing whether a purported right is attributable to the doctrine is that the requirement of definition of subject-matter is not so strict as in the case of easements.

Study material: *Liverpool C.C.* v. *Irwin* [1976] 2 All E.R. 39

Lord Wilberforce's speech is given in full below. It represented the prevailing opinion of the House.

LORD WILBERFORCE. My Lords, this case is of general importance, since it concerns the obligations of local authority, and indeed other, landlords as regards high-rise or multi-storey dwellings towards the tenants of these dwellings. This is a comparatively recent problem though there have been some harbingers of it in previous cases.

50 Haigh Heights, Liverpool, is one of several recently erected tower blocks in the district of Everton. It has some 70 dwelling units in it. It was erected ten years ago, following a slum clearance programme at considerable cost, and was then, no doubt, thought to mark an advance in housing standards. Unfortunately, it has since turned out that effective slum clearance depends on more than expenditure on steel and concrete. There are human factors involved too, and it is these which seem to have failed. The appellants moved into one of the units in this building in July 1966; this was a maisonette of two floors, corresponding to the ninth and tenth floors of the block. Access to it was provided by a staircase and by two electrically operated lifts. Another facility provided was an internal chute into which tenants in the block could discharge rubbish or garbage for collection at the ground level.

There has been a consistent history of trouble in this block, due in part to vandalism, in part to non-cooperation by tenants, in part, it is said, to neglect by the corporation. The appellants, with other tenants, stopped payment of rent so that in May 1973 the corporation had to start proceedings for possession. The appellants put in a counterclaim for damages and for an injunction, alleging that the corporation was in breach of its implied covenant for quiet enjoyment, that it was in breach of the statutory covenant implied by s 32 of the Housing Act 1961 and that it was in breach of an obligation implied by law to keep the 'common parts' in repair. The case came for trial in the Liverpool County Court before his Honour Judge T A Cunliffe. A good deal of evidence was submitted, both orally and in the form of reports. The judge himself visited the block and inspected the premises; he said in his judgment that he was appalled by the general condition of the property. On 10th April 1974 he gave a detailed and careful judgment granting possession to the corporation on the claim and, on the counterclaim, judgment for the appellants for £10 nominal damages. He found that the defects alleged by the appellants were established. These can be summarised as consisting of (i) a number of defects in the maisonette itself—these were significant but not perhaps of major importance; (ii) defects in the common parts, which may be summarised as continual failure of the lifts, sometimes of both at one time, lack of lighting on the stairs, dangerous condition of the staircase with unguarded holes giving access to the rubbish chutes and frequent blockage of the chutes. He found that these had existed or been repeated with considerable frequency throughout the tenancy, had gone from bad to worse, and that while some defects in the common parts could be attributed to vandalism, not all could be so attributed. No doubt also some defects, particularly the blocking of the rubbish chutes, were due to irresponsible action by the tenants themselves. The learned judge decided that there was to be implied a covenant by the corporation to keep the common parts in repair and properly lighted, and that the corporation was in breach of this implied covenant, of the covenant for quiet enjoyment and of the repairing covenant implied by the Housing Act 1961, s 32.

The corporation appealed to the Court of Appeal[1], which allowed the corporation's appeal against the judgment on the counterclaim. While agreeing in the result, the members of that court differed as to their grounds. Roskill and Ormrod LJJ held that no covenant to repair the common parts ought to be implied. Lord Denning MR held that there should be implied a covenant to take reasonable care, not only to keep the lifts and stairs reasonably safe, but also to keep them reasonably fit for use by the tenant and his family and visitors. He held, however, that there was no evidence of any breach of this duty. The court was agreed in holding that there was no breach of the covenant implied under s 32 of the Housing Act 1961; the appellants did not seek to uphold the judge's decision on the covenant for quiet enjoyment, and have not done so in the House.

---

1 [1975] 3 All ER 658, [1975] 3 WLR 663

I consider first the appellants' claim insofar as it is based on contract. The first step must be to ascertain what the contract is. This may look elementary, even naive, but it seems to me to be the essential step and to involve, from the start, an approach different, if simpler, from that taken by the members of the Court of Appeal. We look first at documentary material. As is common with council lettings there is no formal demise or lease or tenancy agreement. There is a document headed 'Liverpool Corporation, Liverpool City Housing Department' and described as 'Conditions of Tenancy'. This contains a list of obligations on the tenant—he shall do this, he shall not do that, or he shall not do that without the corporation's consent. This is an amalgam of obligations added to from time to time, no doubt, to meet complaints, emerging situations, or problems as they appear to the council's officers. In particular there have been added special provisions relating to multi-storey flats which are supposed to make the conditions suitable to such dwellings. We may note under 'Further special notes' some obligations not to obstruct staircases and passages, and not to permit children under ten to operate any lifts. I mention these as a recognition of the existence and relevance of these facilities. At the end there is a form for signature by the tenant stating that he accepts the tenancy. On the landlords' side there is nothing, no signature, no demise, no covenant; the contract takes effect as soon as the tenants sign the form and are let into possession.

We have then a contract which is partly, but not wholly, stated in writing. In order to complete it, in particular to give it a bilateral character, it is necessary to take account of the actions of the parties and the circumstances. As actions of the parties, we must note the granting of possession by the corporation and reservation by it of the 'common parts'—stairs, lifts, chutes etc. As circumstances we must include the nature of the premises, viz a maisonette for family use on the ninth floor of a high block, one which is occupied by a large number of other tenants, all using the common parts and dependent on them, none of them having any expressed obligation to maintain or repair them.

To say that the construction of a complete contract out of these elements involves a process of 'implication' may be correct: it would be so if implication means the supplying of what is not expressed. But there are varieties of implications which the courts think fit to make and they do not necessarily involve the same process. Where there is, on the face of it, a complete, bilateral contract, the courts are sometimes willing to add terms to it, as implied terms; this is very common in mercantile contracts where there is an established usage; in that case the courts are spelling out what both parties know and would, if asked, unhesitatingly agree to be part of the bargain. In other cases, where there is an apparently complete bargain, the courts are willing to add a term on the ground that without it the contract will not work—this is the case, if not of *The Moorcock* itself on its facts, at least of the doctrine of *The Moorcock*[2] as usually applied. This is, as was pointed out by the majority in the Court of Appeal, a strict test—though the degree of strictness seems to vary with the current legal trend, and I think that they were right not to accept it as applicable here. There is a third variety of implication, that which I think Lord Denning MR favours, or at least did favour in this case, and that is the implication of reasonable terms. But though I agree with many of his instances, which in fact fall under one or other of the preceding heads, I cannot go so far as to endorse his principle; indeed, it seems to me, with respect, to extend a long, and undesirable, way beyond sound authority.

The present case, in my opinion, represents a fourth category or, I would rather say, a fourth shade on a continuous spectrum. The court here is simply concerned to establish what the contract is, the parties not having themselves fully stated the terms. In this sense the court is searching for what must be implied.

What then should this contract be held to be? There must first be implied a letting, i e a grant of the right of exclusive possession to the tenants. With this there must, I

2 (1889) 14 PD 64, [1886–90] All ER Rep 530

would suppose, be implied a covenant for quiet enjoyment, as a necessary incident of the letting. The difficulty begins when we consider the common parts. We start with the fact that the demise is useless unless access is obtained by the staircase; we can add that, having regard to the height of the block, and the family nature of the dwellings, the demise would be useless without a lift service; we can continue that there being rubbish chutes built in to the structures and no other means of disposing of light rubbish there must be a right to use the chutes. The question to be answered—and it is the only question in this case—is what is to be the legal relationship between landlord and tenant as regards these matters.

There can be no doubt that there must be implied (i) an easement for the tenants and their licensees to use the stairs, (ii) a right in the nature of an easement to use the lifts and (iii) an easement to use the rubbish chutes.

But are these easements to be accompanied by any obligation on the landlord, and what obligation? There seem to be two alternatives. The first, for which the corporation contends, is for an easement coupled with no legal obligation, except such as may arise under the Occupier's Liability Act 1957 as regards the safety of those using the facilities, and possibly such other liability as might exist under the ordinary law of tort. The alternative is for easements coupled with some obligation on the part of the landlords as regards the maintenance of the subject of them, so that they are available for use.

My Lords, in order to be able to choose between these, it is necessary to define what test is to be applied, and I do not find this difficult. In my opinion such obligation should be read into the contract as the nature of the contract itself implicitly requires, no more, no less; a test in other words of necessity. The relationship accepted by the corporation is that of landlord and tenant; the tenant accepts obligations accordingly, in relation, inter alia, to the stairs, the lifts and the chutes. All these are not just facilities, or conveniences provided at discretion; they are essentials of the tenancy without which life in the dwellings, as a tenant, is not possible. To leave the landlord free of contractual obligation as regards these matters, and subject only to administrative or political pressure, is, in my opinion, totally inconsistent with the nature of this relationship. The subject-matter of the lease (high-rise blocks) and the relationship created by the tenancy demands, of its nature, some contractual obligation on the landlord.

I do not think that this approach involves any innovation as regards the law of contract. The necessity to have regard to the inherent nature of a contract and of the relationship thereby established was stated in this House in *Lister v Romford Ice & Cold Storage Co Ltd*[3]. That was a case between master and servant and of a search for an 'implied term'. Viscount Simonds made a clear distinction between a search for an implied term such as might be necessary to give 'business efficacy' to the particular contract and a search, based on wider considerations, for such a term as the nature of the contract might call for, or as a legal incident of this kind of contract. If the search were for the former, he said[4]: 'I should lose myself in the attempt to formulate it with the necessary precision'. We see an echo of this in the present case, when the majority in the Court of Appeal, considering a 'business efficacy term', i e a '*Moorcock*'[5] term, found themselves faced with five alternative terms and therefore rejected all of them. But that is not, in my opinion, the end, or indeed the object, of the search.

We have some guidance in authority for the kind of term which this typical relationship (of landlord and tenant in multi-occupational dwellings) requires in *Miller v Hancock*. There Bowen LJ said[6]:

'The tenants could only use their flats by using the staircase. The defendant,

3 [1957] 1 All ER 125, [1957] AC 555
4 [1957] 1 All ER at 133, [1957] AC at 576
5 (1889) 14 PD 64, [1886–90] All ER Rep 530
6 [1893] 2 QB 177 at 180, 181, [1891–4] All ER Rep 736 at 738, 739

therefore, when he let the flats, impliedly granted to the tenants an easement over the staircase, which he retained in his own occupation, for the purpose of the enjoyment of the flats so let. Under those circumstances, what is the law as to the repairs of the staircase? It was contended by the defendant's counsel that, according to the common law, the person in enjoyment of an easement is bound to do the necessary repairs himself. That may be true with regard to easements in general, but it is subject to the qualification that the grantor of the easement may undertake to do the repairs either in express terms or by necessary implication. This is not the mere case of a grant of an easement without special circumstances. It appears to me obvious, when one considers what a flat of this kind is, and the only way in which it can be enjoyed, that the parties to the demise of it must have intended by necessary implication, as a basis without which the whole fits the requirements of the case. Such a definition involves—and I think rightly—recognition that the tenants themselves have their responsibilities. What it is reasonable to expect of a landlord has a clear relation to what a reasonable set of tenants should do for themselves.

I add one word as to lighting. In general I would accept that a grant of an easement of passage does not carry with it an obligation on the grantor to light the way. The grantee must take the way accompanied by the primaeval separation of darkness from light and if he passes during the former must bring his own illumination. I think that *Huggett v Miers*[7] was decided on this principle and possibly also *Devine v London Housing Society Ltd*[8]. But the case may be different when the means of passage are constructed, and when natural light is either absent or insufficient. In such a case, to the extent that the easement is useless without some artificial light being provided, the grant should carry with it an obligation to take reasonable care to maintain adequate lighting—comparable to the obligation as regards the lifts. To impose an absolute obligation would be unreasonable; to impose some might be necessary. We have not sufficient material before us to see whether the present case on its facts meets these conditions.

I would hold therefore that the corporation's obligation is as I have described. And in agreement, I believe, with your Lordships, I would hold that it has not been shown in this case that there was any breach of that obligation. On the main point therefore I would hold that the appeal fails.

My Lords, it will be seen that I have reached exactly the same conclusion as that of Lord Denning MR, with most of whose thinking I respectfully agree. I must only differ from the passage in which, more adventurously, he suggested[9] that the courts had power to introduce into contracts any terms they thought reasonable or to anticipate legislative recommendations of the Law Commission. A just result can be reached, if I am right, by a less dangerous route.

As regards the obligation under the Housing Act 1961, s 32, again I am in general agreement with Lord Denning MR. The only possible item which might fall within the covenant implied by this section is that of defective cisterns in the maisonette giving rise to flooding or, if this is prevented, to insufficient flushing. I do not disagree with those of your Lordships who would hold that a breach of the statutory covenant was committed in respect of the matter for which a small sum of damages may be awarded. I would allow the appeal as to this matter and dismiss it for the rest.

---

7 [1908] 2 KB 278, [1908–10] All ER Rep 184
8 [1950] 2 All ER 1173
9 [1975] 3 All ER 666, [1975] 3 WLR at 672

Questions

1 *Consider what reform of the law of easements appears desirable, particularly in regard to:*
subject matter;
section 62 of the Law of Property Act 1925;
prescription.
Compare your answer with the Law Reform Committee Report on Acquisition of Easements and Profits (1966) Cmnd. 3100. See also the Law Commission's Working Paper No. 36 of 1971.

2 *What is meant by 'acquiescence' in regard to enjoyment of an easement 'as of right'?*

3 *Discuss the advantages and disadvantages to a fair and settled law of easements presented by E. R. Ives Investments Ltd. v. High [1967] 1 All E.R. 504.*

4 *To what extent might the law of restrictive covenants be assimilated to the law of easements?*

Chapter Fourteen

Profits à prendre

Introduction

A *profit à prendre* is an interest in the land of another person which gives the right to remove from that land something derived from it. However, in the case of easements, subject-matter alone fails to distinguish profits from other rights, for the same results can be achieved by other methods such as by licence. Like easements, profits are means rather than ends, so that the circumstances and mode of creation are the true distinguishing factors. Since many of the principles applying have already been discussed under the subject of easements, they will be mentioned only briefly here unless there is some variation.

Profits, like easements, can be created to endure for any of the interests for which land can be held, and the same rules apply as to whether these interests are legal or equitable.

Subject-matter may be dealt with swiftly, for it is much more exclusive than that of easements. It is essential that the matter to be taken from the land should be a product of the land. Examples are the rights to take turf or peat (turbary); game; fish (piscary); sand; wood (estovers); ice though not water—for water can only be the subject-matter of an easement—and, of course, the right of pasture. When a profit is enjoyed by one person alone, it is called a 'several profit'; when enjoyed along with other persons it is called a 'profit in common' or simply a 'common'. The most important classification of profits is into profits 'appurtenant' and profits 'in gross'.

A profit appurtenant is one which exists in favour of dominant land. We have already met this principle of dominancy and serviency between two pieces of land in connection with easements, and this class of profits is governed by rules similar to those of easements. Unlike easements, however, profits can also exist in gross, for a person may have the right to enjoy a profit in the land of another person even though he owns no land himself.

The four conditions necessary to the existence of easements apply to profits appurtenant: there must be a dominant and a servient tenement; the profit must accommodate the dominant tenement; those tenements must not be both owned and occupied by the same person and the profit must be capable of forming the subject-matter of a grant. The first three of these rules clearly cannot apply to profits in gross because no dominant tenement exists. The fourth does apply. Thus, in the case of an appurtenant profit the quantity of the profit which can be taken is limited to the needs of the dominant tenement, for the right must accommodate this property. It cannot therefore be founded upon commercial interests (*Harris* v. *Chesterfield* [1911] A.C. 623). A profit in gross, however, is not confined in this way and may be 'without stint'.

Creation of profits

Profits may owe their creation to one of the following methods.

(1) *Statute.* No explanation of this is necessary. The Inclosure Acts provide examples.
(2) *Express grant.* The same principles apply to the express creation of profits as to the express creation of easements, including those relating to agreements, reservations and s.62 of the Law of Property Act 1925.
(3) *Implied grant.* The doctrines of necessity and *Wheeldon* v. *Burrows* do not apply to profits, for their subject-matter is not apt to invoke them, but in olden times, before the Statute *Quia Emptores* of 1290, a conveyance of land would sometimes include by implication of law the right to pasture certain animals on the manorial waste land. Such 'profits appendant' are perhaps best classified under implied grant. Their ancient derivation renders them of no practical importance today.
(4) *Presumed grant.* Once again the same principles apply as in the case of easements, and profits can be acquired by prescription at common law, under the doctrine of lost modern grant, or under the Prescription Act 1832 (see *Tehidy Minerals Ltd.* v. *Norman* [1971] 2 All E.R. 475). The following variations apply, however.

(a) In the case of profits in gross, prescription at common law or under the doctrine of lost modern grant may be proved to accumulate in successive persons irrespective of land ownership, because there is no dominant tenement.
(b) Profits in gross cannot be prescribed for under the Prescription Act because enjoyment of the advantage in question is required to be in favour of a tenement (s.5).
(c) The prescription periods for profits appurtenant under the Act are thirty and sixty years, instead of twenty and forty years as in the case of easements. No longer period is necessary to raise the presumption of the lost grant of a profit than in the case of the lost grant of an easement (*Tehidy Minerals Ltd.* v. *Norman* [1971] 2 All E.R. 475).
(d) Under the Commons Registration Act 1965, s.16, the period during which a right of common was not exercised because of animal health or because the land was requisitioned is to be left out of account in determining whether there has been an interruption within the meaning of the Prescription Act and also in computing the thirty or sixty years period. This provision could clearly be useful where, for instance, movements of stock are restricted because of foot-and-mouth disease.

Extinguishment of profits

Profits can be extinguished in the following ways.

(1) Statute

(a) *Approvement.* Approvement is the release of part of the land from the profit of pasture by the servient owner. This was permitted even in the early law provided that sufficient land was left for the satisfaction of the commoners. Approvement is now regulated by the Law of Commons Act 1893, and government consent is required.

(b) *Inclosure*. Inclosure of land has the effect of discharging the whole of the servient tenement from all rights of common. It was achieved through private Acts of Parliament and later under the provisions of general legislation. The impetus of the movement towards inclosures was the desire to put land to better commercial use which was obviously obstructed by the existence of profits. Compensation was awarded to the profit owners. The loss of open space through inclosure in the eighteenth and early nineteenth centuries led to a reversal of this trend. Inclosures are now regulated by the Commons Act 1876, which requires government and Parliamentary confirmation, and the Commons Amendment Act 1893.

(c) *Registration*. Under the Commons Registration Act 1965, most rights of common had to be registered with the local authority within a certain time which has now expired. Failure to register extinguished the right. The term 'rights of common' has a wide meaning in the Act. The purpose of the legislation is to establish accurately the boundaries of large areas of land, mainly in the north and west of England which are subject to such rights, preparatory to the introduction of further legislation aimed at its better utilization and the preservation of public amenity.

(2) Release

The owner of a profit may release it, expressly by deed or impliedly by clearly showing an intention to release it by such alteration in the use of the dominant tenement as to raise a presumption of abandonment. Mere non-user is probably not enough, although, if lasting a long time, it is no doubt a strong contributory factor (see *Re Yateley Common, Hampshire* [1977] 1 All E.R. 505). If the dominant owner allows the servient owner to incur expense in the belief that the profit has been abandoned, this would also be strong evidence of abandonment.

(3) Unity of ownership and possession

This method of extinguishment has been discussed in relation to easements.

Rights to be distinguished from profits

Because of their more exclusive subject-matter profits are less likely to be confused with other rights than easements are. Nevertheless, the following rights must be carefully distinguished.

(1) Licences

A person may be given a right by contract to take the produce of another person's land. Even if this is done by deed, the resultant advantage will not amount to a profit unless the constituent elements of a profit as described above are present. An example of such a right is a grazing licence authorizing a person to graze cattle upon land.

(2) Public rights

An example of a public right is that of fishing in the sea. This is clearly not a profit since there is no dominant tenement to constitute an appurtenant profit, and no grant to any particular individual, express or presumed, so as to establish a profit in gross.

(3) Rights of indefinite classes

We have already seen that indefinite classes of people cannot own an easement, but that a customary right to similar effect can sometimes be proved on their behalf. A similar problem exists where a fluctuating body of people claim the right to take something from land. The recourse to custom here, however, is not possible since it was ruled a very long time ago that the effect of allowing customary profits would be to exhaust the land. Nevertheless, the law has outflanked this rule in two cases in its eagerness to protect advantages which have been long and peacefully enjoyed.

(a) *Presumed incorporation of the class by the Crown*. The Crown can incorporate a fluctuating class of persons such as the inhabitants of a town. If long enjoyment of the advantage is proved, and if it is shown that the persons in the class have always considered themselves as a corporation and acted as one, by holding meetings for example, then the courts will presume that they were incorporated by the Crown at some date for the particular purpose of enjoying the privilege in question (see *Willingdale* v. *Maitland* (1866), L.R. 3 Eq. 103). The presumption, of course, operates fictionally. In reality few such incorporations have been carried out in this way.

(b) *Presumed charitable trust*. Where the indefinite class of persons cannot claim directly for some reason, such as that they have not acted as a corporation, but where the advantage has long been enjoyed along with an incorporated body such as a local authority, it may be presumed by the court that the advantage was granted to the incorporated body subject to a trust that the indefinite class should be allowed to enjoy it (*Goodman* v. *Saltash Corporation* (1882) 7 App. Cas. 633).

Chapter Fifteen

Mortgages

Introduction

A mortgage is an interest in land created in favour of a creditor as a security for a debt or the performance of an obligation.

Any creditor may sue for the recovery of a debt, but he might be frustrated if the debtor has not enough assets to satisfy the claims of his creditors. In the case of substantial loans, therefore, some form of security is desirable, out of which the debt can be satisfied in preference to other creditors. It might take the form of a pawn, when possession of a chattel is given to the lender on the understanding that he may retain it until the loan is repaid and sell it if it is not. This is not a completely satisfactory solution, because the borrower might be deprived of a very useful or beautiful thing. Yet it would be inviting trouble to allow the debtor to remain in possession of it since he might sell it.

An interest in land, however, is particularly well suited to being a security. The act of constituting an interest in land as a security is a mortgage. It is carried out by the borrower, called the mortgagor, creating a long lease in favour of the creditor, the mortgagee, or, alternatively, by what amounts to the same thing, a 'charge' over the land. However, this lease provides that when the debt is paid the interest in the land shall terminate. If created in the proper way, such an interest is enforceable against the whole world, so that even if the mortgagor later sells the fee simple, the mortgage will, like any lease, adhere to that land as a barnacle sticks to the bottom of a ship wherever that ship goes. The mortgagee, therefore, will be able to enforce the mortgage against the new owner who would have expected to pay a reduced price for the land according to the amount of the mortgage. Usually when land subject to a mortgage is sold, the vendor discharges the debt at the time of completion by repaying the mortgagee out of the purchase-money.

Since the mortgage may thus be made enforceable against the whole world, the mortgagee need not protect his security by taking possession under the lease and so the mortgagor may continue to enjoy his property. Indeed, the mortgagee will not be interested in taking possession, because he is only looking for a security. Nevertheless, he has an estate, and is entitled to possession if he wishes. While the very existence of his interest secures the debt against all who come to the land, the mortgagee will require some ready means of raising the amount due to him, and this is achieved by providing that the mortgagee shall have power to sell the interest of the mortgagor, satisfy his debt and costs from the proceeds of sale and pay the balance of the money to the mortgagor. In most cases there is statutory power to do this, irrespective of agreement.

The law of mortgages has been greatly influenced by history and by the intervention of equity and this has resulted in the application of certain rules, irrespective of the agreement of the parties, once it is clear that a transaction is in essence a mortgage. Consequently, the true rights of the parties may be very different than appears from the terms of their agreement. Equity interfered to protect the mortgagor, who in the past had frequently been open to exploitation. The wastrel landowner gambling into the night and putting himself at the mercy of unscrupulous moneylenders has existed in fact as well as in romantic fiction. Equity intervened in his favour. The doctrines equity evolved in doing so apply today, even though in modified form. The majority of mortgages nowadays are transacted in very different circumstances, for the mortgagor is usually a well-advised commercial firm or a newly-wed with both feet firmly on the ground, and the mortgagee a building society with a high and settled standard of conduct.

When a house is purchased with the aid of a mortgage, the two transactions of purchase and mortgage are telescoped. After negotiating a loan, the purchaser buys the property with the loan and immediately afterwards, on the same day, mortgages it to the mortgagee as security for the loan. Nevertheless, the two transactions are quite separate, a factor which may have important consequences (*Church of England Building Society* v. *Piskor* [1954] 2 All E.R. 85).

Whether a transaction is a mortgage or not is a matter of substance and not one of form, so that if in essence a conveyance is for the purpose of security, then it is a mortgage, even though it is called by some other name. Thus if *A* sells land to *B* and at the same time an option is given to *A* to repurchase upon repayment of the purchase-money, the transaction might be a mortgage. It is a question of the intentions of the parties.

Perhaps more than any other topic in land law, therefore, the mortgage needs a prologue to any discussion of its principles. The following preliminary comments are thus necessary.

(1) The legal forms which mortgages take might give a false impression of the true legal position of the parties and also of the practices they are likely to follow.

(2) The legal rules have been shaped by equity over several centuries so that they justly respond, age by age, to contemporary social and economic considerations. In contrast to the chameleon, the exterior form has remained fairly constant, while the real body has changed. Some of the older authorities are thus no longer reliable. We must curtail history and concisely discuss the judicial restatements for our own generation.

(3) The social background informing a modern account is of enormous importance. The mortgage is no longer merely a means of raising a personal loan. It is the means through which millions of homes are provided for families and by which mighty finance is raised for commercial ventures. In times of recession the financial hardship of borrowers brings problems of breakdown of the mortgage agreement and potential homelessness.

(4) In the present century, statute has supplemented equity in the task of containing the bargains of enthusiastic lenders and borrowers within some imposed bounds. This interference with free will is not new. In modern terms, however, its habitat is within 'consumer protection'. The Law of Property Act 1925, s. 103, recognized the principle in regard to mortgages as it did elsewhere for other transactions. Later examples are the Administration of Justice Act 1973 s.8 and the Consumer Credit Act s. 137.

Considering these factors, the order of treatment of the subject will be as follows. First the classical theory of mortgages will be discussed, since this still underlies all forms of the transaction. This discussion will include: the creation of mortgages; the rights of the mortgagor; the rights of the mortgagee. Then the priority of competing mortgages will be considered. Finally there will follow discussion of some modern mortgage transactions in their contexts with reference to sample documents. References to sections will be to the Law of Property Act 1925 unless otherwise stated.

Creation of mortgages

Mortgages, like leases and certain other interests in land, may exist either as legal or equitable interests. The ways in which legal and equitable mortgages are created will be considered separately. If a legal mortgage is to be created, the estate which is to be mortgaged must itself be legal, that is, either a fee simple absolute in possession or a term of years absolute, and the transaction must be carried out by deed. Equitable mortgages are created when there is only a contract to create a mortgage of a legal estate, when such a mortgage is not accompanied by the required formalities or when the interest itself, which is the subject-matter of the mortgage, is equitable.

Legal mortgages

Given that the subject-matter of the mortgage is a legal estate, there are two ways of creating a legal mortgage, firstly, by a lease 'subject to a provision for cesser on redemption' and secondly, by a 'charge by way of legal mortgage' (ss.85–87). Although the mortgage by lease has now in practice been almost completely replaced by the charge by way of legal mortgage, the mortgage by lease will be discussed first, since the Act explains the effect of a legal charge by reference to it.

(1) *By a lease.* If the estate to be mortgaged is a fee simple, the lease may be of any duration. It must be by deed. This deed will contain the terms of the mortgage and will also contain a clause known as the provision for cesser on redemption. This states that if the loan is repaid in accordance with the terms of the deed and the mortgage thus satisfied or 'redeemed', the term of years shall thereupon cease. Thus, if a term of 3,000 years is created with an agreement that the debt shall be repaid in one year's time and the debt is satisfied at the end of that year, the mortgage term ends then.

If the mortgagor wishes to borrow more money on the security of the same property, he may make a second mortgage, and this is done by creating a second lease in favour of the second mortgagee, usually of one day's greater duration than the first. Third and subsequent mortgages may also be made in the same way. Thus, an indefinite number of legal mortgages may be created on the same property. We shall see later that the rights of these subsequent mortgagees are substantial and are not properly reflected in the fact that nominal reversions only are reserved to them. Subsequent mortgagees should ascertain before advancing their money that the value of the property is enough to support the loans they are to make, as well as the loans of prior mortgagees, because provided that the latter have protected their securities properly, they will have prior right to be satisfied. If the mortgagor's estate is a lease and not a freehold, then a legal mortgage is created by a sub-lease in favour of the mortgagee, with a provision for cesser upon redemption. Again the transaction must be by deed. The length of the sub-lease will, of course, be restricted by the length of the lease out of which it is created, for it must be of less duration. A period of one day less would satisfy this legal requirement, but in practice the mortgage term is made several days less in duration, for second and subsequent mortgages are created by sub-leases of one or more days' longer duration than prior mortgages, and sufficient room in the reversion is thereby provided for these later transactions. The following diagram shows the operation of this procedure in the case of the successive mortgages of a ten-year lease. Once again, an indefinite number of legal mortgages may be created in the same property.

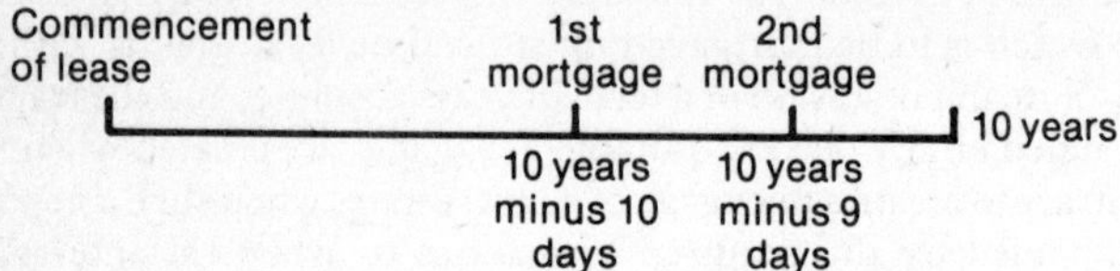

Before 1926, a fee simple was mortgaged by a conveyance of the fee simple itself to the mortgagee, with a provision that when the loan was repaid the estate would be reconveyed to the mortgagor. The mortgagor was left in possession of the property just as he is nowadays. Even leaseholds were occasionally mortgaged by an assignment of the whole term with a similar proviso. Both these methods are now impossible under ss.85 and 86. If an attempt is made to make mortgages in either of these ways, the sections provide what the effect shall be.

A purported mortgage of an estate in fee simple by a conveyance of the fee simple operates as a lease for 3,000 years without impeachment for waste, but subject to cesser on redemption, or, in the case of a second mortgage, as a lease on similar terms for a period of 3,000 years plus one day, or, in the case of subsequent mortgages, of one day's greater duration than the previous mortgage. A purported mortgage of a lease by assignment takes effect as a sub-lease of ten days' less duration than the lease, subject to cesser on redemption. The term taken by second or subsequent mortgagees is one day longer than the mortgage immediately prior to it.

A mortgage term together with its attendant rights is clearly property and as such can itself be mortgaged by the mortgagee if, for instance, he wishes to raise a short term loan without going against the mortgagor to recover his own money. When a mortgage is itself mortgaged, as opposed to being transferred, the transaction is called a sub-mortgage. It is created by the grant of a sub-lease out of the mortgage term or by a charge by way of legal mortgage, which is dealt with below (s.87). The general effect of a sub-mortgage is to place the sub-mortgagee in the position of the mortgagee so far as rights of enforcement of repayment of the original mortgage debt are concerned.

(2) *By a charge by way of legal mortgage.* An alternative way of creating a legal mortgage which applies identically to both the fee simple and to leaseholds is by a 'charge by way of legal mortgage'. After dealing with mortgages by means of leases, the nature of a charge might seem rather elusive. No estate is created and we seem to meet a new concept. In fact, it is a more rational and

elegant means of achieving the desired effect of a security than is the grant of a leasehold, which is a makeshift use of an estate really designed to endow a person with possession of land for a definite period.

The legal charge, as it is usually called, is really easy to understand now that we have discussed mortgages by leasing. Section 87 enacts that a mortgagee by charge of a fee simple shall have the same protection, powers and remedies as if he held a mortgage term of 3,000 years without impeachment of waste, and that a mortgagee by legal charge of a lease shall have the same protection, powers and remedies as if he held a sub-lease of one day's duration less than the lease which was charged. In short, although the charge is different in form from a mortgage by lease, bringing to the mortgage transaction clothing of its own, unborrowed from other wardrobes, its effect is the same (see *Regent Oil Co. Ltd.* v. *J. A. Gregory (Hatch End) Ltd.* [1966] Ch. 402).

The legal charge has grown in popularity amongst practitioners since 1926 and has now largely superseded the lease. The Act provides a short model form of the charge which, however, is optional only. Additional provisions are usually included in practice (Fifth Schedule). The charge must be created by deed.

This new form of legal mortgage has certain advantages over a mortgage by lease besides that of simplicity of appearance. Firstly, since it applies in the same way to both freehold and leasehold estates, both kinds of property can be mortgaged together by a legal charge. Secondly, if a lease contains a covenant against sub-letting, then a mortgage by means of a legal charge, since it does not create a term of years, probably does not constitute a breach of that covenant, even though the landlord's consent is not sought (*Grand Junction Co. Ltd.* v. *Bates* [1954] 2 Q.B. 160, at p. 168). In the case of a mortgage by lease, consent is clearly required, although it is enacted that such consent shall not be unreasonably refused (s.86).

Equitable mortgages

Mortgages may exist as equitable interests in land and are created in the following circumstances.

(1) *Mortgage of an equitable interest.* If the subject-matter of the mortgage is an equitable interest, then the mortgage itself must necessarily be equitable. A mortgage of an equitable interest is created by assigning the interest to the mortgagee with a provision for redemption and reassignment. No deed is necessary, but the transaction must be in writing, signed by the mortgagor or his agent (s.53(I)(c)). It may also be created by will.

(2) *Agreement for mortgage.* We discussed in relation to leaseholds how equity looks on that as done which ought to be done. Thus a contract for a lease is treated as a lease, provided that certain conditions are satisfied. The same principle applies to agreements to create mortgages. There must be a sufficient memorandum in writing or an act of part performance to satisfy s.40 of the Law of Property Act 1925. An imperfect purported legal mortgage which, though in writing, is not under seal, will be treated as a contract for a mortgage.

A deposit of title deeds with the intention that they shall be retained as a security for a loan creates an equitable mortgage (*Russel* v. *Russel* (1783) 1 Bro. C.C. 269). Furthermore, no written memorandum is required, because the deposit is treated as a sufficient act of part performance. In practice, such a deposit is usually accompanied by a deed containing the terms of the mortgage. This makes the transaction a mortgage 'by deed' which, we shall see, enables the mortgagee to exercise certain statutory powers and remedies. The deed might also include a power of attorney or a declaration of trust so as to empower the mortgagee to pass the legal estate in the event of the sale of the security by him. This would otherwise be impossible, because he only holds an equitable interest.

(3) *Equitable charge*. When a person expresses the intention in signed writing that certain land is to stand responsible for the payment of some debt or other obligation, without intending to create or agreeing to create any legal or equitable interest in that land, an equitable charge results. Such a charge would be created, for example, if a man signed a written contract agreeing to charge his land with the payment of a sum of money to another (see *Matthews* v. *Goodday* (1861) 31 L.J. Ch. 282, at p.282).

The rights of the mortgagor

The principal rights of the mortgagor are his beneficial interest in the mortgaged property, the right to redeem, protection in some cases under the Consumer Credit Act 1974 and the right, in certain circumstances, to grant and accept surrenders of leases.

Beneficial interest in the mortgaged property

Since the essence of a mortgage is that it is a security, the mortgagor retains the beneficial interest in the estate or interest which is passed to the mortgagee, subject to the rights of the mortgagee under the mortgage contract. The changes made by the 1925 legislation with regard to the creation of mortgages are skin deep only, and do not affect this substantive interest of the mortgagor, which was taken for granted before the Acts (see the judgment of Lord Parker in *Kreglinger* v. *New Patagonia Meat & Cold Storage Co. Ltd.* [1914] A.C. 25). This beneficial interest arises at the moment the mortgage is created and continues until its end. It explains why a mortgagee who enters into possession of the property must account strictly for the profits of the land, why he must return any surplus money to the mortgagor after his own debt and expenses have been satisfied, following a sale of the property by him, and why a mortgagor can bring actions in his own name for possession or for rents and profits (s.98), although he may only own a reversionary interest. The mortgagor also continues to own the reversion behind the term or sub-term which he has created in favour of the mortgagee.

Right to redeem

In the early days of mortgages, if the mortgagor did not repay the loan upon the very day agreed, the mortgagee was entitled to keep the mortgaged property, even though its value far exceeded the loan. The mortgagor had thus a short-lived contractual right to redeem. Equity intervened against this harsh doctrine and, emphasizing that a mortgage was only a security and that a failure to repay on the agreed day could be remedied, it allowed that mortgagor to redeem at an indefinite time after the contractual right to redeem had passed, provided that the mortgagor, who was thereby invoking equitable principles, was himself prepared to act equitably. This means that, since he has not repaid upon the date agreed, he must give the mortgagee either six months' notice or six months' interest before he enforces his equitable right to redeem, because it is only fair to allow the mortgagee a reasonable time to investigate other ways in which to invest his money. If the loan is not repaid even upon this new date, then a further six months' notice or interest must be given, unless there is some good explanation to account for the failure to pay. Then reasonable notice must be given (*Cromwell Property Investment Co. Ltd.* v. *Western* [1934] Ch. 322). This equitable right to redeem lasts from the day after the contractual right to redeem has passed, until the mortgage itself ends, whether this occurs through repayment, sale of the security or other means. A diagram will illustrate the rights of the mortgagor discussed up to this point and their duration.

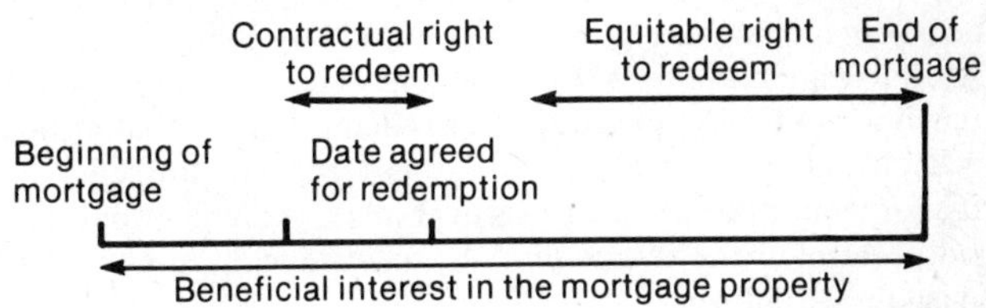

Terminology has not always been consistent or precise in this topic, but the expression 'equity of redemption', as distinguished from the 'equitable right to redeem', is properly reserved to describe the whole of the mortgagor's rights, so as to embrace all the three rights shown in the diagram. As such, it is an interest in land which can be conveyed or devised. Once the equitable right to redeem became established, the date stated in the deed for repayment of the loan as the contractual date for redemption, lost some of its previous importance. As a result, the merely nominal date of redemption six months after the date of the mortgage, which often appears in the mortgage deed, gives no true indication of the mortgagor's right. This is but one reason why it has been remarked that no one ever understood a mortgage deed by the light of nature, or, as Maitland said, it is 'one long *suppressio veri* and *suggestio falsi*'. So much for the incidence of the right of redemption, legal and equitable. We must now examine how it operates.

Historically, the mortgagor has usually been in a weak position, urgently needing money on such terms as are offered, as against the mortgagee who has generally been in such a position of strength that he could press the mortgagor into an unfair bargain. The mortgagee often took advantage of this and, demanding more than the return of his loan with interest tried to exact further profit by fettering or 'clogging' the mortgagor's right to redeem the property, either completely or substantially.

Equity, recognizing the unequal positions of the parties, and affirming that the real purpose of a mortgage is simply to secure a debt, evolved the doctrine that any provision in a mortgage which directly or indirectly had the effect of clogging the right to redeem was void. In the present century, the positions of mortgagors and mortgagees have been re-examined, and it has been recognized that this degree of protection afforded to the mortgagor is not always necessary or deserved. More often, the transaction is one in which the parties are well advised and which embodies a carefully balanced contract which both parties freely entered into as a fair bargain. The repeal of the usury laws has also left the parties freer to compose their own loan terms. While such contracts will still be scrutinized when there is an allegation of fraud, oppression or unconscionable dealing, the dogmatic assertion that every provision which inhibits the right to redeem is void is nowadays too wide. Indeed, some of the older cases have lost most of their authority. We have already noted how the social context in which mortgages now generally occur has changed during recent years.

There are several ways in which a mortgagee, to achieve a bargain suitable to himself, might attempt to affect the right to redeem. Firstly, he might try to make the mortgage irredeemable upon the happening of certain events, or delay the right to redeem for a long period. Secondly, he might include a term that he should be entitled to some advantage in the mortgaged property, such as that the mortgagor should for a certain period buy all his beer or petrol for sale on the mortgaged premises from the mortgagee. He might even attempt to make such a condition operative after redemption, so that although the right to redeem is not affected in theory, it is practically threatened because the mortgagor would be entitled to recover a less valuable property than he mortgaged because of the restriction. We must now discuss to what extent such provisions are enforceable.

(1) *A term must not be oppressive or unconscionable*. Relief will be granted upon equitable principles against terms in a mortgage which are oppressive, unconscionable or secured by fraud (*Knightsbridge Estates Trust Ltd.* v. *Byrne* [1939] Ch. 441, per Greene, M.R. at p.457). These grounds for relief are not restricted to mortgages. It was emphasized in the Knightsbridge case that they do not empower the courts to declare mortgage terms unenforceable merely because they are not reasonable. Freedom of contract is not affected, but when any of these elements is present, one of the parties is not really in a position of freedom. Thus it was held in *Multiservice Bookbinding Ltd.* v. *Marden* [1979] Ch. 84 that an obligation to pay interest on the whole loan throughout the period of the loan, notwithstanding any interim repayment of capital and the linking of the obligation to repay capital and interest to the Swiss franc, was valid, even though the bargain was a hard one. There was no unconscionable behaviour in the sense of the exploitation of a young, inexperienced or ignorant person, or the striking of a bargain which no sensible well-balanced person would have entered (but see *Cityland and Property (Holdings) Ltd.* v. *Dabrah* [1968] Ch. 166).

(2) *A term must not be repugnant to the right to redeem*. Once decided that a transaction is a mortgage, the right to redeem is an integral part of that transaction and cannot be excluded. The one exception is a mortgage by a limited company, which is called a 'debenture' (Companies Act 1948, s.89).

Provisions, therefore, which purport to prevent the right of redemption altogether, or to restrict it to part of the property (*Davis* v. *Symons* [1934] 1 Ch. 442), or to a certain person or persons or time (*Salt* v. *Northampton* [1892] A.C. 1), are void. A provision that the mortgagee shall have an option to purchase the property is similarly inconsistent with a mortgage and is void, though this is not so if the option is agreed upon in a separate and independent transaction, for then the later transaction is not a mortgage (*Reeve* v. *Lisle* [1902] A.C. 461). Furthermore, a right of pre-emption only is always good (*London Rosemex Service Station Ltd.* v. *Shell Mex and B.P. Ltd.* (1969), 20 P. & C.R. 1).

A term postponing the contractual right to redeem for a considerable time is not repugnant to the mortgage transaction unless it has the effect of making the right to redeem merely illusory. In *Fairclough* v. *Swan Brewery Co. Ltd.* [1912] A.C. 565, a lease of twenty years was mortgaged and there was a provision delaying the contractual right to redeem for the whole of this period minus six weeks. The Privy Council held that this provision was void. In substance it attempted to deprive the mortgagor of his lease, and the right to redeem was illusory. In *Knightsbridge Estates Trust Ltd.* v. *Byrne,* above, freehold property was mortgaged and it was agreed that the loan should be repaid over a period of forty years and that there should be no right to redeem before that time. It was held by the Court of Appeal that the mortgagors could not insist upon redemption at an earlier date, because the right to redeem was not illusory. Neither was the transaction oppressive or unconscionable. These two factors being satisfied, the court was not going to inhibit freedom of contract by making further demands such as that the transaction should be 'reasonable'.

An advantage which is restricted in duration to the time of redemption is not inconsistent with the right to redeem and is therefore enforceable. Thus if a publican mortgages his public-house to a brewery, a provision that only the products of that brewery shall be sold in that house until the mortgage is redeemed is enforceable (*Biggs* v. *Hoddinott* [1898] 2 Ch. 307). Similarly, a provision in a mortgage by a garage proprietor (the mortgagor) to a petrol company that only the latter's petrol shall be sold during the continuance of the mortgage may be valid, even though the mortgage is to last for nineteen years (*London Rosemex Service Station Ltd.* v. *Shell Mex and B.P. Ltd.*, above). Once again, as in all mortgage transactions, the agreement must not be oppressive or unconscionable. Such agreements may also be void, however, on the additional ground that they are in unreasonable restraint of trade. This is a matter of the ordinary law of contract and will not be pursued here (see *Esso Petroleum Co. Ltd.* v. *Harper's Garage (Stourport) Ltd.* [1968] A.C. 269). Thus a mortgage may be a security not merely for the repayment of a loan and interest, but also for the performance of an act or obligation.

The final question is whether an advantage, covenanted to be enjoyed by the mortgagee not merely during the mortgage but even after redemption, is repugnant to the right to redeem in that the mortgagor would otherwise take back a less valuable property. This might amount to a partial irredeemability.

The general rule is that an advantage designed to last beyond the time when the mortgage is redeemed is repugnant to the right to redeem and unenforceable beyond that time. Thus in *Noakes* v. *Rice* [1902] A.C. 24 a provision in a mortgage of a public-house that the mortgagor should buy his liquors only from the mortgagees, who were brewers, even after redemption was held by the House of Lords to be unenforceable once the loan had been paid off. The principle was further illustrated in *Bradley* v. *Carritt* [1903] A.C. 253. In that case, tea shares were mortgaged, the mortgagor undertaking that he would always afterwards use the controlling interest which the shares gave him to secure to the mortgagee, a tea broker, the right to sell the company's tea, or, upon failure to do so, the amount of commission which he would have earned as broker if he had sold the tea. A divided House of Lords held that this agreement was repugnant to the right to redeem because, since the value of the shares consisted in their power to secure sale of the company's tea, the agreement would have deprived them of their most desirable characteristic, even after redemption.

In two cases, however, advantages associated with mortgage transactions may remain enforceable even after redemption. The first exception is most difficult to recognize, and is represented by probably only one decided case, *Santley* v. *Wilde* [1899] 2 Ch. 474, a remarkable example of the dangers of sound justice unsupported by adequate conceptualization. A lease of a theatre was mortgaged, the agreement providing that a third of the net profits of the lease should be paid to the mortgagee during the whole of the remainder of the lease, even after repayment of the loan and interest.

The Court of Appeal held that this agreement was binding. The judgment of Lindley, M.R., proceeded mainly on the reasoning that the security of the lease was 'absolutely insufficient' and that it needed bolstering by the covenant for the payment of rents, which thus constituted part of the security. It is difficult to see, however, what purpose such a security can serve after the loan has been paid. It would, of course, be possible and reasonable to construe the payment of a third of the rents for the whole remainder of the lease as part of the price of the loan, along with the payment of interest. Yet the same could be said of the advantage of the liquor sales in *Noakes* v. *Rice*, above. This case seems inconsistent with *Santley* v. *Wilde* unless it can be distinguished on the grounds that in the former the covenant threatened the mortgaged property, whereas in the latter it only concerned the mortgagor's pocket.

The second case of enforceable associated advantages is not strictly an exception to the rule that an advantage designed to last beyond the time of redemption is repugnant to the right to redeem. The advantage is truly collateral to the mortgage and not part of it, even though it might have been concluded in the same instrument. It is possible that the parties, particularly if they are business men, wish to come to an agreement upon a number of matters at the same time and one of these matters might be a loan. The consideration which they give each other in respect of one particular transaction might well be partly expressed in some of the others. The collateral advantage in question might have been an independent aim irrespective of the loan. Indeed, the mortgagee might only have lent the money in order to achieve it. In such a case, that part of the transaction is not a mortgage at all.

In the leading case of *Kreglinger* v. *New Patagonia Meat and Cold Storage Co. Ltd.* [1914] A.C. 25, a firm of woolbrokers agreed to lend money to a firm of meat packers. The loan was for a period of five years, though the mortgagors were entitled to end the mortgage within that period by paying the principal and interest. The security for the loan was the premises and stock of the meat company. The agreement also provided that the mortgagors would, for a period of five years, irrespective of whether the mortgage ended within that time, sell their sheepskins only to the mortgagees, who would offer the best price. The House of Lords held that the mortgagors were bound by this agreement, even though they redeemed the mortgage after two years.

The whole transaction was more than a mere loan. It was an agreement concerning several different matters, including the sale of sheepskins and the granting of a loan, both of which were independently important to the parties. The loan was no more the pivotal part of the transaction than the agreement as to the sheepskins. However, whether the advantage is truly the result of a separate transaction, even though concluded at the same time, is a question of construction and finally depends upon the form in which it is expressed. Viscount Haldane intimated this in the words

> 'I cannot but think that the validity of the bargain in such cases as *Bradley* v *Carritt* and *Santley* v. *Wilde* might have been made free from serious question if the parties had chosen to seek what would have been substantially the same result in a different form . . .' (at p.43).

A short summary of the principles governing the right to redeem may now be attempted as follows. The right to redeem is an integral part of a mortgage transaction and any provision repugnant to this is void. This principle is not offended, however, by mere postponement of the right to redeem unless it renders the right illusory, or by the mortgagee obtaining an advantage which either ends upon redemption or is part of the security itself or is collateral to the mortgage transaction, provided that in each of these cases the provision has not been achieved by fraud, oppression or unconscionable behaviour.

Judicial decisions should derive directly from these sound principles, applied in the light of the practical necessities of the time and of their underlying spirit and purpose. Otherwise, there is a danger that these principles will be overlaid and obscured by the particular problems of past ages. 'The rules as to collateral advantages, for example, have been much modified by the repeal of the usury laws and by the recognition of modern varieties of commercial bargaining . . .' (per Viscount Haldane in *Kreglinger's Case*, at p.38).

(3) *The act of redemption.* The mortgagor redeems the mortgage by tendering the amount due. This amount includes all arrears of interest, even such arrears as would be irrecoverable under the Limitation Act 1980, s.20(5), in an action by the mortgagee (*Holmes* v. *Cowcher* [1970] 1 All E.R. 1224). The right of redemption is also exercisable by an alienee of the equity of redemption or by any person who has an interest in it, such as second or subsequent mortgagees. In the latter case, if several persons compete to redeem, their rights to do so rank in the order in which they were created.

If there is only one mortgage and the mortgagor redeems, the mortgage is discharged and the interest of the mortgagee extinguished (s.116). The indorsement upon the deed by the mortgagee or other person in whom the mortgage is vested of a signed receipt stating the name of the person who pays the money is adequate to document this event (s.115(1)). This is known as a 'vacating receipt'.

If the mortgage in question is redeemed not by the mortgagor but by a second or subsequent mortgagee, the mortgage is not discharged but is transferred to the person who redeems (s.115(2)). He thus stands in the shoes of the mortgagee whose mortgage he has redeemed. The mortgagor may in turn redeem the mortgage by paying off the transferee of the mortgagee, if he wishes to free his property of this incumbrance.

Redemption usually takes place non-contentiously, but may also take place in court if redemption is wrongfully refused. If a subsequent mortgagee seeks to redeem a prior mortgage in court, the doctrine 'redeem up, foreclose down' applies. Reference books should be consulted for further information regarding this uncommon event.

The right to redeem which arises upon the day named in the mortgage deed continues, as we have seen, for an indefinite time after that day. It is, however, extinguished by any one of four events, with the result that the mortgagor loses his right to the mortgaged property.

Firstly, it may be extinguished by foreclosure; secondly, by sale. These are dealt with later in this chapter. Thirdly, the right to redeem is lost by lapse of time under the Limitation Act 1980, s.16, which enacts that when a mortgagee has been in possession of any of the mortgaged land for twelve years, the right of redemption ceases to exist. If the mortgagee receives any payment of the sum of money due to him, or signs any acknowledgement of the mortgagor's title, the period begins afresh. Fourthly, the right to redeem is ended if the mortgagor releases it to the mortgagee. This he might do, for instance, in return for a release of the debt. If the transaction is separate from the mortgage itself, it is not void as being repugnant to the right to redeem.

Protection under the Consumer Credit Act 1974

This Act protects borrowers under a wide range of credit agreements, including mortgages. It was remarked earlier that most modern mortgages are made either between building societies and home buyers or between well advised commercial firms, and that the great sensitivity, expressed in the old cases, in regard to the vulnerable position of the mortgagor is no longer appropriate in these contexts. New classes of people in need of financial protection, and novel ways of parting them from their money are always emerging, even in affluent societies. The pawn shop has gone, but the finance company is very much with us. Its agents have not waited passively in the High Street. They have knocked on doors.

The most important general provision affects all mortgages made by private individuals. Under ss.137–139, the court may reopen a credit agreement which is 'extortionate', that is if the payments to be paid under it are 'grossly exorbitant' or if the agreement 'otherwise contravenes ordinary principles of fair dealing'. In determining these matters, the court must take account of the interest rates prevailing at the time of the agreement, the age, experience, business capacity and health of the debtor and the financial pressure he suffered at the time of the bargain, the degree of risk accepted by the creditor, his relationship with the debtor and 'any other relevant considerations'. The court is empowered to set aside obligations wholly or in part, alter the agreement and to direct the return of property.

Other provisions control a wide range of activities connected with credit agreements such as advertising, licensing of business and enforcement of agreements. A mortgage will not be affected by these provisions if:

(1) The credit provided exceeds £5,000 (s.8), or
(2) The creditor is one of the bodies specified by the Act as being exempt if the loan is made for house purchase. The most important of these bodies mentioned are building societies and local authorities.

These provisions are clearly aimed at second mortgages to finance companies.

Right to grant leases

The mortgagee, by virtue of his estate, has the right to possession of the mortgaged property, so that the mortgagor has no power, apart from his contract or statute, to grant any lease entitling the lessee to possession. Since the mortgagor is usually left in possession, however, it is settled, even at common law, that he may grant a lease which, though not binding on the mortgagee, is binding as between himself and his lessee under the doctrine of estoppel. The mortgagee may, if he wishes, accept the lessee as his own, or refuse to do so and evict him. In the latter case, the lessee may save his position by redeeming the mortgage (*Tarn* v. *Turner* (1888), 39 Ch.D. 456). Of course, if the mortgagee so agrees in writing, the mortgagor may grant leases which bind the mortgagee also (see s.99 (14)).

Quite apart from these powers, a mortgagor, provided that he is in possession and that the contrary intention has not been expressed in the deed or other writing, has power under the Act to grant certain leases which bind not only himself but also the mortgagee (s.99). Such a lease must conform with the following conditions:

(1) If the lease is for agricultural or occupation purposes, the maximum period is for fifty years; if for building purposes, 999 years.
(2) It must be made to take effect in possession not later than twelve months after its date.
(3) It must reserve the best rent reasonably obtainable, regard being paid to the circumstances, but with no fine. This provision is included to safeguard the mortgagee. If the mortgagor defaults in his payments and the mortgagee wishes to take possession of the profits of the property by the appointment of a receiver, these profits will, as a result of this enactment, be substantial.
(4) It must contain a covenant by the lessee for payment of rent and a condition of re-entry on the rent not being paid within a time therein specified not exceeding thirty days.
(5) A counterpart of the lease must be executed by the lessee and the mortgagor must deliver this to the mortgagee, or, in the case of several mortgages, to the first mortgagee in priority, within one month of making it.

If any of these requirements is not obeyed, the lease may be validated under s.152 upon the conditions mentioned there.

It is appropriate to note here a rule of general application. Section 172 of the Law of Property Act 1925 enacts that, with certain exceptions, conveyances made with the intention of defrauding creditors are voidable at the instance of persons thereby prejudiced. A mortgagor who exercises his powers of leasing in order to deprive the mortgagee of possession infringes this rule (*Lloyds Bank Ltd.* v. *Marcan* [1973] 3 All E.R. 754).

Even if these powers are excluded by the mortgage deed, as they frequently are, the mortgagor may still exercise his common-law power of leasing described above, with its limited effect.

As a complement to his statutory power to create leases binding on the mortgagee, the mortgagor is also authorized by the Act to accept surrenders of leases in the following circumstances, provided that the contrary intention has not been expressed in the deed or in other writing (s. 100). The mortgagor may, if in possession of the rents, accept a surrender for the purpose of granting a new lease under the statutory or contractual powers. The surrender is not valid unless the new lease is granted to take effect in possession within one month of the surrender for a term not shorter than the unexpired term of the surrendered lease, and at a rent no less than the original rent.

The rights of the mortgagee

The rights of the mortgagee are varied and formidable and make the mortgage a very desirable form of security. These rights can be exercised concurrently and consecutively insofar as they are not self-contradictory. The order in which they are discussed below is roughly that of increasing finality. The first two mentioned are in the nature of precautions which will often be exercised as a matter of course as soon as the mortgage is created. Then follow rights which are remedies to be exercised when the mortgagor defaults.

Rights to the title deeds

A first mortgagee or chargee of a legal estate, whether taking a legal or equitable mortgage, has a right to take the title deeds relating to the interest mortgaged (ss.85(1) and 86(1)). Section 65 of the Land Registration Act 1925 provides similarly for the deposit of the mortgagor's land certificate in the Land Registry. A mortgagee of a fee simple estate who takes, for instance, a term of 3,000 years or a legal charge, will take home with him the mortgage deed itself and also the title deeds of the fee simple. This has the indirect effect of giving notice to all other persons that the mortgagor's property is subject to a mortgage, for he will have to explain the absence of the deeds to any prospective purchaser. The mortgagor, however, has the right to inspect them and make extracts or abstracts from them from time to time at his own cost (s.96(1)).

When the first mortgage is redeemed, the mortgagee must deliver the deeds to the person next entitled of whom he has notice. In the case of a single mortgage, this person will be the mortgagor; if further mortgages exist it will be the second mortgagee. Although, as we shall see, registration of a mortgage is notice of its existence for other purposes, for the purpose now being discussed it is not. The mortgagee is not required to hand deeds to the person next entitled to them unless he has actual or constructive notice of the superior right (s.96(2), as amended by the Law of Property (Amendment) Act 1926, Sched.). A subsequent mortgagee should, therefore, protect his possible future right to the deeds by giving notice in writing of his interest to prior mortgagees.

Right to insure against fire (sections 101, 108)

If the mortgage, legal or equitable, is by deed, the mortgagee may insure the property against fire and add the cost to the mortgage debt. The amount of insurance must not exceed that mentioned in the deed, or, if none is mentioned, two-thirds of the total replacement cost. If the mortgage is not by deed, there is no such power to insure unless expressly stipulated. Even if the transaction is by deed, the mortgagee cannot exercise this right if the deed states that insurance is not required, or the mortgagor keeps it up in accordance with the deed, or, if there is no provision for insurance, the mortgagor insures with the mortgagee's consent to the amount allowed by the Act.

Right to sue for the sum due

The mortgagee may sue for the sum due as soon as the date for repayment has passed. An action to recover the principal sum is barred under the Limitation Act 1980, s.58(1),(2) after twelve years from that date unless some part-payment of principal or interest or written acknowledgement of the debt causes the time to run afresh. Only six years' arrears of interest may, however, be recovered under the Act. The right to sue belongs to both legal and equitable mortgagees.

Right to possession

> The mortgagee may go into possession before the ink is dry on the mortgage unless there is something in the contract, express or by implication, whereby he has contracted himself out of that right. He has the right because he has a legal term of years in the property or its statutory equivalent.

No default on the part of the mortgagor is necessary (*Four-Maids Ltd.* v. *Dudley Marshall (Properties) Ltd.* [1957] Ch. 317, at p.320, per Harman, J.).

Upon the principles expressed in *Walsh* v. *Lonsdale* (1882), 21 Ch.D. 9, an equitable mortgagee is probably similarly entitled. Generally, a mortgagee will not seek possession but there are three principal occasions when he might have a motive to do so.

The first is that he might wish to take the income of the property because the mortgage repayments are in arrears. The stringency of the rules which apply when he does so, however, discourage the exercise of this right and make the appointment of a receiver more desirable. The appointment of receivers is dealt with below, but here it may be noticed that it amounts to a vicarious possession of the premises under which the mortgagee is not affected by the strict rules just mentioned. These rules, applying to a mortgagee in possession, call him to account not only for the profits which he receives from the property, but also for those which he ought to have received had he acted as a prudent manager of that property. Thus in *White* v. *City of London Brewery Co.* (1889), 42 Ch.D. 237, a mortgagee entered into possession of the property, which was a public house, and then leased it to a tenant who covenanted to buy his liquors from the mortgagee. Previously, it had been a free house. It was held that the mortgagee must account for the additional rent he would have received had it been let as a free house.

The second reason why a mortgagee might desire possession is as a preliminary to exercising his power of sale, for this is greatly facilitated if vacant possession can be offered to a purchaser. The third reason is that the mortgagee might wish to protect his security; it was held in *Western Bank Ltd.* v.

Schindler [1977] Ch. 1 that the mortgagee was entitled to enter possession even before the mortgagor was in default of his repayment obligations.

Mortgages have frequently contained a clause under which the mortgagor 'attorns' tenant to the mortgagee, that is, constitutes himself the mortgagee's tenant. This formerly was a convenient device for the mortgagee for purposes which have now become obsolete and which need not detain us.

The plight of the dispossessed mortgagor, particularly when the property in question is his home, has caused both judges and Parliament to attenuate the harsh consequences of the mortgagees right to possession.

(1) *Judicial relief.* There is inherent jurisdiction in the court to adjourn an application for a short time to afford the mortgagor a chance of performing his obligations if there is a reasonable prospect of this occurring (*Birmingham Citizens Permanent Building Society* v. *Caunt* [1962] Ch. 883). An adjournment will hardly exceed 28 days. The reason for the exception is that the court will not allow a mortgagee to enforce rights in the face of a concrete offer by the mortgagor. This rule applies to all forms of mortgage (*Mobil Oil Co. Ltd.* v. *Rawlinson* [1982] 43 P. & C.R. 221). We shall see below that additional statutory powers are available in the case of a dwelling house.

Before examining those statutory powers, an extraordinary dictum of Lord Denning must be noted. In *Quennell* v. *Maltby* [1979] 1 W.L.R. 318 at p.322, he stated that a mortgagee would be refused possession of a house when it would be contrary to the justice of the case. This statement must be considered strictly within the context of the unusual facts of the case. Space does not allow an examination of this freak authority, but Lord Denning was in effect merely saying that the machinery of mortgages cannot be used to circumvent the Rent Acts. He was saying nothing about possession by mortgagees.

(2) *Statutory relief.* Under the Administration of Justice Act 1970, ss.36–39 and the Administration of Justice Act 1973, s.8, the court may, where a mortgagee claims possession of a dwelling-house, adjourn the case, or stay, suspend or postpone an order for possession for such period as it thinks reasonable if the mortgagor is likely to be able to pay the sum in respect of which he is in default, or to remedy a breach of any other obligation under the mortgage within a reasonable period. In the case of a mortgage debt repayable by instalments, the agreement might make the whole debt become due when there is default in payment of an instalment. In such cases, the Acts do not require the likelihood of repayment of the whole as a condition of relief, but only repayment of the instalment initially due and any further sums falling due during the period of relief. A liberal interpretation of the sections has avoided the absurd possibility that relief might only be available where there has been some default and that a mortgagee might freely exercise his right to possession against a mortgagor who has performed all his obligation (*Western Bank Ltd.* v. *Schindler* [1976] 3 W.L.R. 341).

A spouse who has no proprietary interest but who has registered rights of occupation as a Class F land charge or as a caution or notice must now be notified of the proceedings. The spouse can then apply to be made a party to those proceedings (Matrimonial Homes and Property Act 1981).

Right to appoint a receiver

A receiver is a person who intercepts the rents and profits of property before they reach the owner. We noticed above that strict rules apply when a mortgagee takes possession, but an effect similar to that of taking possession can be achieved by the appointment of a receiver to collect the profits on behalf of the mortgagee. The advantage of this remedy is that the receiver is deemed to be the agent of the mortgagor, so that the mortgagee is not called upon to account for the receiver's acts. The power to appoint a receiver and the rules regulating his authority may be conferred by the mortgage instrument but, irrespective of this, a power so to appoint is given by the Act in the case of all mortgages, legal or equitable, which are made 'by deed' (s.101).

The power arises as soon as 'the mortgage money has become due', that is, when the contractual date for redemption has passed, or, if the mortgage debt is repayable by instalments, when an instalment is overdue. Although the power arises at this time, the mortgagee may not exercise it until one of the following has occurred:

(1) Notice requiring payment of the mortgage money has been served on the mortgagor and default has been made in payment of all or part of it for three months after service.
(2) Some interest is two months or more in arrears.
(3) There has been breach of some provision, other than for payment of the mortgage money or interest, contained in the mortgage deed or in the Act (ss.109 and 103).

In short, the 'count down' begins when the mortgage money is due, but 'blast off' cannot occur until one of the three events mentioned above happens.

Once appointed, the receiver has power to intercept the income of the property. This he may do by action, distress or otherwise. The money thus recovered must be applied by him firstly in discharge of rents, taxes, rates and other outgoings; secondly in keeping down interest on prior mortgages; thirdly in payment of his own commission, of insurance premiums due and of the cost of proper repairs directed by the mortgagee; fourthly in payment of the mortgage interest and fifthly in discharging the principal sum, if so directed by the mortgagee. Any surplus must be paid to the person who would have been entitled to the income if no receiver had been appointed (s.109).

A receiver will often be appointed where the market value of the property has fallen so low as to render it unwise to enforce the remedy of sale, or where the property is tenanted.

Right to sell

A mortgagee can clearly sell the mortgage subject to the right of redemption, but here we are concerned with the right to sell the mortgaged property itself, that is the fee simple or other interest owned by the mortgagor freed of the right to redeem and other rights of the mortgagor.

This right is given by the Act in the case of every mortgage, legal or equitable, which is 'by deed', subject to any express contrary intention or variation of the right contained in the deed (s.101). The power arises and then becomes exercisable upon the same events as in the case of the appointment of a receiver (ss.103 and 109). Provided that the power of sale has arisen, however, a conveyance to a purchaser is effective even though the power has not become exercisable and therefore is wrongful on the part of the mortgagee. An action against him may be brought by a person prejudiced by it (s.104(2)). A purchaser, therefore, is only concerned to see that the power has arisen. Any purported conveyance made before the power has arisen passes no title. A contract to sell by the mortgagee after the power has arisen, but before it has become exercisable, is similarly effective, provided there is no bad faith (*Waring* v. *London and Manchester Assurance Co. Ltd.* [1935] Ch. 310).

The mortgagee may sell either by auction or by private contract subject to such conditions as he thinks fit. 'A mortgagee is strictly speaking not a trustee of the power of sale. It is a power given to him for his own benefit, to enable him the better to realise his debt' (*Warner* v. *Jacob* (1882) 20 Ch.D. 220, at p.224). He has a duty, however, to take reasonable care to obtain the true market value of the property at the date of sale (*Cuckmere Brick Co. Ltd.* v. *Mutual Finance Ltd.* [1971] 2 All E.R. 633). He cannot 'sell' to himself, either directly or indirectly. The juridical nature of this duty remains to be settled. If it is contractual, it can be sued upon only by the mortgagor or his representatives. If it is tortious, then a wider circle of injured persons, including for instance guarantors of loans, might do so. In the latter case, the restrictions on the recovery of damages for economic loss in tort might exert influence (see *Barclays Bank* v. *Thiernal* (1978), 247 E.G. 385 [1981] Conveyancer 329.

Mortgagees who are building societies have a duty to obtain the best price reasonably obtainable under the Building Societies Act 1962, s.36.

The effect of sale when the mortgage is of a fee simple estate is to vest the fee simple in the purchaser and the conveyance may be made in the name of the mortgagor. In the case of the mortgage of a leasehold interest, the effect is to vest the whole leasehold estate in the purchaser. In both cases, the mortgage terms or charges are extinguished (ss.88 and 89), and the rights to redeem are ended.

If several mortgages exist in the property, any of the mortgagees can exercise the power of sale. The sale passes the interest of the mortgagor to the purchaser, subject to any mortgages prior to that of the mortgagee who sells, but freed from any subsequent mortgages which are overreached and are satisfied out of the purchase-money. Thus, if a second mortgagee sells, the purchaser will take the property freed of the second and subsequent mortgages, but subject to the first. This first mortgagee may still exercise his power of sale, in which case the purchaser will lose the property, though he will be entitled to the surplus proceeds of sale after the first mortgagee has been satisfied. Obviously a purchaser from a second mortgagee will expect to pay a reduced price for the property. If a mortgagor has contracted to sell the mortgaged property, the mortgagee's power of sale will nevertheless predominate over the rights of the person who has contracted to buy from the mortgagor, whether or not these are registered, for the mortgagor cannot pass to a purchaser greater rights than he himself owns. The registration would affect only the mortgagor's equity of redemption (see ss.2 and 104 and *Duke* v. *Robson* [1973] 1 All E.R. 486).

Although a mortgagee who sells is not trustee of the power of sale, he is trustee of the proceeds of sale. Under s.105, he must apply them in the following order:

(1) In discharge of any prior incumbrances if the sale was made free of them. This would apply, for instance, if a second mortgagee sold and the first mortgagee agreed to the discharge of his mortgage upon that sale.

(2) In payment of the expenses of sale.
(3) In discharge of the money due to him under his own mortgage.
(4) The residue must then be paid 'to the person next entitled to the mortgaged property'. This person will be the mortgagee next in priority or, if there is no other mortgagee, the mortgagor.

Having satisfied his own and any prior claims out of the proceeds, the mortgagee must discover whether there is a subsequent mortgagee and for this purpose he has a duty to search in the Land Charges Register. In turn, that subsequent mortgagee, having received the surplus proceeds, must likewise make a search and, after satisfaction of his own debt, pass any remaining money to the mortgagee next in priority, or, if there is no later mortgagee, to the mortgagor.

The power of sale extends to equitable mortgages, provided that they are 'by deed'. For this purpose, an equitable mortgage created by mere deposit of deeds is frequently accompanied by a memorandum under seal, for the latter satisfies the statutory description of a mortgage by deed. Since the power of sale under s.101(1) is a power to sell 'the mortgaged property', an equitable mortgagee cannot pass the legal estate to the purchaser (*Re Hodson and Howes' Contract* (1887), 35 Ch.D. 668). Consequently, it is common to include special machinery, such as a power of attorney, in the deed to enable him to convey the legal estate.

However, the view was expressed, by the Court of Appeal in *Re White Rose Cottage* [1965] Ch. 940 that an equitable mortgagee by deed could pass the legal estate under the Act. Whether a broad or even a pedantic approach is taken to ss.101 and 104, this latter view is surely preferable. The power given is to sell 'the mortgaged property'. If this subject-matter of the mortgage in the hands of the mortgagor is legal, it does not cease to become so simple because it was mortgaged in the equitable mode. The fact that the equitable mortgagee does not hold a legal estate is immaterial, for statute can accomplish anything. In any case, even a legal mortgagee upon sale disposes of an interest which he himself does not own.

Right to foreclosure

This classical remedy of the mortgagee has disadvantages which make it less desirable today than the remedy of sale.

Foreclosure is the removal by the court of the mortgagor's equitable right to redeem and the vesting of the interest of the mortgagor absolutely in the mortgagee (see ss.88 and 89).

The right to redeem after the contractual date for redemption has passed is given upon equitable principles and a foreclosure decree marks the termination of this indulgence, which clearly must have limits. The remedy might appear unfair if the mortgaged property is worth more than the mortgage debt, but it is hedged about by rules which protect the mortgagor against harsh results.

The right to bring foreclosure proceedings belong to any mortgagee, legal or equitable, once the contractual date to redeem has lapsed, and with no default by the mortgagor, unless he has agreed not to do so. The effect of foreclosure is to vest the interest of the mortgagor absolutely in the mortgagee, freed from the interests of any subsequent mortgagees and the mortgagor, but subject to any prior mortgages. Since prior mortgagees are not affected, they need not be joined in a foreclosure action. Since subsequent mortgagees and the mortgagor are affected, they must be joined. The action proceeds in two stages.

Firstly, the court issues a foreclosure decree nisi. This states that if the money is not paid by a certain date, usually six months ahead, the mortgagor will be foreclosed. The court now also has power to allow the mortgagor reasonable time to pay under s.36 of the Administration of Justice Act 1970 and s.8 of the Administration of Justice Act 1973, when foreclosure is sought, as it may be, when the mortgagee seeks possession. This power was described above when the mortgagee's right to possession was being considered.

If there are two or more mortgages, each mortgagee is given the chance to pay off and thus redeem the mortgage which is the subject of the action. Otherwise, they are foreclosed. If, on the appointed day, none of the parties so entitled appears and redeems, the foreclosure decree is made absolute. The court may, at the request of any of the parties to a foreclosure action, order a sale of the property (s.91). This action is clearly desirable when the property is worth more than the mortgage debts, as subsequent mortgagees and the mortgagor will be entitled to the surplus according to priority.

Sometimes, even a decree of foreclosure absolute might not be final, for the court has power to re-open the decree. The court has declined to commit to words the terms upon which its discretion to re-open the foreclosure will be exercised, for too much depends upon the circumstances of each case. The mortgagor must apply, however, within a reasonable time. Examples of matters which might weigh with the court are the mortgagor being disappointed at the last moment in his expectation of a loan of money with which to redeem, a large difference between the values of the debt and the mortgaged property, and any special value the property had for the mortgagor. Furthermore, even a purchaser from the mortgagee is deemed to know the law and that foreclosure might be re-opened (see *Campbell* v. *Holyland* (1877), 7 Ch.D. 166). Foreclosure is no longer an important remedy. More detailed accounts may be found in the reference books.

Right to tack

The right to tack is the right to promote a mortgage debt in the order in which several mortgages in the same property must be paid. It concerns the question of priorities and will be discussed below.

Right to consolidate

The right of consolidation is the right of a person who holds two or more mortgages to refuse redemption of one unless the others are also redeemed.

It is fundamentally an illustration of the principle that he who comes to equity must do equity, but the doctrine has been developed to such a point of technicality that it does not always work justly. In its simplest and unspoilt form, it is illustrated by the following example. If *M* mortgages two properties 'Blackacre' and 'Whiteacre', to *A*, for £1,000 each, and each property is worth, say, £2,000, then if the value of 'Blackacre' depreciates while that of 'Whiteacre' perhaps increases, it would be unfair if *M* were allowed to redeem 'Whiteacre' and leave *A* with a security which might not cover the remaining debt. The right can only exist under the following conditions:

(1) The intention to enjoy the right to consolidate must appear in the deeds of at least one of the mortgages in respect of which consolidation is claimed (s.93).
(2) A mortgage cannot be the subject of consolidation unless the contractual date for redemption has passed (*Cummins* v. *Fletcher* (1880), 14 Ch.D. 699). Since the maxim that he who comes to equity must do equity is the root of the right to consolidate, a person who seeks to redeem under his contractual rights is not seeking the assistance of equity at all. Thus, if *M* mortgages three properties, *A*, *B* and *C*, to *X* and the contractual dates for redemption have passed in the cases of *B* and *C*, but not in the case of *A*, then although *X* can insist that *C* cannot be redeemed without *B* being redeemed and vice versa, *M* may redeem *A* on the date agreed for redemption without also having to redeem mortgages *B* and *C*.
(3) The mortgages in respect of which consolidation is claimed must originally have been made by the same mortgagor (*Sharp* v. *Rickards* [1909] 1 Ch. 109). Thus, if M^1 mortgaged property *A* to *X* and M^2 mortgaged property *B* to *X* and later M^1 purchased property *B*, *X* cannot require the two mortgages to be consolidated against M^1.
(4) At the date when redemption is sought, all the equities of redemption must be in one hand and at the same time all the mortgages must be in one hand, or this state of things must have occurred at some time, even though the equities of redemptions have become separated. Of course, the mortgages must always be in the same hands at the date when consolidation is sought, for otherwise there would be no purpose in the owner of a mortgage desiring it. This rule lays the limits to the doctrine of consolidation, which had been growing rankly, and was finally established in *Pledge* v. *White* 1896, A.C. 187.

The following diagram might clarify the doctrine.

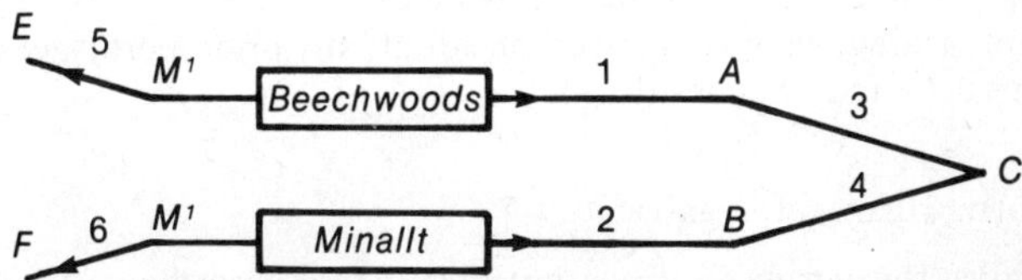

M^1 is the original mortgagor of both properties, 'Beechwoods' and 'Minallt'. Mortgages and assignments of mortgages are shown to the right of the boxes and the assignments of the equities of redemption are shown to the left. The order in which the transactions took place is shown by the numbers placed near the lines denoting the transactions. *E* is seeking to redeem the mortgage on 'Beechwoods' by paying off *C*. But *C* may consolidate the mortgage on 'Minallt' against him, and require both mortgages to be redeemed at the same time, so that *E* may be required to redeem it as a condition of redeeming 'Beechwoods', assuming the right to consolidate was reserved in either of the mortgage deeds. The mortgages were both made by M^1 and there was a time, namely at stage 4, when the mortgages were owned by one person, C, and simultaneously the equities of redemption were owned by one person, M^1. If there are three or more properties concerned, the problem can be solved by playing each property against each other separately in the way described above.

The doctrine applies to both legal and equitable mortgages and against persons such as second mortgagees who have only a limited interest in the equity of redemption.

Priority of mortgages

When the same property has been mortgaged more than once by the mortgagor to different mortgagees and when the mortgagor defaults in paying his debts to these mortgagees, the property might not realize enough money to pay all the mortgagees. The subject of priorities is concerned with the order in which the mortgagees shall be paid and, consequently, who shall be disappointed.

The simple solution that the mortgages should rank for payment in the order of their creation would sometimes produce unfair results, as, for instance, when a first mortgagee conspires with the mortgagor to conceal his mortgage, thus encouraging a second mortgagee to lend a further loan on the security of the property. The demands of justice have, therefore, resulted in a more complex code of rules. The rules applying before 1926 have been considerably modified by the 1925 legislation, largely because of the extension of the system of land charges. The account given below is that of the law applying to mortgages created after 1925.

There are two codes of rules, one applying to all mortgages, legal or equitable, of legal estates in land, the other to all mortgages of equitable interests in land, which, of course, must necessarily be equitable. What is important is the subject-matter of the mortgage, not the mode in which it is transacted. Thus the same code applies to a legal mortgage of a legal estate as to an equitable mortgage of a legal estate, such as one by deposit of deeds. The second code only applies when an equitable interest such as a life interest is mortgaged. These two codes must now be examined separately. Then the doctrine of tacking, which empowers an admittedly prior mortgagee to swell a mortgage debt, must be considered.

Priority of mortgages of a legal estate

The law gives the mortgagee the opportunity to rank according to the order of creation, but also recognizes the duty he owes to later prospective mortgagees to make the presence of his own mortgage discoverable by them. All mortgagees must, in order to preserve their priority, take certain action to make their mortgages discoverable.

A first mortgagee, whether legal or equitable, of a legal estate has the right to call for the title deeds of the property (ss.85 and 86). If a prospective purchaser or second mortgagee later negotiates with the mortgagor, the absence of the deeds will put him on his guard. A first mortgagee should, therefore, take the deeds. Having done so, he cannot register his mortgage under the provisions mentioned below.

All other mortgagees of a legal estate can register their mortgages under the Land Charges Act 1972 (or under the Land Registration Act 1925, s.26). If such a mortgage is legal, it is registrable in Class C (i). These legal mortgages, not protected by deposit of the title deeds, are called '*puisne*' mortgages. If the mortgage is equitable, it is registrable under Class C (iii) (or, in the case of unregistered land, by a notice or caution). The Act then declares the consequences of failure to register. Since there are two ways of protecting mortgages, three types of problem might arise. Firstly, the priority of registrable mortgages between themselves might have to be resolved; secondly, the same problem might occur between two unregistrable mortgages; thirdly, there might be a dispute between a registrable mortgage and an unregistrable one. These must now be separately dealt with.

(1) *Priority of registrable mortgages as between themselves.* The priority of these mortgages between themselves is controlled by two statutory provisions which, due presumably to an oversight, are contradictory.

Firstly, s.97 of the Law of Property Act 1925 enacts that a mortgage not protected by deposit of deeds shall rank 'according to its date of registration as a land charge pursuant to the Land Charges Act 1972'.

Secondly, s.4 of the Land Charges Act 1972 states that such mortgages shall 'be void against a purchaser of the land charged therewith, or of any interest in such land, unless the land charge is registered in the appropriate register before the completion of the purchase'. Another mortgagee is, of course, a 'purchaser', provided that he gives valuable consideration (Land Charges Act 1972, s.17).

An example will illustrate their apparent incompatibility. Let us say that *M* mortgaged 'Blackacre' on 1st January to *A*, who took the title deeds, then on 2nd January to *B*, and then on 3rd January to *C*. Then suppose that *B* did not register his mortgage until 4th January and *C* registered on 5th January. An assessment of the priorities of the two registrable incumbrances, those of *B* and *C*, under s.97, would place *B* before *C*, because he had registered his mortgage before *C* had registered his. Yet under s.4, *C* would be placed before *B*, because *B*'s mortgage had not been registered before *C*'s mortgage had been 'completed' and would, therefore, be void as against it. This does not, of course, mean that *B*'s mortgage is void altogether; it is valid against the mortgagor and indeed any other mortgage created after it has been registered. The section merely makes it void as against interests purchased before it was registered. It makes no difference, however, that a purchaser such as *C* had actual notice of *B*'s interest. Although there is no decisive case upon the matter yet, and there are arguments in favour of the prevalence of either section, probably the better view is that s.4 predominates (see Megarry and Wade, *The Law of Real Property*, 4th edn, p.972). In the case of registered land there is no such conflict, priority depending upon order of registration (Land Registration Act 1925, s.29).

Even if s.4 prevails, it is theoretically capable of producing strange results. Suppose that in June *M* makes registrable mortgages in favour of *A* on the 1st, *B* on the 2nd and *C* on the 4th. Then suppose that *A* registers on the 3rd, *C* on the 5th and *B* on the 6th. *A*'s mortgage is void against *B*'s because *B*'s was made before *A*'s was registered. Therefore *B* ranks before *A*. The mortgage of *A*, however, ranks prior to *C*'s because it was registered before *C*'s was created. Yet *C*'s must rank before *B*'s, because *B*'s was not registered when *C*'s was made. It is impossible to express the general results as any lineal order of priority, but the following diagram reveals that the section is not rationally perfect.

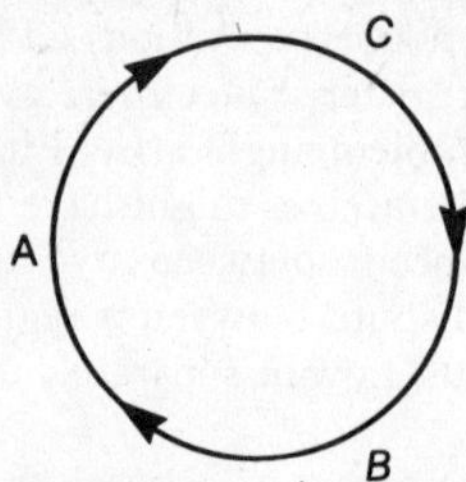

If each mortgagee is owed £1,000 and the property is worth only £2,000, a rather desperate problem could arise if a solution is to be sought within the four corners of the section.

A mortgagee can, however, protect himself against the risk of a further mortgage being created before he has had time to register his own incumbrance by the registration of a priority notice before his own mortgage is created. This matter is explained more fully when land charges are discussed.

(2) *Priority of unregistrable mortgages as between themselves.* Normally there should be no question of the priorities of two or more unregistrable mortgages of a legal estate, since if a mortgagee takes possession of the title deeds, he should take all of them. There would then obviously be no chance of another mortgagee taking deeds. All such later mortgages would then be registrable. There seems, however, to be no duty on a mortgagee who protects himself by taking the deeds to take them all, provided that he takes one or more which are vital to the proof of title.

Questions of the priority of mortgages protected by deposit of deeds may, therefore, arise as between themselves. These questions are resolved by the following common-law principles which are expressly preserved by the Act (s.13).

The fundamental rule is that such mortgages rank in the order of creation, but this order might be displaced if either

(a) a legal mortgagee for value has no notice at the time of the creation of his interest of an earlier equitable mortgage, in which case the legal mortgage is preferred, or

(b) an earlier mortgagee has, by his conduct, deserved, in the eyes of the law, to be postponed to a later one.

These principles of displacement must now be examined. The first is, of course, a doctrine of general application and is not restricted to mortgages. Little need be added here, except to say that, in regard to notice, the law has been much more indulgent to the purchaser of the legal estate when that legal estate has been a mortgage. Thus, in *Hewitt* v. *Loosemore* (1851), 9 Hare 449, *M* made an equitable mortgage by deposit of deeds in favour of *A* and later made a legal mortgage in favour of *B*, a farmer who claimed to be unversed in such legal processes. When *B* asked for the deeds, *M* told him that he was busy and would give them to him later. It was held that the legal mortgage enjoyed priority. Indeed, some of these cases seem to have been decided on the grounds of 'gross negligence', a factor which is relevant to the second of the principles mentioned above, rather than to the ordinary doctrine of notice. (See also *Oliver* v. *Hinton* [1899] 2 Ch. 264).

The conduct referred to in the second of the principles which will displace the fundamental rule governing the priority of unregistrable mortgages of legal estates as between themselves is constituted by fraud, gross negligence, or some act which, because it helps to deceive another person into taking a mortgage, estops the first mortgagee from claiming his priority over him. Such conduct is usually related to the title deeds. Thus a first mortgagee, who leaves the title deeds in the hands of the mortgagor to enable him to create further mortgages, will be postponed to a later mortgagee, who does not know of the first mortgage. This is because the first mortgagee has, even though in good faith, enabled the mortgagor to present himself as the owner of an unencumbered property, and will therefore be estopped from claiming the priority which otherwise would have been his (*Perry Herrick* v. *Attwood* (1857), 2 De G. & J. 21).

If the earlier mortgagee takes the deeds but then releases them, or fails for some other reason to retain them, and this is due to fraud or gross negligence, on principle similar results ought to follow. Yet it was decided in *Northern Counties of England Fire Insurance Co.* v. *Whipp* (1884), 26 Ch.D. 482, that only fraud would cause a postponement.

It has been suggested in one case that the degree of negligence required to postpone an equitable mortgage is less than that needed to postpone a legal one (*Taylor* v. *Russell* [1891] 1 Ch. 1, at p.17), but there seems to be no decisive authority to support this view.

Such are the principles governing the priority of unregistrable mortgages of a legal estate. As mentioned earlier, a competition between two such mortgagees could only occur if each mortgagee took some but not all the deeds; otherwise, the mortgage would be registrable. The allocation of negligence in such a case must be a difficult task. On the one hand, the first mortgagee might be considered negligent in not taking all the deeds relevant to the title, unless he had a reasonable excuse for not so doing (see *Walker* v. *Linom* [1907] 2 Ch. 104, which concerned a purchaser and a mortgagee). On the other hand, it could be argued that the second mortgagee can hardly claim to have been misled when the absence of some of the deeds would have occurred to him if he had taken the trouble to check (see also *Colyer* v. *Finch* (1856), 5 H.L. Cas. 905).

(3) *Priority of unregistrable mortgage as against registrable mortgage.* Two types of contest are possible.

(a) The first mortgage is unregistrable and the second is registrable—In a competition between a mortgagee, legal or equitable, who takes the deeds and a later one who does not, the common-law principles described above apply, for they are expressly preserved by the Act (s.13). The earlier mortgage protected by deposit of deeds will rank first by virtue of its earlier creation, unless this order is displaced by the mortgagee's fraud, gross negligence or estoppel, or, being equitable, by the later one being a legal mortgage for value without notice of the first. 'Notice' in this context means actual or constructive notice and not notice by registration, for the earlier mortgage is, of course, unregistrable. In regard to gross negligence, this will hardly be constituted by failure to get in the deeds, for by definition the earlier mortgagee has accomplished this. Other acts of gross negligence and fraud, such as might occur through a later release of the deeds, would remain in point.

(b) The first mortgage is registrable and the second is unregistrable—The priority of two such mortgages depends entirely upon whether the first one is registered before the second one is created (L.P.A. 1925, s.97, and Land Charges Act 1972, s.4). If it is so registered, the first mortgage will rank first in priority. If it is not, it will be void as against the second, which will therefore rank before it in priority.

Finally, an example might illustrate the operation of these interacting rules. In the following series of mortgages, all were registrable except that of *A*, who took the title deeds on the date of the creation of the mortgage and then fraudulently released them to the mortgagor, thereby inducing *B* and *C* to take subsequent mortgages. The deeds were handed back after this time, and before the mortgagor had opened negotiations for a mortgage with *D*. Our approach will be to take each mortgage in turn and test its priority against each other one individually.

Mortgage	*Date of creation*	*Date of registration or possession of deeds*	
A	1.1.71	Taken	1.1.71
		Released	25.1.71
		Taken back	15.2.71
B	1.2.71	15.2.71	
C	14.2.71	17.2.71	
D	18.2.71		

Prima facie, *A* ranks first, but loses this priority to *B* and *C* on the common-law principles discussed above, because his fraud has helped to deceive *B* and *C* into making mortgages. *A* will, however, rank before *D*, because as against him he has not done any act which will displace the fundamental rule that priority is governed by the order of creation of the mortgages. In all the three competitions that we have just observed, the contest has been between an unregistrable mortgage followed by a registrable mortgage.

B's mortgage ranks after *C*'s. Since it was not registered before *C*'s was created, it is void as against it, though not, of course, against the mortgagor. However, it loses no priority as against that of *D*, because it was registered before *D*'s was created. *C*'s mortgage ranks before *D*'s because it too was registered before *D*'s was created. *D*'s mortgage, therefore, ranks last, although, despite *D*'s failure to register, it is still good against the mortgagor. The latter will only be entitled to any part of the proceeds of a sale after all the mortgagees have been fully satisfied. These last three contests were between registrable mortgages. The question of priority notices has been deliberately ignored in the interests of clarity.

Thus, the final order of priority will be *C, B, A, D.*

Priority of mortgages of an equitable interest

The doctrine known as the rule in *Dearle* v. *Hall* (1828), 3 Russ. 1, which formerly only applied to the priority of successive dealings with equitable interests in pure personalty, was extended by the Act to govern the priority of successive mortgages of an equitable interest in land also (s.137). The Act made certain modifications as to the way notice may be served in accordance with the doctrine. Examples of the occasions when it applies would be successive mortgages of a life interest or an interest under a trust for sale.

Under the rule, priority depends upon the order in which notice of the mortgages is received by the owner of the legal interest in accordance with the rule, provided only that a mortgagee who has actual or constructive notice of an earlier mortgage at the time when he made his own cannot gain priority over that mortgage merely by giving notice first. Therefore the fundamental rule is that the mortgages rank not *prima facie* in order of creation, but in the order in which notice is given. The detailed operation of the rule must now be examined.

(1) *Form of notice.* The notice must be in writing. Otherwise, it has no effect upon priority (s.137 (3)). Provided that it is in writing, there is no requirement that it must be served by the mortgagee himself. Indeed, it has been held that notice gained by casually reading about a mortgage or assignment constitutes notice for this purpose (*Lloyd* v. *Banks* (1868), L.R. 3 Ch. 488).

(2) *Persons entitled to receive notice.* The notice may be served upon the following persons:

(a) in the case of a dealing with an interest in settled land, capital money, or securities representing capital money, the trustees of the settlement;
(b) in the case of an interest under a trust for sale, the trustees for sale; and
(c) in any other case the estate owner (s.137 (2)).

Where the trustees are not persons to whom a valid notice can be given—or there are no trustees to whom notice can be given, or where for any other reason a valid notice cannot be served at all without unreasonable cost or delay—then a mortgagee may require a memorandum to be written on or annexed to the instrument creating the trust. In the case of settled land, this would be the trust instrument, and this operates in the same way as notice to the trustees (s.137 (4) and (5)). There is also an alternative provision for nominating a trust corporation to receive notices.

The notice should be served upon all the trustees in existence at the time of the notice. If this is done, the notice remains permanently effective, even when these trustees have been replaced by others (*Re Wasdale* [1899] 1 Ch. 163). If notice is given only to one of several trustees, it is effective against all mortgages created while that trustee remains in office, but not against those created after his trusteeship ends (*Re Phillips' Trusts* [1903] 1 Ch. 183).

Tacking

Tacking is the advancement of a further sum of money by a mortgagee upon the security of his mortgage in such circumstances that it enjoys the same priority as the original debt. If, for instance, *A* lends £100 to *X* upon the security of 'Blackacre', then *B* lends *X* £100, taking a second mortgage of the land, and then *A* lends a further sum of £100 to *X* upon the same security, this last loan will generally rank for payment after that of *B*. But where the doctrine of tacking operates, *A* has a right to a repayment of his total advance of £200 in priority to that of *B*.

The process must be distinguished from that of mortgaging the property a second time to the same person. In tacking, the original mortgage debt is merely swollen at a later time. It must also be distinguished from consolidation of mortgages, which, unlike tacking, involves mortgages on different properties. The doctrine was regulated by the Law of Property Act 1925, and a mortgagee can now only tack so as to achieve the same priority for the later advances as for the original loan in any of the following circumstances (s.94). The doctrine applies irrespective of whether the property mortgaged is a legal estate or an equitable interest or whether in the former case the mortgage is legal or equitable.

(1) *If the later mortgagees agree*. Suppose that *M* mortgages property to *A for* £1,000 and then to *B* for £1,000, then finds that he needs more money. If the land appears valuable enough to cover the total of all the loans, *B* might agree that if *A* lends a further £1,000 then he shall rank first for the payment of the full sum of £2,000, although only £1,000 was advanced before his own loan.
(2) *If the mortgagee has no notice of the later mortgage at the time of the further advance*. If the later mortgage is registered, this constitutes actual notice. If the mortgage is unregistrable, then notice will depend upon the old principles. However, if the mortgage is made expressly 'for securing a current account or other further advances', registration is not deemed to constitute notice unless it has been effected either at the time when the original mortgage was created or when the last search, if any, was made by the original mortgagee, whichever happened last (s.94 (2), as amended by the Law of Property (Amendment) Act 1926, s.7).

This latter provision is to accommodate banks. If a mortgage is made to a bank to secure an overdraft, the amount owing to the bank will fluctuate from time to time as money is paid in and out. If a second mortgage is then made to another person, then it would be fair to fix the sum in respect of which the bank enjoys priority as the amount owing at that time, if the bank then knew that the second mortgage had been created. If registration were to constitute notice, it would mean that the bank, in order to ensure that the loan was adequately secured, would have to search before honouring individual cheques of the mortgagor. Otherwise, it might well find that the amount for which the cheque was drawn was postponed to the debt owed to a second mortgagee. A second or subsequent mortgagee should, therefore, send written notice to earlier mortgagees, even though his own mortgage is registered, so that the priority of such further advances can be stemmed. Such notice is also desirable to ensure that, on the repayment of the earlier mortgage, the title deeds are not returned to the mortgagor.

(3) *If the mortgage imposes an obligation to make further advances.* If the mortgage does not merely empower the mortgagee to make further advances, but obliges him to do so, if required by the mortgagor, then these further advances may be tacked to the original debt, even though the mortgagee has express notice of a later mortgage at the time when the further sum is lent. Prospective second or later mortgagees, therefore, having discovered the existence of an earlier mortgage, should enquire whether further advances are made obligatory under its terms.

An example will illustrate these principles. Suppose that *M* mortgages 'Blackacre' to *A* for £1,000 and then for £1,000 to *B*, who registers. Then let us say *A* advances a further £1,000 to *M* on the security of the same property. This second advance will take priority over *B*'s mortgage in any event if there was an obligation to advance it. If there was not, then it ranks below *B*'s debt, since the latter's mortgage was registered when the second advance was made, unless *A*'s mortgage was made expressly for securing further advances. In the latter case, the later advance will rank before *B*'s mortgage, unless at the time of that advance *A* had actual or constructive notice of *B*'s mortgage, or happens to have made a search before making the second advance and discovered *B*'s mortgage. In that case, the advance will rank below *B*'s debt.

The mortgage in its modern context

Introduction

The general law of mortgages developed in the context of business loans. Many of the cases cited in this chapter concern independently struck bargains between brewers and pub owners, large-scale property owners and those who finance them and other commercial organizations. Such transactions are still important today. Yet during the last fifty years another type of mortgage transaction has assumed enormous importance, not only in economic but also in social terms, since many millions of people and their family lives are concerned. House purchase mortgages operate in a different social and financial climate from those which were scrutinized by the appellate courts a century or so ago and which helped to forge the doctrines described earlier. Furthermore, statute has intervened to protect the mortgagor as a consumer. House purchase mortgages have transformed the lives of millions of people. They have given them a real financial stake in property they cannot afford to purchase; afforded them mobility of home address; enabled them to spread their indebtedness over nearly half their life spans and thus enjoy material benefits at an earlier age than formerly.

The purpose of this part of the chapter is simply to show how the classical principles of the mortgage reach down to accommodate the modern domestic mortgage. In short, the doctrines described earlier generally apply, though statutory rules provide a background control. Yet, as is so often the case with the mortgage, forms and appearances change. Examples of the domestic mortgage transaction will be given. Then some possible new developments in the financing of home purchase will be mentioned.

Examples of modern mortgage transactions

With their kind permission, the complete deed used by the National Provincial Building Society and pages 3–12 of their Mortgage Conditions (1983

Edition) are reproduced in the appendix to this book. Its simple elegance is outstanding. The following comments upon these are only intended to assist the reader in relating the transaction to the survey of mortgage doctrines attempted earlier in this chapter.

(1) Two matters may be disposed of quickly: (a) The acknowledgement of receipt of the loan repayment is printed on the mortgage deed itself. This is done so that on final repayment the settlement of the debt can be indorsed on the loan instrument. This 'vacating receipt' is thus made to keep permanent company with the contract of loan. Once executed, it cancels the mortgage, (b) The declaration as to overriding interests concerns third party rights in regard to registered land. The problem is discussed in Chapter 18.
(2) Otherwise the prominent feature of the deed is that it incorporates rights and duties by reference to conditions which are contained in a separate book of conditions. Before these are examined some matters of fundamental importance to the home-buyer might be mentioned.

(a) The obligation to repay the loan after a few months becomes even less a reality than earlier described. Yet for technical reasons the obligation is kept alive (see Condition 7.1). The true position is as follows. The loan and the estimated interest accruing upon it over the agreed loan period, say thirty years, are aggregated in one sum. That sum is divided into equal monthly payments over that period. The true obligations of the borrower are expressed in the monthly payments.

(b) The right to change the rates of interest and therefore the total and monthly repayment sums is reserved to the Society (see Condition 3.3). This right should be considered in relation to the general doctrine that mortgage transactions must not be oppressive. In practice the interest rate is linked to the bank rate.

Possible new developments in mortgage transactions

Revolutionary though the impact of building society loans has been upon home ownership, some classes of people nevertheless suffer from the rather exclusive favour shown towards young couples earning good salaries. Amongst those less favoured by the mortgage market are: elderly people owning unmortgaged or lightly mortgaged property who are in need of increased income; divorced women owning the matrimonial home subject to substantial mortgage repayments but, with growing children off their hands, faced with decreasing payments from their former husbands; older people wishing to own homes for the first time.

On the other hand, safe investment is being sought for large pension funds. Mortgages are sound investments. Index-linked mortgages might provide solutions to some of these problems. These take account of the improvement of value of houses whilst taking adequate profits. A house buyer can buy at four times his annual salary, as opposed to the ordinary building society rate of two and a half times that figure. It is not unconscionable or contrary to public policy to link repayment of capital and interest to rates of exchange (see *Multiservice Bookbinding Ltd.* v. *Marden* [1979] Ch. 84). On redemption, the advance is multiplied by a fraction of the rise in house prices, thus enabling the lender to take his benefit at that stage rather than through interest rates.

Questions

1 *Since the essence of a mortgage is the securing of a loan on property owned by the borrower, why should it be difficult for older people and women to obtain mortgage loans despite property ownership?*

The use of mortgages for purposes other than home-provision, e.g. for home maintenance and improvement should be considered.

Compare your answer with the comments made in:

(1) *The Times, 8th May 1982: 'Elderly may cash in on houses';*

(2) *The Solicitors' Journal* and *Property Law Bulletin, 30th April 1982, p.13: 'Index-linked mortgages: the building trust';*

(3) *New Law Journal, 10th June 1982: 'Competition in the mortgage market'.*

2 *To what extent do equity and statute law protect the modern domestic mortgagor from the possible exactions of the mortgagee?*

3 *Can you reconcile the raising of interest rates after the conclusion of a mortgage agreement with the right to redeem the mortgaged property?*

Chapter Sixteen

Rentcharges

Nature

A rentcharge is a periodical sum of money payable out of land and not attributable to tenure. These last words distinguish it from a rent service, which is the rent payable by a tenant to his landlord, and which derives from tenure. A rentcharge is an interest in land, the burden running with the land upon which it is charged and the benefit being enforceable by whoever owns the rentcharge for the time being. Thus its effectiveness does not depend upon either privity of contract or upon tenure. If I grant the fee simple of 'Blackacre' to *A*, subject to the payment of an annual sum of £1,000 to *B*, *B* owns a rentcharge which *A* must satisfy, even though there is no relationship of contract or tenure between him and *B*.

Like other interests in or over the land of another person, rentcharges can be made to endure for the usual periods of time available for estates and interests in land, and can exist either as legal or equitable interests. They can only be legal interests, however, if they are in possession, created to last either in perpetuity or for a term of years absolute (L.P.A. 1925, s.1(2)(b)), and made with the formalities required by the law. In all other cases they are equitable. If they are made voluntarily, or in consideration of marriage, or by way of family arrangement, for the life of any person or for less period, a settlement results (Settled Land Act 1925, s.1(1)(v)). Such an equitable rentcharge is used in a settlement to provide a jointure for a wife after the death of her husband. In Chapter 5, we noticed a common use of a legal rentcharge when a fee simple is sold and a rentcharge reserved in place of the lump sum usually taken as purchase price. These rentcharges are sometimes called fee farm rents.

A rentcharge can be charged upon or created out of another rentcharge (L.P.A. 1925, s.122).

Creation

A legal rentcharge must be created by deed if *inter vivos*, but may be created by will. However, the doctrine of *Walsh* v. *Lonsdale* (1882), 21 Ch.D. 9, applies, so that specific performance can be demanded of a contract to create a rentcharge, provided that it is evidenced by sufficient memorandum to satisfy s.40 of the Law of Property Act 1925. The creation of new rentcharges is prohibited by the Rentcharges Act 1977 s.2(1), with certain exceptions including those which cause or are associated with settlements, 'estate' rentcharges and those arising under a statute providing for the creation of rentcharges in connection with the execution of works on land. The Act should be consulted for details.

Enforcement

If a rentcharge is not paid, the following remedies are available. If the rentcharge is created out of another rentcharge, the only one of these which is apt is an action for recovery of the money, but there is the additional remedy under the Law of Property Act 1925, s.122(2), which authorizes the appointment of a receiver.

(1) *Right of re-entry*. The right to forfeit the land upon which the rentcharge is imposed is only available if expressly reserved in the instrument of creation. The following remedies may be used irrespective of reservation.
(2) *Action for recovery of the money*. This action may be brought against the person who is entitled to the rents and profits of the land, known in this context as the '*terre* tenant'.
(3) *Distress (L.P.A. 1925, s.121(2))*. Subject to any contrary intention expressed in the instrument of creation, the owner of a rentcharge created after 1881 can distrain on the land or part of it if the sum or any part of it is twenty-one days in arrears.
(4) *Entry into possession (L.P.A. 1925, s.121 (3))*. Subject to any contrary intention expressed in the instrument of creation the rent owner can, if any part of the sum is forty days in arrears, enter into possession of the land or part of it and satisfy the debt out of the profits.
(5) *Lease to a trustee (L.P.A. 1925, s.121 (4))*. Subject again to any expressed contrary intention, if any part of the sum is forty days in arrears, the owner of a rentcharge created after 1881 can lease the land or part of it to a trustee on trust to raise the sum due or to become due by creating a mortgage.

Extinguishment

A rentcharge may be extinguished in the following ways:

(1) *Release*. The owner of the rentcharge may release the land from liability either wholly or partly (see L.P.A. 1925, s.70).
(2) *Merger*. The rentcharge might disappear through merger if the rentcharge owner acquires the land upon which it is charged, but this ultimately depends upon his intention (L.P.A. 1925, s.185).
(3) *Limitation Act 1980*. If a rentcharge is unpaid for twelve years it is extinguished by the Act, though if during this time it is paid to a third party it remains recoverable by him though not by the original owner.
(4) *Section 3(1) of the 1977 Act*. This provides that, subject to certain exceptions, rentcharges, if not otherwise extinguished, shall cease to have effect at the expiry of sixty years beginning either with the passing of the Act or with the date on which the rentcharge first became payable, whichever is later.
(5) *Statutory discharge*. Under the Rentcharges Act 1977, a landowner may discharge the land from a rentcharge upon payment of the capital value of the rentcharge (see ss.8, 9 and 10).

Registration

Certain rentcharges are capable of substantive registration; others can be protected by notice. See Wontner's *Guide to Land Registry Practice* (J. J. Wontner and F. Quickfall, 13th edn, Oyez 1979, Chapter IX).

Chapter Seventeen

Registration of incumbrances

Introduction

We have already seen that a prospective purchaser of land not only investigates the vendor's title to the land, but also seeks to discover what interests third parties have in the land. The general principle has always been that if such interests are legal they will bind the purchaser whether he knows of them or not, and if they are equitable they will bind everyone except a purchaser in good faith of a legal estate in the land without notice of them.

This principle was greatly effected by the Land Charges Act 1925, the provisions of which, as amended, are now consolidated in the Land Charges Act, 1972, except for the rules relating to local land charges. This provides that many equitable interests are registrable. Since registration constitutes actual notice of the interest to all persons (L.P.A. 1925, s.198), these equitable interests can be endowed with all the inviolability of legal interests by the simple act of registration. On the other hand, certain legal interests are made registrable, and failure to register may cause them to fail against purchasers. The principle mentioned above, therefore, has had both its wings clipped.

Five registers are maintained at the Land Charges Registry at Plymouth. They are computerized and are concerned with the registration of incumbrances on land the title to which is unregistered. Some of these registers are of only minor importance. A sixth, the local land charges register, is kept by local authorities under the Land Charges Act 1975, for all land, registered or otherwise, in their areas. The land charges registrar does not question the validity of an interest when the owner of it applies to register, so that registration is no guarantee of its validity. Registration will not help in the enforcement of an alleged restrictive covenant, for instance, if no land or reversion was retained by the covenantee. All the register really declares is: 'If this interest is valid here is notice of it.' Brief references will later be made to two further registers one affecting companies, the other affecting common land.

The plan for this chapter will be firstly to describe the six registers and the matters which can be entered in them, and secondly, to explain the effects of registration and non-registration. References to sections are to those of the Land Charges Act 1972, unless otherwise stated.

The registers and their contents

The registers and the matters eligible to be entered in them are as follows:

(1) *Register of pending actions (s.5)*. Any action in relation to any interest in land which is pending or any petition in bankruptcy may be entered in this register. An entry is effective for five years but may be renewed (s.8). The court may order it to be 'vacated', that is struck out, if, during the pendency

of the action, it believes the proceedings are not prosecuted in good faith (see *Taylor* v. *Taylor* [1968] 1 W.L.R. 378). Section 1 (6) confers on the court a general power to vacate registrations and this extends to all the registers, notwithstanding this special provision. So the grounds for vacating registration of pending actions are not limited to lack of good faith (*Northern Development (Holdings) Ltd.* v. *U.D.T. Securities* [1977] 1 All E.R. 747). The purpose of the provision is to warn any person to whom the owner of the interest may sell before the case has been decided that a case is on foot and that, if he buys, he does so at his own risk and subject to any decision the court might reach. It has been held that the claim must be to some proprietary right in the land (*Calgary and Edmonton Land Co. Ltd.* v. *Dobinson* [1974] 1 All E.R. 484).

(2) *Register of annuities (s.1 and Sched. I).* This register is moribund. Before 1926 certain annuities were registrable under earlier legislation. The present section simply enacts that no more entries in that register shall be made after the Act and that, when all the existing entries have been satisfied, the register shall be closed. If such annuities, though made before 1926, were not registered, they become registrable as Class E land charges mentioned below. The days of that class also are numbered. Annuities which are created after 1925 may be registered as Class C (iii) land charges provided that they do not arise under a strict settlement or trust for sale. If they do so, they are not registrable at all but are protected by the conveyancing machinery provided for settlements and trusts for sale. They can of course be overreached.

(3) *Register of writs and orders affecting the land (s.6).* In this register may be entered writs and orders made by any court for enforcing judgments, or recognizances or any orders appointing receivers of land or receiving orders in bankruptcy. These entries expire after five years but are renewable. They are to be distinguished from the pending actions dealt with above, because they are concerned with the results and enforcements of the court's decisions.

(4) *Register of deeds of arrangement (s.7).* Deeds of arrangement may be registered here by the trustee of the deed or by a creditor assenting to or taking the benefit of the deed. A deed of arrangement is a document under which a debtor surrenders control of his property in favour of his creditors, in return for a release from his debts (see the Deeds of Arrangement Act 1914).

(5) *Register of land charges (s.2).* The matters which can be entered in this register are divided into six classes, A, B, C, D, E and F, Classes C and D containing sub-divisions. It relates only to unregistered land.

Class A consists of charges on land arising under statute when some person makes an application to have the charge created. A life tenant, who has to pay compensation under the Agricultural Holdings Act 1948 to an outgoing tenant, may apply to the Minister for the amount to be charged on the land, and the resultant charge would fall into this class.

Class B consists of charges imposed by statute without any person applying for their creation and not being registrable in the local land charges register. An example is a charge on land to cover contributions payable by a legally assisted person under the Legal Aid Act 1974, s.9.

Class C is subdivided into the following categories:

(i) Puisne mortgages (legal mortgages not protected by deposit of the deeds).

(ii) Limited owners' charges—These are equitable charges acquired by tenants for life or statutory owners, under statute, because they have paid death duties or other liabilities, and to which special priority is given by the statute. Where liabilities relate to the value of the land itself in this way, it is fair that a person having a limited interest only in it should be allowed to spread the ultimate burden of it on the settled property.

(iii) General equitable charges—This category sweeps up equitable charges which are not registrable in other categories, provided that they are not protected by a deposit of documents relating to the legal estate affected, and do not arise, or affect interests arising, under a settlement or a trust for sale. An example is an equitable mortgage of a legal estate in land not protected by a deposit of deeds.

(iv) Estate contracts—This category comprises any contract by a person who owns a legal estate, or is entitled to have a legal estate conveyed to him, to convey or create some legal estate, any option to purchase, right of pre-emption or other like right. It has been held to include a covenant in a lease requiring the tenant to offer to surrender the lease to the landlord before seeking his consent to assignment or sub-letting (*Greene* v. *Church Commissioners for England* [1974] Ch. 467). Such contracts raise an equitable interest in the person contracting to buy the estate (see *Beesly* v. *Hallwood Estates Ltd* [1960] 2 All E.R. 314; *Turley* v. *Mackay* [1944] Ch. 37). A notice of desire to purchase the reversion or to acquire a new lease under the Leasehold Reform Act 1967 comes under this head.

With regard to rights of pre-emption, a recent decision of the Court of Appeal has virtually denuded them of any benefit through registration. *A* granted a right of pre-emption during *A*'s life to *P*, which *P* registered. *A* later granted an option to purchase the same land to *O* which *O* registered. The intention appears to have been that *O* should be entitled to exercise his option if *P* failed to take the land through pre-emption during *A*'s lifetime. Next, *A* sold the land to *P*, though on slightly altered terms than agreed in the original agreement for pre-emption. After *A*'s death, *O* attempted to exercise his option. The Court held that he could do so, despite the facts that *P* had registered his right before *O* had negotiated his option with *A*, and that this would entitle him to take the land from *P* at a price considerably less than that which *P* had paid for it.

The reason was that a right of pre-emption is not an interest in land and therefore cannot bind a purchaser, even though the latter has notice of it. It could not be an interest in land because whether the grantee ever took any benefit under it depended entirely on the will of the grantor. Only when the latter decided to sell could the right become an interest (*Pritchard* v. *Briggs* [1979] 3 W.L.R. 868).

This reasoning is open to criticism. Contingent interests in land which depend upon the volition of the grantor can exist in the family context. An example is a settlement by *S* under which he grants the fee simple interest in land to 'such child of mine as I shall appoint'. If the land is then sold, the resultant purchase money will still remain subject to the settlement—even though *S* might never exercise his power of appointment. The example is given merely to show that the 1925 legislation protects contingent interests of all types. If they occur in the 'family' field, the machinery of the strict settlement or trust for sale shields them. If they arise in the 'commercial' field, the system of registration is available to protect them.

It is difficult to see upon what grounds of justice any distinction can be drawn between the two categories.

Class D is subdivided into the following categories:

(i) Charges for death duties—Any charge acquired by the Commissioners of Inland Revenue under any statute for death duties may be registered under this head.

(ii) Restrictive covenants—Restrictive covenants are registrable if entered into after 1925, unless made between lessors and lessees. Restrictive covenants are the second most numerous of all entries on the land charges register.

(iii) Equitable easements and other equitable rights or privileges over or affecting land. These are registrable if they were created after 1925. The vagueness of this class has proved troublesome to the extent that its abolition has been advocated. Identification of the equitable rights capable of registration under this head has been rendered more difficult by *Ives Investment Ltd.* v. *High* [1967] 2 Q.B. 379. This was discussed in Chapter 7. The wording is probably wide enough to include equitable profits also, but has been held not to include equitable rights of re-entry (*Shiloh Spinners Ltd.* v. *Harding* [1973] 1 All E.R. 90, nor a tenant's right to remove fixtures at the end of a lease (*Poster* v. *Slough Estates Ltd.* [1968] 3 All E.R. 257). Licences, although often protected by equitable remedies and sometimes binding upon third parties, cannot be registered, unless, presumably, they amount to easements by estoppel. Even in the latter case, *Ives Investment Ltd.* v. *High* could present a barrier in many cases. Considering, however, that licences are frequently informal transactions, undertaken without legal advice, ineligibility to register could be helpful to the licensee. Since it will seldom occur to him to register, his failure to do so will not have the drastic effect upon his rights which failure to register eligible rights entails.

Class E: this class is of little importance and has already been discussed as far as necessary.

Class F: this class was added by the Matrimonial Homes Act 1967, and in it may be registered a spouse's rights of occupation under the Act.

(6) *Local land charges (Local Land Charges Act 1975)*. Local authorities keep registers in which they enter certain charges arising under various statutes which affect land in their area. Examples of this are refusals of planning permission and unpaid road-making charges payable by frontagers to a street which was made up at the expense of the local authority. The register covers both registered and unregistered land. Purchase of land should invariably be preceded by a search in the local land charges register as it by a search of the registers maintained under the Land Charges Act 1972 for unregistered land.

(7) Companies: under the Companies Act 1948, a register is maintained by the Registrar of Companies for the registration of charges over land created by companies for securing money. If such a charge was created before 1st January 1970, or at any time in the case of a floating charge, registration shall be sufficient in place of registration under the 1972 Act (see s.3 of the 1972 Act). In other cases, registration under both schemes is required if a purchaser from the company is to be bound by it.

The alternative registration under the 1948 Act can produce a curious result in that the name registered might not be the name of the estate owner against whom registration would have been appropriate under the 1972 Act. (*Property Discount Corporation Ltd.* v. *Lyon Group Ltd.* [1981] 1 All E.R. 379).

(8) Common rights: under the Commons Registration Act 1965, two registers are maintained for the registration of commons and town or village greens and for the ownership of and rights over them. The registration authority is the appropriate county council or, in the case of land situated in Greater London, the Greater London Council.

Effects of non-registration

Interests eligible for entry under Classes C (iv) or D or as local land charges are void against a purchaser of a legal estate in the land for money or money's worth unless registered before the completion of the purchase (s.4(6) and see *McCarthy & Stone Ltd.* v. *Julian S. Hodge & Co. Ltd.* [1971] 2 All E.R. 973). All the other charges and matters registrable under the Act, with two minor exceptions, are void against a purchaser for value of any interest in the land. It was remarked earlier in this book that the statutory doctrine of notice introduced in 1925 brought certainty to conveyancing transactions where some third party rights are concerned, but that it did so at the expense of ethical standards. The House of Lords have recently underlined that there is to be no softening of this principle. In *Midland Bank Trust Co. Ltd.* v. *Green* [1981] 1 All E.R. 153, *F* granted *S* an option to buy 'Blackacre'. *S* failed to register. Several years later, *F*, with the purpose of defeating the option, conveyed the land to his wife for £500, although its true value was £40,000. *S* had been in occupation of the land under a lease at all material times. It was held that the wife was a purchaser of the legal estate for money or money's worth and therefore took free of the option. Bad faith was not relevant because it was not required and had no doubt been deliberately omitted from s.4(6) and 'money or money's worth' required no adequacy of consideration. Lord Wilberforce delivered the judgment of the House. The other four Law Lords agreed unreservedly. We might note that even those in actual occupation suffer if they fail to register their rights. We shall see that in the case of registered titles, persons in actual occupation of land do enjoy particular consideration although the severe effects of failure to register prevail under that system too.

The differences between the two principles, namely the kind of interest required to be taken by the purchaser and the type of consideration necessary, should be carefully noted (see 38 Conveyancer 8). The two exceptions separately dealt with need only be mentioned here. They concern pending actions (s.5(7) and (8)) and certain writs and orders (s.6(4) and (5)). The word 'purchaser' is given a wide definition under s.17 so as to include any person, including a lessee or mortgagee, who takes any interest or charge for valuable consideration.

If a registrable interest is created in land and is very shortly followed by the creation of another interest, there may not be time to register the first interest before the second is created. The first would therefore be void as against the purchaser of the second. Thus, if *A* makes a restrictive covenant with his neighbour *B* not to build on his land, 'Blackacre', and later the same day sells or mortgages the land to *C*, there would clearly not be time for *B* to register, and therefore the covenant would be void as against *C*. Section 11 provides a solution to this dilemma by enabling any person who intends to apply to register any contemplated charge or other matter registrable under the Act, to register a 'priority notice' at least fifteen days before the registration is to take effect, that is, before the creation of the interest to be protected. If the charge or matter itself is then registered within thirty days after the priority notice, the registration takes effect as if it had been made at the time of the creation of the charge.

A prospective purchaser may discover entries on the registers by obtaining an official certificate of search. If the purchase is completed within fifteen days after the date of the certificate, he will not be affected by any entry made after the date of the certificate and before completion of the purchase, unless it is made pursuant to a priority notice (s.11). If this were not so, a purchaser could never be sure that some charge had not been registered in the short time between the arrival of the certificate from the registry and the completion of the transaction. There is no priority period with company searches, local land charge searches or commons registration searches.

Incumbrances are registered against the name of the estate owner and not against the land, although the identity of the land affected is recorded with the entry (see *Oak Co-Operative Building Society* v. *Blackburn* [1968] 2 All E.R. 117). This means that the reference for a search requested by a prospective purchaser is to a name and not land. Consequently the names of all the estate owners in the past must, in theory, be known if all the incumbrances are to be discovered. In practice this is not necessary; a search is made before every successive transaction transferring ownership and the certificates resulting from these searches are generally kept with the title deeds, so that, together with the certificate against the outgoing estate owner (the vendor), they will provide a purchaser with a complete record.

The Law of Property Act 1969, in reducing the period of commencement of titles under open contracts to fifteen years, accentuates the problem because it might sometimes preclude a purchaser discovering the names of previous estate owners and perhaps old land charges which will nevertheless bind him. However, the Act does provide for compensation in certain cases where loss is occasioned by the existence of 'old land charges' (s.25).

Although s.198 of the Law of Property Act 1925 fixes a purchaser with notice of all matters registered under the Land Charges Act, there was previously doubt as to whether this notice operated at the moment of the contract or at the moment of completion (see *Re Forsey and Hollebone's Contract* [1927] 2 Ch. 379). However, the Law of Property Act 1969, s.24, enacted that the question whether a prospective purchaser has notice at the time of the contract of a registered land charge is to be determined by reference to his actual knowledge. An example might illustrate this.

If *P* contracts to buy 'Blackacre' from *V* and a restrictive covenant is already registered against the land at that time, and later the conveyance is completed, there is no doubt that *P* takes the land subject to the covenant. This principle remains quite undisturbed. Yet he might be able to proceed against *V* or refuse to complete on the grounds that he was, at the moment of contract, unaware of the covenant, despite the fact that it was registered at that time.

Study material: *Caunce* v. *Caunce* [1969] 1 All E.R. 722

STAMP, J.: The plaintiff and the first defendant, now a bankrupt, to this action, are and were at all material times husband and wife and living together. On 3rd November 1959, there was a conveyance on sale to the husband in fee simple of a house at Leamington Spa, and on the same day the husband charged the property by way of legal mortgage in favour of the Leicester Permanent Building Society to secure the principal sum of £2,020 advanced for the purpose of meeting the capital asked of the property. Neither the husband nor his trustee in bankruptcy (the second defendant) has served a defence in this action and the husband is, I understand, in default of appearance. This being so and on the evidence of the wife, I find as a fact that, in addition to the £2,020 advanced by the building society, the wife provided out of her own money the sum of £479 odd in respect of the cost of the acquisition, including legal costs. I refer to the cost of the acquisition rather than to the purchase price because at the time of the acquisition the house was in the course of erection and part of the money was, I think, paid direct to the builders. However, nothing turns on this.

I find as a fact that on the wife's evidence the property was acquired as and for and became the matrimonial home. The wife claims—and I find as a fact—that the property was acquired on the terms as between her and the husband that the cost of that acquisition, so far as not obtained from the building society, should be provided by the wife, and that the property was to be vested in the wife and the husband as joint tenants at law. I also find that the husband wrongfully and in breach of those terms procured that the property should be conveyed to him alone. Subsequently to the date of the conveyance and down to the time of his bankruptcy, the husband provided, so far as it did not fall into arrear, the instalments payable in respect of the building society mortgage. At the date of the receiving order made on 7th July 1966, there were, I think, some arrears and thereafter the wife paid off the arrears and she has kept down the instalments of principal and interest since that date.

The court is not being asked at this stage to specify the shares in which the wife and the trustee in bankruptcy are entitled to the net rents and profits until sale or the net proceeds of sale, but to declare that they are entitled to the same in the proportions in which the wife and husband respectively provided the capital cost and the repayment of the amount secured by the building society mortgage, and this, as between the wife and the husband and his trustee in bankruptcy, I will do. Having held that the wife has an equitable interest in the property, the question I have to decide (and the only substantial question argued before me) is whether the third defendant, Lloyds Bank, Ltd. which, subsequently to the purchase, advanced money on the security of the property, has priority over that equitable interest.

By several mortgages dated respectively 17th June 1964, 24th December 1964 and 22nd February 1966, the husband charged the property by way of legal mortgage in favour of the bank to secure the respective sums of £500, £500 and £200 advanced to the husband and other moneys therein mentioned. The wife claims, and I find as a fact, that she was unaware of the creation of any of these three mortgages. Shortly after the receiving order the husband left the premises and has not lived there since and he left the wife living there without him. The bank being in the same position as if it had obtained a legal estate (see s.87 (1) of the Law of Property Act 1925) and there being no suggestion that the bank acted otherwise than bona fide, it took the property free from the wife's equitable interest unless it had constructive notice of the existence of that interest.

The wife seeks to fix the bank with notice of her interest on several grounds. It is urged—and this is really in the forefront of the wife's argument—that today when so many matrimonial homes are purchased out of moneys provided in part by the wife, a purchaser, by which expression I include a mortgagee, who finds the matrimonial home vested in one of these spouses, more particularly in this case a husband, is put on enquiry whether the other spouse has an equitable interest in the property and that, if he does not enquire of the other spouse whether such an interest is claimed, he takes subject to the interest. As a bare proposition of law no authority has been cited for that proposition, and in view of the disinclination of the courts to extend the doctrine of constructive notice (see *Hunt* v. *Luck*[1]), I am not persuaded that it ought to be accepted. More particularly is this the case where, as was the fact, the wife knew almost at the outset that the property was in the sole name of the husband and had taken no step to assert her rights.

In coming to this conclusion I would guard myself from expressing any view whether it would make any difference if, at the time of the advance or purchase, the wife was in occupation of the property to the exclusion of the husband, a circumstance which, in *National Provincial Bank, Ltd.* v. *Hastings Car Mart, Ltd.*[2], the majority of the Court of Appeal thought put the lender on enquiry whether the wife had what was then known as a deserted wife's equity. Here the wife was living in the house with the husband at the time of each of the bank's advances and, in the absence of other facts, I could not hold that the mere fact that the house was the matrimonial home put the bank on enquiry whether the wife had or had not an equitable interest in it. I shall say more about this later.

Then it is said that there were facts known to the bank which suggested that the wife, in fact, had an equitable interest in the property. The wife was their customer. In April 1959, she had withdrawn £50 from her deposit account with the bank, the withdrawal taking the form of a cheque drawn by the bank in favour of Orange & Co. who were the agents through whom the purchase of the property was negotiated. Then on about 26th October 1959, £289 13s. was drawn on the wife's account in favour of Wright, Hassall & Co., solicitors, who were acting in connection with the purchase. Then, in June 1960, an additional sum was required by the builders for alterations to the specifications of the house which was to be built, and a sum of £139 10s. was transferred by the wife from her deposit account with the bank to a current business account and a cheque for £139 10s. was drawn on the business account in favour of A.C. Lloyd, Ltd. There is no evidence that the bank knew at that time that Orange & Co. were acting in relation to the purchase of the matrimonial home; there is no evidence that at that time the bank knew that Wright, Hassall & Co. were acting in the purchase or, indeed, that at that stage it had any actual knowledge of the purchase. Of course, a bank manager or a bank clerk may be sufficiently interested in the affairs of the bank's customers to examine the nature of the payments drawn on the customers' accounts and he may draw inferences from those payments regarding the activities of the customer. But in the absence of authority constraining me to hold otherwise, I cannot find that a bank has a duty to do so or that when, five years later, the customer's husband asks for a loan on the security of the matrimonial home, the bank has a duty to the customer either to remember the details or the inferences to be drawn from them, or to examine the customer's account of five years earlier to see if there was ground for supposing that the customer provided the purchase price or any part of it.

There is here, however, a further fact which was sought to be added to what appears to me to be a somewhat flimsy structure. There is, in the possession of the bank, a note of an interview with the wife dated 7th November 1960. According to that note the wife called at the bank on that day "to request a loan of £240 for purchase of furniture for new house at Radford Semele". From that note it appears that the bank knew that the house had been bought, but one may peruse the note in vain to discover the slightest suggestion that the wife had provided any part of the purchase money. The note is a fairly long one and I will not read it in detail, it being sufficient to say that there was a discussion about the security which the wife could offer. She was at that time the owner of a small business which appears to have been doing reasonably well; it was a sweet shop, I think, and there was a discussion between her and the official of the bank regarding the takings from that business and what arrangements she could make

---

1 [1901] 1 Ch. 45.
2 [1964] 1 All E.R. 688; [1964] Ch. 665.

to repay the amount borrowed for the purchase of the furniture. On behalf of the wife counsel is entitled to say that, as from that date, the bank knew that the house had been purchased, and had the manager or one of his staff then examined the wife's account at the bank for the previous 12 months or so, he would or might have appreciated the probability that the wife had put up part of the purchase price.

At a somewhat late stage of counsel's opening on behalf of the wife, a further point was added and the case was put in a somewhat different, alternative way. It is the fact that the husband had not always proved to be a very satisfactory customer from the point of view of the bank. There were record cards which, I think, must have been brought to the attention of the manager of the bank at the time of the first of the three legal charges, and from which it appears that at the time of the purchase the husband was hard put to it to find a few pounds; knowing that he was so low in funds, the bank should, so the argument goes, have taken advantage of what appears to me to be the wholly fortuitous fact that the wife's account was with the bank which could refresh its memory by looking at that account to see if there was not ground for supposing that the wife had in truth provided the money for the purchase. Had it done so and observed the withdrawals to which I have adverted, and particularly the payment of £289 to the solicitors and the fact that the wife had a small business of her own and had raised money to buy the furniture for the new house, the source of the purchase money of the house would have become tolerably clear. Ergo, so the argument runs, the bank is fixed with constructive notice of the wife's equitable interest. How far the bank would have been fixed with notice of the equitable interest if it had made the enquiry which it is said it ought to have made, is a matter which I need not decide, for, in my judgment, the bank never came under an obligation to make the enquiry. But I would, in passing, observe that it does not in the least follow that because £200 or £300 are found by a wife on the purchase of the matrimonial home that she has an equitable interest in it. It must be the commonest thing in the world for a wife to lend her husband a few hundred pounds in order that the house should be bought and for the loan to be repaid in a comparatively short time. As I have indicated, however, I cannot hold that the bank was bound to make any such enquiry as has been urged it ought to have done. So to hold would, in my judgment, be to place on a bank an intolerable burden and would stretch the doctrine of constructive notice to a point beyond its proper limits.

In this connection I would borrow two passages from the judgment of FARWELL, J., in *Hunt* v. *Luck*[3]. The first of them is as follows[4]:

> "This doctrine of constructive notice, imputing as it does knowledge which the person affected does not actually possess, is one which the courts of late years have been unwilling to extend. I am not referring to cases where a man wilfully shuts his eyes so as to avoid notice but to cases like the present, where honest men are to be affected by knowledge which every one admits they did not in fact possess. So far as regards the merits of the case, even assuming both parties to the action to be equally innocent, the man who has been swindled by too great confidence in his own agent has surely less claim to the assistance of a court of equity than a purchaser for value who gets the legal estate, and pays his money without notice. Granted that the vendor has every reason to believe his agent an honest man, still, if he is mistaken and trusts a rogue, he, rather than the purchaser for value without notice who is misled by his having so trusted, ought to bear the burden."

And so it appears to me as between a wife who has trusted her husband to have the property vested in his sole name or who has not taken steps to get it vested in joint names, on the one hand, and a mortgagee bank on the other.

3 [1901] 1 Ch. 45.
4 [1901] 1 Ch. at p.48.

The second passage of FARWELL, J.'s judgment is as follows[5]:

> "Constructive notice is the knowledge which the Courts impute to a person upon a presumption so strong of the existence of the knowledge that it cannot be allowed to be rebutted, either from his knowing something which ought to have put him to further inquiry or from his wilfully abstaining from inquiry, to avoid notice. How can I hold that the mortgagees here wilfully neglected to make some inquiry which is usual in cases of mortgages or sales of real estate in order to avoid acquiring some knowledge which they would thereby have obtained."

The last sentence of that passage appears to be applicable to the facts of the present case. Nor do I find the suggestion that a bank mortgagee should, at its peril, be bound to conduct an enquiry into the financial relations between husband and wife before it can advance money on security of property vested in the husband, at all an attractive one and, in my view, in this day and age husbands and wives ought to be able to bank at the same bank without having their accounts analysed by the bank in order to find out if one of them is deceiving the other.

The exercise which, it is submitted, ought to have been conducted in the present case would, it seems to me, have been more appropriate to a police enquiry or that of a detective agency than to a bank manager who no doubt often arranges advances daily in the ordinary course of business. And one may ask the rhetorical question, "At what point are such enquiries to end?" Such enquiries, perhaps, lie within a small compass in the case of a country branch of a bank but would assume a most complicated and difficult character when embarked on in a bank which carries many thousands of accounts. Is the bank, being uncertain how the borrower can have found the money, to search not only his wife's account but also, perhaps, his father's account? As LORD UPJOHN pointed out in his speech in *National Provincial Bank, Ltd.* v. *Ainsworth*[6]:

> "It has been the policy of the law for over a hundred years to simplify and facilitate transactions in real property. It is of great importance that persons should be able freely and easily to raise money on the security of their property."

I can, perhaps, most conveniently summarise my judgment on this part of the case by referring to s. 199 of the Law of Property Act 1925, and say that at the times of the several advances to the husband an enquiry into the details of the wife's bank account with a view to ascertaining whether she had provided a part of the purchase price was not an enquiry which ought reasonably to have been made within the meaning of sub-s. (1) (ii) of that section.

I must now consider a further argument advanced on behalf of the wife. It is contended that an enquiry ought to have been made on the property and that if such an enquiry had been made the wife would have asserted her equitable interest, ergo, so the argument runs, the bank had constructive notice of that interest. Before going on to consider this contention it is, perhaps, convenient that I should remark by way of warning that s. 199 is a section designed not to extend but to limit the doctrine of constructive notice. The section does not operate so as to fix a purchaser with constructive notice of a matter of which he would not have had constructive notice prior to the coming into force of the Law of Property Act 1925. The law, as I understand it, is this: if there be in possession or occupation of the property contracted to be sold or mortgaged a person other than the vendor or, as in this case, other than the mortgagor, and the purchaser makes no enquiry of that person, he takes the property fixed with notice of that person's rights and interests, however that may be. (See the judgment of VAUGHAN WILLIAMS, L.J., in *Hunt* v. *Luck*[7] in the Court of Appeal.) Here it is said that the wife was in possession or occupation. No enquiry was made of her and,

---

5 [1901] 1 Ch. at p.52.
6 [1965] 2 All E.R. 472 at p.485; [1965] A.C. 1175 at p.1233.
7 [1902] 1 Ch. 428 at p.433; [1900-03] All E.R. Rep. 295 at p.297.

therefore, the bank is fixed with notice of her equitable interest. In my judgment it is here that the fallacy arises for the wife in this case, unlike the deserted wife, was not in apparent occupation or possession. She was there ostensibly because she was the husband's wife and her presence there was wholly consistent with the title offered by the husband to the bank.

A similar point was touched on by LORD WILBERFORCE in *National Provincial Bank, Ltd.* v. *Ainsworth*[8] when he said:

> "For to hold that the wife acquires on marriage a right valid against third parties to remain in the house where she lives with her husband would not only fly in the face of the reality of the marriage relationship which requires the spouses to live together, as they can agree, wherever circumstances may prescribe, but would create impossible difficulties for those dealing with the property of a married man. It would mean that the concurrence of the wife would be necessary for all dealings."

In my judgment, where the vendor or mortgagor is himself in possession and occupation of the property, the purchaser or the mortgagee is not affected with notice of the equitable interests of any other person who may be resident there, and whose presence is wholly consistent with the title offered. If one buys with vacant possession on completion and one knows or finds out that the vendor is himself in possession and occupation of the property, one is, in my judgment, by reason of one's failure to make further enquiries on the premises, no more fixed with notice of the equitable interest of the vendor's wife who is living there with him than one would be affected with notice of the equitable interest of any other person who might also be resident on the premises, e.g., the vendor's father, his Uncle Harry or his Aunt Matilda, any of whom, be it observed, might have contributed money towards the purchase of the property. The reason is that the vendor being in possession, the presence of his wife or guest or lodger implies nothing to negative the title offered. It is otherwise if the vendor is not in occupation and one finds another party whose presence demands an explanation and whose presence one ignores at one's peril.

I would add this: counsel for the bank in his very clear argument has called attention to the fact that this is a conveyancing question, and I accept the point he makes that in such a matter the practice of conveyancers carries great weight. I have never heard it suggested, and no textbook or judicial utterance has been cited which suggests, that where one finds a vendor and his wife living together on the property a prudent solicitor acting for the purchaser ought to enquire of the wife whether she claims an interest in the house. Counsel for the bank also points out, by reference to remarks made by RUSSELL, L.J., in the Court of Appeal in *National Provincial Bank, Ltd.* v. *Hastings Car Mart, Ltd.*[9] and to the speeches of LORD UPJOHN and LORD WILBERFORCE in the House of Lords in that case[10], how unworkable and undesirable it would be if the law required such an enquiry—an enquiry, let me add, which would be as embarrassing to the enquirer as it would be, in my view, intolerable to the wife and the husband. Counsel for the bank put it well when, in commenting on the whole of the wife's case, he said it is not in the public interest that bank mortgagees should be snoopers and busybodies in relation to wholly normal transactions of mortgages. I must, make it clear, because much reliance was placed by the wife's evidence on what was said by the majority of the Court of Appeal in the *Hastings Car Mart* case[9] regarding the duty of a purchaser to make enquiries on the premises where the wife is living alone in the matrimonial home after her husband has left her, that about such a situation I say nothing whatsoever. Here the wife was living with her husband.

---

8 [1965] 2 All E.R. at p.494; [1965] A.C. at p.1248.
9 [1964] 1 All E.R. 688; [1964] Ch. 665.
10 [1965] 2 All E.R. 472; [1965] A.C. 1175.

Finally, I must refer to an argument which was at first mooted in reply on behalf of the wife to the effect that the standard of duty required of a bank in such a case as this is to be equated with the standard of duty which is required of a bank when it seeks to excuse itself from what otherwise would be a conversion or is a conversion of a cheque. But this is not an action for breach of contract or an action for tort and I can see no kind of analogy between the two classes of case. The cases depending on the doctrine of equitable constructive notice appear to me to be as different as chalk from cheese.

Declaration accordingly.

Extract reproduced by permission of the All England Law Reports.

Questions

1 *Note on the two systems of conveyancing:*

We have seen that the principles of enjoyment and ownership under the unregistered and registered systems concur. Enjoyment of the fee simple estate, or of any other interest, is the same under both systems, once transfer has run its course. Yet the act of transfer differs under the two systems. This divergence is illustrated by the cases of Caunce v. Caunce [1969] 1 All E.R. 722 and Williams & Glyn's Bank v. Boland [1979] 2 All E.R. 697. The former case is considered above, the latter at the end of the next chapter. The question may be put now and answered when Chapter 18 has been studied.

In what ways does the existence of two systems of transfer affect substantive rights?

2 *What difficulties might follow as a result of charges being registered against names rather than against the land under the Land Charges Act 1972?*

3 *What is meant by 'money or money's worth' in section 4(6) of the Land Charges Act 1972?*

4 *What is the modern role of the doctrines of actual and constructive notice?*

Chapter Eighteen

Registration of title

Introduction

In Chapter 2 an elementary account was given of the way in which land has been conveyed in this country for several centuries. The vendor's aim has been to produce documentary evidence of past transactions over such a period of time as to raise the overwhelming inference that he owns the estate which the purchaser wishes to buy. Besides being satisfied as to the vendor's title to the land, the purchaser will also wish to know what rights exist in it in favour of third parties or the general public. This he will establish by inspecting the documents of title referred to above, by making searches in the Land Charges Register and the local land charges register, by making enquiries of the vendor and by a physical inspection of the land.

Some of the weaknesses of the system were mentioned, but outstanding amongst them is the wastefulness of making separate investigations of title on each successive occasion when the land is sold. Thus, I might take a conveyance of 'Blackacre' today in 1983 having investigated the title back to, say, 1960. If I sell the land tomorrow, the purchaser will repeat this investigation over more or less the same period of time.

The main purpose behind the introduction of registration of title is to make this repetitive work unnecessary. This is achieved by making one final proof of the title to the satisfaction of the Chief Land Registrar, who then records the title in a register in the name of the proprietor. Thereafter the register constitutes the sole proof of that title, which is guaranteed by the state. Many third-party rights may also be protected by entries in the register, so that once a title is registered the Land Charges Register has no longer any part to play in relation to it. Not all such third-party or public rights can, however, be entered in the register so that enquiries and inspections still must be made. Furthermore, searches must still be made in the local land charges register. To this extent the new system falls short of any ideal that the register should be a perfect mirror to a title. This failure to give an exhaustive record of rights in or over the land is partly due to the very nature of land enjoyment. As to proposals for improvements to the system, see the Law Commission's Working Paper (No. 32) and 34 Conveyancer 369.

The system of registered conveyancing does not affect the pattern of estates and interests which can exist in land (see *Murray* v. *Two Strokes Ltd.* [1973] 3 All E.R. 357). Similarly, the rules as to trusts for sale, strict settlements, co-ownership and so on, remain the same as in the case of unregistered title. It is simply that the ways in which title to these estates and interests are proved, the way in which they are transferred and the way in which third party rights are protected are altered. As to this last factor, we shall see that the different means of protection in the two systems can occasionally result in an interest being better protected under one system than under the other. In the course of time, procedural rules can create substantive law, as our medieval writ system showed. Perhaps this might be so with registered land in the future.

The registered system is applied to a particular district compulsorily by Order in Council. Formerly, titles could be registered voluntarily in any district, but this is no longer allowed, except where it is especially convenient to register, such as in the cases of lost deeds or large estate development. This was enacted by the Land Registration Act 1966, so that compulsory registration could be speeded up. At present, more than a half of conveyances are of registered title. Even within a compulsory area, the obligation to register title only arises on the first sale of the fee simple, or upon the first creation or assignment of a leasehold term of forty years or more. Once a title is registered, all subsequent dealings with the estate are carried out under the system.

The Land Registry has its headquarters at Lincoln's Inn Fields in London, but twelve district registries carry out the duties of registration in their own areas. The chief officer is called the Chief Land Registrar. The law concerning registration of title is contained in the Land Registration Acts 1925–71 and in the Rules of 1925–78. The legislation, though somewhat imperfect, has not been greatly litigated.

The order in which the various topics will be discussed is as follows: the register and its contents, the procedure of registration, the transfer of interests after registration of title and the guarantee of the title. References to sections in this chapter will be to sections of the Land Registration Act 1925, unless otherwise stated.

The register and its contents

In this part, three matters must be discussed. Firstly, there is the classification of interests in land drawn by the Act which govern whether an interest may be protected by registration, and, if so, how. Secondly, there is the way in which the register is structured so as to accommodate the various registrable interests. Thirdly, there is the marriage of the two matters mentioned above, namely, the way in which registrable interests are protected by the register.

Classification of interests

The classification of interests drawn by the Act is threefold.

(1) *The legal estate.* There are only two principal interests which may be registered in the sense that new sections of the register may be opened up for them, and these are the two legal estates (s.2). A fee simple absolute in possession may therefore be registered. So may certain terms of years absolute, but in this case only provided that more than twenty-one years are unexpired, that there is no absolute prohibition against assignment and that they are not merely mortgage terms subject to a right of redemption (s.8). Certain legal rentcharges are capable of substantive registration. We shall see below that many other interests are capable of registration in the sense of being entered on the register which has already been opened for these legal estates, but they cannot be registered independently if the legal estate is not

registered. The legal estate, therefore, is the germ cell of registration and all other registrable interests are merely registered against it. These other interests are like apples hanging from a tree. The registered legal estate is the tree itself. No tree, no apples. In other words, if there is no legal estate registered other interests must look for their protection under the unregistered system.

Since more than one legal estate may exist in the same land, as where the fee simple is subject to a lease, and perhaps even a sub-lease, then several separate registered titles and, therefore, independent sections of the register, may exist in respect of the same land. Such separate sections may however allude to each other by cross-references on the register.

(2) *Minor interests.* If a legal estate is registered, then certain third party rights affecting the property may be entered upon that register against it. These are called minor interests. Although their definition in s.3 is oblique, they are identifiable as follows. We saw above that the legal estate is, with some exceptions, independently registrable and in this case the act of registration is the source of its protection. Below we shall find that certain interests listed by the Act are fully effective without being entered on the register, even though the legal estate which they affect is registered. Because of this characteristic, these are called 'overriding interests'. All other interests—the residue left by these two classifications—are minor interests and require entry on the register for their protection. The symmetry of this threefold classification is, however, slightly marred by the fact that certain rights which are expressly rendered capable of registration such as matters which would, in the case of unregistered land, be protected under the Land Charges Act 1972 (see s.59), are also capable of being overriding interests. The classification attempted by the Act is thus imperfect since two of the categories are not mutually exclusive. The manner in which they are so entered and the nature of their protection will be discussed later.

Examples of minor interests are equitable interests such as life interests arising under strict settlements and trusts for sale and restrictive covenants. They must possess the true characteristics of interests in land, as opposed to merely personal rights, for the Act does not extend the area of rights in respect of which protection against third parties would be afforded under the unregistered system (see *Murray* v. *Two Strokes Ltd.* [1973] 3 All E.R. 357). The hallmark of these interests, however, is not their equitable nature. Generally they are characterized by not being readily discoverable from an inspection of the land, but their true identity stems from their residuary nature.

(3) *Overriding interests (ss.3, 70).* These are interests which bind a registered proprietor or his alienee irrespective of registration and irrespective of notice. They can, however, appear on the register and then they cease to be overriding interests and take their protection from the register. They are listed in s.70. The principal ones are as follows:

(a) Rights of common; drainage rights; customary rights (until extinguished); public rights; *profits à prendre*; rights of sheep-walk; rights of way; watercourses; rights of water, and other easements not being equitable easements required to be protected by notice on the register;

(b) Liability to repair highways by reason of tenure; quit-rents; crown rents; heriots, and other rents and charges (until extinguished) having their origin in tenure;

(c) Liability to repair the chancel of any church;
(d) Liability in respect of embankments, and sea and river walls;
(e) [Extinguished effect];
(f) Subject to the provisions of the Act, rights acquired or in course of being acquired under the Limitation Acts;
(g) The rights of every person in actual occupation of the land or in receipt of the rents and profits thereof, save where enquiry is made of such person and the rights are not disclosed. This category will be discussed shortly;
(h) In the case of a possessory, qualified, or good leasehold title; all estates, rights, interests, and powers excepted from the effect of registration. The nature of these titles is explained below;
(i) Rights under local land charges unless and until registered or protected on the register in the prescribed manner;
(j) Rights of fishing and sporting; seignorial and manorial rights of all descriptions (until extinguished), and franchises;
(k) Leases for any term or interest not exceeding twenty-one years, granted at a rent without taking a fine. A 'grant' is not constituted by an agreement to grant a lease (*City Permanent B.S.* v. *Miller* [1952] Ch. 840). If possession is taken under the agreement however, an overriding interest will occur under (g) above.

The list of overriding interests has been added to by subsequent Acts, such as rights in respect of coal vested in the National Coal Board by the Coal Act 1938, s.41.

The rights under (g) were widely drawn so as to protect persons who in terms of ordinary justice deserve protection, but whose interests are either inappropriate for registration or, if appropriate, are often informally created and thus unlikely to be registered by unsuspecting laymen. This policy led to the overlapping of categories mentioned above. It has been by far the most controversial of all the classes of overriding interests and has been subject to judicial decisions which have far-reaching consequences in the fields both of conveyancing and land enjoyment. The following elements of the provision call for some discussion: the nature of the 'rights', 'actual occupation' and 'inquiry'.

To ascertain what 'rights' come within this provision we must have regard to the general law of land, irrespective of the Act, for the enactment does not augment but merely protects rights for what they are. Rights of a merely personal character do not, therefore, rise above their ordinary station merely because they occur where title is registered. Thus the right of a deserted wife against her husband to live in the matrimonial home is not an overriding interest, even though she is in occupation of the property, for to qualify as an overriding interest the right must be 'capable of enduring through different ownerships of the land according to normal conceptions of title to real property' (*National Provincial Bank Ltd.* v. *Ainsworth* [1965] A.C. 1175). We shall see, however, that such a right is a minor interest and may be protected by a notice.

The provision does not apply to rights of persons in occupation of land under a strict settlement, because they are designated exclusively minor interests under the Act (s.86(2)). Whether the interests of persons enjoying occupation under an express trust for sale are overriding interests is not so clear (see 22 Conveyancer 24 and 33 Conveyancer 254). Equitable as well as legal interests are included, so that persons in occupation under agreements for leases or options to purchase the freehold granted to a lessee in occupation are protected, even though they are capable of registration by entry on the register but have not been so registered (*Webb* v. *Pollmount Ltd.* [1966] Ch. 584; and see *London and Cheshire Insurance Co. Ltd.* v. *Laplagrene Property Co. Ltd.* [1971] 2 W.L.R. 257).

The meaning of 'actual occupation' has been the subject of two major judicial decisions in recent years. In *Hodgson* v. *Marks* [1971] 2 All E.R. 684, *H*, a widow voluntarily conveyed her house to her lodger, *E*, on the oral understanding that though it was to be registered in his name for the purpose of his management of her affairs it was to be held upon trust for her. Both parties continued to live, sleep and eat in the house after the transfer in exactly the same way as before it. The financial arrangements for *E*'s board remained unchanged. *E* later sold the house to *M* without the knowledge of *H*. *M* mortgaged it to a building society. After *E*'s death, the question arose whether *H*'s rights enjoyed protection under section 70(1)(g). The Court of Appeal held that her interest was protected because she was in 'actual occupation' of the house. Such occupation was a matter of physical presence.

In *Williams and Glyn's Bank Ltd.* v. *Boland* [1979] 2 All E.R. 697, *H* was the sole registered proprietor of the home where he and his wife *W* lived. However, *W* was a part-owner in equity but had not protected her interest by any entry on the register. *H*, without *W*'s knowledge, mortgaged the house to the bank for a loan for business purposes. The bank made no inquiry as to *W*'s interest or even as to her existence. The bank later sought to enforce the loan and the question was whether *W*'s interest was an overriding one against them. This depended upon whether she was in 'actual occupation'. The House of Lords held that she was. The criterion of physical presence, emphasized in *Hodgson* v. *Marks* was confirmed. The question is one of fact not law. 'Actual occupation' is not necessarily confined to one person. The expression is to be read in the context of the Act and meanings attached to 'occupation' in other Acts are not to be imported. Although occupation will usually produce visible signs, it is important to banish any trace of the doctrine of notice from the test we are discussing. That principle belongs exclusively to the unregistered system. In *Caunce* v. *Caunce* [1969] 1 All E.R. 722 it was held that the presence in the home of a beneficially entitled wife did not constitute notice to a purchaser from the husband who was sole owner of an unregistered legal estate. The wife's interest was therefore defeated. Thus identical fact situations can produce different legal consequences in the two systems. 'Actual occupation', however, has nothing to do with the state of mind of a purchaser, only with the state of mind and presence of the body of the occupier.

Problems of construction of words are commonplace in law. The significance of the decision in *Boland* is that the House of Lords chose to prefer the interests of occupiers against those of banks, building societies and conveyancing solicitors in a field of considerable economic activity. There is nothing in the judgments which limits the decision to matrimonial homes however. The decision is thus of social importance because of the quantity of transactions it will influence.

Finally, a purchaser can take free of an otherwise overriding interest if he makes 'enquiry' and the interest is not disclosed. Such enquiry will only have this effect however if it is addressed to the person who owns the interest in question (see *Hodgson* v. *Marks*, above). This requirement presents the principal difficulty for the purchaser, the lender and the conveyancer—the potential difficulty of discovering all the appropriate persons to whom to put enquiries.

Lenders and conveyancers have criticized the decision in *Boland*. On the other hand, the House of Lords hinted that the difficulties anticipated by these groups have been overstated. It is perhaps too early to distinguish froth and water in the immediate wake of the decision. A brief and uncritical statement of some of the apparent advantages and anxieties raised by the decision might be attempted.

Some of the advantages are:

(1) The primary use of property as a unit of human shelter and sustenance is confirmed;
(2) the absence of a general code of ownership of the matrimonial home is rendered less urgent.

The danger of injustice remains, however, as in the case of a spouse who is no longer in occupation and possibly in even greater need of protection (see N.L.J., 2nd Oct. 1980, 896).

Some of the disadvantages are:

(1) Conveyancers will sometimes experience difficulties in locating all owners of interests for enquiry;
(2) collusion between equitable co-owners might unjustly prejudice purchasers where the interest of one co-owner is deliberately concealed by the other;
(3) the incentive to enter notice of certain registrable interests on the register is reduced.

The structure of the register

The register is in three parts: the property register, the proprietorship register and the charges register. The document of title which the registered proprietor is given, known as a 'land certificate', is simply a copy of these three parts of the register relating to his land. His true proof of title, however, is the register itself and not the certificate. The register is kept on a card index system; each title is identified by title number and has a separate card. The three parts of the register concerning a particular property title all appear on that card. Although the register itself is not open to inspection without the permission of the registered owner, it is possible to discover without such permission whether a particular property is registered or whether application for registration has been made in respect of it. This can be done by an appropriate search of the Index Map and Parcels Index. The search will not reveal the name of the owner, merely whether the land is registered or registration is pending. A prospective purchaser or chargee will clearly wish to ascertain this as a safeguard against fraud. A vendor might, for instance, represent the land as being unregistered, when it is in fact registered, in order to conceal incumbrances.

The contents of the three parts are as follows.

(1) *The property register.* This describes the land and the estate for which it is held by reference to a plan or map. It also contains notes of interests, such as easements, or even covenants which exist in favour of the registered land. It may also record its freedom from the burden of certain interests such as easements. Noting of such appurtenant rights upon the register is, however, at the option of the Chief Land Registrar.
(2) *The proprietorship register.* This part of the register contains the name and address of the proprietor, the nature of the title registered—that is, whether it is absolute, good leasehold, qualified or possessory—and any cautions, inhibitions and restrictions affecting the proprietor's right to deal with the estate. These matters are dealt with below.
(3) *The charges register.* This contains incumbrances running against the registered land such as mortgages and restrictive covenants. Below are fictitious examples of a land certificate and the appropriate entries on the register which are attached to it.

How registrable interests are protected by the register

We have seen that of the three classes of interests, one class, that of overriding interests, binds a purchaser, even though normally the interests are not registered. One of the two remaining classes, the legal estate, which is the subject-matter of registration, receives its protection from the act of registration. We must now discuss how the third class, that of minor interests, receives its protection.

Minor interests are protected in one of two ways according to their subject-matter. Some are protected by entries on the proprietorship register, in which case dealing with the land is prevented altogether for a certain time, or is only permitted if carried out in a certain way which will protect the interest in question. This is achieved through the machinery of 'restrictions', 'cautions' and 'inhibitions'. Others are protected by the entry of a notice on the charges register. This does not prevent dealing with the estate but fixes the world with notice of the incumbrance, so that if the incumbrance is otherwise valid, alienees of the property will take subject to it. Notices perform, therefore, the same function as registration of charges under the Land Charges Act 1972, in respect of unregistered land. The cases to which these two methods apply must now be considered.

A restriction is entered on the proprietorship register by or with the agreement of the registered proprietor, and prevents any transaction being carried out except according to the conditions or in the manner specified by the restriction (s.58). It is thus a voluntary or friendly entry and is appropriate in the case of strict settlements, express trusts for sale and co-ownership, where equitable interests arising under them require protection. A tenant for life under a strict settlement, for instance, will be the registered proprietor of the fee simple, but restrictions will be placed on the register firstly preventing the registration of any disposition *ultra vires* the Settled Land Act 1925, and secondly prohibiting any disposition involving capital money being registered unless the money is paid to the trustees. The demands of both Acts are thereby satisfied. The curtain principle is maintained, for the details of the

H.M. LAND REGISTRY — LAND REGISTRATION ACTS, 1925 TO 1971

LAND CERTIFICATE

This is to certify that the land described in the office copy of the register and shown on the official plan within is registered at H.M. Land Registry under the Title Number endorsed hereon.

Seal

H.M. LAND REGISTRY

TITLE NUMBER XYZ 1234

A. PROPERTY REGISTER

COUNTY OR COUNTY BOROUGH	PARISH OR PLACE
Solihull	Solihull

The freehold land shown and edged with red on the plan of the above Title filed at the Registry registered on 20th February 1982 known as 98 Withered Heath Road.

B. PROPRIETORSHIP REGISTER TITLE ABSOLUTE

ENTRY NUMBER	PROPRIETOR, ETC.	APPLICATION NUMBER AND REMARKS
I	Margaret Morley of 10 Withered Heath Road, Solihull, Warwickshire, registered 20th February 1982.	Price paid £30000

C. CHARGES REGISTER

ENTRY NUMBER	Date at beginning of each entry is date of entry on register.	APPLICATION NUMBER AND REMARKS
I	20th February 1982 – A conveyance of the land in this title dated 1st July 1970 and made between (I) James Desmond (Vendor) and John Largedy (Purchaser) contains the following covenant: No building shall be erected within 25 yards of the southern boundary of the land conveyed.	

This is a model Land Certificate prepared by the author and based on certificates in use.

trust are not entered on the register, and the invalidating effect of s.18 of the Settled Land Act is reconciled with the confirmatory effects of registration of title.

A caution has a similar effect of preventing dealings with the property until the person lodging the caution has been notified. Unlike a restriction, however, a caution is hostile and its purpose is to prevent dealings with the estate until the cautioner has had the opportunity of disputing the right to do so when that cautioner claims an interest in the land not already protected by the register (ss.53–55; and see 35 Conveyancer 21). For instance, in *Elias* v. *Mitchell* [1972] 2 All E.R. 153 a co-owner in equity was held entitled to enter a caution to prevent a sale of the land by the sole registered proprietor of the legal estate. Cautions may be entered against first registration of title, as where the cautioner alleges that a conveyance of unregistered property was illegally obtained from him. This is an exception to the principle mentioned earlier that title to land must be registered before third party claims can be entered on the register. The Registrar will fix a time limit within which the cautioner must dispute the right of the owner to register, or to dispose of the land if it is already registered, as the case may be.

Inhibitions also prevent dealings with the registered property until the occurrence of a certain event or until further order (s.57). They may be entered on the proprietorship register by the court or the Registrar on the application of any person interested. They are thus hostile. They are intended to be used, rather than the other methods mentioned above, in cases of emergency, since they are speedier in effect. Sometimes they are used as a matter of course, for instance, in cases of bankruptcy where inhibitions are entered to prevent the registered proprietor dealing with his land.

The two legal estates, with certain exceptions	*The Property Register*
Minor interests: sometimes (a) by paralysing dealings or regulating how they are carried out, and sometimes (b) by fixing prospective alienees with notice. Sometimes there is the alternative between (a) and (b).	*The Proprietorship Register* *The Charges Register*

Overriding interests are effective irrespective of entry on the register.

Many minor interests may be protected by notice. A notice is entered on the charges register and, as mentioned above, its effect is that universal notice of the interest concerned is thereby given so that dispositions take effect subject to it (see ss.48–53 and 59). Unlike registration of the title itself, entry has no confirmatory effect on the interest; if it is not otherwise valid, notice will not make it so. Matters which can be protected by notice in this way embrace all those rights which can be protected under the Land Charges Act 1972, including a spouse's right of occupation under the Matrimonial Homes Act 1967, a tenant's notice of his desire to acquire the freehold or an extended lease under the Leasehold Reform Act 1967, and even leases when they are not overriding interests and whether or not the title to the lease has been independently registered. The most common entries are restrictive covenants.

Generally, notices require the consent of the registered proprietor, but if this is not given, a caution may be lodged until it is. The diagram on page 338 might help to summarize the way in which the Act provides for the protection of the three classes of interests.

The procedure of registration

In this section we must discuss compulsory registration of title. The process of registration, the types of title granted on registration and the conversion of one type of title into another.

Compulsory registration

We have already noticed which estates may be registered in areas where registration is compulsory. Now we must see what estates not merely may, but must, have their titles registered, and when registration takes place. They are as follows (s.123):

(1) Title to the fee simple absolute in possession must be registered on its first 'sale' after compulsory registration has been introduced into an area. No doubt the use of the word 'sale' excludes transactions without consideration or where the only consideration is marriage.
(2) Title to a term of years absolute must be registered on the 'grant' of a term not being less than forty years from the date of the delivery of the grant as must every assignment on 'sale' of a term of years absolute having not less than forty years to run from the date of the delivery of the assignment. If the title to freehold or leasehold land is already registered, a lease for more than twenty-one years must be registered.

An application for first registration must generally be made within two months of the transaction; otherwise the transaction becomes void so far as the passing of the legal estate is concerned. Once registration has been carried out, all subsequent dealings with the estate must be effected under the system. This is so even when the title has been registered voluntarily.

The process of registration

The person entitled to apply for registration is the estate owner or person entitled to have the registrable estate vested in him. In the case of settled land, for instance, this will be the tenant for life. The application is made to the appropriate district registry and must be accompanied, unless the Registrar directs otherwise, by such original deeds and documents relating to the title as the applicant has in his possession, abstract of title and sufficient particulars by which to identify the land on the registry maps. The title is then examined by the Registrar, who may make requisitions of the applicant regarding the title. There is also machinery for the making of objections to registration (Land Registration Rules 1925, rr.34, 35). When the Registrar has completed his investigations the land certificate will be issued to the registered proprietor.

This certificate states the nature of the title which has been registered. The different types of title which may be awarded must now be explained.

Types of title

There are four types of title: absolute; qualified; possessory and good leasehold. The last only applies to leases. Qualified title cannot be applied for, but may be granted unilaterally by the Registrar. The word 'absolute' here has no connection with its use in the expressions 'fee simple absolute' and 'term of years absolute'. It relates to the title to an estate and not to the nature of the estate itself. These titles must now be discussed individually.

(1) *Absolute title.* In the case of freehold registration, an absolute title will be granted where the Registrar is satisfied that the title cannot be successfully challenged. It is the title normally sought and granted. Registration vests in the first registered proprietor the fee simple together with all rights and privileges existing in favour of the land, and subject only to any entries on the register, to overriding interests unless the contrary is stated on the register, and, where he is not entitled for his own benefit, to minor interests of which he has notice. This last proviso ensures that trustees of the legal estate hold subject to the interests of the beneficiaries (s.5). In short, registration guarantees that the person in whose name the title is registered is the owner.

Absolute title to leasehold property may be granted if the Registrar is satisfied not only as to the validity of the title to the lease, but also as to the validity of the titles to the freehold and any reversionary leases behind the lease registered. Registration vests the title to the lease in the first registered proprietor subject to those rights mentioned above subject to which a registered freeholder takes, and also to all the obligations and liabilities in the lease (see s.9).

(2) *Good leasehold title.* This title is only granted for leases. Its effect is the same as that of an absolute title to a lease except that it does not guarantee that the landlord had the right to grant the lease and does not indicate matters affecting the freehold, such as restrictive covenants, which will bind the lessee. The need for such a title arises because a lessee cannot investigate the freeholder's title unless there is provision to do so in the contract (L.P.A. 1925, s.44(2)). If, however, unknown to the lessee, the freehold title is already registered, the Registrar may grant absolute title to a lessee even though he has only applied for good leasehold title.

(3) *Qualified title.* In the case of freeholds, this title is the same as absolute title except that it is made subject to some defect specified in the register, and therefore registration does not prejudice the enforcement of the estate or right constituting the defect (s.7).

In the case of leaseholds, a qualified title has the same effect as an absolute title or good leasehold title, according to the title applied for, but again subject to some specified defect (ss.7, 12).

The grant of qualified title is of very rare occurrence.

(4) *Possessory title.* In Chapter 8 it was explained that possession of land is a source of title to it. The ultimate acceptability of a title based on recent possession depends upon the passage of time and the extinction of any oustanding superior rights to possession under the Limitation Act.

Applications based only upon possession of land may be made in respect of both freeholds and leaseholds. What must be proved is possession of land or receipt of its rents and profits, and, of course, there is no investigation of title in the sense of documents, for indeed there may be no documents to support the claim. As might be expected, the registration of such a title makes no guarantee against the enforcement of any rights contrary to the title which existed or where capable of existing at the time of first registration (ss.6 and 11).

Conversion of titles

The act provides for the conversion of inferior titles into superior or absolute titles (s.77).

The Registrar has a discretion to convert a title registered as qualified, good leasehold or possessory into absolute or good leasehold title when it has been transferred for valuable consideration, and to convert a title which has been registered as good leasehold title for at least ten years into absolute title, provided that he is satisfied that the proprietor or successive proprietors have been in possession during that period.

The registrar must convert a freehold possessory title to absolute title after fifteen years and a leasehold possessory title to absolute after ten years, provided that he is satisfied in both cases that the proprietor is in possession.

The transfer of interests after registration

The title is now registered. We must next see how estates and interests are transferred to or acquired by others in future. The following cases must be considered: the transfer of the registered estate *inter vivos*, upon death, and upon bankruptcy, the loss of title under the Limitation Act 1980, and the way in which minor and overriding interests may be created or dealt with after registration.

Transfer *inter vivos*

The purchaser has no need to trace the devolution of the title as in the case of unregistered conveyancing, for registration is all that need be proved. Instead of an abstract of title, therefore, the vendor supplies him with an office copy of the entries on the register, extract from filed plan, and an authority to inspect the register. The purchaser must, however, make the usual enquiries, including a search in the local land charges register, and inspection of the land, for, as we have seen, the register is not conclusive as to third party rights.

The conveyance is carried out by a form of transfer specified in the Rules. This must be deposited at the Registry with the land certificate. When the Registrar registers the necessary changes on the register, the legal estate passes (ss.19–23). The amended land certificate is then returned to the new proprietor. There is, of course, provision for the conveyance of part only of the property.

The transferee, once his name is on the register, takes the estate together with the benefit of rights existing in its favour, including those implied under s.62 of the Law of Property Act 1925, so far as appropriate (ss.19(3),20), but subject to:

(a) Overriding interests.

(b) Minor interests entered on the register. In the case of certain minor interests, such as restrictive covenants, the effect of entry on the register is that the transferee takes the land burdened with the interest. In the case of others, such as beneficial interests under a settlement, the effect of entry is simply that the land must be transferred in a particular way designed to safeguard the rights of the beneficiaries. If this is done, however, the interest is overreached. If the disposition is not made for valuable consideration, however, a transferee takes subject to such minor interests as bound the transferor even if they are not entered on the register (s.20).

The effect of failure to register any registrable incumbrance which is not an overriding interest is, under the section, that the purchaser takes 'free' of it. The clear cut severity of this consequence matches that which prevails in the case of unregistered land. The doctrine of actual or constructive notice is banished in favour of the much more easily ascertainable state of the register (see also s.59(6)).

However, a decision of the High Court has cast some doubts upon the remorselessness of this statutory policy. In *Peffer* v. *Rigg* [1977] 3 All E.R. 745, *P* and *R* purchased a home for their mother-in-law. *R* was the sole registered proprietor but there was an agreement that it should be held on a tenancy in common beneficially. *P*'s interest was not entered on the register. The marriage of *R* and his wife *W* broke down and *R* transferred the house to *W* for £1 as part of the divorce settlement, the mother-in-law having already died. *W* was aware of all the facts mentioned above. *P* had no overriding interest. It was held that *P* was entitled to a half-share in the property. *W* could not claim the immunity from unregistered minor interests bestowed by s.20(1) upon dispositions 'for valuable consideration' since the parties had described the consideration as nominal only. A second reason was that under s.59(6), where immunity is further stated, it is expressed to run in favour of a 'purchaser'. Under section 3 (XXi) 'purchaser' means a purchaser 'in good faith'. *W* could scarcely claim to possess good faith since she had knowledge of *P*'s interest. Yet a further reason was that a new trust was imposed when transfer was made to her. This was a constructive trust brought about by her knowledge of the existing trust. However just the decision, it was surely reached by doing violence to the principles of the Act. The case may be compared in this respect with *Ives Investment Ltd*. v. *High* [1967] 1 All E.R. 504, a decision discussed in relation to easements.

Transfer on bankruptcy

When the proprietor is adjudicated bankrupt, the trustee in bankruptcy may be registered as proprietor. Before this event, creditors may be protected by a creditor's notice and a bankruptcy inhibition (see s.42).

Transfer on death

The personal representatives of a deceased proprietor may be registered in the place of the deceased, or alternatively they may have the person entitled under the will or intestacy, or purchaser, registered directly in place of the deceased (ss.37 and 41).

Loss of title under the Limitation Act 1980

Time runs against a registered proprietor under the Limitation Act 1980, in the same way that it runs in the case of unregistered land. The title of a registered proprietor, however, is not extinguished until the adverse possessor has been registered as proprietor. Until registration, which is treated as a first registration of a new title, the registered proprietor is deemed to hold the estate upon trust for the adverse possessor. This is without prejudice to the estates and interests of any other person interested in the land whose estate or interest is not extinguished by the Act.

Easements and other rights affecting land may be created in the same ways, including prescription, as in the case of unregistered land.

Dealings with interests other than the registered estate

When beneficial interests arising under strict settlements or trusts for sale are assigned or mortgaged, their priority is protected by 'priority inhibitions' and 'priority cautions' which may be registered in the minor interests index. Priority depends upon the order in which they are entered, and not upon the doctrine of *Dearle* v. *Hall* (1828), 3 Russ. 1 (see s.102). This index is not part of the register and, despite its misleading name, is used only for the purpose of establishing priorities. A person taking a conveyance of the land is therefore not affected by it. The mode of transfer of the interests mentioned above does not differ from that which prevails in the case of unregistered title and calls for no special treatment here. The same applies to the transfer of overriding interests.

A mortgage of an estate the title to which is registered may be carried out in three ways:

(1) *By registered charge (s.25)*. This is created by a deed describing the land by reference to the register, or in any other manner which enables the Registrar to identify it without reference to any other document. The land certificate must be deposited at the Registry during the currency of the charge. It is protected by entry on the charges register, and the registered chargee acquires the powers of a legal mortgagee, unless the register declares otherwise (s.34). A charge certificate issued to the chargee constitutes his document of title. It carries the same information as the land certificate and the mortgage deed is bound up with it.

Successive registered charges of the same land rank for the purposes of priority in the order in which they are entered on the register and not in order of their creation (s.29). (For a discussion of the priorities of interests in registered land see 35 Conveyancer 100). Further advances may be tacked only if such advances are obligatory and if either the obligation is entered on the register, or if made before notice of any intended entry on the register which would affect the priority of a further advance, sent by the registrar by registered post, ought to have been received by the chargee (s.30, as amended by the Law of Property (Amendment) Act 1926).

(2) *By unregistered mortgage (see Administration of Justice Act 1977, s.26)*. The registered proprietor may mortgage the land as if the land were unregistered. This practice is now rare however. Protection may be given to it by the entry of a 'mortgage caution' on the register. Before the caution is entered, the mortgage takes effect in equity only and may be overridden as a minor interest. (See *Schwab (E.S.) & Co.* v. *McCarthy* [1975] P. & C.R. 196). Such

mortgages can be subsequently converted into registered charges. It is common practice, however, to protect such mortgages by a notice of deposit of the land certificate in order to save the *ad valorem* fees required on the registration of a charge or the entry of a mortgage caution (see *Barclays Bank Ltd.* v. *Taylor* [1973] 2 W.L.R. 293).

(3) *By deposit of the land certificate (s.66).* The proprietor may create an equitable mortgage by depositing the land certificate with the person advancing the loan, who may then protect his interest by having notice of it entered on the charges register. This method of charging is favoured by banks to protect short-term or fluctuating loans secured on the property.

The guarantee of title

We have seen that it is of the essence of the registered system that the very act of registration vests the estate in the person registered as its proprietor. But there are occasions when, due to fraud or mistake, a person other than the true owner has been registered, and it would be unjust dogmatically to refuse to alter the register. There is, therefore, machinery for its rectification. The principle of guarantee of title is in such cases maintained by a right of indemnity in favour of those who suffer loss through rectification. These two matters will now be discussed.

Rectification (section 82, as amended by the Administration of Justice Act 1977, section 24)

The register may be rectified by order of the Registrar or of the court in the circumstances mentioned in the section: such as where an entry has been obtained by fraud, where there has been a mistake or omission or where a legal estate has been registered in the name of a person who, if the land had not been registered, would not have been the estate owner. The register cannot, however, be rectified, except for the purpose of giving effect to an overriding interest, so as to affect the title of the registered proprietor if he is in possession unless:

(1) that proprietor has been party to or has substantially contributed to the fraud, mistake or omission which makes the rectification necessary, or
(2) it would be unjust not to rectify the register against him (see generally, *Epps* v. *Esso Petroleum Co. Ltd.* [1973] 2 All E.R. 465).

In *Re 139 Deptford High Street* [1951] Ch. 884, the premises were described in the application for first registration simply as '139 High Street, Deptford' and no plan was provided. The Land Registry mistakenly thought the property included some adjacent land which had every appearance of being part of it, and indeed the applicant was under the same impression. Rectification was ordered on the grounds that the proprietor had contributed to the mistake as mentioned under (1) above.

Indemnity (section 83)

A person 'suffering loss' by reason of rectification, or by any error or omission on the register which is not rectified, or by the loss or destruction of any document lodged at the registry for inspection or safe custody, or because of an error in any official search, is entitled to be indemnified. No indemnity is payable, however

> where the applicant or a person through whom he derives title (otherwise than under a disposition for valuable consideration which is registered or protected on the register) has caused or substantially contributed to the loss by fraud or lack of proper care (Land Registration and Land Charges Act 1971, amending s.83; see also *Re 139 Deptford High Street*, above).

In *Re Chowood's Registered Land* [1933] Ch. 574 a squatter had, unknown to the purchaser of that land, acquired a predominant title to part of certain land under the Limitation Acts. The register was accordingly rectified, since the squatter's right was an overriding interest. The purchaser was held not to be entitled to an indemnity because his loss did not arise from rectification of the register but from the fact that he paid for property which was not the vendor's to sell (see also *Hodgson* v. *Marks* [1971] 2 All E.R. 684).

Study material: *Williams & Glyn's Bank Ltd.* v. *Boland and Another* [1980] 2 All E.R. 408

The House of Lords was unanimous in this case. The principal speech was that of Lord Wilberforce which is reproduced entirely below.

LORD WILBERFORCE. My Lords, these appeals, apart from one special point affecting only Mr Boland, raise for decision the same question: whether a husband or a wife (in each actual case a wife) who has a beneficial interest in the matrimonial home, by virtue of having contributed to its purchase price, but whose spouse is the legal and registered owner, has an 'overriding interest' binding on a mortgagee who claims possession of the matrimonial home under a mortgage granted by that spouse alone. Although this statement of the issue uses the words 'spouse', 'husband and wife', 'matrimonial home', the appeals do not, in my understanding, involve any question of matrimonial law, or of the rights of married women or of women as such. Exactly the same issue could arise if the roles of husband and wife were reversed, or if the persons interested in the house were not married to each other. The solution must be derived from a consideration in the light of current social conditions of the Land Registration Act 1925 and other property statutes.

The essential facts behind this legal formulation are as follows. Each wife contributed a substantial sum of her own money toward the purchase of the matrimonial home or to paying off a mortgage on it. This, indisputably, made her an equitable tenant in common to the extent of her contribution. Each house being registered land was transferred into the sole name of the husband who became its registered proprietor. Later, each husband mortgaged the house by legal mortgage to the appellant bank, which made no inquiries of either wife. Default being made, the bank started proceedings, in the *Boland* case in the High Court and in the *Brown* case in the Dartford County Court, for possession, with a view to sale. In each case the judge made an order for possession but his decision was reversed by the Court of Appeal ([1979] 2 All ER 697, [1979] Ch 312. So the question is whether the legal and registered mortgage takes effect against the matrimonial home, or whether the wife's beneficial interest has priority over it.

The legal framework within which the appeals are to be decided can be summarised as follows. Under the Land Registration Act 1925, legal estates in land are the only interests in respect of which a proprietor can be registered. Other interests take effect in equity as 'minor interests', which are overridden by a registered transfer. But the Act recognises also an intermediate, or hybrid, class of what are called 'overriding interests'; though these are not registered, legal dispositions take effect subject to them. The list of overriding interests is contained in s 70 and it includes such matters as easements, liabilities having their origin in tenure, land tax and tithe rentcharges, seignorial and manorial rights, leases for terms not exceeding 21 years, and, finally, the relevant paragraph being s 70(1)(*g*)—

> 'The rights of every person in actual occupation of the land or in receipt of the rents and profits thereof, save where enquiry is made of such person and the rights are not disclosed.'

The first question is whether the wife is a 'person in actual occupation', and, if so, whether her right as a tenant in common in equity is a right protected by this provision.

The other main legal element arises out of the Law of Property Act 1925. Since that Act, undivided shares in land can only take effect in equity, behind a trust for sale on which the legal owner is to hold the land. Dispositions of the land, including mortgages, may be made under this trust, and provided that there are at least two trustees, or a trust corporation, 'overreach' the trusts. This means that the 'purchaser' takes free from them, whether or not he has notice of them, and that the trusts are enforceable against the proceeds of sale: see s 2(2) of the Law of Property Act 1925, and s 2 (3) which lists certain exceptions.

The second question is whether the wife's equitable interest under the trust for sale, if she is in occupation of the land, is capable of being an overriding interest, or whether, as is generally the rule as regards equitable interests, it can only take effect as a 'minor interest'. In the latter event a registered transferee, including a legal mortgagee, would take free from it.

The system of land registration, as it exists in England, which long antedates the Land Registration Act 1925, is designed to simplify and to cheapen conveyancing. It is intended to replace the often complicated and voluminous title deeds of property by a single land certificate, on the strength of which land can be dealt with. In place of the lengthy and often technical investigation of title to which a purchaser was committed, all he has to do is to consult the register; from any burden not entered on the register, with one exception, he takes free. Above all, the system is designed to free the purchaser from the hazards of notice, real or constructive, which, in the case of unregistered land, involved him in inquiries, often quite elaborate, failing which he might be bound by equities. The Law of Property Act 1925 contains provisions limiting the effect of the doctrine of notice, but it still remains a potential source of danger to purchasers. By contrast, the only provisions in the Land Registration Act 1925 with regard to notice are provisions which enable a purchaser to take the estate free from equitable interests or equities whether he has notice or not (see, for example, s 3(xv) sv 'minor interests'.) The only kind of notice recognised is by entry on the register.

The exception just mentioned consists of 'overriding interests' listed in s 70. As to these, all registered land is stated to be deemed to be subject to such of them as may be subsisting in reference to the land, unless the contrary is expressed on the register. The land is so subject regardless of notice actual or constructive. In my opinion, therefore, the law as to notice as it may affect purchasers of unregistered land, whether contained in decided cases or in a statute (eg the Conveyancing Act 1882, s 3 and the Law of Property Act 1925, s 199) has no application even by analogy to registered land. Whether a particular right is an overriding interest, and whether it affects a purchaser, is to be decided on the terms of s 70, and other relevant provisions of the Land Registration Act 1925, and on nothing else.

In relation to rights connected with occupation, it has been said that the purpose and effect of s 70(1)(*g*) of the Land Registration Act 1925 was to make applicable to registered land the same rule as previously had been held to apply to unregistered land (see *National Provincial Bank Ltd v Ainsworth*, [1964] 1 All ER 688 at 697, [1964] Ch 665 at 689 (per Lord Denning MR) and [1965] 2 All ER 472 at 501–502, [1965] AC 1175 at 1259 (in this House)).

I adhere to this, but I do not accept the argument which counsel for the appellant sought to draw from it. His submission was that, in applying s 70(1)(*g*), we should have regard to and limit the application of the paragraph in the light of the doctrine of notice. But this would run counter to the whole purpose of the Act. The purpose, in each system, is the same, namely, to safeguard the rights of persons in occupation, but the method used differs. In the case of unregistered land, the purchaser's obligation depends on what he has notice of, notice actual or constructive. In the case of registered land, it is the fact of occupation that matters. If there is actual occupation, and the occupier has rights, the purchaser takes subject to them. If not, he does not. No further element is material.

I now deal with the first question. Were the wives here in 'actual occupation'? These words are ordinary words of plain English, and should, in my opinion, be interpreted as such. Historically they appear to have emerged in the judgment of Lord Loughborough LC in *Taylor* v *Stibbert* (1794) 2 Ves 437 at 440, 30 ER 713 at 714 in a passage which repays quotation:

> '. . . whoever purchases an estate from the owner, knowing it to be in possession of tenants, is bound to inquire into the estates, those tenants have. It has been determined, that a purchaser being told, particular parts of the estate were in possession of a tenant, without any information as to his interest, and taking it for granted it was only from year to year, was bound by a lease, that tenant had, which was a surprise upon him. That was rightly determined; for it was sufficient to put the purchaser upon inquiry, that he was informed the estate was not in the *actual possession* of the person with whom he contracted; that he could not transfer the ownership and possession at the same time; that there were interests, as to the extent and terms of which it was his duty to inquire.' (My emphasis.)

They were taken up in the judgment of the Privy Council in *Barnhart v Greenshields* (1853) 9 Moo PC 18, 14 ER 204. The purpose for which they were used, in that case, was evidently to distinguish the case of a person who was in some kind of legal possession, as by receipt of the rents and profits, from that of a person actually in occupation as tenant. Given occupation, i e presence on the land, I do not think that the word 'actual' was intended to introduce any additional qualification, certainly not to suggest that possession must be 'adverse': it merely emphasises that what is required is physical presence, not some entitlement in law. So, even if it were necessary to look behind these plain words into history, I would find no reason for denying them their plain meaning.

Then, were the wives in actual occupation? I ask: why not? There was physical presence, with all the rights that occupiers have, including the right to exclude all others except those having similar rights. The house was a matrimonial home, intended to be occupied, and in fact occupied, by both spouses, both of whom have an interest in it; it would require some special doctrine of law to avoid the result that each is in occupation. Three arguments were used for a contrary conclusion. First, it was said that if the vendor (I use this word to include a mortgagor) is in occupation, that is enough to prevent the application of the paragraph. This seems to be a proposition of general application, not limited to the case of husbands, and no doubt, if correct, would be very convenient for purchasers and intending mortgagees. But the presence of the vendor, with occupation, does not exclude the possibility of occupation of others. There are observations which suggest the contrary in the unregistered land case of *Caunce v Caunce* [1969] 1 All ER 722, [1969] 1 WLR 286, but I agree with the disapproval of these and with the assertion of the proposition I have just stated by Russell LJ in *Hodgson v Marks* [1971] 2 All ER 684 at 690, [1971] Ch 892 at 934–935. Then it was suggested that the wife's 'occupation' was nothing but the shadow of the husband's, a version I suppose of the doctrine of unity of husband and wife. This expression and the argument flowing from it was used by Templeman J in *Bird v Syme Thomson* [1978] 3 All ER 1027 at 1030, [1979] 1 WLR 440 at 444, a decision preceding and which he followed in the present case. The argument was also inherent in the judgment in *Caunce v Caunce* which influenced the decisions of Templeman J. It somewhat faded from the arguments in the present case and appears to me to be heavily obsolete.

The appellants' main and final position became in the end this: that, to come within the paragraph, the occupation in question must be apparently inconsistent with the title of the vendor. This, it was suggested, would exclude the wife of a husband-vendor because her apparent occupation would be satisfactorily accounted for by his. But, apart from the rewriting of the paragraph which this would involve, the suggestion is unacceptable. Consistency, or inconsistency, involves the absence, or presence, of an independent right to occupy, though I must observe that 'inconsistency' in this context is an inappropriate word. But how can either quality be predicated of a wife, simply qua wife? A wife may, and everyone knows this, have rights of her own; particularly, many wives have a share in a matrimonial home. How can it be said that the presence of a wife in the house, as occupier, is consistent or inconsistent with the husband's rights until one knows what rights she has? And if she has rights, why, just because she is a wife (or in the converse case, just because an occupier is the husband), should these rights be denied protection under the paragraph? If one looks beyond the case of husband and wife, the difficulty of all these arguments stands out if one considers the case of a man living with a mistress, or of a man and a woman (or for that matter two persons of the same sex) living in a house in separate or partially shared rooms. Are these cases of apparently consistent occupation, so that the rights of the other person (other than the vendor) can be disregarded? The only solution which is consistent with the Act (s 70(1)(*g*)) and with common sense is to read the paragraph for what it says. Occupation, existing as a fact, may protect rights if the person in occupation has rights. On this part of the case I have no difficulty in concluding that a spouse, living in a house, has an actual occupation capable of conferring protection, as an overriding interest, on rights of that spouse.

This brings me to the second question, which is whether such rights as a spouse has under a trust for sale are capable of recognition as overriding interests, a question to my mind of some difficulty. The argument against this is based on the structure of the Land Registration Act 1925 and on specific provisions in it.

As to structure, it is said that the Act recognises three things: (a) legal estates, (b) minor interests, which take effect in equity, and (c) overriding interests. These are mutually exclusive: an equitable interest, which is a minor interest, is incapable of being at the same time an overriding interest. The wife's interest, existing under, or behind, a trust for sale, is an equitable interest and nothing more. To give it the protection of an overriding interest would, moreover, contradict the principle according to which such an equitable interest can be overreached by an exercise of the trust for sale. As to the provisions of the Act, particular emphasis is placed on s 3(xv) which, in defining 'Minor interests', specifically includes in the case of land held on trust for sale 'all interests and powers which are under the Law of Property Act, 1925, capable of being overridden by the trustees for sale' and excludes, expressly, overriding interests. Reliance is also placed on s 86, which, dealing analogously, so it is said, with settled land, prescribes that successive or other interests created by or arising under a settlement take effect as minor interests and not otherwise, and on s 101, which, it is argued, recognises the exclusive character of minor interests, which in all cases can be overridden.

My Lords, I find this argument formidable. To reach a conclusion on it involves some further consideration of the nature of trusts for sale, in relation to undivided shares. The trusts on which, in this case, the land is to be held are defined (as 'statutory trusts') in s 35 of the Law of Property Act 1925, i e—

> '. . . upon trust to sell the same and to stand possessed of the net proceeds of sale, after payment of costs, and of the net rents and profits until sale after payment of rates, taxes, costs of insurance, repairs, and other outgoings, upon

> such trusts, and subject to such powers and provisions, as may be requisite for giving effect to the rights of the persons . . . interested in the land.'

In addition to this specific disposition, the general provisions as to trusts for sale in ss 23 to 31, where not inconsistent, appear to apply. The right of occupation of the land pending sale is not explicitly dealt with in these sections and the position as to it is obscure. Before the Act the position was that owners of undivided shares (which could exist at law) had concurrent rights of occupation. In *Bull v Bull* [1955] 1 All ER 253, [1955] 1 QB 234 it was held by the Court of Appeal, applying *Re Warren, Warren v Warren* [1932] 1 Ch 42, [1931] All ER Rep 702, that the conversion of these legal estates into equitable interests by the Law of Property Act 1925 should not affect the mutual rights of the owners. Denning LJ, in a judgment which I find most illuminating, there held, in a factual situation similar to that of the instant cases, that 'when there are two equitable tenants in common, then, until the place is sold, each of them is entitled concurrently with the other to the possession of the land and to the use and enjoyment of it in a proper manner' ([1955] 1 All ER 253 at 255, [1955] 1 QB 234 at 238). And he referred to s 14 of the Law of Property Act 1925 which provides that the Act 'shall not prejudicially affect the interest of any person in possession or in actual occupation of land to which he may be entitled in right of such possession or occupation'.

How then are these various rights to be fitted into the scheme of the Land Registration Act 1925? It is clear, at least, that the interests of the co-owners under the 'statutory trusts' are minor interests: this fits with the definition in s 3(xv). But I can see no reason why, if these interests, or that of any one of them, are or is protected by 'actual occupation' they should remain merely as 'minor interests'. On the contrary, I see every reason why, in that event, they should acquire the status of overriding interests. And, moreover, I find it easy to accept that they satisfy the opening, and governing, words of s 70, namely, interests subsisting in reference to the land. As Lord Denning MR points out, to describe the interests of spouses in a house jointly bought to be lived in as a matrimonial home as merely an interest in the proceeds of sale, or rents and profits until sale, is just a little unreal; see also *Elias v Mitchell* [1972] 2 All ER 153, [1972] Ch 652 per Pennycuick V-C, with whose analysis I agree, and contrast *Cedar Holdings Ltd v Green* [1979] 3 All ER 117, [1979] 3 WLR 31 (which I consider to have been wrongly decided).

There are decisions, in relation to other equitable interests than those of tenants in common, which confirm this line of argument. In *Bridges v Mees* [1957] 2 All ER 577, [1957] Ch 475 Harman J decided that a purchaser of land under a contract for sale, who had paid the price and so was entitled to the land in equity, could acquire an overriding interest by virtue of actual occupation, and a similar position was held by the Court of Appeal to arise in relation to a resulting trust (see *Hodgson v Marks* [1971] 2 All ER 684, [1971] Ch 892). These decisions following the law as it undoubtedly existed before 1925: see *Barnhart v Greenshields* (1853) 9 Moo PCC 18 at 32, 14 ER 204 at 209, *Daniels v Davison* (1809) 16 Ves 249, 33 ER 978, *Allen v Anthony* (1816) 1 Mer 282 at 284, 35 ER 679 per Lord Eldon LC) provide an answer to the argument that there is a firm dividing line, or an unbridgeable gulf, between minor interests and overriding interests, and, on the contrary, confirm that the fact of occupation enables protection of the latter to extend to what without it would be the former. In my opinion, the wives' equitable interests, subsisting in reference to the land, were by the fact of occupation, made into overriding interests, and so protected by s 70(1)(*g*). I should add that it makes no difference to this that these same interests might also have been capable of protection by the registration of a caution (see *Bridges v Mees* [1957] 2 All ER 577 at 582, [1957] Ch 475 at 487 and the Land Registration Act 1925, s 59(6)).

There was finally an argument based on s 74 of the Land Registration Act 1925. Section 74 provides:

> 'Subject to the provisions of this Act as to settled land, neither the registrar nor

> any person dealing with a registered estate or charge shall be affected with notice of a trust express implied or constructive, and references to trusts shall, so far as possible, be excluded from the register.'

The argument was that, if the overriding interest sought to be protected is, under the general law, only binding on a purchaser by virtue of notice, the section has the effect of denying the protection. It is obvious, and indeed conceded, that if this is right, *Hodgson v Marks* and *Bridges v Mees* must have been wrongly decided.

I am of opinion that this section has no such effect. Its purpose is to make clear, as I have already explained, that the doctrine of notice has no application to registered conveyancing, and accordingly to establish, as an administrative measure, that entries may not be made in the register which would only be appropriate if that doctrine were applicable. It cannot have the effect of cutting down the general application of s 70(1).

I would only add, in conclusion, on the appeal as it concerns the wives a brief observation on the conveyancing consequences of dismissing the appeal. These were alarming to Templeman J, and I can agree with him to the extent that whereas the object of a land registration system is to reduce the risks to purchasers from anything not on the register, to extend (if it be an extension) the area of risk so as to include possible interests of spouses, and indeed, in theory, of other members of the family or even outside it, may add to the burdens of purchasers, and involve them in inquiries which in some cases may be troublesome.

But conceded, as it must be, that the Act, following established practice, gives protection to occupation, the extension of the risk area follows necessarily from the extension, beyond the paterfamilias, of rights of ownership, itself following from the diffusion of property and earning capacity. What is involved is a departure from an easy-going practice of dispensing with inquiries as to occupation beyond that of the vendor and accepting the risks of doing so. To substitute for this a practice of more careful inquiry as to the fact of occupation, and, if necessary, as to the rights of occupiers, cannot, in my view of the matter, be considered as unacceptable except at the price of overlooking the widespread development of shared interests of ownership. In the light of s 70 of the Act, I cannot believe that Parliament intended this, though it may be true that in 1925 it did not foresee the full extent of this development.

Mr Boland's appeal

The special point taken by Mr Boland arises out of the facts of this case and the nature of the bank's proceeding against him. This was brought under RSC Ord 88 for summary judgment. Mr Boland contended that there was a dispute as to the amount actually owed by him to the bank, and that until this dispute was resolved by trial, judgment for possession ought not to be granted against him before he had had an opportunity of invoking the discretion of the court under the Administration of Justice Act 1970, s 36. The judgment of Templeman J, who fully considered this point, provides a complete answer to this contention. It is clear that, on the view of the matter most favourable to Mr Boland, he owes a substantial sum, of the order of £40,000, to the bank. He has, on the other hand, put forward no material evidence as to the likelihood, or possibility, of discharging or refinancing this indebtedness, on which to invoke the court's discretion under the section, and the judge was undoubtedly right in refusing to exercise it in the absence of such material evidence. In any case, there was no basis on which the Court of Appeal could legitimately interfere with the decision of the judge, and indeed no substantial reason was given for doing so. In my opinion this part of the decision of the Court of Appeal cannot be supported.

However, on the main issue on both appeals, as they affect the wives, the decision of the Court of Appeal was, in my opinion, right, and an order for possession cannot be made in either case. I would dismiss the appeals.

Questions

1 *Suppose that you propose to lend money to a borrower on the security of his land. What precautions would you take to protect yourself against the possible consequences revealed by Boland's Case?*
Then read [1980] Conv. 361.

2 *What is meant by 'overriding interests'?*

3 *How is the equitable interest of a life tenant under the Settled Land Act 1925 protected in the case of registered land?*

4 *Describe briefly how title is proved in regard to registered land.*

Appendix

National and Provincial Building Society Legal Charge

National and Provincial Building Society Mortgage Conditions

This deed secures further advances

National & Provincial

Account number

NATIONAL AND PROVINCIAL BUILDING SOCIETY

Legal Charge

A legal charge made the day of 19 between

The Borrower:

The Guarantor (if any):

The Society: National and Provincial Building Society of Provincial House Bradford West Yorkshire BD1 1NL

1 The Borrower is a member of the Society.
2 This Mortgage incorporates the National and Provincial Building Society Mortgage Conditions 1983 Edition and the Rules and the Borrower (and the Guarantor (if any)) have received copies of the said Mortgage Conditions and the Rules.
3 The Society has paid to the Borrower the Advance mentioned below the receipt of which the Borrower acknowledges.
4 The Borrower as beneficial owner charges the property hereinafter described by way of legal mortgage with payment to the Society of the Advance and all Interest and other moneys payable or becoming payable by the Borrower to the Society howsoever being or becoming so payable.
5 If a Guarantor is named in this deed then his obligations to the Society appear from the provisions of clause 13 of the said Conditions

Land Registry title number	County and District (or London Borough)	Advance

The Mortgaged Property

Signed sealed and delivered by the Borrower and the Guarantor (if any) Signatures:	Seals	Signatures addresses and occupations of witnesses:

L-100-0

National & Provincial

NATIONAL AND PROVINCIAL BUILDING SOCIETY

Legal Charge

To the Society: Declaration and Request

I/We declare that I/we will assert no right to any overriding interest by occupation adverse to the Society's rights under the Mortgage overleaf and I/we request you to make the advance accordingly.

Name	Signature

Solicitor

National and Provincial Building Society hereby acknowledges to have received all moneys intended to be secured by the within written deed

In witness whereof the Seal of National and Provincial Building Society is hereto affixed this
day of one thousand nine hundred and
by order of the Board of Directors in the presence of:

By authority of the Board of Directors

National and Provincial Building Society Mortgage Conditions 1983 Edition

1 Definitions

1.1 'Advance' means any sum advanced by the Society to the Borrower and shall include any further advance or re-advance to the Borrower and the Mortgage shall secure such further advances and re-advances and constitute a continuing security accordingly.

1.2 'Assignor' means any person to whom the Policy Conditions below apply as an assignor.

1.3 'Borrower' means the person to whom an Advance has been made and includes his successors in title.

1.4 'Guarantor' includes the personal representatives of any Guarantor.

1.5 'Interest' means interest at the rate applicable to the Mortgage from time to time.

1.6 'Month' means a calendar month.

1.7 'Mortgage' means any legal charge or other mortgage deed into which these conditions have been incorporated and includes (unless the context otherwise requires) any further charge.

1.8 'Mortgaged Property' means all freehold and leasehold property charged to the Society by the Borrower and shall include all fixtures thereon and additions thereto: references to the mortgaged property shall (unless the context otherwise requires) include a reference to any part or parts or the whole thereof.

1.9 'Person' includes company the masculine gender includes the feminine the singular includes the plural and vice versa and if two or more persons constitute the Borrower or the Guarantor then all covenants by the Borrower or Guarantor contained in or implied by the Mortgage shall be joint and several covenants by such persons.

1.10 'Policy' means any policy to which the Policy Conditions below apply.

1.11 'Receiver' means any person appointed by the Society pursuant to Section 109 of the Law of Property Act, 1925.

1.12 'Repayment' means the monthly repayment notified to the Borrower as constituting the Repayment for the time being by notice given by the Society whether by any offer of advance or revision thereof prior to or at the time of the Mortgage or under these Conditions thereafter.

1.13 'Rules' means the Rules of the Society in force from time to time.

1.14 'Society' means National and Provincial Building Society and includes the persons deriving title under it.

1.15 'Year' means the year commencing 1 January to the following 31 December

2 Payments

2.1 The Borrower covenants that he will pay to the Society

2.1.1 The Repayment commencing with a payment on such date in the Month next following the date of the Mortgage as (subject to clause 12) may be notified by the Society to the Borrower and whether prior to or at the time of the Mortgage or under these Conditions thereafter and continuing monthly thereafter until all moneys secured to the Society under the Mortgage have been paid.

2.1.2 Upon the expiration of two Months' notice given at any time to this effect or on such earlier date being the date upon which the power of sale under the Mortgage becomes exercisable all moneys then owing and all other sums secured to the Society on the security of the Mortgage including interest both before and after any judgment.

2.1.3 The costs expenses and liabilities and other moneys recoverable or payable from time to time from or by the Borrower under the Rules.

2.1.4 Premiums on insurances effected by the Society for or in relation to the Borrower, the Advance, the Mortgaged Property or its contents and all sums expended and costs and expenses incurred by the Society pursuant to clause 14.4.

2.1.5 Interest in accordance with the provision in that behalf hereinafter contained.

2.2 The Repayment may be calculated so as to include all or any part of capital, interest and such costs, expenses, liabilities and moneys recoverable or payable and premiums, sums expended and costs and expenses incurred as aforesaid and may be varied to take account from time to time of any increase or decrease in any of the same.

2.3 Each payment made by the Borrower to the Society shall be applied towards satisfying any moneys secured to the Society under the Mortgage in such order as the Society in its absolute discretion thinks fit save where otherwise agreed.

3 Interest

3.1 Where an Advance is made by instalments Interest shall not be charged in respect of any part of an Advance which is withheld by the Society until such time as the completion of that part of the Advance takes place.

3.2 Subject to sub clause 3.1 hereof Interest shall be charged in any Year

3.2.1 on all moneys including Interest owing to the Society by the Borrower on the last day of the preceding Year and

3.2.2 in respect of any moneys becoming payable to the Society by the Borrower as from the date upon which such moneys became payable or the date of completion as the case may be.

3.3 Interest shall be charged at such rate as the Society shall from time to time apply to the category of business to which the Society shall consider the Mortgage belongs and may accordingly be increased or decreased by the Society at any time and with effect from such date or dates as the Society shall determine provided that

3.3.1 The Society will take such steps as it considers to be reasonable and appropriate to bring any such increase or decrease to the attention of the Borrower provided that without prejudice to the generality of the foregoing either written notice given in accordance with the provisions in that behalf hereinafter contained or publication of such notice in at least two national daily newspapers shall constitute reasonable and appropriate notice for the purposes of this clause.

3.3.2 The Borrower may by notice given to the Society within one Month from the date upon which any increase is to take effect in respect of the Mortgage and referring to this provision be entitled to redeem the Mortgage without liability for payment of any additional Interest at the increased rate provided that such redemption is effected within three Months of the said date.

4 Insurance

4.1 The Society shall have power to insure the Mortgaged Property at the Borrower's expense for such amounts against such risks in such office through such agency and in such manner as the Society may from time to time determine.

4.2 If the Mortgaged Property is insured through the agency of the Society then the Society shall be entitled to retain any commission that it receives.

4.3 The Borrower shall not insure the Mortgaged Property himself except with the Society's prior written approval which the Society may give or decline in its absolute discretion.

4.4 The Borrower shall deliver to the Society on demand all policies of insurance and premium receipts relating to the Mortgaged Property whenever required to do so by the Society and will stand possessed of any insurance moneys received under such policies as trustee for the Society.

5 Consolidation

Section 93 of the Law of Property Act, 1925 shall not apply to the Mortgage.

6 Borrower's Power to Lease

The Mortgagor's powers to let or to take surrenders of leases contained in Section 99 of the Law of Property Act, 1925 are excluded from the Mortgage and the Borrower covenants that he will not without the Society's prior written consent (which it may give or decline in its absolute discretion) charge let licence mortgage or part with or share possession or occupation of the Mortgaged Property.

7 Society's Remedies

7.1 For the purpose of Section 101 of the Law of Property Act, 1925 the mortgage money shall become due 28 days after the date of the Mortgage and in particular in favour of a purchaser the power of sale shall become exercisable 28 days after the date of the Mortgage.

7.2 The power of sale applies to the Mortgage free from the restrictions or conditions precedent contained in Section 103 of the Law of Property Act, 1925 and is extended so as to authorise a sale for a price payable with or without interest by instalments over such period and in such manner as the Society may think fit.

7.3 If the Borrower

7.3.1 is in default of the payment of any two Repayments in whole or in part or for two Months in the payment of any sums payable whether under the Mortgage or the Rules or

7.3.2 commits any act of bankruptcy or enters into any arrangement with or for the benefit of his creditors or

7.3.3 being a company has an order made or resolution passed for winding up or has a receiver appointed on behalf of debenture holders or stockholders of the company or

7.3.4 fails to perform and observe all or any of the covenants contained in or implied by the Mortgage or

7.4 If the Mortgaged Property or any part of it shall become subject to a compulsory purchase order or be requisitioned by any appropriate authority

then in any such case as is mentioned in sub clauses 7.3 and 7.4 all moneys secured by the Mortgage including Interest shall become immediately due and payable and all mortgagees powers by statute as hereby applied shall immediately become exercisable by the Society and the Society may at any time thereafter and without previous notice to the Borrower and without the Borrower's agreement exercise all or any of such powers.

8 Receiver

8.1 A Receiver shall have power in respect of any work incidental to the receivership to employ and pay agents.

8.2 A Receiver may be either an officer or employee of the Society or any other person at the Society's discretion.

8.3 A Receiver appointed by the Society in the exercise of its statutory powers on its behalf shall have the powers set forth in sub clauses 1-5 of clause 9 hereof in addition to his statutory powers.

8.4 Section 109 of the Law of Property Act, 1925 applies to the Mortgage as if subsection (8) (iv) thereof said 'In payment of the moneys of whatsoever nature other than principal money due or accruing due under the Mortgage'.

9 Additional Powers of the Society

In addition to all other powers available to it the Society shall be able

9.1 If the Borrower fails to perform any of his obligations and in particular is in breach of any of the covenants on the part of the Borrower incorporated in the Mortgage to perform the same and to pay all costs and claims arising from such breach and to repair or continue the erection and completion of buildings comprising the Mortgaged Property and to enter upon the Mortgaged Property for that purpose and so that all moneys expended by the Society for such purposes or any of them and all costs and expenses incurred by the Society in relation to the Mortgaged Property and the security constituted by the Mortgage shall be payable by the Borrower on demand and until paid shall be a charge upon the Mortgaged Property.

9.2 To eject from the Mortgaged Property the Borrower or any tenants of the Borrower, workmen or other persons at or in possession of the Mortgaged Property who are there otherwise than with the written consent of the Society upon such date as the Society may enter into possession of the Mortgaged Property or cause a Receiver to be appointed in the exercise of its statutory powers.

9.3 To do such works of repair alteration or cause such additions to the Mortgaged Property as the Society decides are necessary to protect or improve the Mortgaged Property and in the Borrower's name if this shall be necessary to obtain all necessary consents and permissions in connection therewith.

9.4 To grant leases or tenancies of the Mortgaged Property upon such terms and subject to such conditions as the Society shall think fit.

9.5 To apply as between the Borrower and the Society all moneys received from a tenant of any furnished letting of the Mortgaged Property as being a payment made in respect of the Mortgaged Property and not in any part as being attributable to any furniture or fittings comprised in such letting in any case where such letting is or becomes binding upon the Society.

9.6 To remove from the Mortgaged Property any furniture or chattels of or belonging to the Borrower contained in or found upon the Mortgaged Property by the Society upon its entering into possession of the whole or any part thereof if the Borrower fails to remove the same within 28 days of a request by the Society to do so and the Society shall become and is hereby appointed the agent of the Borrower with the Borrower's full authority to deal with such furniture or chattels in such manner as the Society shall think fit in the event of such failure on the part of the Borrower with effect from the expiration of the said period of 28 days provided that nothing contained in the Mortgage shall give to or confer upon the Society any charge or right in respect of any such furniture or chattels or the proceeds of sale thereof which would otherwise constitute the Mortgage as a bill of sale.

9.7 To transfer as attorney of the Borrower any share held by the Borrower in any Residents Society or Management Company registered under the Companies Acts, 1948 to 1967 or the Industrial and Provident Societies Acts, 1965 to 1968 or any similar Acts where the Borrower is a member thereof by reason of his being the owner or lessee of the Mortgaged Property to any person to whom the Society has sold the Mortgaged Property in exercise of its power of sale and to receive any consideration paid in respect of such a transfer but so that the Society shall not have any charge over such share.

9.8 To transfer the benefit of the Mortgage

9.8.1 to any person at any time

9.8.1.1 after the moneys secured thereby shall have become immediately due and payable for whatsoever reason, or,

9.8.1.2 without the Borrower's consent at any time before such event as aforesaid on giving to the Borrower not less than three Months' notice in writing of its intention to do so or,

9.8.1.3 with the Borrower's consent.

9.8.2 And where any such transfer is made all moneys remaining owing by the Borrower to the Society under the Mortgage shall at the date of such transfer be treated as principal money and shall become payable to the transferee on demand with interest thereon in the meantime from the date of the transfer at the rate of interest which was payable to the Society by the Borrower immediately before the date of the transfer and so that the provisions incorporated in the Mortgage enabling the Society to alter the rate of interest shall not be exercisable after the date of such transfer.

9.8.3 And after such transfer the Rules shall cease to apply to the Mortgage but all the rights and powers vested in and discretions exercisable by the Society under the Mortgage will (mutatis mutandis) be exercisable by the transferee.

9.8.4 And in any such transfer by the Society every statement of fact made in good faith shall be conclusive and binding on the Borrower.

9.9 At any time after taking possession of the Mortgaged Property or appointing a Receiver the Society may on notice to the Borrower give up possession or determine the appointment of the Receiver.

10 Further Borrower's Covenants

The Borrower covenants with the Society

10.1 To observe perform and be bound by the Rules.

10.2 To keep the Mortgaged Property in good and substantial repair and condition.

10.3 Without delay and in a good and workmanlike manner to the Society's satisfaction to complete all unfinished buildings (if any) upon the Mortgaged Property together with all drains, fences, gates, pathways and any other works comprised in the Mortgaged Property.

10.4 To permit the Society to inspect the condition of the Mortgaged Property at any time subject to the reasonable convenience of the Borrower and without making the Society liable as mortgagee in possession.

10.5 Not without the written consent of the Society to carry out any structural or other alterations to the Mortgaged Property nor to apply to any Planning Authority to change the use thereof.

10.6 To comply with the Town and Country Planning Act, 1971 or any Act or Acts amending re-enacting or revising the same for the time being in force or any Regulation or Order made thereunder and within seven days of the receipt by the Borrower of any notice, order or proposal made given or issued by any planning or other authority affecting or concerning the Mortgaged Property to send a copy thereof to the Society and also forthwith to take all reasonable and necessary steps to comply therewith and to keep the Society informed thereon.

10.7 To observe and perform all covenants stipulations regulations and agreements affecting the Mortgaged Property.

10.8 To pay the rent and other outgoings reserved or payable under any lease under which the Mortgaged Property is held by the Borrower and any rentcharge or other outgoing charged upon the Mortgaged Property and whenever requested to do so to produce to the Society on demand any receipt for such payment and further to perform and observe all covenants regulations and agreements on the part of the lessee and conditions contained in any such lease as aforesaid.

10.9 To pay all sums due from time to time in connection with the insurance of the Mortgaged Property.

11 Re-Advance

The Society may if it in its absolute discretion so determines from time to time at the request of the Borrower return to the Borrower by way of further advance any amount which may have been paid to the Society in reduction of the Advance and the Mortgage shall thereafter operate (mutatis mutandis) as if such sum so returned had not been paid to the Society and all Interest on such sum had been paid to the Society up to the commencement of the Month in which such return is made.

12 Miscellaneous

In default and until notification under clause 2.1.1 (which notification may be at any time during the subsistence of this security) the due date for the purposes of that clause shall be the last day of the Month.

13 Guarantor

If there is a Guarantor named in the Mortgage then

13.1 The Guarantor covenants with the Society to observe and perform all the obligations of the Borrower under the Mortgage.

13.2 The Guarantor waives the right to participate in the proceeds of any security held or acquired by the Society or in any money received by the Society whether from the Borrower or from any other source in or towards the reduction of the moneys secured by the Mortgage unless and until all money secured by the Mortgage has been received by the Society in full.

13.3 The liability of the Guarantor shall not be affected by any further or future advance, re-advance security giving of time or any other act, omission or means whatsoever whereby his liability would not have been discharged if he had been the principal debtor.

13.4 As between the Society and the Guarantor the Guarantor shall be deemed to be the principal debtor.

14 Policy Conditions (where applicable)

14.1 The expression 'the Policy' shall include any new or exchange policy.

14.2 Unless and until a Policy has been legally assigned to the Society, the Society, having the Policy deposited with it, shall have an equitable charge on the Policy on the terms of these Policy Conditions; and the Borrower appoints the Society irrevocably (but subject to redemption) to be the attorney of the Borrower in his name to assign, transfer, surrender or otherwise deal with the Policy and the full benefit thereof.

14.3 The Society may at any time apply the Policy and the full benefit thereof (including any surrender moneys) towards the discharge of any obligation to the Society of the Borrower (including any obligation in respect of any further or future advance upon the same or other security and interest thereon and whether alone or jointly with another or others) and of the Assignor or either of them and the Policy and the full benefit thereof shall constitute a continuing security and are charged hereby accordingly.

14.4 The Assignor covenants with the Society

14.4.1 That so long as any money remains due to the Society from the Borrower the Assignor will not without the prior consent in writing of the Society do or permit or suffer any act omission matter or thing in consequence whereof payment under the Policy may be declined or limited and will not do or permit or suffer anything whereby the Policy may become void or voidable or whereby the Society may be prevented from receiving any money thereunder and that the Assignor will immediately at his own cost in case the Policy shall become voidable do all things necessary for restoring the same and in case the Policy shall become void also do everything necessary to enable the Society to effect a new Policy on the life of the life assured in the name of the Society for the amount which would have become payable under the Policy if the life assured had died immediately before it became void.

14.4.2 To pay all sums necessary to keep the Policy on foot within seven days after they shall become payable and to deliver the receipt or sufficient evidence of every payment to the Society whenever the Society requires sight thereof.

14.4.3 To pay all sums paid and costs and expenses incurred by the Society and interest as provided for by clause 14.5.

14.5 In default of payment of any sums necessary to keep the Policy on foot the Society may pay the same and all sums so paid and all costs and expenses incurred in restoring the Policy shall be repaid to the Society together with interest thereon at the rate from time to time payable under the Mortgage and until repayment the Policy shall stand charged with the amount to be repaid and the interest thereon.

14.6 The Policy may at any time be surrendered by the Society to the insurers by whom it was granted for a sum which shall not be less than the surrender value of the Policy according to the tables for the time being in use by such insurers, or exchanged for a fully paid up Policy, or such arrangements may be made with the insurers as the Society may think fit.

14.7 Upon payment to the Society of all moneys for which the Policy is security the Society will at the request and cost of the Assignor reassign it or assign it as he shall direct.

14.8 If there is a Guarantor named in any assignment of a Policy to the Society

14.8.1 The Guarantor covenants with the Society to observe and perform all the obligations of the Assignor.

14.8.2 The Guarantor waives the right to participate in the proceeds of any security held or acquired by the Society or in any moneys received by the Society from any source in or towards reduction of the moneys for which the Policy is security unless and until all such moneys have been received by the Society in full.

14.8.3 The liability of the Guarantor shall not be affected by any further or future advance, re-advance, security, giving of time or any other act, omission or means whatsoever whereby his liability would not have been discharged if he had been the principal debtor.

14.8.4 As between the Society and the Guarantor the Guarantor shall be deemed to be the principal debtor.

14.9 The provisions as to the giving of notice (including deemed service) which under clause 15 apply to the Borrower and the Guarantor shall also respectively apply to the Assignor and any Guarantor of a Policy.

15 Notices

Without prejudice to clause 3.3.1 any notice to be given by the Society shall be in writing and shall be sufficiently given, if served in any manner in which a notice may be served on a mortgagor under Section 196 of the Law of Property Act, 1925, or if it is sent by any ordinary prepaid post addressed to the Borrower or the Guarantor by name or by that designation at his address last known to the Society, or (in the case of notice to the Borrower) at the address of the Mortgaged Property and if the letter is not returned through the Post Office undelivered any notice so served (whether as to the Repayment or howsoever otherwise) shall be deemed to have been served at the time at which the letter should have been delivered in the ordinary course. Any request by the Society may be made in like manner and to like effect.

16 Conflict

In the event of conflict between the Mortgage (including these Conditions) and the Rules the Mortgage shall prevail.

The deed and mortgage conditions are reproduced by permission of the National and Provincial Building Society.

Glossary

Absolute Free from determining factors; commonly used in expression 'fee simple absolute'.

Abstract of title A summary of documents of title; abstracts of title are used to prove title to land.

Acquiescence A failure to resist the infringement of a right.

Administrator See **'Personal representatives'**.

Advowson A right to present a parson to a living. The right can be annexed to land, or exist independently. In either case, it is classified as 'land'.

Alienation A transfer of property, whether by sale gift or other transaction.

Appurtenant Attached to land by agreement of parties; an example of an appurtenant right is an easement; contrast 'appendant' which means attached by operation of law; appendant rights are an archaic class, principally affecting *profits à prendre*.

Assent A transfer of property by personal representatives to beneficiaries under a will or intestacy; a deed is not necessary here; hence the special term.

Assignment A transfer of property; commonly used in the transfer of a lease.

Base fee An incompletely barred entail which endures only for so long as the entail would have endured, but which is good as against those who would have inherited the entail.

Beneficial owner An owner of interest who does not hold it on trust for others.

Charge An interest in land created either by act of parties or by operation of law for securing a debt or other obligation; for example, a mortgage.

Chattel Any property other than freehold land; 'personal' chattels are movable items of property.

Consolidation An obligation, arising on the right to redemption of one mortgage, to redeem one or other mortgages of other properties.

Contingent Not presently owned; a key term in the rule against perpetuities.

Conversion	Treating land as money, or money as land; the topic gains most of its importance in the context of express and statutory trusts for sale.
Conveyance	A document transferring property during the lifetime of the transferor.
Co-ownership	Ownership shared by two or more persons at the same time.
Corporeal	Tangible: e.g. soil, bricks; see also **'Incorporeal'.**
Covenant	A contract under seal.
Deed	A document under seal; it is the principal means through which interests in land are transferred.
Demise	A grant of a lease.
Devise	A grant of a freehold interest by will.
Dominant tenement	Land benefiting from a burden placed upon other land; usually an easement or restrictive covenant is concerned.
Entail	An interest in land which lasts as long as descendant heirs of the original grantee of the interest are born.
Estate	Generally an interest giving the right to the land itself; particularly applied to legal interests having this effect.
Estoppel	Preclusion from denying facts which have been stated or inferred and upon which another person has acted.
Execute	Complete a transfer of property.
Executor	See **'Personal representatives'**.
Fee simple	Ownership.
Fine	A capital payment.
Foreclosure	The lifting of the right of redemption from mortgaged property.
Freehold	A fee simple, absolute ownership.
Hereditament	Land.
Incumbrance	A burden upon property.
Incorporeal hereditament	Intangible 'land'; e.g. an easement.
Indenture	Archaic word to describe a deed.
Instrument	Any legal document.
Intestacy	Failure to dispose of property by will.
Jus accrescendi	See **'Survivorship'**.
Land	A word of variable meaning—see Chapter 3.
Licence	Permission.

Minor interest — An interest in registered land which requires entry on the Register for its protection against purchasers.

Next of kin — Persons entitled to the property of an intestate person.

Oral — By word of mouth; distinguish 'verbal' which means by words, whether written or oral; a common confusion.

Overreach — To convert an interest in land to an interest in purchase money upon sale of the land.

Override — To defeat an interest in land by receiving a conveyance of an interest in that land.

Overriding interest — An interest in registered land which is binding upon purchasers even though it is not entered on the Register.

Personal representatives — Executors or administrators; both types of personal representatives deal with the property of deceased persons; the former are appointed by the will and confirmed by the court (normally a merely administrative procedure); the latter receive their authority from the court because of close relationship to the deceased.

Possession — Occupation of land or receipt of its rents and profits.

Prescription — The process of acquiring easements and profits by long use.

Privity of contract — The relationship of contracting parties.

Privity of estate — The relationship of landlord and tenant.

Probate — Grant of approval of a will by the court (normally an administrative procedure).

Puisne mortgage — A legal mortgage not protected by deposit of deeds.

Purchaser — One who acquires property by act of parties rather than operation of law; e.g. a donnee.

Remainder — An interest in land which follows another interest; e.g. *B*'s interest in a grant to *A* for life and *B* in fee simple.

Resulting trust — A trust arising in favour of a grantor whose attempted transfer fails or partially fails.

Rent service — A rent due from a tenant to a landlord.

Rentcharge — A rent payable where there is no landlord/tenant relationship.

Reversion — A remainder retained by a grantor of a prior interest.

Restrictive covenant — A covenant not to use land in a particular way;

	such agreements are capable of binding land permanently as do easements.
Root of title	The earliest of the series of documents upon which proof of title to land is based.
Seisin	Possession by a freeholder.
Settlement	A structure of consecutive interests in land other than those of landlord and tenant but including absolute ownership by a minor.
Survivorship	The coalescence of property on the death of one joint owner into the hands of the other joint tenants.
Tenure	Holding land of another—usually relating to landlord and tenant.
Term of years	A lease or tenancy.
Trust for sale	A duty to sell land derived either from the terms of an instrument or of an Act of Parliament; the former is called an 'express trust for sale'; the latter is a 'statutory trust for sale'.
Words of limitation	Formal words legally required for the creation of interests in land; the doctrine now applies only to entailed interests.

Index